ESSAYS
ON JEWISH LIFE
AND THOUGHT

ESSAYS ON JEWISH LIFE AND THOUGHT

PRESENTED IN HONOR OF

SALO WITTMAYER BARON

Edited by

Joseph L. Blau Philip Friedman
Arthur Hertzberg Isaac Mendelsohn

COLUMBIA UNIVERSITY PRESS
New York 1959

The publication of this volume was made possible by
the Conference on Jewish Social Studies
through its Meisel Fund.

Library of Congress Catalog Card Number: *57—11757*

Published in Great Britain, Canada, India, and Pakistan
By the Oxford University Press
London, Toronto, Bombay, and Karachi

Manufactured in the Netherlands

EDITORS' PREFACE

THOUGH THIS VOLUME has been edited by the four men whose names appear on the title page, the Board of Editors cannot claim the credit for the initial impulse toward this *Festschrift*. As Dr. Baron's sixtieth birthday was approaching, the idea arose spontaneously in several circles that such a collection of scholarly studies would be the "birthday present" that he might most enjoy. The editors do, however, bear the responsibility for the manner in which this thought has been realized. To "raise up many disciples" is one of the commandments of the Mishnah; we felt that a volume representing exclusively former students of Dr. Baron would be more than the usual tribute, for it underscores an aspect of his work which is perhaps less immediately apparent than the magisterial range and depth of his own writings—that in over thirty-five years of teaching Salo Wittmayer Baron has, indeed, more than fulfilled the ancient injunction. Only one regret attended this decision: it required the refusal of many offers by eminent colleagues and friends of our teacher to share in this tribute with essays they wished to prepare in his honor.

It remains for the editors to express their thanks to the Conference on Jewish Social Studies, which, through its Meisel Fund, made the publication of this book possible, and to the Columbia University Press and its able staff for many kindnesses and courtesies in the various stages of seeing this volume through the press.

THE BOARD OF EDITORS

THE HISTORIC QUEST

TO ACHIEVE DISTINCTION in any field, to stand out decisively from the majority, is not given to many. It is a rare gift, one that endows its fortunate possessor with a special, recognizable light. But it is also a demanding gift, one that requires total service and devotion. All human ties and human weaknesses must be resolutely transcended to give full scope to the talent that is forever surging on and on. The distinguished man is not often also beloved.

Yet the distinguished historian can be, indeed he must be, an exception to this rule. For to gain distinction as an historian requires a deep and sympathetic understanding of men. The historic quest is the unremitting struggle to comprehend the fullness of human experience from the sparse and scattered records that men have left behind. The validity of the inferences that any historian makes may be a matter of logic; their truth and their consequent acceptability rests on the historian's understanding of what people are, how people live and think and love. To gain this understanding, the historian must be a humanist. Nay, more, the distinguished historian must be a full human being. His greatness as an historian and his greatness as a man cannot be separated.

It is not a fitting thing for the editors and contributors to this volume of tribute to Salo Wittmayer Baron, in honor of his sixtieth birthday, to pass final judgment on our teacher's rank as an historian. Yet in bringing this offering to him, we are bearing testimony to our regard for him as a person and our respect for him as a teacher. And this, by implication, suggests the high place that we would assign to him in the long line of Jewish historians from the anonymous writers of the historical sections of the Bible down to the present generation.

Salo W. Baron's stature as an historian rests on his projected but still incomplete reworking not of any fragmentary epoch of Jewish history, but of its entire millennial course. In this reconsideration he has utilized to the full the techniques and conclusions that modern social sciences have made available to the student of history. His capacity to use this material did not come by accident; he prepared himself deliberately for the work he was to do. Born in 1895, in Tarnow, Austria, he was inspired by the comprehensive Jewish history of Heinrich Graetz to make his career as a Jewish historian. In his early teens, Salo Baron had already committed much of Graetz's history to memory.

Then he studied in Vienna, receiving three degrees—Ph. D., Pol. Sc. D., and Jur. D.—from the University of Vienna and a rabbinical degree from the Jewish Theological Seminary in Vienna, all during the years between 1917 and 1923. For part of this time, from 1919 on, Baron was also beginning his career as a teacher, at the Jüdisches Pädagogium in Vienna. A number of his early publications were written in this period, as the bibliography included in this volume shows. Thus it is clear that the phenomenal capacity for concentrated work which is the envy and admiration of all who know Baron and have tried to work with him was characteristic of him from his early days as a scholar.

Baron continued to teach in Vienna, at the Jüdisches Pädagogium, until 1926. Some of the contributors to this volume were among his students there. In 1926 and 1927, he was twice invited to serve as Visiting Lecturer in the Jewish Institute of Religion in New York, and in the latter year was appointed Professor of History, Librarian, and Director of the Department of Advanced Studies there, retaining these multiple responsibilities until 1930. Then the Miller Foundation established a chair of Jewish History, Literature, and Institutions at Columbia University, and Professor Baron was invited to be its first incumbent. In 1950, when a Center of Israeli Studies was opened at Columbia, Baron assumed the position of Director of this Center. Most of the studies in this volume were written by those who have been his students during his long tenure—more than a quarter of a century—of this chair at Columbia University. In addition to his duties at Columbia, Baron taught for several years at the Graduate School for Jewish Social Work in New York, and, since 1954, has served as Visiting Professor at the Jewish Theological Seminary of America. In 1944 he was named as Rauschenbusch Lecturer at the Colgate-Rochester Divinity School.

Some of the themes of Professor Baron's teaching of Jewish history are especially worthy of mention here. First and most important of these is that he has emphasized and exemplified a pluralistic approach to the study of Jewish history. Recognizing and accepting the continuity in the historical life of the Jewish people from earliest days—for Baron is one of those who has most gladly welcomed the evidence of archaeology for the trustworthiness of biblical narrative—he has, nevertheless, seen that Jewish life in modern times cannot be explained solely on the basis of an internal evolution. There has been, at all times, a process of interaction between the Jews and their neighbors. If it can be said with truth that the

Jewish people has influenced the world, it must be added, with equal truth, that the world has influenced the Jewish people. For the historian this implies the relevance of all history to Jewish history.

Second, although as a sociologist Baron has made original contributions to the understanding of Jewish history, he does not insist that such understanding can come about only through sociology. Nor is he prepared to admit that any other single key will suffice for the purpose. The history of the Jewish people is many-faceted. To account foı its complexities by an exclusive attention to religion or economics or social patterns or demography—the list of possible alternatives is endless and easy to document—is to introduce a specious simplicity that does not satisfy the facts. Any historian, and especially any historian of the Jews, must be as many-sided as his material.

For all this, Baron's historical interpretations tend to be conservative. Many of his most original and even radical innovations of approach are used to bolster up or to restore the most traditional of interpretations. No one who has been a student in his classes will easily forget his marshaling of demographic evidence of the Jewish population in Palestine and the Roman provinces in A.D. 112 to prove, with glowing dramatic fervor, that only the failure of the provincial Jews to revolt simultaneously with the Jews of Palestine turned the rebellion into a lost cause. Even for a more recent period, the era of Jewish emancipation from the French Revolution to the present, Baron's vast collection of materials is bent to prove that from the internal viewpoint of the Jewish people, their solidarity and the development of their culture, emancipation was a tragic and possibly a fatal mistake.

It is not only by the wealth of information and the solidity of his interpretations that Salo Baron as a teacher has impressed his students. His presentations are vigorous and dynamic. His entry into the lecture room is quiet. His appearance gives no suggestion of his vitality as a lecturer. He rarely uses gesture to reenfoıce his points. Yet to hear his lectures is to feel the driving force of a powerful personality masterfully dominating his subject. Baron as a teacher inspires students to strive to emulate his own mastery; few succeed, but all are the better foı the striving. To add to this all too brief characterization of his teaching, it remains to be said that the student grapevine, that altogether admirable recorder of judgment, recommends to the young student and potential teacher of other fields of history the auditing of Baron's lectures, for a demonstration of creative historical imagination.

Much of Baron's traditionalism arises from a regard for the integıity of the Jewish community as it developed over the centuries, especially in Europe. His feeling is both intellectual and practical. Baron has expressed his intellectual conviction as a social historian by his monumental three-volume study of *The Jewish Community: Its History and Structure to the American Revolution* (Philadelphia, 1942). This is in many respects the most original of his major works because in it the fusion of historian and sociologist is most clearly evinced.

The practical aspects of Baron's regard for the Jewish community are firmly grounded in the experiences of his boyhood in Tarnow, strengthened by his historical studies, and given point by the chaos of American Jewish organizational life without the controlling element of community. He has expressed his practical sense of the necessity for finding some equivalents for the traditional community to serve the needs of the modern Jewish world. His record of public service toward this end has been full and consistent. From 1925 to 1927 he was a member of both the Permanent Minorities Commission and the Governing Council of the International Federation of the League of Nations Unions. Since 1952, he has been a Corresponding Member of the UNESCO-sponsored International Commission for a Scientific and Cultural History of Mankind. He was the Founder, and has been President, of Jewish Cultural Reconstruction, Inc., a chartered corporation for the recovery and redistribution of Jewish religious and cultural treasures seized by the Nazis. He has also been Chairman of the Cultural Advisory Committee of the Conference on Jewish Material Claims against Germany. From 1945 to 1948, he was Chairman of the Commission on Survey of the National Jewish Welfare Board, and from 1947 to 1952, a member of the Citizens Federal Committee on Education, an activity of the United States Department of Education.

In addition, Baron has been an active participant in the work of various cultural organizations serving the intellectual needs of the American Jewish people. He is a Fellow of the American Academy for Jewish Research, and served as its president from 1940 to 1943. He has been President (and, more recently, Honorary President) since 1941 of the Conference on Jewish Relations (now called the Conference on Jewish Social Studies). He has been President of the American Jewish Historical Society. The American Jewish Committee, the American Jewish Congress, the Jewish Publication Society of America, and the American Jewish Tercentenary Committee have all called upon Baron for various forms of service. Small wonder that, in 1944, the Hebrew Union College of Cincinnati, the oldest Jewish theological seminary in America, bestowed upon Salo W. Baron the degree of D.H.L., *honoris causa.*

The editors and contributors to this volume, and those whose sponsorship have made possible its publication, wish to present this tribute to Salo Wittmayer Baron *honoris causa*, but, more importantly, they wish to present it *amoris causa.* Baron has been our teacher, and he has taught us more than Jewish history. He has taught us also the importance of participating in the life of the world around us, if our intellectual activity is not to be sterile. He has taught us by his example that an understanding of men can be gained, in the last analysis, only by living with men and sharing with them in the tasks of everyday life.

We dare not presume that any of the essays we present here to our teacher is truly worthy of his own achievement. We hope that he will feel a sense of pride in having stimulated and inspired the writing of these essays, whatever their limitations. We hope, too, that their variety may suggest the breadth of Baron's interests and his comprehensive approach to Jewish history and culture. Finally, we hope that Salo Baron will accept this *Festschrift* in the spirit in which it is offered, a spirit of respect, of esteem, and of love.

JOSEPH L. BLAU
for the Board of Editors

CONTENTS

BIBLIOGRAPHY OF THE WRITINGS OF SALO WITTMAYER BARON

1912

1. ״חזיון מעציב״ (A Sad Phenomenon), *Hamicpe*, IX, No. 43 (November 8), 3. Under the pseudonym שבא.
2. ״משבר־הכסף״ (Financial Crisis), *Hamicpe*, IX, No. 44 (November 15), 2–3. Under the pseudonym שבא.
3. ״שאלת הצדקה ותקוניה״ (The Problem of Social Welfare and Its Reforms), *Hamicpe*, IX, No. 46 (November 29), 1–2. Under the pseudonym שבא.
4. ״תקון סדר הבחירה לסים הגליצאי״ (Reform of the Electoral System for the Galician Diet), *Hamicpe*, IX, No. 49 (December 20), 1–2. Under the pseudonym שבא.

1913

5. ״אותות הזמן״ (Portents of the Day), *Hamicpe*, X, No. 27 (July 11), 2–3.
6. ״הבויקוט הפולני״ (The Polish Boycott), 5 parts, *Hamicpe*, X, No. 7 (February 14), 1–2; No. 8 (February 21), pp. 1–2; No. 9 (February 28), pp. 3–4; No. 10 (March 7), pp. 2–3; No. 11 (March 14), pp. 3–4. Under the pseudonym שבא.
7. ״על מפתן התקופה״ (On the Threshold of a New Period), *Hamicpe*, X, No. 36 (September 12) 4–5. Under the pseudonym שבא.

1914

8. ״ליובלו של ׳המצפה׳״ (On the Anniversary of the *Hamicpe*), 2 parts, *Hamicpe*, XI, No. 17 (April 24), 2–3; No. 18 (May 1), p. 3.
9. ״מרדכי דוד ברנדשטטר (ליובל השבעים שלו)״ (Mordecai David Brandstaetter), 3 parts, *Haṣefirah*, XL, No. 94 (May 7), 1; No. 95 (May 8), p. 4; No. 97 (May 11), pp. 1–2.
10. ״שאלת הזמן״ (The Problem of the Day), 2 parts, *Hamicpe*, XI, No. 3 (January 16), 2–3; No. 4 (January 23), pp. 2–3.

1918

11. "Graetzens Geschichtsschreibung," *Monatsschrift für Geschichte und Wissenschaft des Judentums* (*MGWJ*), LXII, 5–15.
12. "Nation oder Sprache?" *Die Wage*, XXI, No. 18 (May 4), 276–80.

1920

13. *Die Judenfrage auf dem Wiener Kongress, Auf Grund von zum Teil ungedruckten Quellen dargestellt*. Vienna and Berlin. 211 pp.

1923

14. *Die politische Theorie Ferdinand Lassalles.* Leipzig, 122 pp. Beihefte zum Archiv für die Geschichte des Sozialismus und der Arbeiterbewegung, hrsg. von Carl Grünberg, Heft 2.

1925

15. "פרדינד לסל היהודי" (Ferdinand Lassalle, the Jew), *Hatekufah*, XXIII' 347–62.
16. Interview with Japanese diplomat, *Revue Internationale*, 1925–26, p. 106.
17. Review of Josef Klausner, *Historia Yisraelit*, Vols. II–IV (Berlin, 1924–25). In *Literarische Wochenschrift*, No. 27 (December 5), pp. 840–41.

1926

18. "Jüdische und Palästina Fragen auf dem Zehnten Kongress der Internationalen Union der Völkerbundligen," *Zionistische Korrespondenz*, VI, No. 27 (July 9), 1–5.
19. "Unveröffentlichte Aktenstücke zur Judenfrage auf dem Wiener Kongress," *MGWJ*, LXX, 457–75.
20. "אדמים, עזריה מן" (De'Rossi, Azariah), *Eshkol, Hebrew Encyclopaedia*, קונטרס לדוגמה Berlin, pp. 28–29.
21. "Für den Schutz der Minderheiten. Der Kongress der Völkerbundligen," *Wiener Morgenzeitung*, VIII, No. 2644 (July 4), 2.
22. "Eine Palästinadebatte auf dem Kongress der Völkerbundligen," *Wiener Morgenzeitung*, VIII, No. 2646 (July 6), 2.
23. "Der zehnte Kongress der Internationalen Union der Völkerbundligen," *Wiener Morgenzeitung*, VIII, No. 2650 (July 10), 2.
24. Review of Simon Dubnow, *Weltgeschichte des jüdischen Volkes*, Vol. I (Berlin, 1925). In *Literarische Wochenschrift*, Nos. 3–4 (January 20), pp. 72–73.
25. Review of N. M. Gelber, *Aus zwei Jahrhunderten* (Vienna, 1924); and *Die Juden und der polnische Aufstand 1863* (Vienna, 1923). In *MGWJ*, LXX, 134–35.
26. Review of Ferdinand Lassalle, *Nachgelassene Briefe und Schriften*, hrsg. v. Gustav Mayer, V. Bd. (Stuttgart, 1925). In *Archiv für Geschichte des Sozialismus*, XII, 449–50.

1927

27. "Azariah de' Rossi's Attitude to Life," in *Jewish Studies in Memory of Israel Abrahams*, New York, pp. 12–52.
28. "Artom, Isacco," *Jüdisches Lexikon*, Berlin, I, 486–87.
29. Review of I[sidor] Kracauer, *Geschichte der Juden in Frankfurt a. M. (1150–1824)*, Vol. I (Frankfort, 1925). In *Literarische Wochenschrift*, No. 7 (February 13), pp. 166–67.

1928

30. "Ghetto and Emancipation," *Menorah Journal* (*MJ*), XIV, 515–26.
31. "La Méthode Historique d'Azaria de' Rossi," *Révue des études juives* (*REJ*), LXXXVI, 151–75; LXXXVII, 43–78. Also as a pamphlet, Paris, 1929, 61 pp. (Publications de la Société des études juives).
32. "על קבר מרדכי דוד בראנדשטטר ז״ל, האי״ש" (Obituary of Mordecai David Brandstaetter), *Hadoar*, VIII, No. 28 (June 3), 440–41.
33. "הרב צ·פ· חיות בתור חוקר ומורה" (Rabbi H. P. Chajes as Scholar and Teacher), *Shebile ha-Hinnuk*, IV, No. 1, 37–45.
34. "The Study of Jewish History," *Jewish Institute Quarterly*, IV, No. 2 (January), 7–14.
35. "Research in Jewish History," *Jewish Institute Quarterly*, IV, No. 4 (May), 1–8.
36. "Fischhof, Adolf (Abraham)," *Jüdisches Lexikon*, II, 673–74.
37. "Friedjung, Heinrich," *Jüdisches Lexikon, II*, 822–23.
38. Review of *The Legacy of Israel*, ed. by Edwyn R. Bevan and Charles Singer (Oxford, 1927). In *Journal of Religion*, VIII, No. 3 (July), 477–79.

1929

39. "Nationalism and Intolerance," *MJ*, XVI (June), 405–15; XVII (November), 148–58. Also reprint, New York, 22 pp.
40. "אדמים ׳עזריה מן" (De'Rossi, Azariah), *Eshkol, Hebrew Encyclopaedia*, I, 689–93. Revised from No. 20.
41. "תשובה בשפה איטלקית מאת ר׳ אברהם גראציאנו" (An Italian Responsum of Abraham Graziano), in *Studies in Jewish Bibliography and Related Subjects in Memory of Abraham Solomon Freidus*, New York and Vienna, pp. 122–37.
42. Introduction to Filip Friedmann, *Die galizischen Juden im Kampfe um ihre Gleichberechtigung* (*1848–1868*), Frankfurt a. M.

1930

43. *The Jews in Roumania. Report Submitted to the Eighth Session of the American Jewish Congress.* New York, 15 pp. An extract of this Report appeared under the title, "The Situation of the Jews in Roumania," in *Jewish Tribune*, XLVII, No. 17 (October 24), 2.
44. "The Authenticity of the Numbers in the Historical Books of O.T.," *Journal of Biblical Literature* (*JBL*), XLIX, Part 3, pp. 287–91.
45. "I. M. Jost, the Historian," *Proceedings of the American Academy for Jewish Research* (*PAAJR*), I, 7–32.
46. "Teaching Jewish History." Interview by Dr. Dora Askowith. In *Jewish Tribune*, XLVI, No. 7 (February 14), 2, 7. Appeared also in Polish transl. in the literary supplement to *Chwila*, No. 3988 (Low, May 4, 1930), pp. 9–10.
47. "Berliner, Abraham," *Encyclopaedia of Social Sciences*, II, 523.

1931

48. "Zur ostjüdischen Einwanderung in Preussen, Aktenstücke," *Zeitschrift für die Geschichte der Juden in Deutschland*, N. S., III, 193–203.
49. "Żydzi w Rumunji," *Miesięcznik żydowski*, I, No. 4 (March), 322–35. Transl. of No. 43.
50. "Frankel, Zecharias," *Encyclopaedia of Social Sciences*, VI, 418–19.
51. "Graetz, Heinrich," *Encyclopaedia Judaica*, VII, 645–52.
52. Review of George A. Barton, *A History of the Hebrew People from the Earliest Times to the Year 70 A.D.* (New York, 1930). In *Historical Outlook*, October, p. 305.

1932

53. "Jewish Emancipation," *Encyclopaedia of Social Sciences*, VIII, 394–99.
54. "Karo, Joseph," *Encyclopaedia of Social Sciences*, VIII, 547–48.
55. Interview in *Der Wiener Tag*, July 3.
56. "אוכלוסי ישראל בימי המלכים" (The Israelitic Population under the Kings, in *Abhandlungen zur Erinnerung an Hirsch Perez Chajes*, Vienna, pp. 76–163.
57. "Jewish Influence on Christian Reform Movements," *Jewish Quarterly Review* (*JQR*), XXIII, 405–10. Review of L. I. Newman's work on this subject.
58. "Jews and the Syrian Massacres of 1860," *PAAJR*, IV, 3–31.
59. "Żydzi a żydowstwo" (Jews and Judaism), *Miesięcznik żydowski*, III, Part 2, Nos. 11–12 (November–December), 193–207. Essentially transl. from ms. of Chap. I in No. 71.
60. Review of Fannie A. Andrews, *The Holy Land under Mandate* (2 vols., Boston, 1931); and of Angelo S. Rappoport, *History of Palestine* (London, 1931). In *Historical Outlook*, XXIV (March), 160–161.

1935

61. *Jewish Studies in Memory of George A. Kohut*. Edited by Salo W. Baron and Alexander Marx. New York: Bloch Publishing Co.
62. "Abraham Benisch's Project for Jewish Colonization in Palestine (1842)," in *Jewish Studies in Memory of George A. Kohut*, New York, pp. 72–85.
63. "Germany's Ghetto, Past and Present," *Independent Journal of Columbia University*, III, No. 3 (November 15), 3–4.
64. "An Historical Critique of the Jewish Community," *Jewish Social Service Quarterly* (*JSSQ*), XI, 44–49. Also in *Jewish Education*, X, (1936), 2–8.
65. "The Historical Outlook of Maimonides," *PAAJR*, VI, 5–113.
66. "Maimonides, Guia y Legislador de su Pueblo," *Revista Hispanica Moderna*, I, No. 4 (July), 303–7. Transl. of Address at Maimonides Celebration.
67. "לתולדות יהודי גרמניה בא"י" (On the History of German Jews in Palestine), in *Minhah le-David* (The David Yellin Jubilee Volume), Jerusalem, pp. 113–28.

68. Review of Jacob de Haas, *Palestine, the Last Two Thousand Years* (New York, 1934), In *Annals of the American Academy of Political and Social Science*, Vol. 178 (March), pp. 235–36.
69. Another review of the same work. In *American Historical Review*, XL, No. 3 (April), 545–46.
70. Review of M. I. Zwick, *Berthold Auerbachs sozialpolitischer und ethischer Liberalismus* (Stuttgart, 1933). In *Germanic Review*, No. 1 (January), pp. 50–51.

1937

71. *A Social and Religious History of the Jews.* 3 vols. New York: Columbia University Press. Pp. xii + 377; ix + 462; xi + 406. 2d Impression, 1938–39.
72. "מתולדות הישוב היהודי בירושלים" (From the History of the Jewish Settlement in Jerusalem), in *Sefer Klausner* (Josef Klausner Jubilee Volume), Jerusalem, pp. 302–12.
73. "סכסוך תקהלות בוירונה עפ"י תשובת ר' מרדכי בשאן בסוף המאה השבע עשרה" (A Communal Controversy in Verona), in *Sefer ha-Yobel le-Professor Shemuel Krauss*, Jerusalem, pp. 217–54. Also reprint with 2 pages of corrections.
74. Review of Fritz Baer, *Die Juden im christlichen Spanien.* Erster Teil, Urkunden und Regesten. Zweiter Band, Kastilien, Inquisitionsakten (Berlin, 1936). In *American Historical Review*, XLIII, No. 1 (October), 101–3.

1938

75. "A propos de mon 'A Social and Religious History of the Jews,' " *REJ*, N. S., IV (CIV), Nos. 1–2 (July–December), 139–46. Answer to Solomon Zeitlin's review, *ibid.*, N. S., II, 141–43.
76. "Democracy and Judaism," *Hadassah Newsletter*, January, pp. 66–67.
77. "Freedom and Constraint in the Jewish Community," in *Essays and Studies in Memory of Linda R. Miller*, New York, pp. 9–23.
78. "The Jewish Question in the Nineteenth Century," *Journal of Modern History*, X, No. 1 (March), 51–65.
79. "Palestine and the Refugee Problem," *Story Behind the Headlines*, December 6, 23 pp. [Collaborated with Caesar Searchinger's broadcast.]
80. "לתולדות ההשכלה והחינוך בווינה" (A Study in the History of Jewish Enlightenment and Education in Vienna), in *Sepher Touroff Anniversary Volume*, New York, pp. 167–83, 374–79.
81. "סאציאל־רעליגעזע פארשונגען אין אידישער געשיכטע" (Socioreligious Research in Jewish History: A Lecture), *Di Zukunft*, XLIII, No. 5 (June), 341–47.
82. Review of Isaac Da Costa, *Noble Families among Sephardic Jews* (New York, 1936). In *American Historical Review*, XLIII, No. 3 (April), 608–10.
83. Review of Franz Kobler, *Juden und Judentum in deutschen Briefen aus*

drei Jahrhunderten (Vienna, 1935). In *Historia Judaica*, I, No. 1 (November), 74–75.

1939

84. "Emphases in Jewish History," *Jewish Social Studies* (*JSS*), I, No. 1 (January), 15–38. Appeared also in *Jewish Education*, XI, No. 1 (April), 8–22; and, with some variations, in *JSSQ*, XV, No. 2 (December 1938), 219–35.
85. "Cultural Problems of American Jewry," in *Harry L. Glucksman Annual Lectures*, No. 1, New York: Jewish Welfare Board, pp. 16–26. Also appeared in *Jewish Center*, XVII, No. 2 (June), 7–11.
86. "משה כהן בעלאינפאנטע א משכיל פון נאפאלעאנס צייטן" (Moses Cohen Belinfante, a Maskil of the Napoleonic Period), *Jiwobleter*, XIII, Nos. 5–6 [Wachstein Memorial Volume] (September–October), 429–59. An abridged transl. under the title of "Un iluminista sefardi de la época napoleonica" appeared in *Judaica*, VII, Nos. 73–75 (July–September), 68–77.
87. Review of Mortimer Cohen, *Jacob Emden: A Man of Controversy* (Philadelphia, 1937). In *JSS*, I, No. 4 (October), 483–87. Supplemented by comments of author and reviewer, *ibid.*, II, No. 1 (January 1940), 117–23.
88. Review of Sigmund Freud, *Moses and Monotheism* (New York, 1939). In *American Journal of Sociology*, XLV, No. 3 (November), 471–77.
89. Review of Jewish Historical Society of England, *Transactions, 1932–35* (London, 1936); and *Miscellanies*, Vol. III (London, 1937). In *JSS*, I, No. 4 (October), 467–69.
90. Review of Jacob R. Marcus, *The Jew in the Medieval World, a Source Book, 315–1791* (Cincinnati, 1938). In *American Historical Review*, XLIV, No. 2 (January), 421–22.
91. Review of *Occident and Orient* (ed. by Bruno Schindler and A. Marmorstein). Studies in honor of Haham Dr. M. Gaster's 80th Birthday (London, 1936). In *JSS*, I, No. 3 (July), 370–73.
92. Review of James Parkes, *The Jew in the Medieval Community* (London, 1938). In *MJ*, XXVII, No. 1, 102–7.
93. Review of Hans Zucker, *Studien zur jüdischen Selbstverwaltung im Altertum* (Berlin, 1936). In *JSS*, I, No. 2 (April), 264–65.
94. Booknote on Joshua Bloch, *Early Hebrew Printing in Spain and Portugal* (New York, 1938). In *JSS*, I, No. 3 (July), 391–92.
95. Booknote on Ernst Hoffman, *Die Liebe zu Gott bei Moses Ben Maimon* (Breslau, 1937). In *JSS*, I, No. 3 (July), 391.
96. Booknote on W. O. E. Oesterley, *Sacrifices in Ancient Israel* (New York), 1938). In *JSS*, I, No. 3 (July), 389–90.
97. Booknote on Michael Traub, *Die jüdische Auswanderung aus Deutschland*, etc. (Berlin, 1936). In *JSS*, I, No. 3 (July), 392.

1940

98. "Bibliography of Jewish Social Studies, 1938–39," *JSS*, II, No. 3 (July), 305–88; No. 4 (October), pp. 481–605.

99. "The Future of European Jewry," *Jewish Forum*, XXIII, No. 9 (October), 164–65, 171. A radio address.

100. "Great Britain and Damascus Jewry in 1860–61 — an Archival Study," *JSS*, II, No. 2 (April), 179–208.

101. Necrology: Zevi Diesendruck, *PAAJR*, X, 3–4 (signed by Salo W. Baron and Shalom Spiegel).

102. Necrology: Zevi Diesendruck, *American Historical Review*, XLVI, 255–56.

103. "Reflections on the Future of the Jews of Europe," *Contemporary Jewish Record*, III (July–August), 355–69. Appeared also, with some variations, in *JSSQ*, Vol. XX.

104. "על שיטתו ההיסטורית של שמעון דובנוב" (Simon Dubnow's Historical Approach), *Bitzaron*, II, No. 3 (December), 212–15.

105. Review of Louis Finkelstein, *The Pharisees* (2 vols., Philadelphia, 1938). In *Review of Religion*, IV, No. 2 (January), 196–99.

106. Another review of the same work. In *JBL*, LIX, No. 1 (March), 60–67.

107. Review of *Judaism and Christianity*, 3 vols., ed. by W. O. E. Oesterley, H. Loewe, and Erwin I. J. Rosenthal (New York, 1937–38). In *American Historical Review*, XLV, No. 2 (January), 358–61.

108. Review of *Letters to Emma Lazarus*, ed. by Ralph L. Rusk (New York, 1939). In *JSS*, II, No. 1 (January), 108–9.

109. Review of מסעות חבשוש, transl. by S. D. Goitein from Arabic into Hebrew (Tel-Aviv, 1939). In *JSS*, II, No. 2 (April), 226–27.

110. Review of Manfred Reifer, *Ausgewählte historische Schriften* (Cernauti, 1938). In *JSS*, II, No. 2 (April), 220.

111. Review of Cecil Roth, *Magna bibliotheca Anglo-Judaica* (London, 1937). In *JSS*, II, No. 1 (January), 97–99.

112. Review of *Scritti in Onore di Dante Lattes*, ed. by Guido Bedarida (Città di Castella, 1938). In *JSS*, II, No. 2 (April), 223–26.

113. Review of Oskar Wolfsberg, *Zur Zeit- und Geistesgeschichte des Judentums* (Zurich, 1938). In *Historia Judaica*, II, No. 2 (October), 119–20.

114. Booknote on Saul Mézan, *De Gabirol à Abravanel* (Paris, 1936). In *JSS*, II, No. 1 (January), 113.

115. Booknote on D. Sidersky, *Quelques portraits de nos maîtres des études semitiques* (Paris, 1937). In *JSS*, II, No. 1 (January), 112–13.

116. Booknote on הרפתקאותיו של אשר הלוי: ספר–מסעות כתוב בידי עצמו (Book of Travels Written by Himself), ed. by Abraham Yaari (Jerusalem, 1938). In *JSS*, II, No. 1 (January), 114.

117. Introduction to Manoah L. Bialik, *The Cooperative Credit Movement in Palestine*, Ann Arbor, Michigan.

1941

118. *Bibliography of Jewish Social Studies, 1938–39*. New York. Jewish Social Studies, Publications, No. 1, iv + 291 pp. Revised edition of no. 97 with Additions, Corrections, and Index, pp. 213–91.

119. Ed., *Essays on Maimonides; an Octocentennial Volume*. New York: Columbia University Press.

120. "The Economic Views of Maimonides," in *Essays on Maimonides*, pp. 127–264.

121. "Maimonides, the Leader and Lawgiver," in *Essays on Maimonides*, pp. 12–18.

122. "Rashi and the Community of Troyes," in *Rashi Anniversary Volume* of the American Academy for Jewish Research (Texts and Studies, I), New York, pp. 47–71.

123. "Yehudah Halevi: An Answer to a Historic Challenge," *JSS*, III, No. 3 (July), 243–72.

124. Review of Albert M. Hyamson, *The British Consulate in Jerusalem in Relation to the Jews of Palestine, 1838–1914* (London, 1939). In *JSS*, III, No. 3 (July), 343. See No. 138.

125. Review of *Jewish Theological Seminary*, ed. by Cyrus Adler (New York, 1939); and *The Hebrew University* (Jerusalem, 1939). In *JSS*, III, No. 1 (January), 99–102.

126. Review of Israel Klauzner, תולדות הקהילה העברית בווילנה (History of the Jewish Community in Wilno) (Wilno, 1938). In *JSS*, III, No. 4 (October), 419–20.

127. Review of Arthur Ruppin, *Jewish Fate and Future* (New York, 1940). In *Jewish Digest*, January, pp. 89–92.

128. Review of A. L. Sachar, *The Jew in the Cotenmporary World* (New York, 1939). In *American Historical Review*, XLVI, 455–56.

129. Review of Joseph Vogt, *Kaiser Julian und das Judentum* (Leipzig, 1939). In *JSS*, III, No. 2 (April), 220.

130. Booknote on Solomon F. Bloom, *World of Nations* (New York, 1941). In *JSS*, III, No. 4 (October), 438–39.

131. Booknote on H. Wheeler Robinson, *The History of Israel* (New York, 1938). In *JSS*, III, No. 1 (January), 118–19.

132. Booknote on Royal Institute of International Affairs, *Great Britain and Palestine, 1915–39* (London, 1939); and Ben M. Edidin, *Rebuilding Palestine* (New York, 1939). In *JSS*, III, No. 1 (January), 121–22.

133. Booknote on *Cultural Approaches to History*, ed. by Caroline F. Ware (New York, 1940). In *JSS*, III, No. 4 (October), 439–40.

1942

134. *The Jewish Community: Its History and Structure to the American Revolution.* 3 vols. Philadelphia: Jewish Publication Society of America. 1942–5702. The Morris Loeb Series. Pp. xii + 374; 366; 572. 2d Impression, 1945.

135. *American and Jewish Destiny: A Semimillennial Experience.* Address delivered under auspices of the Synagogue Council of America on Monday Evening, October 12, 1942, at Spanish and Portuguese Congregation Shearith Israel of New York. 12 pp.

136. *Effect of War on Jewish Community Life.* Harry L. Gluckman Memorial Lecture for 1942, New York. 15 pp.

137. ׳לתולדות החלוקה ופדיון השבויים במאה הי״ז״ (A Contribution to the History of Palestine Relief and the Ransom of Captives), *Sefer ha-Shanah*

li Yehude Amerika (American Hebrew Year Book), [VI], 5702, pp. 168–80.

138. "Jewish Factor in Medieval Civilization," *PAAJR*, XII, 1–48.
139. "Modern Capitalism and Jewish Fate," *MJ*, XXX, No. 2, 116–38.
140. "Prospects for Peace in Palestine," in *The Near East; Problems and Prospects*, ed. by Philip W. Ireland, Chicago (Lectures on the Harris Foundation), pp. 103–40.
141. "David Yellin" (Obituary). In *JSS*, IV, No. 2 (April), 191.
142. Correspondence, *JQR*, XXXII, No. 3 (January), 321–25. Answer to Zeitlin's revies of *Essays on Maimonides*, *ibid.*, No. 1, pp. 107–14.
143. Review of Cecil Roth, *A History of the Jews in England* (Oxford, 1941). In *Journal of Modern History*, XIV, 522–23. See also No. 145.
144. Review of *Transactions of the Jewish Historical Society of England, 1935–39*, Vol. XIV (London, 1940); and of Albert M. Hyamson, *The British Consulate in Jerusalem*, Part II (London, 1941). In *JSS*, IV, No. 4 (October), 403–7. Cf. Nos. 83 and 118.
145. Booknote on David Druck, *Yehuda Halevy* (New York, 1941). In *JSS*, IV, No. 3 (July), 286.
146. Booknote on George Vernadsky, *Bohdan, Hetman of Ukraine* (New Haven, 1941). In *JSS*, IV, No. 3 (July), 286.
147. Foreword to *Essays on Antisemitism*, ed. by Koppel S. Pinson. Jewish Social Studies, Publications, No. 2, New York.

1943

148. *Palestinian Messengers in America, 1849–79 . . . A Record of Four Journeys*. New York: Conference on Jewish Relations, 116 pp. Together with Jeannette M. Baron. Reprinted from *JSS*, Vol. V, Nos. 2–3.
149. *President's Report 1940–1943*. Conference on Jewish Relations, New York.
150. "Israel's Present" (Symposium on "Israel's Present and Future"), in *Man's Faith and This Crisis* (Addresses delivered at 38th Council of Union of American Hebrew Congregations, April 2–4, 1943), New York, pp. 78–82.
151. "Moses Cohen Belinfante: A Leader of Dutch-Jewish Enlightenment," *Historia Judaica*, V, No. 1 (April), 1–26. Revised transl. of No. 86 with supplementary documents.
152. ״לתולדות הישוב היהודי בטבריה בשנות תק״ב–ד״ (On the History of the Jewish Settlement in Tiberias in 1742–44), in *Sepher ha-Yobel*, a Tribute to Professor Alexander Marx, New York, pp. 79–88.
153. "Saadia's Communal Activities," in *Saadia Anniversary Volume* of the American Academy for Jewish Research (Texts and Studies, II), pp. 9–74.
154. Review of Cecil Roth, *A History of the Jews in England* (Oxford, 1941). In *JSS*, V, No. 1 (January), 61–63.
155. Review of יידן אין פראנקרייך (The Jews in France), ed. by E. Tcherikower (New York, 1942). In *JSS*, V, No. 1 (January), 67–70.
156. Booknote on *The Jewish Quarterly Review*, N. S., XXXIII, Nos. 2–3 (Saadia Anniversary Issue) (Philadelphia, 1943). In *JSS*, V, No. 4 (October), 408.

157. Booknote on F. A. Teilhaber, *The Graphic Historical Atlas of Palestine* (Tel-Aviv, 1941). In *JSS*, V, No. 4 (October), 407–8.

1944

158. "Migration Speeds Progress," *Rescue: Information Bulletin of the HIAS*, I, Nos. 3–4 (March-April), 3, 15–16.
159. "לתולדות קהלות קורפו וארגונן" (On the History of the Corfù Communities and Their Organization), in *Kobeṣ Madda'i*, Studies in Memory of Moses Schorr, ed. by Louis Ginzberg and Abraham Weiss, New York, pp. 25–41.
160. "Bernstein, Herman," *Dictionary of American Biography*, Vol. XXI, Supplement One, New York, pp. 77–79.
161. Review of ספר זכרון לאשר גולאק ולשמואל קליין ז"ל (Studies in Memory of Asher Gulak and Samuel Klein) (Jerusalem, 1942). In *JSS*, VI, No. 3 (July), 275–78.
162. Review of Hans Kohn, *The Idea of Nationalism* (New York, 1944). In *JSS*, VI, No. 4 (October), 408–11.

1945

163. "The Jewish Community of Tomorrow," in *Moral and Spiritual Foundations for the World of Tomorrow*. The Centenary Series of Addresses and Other Papers Prepared for the Celebration of the Hundredth Anniversary of Congregation Emanu-El, 1845–1945. New York, pp. 75–83.
164. "Levi Herzfeld, the First Jewish Economic Historian," in *Louis Ginzberg Jubilee Volume*. On the Occasion of His Seventieth Birthday, English section. New York, pp. 75–104.
165. "The Spiritual Reconstruction of European Jewry," *Commentary*, I, No. 1 (November), 4–12. Appeared also in a different form in the *Yearbook of the Central Conference of American Rabbis*, LV, 193–206.
166. Booknote on Henry Charles Lea, *Minor Historical Writings and Other Essays*, ed. by Arthur C. Howland (Philadelphia, 1942). In *JSS*, VII, No. 1 (January), 94.

1946

167. Foreword to *Essays on Antisemitism*, ed. by Koppel S. Pinson. Second edition, revised and enlarged. Jewish Social Studies, Publications, No. 2, New York.

1947

168. *Modern Nationalism and Religion*. The Rauschenbusch Lectures for 1944 (Colgate-Rochester Divinity School, Rochester, N. Y.). New York: Harper and Brothers. Pp. x + 363.

169. *President's Report 1943–1946.* Conference on Jewish Relations, New York.

170. "How S. A. Jewry Should Plan Its Future," *Jewish Affairs*, II, No. 4 (April), 4–9.

171. "Prospects for the Diaspora," *New Palestine*, XXXVII, No. 20 (June 20), 143–46.

172. "Work Among Our Youth," *Proceedings Canadian Jewish Congress of the Plenary Session, May 31 June 2, 1947*, Montreal, pp. 55, 61–64.

173. "The Year in Retrospect," *American Jewish Yearbook*, XLIX (1947–48), 103–22.

174. Opening Address at JWB Annual Meeting in Pittsburgh, May 10, 1947 (Chairman of Survey Commission). In JWB *Circle*, II, No. 6, pp. 5, 14.

175. Booknote on George Antonius, *The Arab Awakening: The Story of the Arab National Movement* (New York, 1946). In *JSS*, IX, No. 2 (April), 191–92.

176. Booknote on Corliss Lamont, *Peoples of the Soviet Union* (New York, 1946). In *JSS*, IX, No. 2 (April), 190–91.

177. Booknote on C. J. Friedrich, *American Policy toward Palestine* (Washington, D. C., American Council on Public Affairs, 1944). In *Journal of Modern History*, XIX, 386.

1948

178. *The Jewish Community and Jewish Education.* American Association for Jewish Education, New York, 17 pp. Also appeared in *Jewish Education*, XIX, No. 2 (March), 7–13, 42. (Paper read before a special session on "Communal Responsibility for Jewish Education" at a meeting of the Board of Governors of the American Association for Jewish Education in New York City, October 19, 1947.)

179. Foreword to "Religion and Democracy," Papers from the University Seminar on Religion, Columbia University, 1946–47, *Review of Religion*, January, p. 116.

180. Review of Mordecai M. Kaplan, *The Future of the American Jew* (New York, 1948). In New York *Times*, Book Review, May 2, p. 12.

181. Review of James Parkes, *The Emergence of the Jewish Problem 1878–1939* (London, 1946, under the auspices of the Royal Institute of International Affairs). In *Middle East Journal*, II (January), 96–97.

182. Booknote on Kuno Trau and Michael Karyan, אדם בעולם צבי פרץ חיות (Biographical Sketch of H. P. Chajes) (Tel-Aviv, 1947). In *JSS*, X, No. 1 (January), 97–98.

183. Introduction to *Tentative List of Jewish Publishers of Judaica and Hebraica in Axis Occupied Countries.* Supplement to *JSS*, X, No. 2 (April), 5–7.

184. Letter of Transmittal to Frank L. Weil, in *JWB Survey*, by O. I. Janowsky, New York: The Dial Press, pp. vii–ix.

1949

185. "A Diplomatic Episode in the Spanish-Portuguese Community of London (1841)," *Bulletin Congregation Habonim*, IX, No. 9 (September), 12–16.

Issue dedicated to Dr. Adolf Kober on occasion of his 70th Birthday. Mimeographed.

186. "The Impact of the Revolution of 1848 on Jewish Emancipation," *JSS*, XI, No. 3 (July), 195–248.
187. "The Revolution of 1848 and Jewish Scholarship, Part I," *PAAJR*, XVIII, 1–66.
188. Review of Arnold J. Toynbee, *Civilization on Trial* (New York, 1948). In *Political Science Quarterly*, LXIV, No. 1 (March), 110–13.
189. Review of Chaim Weizmann, *Trial and Error* (2 vols., New York, 1949) In New York *Times*, Book Review, January 23, p. 1.

1950

190. "American Jewish History: Problems and Methods," *Publications of the American Jewish Historical Society* (*PAJHS*), XXXIX, No. 3 (March), 207–66.
191. "Moritz Steinschneider's Contribution to Jewish Historiography," in *Alexander Marx Jubilee Volume*, New York, pp. 83–148.
192. "Opening Remarks" to the Conference on "Problems of Research in the Study of the Jewish Catastrophe 1939–45" held at the New School for Social Research, New York City. In *JSS*, XII, No. 1 (January), 13–16.

1951

193. "New Horizons in Jewish History," in *Freedom and Reason: Studies in Philosophy and Jewish Culture in Memory of Morris Raphael Cohen*, Glencoe, Ill., pp. 337–53.
194. "The Revolution of 1848 and Jewish Scholarship, Part II," *PAAJR*, XX, 1–100.
195. Review of Ben Zion Bokser, *The Legacy of Maimonides* (New York, Philosophical Library, 1950). In New York *Times*, Book Review, February 18, p. 25.
196. Review of Saul Lieberman, *Hellenism in Jewish Palestine: Studies in the Literary Transmission Beliefs and Manners of Palestine in the I Century B. C.E-IV Century C. E.* (Texts and Studies of the Jewish Theological Seminary of America, Vol. XVIII, New York, 1950). In New York *Times*, Book Review, July 29, p. 7.
197. Review of Cecil Roth, *The Great Synagogue, London, 1690–1940* (London, 1950). In *JSS*, XIII, No. 3 (July), 261–62.
198. Review of Jean Stengers, *Les Juifs dans les pays-bas au moyen-âge* (Académie Royale de Belgique, Classe des lettres, et des sciences morales et politiques, Mémoires, XLV, 2, Brussels, 1950). In *Speculum*, XXVI, No. 2 (April), 407–9.
199. Review of *A Documentary History of the Jews in the United States 1654–1875*, ed. by Morris U. Schappes (New York, 1950). In *JSS*, XIII, No. 1 (January), 77–80.
200. Review of R. Walzer, *Galen on Jews and Christians* (London, 1949,

Oxford Classical and Philosophical Monographs). In *Journal of the History of Medicine and Allied Sciences*, VI, 428–29.

201. Booknote on Louis Gottschalk, *Understanding History; a Primer of Historical Method* (New York, 1950). In *JSS*, XIII, No. 3 (July), 280–81.
202. Booknote on *Hitler Directs His War; the Secret Records of His Daily Military Conferences, Selected and Annotated . . . from the Manuscript in the University of Pennsylvania Library*, ed. by Felix Gilbert (New York, 1950). In *JSS*, XIII, No. 3 (July), 283.
203. Booknote on Jacques Petitpierre, *The Romance of the Mendelssohns* (New York, 1950). In *JSS*, XIII, No. 3 (July), 282.
204. Booknote on Walter A. Kaufmann, *Nietzsche: Philosopher, Psychologist, Anti-Christ* (Princeton, 1950). In *JSS*, XIII, No. 3 (July), 283–84.
205. Booknote on Manfred Reifer, *Dr. Mayer Ebner, ein juedisches Leben* (Tel-Aviv, 1949). In *JSS*, XIII, No. 3 (July), 284–85.
206. Booknote on *South African Jews in World War II* (Published by the South African Jewish Board of Deputies, Johannesburg, 1950). In *JSS*, XIII, No. 3 (July), 285–86.

1952

207. *A Social and Religious History of the Jews.* Second edition, revised and enlarged. Vols. I–II: Ancient Times. New York: Columbia University Press, and Philadelphia: The Jewish Publication Society of America. Pp. ix + 415; vi + 493.
208. "Aspects of the Jewish Communal Crisis in 1848," *JSS*, XIV, No. 2 (April), 99–144.
209. "Hebrew Civilization," *Encyclopedia Americana* (1952) under *Middle East*, Section No. 5, Vol. XIX, 38k-38n. Also in *Background of the Middle East*, Cornell University Press. Chap. V, pp. 33–42.
210. "Impact of Wars on Religion," *Political Science Quarterly*, LXVII, No. 4 (December), 534–72.
211. "A Revolutionary Transformation of Jewish Community," *ADL Bulletin*, May, p. 2.
212. Review of Rufus Learsi, *Fulfillment: The Epic Story of Zionism* (Cleveland and New York, 1951). In *Saturday Review*, April 12, p. 37.
213. Review of Malcolm Hay, *The Foot of Pride* (Boston, 1950); and Ludwig Lewisohn, *The American Jew: Character and Destiny* (New York, 1950). In *New Republic*, January 21, pp. 19–20.
214. Booknote on Moses Hadas, *A History of Greek Literature* (New York, 1950); and *A History of Latin Literature* (New York, 1952). In *JSS*, XIV, No. 3, (July), 277–78.

1953

215. "Church and State Debates in the Jewish Community of 1848," in *Mordecai M. Kaplan Jubilee Volume*, the Jewish Theological Seminary of America, New York, pp. 49–72.
216. "The Cold War and Jewry," *American Zionist*, Abba Hillel Silver Anniversary Issue, XLIII, No. 7 (February 5), 21–24.
217. "Jewish Immigration and Communal Conflicts in Seventeenth-Century

Corfù," in *The Joshua Starr Memorial Volume: Studies in History and Philology*. Jewish Social Studies, Publications, No. 5, New York, Conference on Jewish Relations, pp. 169–82.

218. "שד"ל והמהפכה בשנות התר"ח–ט" (Samuel David Luzzatto and the Revolution of 1848), *Sefer Assaf*, pp. 40–63.

219. Review of Israel Cohen, *Contemporary Jewry, a Survey of Social, Cultural, Economic and Political Conditions* (London, 1950). in *JSS* XV, No. 1 (January), 90–92.

220. Review of Gerald de Gaury, *The New State of Israel* (New York, 1952). In *Political Science Quarterly*, LXVIII, No. 2 (June), 287-88.

221. Review of David Hedegard, *Seder R. Amram Gaon*, Part. I. Hebrew Text with Critical Apparatus Translation with Notes and Introduction (Motala, Sweden, 1951). In *JSS*, XV, No. 2 (April), 178–79.

222. Review of Simha (Simone) Luzzatto, מאמר על יהודי ויניציה (Discourse on the Status of Jews in Venice), translated from the Italian by Dante Lattes, with introduction by Riccardo Benjamin Bachi and M. S. Shulvass, edited by the late A. Z. Aeshcoly (Jerusalem, Sifriah historiografit [Historiographic Library], Mosad Bialik, 1951). In *JSS*, XV, Nos. 3–4 (July–October), 313–14.

223. Review of Abraham A. Neuman, *Landmarks and Goals: Historical Studies and Addresses* (Philadelphia, Dropsie College Press, 1953). In New York *Times*, Book Review, October 25, p. 46.

224. Booknote on Ray Allen Billington, *The Protestant Crusade 1800–1860: The Growth of Bigotry and the Anti-Catholic Movement in America* (New York, 1938; second printing, 1952). In *JSS*, XV, Nos. 3–4 (July-October), 331–32.

225. Booknote on S. G. F. Brandon, *The Fall of Jerusalem and the Christian Church: A Study of the Effects of the Jewish Overthrow of A.D. 70 on Christianity* (London, Society for the Promotion of Christian Knowledge, 1951). In *JSS*, XV, No. 1 (January), 93.

226. Booknote on Zevi (Hirsch) Perez Chayes, נאומים והרצאות (Addresses and Lectures) (Boston, Hebrew Teachers College, 1953). In *JSS*, XV, Nos. 3–4 (July–October), 329.

227. Booknote on William Chomsky, *David Kimhi's Hebrew Grammar (Mikhlol): Systematically Presented and Critically Annotated* (New York, 1952). In *JSS*, XV, Nos. 3–4 (July–October), 328.

228. Booknote on Frank S. Mead, *Handbook of Denominations in the United States* (New York and Nashville, 1951). In *JSS*, XV, Nos. 3–4 (July October), 332.

229. Booknote on Manfred Reifer, *Menschen und Ideen. Erinnerungen* (Tel-Aviv, n.d.). In *JSS*, XV, Nos. 3–4 (July–October), 329.

230. Booknote on Priscilla Robertson, *Revolutions of 1848: A Social History* (Princeton, 1952). In *JSS*, XV, Nos. 3–4 (July–October), 330.

1954

231. *Historic Jerusalem: City Holy and Eternal.* New York: Hemisphere Publications, Inc. Pp. 32 + 63 plates.

232. *Judaism: Postbiblical and Talmudic Period* (in collaboration with Joseph L. Blau). Library of Religion, Series of Readings in Sacred Scriptures and Basic Writings of the World's Religions, Past and Present, New York: Liberal Arts Press. Pp. xxvi + 245.

233. "American Jewish Communal Pioneering," Presidential Address, American Jewish Historical Society, February 20, 1954, *PAJHS*, XLIII, No. 3 (March), 133–50. Also appeared in Yiddish transl. in *Zunkunft*, LIX, 251–59.

234. "עתידה של יהדות אמריקה" (The Future of American Jewry), *Gesher*, Nos. 2–3, pp. 9–17.

235. "אמונה והיסטוריה בתולדות ישראל" (Faith and History in the Jewish Past), *Megillot*, March, pp. 5–14.

236. Address: "Report on Israel," delivered at Fourth Session, Part II, Saturday morning, March 7, 1953, Seventh Annual Conference on Middle East Affairs sponsored by the Middle East Institute. Published in *Evolution in the Middle East-Reform, Revolt and Change*, Washington, D. C., pp. 77–85.

237. "Three Hundred Years of American Jewry," "*300*," September, pp. 3, 5.

238. "Eugen Täubler," *PAAJR*, XXII, 1953 (appeared early in 1954), pp. xxxi–xxxiv (cosigner, Ralph Marcus).

239. Review of Oscar Handlin, *Adventure in Freedom*, and Rufus Learsi, *The Jews in America: A History*. In New York *Times*, Book Review, September 12, p. 6.

240. Foreword to Stuart Rosenberg, *The Jewish Community in Rochester, 1843–1925*, New York.

241. Foreword to Arnold Wiznitzer, *The Records of the Earliest Jewish Community in the New World*, New York.

1955

242. *Are the Jews Still the People of the Book?* Oscar Hillel Plotkin Lecture, 1955, Glencoe, Ill.

243. **היסטוריה חברותית ודתית של עם ישראל** (Tel-Aviv, Massada, 1955–). Vol. I (Translation of *A Social and Religious History of the Jews*, second edition.)

244. "Some of the Tercentenary's Historic Lessons," *PAJHS*, No. 44 (June), pp. 199–209.

245. "President's Report 1953–1955," *PAJHS*, No. 44 (June), pp. 243–47.

246. Review of Erwin R. Goodenough, *Jewish Symbols in the Greco-Roman Period* (New York, 1953, Bollingen Series XXXVII). Vol. I: The Archeological Evidence from Palestine; Vol. II: The Archeological Evidence from the Diaspora; Vol. III: Illustrations. In *JBL*, LXXIV, 196–99.

247. Review of Moses Hadas, *Third and Fourth Books of the Maccabees* (New York, Dropsie College Edition, Jewish Apocryphal Literature, (1953). In *JBL*, LXXIV, 280–81.

248. **היסטוריה חברותית ודתית של עם ישראל** (Tel-Aviv, Massada, 1956). Vol. II (Translation of *A Social and Religious History of the Jews*, second edition). 230 pp.

249. *Histoire d'Israël vie sociale et religieuse* (Paris, Presses Universitaires de France). Vol. I (French translation of *A Social and Religious History of the Jews*). 589 pp.

1956

250. *Great Ages and Ideas of the Jewish People*, by Salo W. Baron [and others], ed. by Leo W. Schwarz. New York, Random House. Pp. xxvi + 515.
251. "The Emancipation Movement and American Jewry" (Hebrew), in *Eretz-Israel*, Vol. IV (Ben Zvi Jubilee Volume), Jerusalem, Israel Exploration Society, pp. 205–14.
252. "Maimonides' Significance to Our Generation," in *Maimonides: His Teachings and Personality*. ed. by Simon Federbusch, New York, pp. 7–16.
253. "Second and Third Commonwealth: Parallels and Differences," in *Israel: Its Role in Civilization*, ed. by Moshe Davis, New York, pp. 58–66.
254. "A Vilna Excommunication and the Great Powers" (Hebrew), *Horeb*, XII (September), pp. 62–69.
255. Review of Izhak Ben-Zvi, *Eres-Yisrael ve-Yishubah bi-yeme ha-shilton ha-'otmani* (Eretz-Israel under Ottoman Rule: Four Centuries of History) (Jerusalem, 1955). In *Middle Eastern Affairs*, VII, Nos. 8–9 (August-September), 302.
256. Review of Justine Wise Polier and James Waterman Wise, eds., *The Personal Letters of Stephen Wise* (Boston, 1956). In New York *Times*, Book Review, July 8, p. 18.

1957–58

257. *Histoire d'Israël vie sociale et religieuse* (Paris, Presses Universitaires de France). Vol. II (French translation of *A Social and Religious History of the Jews*). 727 pp.
258. היסטוריה חבדותית ורתית של עם ישראל (Tel-Aviv, Massada, 1957), Vol. III (Translation of *A Social and Religious History of the Jews*, second edition). 254 pp.
259. *A Social and Religious History of the Jews*. Second edition, revised and enlarged. Vols. III–VIII: High Middle Ages, 500–1200. Vol. III: Heirs of Rome and Persia. Vol. IV: Meeting of East and West. Vol. V: Religious Controls and Dissensions. Vol. VI: Laws, Homilies, and the Bible. Vol. VII: Hebrew Language and Letters. Vol. VIII: Philosophy and Science. New York: Columbia University Press, and Philadelphia: The Jewish Publication Society of America. Pp. xii + 340; vi + 352; vi + 416; vi + 486; vi + 321; vi + 405.

ESSAYS
ON JEWISH LIFE
AND THOUGHT

THE CORRESPONDENCE OF TOBIAS BEN MOSES THE KARAITE OF CONSTANTINOPLE

By Zvi Ankori

FOR LACK OF documentary evidence stemming directly from the Karaite communities in the Empire, the prevailing reconstruction of early Karaite history in Byzantium had to rely solely on casual historical references in the literary productions of the sect and on testimonies of later Karaite authorities. The former, however, did not make their appearance on Byzantine soil before the second half of the eleventh century, whereas the latter were, oftener than not, based on mere inferences from rather inferior manuscript materials,[1] as well as on traditions which, when submitted to closer scrutiny, proved to be of dubious authenticity.[2]

A tradition of this kind, embodied in a statement by the fifteenth-century "last codifier" of Karaite lore, Elijah Bashyachi,[3] credits Tobias

[1] The deterioration of Byzantine Karaite manuscripts in the later Middle Ages can be gauged, for instance, from the sorry condition of the one and only MS of Hadassi's twelfth-century encyclopedic opus *Eshkol hak-Kofer*, as reported by Shabbetai of Pravado, who copied the book in 1482, and by Kaleb Afendopolo, who compiled an index to it in 1497. Cf. Shabbetai's account in Frankl's "Karäische Studien," *MGWJ*, XXXI (1882), 271, and Afendopolo's introduction, *Naḥal ha-Eshkol*, fol. lc-d, preceding the Gozlow edition of Hadassi's work. The inferior quality of the MS material at hand was held responsible by Frankl for the chronological error committed by Bashyachi and others with reference to Nisi b. Noaḥ. Cf. his Hebrew critique in *Hashshaḥar*, VIII (1876-77), 182. The misrepresentations, committed for the same reason in regard to the literary activity of the eleventh-century Tobias b. Moses, have been listed in my Hebrew essay on "Elijah Bashyachi: An Inquiry into His Traditions concerning the Beginnings of Karaism in Byzantium," *Tarbiz*, XXV (1955-56), 44-65, 183-201 (with an English résumé).

[2] Most drastic examples of such traditions are, of course, the various accounts of the antiquity of the sect, or, in a different direction, the claim that Abraham b. Ezra was the pupil of the late tenth-century Eastern Karaite exegete Yefeth b. ʻAlī. Surely, hardly any purpose is served, from the point of view of historical research, in merely recording lack of historical sense and exaggerated absorption in matters of law and ritual on the part of the Karaites. While it is the duty of the modern student to unravel these distortions of history, the distortions become in themselves a historical factor worthy of consideration.

[3] See on him Markon, *Enc. Judaica (EJ)*, III, 1130-32, and most recently Leon

ben Moses—variously called "the Mourner," "the Servant," "the Proficient," "the Translator"—with the distinction of having carried Byzantine Karaism into the light of history.[4] It asserts, in effect, that this Karaite disciple from Constantinople introduced in Byzantium, by way of Hebrew translations from the Arabic, the bulk of Karaite teachings which he acquired during years of study at the Sectarian Academy in Jerusalem, notably under the guidance of the great Yeshūʻah ben Yehūdah.[5] Coupled with a somewhat mechanical juxtaposition to the frequently quoted report by the twelfth-century Abraham ibn Daūd on the establishment of the sect in Spain, allegedly by another pupil of Yeshūʻah,[6] and blended with unwarranted textual deductions, this tradition has strongly colored the conception of Byzantine Karaite beginnings as subsequently expounded by modern students of Karaism.[7]

The preponderant interest in the *literary* expressions of the sect's ways and beliefs dwarfed into pitiful insignificance the exasperatingly inadequate number—three in all—of Genizah documents pertaining to the *preliterary* stage of Byzantine Karaism. Thus, the casual bit of information, published almost half a century ago, about Karaite captives from Byzantium ransomed in Egypt as early as 1028 C.E., remains to this day a barren chronological curio, dutifully repeated in major studies, yet with no serious bearing on the subsequent literary-historical accounts.[8]

Nemoy, in his brief introduction to an English selection from Bashyachi's writings, *Karaite Anthology* (New Haven, 1952), pp. 236 ff. Cf. also my Hebrew sketch in *Enṣiḳlopedyah ʻIvrith* (Enc. Hebraica), Vol. IX, *s.v.*

[4] האבל, העובד, הבקי, המעתיק. For a résumé of Tobias's literary activity, see Poznański, *Oṣar Yisrael*, V, 12a-14a. The most important additions to the bibliography given there are, of course, Mann's occasional references to Tobias in his two volumes of *Texts and Studies* (Cincinnati, 1931-35); consult index at the end of Vol. II, p. 1591, *s.v.* Tob. b. Moses, Kar. scholar.

[5] For quotation and full discussion of the statement by Elijah Bashyachi in *Iggereth Gid han-Nasheh* (preceding the Gozlow edition of his code *Addereth Eliyyahū*) and for a critical evaluation of the authenticity of traditions reported by this sage, consult my Hebrew essay cited above, end of note 1. On the Karaite Center in Jerusalem in the period under review see Poznański, "Beginnings of Karaite Settlement in Jerusalem" (Hebrew), in Luncz's *Jerusalem*, X (1913), 83 ff., and, ultimately, Mann's "The Karaite Settlement in Palestine till the First Crusade," *Texts and Studies*, II, 3 ff. For a summary of Yeshūʻah's activities, see Markon, *EJ*, IX, 42 f.; also the recent popular introduction by Nemoy to his English translation of excerpts from Yeshūʻah's writings, *Karaite Anthology*, pp. 123 ff.

[6] *Seder haḳ-Ḳabbalah* in *Medieval Jewish Chronicles*, ed. Adolf Neubauer (2 vols., Oxford, 1887-95), I, 79. For a critique of this historical analogy see the closing sections of my aforementioned Hebrew study.

[7] See ultimately Mann, *Texts and Studies*, II, 3, 287, and *passim.*

[8] A. Cowley, "Bodleian Genizah Fragments—IV," *JQR* (O.S.), XIX (1906), 250-54; Joshua Starr, *Jews in the Byzantine Empire* (Athens, 1939), pp. 190 f., No. 132. For

Similarly, two epistles from the pen of Tobias ben Moses himself, brought to light within the last three decades, were not even utilized later by the very scholar who edited one of them and interpreted both for the first time. His summary of early Byzantine experience in the life story of Karaism does not mention the correspondence at all.[9]

In the light of this hardly satisfactory situation in Byzantine Karaite historical research[10] an attempt will be made here to reinterpret and reappraise the two Genizah epistles just mentioned, without however engaging in a critical appreciation of Tobias's somewhat more familiar literary activity. The revealing insights into the writer's personality that these letters afford, the unexpected glimpses they allow into the initial successes and setbacks of his communal career, the disclosures that they offer of his unsuspected connections with Rabbanites and his feuds with fellow Karaites in Palestine and Egypt, and, first and above all, the weighty chronological clues they indirectly convey make the correct understanding and dating of these letters crucial for the reconstruction and historical evaluation of early Byzantine Karaism.[11]

Letter I (MS 12.347 of the Taylor-Schechter Collection in Cambridge) was published for the first time by J. Mann in his *Texts and Studies*, Vol. I (1931), pp. 383-85, and interpreted there, pp. 372-74, jointly with Letter II, which was edited still earlier (1927) by R. Gottheil and W. H. Worrell as Nos. XXXI and XXXII of the *Fragments from the Cairo Genizah in the Freer Collection*, pp. 142-49, along with facsimiles, scanty

---

a discussion of content and background see Jacob Mann, *The Jews in Egypt and Palestine under the Fāṭimid Caliphs* (2 vols., London, 1920-22), I, 87 ff. (esp. p. 89); Mann, *Texts and Studies*, II, 287; Starr, *Jews in the Byzantine Empire*, pp. 32, 242 (App. A), and "The Place-Name Italya-Antaliyah," *Rivista degli Studi Orientali*, XVII (1937-38), 475 ff.

[9] Bibliographical details concerning the Genizah epistles in question are offered at the end of the present introduction. The corresponding references given by Starr in App. A to his *Jews in the Byzantine Empire*, p. 242, have to be reversed. An excerpt from the first of the said epistles was included by Assaf-Mayer in *Sefer hay-Yishshūb*, II, 47a, No. 20. The summary by Mann appears in his *Texts and Studies*, II, 287-93, of which the first page only is devoted to the eleventh century.

[10] The 18-line paragraph on the Karaites in Samuel Krauss's *Studien zur byzantinisch-jüdischen Geschichte* (Leipzig, 1914), p. 98, does not deal with the early stages at all. Mann's résumé was cited in the preceding note. Starr's two-and-a-half page appendix on the "Karaites in the Empire," *Jews in the Byzantine Empire*, pp. 242-44, is, in a way, the best available summary of conclusions reached so far in the field of Byzantine Karaite research, although some of its details need rectification.

[11] The conclusions reached here are utilized in this writer's *Karaites in Byzantium: The Formative Years (970-1100)* (Jerusalem and New York, 1959), prepared as a doctoral dissertation under the guidance of Professor Salo W. Baron at Columbia University.

notes, and an English translation. Mann later added some corrections to the Gottheil-Worrell edition (pp. 373 f., n. 3); these have been partly incorporated in our reading here. In the Appendix to the present study the pertinent texts have been conveniently assembled and reedited. The new readings and restorations are based on a photostatic copy of Letter I from the Cambridge University Library as well as on a reexamination of the original manuscripts of Letter II in the Freer Collection in Washington.[12]

I

Whereas in Letter I the person of the writer and of the addressee and their respective whereabouts do not leave room for doubt (Tobias "the Mourner" of Jerusalem to Rabbi Peraḥ ben Mūmal or Muammil in Fusṭāṭ), an identification is necessary in regard to the correspondents of Letter II. Though the editors of the fragments did not venture any suggestion as to the identity of the writer, Mann's solution can be accepted without reservations. True, the name "Ṭobiyah" appears both in the introduction (B/I/6-10, acrostic) and in the business part of the letter (B/I/21) accompanied by no further details; yet, on the basis of context, epigraphy, and circumstantial evidence it is quite plausible to identify this "Ṭobiyah" with the Byzantine Karaite Tobias ben Moses, the writer of Letter I. The country of provenance of the correspondent is very

[12] Letter I will be designated henceforth as A; when quoted, the number of the line (or lines) referred to will also be given. (Since the first line of the letter was omitted by Mann, there is a constant discrepancy of one between our references, which quote the edition offered in the Appendix to the present study, and the serial numbers of corresponding lines in Mann's reproduction.) Letter II, consisting of two leaves, will be designated as B/I and B/II, corresponding to Fragments XXXI and XXXII respectively of the Gottheil-Worrell edition. Separate numbering has been preserved for the quoted lines of each page. The two leaves, pasted together and prepared as one sheet *before* the writing was started, subsequently fell apart after the glue had dried out in the course of ages. This is clearly visible in the original MS. There is a pale, narrow stripe at the top of B/II, where B/I was originally pasted on; on the other hand, one has no difficulty in discovering at the bottom of B/I (which, as we know, overlapped B/II) the protruding limbs of two letters belonging to line 1 of B/II. This, incidentally, caused the first editors to misread that line and assume a (nonexistent) lacuna between the two leaves. The matter in general has already been recognized and rectified by Mann, *Texts and Studies*, I, 373 f., n. 3. Still, there must have been an additional sheet attached to the extant documents, for there is a specific mention in B/I/23-24 of "two columns," and the text in our possession is obviously incomplete. Since, however, the impression one gains from the last lines of the available text is that the end of the epistle is close at hand, one may assume that the missing sheet contained merely some wind-up phrases and greetings, as well as (unfortunately) the address, date, and full signature of the writer.

clearly stated: it is "The Land of Edom," i.e., the Byzantine Empire.[13] It is lovingly remembered as "my country," "my fatherland," and as the place where the writer's family still dwells, although he himself has been away for more than a year (B/II/12-13). In fact, the desire to return to that country is one of the motives which prompted Tobias to write his letter, and one of the things he asks of his benefactor is to procure the indispensable safe-conduct that will enable him to leave Egypt for his native land.

The recipient of the appeal is Abū Sa'ad ben Abū'l Fadhl Sahl (= Abraham ben Abī Ḥesed Yashar) at-Tustarī, whose generous contributions to the welfare of Jewish communities and individuals in distress are mentioned many a time in Genizah documents along with those of his brother Abū Naṣr Fadhl (= Ḥesed), the latter being referred to also in our Letter I. This famous Fusṭāṭ family has been the subject of studies, especially with regard to the controversial point of its religious and communal allegiance, and it is beyond the scope of this paper to elaborate on the matter.[14]

It is unfortunate that the closing part of Letter II is missing, thus

[13] For the identification of "Edom," in the early Byzantine Karaite literature, with Byzantium proper and not just with Christianity in general or with the Roman Empire at large, cf., e.g., Jacob ben Reuben's Commentary on Obadiah. On "The vision of Obadiah, thus saith the Lord God concerning Edom" (Ob. 1:1), Jacob remarks: "By this is meant Edom, to whom [or: whereto] the children of Esau [= Christians] have come and crowned him over them as king of *Greece*—and it is in regard to them that Obadiah had prophesied" (*Sefer ha-'Osher*, fol. 16c). Developing this identification further, Jacob comments on Ob. 1:3: "'[Whose habitation is] high'—i.e., Constantinople and Romania" (*ibid.*). How deeply this connotation was ingrained in Karaite exegesis of the time can be gauged from Jacob's Commentary on Ezekiel (Ez. 35:2; Starr's note to No. 146, *Jews in the Byzantine Empire*, p. 200, has to be corrected accordingly). The verse in question does not even use the term "Edom" but the strictly geographical "Mount Se'īr," synonymous with the ancient site of the Idumeans. Nevertheless, the Byzantine Karaite commentator says: "'And I will lay my vengeance upon Edom [by the hand of my people Israel]' (Ez. 25:14)—i.e., what they shall do to Constantinople and her people; and this is the meaning of '[Son of man, set thy face] against Mount Se'īr [and prophesy against it]' (Ez. 35:2)" (*Sefer ha-'Osher*, fol. 9c, beginning of Ch. 35).

[14] On the Banū Sahl of Tustar see Walter Fischel, *Jews in the Economic and Political Life of Medieval Islām* (London, 1937), pp. 68-89. Cf. also Mann, *Texts and Studies*, I, 371 ff., where Mann's earlier studies on the matter are indicated. See also, most recently, Goitein's "Petitions to Fāṭimid Caliphs from the Cairo Genizah," *JQR* (N.S.), XLV (1954), 36 f., where, against Mann's insistence on the Tustarīs' Rabbinism, new evidence is advanced in favor of the earlier thesis by Poznański, suggesting that the Banū Tustar were of Karaite persuasion. The whole problem indeed merits renewed consideration of the available material; albeit proof of the Tustarīs' Karaism would strengthen the exposition offered here, arguments based thereon have deliberately been refrained from in the present study, pending such an over-all reconsideration of the question.

depriving us of the knowledge where exactly Tobias was staying in Egypt (Alexandria? Fusṭāṭ?) and when he wrote his plea. The editors of the fragment rightly recall 1048 C.E. as the year in which Abraham at-Tustarī was assassinated, and decide that the letter "can safely be dated A.D. 1048." Mann does not attempt to date the letter, but, in accord with his general interpretation of both epistles, to be discussed presently, he considers the year of Abraham's assassination as the *terminus ad quem* for Tobias's return home from Palestine.

In the interpretation of the contents of our epistles Mann was confronted with a dilemma which he left unsolved. For, on the one hand, he accepted the aforementioned general view that Tobias went to Palestine to study under Yeshū'ah ben Yehūdah, and thus had to assign him to the *second* half of the eleventh century, whereas, on the other hand, he was compelled by the evidence of the Genizah letters to advance Tobias to the *first* half of that century.[15] Taking recourse to what seemed to him the only way of reconciling the two divergent dates, Mann connected the two letters chronologically and tried to push them as close to the middle of the eleventh century as possible, 1048 C.E. being of course the limit. This, in turn, called for strange vagueness in reference to the length of time Tobias spent in Palestine.

The reconstruction of the Tobias story, on the basis of the two Genizah letters taken in close succession, runs, according to Mann, as follows:

On his way to Palestine from Byzantium Tobias first landed at Damietta (B/II/18-19).[16] There he was arrested as a Byzantine subject and released later by bribing the port officials, both using funds of his own and securing help from Abraham at-Tustarī (B/II/19-20). In Jerusalem, where he "stayed for some time" (??), Tobias lived under great economic hardships as well as in a state of spiritual dejection. He was omitted from the list of the recipients of funds forthcoming from Egypt (from Abraham's brother, Abū Naṣr Ḥesed, and from an Abū 'Alī Yefeth) for distribution among the poor and the "Mourners of Zion" (*Abelē Ṣiyyon*), of whom he was a member (A/20, 24 ff.). Moreover, he was befriended by no one, save for Abū'l-Faraj Harūn, the well-known Karaite grammarian, who occasionally inquired about his welfare (A/19-20, 23-24).[17]

[15] See above, pp. 1-2. The latter alternative was, indeed, without much ado, accepted by Assaf in his descriptive note to the excerpt from Tobias's Letter II, published in *Sefer hay-Yishshūb* (see note 9, above).

[16] For identification of חִינֵּס with Damietta see Mann, *Jews in Egypt and Palestine*, II, 69, n. 1, and the documentation therein.

[17] On this "Jerusalem grammarian" see Bacher, "Le Grammairien anonyme de Jérusalem et son livre," *REJ*, XXX (1895), 232-56; Poznański, "Aboul-Faradj Haroun

To add grief to disaster, Tobias probably sustained a loss in his family (A/18-19 and the restored A/6). There is also an obscure hint concerning his grief over his only daughter who stayed with "that adulterous woman" (A/34-35). Tobias's sole desire now is to return home, and it is in connection with the necessary travel expenses that he appeals to the Rabbanite scholar in Fusṭāṭ, Abū Surūr Peraḥ ben Mūmal. Finally he returns home, via Egypt. Here, however, he stays for over a year in the employment of Abraham at-Tustarī (B/II/2 ff.), possibly as scribe.[18] In Egypt Tobias was reduced to a meager allowance, and his family (of three in all) lived through a hard time. When, however, his patron got tired of him, Tobias decided to go home and asked Tustarī to provide him with the necessary papers so that his sad experience of the past in Damietta should not be repeated. Not later than 1048 C.E. Tobias returned to his native land.

Thus far, Mann's reconstruction. The contribution Mann has made, in identifying the writer of the letters in question as the Karaite Tobias ben Moses of Constantinople, cannot be overestimated. It shifts, for the first time, Byzantine Karaism, led by Tobias, from a position of *literary* (Hebrew) epigone to the so-called creative (Arabic) Golden Age of Karaism into a *historical* context of actions and broader group-relationships. Yet Mann's rendering fails to indicate the exact context in which the reported events could be set organically. Indeed, in its sum total, it raises more questions than it actually answers.

In the first place, Mann's account cannot be squared with the whole pattern of activity with which Tobias's name has been identified so far in the presentation of eleventh-century Karaism and which Mann himself unreservedly accepts. This pattern envisages a Byzantine student coming, with other young enthusiasts, to Jerusalem under the auspices of an ambitious propaganda scheme sponsored by the sectarian center in Palestine;

---

ben al-Faradj le grammairien de Jérusalem et son Mouschtamil," *REJ*, XXXIII (1896), 24-39 and 197-218, as well as "Nouveaux renseignements sur Abou-l-Faradj Haroun ben al-Faradj et ses ouvrages," *REJ*, LVI (1908), 42-69, and the aforementioned Hebrew essay in *Jerusalem*; Hartwig Hirschfeld, *Literary History of Hebrew Grammarians and Lexicographers* (Oxford, 1926), pp. 50-53; Solomon L. Skoss, *The Arabic Commentary of ʿAlī ben Suleimān the Karaite on the Book of Genesis* (Philadelphia, 1928), pp. 11-27.

18 While the elegant writing in Letter II (as already observed by Mann) speaks for itself, one could add in support thereof that in his *Oṣar Neḥmad* Tobias indeed introduces himself as scribe. Cf. the text communicated by Neubauer from a Bodleian fragment, *Catalogue*, I, 58, No. 290: אני טוביה הסופר (see below, n. 54). It is not surprising that precisely this professional accomplishment was the cause of slight graphic differences between the hastily written informal Letter I and the elaborate performance in Letter II, addressed to a notable of Tustarī's stature.

here, after years of study and indoctrination, the students set out to translate the choice of Karaite exegetic, philosophic, and legalistic lore from Arabic into Hebrew, in order to introduce it into their native lands as a springboard for Karaite expansion.[19] The picture that we get from Mann's interpretation of the letters is not only diametrically different, but, even discarding, as I do, the above conception as a romantic idealization, it cannot possibly be reconciled with Tobias's literary undertakings that all may see and that Mann would be the last to underestimate. The Tobias we get acquainted with here is indeed a sorry failure. He comes to Jerusalem where nobody cares whether he is dead or alive; his share in the fund for the poor is cut off from him; no one befriends him except the teacher of his teacher, the old Abū'l-Faraj Harūn. Now, where is the great Yeshū'ah ben Yehūdah, allegedly Tobias's own teacher and master? Is he not supposed to take interest in the student who admittedly translated many of his books and traveled to him from afar for the express purpose of carrying Yeshū'ah's doctrines back to his native community? Why is the name of Yeshū'ah not mentioned at all, for better or worse? And why, of all people, does the future missionary of Karaism to Byzantium carry his grievances to an Egyptian Rabbanite, after years of sojourn and study in the spiritual capital of Karaism?

Even more difficult is the question of chronology. We have stressed the fact that Mann subscribes to the general view that Tobias was a pupil of Yeshū'ah. The latter is known to have written about 1050 C.E. and later, whereas in Mann's account, Tobias must have completed his education before 1048.[20] Even granted that Yeshū'ah was already a scholar of note in the early forties of the eleventh century, it is still very unlikely that he gained such fame in the first half of the century that students flocked to him from abroad while his own teachers, e.g., Abū'l-Faraj Harūn, were still very much alive and active.[21]

[19] See Mann, *Texts and Studies*, I, 372, and II, 3, 39, 287, 289 f.

[20] Yeshū'ah's long commentary on the Pentateuch was written about 1050 C.E., as follows from the sources referred to by Samuel Poznański, *The Karaite Literary Opponents of Saadiah Gaon* (London, 1908), p. 50. The abridgment thereof was started in 1054. Cf. Margoliouth, "Ibn al-Hītī's Arabic Chronicle of Karaite Doctors," *JQR* (O.S.), IX (1896-97), 429-43 (the date is mentioned in the Arabic text on p. 434 and in the English translation on p. 440); cf. also Nemoy's translation of the chronicle in *Karaite Anthology*, pp. 230 ff., the pertinent passage appearing in § 12, p. 233. See also Poznański, *The Karaite Literary Opponents of Saadiah Gaon*, pp. 48 f., and the additional information in Mann, *Texts and Studies*, II, 34 f.

[21] This argument is, of course, valid only in regard to the first half of the eleventh century, i.e., the formative years of Yeshū'ah's career. Surely, close to 1050 C.E. Yeshū'ah acquired independent standing and reputation, although Abū'l-Faraj Harūn

Logically, only three ways may possibly lead out of the present difficulty: either (a) the Tobias of our letters is not identical with the Karaite student of Byzantium going by the same name—Mann excludes this possibility; or (b) our Genizah letters tell us of an early pilgrimage to Palestine by Tobias and of his sojourn in Egypt on his way home, whereas the long period of his actual study under Yeshū'ah was still to come at a later date, some time in the second half of the century, when the academy of Yeshū'ah became the Mecca of diligent Karaite students from abroad—Mann does not mention this possibility in any of his voluminous writings on Karaism; or finally (c) the Byzantine Tobias ben Moses was not a pupil of Yeshū'ah ben Yehūdah—Mann does not explore this possibility either. He simply does not raise the question at all.

In addition to these broader difficulties of chronology and background, the internal evidence of details, contained in the letters, also militates against Mann's reconstruction.

In the first place, there is nothing that ties the two letters together except the person of their writer and a casual mention in Letter I of the brother of the recipient of Letter II as a benefactor of *Abelē Ṣiyyon*. The time-sequence that Mann imposes on the documents and the conclusion that he draws from this contiguity, namely, that Tobias's sojourn in Egypt was on his way home from Palestine, are entirely arbitrary and, indeed, against the letter and spirit of the text. What a far cry between the two epistles! While the first is a complaint of a proud, yet downhearted *Abel*, who suddenly found himself alienated from his surroundings and reduced to economic straits, the second is a plea of a no less proud but independent man. True, he is again badly off financially (B/II/6-7); he had known misfortune in life (B/I/21). Yet, in spite of the conventional panegyrics in the introduction, a sense of proud consciousness permeates the whole letter, consciousness of the fact that he is in the position to make his own decisions and also to offer something in return for favors. There can even be detected an unmistakable tone of reproach when he states:

A full year I have stayed in the employment of my illustrious master, yet no profit have I seen of the work of my hands (B/II/2-3).

It would be below his dignity and against his sense of loyalty to ask others for support:

---

is still heard of in 1065-66 (cf. Margoliouth, "Ibn al-Hītī's Chronicle," *JQR* [O.S.], IX [1896-97], 434).

Yet I have not stood before any man to ask him for support; neither have I begged of any man nor has any man ever given me anything (B/II/3-5).

In fact, even when pleading with his master he mentions neither Palestine nor his being a "Mourner of Zion," although, knowing the Tustarīs' interest in the *Abelim*, a reference to his status might enhance his prospects for financial support. There is no feeling that he is in Egypt *on his way home* from Palestine, but that he came to that country specially, on a good and proud purpose:

For I did not come hither to the Land of Egypt to beg anything of the elders, so that I might support myself and make a living, but I have come for one thing [or: for something else] (B/I/24-25 and B/II/1).

This special purpose must have been very well known to Tustarī, for Tobias does not bother to elaborate, or perhaps he prefers, for some reason or other, not to expatiate on the subject. He surely could not have meant his personal employment; it seems, rather, that he accepted employment from Tustarī to keep him going as long as nothing substantial had been done to further the real cause of his visit to Egypt. Day after day Tobias made his entreaties anew, so much so that he suspects now that his insistence caused Tustarī to get tired of him (B/II/9-10). Be this as it may, the real objective of his prolonged visit has not been achieved, and Tobias addresses a last plea before his intended departure:

And so I implore my Lord, the Elder, the honored Prince, that he perform my request on account of which I have come down to this place (B/II/13-15).

Incidentally, this last wording definitely points to an intentional visit to Egypt, the objective of which had not yet been attained. It would have benefited our knowledge of early Byzantine Karaite affairs had Tobias been more outspoken about the things he had expected to achieve in Egypt. In any case, the time has come, so he feels, to pack up and leave for home. His disappointment over the failure of the "request on account of which he has come down to this place" and the economic hardships that he and his family (or two other members of his party?) had to endure for over a year of waiting appear now even more painful with the unexpected deterioration of his patron's relation to him, of which he learned from an Abū'l-Faraj Hībah, probably one of Tustarī's associates or officials kindly disposed to Tobias. The reason for Tustarī's anger is hard to fathom. If my rendering of the text is correct, Tobias suspects that some slanderous rumors about him have reached his patron's ear (B/II/10-11 and our note *ad loc.*), which could perhaps be connected with Tobias's own reference, at the end of Letter I (A/34-35), to some family troubles.

As already noted, Tobias admits that his insistence, too, may have tired his benefactor's patience. Finally, to Tobias's general feeling of frustration there was now added his particular disappointment with members of Tustarī's inner circle with whom he has come in touch (B/II/15). The only person to whom he still could turn in full confidence is, in spite of the mild reproach earlier, Abraham at-Tustarī.

In addition to the last plea for fulfillment of his principal request, Tobias asks for a safe-conduct home (B/II/16-19). Here we learn that "in those days" (B/II/20) Tobias was imprisoned in Damietta. It was, we recall, suggested that the event happened when Tobias was on his way to Palestine. Although there is nothing in the text to oppose this interpretation, there is also nothing that necessitates a reference to the far-off past. The unfortunate experience might have occurred a year or so before the letter was written, when Tobias reached Egypt directly from Byzantium, and so an allusion to it was designed to recall things still fresh in the minds of the correspondents. In fact, it thus becomes even more obvious why the petitioner, who has come to Egypt for a specific purpose with limited funds only, not expecting his visit to extend for over a year, was compelled to engage in some sort of temporary employment, especially after having spent part of his money on bribing the Damietta authorities.

The last part of Letter II is perhaps the most illuminating. In return for the favors, Tobias promises to spread the fame of his benefactor "in all the communities of the Land of Edom, whether near or far" (B/II/22-24). If a statement of this kind could perhaps be taken as a conventional figure of speech by a writer seeking patronage, the next sentence defies any such assumption and, conversely, sheds new light on the former wording, too. For this is what Tobias declares:

> And I shall decree [ואתקן] that every Monday and Thursday people should recite [שיברכו] a blessing for my honored Lord in synagogues (B/II/24-25).

Now, such an assurance given to a man of great power in worldly and Jewish communal affairs, who knew very well whether it was backed by the necessary authority or not, could not have been a vain boast, for, after all, in that case it would have defeated the petitioner's own purpose, namely, the desire to win Tustarī's earnest attention. The fact that a pledge of this kind was given at the end of the letter, so that it might be taken as a solemn obligation in return for favors, proves that Tobias at the time of his writing to Tustarī, i.e., before 1048 C.E., already held a position of authority such as to enable him to issue liturgical instructions which would be valid in Karaite synagogues of his country. He does not assure Tustarī that he personally will recite prayers for him in the synagogue (he would then say: ואברך שני וחמישי לאדוני etc.), nor does he promise to endow certain synagogues with funds so that, as is customary, the poor could be entrusted with the pronouncement of such blessings (this might have been formulated, e.g.: ואנדב שני וחמישי שיברכו לאדוני), but he takes it upon himself to enact (ואתקן i.e., to issue a *takkanah* or ordinance) that blessing be recited in synagogues. Moreover, the promulgation of the said decree is pledged not only in respect to the synagogue of which he might have been a member or even an officeholder, but for synagogues at large (בבתי כנסיות —expressed in the plural and without the definite article!), and not for one special occasion but as a routine procedure to be introduced on every Monday and Thursday, when the pious fast and the Scripture portion is read in public and the House of God is filled with believers.[22] In view of the authority that Tobias displays here, his proud independence, despite poverty, stressed earlier in this discussion, becomes completely understandable. It is the usual proud, though very respectful and, depending on the need, panegyrical appeal of one of the "aristocracy of learning" to one of the "aristocracy of wealth," exchanging spiritual gratitude, expressed in public prayers, for grants and favors of a material character—a feature so familiar to us from scores of Genizah fragments published in the last fifty years.

It would, of course, be far-fetched to try to decide whether, in view of Tobias's official authority, his mission to Egypt was of a personal character or perhaps on behalf of the Karaite communities in Byzantium. The fact that he promises in return an enactment that will impose liturgical duties on the communities as a whole speaks rather in favor of a mission in the public interest. We shall have to reserve judgment in the matter, however, until a new lucky find sheds additional light on this highly intriguing problem.[23]

[22] What Tobias promised Tustarī was, in fact, the introduction into Byzantine Karaite ritual of a procedure well established among his coreligionists in the Karaite communities of Egypt in regard to the Tustarī brothers. Even long after the death of these generous notables their names were remembered and their deeds recounted in Karaite Memorial Services, as we gather from a Fusṭāṭ Memorial List published by M. Ginsburger, "Deux manuscripts caraïtes," *REJ*, LXXII (1921), 40 ff. (see esp. p. 41, where the generosity of Yashar, the father, and of Abraham, the son, is extolled); cf. also Mann, *Jews in Egypt and Palestine*, II (Addenda), 376. On Karaite Memorial Lists in general see Mann, *Texts and Studies*, II, 256 f., and the literature quoted there on p. 257, n. 4.

[23] Chances are that the reading at the end of B/II/1 is not בעבור דָּבָר אֶחָד (or: אַחֵר), but בעבור דְּבַר אֲחֵרִים, meaning, "But I have come hither in the interest [or: for the

There is another lesson to be drawn from the closing paragraph of the letter under discussion. The functioning in Byzantium, before 1048 C.E., of a Karaite authority enacting decrees in matters religious and ritual presupposes not only the existence of Karaism in the country in the first half of the eleventh century—this we know from a still earlier document (dated 1028 C.E.) mentioned in our introductory remarks above—but a definite organizational system on which the said authority was based. In fact, the wording "in all the communities of the Land of Edom whether near of far" may very well mean a network of Karaite communal units spread over a considerable territory of the Byzantine Empire, with synagogues as their local centers of assembly and prayer, and with a central authority, probably in Constantinople, exerting binding influence, at least in matters of ritual and religious jurisdiction, over all the congregations of the country. I discuss the problem of communal government in Byzantine Karaism in a different connection, where evidence is produced for its activity in the second part of the eleventh century and in later times. It is important, however, to note here that our letter offers *contemporary testimony to the existence of this system, embracing no doubt a great many communities, as early as the mid-forties of the eleventh century*. It also indicates, contrary to the accepted view, that *Tobias already wielded such an authority before 1048*—consequently, the period of his studies in Jerusalem ought to be advanced to not later than the thirties, and perhaps even beginning with the latter part of the twenties, of the century under discussion.

In view of our preceding findings, the content of Letter I, Mann's interpretation of which has been summarized above, will also have to be seen in a new light. The epistle unmistakably was written by Tobias ben Moses, the "Mourner" or the "Servant" (line 4 of the address and A/6), in the time when Tobias stayed in Jerusalem (last line of the address) as student of the Jerusalem Karaite Academy (A/6). Tobias's membership in the Order of the "Mourners of Zion" is not only stated in the address (line 4), but also follows from the spirit and phraseology of the whole epistle (A/7-8, 10-11, 13-14, 16). A series of appropriate biblical verses is

---

sake] of OTHERS." The space left for the last word surely warrants, even demands, more than three letters, while, as shown in our note *ad loc.* (see App., n. 141), Mann's five-letter correction בעבור דְבַר אֲדוֹנִי (to mean: "for the sake of MY MASTER'S business," or "summoned by MY MASTER") is both graphically as well as through the context unwarranted. The "three souls" (including Tobias himself), in B/II/6, would then refer not to Tobias's own family, of which he indeed reports (in B/II/13) that it remained in his native land, but to a delegation that he led to Egypt, or to two petitioners he accompanied abroad in his official capacity, in order to support their plea.

used to convey the idea of undying national hope for redemption, and local events assume a meaning that can best be expressed in the inexhaustible terms of the Holy Scriptures (cf. the quotations from Lev. 26:44, Jer. 14:8 and 17:13, and Is. 63:9 and 66:13). Since the letter was addressed to a Rabbanite scholar, even an aggadic comment on a verse from Isaiah is not wanting (A/14-15).[24]

In the letter Tobias requests his correspondent to dispatch to him, as soon as possible, instructions regarding the disposition of funds he probably borrowed from Peraḥ, for he is about to leave for home soon (A/31-33 and our note *ad loc.*); hence it may be inferred that the letter was written in the last year of Tobias's sojourn in Jerusalem. Indeed, a similar conclusion has been reached by Mann, although, as we recall, his interpretation of the passage differed from the one just presented. This correct inference, however, calls for an explanation of the strange alienation of Tobias from his surrounding in the last year of his stay in Jerusalem—an explanation that will, at the same time, not derogate from the stature of the man. For, to begin with, Tobias must already have been at that time an important, or at least a promising, figure, corresponding with leading personalities of his generation, some even of the Rabbanite camp. Secondly, the estrangement Tobias complains of, and especially the drastic pecuniary measures that left him out of the list of *Abelim* eligible for financial support, seem to mark a new development. Earlier, Tobias wrote dirges in memory of the father of one of the explicitly mentioned philanthropists (A/26-27)—surely a sign of friendliness, even though some kind of reward was expected. Indeed, estranged were now certain persons in positions of power in the community—alas, those who administered the fund distribution!—nevertheless, the text, though badly

[24] This midrashic quotation, by the way, should not necessarily be viewed as a mere matter of expediency in respect to the person on the receiving end. Tobias's writings in general show a considerable familiarity with Rabbinic literature; see on it Poznański, *Oṣar Yisrael*, V, 13b. One may perhaps surmise that, in addition to acquainting themselves consciously with talmudic material for scholastic and polemical reasons—a fact which we have ample evidence of throughout the history of Karaism—Karaite *Abelim* might have adopted from their Rabbanite colleagues some Rabbinic homilies connected with the idea of national mourning, much the same as several Karaite customs of the *Abelim* enjoyed popularity in the Rabbanite camp. Cf., for instance, the frank statement by Levi ben Yefeth, in his Book of Precepts (in Pinsker's *Liḳḳūṭē Ḳadmoniyyoth*, App., p. 89), and, conversely, the account by Sahl b. Maṣliaḥ (*ibid.*, p. 33; also in an abridged English version, in Nemoy, *Karaite Anthology*, pp. 117 f., § 15). Thus, "acceptable" Midrashim of the type invoked by Tobias in his letter might have tacitly been acknowledged and possibly quoted *bona fide* by the Karaites, unlike the crude anthropomorphic Aggadoth which were the object of biting ridicule and were—as a cursory glance at Karaite polemical literature will immediately reveal—studied and collected by the dissident scholars for the express purpose of refuting them.

mutilated, does not seem to indicate that the resentment was general:

And there is no one to comfort, and were it not for the mercy of God and for [= the fact that] people have come ... [probably: and cheered my heart] ... with kind words, I should have died (A/20-21).

Hence, not all the members of the community gave Tobias the cold shoulder. Rather, it looks as if in the petty feuds within the Jerusalem Center Tobias landed on the wrong side and drew some scornful glances from the victorious faction which held a tight grip on the funds destined for the *Abelim.* In brief, our letter, painfully obscure at first glance, hints at certain events and actions which, no doubt, had an important bearing on Tobias's career. Consequently, our understanding of it is decisive for the reconstruction of Tobias's transition from service under the tutelage of the Jerusalem Center to independent leadership of the Karaite communities in Byzantium.

The interpretation that follows seems capable of solving these difficulties of detail and, at the same time, of integrating the account of Tobias's misfortune in the broader historical context of the period.

II

The fact that, contrary to the once prevailing conceptions, communal feuds and alliances within tenth- and eleventh-century Jewry failed, oftener than not, to align automatically in accord with sectarian allegiance provides a decisive key to the understanding of the internal history of Karaism in the period under review and, for that matter, in later periods too. True, the full import of the interests and ambitions involved in these wrangles and confederacies is often lost to us for lack of sufficient background information. Still, it is a matter of record that no less a foe of the sect than Sa'adyah Gaon could with no difficulty be found embattled, hand in hand with the Karaites, against the claims to ascendancy of the Palestinian gaon Ben Meir and against the Babylonian exilarch Ben Zakkai,[25] while, a century and a half later, another gaon, Daniel ben 'Azaryah, attained the chair of Palestinian Gaonate and Patriarchate with considerable help from the sectarians[26] and had his son David marry the daughter of a Karaite potentate of Fusṭāṭ.[27]

[25] Mann, *Texts and Studies*, II, 46, 132, 134. Cf. also S. W. Baron, "Saadiah's Communal Activities," in *Saadiah Anniversary Volume of the American Academy for Jewish Research* (Philadelphia, 1943), p. 9.

[26] Mann, *Jews in Egypt and Palestine*, I, 178, 274.

[27] The marriage contract was published by S. Schechter in "Genizah Specimens,"

A heated communal feud along such nondefined lines burst into the open in the late thirties of the eleventh century, when Nathan ben Abraham was involved in a severe conflict with his superior, the Palestinian gaon Solomon ben Yehūdah, and finally proclaimed a rival Gaonate in Ramleh. For details of motives and events the reader will have to be referred elsewhere;[28] suffice it to stress here that the strife split the Rabbanite camp in Palestine into two parties, which fact, in turn, divided Egyptian Jewry, the financial and political mainstay of Jewish Palestine, into supporters and opponents of either side. We are not concerned here with the over-all strategy of the two rivals but with those specific moves which had an effect on the Karaite community in Palestine, and, I believe, on Byzantine Karaism, too.

The sheer numerical weight of the Karaites in Palestine, and, through them, the attitude of the numerous Karaites in Damascus and especially of their wealthy and influential brethern in Fusṭāṭ, were strategic factors that neither side could lightheartedly afford to neglect. Consequently, the Karaite Center in Palestine was also plunged into the thick of battle, though by no means united in its decision as to which of the sides deserved its support. It seems, however, that the expediency of local politics and cognate reasons caused a great many Karaites to side with the rival gaon of Ramleh, and even some of them, who outwardly remained steadfast in their support of the legitimate gaon Solomon ben Yehūdah, in reality favored his opponent.[29] Whether it is true that this support was solicited by Nathan through a promise of certain legalistic concessions to Karaite practices[30] or whether a rumor to this effect was merely one of the indiscriminate missiles hurled in the heat of battle is impossible to ascertain from the available evidence. Solomon's sober explanation that

> they [viz., the Karaites] are favorably inclined towards him [= Nathan], for all that causeth them joy is to fight the Rabbanites, for there is no faith [i.e., in their hearts],[31]

proves only that he was quite aware of the fact that in the seemingly

---

JQR (O.S.), XIII (1900-1901), 220-21 (with an introduction, pp. 218 ff.), and reproduced in Gulak's *Oṣar hash-Sheṭaroth*, pp. 33 f., No. 29. Cf. Mann, *Jews in Egypt and Palestine*, I, 138, 177, 188.

[28] See Mann's "The Affair of Nathan b. Abraham as Rival Gaon in Palestine to Solomon b. Yehūdah," in *Texts and Studies*, I, 323 ff., where references to his earlier research on the subject are also given.

[29] This is, anyhow, the tenor of Solomon's complaint to Ephraim ben Shemaryah of Fusṭāṭ, published by Mann, *Jews in Egypt and Palestine*, II, 162, ll. 24-25.

[30] Mann, *Jews in Egypt and Palestine*, II, 161, ll. 13-14.

[31] *Ibid.*, ll. 14-15.

extraneous conflict the Karaites pursued interests of their own. He was not slow, therefore, in forging weapons which would prove to the Karaites that their interests did not necessarily coincide with those of his opponent. Whatever the reason, Nathan himself admits of weighty Karaite support. In a communication to a disciple of his in Fusṭāṭ he describes the overwhelming success of his cause in Damascus and a celebration of unparalleled dimensions at his school, attended by both Rabbanites and Karaites.[32]

To what extent the Karaites were a force to be reckoned with in this intra-Rabbanite feud we learn from the fact that, when the matter was finally brought to a close, the Karaite Nasī Ḥezeḳiah (ben Solomon ben David) was among the signatories of the agreement concluded between the rival parties.[33] The very fact, however, that the leading Karaite dignitary of Jerusalem was a party to an agreement which deprived Nathan of his usurped office and compelled him and his followers to revert to their old rank and position proves that the official Karaite leadership must have joined hands with Solomon at a certain juncture of the controversy.

Following his happy identification of our Nathan ben Abraham as the author of an infamous Arabic composition in which the legitimacy of the highest-ranking (Babylonian) Rabbanite and Karaite dignitaries was outrightly challenged,[34] Mann has offered an ingenious suggestion as to the reason for the change of heart among the leading Karaite authorities in Palestine. It seems that when the rival gaon was at the height of his career, some time about 1040-41, the Solomon ben Yehūdah faction dug up an early pamphlet of his, in which the notorious episode from the seventh century, about the Babylonian exilarch Bustanai and the captive Persian princess presented to him by the Arab conqueror, was retold with a shockingly anti-Karaite slant. This, perforce shattered to

[32] Cf. his letter to Berakha ben Rewaḥ, *ibid.*, p. 172, ll. 15-18.

[33] Richard Gottheil and William H. Worrell, *Fragments from the Cairo Genizah in the Freer Collection* (New York, 1927), p. 200, l. 4 of verso, and the corrections by Assaf, in *Zion* (O.S.), II (1927-28), 116, and by Mann, *Texts and Studies*, I, 332. Cf. also Assaf, in *Tarbiz*, III (1931), 345 f. The corrected Arabic text was reproduced, along with a Hebrew translation, in Assaf-Mayer's *Sefer hay-Yishshūb*, II, 27a-28b, No. 56.

[34] First published by Margoliouth as § 1 ("On the Exilarch Bustanī") of "Some British Museum Genizah Texts," *JQR* (O.S.), XIV (1901-2), 303-7; cf. also Worman, "The Exilarch Bustani," *JQR* (O.S.), XX (1907-8), 211-15; Tykocinski, "Bustanai the Exilarch" (Hebrew), *Debir*, I (1923), 145-79 (esp. pp. 152-53); A. Marx, "Der arabische Bustanai-Bericht und Nathan ha-Babli," in *Livre d'hommage à la mémoire du S. Poznański* (Warsaw, 1927), pp. 76-81; and finally Mann, *Texts and Studies*, I, 334 ff.

pieces the alliance with the Karaites, so instrumental to the usurper's success.

The leitmotif of Nathan's Bustanai report was by no means a novelty on Palestinian soil. While the well-known version of the Babylonian schools traced the descent of the Babylonian exilarchs to the Davidide Bustanai and his Jewish wife, a different story was current in the Jerusalem Academy. Here the Palestinian geonim, locked in an uneven struggle with Babylonian hegemony (e.g., the tenth-century Sa'adyah–Ben Meir controversy) and, at the same time and earlier, with the Karaite Nesiim of the (Davidic) House of 'Anan, considered it particularly effective to discredit the Davidic ancestry of the Baghdād Rosh hag-Golah and of the Karaite leaders by linking their line with the *non*-Jewish wife of Bustanai, whom the seventh-century Jewish prince allegedly failed to manumit.[35] These invectives, to be sure, would be employed either way, depending on what direction the political wind was blowing, leading sometimes to rather odd combinations of friend and foe. And so, the gaonic family of Ben Meir, priding itself on direct descent from Yehūdah han-Nasī, a scion of the House of David, would put in one company the Bnē Zakkai of Baghdād and the Karaite Davidides 'Anan ben David and Bo'az as illegitimate offspring of Bustanai. On the other hand, the Baghdādian Khalāf ben Sarjādo, who was on the same side of the political fence as David ben Zakkai (and, thus, not interested in slandering the name of the exilarch's family) but at odds with Sa'adyah, would throw in this arch-enemy of Karaism with the dissident Nesiim, "the sons of the prostitute and the slave."[36]

The slanderous Bustanai account found its way to Kairowān, the original seat of Nathan ben Abraham. There it was incorporated by the latter into one of his writings, composed, of course, many years before his Palestinian romance with the Karaites. When the quoted report was floated in Fusṭāṭ in 1040-41 by the Solomon party with the obvious purpose of showing to the Karaite leadership in Palestine and Egypt what their political favorite thought of the blood purity of their Davidic aristocracy, a reversal in the official attitude of the Karaite dignitaries to Nathan could not fail to be forthcoming. In the fall of 1041 an agreement was signed giving victory to the veteran Solomon ben Yehūdah. The Karaite Nasī Ḥezeḳiah (of whom we already know that he was instrumental

[35] Cf. the pertinent passage in Margoliouth, *JQR* (O.S.), XIV (1901-2), 304 f. (and in Eng. tr., p. 306).

[36] See the references and quotations conveniently recalled by Mann, *Texts and Studies*, I, 335, n. 21.

in drawing up the terms) could surely not tolerate a situation in which a shadow was cast on the legitimacy of his own line.

Yet, continuing from where Mann left off, it will not be difficult to see that the action of the Karaite Nasī in switching his support to Solomon ben Yehūdah, when his vested interests were endangered, was not immediately and unanimously taken up by all the members of the Karaite community. While strife and communal feud were raging in the Rabbanite camp, the Karaite community was no less torn from within by controversy and dissension. Although the famous dictum of Ḳirḳisānī, that there are no two Karaites who agree with each other,[37] is usually quoted in regard to the sectarians' bickerings in the *legalistic* and *exegetic* field, a careful study of Karaism in the tenth and eleventh centuries also reveals a picture of anything but *communal* unity. There must especially have been a deep-seated annoyance on the part of many pious *Abelē Ṣiyyon* with the worldly practices of, at least, some Karaite Nesiim. It is only human to suppose that favoritism and political whip-tactics, affecting the distribution of funds which were destined for the *Abelim* and allocated to them probably through the office of the Nasī or his officials, were not infrequent. The complaint of Tobias in the very Genizah letter under discussion testifies quite clearly that such practices were indeed employed. It is in the light of this situation within the Karaite camp that one ought to read the statement of Salman ben Yerūḥam, a champion of the *Abelim* Order some two or three generations earlier,[38] in his Arabic Commentary to the Psalms. Elaborating on the last verse (v. 176) of Chapter 119, Salman asserts:

> This psalm was in its entirety pronounced in regard to the People of the Diaspora-period, there is no doubt about it. So by saying, "My people hath been lost sheep" (Jer. 50:6), the Scripture intended to inform us that the misfortune of Israel, from beginning to end, stems from their shepherds. And this is why the Karaites, may their Rock guard them, seceded from the Exilarchate of the Rabbanites and imposed on themselves that there will be no Rosh (Raīs = Nasī) over them in the time of the Galuth, even as the Lord, may He be exalted, said, "For the children of Israel shall abide many days without a king and without a prince" (Hos. 3:4).[39]

[37] *Kitāb al-Anwār wa-l-Marāḳib*, ed. Nemoy, I, 14, ll. 11-13. On Ḳirḳisānī see most recently Nemoy's introduction to English excerpts from his writings, in *Karaite Anthology*, pp. 42 ff., and G. Vajda, in *REJ*, CVI (1941-45), 87-123, CVII (1946-47), 52-98, CVIII (1948), 63-91.

[38] A popular introduction to Salman ben Yeruḥam precedes Nemoy's translation from his writings, *Karaite Anthology*, pp. 69 ff.

[39] Pinsker, *Liḳḳūṭē Ḳadmoniyyoth*, App., pp. 51 f., n. 2; also in Mann's excerpts from the Arabic translation and commentary on Psalms by Salman, *Texts and Studies*, II, 84.

This statement caused much uneasiness to Pinsker, who was aware of the existence of Karaite Nesiim in the very time and in the very city in which Salman wrote the above words. He, therefore, labeled it an outright lie, of the kind that was not unusual in the heat of controversy. Indeed, he placed it as the counterpart of another distortion of history committed by no other than Sa'adyah Gaon in the course of an anti-Karaite argument, when he claimed biblical antiquity for the Rabbanite system of calendar calculation—an assertion which, incidentally, made the later Rabbanite authorities very uncomfortable.[40]

This line of reasoning, followed also by later scholars,[41] seems to me untenable. For, if Sa'adyah's pronouncement, which, after all, could be checked only against literary references and oral traditions, was immediately singled out by Karaite polemicists as unfounded, how much more so would Salman's statement not have been left unchallenged. Surely, a falsehood in this field would have boomeranged against Salman instantaneously, with the Rabbanites having no difficulty whatsoever in pointing to contemporary realities.

Salman's comment, viewed in the light of our preceding discussion, makes perfect sense. It does not, by any means, claim the nonexistence of Karaite Nesiim in his time; rather, it takes pains to remind the Karaites of a sacred obligation they have taken upon themselves and have failed to fulfill. In accord with the political and religious philosophy of *Abelē Ṣiyyon*, Salman argues that the establishment of a *Karaite Nesiūth* not only leaves one of the basic reasons of the Karaite revolt against Rabbanite institutionalism an empty shell, but is also an outright religious sin; for it was the express will of God, revealed in the Scriptures, to leave the

[40] Pinsker, *Liḳḳūṭē Ḳadmoniyyoth*, pp. 51 f. and 13 ff. We may, parenthetically, add here that the claim of biblical antiquity for the precalculated calendar, going even beyond Sa'adyah's assertion back to the times of Adam, has since been traced to earlier midrashic and apocryphal literature, as well as shown to have persisted in post-Sa'adyan writings in spite of the uneasiness of some scholars in the matter. Cf. on it M. Kasher, *Torah Shelēmah*, XIII, 5a ff.

[41] Julius Fürst, *Geschichte des Karäerthums* (Leipzig, 1862-69), II, 81, and notes. Adolf Neubauer, *Aus der Petersburger Bibliothek* (Leipzig, 1866), pp. 13 f., makes no effort to soften up his real opinion of Salman's statement: "Seine Wuth," says Neubauer, "und sein Parteigeist gegen die Rabbaniten scheint so weit zu gehen, dass er ihnen Sachen aufbindet, die gerade die Karäer hatten; so wirft er ihnen vor, dass sie sich ein Oberhaupt im Exil gewählt hatten, weswegen die Karäer aus ihrem Verbande getreten sind. Nun betrachtet man die genealogischen Tafeln der Karäer, so wird man doch so viel Nesiim finden, mehr als man deren wünscht." So, too, P. F. Frankl terms Salman's comment an "offenkundige Entstellung des Sachverhalts"; cf. *Ersch und Gruber Enz.*, Section II, Vol. XXXIII (1883), p. 13, n. 14.

children of Israel for many days "without a king and without a prince."[42]

Even more outspoken than Salman was his younger contemporary Yefeth ben 'Alī, who exerted a tremendous influence on Tobias ben Moses and on Byzantine Karaism at large.[43] He even went so far as to indicate clearly whom in Dispersion he considered fit to replace princes and exilarchs in a position of authority. Interpreting the very verse of Hosea (3:4) with which Salman concluded the above-quoted passage in a vein similar to that of his predecessor, Yefeth says:

> He points out that they shall remain without a king and without a prince, neither of the house of David nor of any other, since the cause of their ruin lay in their kings and princes who transgressed and corrupted the people. But if anyone were to say, "Behold they do have in Captivity exilarchs and presidents of academies," we should say to him: "These are transgressors; God has not invested them with authority. Only TEACHERS are requisite in Captivity and NONE ELSE."[44]

The implication is clear: only teachers and spiritual leaders in their own right, and not vain heirs to the Davidic title, imitating the Rabbanite aristocratic elite of "exilarchs and presidents of academies," are in line with true Karaite tradition and with the letter and spirit of Divine Law. Indeed, the title bestowed by posterity on this greatest of Karaite Bible exegetes was "Teacher"—precisely the one which alone, in Yefeth's opinion, befitted a Karaite leader in Captivity.[45]

This opposition of all or part of *Abelē Ṣiyyon* to *Nesiūth* must also, to a great extent, be attributed to their resentment of 'Anan, whose descendants claimed the privilege of leadership, and of the 'Ananite faction within Karaism.[46] It will take us too far to expatiate on this subject;

[42] Mann, *Texts and Studies*, II, 84, n. 85a, already had an inkling of the thesis developed here, though he did not care to pursue it further. Accepting the position of Pinsker and of all the other scholars (see the preceding note) that "here again Salman does not state the truth since the sectaries regarded as their Raīs any members of 'Anan's family," he wonders for a moment: "Or does Salman express here his opposition to the Karaite Nesiim of Jerusalem?"

[43] See on him, recently, Philip Birnbaum's introduction to his edition of *The Arabic Commentary of Yefet ben 'Alī the Karaite on the Book of Hosea* (Philadelphia, 1942), as well as the short popular summary of Nemoy preceding his selections from Yefeth's writings, *Karaite Anthology*, pp. 83 f.

[44] Birnbaum, *The Arabic Commentary*, p. 53, ll. 7-14.

[45] In fact, the whole circle of scholars identified with the Karaite Academy in the Bakhtawī court in Jerusalem bore the title of "Teachers." Cf. the Rabbanite (!) text published by Mann, *Texts and Studies*, II, 95, ll. 13 ff.; similarly in the Karaite passage, already referred to above (note 24), from the Book of Precepts by Levi b. Yefeth (in Pinsker's *Liḳḳūṭē Ḳadmoniyyoth*, App., p. 89).

[46] E.g., Daniel al-Ḳūmisī, of the late ninth and the early tenth century, as reported by Ḳirḳisānī (*Kitāb al-Anwār*, ed. Nemoy, I, 5; Engl. version in *Karaite Anthology*,

suffice it to recall here that, as we know from both Karaite and extraneous sources, these differences were still a living reality in the first half of the eleventh century, and no common denominator had yet been found for all the trends and sub-trends mushrooming in the charged climate of the period.[47] It was left to the generations immediately following the eclipse of the Jerusalem Center to attain, under the prompting of special historic circumstances in a changing world, such a measure of external uniformity that, at last, it did not seem strange to attribute to ʻAnan himself the very leadership of his one-time opponents, the "Mourners of Zion."[48]

---

p. 330, n. III/1), and as expressed also in the Commentary on Daniel attributed to al-Ḳūmisī (published by Mann, *JQR* [N.S.], XII [1921-22], 519; *Karaite Anthology*, p. 39); the tenth-century Ḳirḳisānī himself (*Kitāb al-Anwār*, V, 1145; *Karaite Anthology*, p. 44, n. 7), despite his earlier stricture against al-Ḳūmisī's too outspoken contempt, unbecoming a learned and pious man; his contemporary, Salman b. Yerūḥam (in Pinsker's *Liḳḳūṭē Ḳadmoniyyoth*, pp. 21 f.). The very theory of successive purification-stages, from the crude doctrines of ʻAnan b. David to Karaism par excellence, symbolized by the "Lilies" of the *Abelē Ṣiyyon* type—a theory first expounded by Salman and continued through Yefeth b.ʻ Alī into the Byzantine Karaite conception of history, such as expressed by Jacob b. Reuben—serves, despite Frankl's objections (*Ersch u. Gruber Enz.*, Section II, Vol. XXXIII, p. 13, n. 18), as a drastic illustration of the tenth- and eleventh-century signal dissociation from ʻAnan, his descendants, and his orthodox followers, by spokesmen of the scholarly center in Jerusalem and by their Byzantine pupils. Indeed, in a different connection I have elaborated more fully on the broader implications of what seems to me the coexistence, until the twelfth century, of two well-defined, at times mutually exclusive and always bitterly opposed, trends within Karaism: the institutionalist trend, quite naturally hinged on the different branches of the Davidic House of ʻAnan, and the intellectualist-ascetic trend, best manifested in the Jerusalem circle of "Mourners" and scholars.

[47] Note, for instance, the early eleventh-century Levi b. Yefeth (in Pinsker, *Liḳḳūṭē Ḳadmoniyyoth*, p. 22, and App., p. 92); later in the same century, Yeshūʻah b. Yehūdah (as reported by Bashyachi, *Addereth Eliyyahū*, ed. Gozlow, fol. 63a); the late eleventh- (or early twelfth-) century Jacob b. Reuben, in his Commentary on the Song of Songs (*Sefer ha-ʻOsher*, fol. 12b; cf. Pinsker, *Liḳḳūṭē Ḳadmoniyyoth*, p. 22). For Ibn Ḥazm's mention of ʻAnanites in Toledo and Talavera, cf. his *Kitāb al-Faṣl fī-Milal wa-l-Ahwā' wa-n-Niḥal* (ed. Cairo, A.H. 1317), I, 99, and, still earlier, Schreiner, "Miscellen (2): Aus Ibn Ḥazms Kitāb etc.," *MGWJ*, XXXIV (1885), 139 f. (in Hebrew characters). The corrupt transcription of both editions was partially corrected by Poznański, in "Ibn Ḥazm über jüdische Secten," *JQR* (O.S.), XVI (1903-4), 767, and, ultimately, by Perlmann's happy restoration of the diacritic marks, in "Eleventh-century Andalusian Authors on the Jews of Granada," *PAAJR*, XVIII (1948-49), 280, n. 44.

[48] Cf. the statement by the twelfth-century Byzantine Karaite Elijah ben Abraham, in "Ḥillūḳ haḳ-Ḳara'īm we ha-Rabbanim" (Pinsker, *Liḳḳūṭē Ḳadmoniyyoth*, App., p. 104). The author of the *Ḥillūḳ* was, of course, in no position to ignore the still persisting opposition to ʻAnan (*Liḳḳūṭē*, p. 101); his apology, however, is immaterial to our discussion. This idealistic presentation of ʻAnan's ties with Jerusalem and with the "Mourners of Zion" becomes a matter of fact to a fourteenth-century Karaite Anonymous (reported first by Harkavy, *Voskhod*, XVIII [1898], Part 2, p. 9, n. 4, then reproduced more

I have elaborated at great length on the effect that the Solomon-Nathan affair had on the Karaite community, for it is my contention that Letter I by Tobias the "Mourner" has to be read within the chronological framework of the events connected with that affair and against the background of the atmosphere and relations within the Karaite camp as depicted in the preceding pages.

In the first place, the recipient of Tobias's letter merits our attention. He is Abū Surūr Peraḥ ben Mūmal (or Muammil). We learn that the two men had maintained a correspondence before this letter, and that theirs is not a passing acquaintance but a relationship based on a broader

---

fully by Mann, *Texts and Studies*, II, 108), and gathers momentum with the flow of centuries. In the relatively modern period it appears fully embellished in Simḥah Lutzki's *Oraḥ Ṣaddiḳim*, fol. 19a. Needless to say, the role of 'Anan as an alleged pioneer of Karaite rebuilding of the Holy City and as leader of the "Mourners of Zion" is completely unhistorical (cf. Poznański, in his already quoted Hebrew essay, *Jerusalem*, X, [1913], 85 ff.; Poznański, in *Hastings' Encyclopedia of Religion and Ethics*, VII, 663b-664a; Mann, *Jews in Egypt and Palestine*, I, 60 f.; Mann, *Texts and Studies*, II, 4; Salo W. Baron, *Social and Religious History of the Jews* [2d ed., New York, 1957], V, 221). True, this critical position has been challenged recently by R. Mahler in his historico-materialistic interpretation of Karaite history (first published in Yiddish, *Karaimer—a Yiddishe Geuleh-Bavegung in Mitlalter* [New York, 1947], then in Hebrew, *Haḳ-Ḳara'īm—Tenū'ath Ge'ūlah Yehūdith bi-Ymē hab-Beynayyim* [Merhavyah, 1949]. The present author agrees with Mahler on the basic problem of approach, i.e., on the need of viewing medieval sectarianism, including Jewish, as an expression of a social (but, let us add, also political, communal, and regional) protest. Yet, to limit ourselves to the particular point under discussion now, Mahler failed to grasp the formative process within Karaism, which, at its tenth-century peak, carried the movement a long way off its initial direction. Mahler's determination to prove that nationalism was one of the two leading factors responsible not only for the subsequent molding of the character of Karaism but for the very emergence of the sect led him into a fallacious search for Karaite Palestino-centric ideology of the tenth-century *Abelim*-brand right in the sayings and doctrines of 'Anan, the avowed founder of the movement, whose nationalism shows rather a Diaspora-centric orientation. Thus, in Mahler's reconstruction, Karaite ideology formed, from its earliest exposition by 'Anan till at least the eleventh and twelfth centuries, one solid unit, and, barring a few later formal emendations, could be accepted *in toto* as substantially emanating from its eighth-century founder. *Ipso facto*, the rift between 'Ananism and ninth- and tenth-century Karaism, so outspokenly admitted by the leaders of the "Mourners" Order, was shelved by Mahler in favor of the centuries-later idealizing presentations of 'Anan, mentioned earlier in this note. It is, of course, technically impossible to go into a detailed critique of Mahler's theory in the framework of this study (cf. Ashtor-Strauss's review in *Kirjath Sefer*, XXVI [1950], 122-25; Nemoy's review-article, "Social and Economic Factors in Early Karaism" [Yiddish], in *YIVO Bleter*, XXXIII [1949], 95-112; Ben-Sasson's "The First of the Karaites and the Trend of Their Social Conception" [Hebrew], *Zion*, XV [1950], 42-55). The present writer had already devoted a lengthy paper (unpublished) in 1951 to Mahler's otherwise stimulating contribution, where the above-mentioned interpretation of the 'Anan-*Abelim* relationship was also submitted to a detailed scrutiny and thoroughly refuted.

circle of mutual friends (A/8-9, 36-37). There is even, as already mentioned, a certain amount of money loaned or deposited by Peraḥ for Tobias (A/31). Though the difference of age and rank between the two is unmistakable (cf. the address and A/3-5, 8-9, 37), there is no sense of uneasiness on the part of Tobias, except for the usual poetic conventionalities in the introduction.

Now, who was Peraḥ ben Mūmal?

He was a Rabbanite scholar of Fusṭāṭ, who was already among the signatories of a court-writ of 1018 C.E. preserved in the Genizah.[49] This, incidentally, explains the difference of age and standing between him and Tobias, who some twenty years later was only on the eve of his independent career.

In our case, however, it is most important to note that Peraḥ was one of the staunch supporters of the usurper-gaon Nathan ben Abraham. In fact, it was most probably Nathan who raised Peraḥ ben Mūmal to the rank of Rosh hap-Pereḳ.[50] Thus, an early statement of evidence, presented to the chair of Nathan, shows Peraḥyah ben Mūmal heading the list of signatories with no title attached to his name, while Nathan himself is addressed in a general way as the "Head of the Academy";[51] however, in what must have been (to judge by the titles) a later communication from Nathan to Peraḥ [=Peraḥyah] ben Mūmal, Nathan already styles himself "Gaon," and Peraḥ is addressed as "Rosh hap-Pereḳ."[52]

Now, it seems that, like many other Karaites in Jerusalem, Tobias sided with the party of Nathan Gaon, and possibly in a very active way, too. Whether his acquaintance with Peraḥ ben Mūmal preceded the outbreak of the conflict and influenced Tobias's partisan preference, or whether it resulted from the steps taken by the usurper and his associates to win over to their side the qualitatively important *avant-garde* of the Karaite community, the *Abelē Ṣiyyon*, is impossible to ascertain from the available evidence. In any case, the steadfast support of a brilliant student of the Karaite Academy, already known from some literary attempts (A/26-27) and respected by the rank and file of his coreligionists

[49] See Mann, *Jews in Egypt and Palestine*, II, 174, n. 1.

[50] It is worth while to recall here that the provisions of the Solomon-Nathan agreement of 1041 tacitly admitted the voiding of all promotions emanating from the office of Nathan (including his own title), while those of Solomon retained their validity. Cf. Gottheil-Worrell, *Fragments from the Cairo Genizah in the Freer Collection*, pp. 196 ff., esp. recto, ll. 4-5 and 12-17; see also the summary of the agreement by Mann, *Texts and Studies*, I, 331 f., and the text in Arabic (and in Hebrew translation) as given ultimately in Assaf-Mayer's *Sefer hay-Yishshūb* (cf. above, note 33).

[51] Mann, *Jews in Egypt and Palestine*, II, 173 f.

[52] *Ibid.*, II, 173, ll. 1-3, 12, 14, and in the very opening of the address.

for leading the ascetic life of a "Mourner of Zion," must have been an asset to the rebellious party. It appears, however, that when the change of heart in regard to the favorite gaon had taken place in the entourage of the Karaite Nasī Ḥezeḳiah, following the circulation of the Bustanai pamphlet by the partisans of Solomon, Tobias did not desert Nathan's camp. Again, it is futile to conjecture whether personal motives were involved. We have referred above to a mention of some money deposited by Peraḥ for Tobias's use (A/31). Indeed, in one of his letters Solomon Gaon accuses Nathan of forcing his way through by means of his riches:

> I, it is from God that [authority] was given to me, not through power nor through might nor with riches, whereas he [= Nathan] comes forward with wealth, prides himself therewith, and gets the upper hand.[53]

It is to be doubted whether one can rely on the evidence of an adversary or even on an obscure reference to pecuniary matters in Tobias's own letter so as to question the integrity of an *Abel-Ṣiyyon*, whose firmness of conviction and strength of character speak from every line of the epistle at hand. Rather, we shall be right in explaining Tobias's reluctance to follow the lead of the Karaite Nasī in abandoning Nathan by the above-depicted general opposition of the "Mourners" Order to some Nesiim.[54] (Indeed, Ḥezeḳiah is known to have left the Jerusalem Center permanently in the early second half of the century.)

The bureaucratic machine of the Nasī retaliated by cutting off funds (A/22 and 24-26). This, however, did not break Tobias's will. Most emphatically he impresses upon his correspondent that his recent silence was caused by personal mishaps and by his general dejection and economic distress in the painfully changed atmosphere and should by no means be construed to indicate severance of relations (A/17-18). He preferred leaving the country to conforming. It is to this effect that he writes his letter to Peraḥ. He wishes to wind up his affairs, for very soon he will be on his way home.

We are in a position now to infer exactly, almost to the month, the date

[53] *Ibid.*, II, 162, ll. 22-24; cf. also Nathan's earlier letter on his business background, pp. 169 f.

[54] It seems that those of the past Nesiim who satisfied the requirements set down by Yefeth for spiritual leadership (see above, p. 21), by virtue of their scholastic standing or personal qualities, were held by Tobias in high respect. Such was, for instance, the case with Ḥezeḳiah's grandfather David ben Bo'az, as follows from the statement at the end of the Bodleian MS of Tobias's *Oṣar Neḥmad* on Leviticus (quoted already above, note 18). Cf. Neubauer's *Catalogue*, I, 58, No. 290 (cf. Volume of Facsimiles, Plate XXXV, ll. 1-3 in the second half of the leaf).

of Letter I, and, accordingly, to fix the year of Tobias's return to Byzantium from his sojourn as student and *Abel* in Jerusalem. The conflict between Solomon Gaon and his rival broke out sometime early in 1039 C.E., for in the summer of that year Nathan already styles himself "Gaon."[55] The agreement between the two parties was concluded in the fall (Hoshana Rabba) of 1041. The Bustanai report was copied in Fusṭāṭ in 1040-41, as Mann correctly suggested,[56] and it was in the wake of this publication that the Karaite official leadership changed its position. Now, the epistle to Peraḥ must have been written after this latter event, for it was this very change that provoked Tobias's complaint, although, as manifest from the general mood of the letter, the change was still quite recent and the retaliative measures of the fund administrators painfully new. So much for the *terminus a quo*.

On the other hand, the agreement between the parties seems not to have been concluded yet at the time our letter was written. In an earlier communication to Tobias (so we learn from the reply of the latter) Peraḥ hinted at the panic that had possessed his men in Egypt because of some (obviously non-Jewish) enemies (A/10). Mann could not make out the hint, and halfheartedly suggested that "perhaps the revolt in Palestine in 1024-29 is referred to which also threatened Egypt."[57] This would imply that as early as 1029 (or earlier) Tobias already completed his studies in Jerusalem, which, even ignoring the broader difficulties outlined above, is by any standard untenable.

Now, in the chronological and factual framework of the Solomon-Nathan affair, the allusion, for obvious reasons couched in vague terms, becomes perfectly intelligible. Moreover, it now becomes clear why it was that Peraḥ, at the Fusṭāṭ end of the line, reported the bad news to Tobias in Palestine, and not the other way round, which should have been expected in case the spread of a revolt *from* Palestine *to* Egypt was hinted at. Indeed, Tobias does not seem to be aware of the danger and sends the usual comforting phrases. I believe Peraḥ alludes in his letter to the intervention of Solomon's supporters at the court of the Caliph and of the Wazīr in Cairo in favor of the legitimate gaon. This intervention was successful, as we learn from a triumphant epistle of Solomon. On instructions from Egypt, the Jerusalem Fāṭimid commander and city officials and, above all, the Egyptian governor at Ramleh took sides with

[55] So in two letters written in Tammūz of [1]350 Seleucid Era; cf. Mann, *Jews in Egypt and Palestine*, II, 167 f. and 168 f.

[56] *Texts and Studies*, I, 335 f.

[57] *Ibid.*, I, 373.

the veteran gaon.[58] Surely, the outside power that, being responsible for Solomon's victory, is quoted by the latter in eulogizing terms does not deserve from the defeated party a better label than that of "enemies."[59] Who knows whether this favorable government intervention was not made possible when the Karaite leadership also joined hands with Solomon and moved its influential advocates in Fusṭāṭ to action.

Now, it is obvious from our letter that, while Peraḥ, in Fusṭāṭ, was already aware of the imminent danger to Nathan's cause, Tobias could not yet report any developments of this nature from Palestine, although the change of the official Karaite stand in the conflict had been made known to him in a most drastic fashion. Hence, our letter was written after the beginning of the year 1041, but before the fall of the same year, when the agreement, prompted by government intervention, was signed. It plausible to infer from the statement of Tobias (A/32), announcing that he "wants to leave [Jerusalem] after . . ." (here the text is mutilated, but Mann suggested "after [the festivals]"), that Passover is meant, rather than the far-off Tishri Festivals when the agreement was signed. In fact, it stands to reason that Tobias would decide to undertake the land-and-sea trip in late spring rather than in winter. Consequently, our letter must have been written some time in February, 1041, and, no doubt, about May of the same year Tobias left Jerusalem for good.

Thus, to return for a moment to Letter II, some five or six years could have elapsed between Tobias's return home and his subsequent visit to Egypt. In the course of these years, the Jerusalem-educated scholar, then in his forties, assumed offical leadership over the Karaite communities of Byzantium.[60]

[58] Mann, *Jews in Egypt and Palestine*, II, 166-67 (esp. ll. 12-14). Cf. Assaf-Mayer, *Sefer hay-Yishshūb*, II, 27a, No. 55.

[59] Although this interpretation neither rests nor falls with the reading I suggested for the obviously corrupted וסינגילאת in A/12 (see my note *ad loc.*, App., n. 84), it surely gains strength thereby. Thus, with my proposed *sijillāt*, governmental *writs* and judicial *instructions*—and not rebellious *actions*—are hinted at as prejudicial to the cause common to Tobias and Peraḥ. It is only natural to see the pious and confident *Abel* invoking Divine Writs, contained in the Holy Scriptures, against the frail human-made decrees of an adverse government.

[60] Quite naturally the question should be raised why in Letter II (written, as we concluded, some time in the mid- or late forties of the eleventh century, when he was in Egypt in the capacity of spiritual head of the Karaite communities in the Byzantine Empire) Tobias did not mention his status of *Abel*. This problem, however, as well as that of the evolution of the *Abelūth* doctrine in general in the spiritual climate of the Christian Empire in a crusading age, is discussed by the present writer elsewhere. It is perhaps illuminating to note in this connection that Firkowicz, not being aware of our Letter I, where the epithets *Abel* (= Mourner) and *'Obed* (= Servant of God) appear together, tried to distinguish between two persons going by the name of "Tobias":

We are now finally confronted with the most crucial problem in the reconstruction of the chronology of Tobias ben Moses and, indirectly, of early Byzantine Karaite history. This problem cannot be tacitly avoided; for there is no way, on the one hand, of accepting the conclusions reached from the analysis of the Genizah letters written by the hand of Tobias himself—which compel us to assign the end of his student years to 1041 (and consequently the period of his sojourn in Jerusalem to the thirties, including perhaps the late twenties, of the eleventh century) and his first years in independent leadership of Byzantine Karaism to the mid-forties of the same century—and then, on the other hand, placing him again at the feet of Yeshū'ah ben Yehūdah in Jerusalem in the second half, or, at the earliest, in the middle of the century, as all the Karaite scholars from the fifteenth century on and the consensus of modern students of Karaite history would have it.

Of the three possibilities, outlined at an earlier stage of this analysis, only the last one really remains open to us. It is my contention that *Tobias studied in Jerusalem not under Yeshū'ah ben Yehūdah but under Yōsef al-Baṣīr* (*ha-Roēh*), who, together with Abū'l-Faraj Harūn, mentioned by name in Letter I, raised the scholarly level of the Karaite Academy in Jerusalem in the first half of the eleventh century to unparalleled heights.[61] Although we do not know the exact date of al-Baṣīr's death,

---

he assigned one of them, the *Baḳī* (= Versed in the Law), son of Moses the *Abel*, to the beginning of the eleventh century, and the other, known as *'Obed* or *Ma'atiḳ* (= the Translator) and pupil of Yeshū'ah ben Yehūdah, to the second half of that century (cf. Firkowicz's communication to A. B. Gottlober, in the latter's *Biḳḳoreth le-Tholedoth haḳ-Ḳara'īm*, p. 169, note). True, as Mann has said in a different connection (*Texts and Studies*, I, 375), "we cannot fathom out the skill of Firkowicz when changing or correcting colophons"—for, needless to add, the letter that Firkowicz produced to substantiate his thesis (*Benē Reshef*, p. 15) has proved spurious and the whole theory of two Tobiases unfounded (cf. P. F. Frankl, "Karäische Studien" [First Article], *MGWJ*, XXV [1876], where the alleged letter of David ben Bo'az to Tobias the *Baḳī* is reprinted, pp. 56-59, and analyzed, pp. 59 ff.). Yet, in fairness to the nineteenth-century Karaite politician, manuscript-collector, and editor, one has to admit that he sensed the inevitable difficulties and contradictions, chronological and biographical, inherent in the way Tobias was, and still is, presented in the framework of Karaite history. Also Simḥah Lutzki, in enumerating the early Karaite sages, puts Tobias the *Baḳī* in the first half of the eleventh century, immediately after Yeshū'ah ben Aaron (= Abū'l-Faraj Harūn), as the chronology of our Genizah fragments leads us to do, and then has another Tobias ben Moses (to our mind identical with the first but active as an independent leader in the middle and in the second half of the eleventh century) listed along with later Byzantine Karaite scholars like Jacob ben Simon, Yehūdah Hadassi, etc. Cf. *Oraḥ Ṣaddīḳim*, fol. 21b.

[61] See on Yōsef al-Baṣīr, in general, *Oṣar Yisrael*, V, 134b-135b, and the bibliography given there. In view of the tremendous influence al-Baṣīr had exerted on Tobias and of the important part the works of this sage played in Tobias's literary activity, it may

Poznański, with his fine insight into Karaite history, tentatively fixed it at about 1040 C.E.,[62] the last dated treatise of al-Başīr having been composed in 1036-37.[63] Yeshū'ah ben Yehūdah himself was a pupil of al-Başīr as well as of Abū'l-Faraj Harūn,[64] the latter, incidentally, having survived his colleague.[65]

In this connection I wish to state that, even earlier and independently of the above Genizah evidence, I reached the same conclusion as to who really was the teacher of Tobias on the basis of an over-all investigation of the problem of authorship of Karaite Hebrew translations from the Arabic in the first century of Karaism in Byzantium. A critique of the traditions pertaining to the Tobias problem convinced me of the same

---

be advisable to mention here the foremost studies relating to him. These are, of course, the treatments by P. F. Frankl, beginning with "Die Stellung Joseph al-Başīrs in der jüdischen Religionsphilosophie," *MGWJ*, XX (1871), 114-19, 150-57, and his bibliographical analysis in "Zur karäischen Bibliographie," *MGWJ*, XXI (1872), 207-17, 274-80, culminating in *Ein mu'tazilitischer Kalām aus dem 10. Jahrhundert* and *Beiträge zur Literaturgeschichte der Karäer*, where also our Tobias comes into the picture. Likewise cf. M. Schreiner's *Der Kalām in der jüdischen Literatur*. On Abū'l-Faraj Harūn see the references above, note 17. For the activity of these two sages in Jerusalem, cf. Poznański's already-quoted Hebrew study in *Jerusalem*, X (1913), 102-6.

62 Cf. Poznański, "Nouveaux renseignements sur Abou-l-Faradj Haroun, etc.," *REJ*, LVI (1908), 43 f.; Poznański, *Jerusalem*, X (1913), 104 and 106; Poznański, *Hastings' Encyclopedia of Religion and Ethics*, VII, 666a.

63 So in the familiar chronicle of Ibn al-Hītī, see above, note 20. Our passage appears in *JQR* (O.S.), IX (1896-97), 434, English Version, p. 440, as well as in Nemoy, *Karaite Anthology*, pp. 232 f. Cf. also Poznański's bibliographical note in *The Karaite Literary Opponents of Saadiah Gaon*, p. 46, n. 2. The correctness of Poznański's hypothesis as to the date of al-Başīr's death had been impugned some thirty yeare ago on the basis of a MS allegedly dictated by al-Başīr in 1048. Cf. A. Marx, "The Books and MSS of the Seminary Library in the Exhibition of the N.Y. Public Library," *United Synagogue Recorder*, VI (June, 1926), 20b (also in German tr., *Soncino-Blätter*, II [1927], 116a-b). This finding has subsequently been incorporated into Skoss's *The Arabic Commentary of 'Alī ben Suleimān the Karaite on the Book of Genesis*, pp. 92 f. (note to 1. 8) and p. 191 (addendum to p. 19), as well as in his reply in *Tarbiz*, II (1930-31), 513, to Baneth's discussion of "The Date of 'Ali b. Suleimān," *Tarbiz*, II, 115 ff. This allegation, however, has proved, on closer examination of the MS, entirely unfounded. See my "Ibn al-Hītī and the Chronology of Joseph al-Başīr the Karaite," *Journal of Jewish Studies*, VIII (1957), 71-81.

64 Poznański, *The Karaite Literary Opponents of Saadiah Gaon*, p. 48; Mann, *Texts and Studies*, II, 34. The theory of Pinsker (*Likkūtē Kadmoniyyoth*, App., p. 170) and of Neubauer (*Aus der Petersburger Bibliothek*, p. 19), according to which Yeshū'ah was considered a pupil of al-Başīr in a figurative sense only, grew out of the assumption, prevailing in their days, that al-Başīr was a contemporary of Sa'adyah Gaon. Since this has proven to be a mistaken premise, the aforementioned theory, too, can now unreservedly be discarded.

65 See the above-cited chronicle of Ibn al-Hītī, *JQR* (O.S.), IX (1896-97), pp. 433 f. (English tr., p. 440, as well as in Nemoy's *Karaite Anthology*, p. 232).

point.[66] The fact that identical results were yielded by a study carried out from three different angles is surely not a mere coincidence.

To return now to our analysis of Letter I, we do not, thus, feel any more difficulty in the fact that Yeshūʻah ben Yehūdah is not mentioned. After all, he was more or less of the same age and rank as Tobias, perhaps even on the other side of the fence in the conflict which forms the background of our letter. Neither do we wonder why the name of Tobias's teacher, Yōsef al-Baṣīr, is missing. Quite the contrary, only now can we grasp the full depth of Tobias's feeling of loneliness and dejection. For, as suggested, al-Baṣīr died about 1040, i.e., a year, or perhaps a few months only, before the letter was written. It would be futile to conjecture whether Tobias followed his master in the strife that was raging in the community and whether the fact that Abū'l-Faraj Harūn, al-Baṣīr's colleague, remained steadfast in his care for him had anything to do with it. Harūn's magnanimity and his keeping aloof from the petty feud, whichever party he sympathized with, are only to be expected of the venerated sage, the President of the Karaite Academy in Jerusalem, whose personality and learning commanded respect and honor from Karaites and Rabbanites alike. Be this as it may, Tobias's grief over the death of the man who was his teacher and master and whom he undoubtedly learned to admire and love must also have influenced his decision not to fight it out on the spot, but, now that his studies were over with the death of al-Baṣīr, better to leave Jerusalem for good and return to his native land.

The bitter experience of Tobias in communal politics had a lasting effect on him. Though the events described in the preceding pages occurred beyond the political boundaries of the Byzantine Empire, they had a direct bearing on the history of Karaism in Byzantium not only because an important Karaite leader of Byzantine origin personally participated in them but, even more so, because of the role which independent Karaism on the Bosporus was to play in later developments of the sect. These developments, in turn, form the subject of a separate study.[67]

[66] Cf. my Hebrew essay on "Elijah Bashyachi: An Inquiry into His Traditions concerning the Beginnings of Karaism in Byzantium," *Tarbiz*, XXV (1955), 44 ff., 183 ff., n the first chapter of which have also been incorporated the results of the aforementioned study on the authorship problem of Byzantine Karaite original treatises and translations, insofar as our Tobias b. Moses is concerned.

[67] See my *Karaites in Byzantium: The Formative Years (970-1100)*.

Courtesy of Cambridge University Library

LETTER FROM TOBIAS BEN MOSES TO PERAḤ BEN MŪMAL (RECTO)

Courtesy of Cambridge University Library

LETTER FROM TOBIAS BEN MOSES TO PERAḤ BEN MŪMAL (VERSO)

APPENDIX

Letter I (A): From Tobias, in Jerusalem, to Peraḥ b. Mūmal, in Fusṭāṭ

(recto)

שלום רב לא[הב]י תורתך וג'[68]
שלומות רבות וישועות עצומות· ובשורות נאומות· ושנים נעי[מות]·
ו[בר]כות רשומות· מיודע תעלומות· לאד'[69] ומרי כב' גד' ק[ד][70]
הדרת יקרת· תפארת עטרת מרו'ר[71] הזקן היקר התכ[ם] וה נבון הידוע [אבוסרור][72]
פרת האלהים יש'[73] ויעזרהו וינצרהו· בן כב' גד' [מ]ר' ו[ר'] הזקן מ[ו]מל יר' אל[74]
ממני אני טוביה העובד הת[למ]יד ה[צעיר האב]ל במות א· · ·[75]
ובעד שבר כל יש'[76] ועל ציון וירוש'[77] האלהים ינתמנ[ו] ככת'[78] כא"ש אשר אמו]
תנחמנו כן אנכי אנחמכם ובירוש תנוחמו: [וא]מר ל[אדוני הזקן][79]
היקר כי באה אלי כתבך הנאה והיקרה ושמחתי כי[80] א[תם][81] · · · · · ·
וכי אתם מן פחד האויבים ביראה גדולה ברוך י'י אלהינו אשר · · · · · ·
מעמו כי היה הו[א] יודע מה[82] יעבור על זאת האמה השפלה וכ[תב][83] · · · · · ·
וסינגילאת[84] שאם יבוא לנו צרה נשוב אליהם ונראה[85] ונ[קח] · · · · · ·

68 Ps. 119 : 165. This line is missing in Mann's edition of the epistle.

69 = לאדוני. There is a blank in the MS both before and after these two letters. While the first might be taken as the usual space left between paragraphs, the latter could possibly result from the fading of the remaining letters of the word לאדוני. Indeed, there is no dot above the ד to indicate an abbreviation.

70 Faded. Possibly the word קדושת was written in full.

71 = מרנא ורבנא (or: מורנו ורבנו); added above the line.

72 Supplied by Mann on the basis of the address.

73 = ישמרהו.

74 = ירחמהו אל; supplied by Mann on the basis of the address.

75 The continuation may have possibly contained the word אחי (or אשתי), which would perhaps elucidate the equally faded end of 1. 22 (or the obscure hint to an adulterous woman taking care of his only daughter, in 1. 35). Thus Tobias was mourning after a brother of his or a friend whom he figuratively calls "my brother" (or after his deceased wife). Or, shall we perhaps assume במות א[דוני מורי], pointing to the death of Tobias's teacher Yōsef al-Baṣīr? Mann reads התלמ]יד ה ..... המת[אבל].

76 ישראל; so also twice in 1. 14.

77 = וירושלים.

78 = ככתוב; Is. 66 : 13. The lacuna was restored by Mann on the basis of the extant part of the verse.

79 The reading is doubtful. Mann has [ו]מד[יע אל הזקן].

80 Mann reads בו; Tobias, however, uses the feminine all along in regard to כתב.

81 The faded section possibly contained an expression of joy over the addressee's good health. The following וכי is to be understood, then, in contrast to the earlier phrase: "and [as for the fact] that you are in great fear...."

82 Mann reads כי, which is graphically unwarranted and blurs the meaning of the sentence.

83 Possibly וכתב להם בריתות.

84 Mann mistakenly read וסונגילאת. The reading offered here, clearly following from the facsimile, makes the solution of this obscure expression, suggested later in this note, even more plausible. Indeed, lines 11-13 present great difficulty owing to the unintelligible וסינגילאת of which Mann said in the course of his interpretation (*Texts and Studies*, I, 373), "There is evidently in 1. 11 [i.e., our 1. 12] a Greek word (וסונגילאת)

נפשנו כי לא נאבד ותחלתם[86] ואף גם זאת בהיותם [בארץ איביהם וג׳ מקוה][87] ישׂ וג׳[88] מקוה ישׂ מושיעו בעת צרה וג׳[89] בכל [צרתם לא צר ומלאך פניו וג׳][90] מלמד שאמׂ החכמׂ זכׂ לב״[91] שבכל .... במקרא· ואשרי שיבטח בו ואוי [למי שימ··][92] ....

---

though its meaning is obscure to me"; see also his note 22 to the text. In turn, also the subsequent wording was hardly intelligible, e.g., the last but one word of 1. 12—אליהם (Mann, n. 24: "It is not clear to whom the plural suffix refers. Read perhaps אליו, viz. to God"); or the fifth word of 1. 13— ותחלתם (Mann, n. 25: "This is evidently corrupt for תוחלתם, but here again this plur. suffix is obscure and תוחלתנו would fit in better, viz. our hope is expressed in the following verses"). This presentation is hardly satisfactory. For, in the first place, although Tobias is known to have employed Greek terms in works intended for Byzantine readers, it should seem rather strange to have him follow the same usage in a letter addressed to an Arabic-speaking Jewish worthy in Fusṭāṭ, Egypt, who most probably did not know Greek. Secondly, the last syllable of וסינגילאת betrays rather an Arabic plural ending, although the root is not Arabic and the form we have is no doubt corrupt. Finally, the chain of emendations suggested for the perfect Hebrew wording cannot, in any case, be indulged in without reluctance. It seems to me that by סינגילאת Tobias had in mind the Arabic *sijillāt*, denoting judicial records, writs, or writing rolls (cf. Lane's *Arabic-English Lexicon*, I, 1311b, *s.v.*). In accord with my interpretation of the epistle, Tobias, replying to Peraḥ's hint about the impending writs of the government in favor of Solomon, states, in the confident manner of an *Abel Ṣiyyon*, that God, having been aware in advance of the afflictions that will befall His children in the Diaspora, prepared for them—against the decrees and writs of adverse governments—decrees and writs of His own, "so that in case trouble afflicts us we might return to them (!אליהם, viz., to these Divine Writs) and see [i.e., God's promise therein] and take [cheer and confidence into] our souls that we shall not perish." These Writs, of course, are contained in the Revealed Word—"and their beginning phrases (! ותחלתם) are the following"—here the initial sections of appropriate biblical phrases are given. The misspelling of סִגִּלָּאת might, incidentally, be either due to Tobias's insufficient knowledge of Arabic, or to the fact that the originally non-Arabic term, probably quite diffusedly employed in dealings with governmental agencies, settled in the Judaeo-Arabic jargon in a corrupt form.

85 Missing in Mann's edition.

86 Indeed, only the beginning clause of the Divine Writ from Lev. 26 : 44 is given. The actual promise appears further down the verse: לא מאסתים ולא געלתים לכלתם להפר בריתי אתם אני ה׳ אלהיהם. The choice of a passage which points to the never-expiring validity in the Diaspora of God's *covenant* with His people as a bulwark against their afflictions in the "land of their enemies" falls in very well with our solution of וסינגילאת in note 84, above, and serves as an appropriate preamble to the subsequent prophetic quotations.

87 Supplied by Mann.

88 Jer. 17 : 13.

89 Jer. 14 : 8.

90 Is. 63 : 9. Reconstructed by Mann.

91 = שאמרו החכמים זכרונם לברכה. Note that Tobias, the Karaite, lends to the expression, usually invoked with the pronominal suffix of the first person plural (חכמינו ז״ל), an impersonal bend. Mann recognized in what probably followed a well-known Rabbinic homily that God takes part in the suffering of Israel. Cf., however, the homiletical interpretation of the same verse in Yehūdah Hadassi's *Eshkol hak-Kofer*, fol. 68b, Alphabet 172/ה׳.

92 Mann reads ואשרי שיבטח בו וא[שרי החוסה בו].

כי[93] לא כתבתי לך עד עתה חי נפשך וחי[94] ......
לא עשיתי זה אלא מדאגה גדולה כ[י צרה ושבר][95] גדול .....
את נפשי בבית המת אני ואין איש יסו[ר לשאו]ל ל[שלומי][96] ......
ואין איש מנחם ולולי רחמי שדי ובאו אנש[ים מ]א[ח] ......
בדברים ט[ובים] הייתי אמות: וכל שכן כי ....
ואפילו גרה אחת לא יתנו לי ואני כרתי את נפשי מן העו[לם ללא אח][97] .....
בעולם ולולי כי הזקן אבו אלפרג אהרן שׁ צֿ[98] ישלח אחת לעתים וישאל [לשלומי]
לא הייתי אדע טוב או רע· וכל שכן כי באו לזקן אבונצר חסד באלה הימים
דרכמונים ופיזרום לכל איש וכן לאבועלי יפת בן אברהם יר׳ אל [ו]פיזרו גם אלה
ולא נתנו לי אפילו שעורה אחת· ולא הם זכרו אותי בשאר האנ[שים] ולא ב[עד]
הקִינות שעשיתי עליו[99] וברוך י׳י ואם הם הניחוני ולא זכרו לי[100] האלהים [לא]
יעזוב את יראיו כי אם יכלכלם ברחמיו כי מי אני עתה ומה כחי לול[י כי][101]
מערב עד ערב לא יתסיר לי הקֹבֹה מן פת חרבה שא[וכל] ....
נעימותיו·[102] אבל לא חפצו בברכה ותרחק מהם ....
תחפוץ שאתן[103] הכספים שלך שהם לך עלי ושגר [ל] ....
אצלך ואל תאחר בזה אדוני כי אני חפץ לצאת אחר[104] ....

[93] Meaning "as for the fact that." Cf. above, note 81.

[94] Mann reads וחי נפשי.

[95] Mann reads just כי שבר.

[96] Reconstructed by Mann.

[97] Faded. Mann suggests ואות[ר]. For the implication of the wording offered here see above, note 75.

[98] = שמרהו צורו.

[99] Mann understood the line as recalling dirges that Tobias composed on the death of Abraham, the father of Abū 'Alī Yefeth. The construction "neither . . . nor" (ולא . . . ולא . . .) seems to emphasize here Tobias's feeling of having been doubly mistreated: his right to a regular allowance "amid the other people (= the *Abelim*)" has been violated, and his individual merits and deeds which called for the customary reward were unfairly ignored. See next note.

[100] Continuing the stress on double injustice, indicated in the previous note, the phrase ולא זכרו לי, 'and they did not remember *for my sake*' (i.e., they did not think of rewarding me for all the good that I have done), should be distinguished from a resembling phrase in the preceding line— ולא הם זכרו אותי בשאר האנשים, 'and they did not remember *me* [i.e., did not list my name] with the others.'

[101] Faded.

[102] Mann reads מזימותיו.

[103] Mann reads שֶׁאוֹתָן, which is unwarranted both graphically as well as from the point of view of grammar, and interprets the line as an appeal by Tobias to Peraḥ to send him the funds held by the latter for Tobias's account so that he may pay for his journey home (*Texts and Studies*, I, 373). Though the line is not very clear anyway, it seems that the real implication is of an entirely different nature: Tobias asks for instructions in regard to a certain amount of money which he *owes* Peraḥ and which now, winding up his affairs in Jerusalem, he wishes to forward to the proper party for further transmission to Fusṭāṭ. Proud and scrupulous *Abel* that he is, despite poverty and grief, he is anxious to dispose of his debts before he undertakes the imminent journey home.

[104] Mann inferred that Tobias evidently wished to leave Jerusalem after the festivals. In my reconstruction I suggested that Passover, rather than the Tishri High Holidays, is meant here.

והנמהר אולי ישיבני י׳י אל ביתי ואל נחלת אבותי כ[י]..........
וכל שכן כאב הבת היתידה לא תזוז מלבי[105]
(ma יומם[106] ולילה· ומי היה יתן | והיתה תמות ולא היתה עם | האשה המנאפת·[107]ן
ואם תראה לזקן אבועלי | ו··[108] תתן לו שלום | בחסדך וגם תשאל | לשלום ביתו|
ותכתוב לי שלומם· | ושלום אדוני | הזקן הישר ירבה | לעד אמן·

Addres (verso)
[ל]כ׳[109] גד מר׳ור׳[110] אבוסדור פרח הי[קר]
.....[111] בן הג׳[112] מומל הזקן יר׳ [אל]
...[113]·במצכים· [ישמ׳ אל][114]

ממני טוביה האבל שואל[115] שלומך·
מן עיר הקדש תבנה ות׳ במ׳[116] אמ[ן]·
الفسطاط[117]

Letter II (B): From Tobias, somewhere in Egypt, to Abraham at-Tustarī, in Fusṭāṭ

(B/I)
אשרי שמרי משפט עושה צדקה בכל עת:[118]
אשרי משכיל אל דל ביום רעה ימלט׳ וג׳:[119]
אויה לי כי גרתי משך שכנתי עם אהלי ק[דר]:[120]
ותכ[יתי לי׳י המסתיר פנים וקי׳[ו]יתי לו:[121]

[105] Mann mistakenly assumed that the second half of the line faded. There is no lacuna between מלבי and the text on the margin.

[106] The section that follows appears in the MS in the form of short lines written diagonally on the right-hand margin, beginning with the low corner and continuing up and above the top line of the page. For the sake of easier reference the text is reproduced here in ordinary verses, preserving the serial numbering of lines applied for the whole page (so also in Mann's edition).

[107] The allusion to Tobias's family troubles is obscure. In my restored reading of line 11 in B/II a slanderous gossip against Tobias is implied, which might perhaps have some connection with the present "grief over the only daughter" who stays "with that adulterous woman."

[108] Mann has תין which, he concedes, is doubtful and should better be נָתַן. The first letter, however, is definitely a ו. Possibly read וגם as counterpart of the next clause.

[109] This section, written on the verso of the page, appears in Mann's edition on top of the preceding text.

[110] = לכבוד גדולת מרנא ורבנא. Mann reads לכ׳ גד׳ קד׳ מר׳.

[111] Mann supplied [החכם והנבון], probably imitating l. 4 of the recto. However, the last letter, which is the only extant remnant of the clause, is surely not ן.

[112] = הוד גדולתו. Mann's הרב is graphically impossible.

[113] There is a period (.) preceding במצרים, which perhaps indicates the existence of a word or two in the (damaged) beginning section of the line.

[114] The reading is doubtful. Mann's tentative שלום is graphically impossible.

[115] Mann has [הדורש].

[116] = ותכונן במהרה. Mann missed the abbreviation and reconstructed [ות[כונן.

[117] Missing in Mann's edition. There is of course no telling whether this Arabic word (reading *al-Fusṭāṭ*) was written down by Tobias himself. The rest of the verso is blank, save for an upside-down inscription, added by a different hand (possibly Peraḥ himself or his secretary): כתאב [מן] טוביה, meaning "Letter from Tobias."

[118] Ps. 106 : 3.

[119] Ps. 41 : 2; the first editors read [ימלטה[ו יהוה, in line with the original ending of the biblical verse. The dot over the ט clearly indicates an abbreviation. The next letters, distinctly separated from ימלט, are וג.

[120] Ps. 120 : 5 (last word restored in accord with the scriptural text).

[121] Is. 8 : 12 (the original verse reads פניו). A superfluous י before the ו of קויתי has been marked off by two dots, meaning: deleted.

הדרת[122] יקרת אדיר שרי המלאכת: כבוד הוד אציל חורי ממלכת:[123]
טַּפסר מצא ויחן·[124] בְּרור לבב מתחן·[125] להסליל ול[ק·]ל:
וַּעדי עד יתקיים· במצותיו הוא קיים· [ל]·············
ביַּפה טוב ומיתס· להטיב כל מעש· ב ·····ו ·····
אבַּרותו הא[צי]לו·[126] חסות תחת צילו· כל ק[הל ישראל:]
הַּ·ו ···············ל ··· ·········· ············
כבוד גדולת תהלת· יקר קהלת· המונת מעלת· הדרת יקרת·
צברת כתרת· אדוני ומרי· החכם הנבון· החסיד הנדיב· יש[ר]
בדרכיו· תם במפעליו· השר המיוקר· הזקן המפואר מכ[הג][127]
אברהם הידוע אביסעד שמרו צורו· ויעזרו נוצרו· לא י[ד]ל[128]
עושרו· ולא יכבה נרו· קמיו יפלו· ואויביו יושפלו· תחת שא[ו]ל
יוכפלו·[129] יחדו המה יתהוללו·[130] בן כבֹ גדֹ קהֹ קדו[131]············

[122] The first editors failed to reconstruct the name conveyed in the acrostic and put a dot on the initial ה of l. 5. This dot is of course unnecessary and is conspicuously missing in the MS. The acrostic starts with the next line, reading Ṭ-O-B-iY-aH. Line 9 should precede line 8, as marked by the scribe by means of a small א above the initial letter of l. 9 and a small ב above the initial letter of l. 8. This was rightly indicated by Mann in the corrections he supplied to the text (*Texts and Studies*, I, 373 f., n. 3).

[123] The present reading, clearly evident from the MS, means "Glory of the noblest amid the noblemen of the kingdom"—thus forming a natural counterpart of the earlier hemistich. Mann's correction of Gottheil-Worrell's version, substituting בהלכת for בו לכת (אציל הורי), to serve as a paiṭanic form of the word *halakha*, still makes a clumsy Hebrew and attributes to at-Tustarī scholarly merits that are supported by no other reference in the abundant literature pertaining to him, yielded by the Genizah, beside being also graphically unwarranted.

[124] Both Gottheil-Worrel's מצאר חן (n. 6: "מִצְהַר?") and Mann's מצאוי חן do not make sense and violate the rhyme. My reading means: "The dignitary, he has found [the pure-hearted supplicant, mentioned next] and was gracious (ויחן from חנן) to him."

[125] Mann's correction תַּחַן (= תחִנה), instead of Gottheil-Worrell's בַּת חִן, is right, although the meaning of תחן and תחנה here is not "prayer" (Mann, *Texts and Studies*, I, 373, n. 3, bottom), but "supplication" addressed to a high-ranking personality; cf. B/II, l. 13 and l. 21. The preposition preceding the word is מ and not ב.

[126] An emendation into הצילו (Gottheil-Worrell, n. 8) is unnecessary and graphically impossible.

[127] = מעלת כבוד הוד גדולתו. Last two letters are faded.

[128] This is Mann's correction of Gottheil-Worrell's י[ק]ל. Though still uncertain, it makes good Hebrew and suits the context.

[129] The first editors restored תחת ש[בטו] and joined it in their translation to the former phrase, while leaving the subsequent יוכפלו standing alone. The meaning was thus: ". . . and may his enemies be brought low, under his rod! May they be confounded!" This not only mutilates the original verse-division of the paragraph under discussion and makes an awkward Hebrew, but is also graphically unwarranted. Our rendering means: "May their number be doubled underneath Hell!"

[130] Mann's correction יתהוללו is superfluous and graphically unwarranted. Cf. Jer. 50:38: ובאימים יתהללו (see Gesenius's *Hebrew-English Lexicon*, ed. Tregelles, p. 226, *s.v.* הלל).

[131] = כבוד גדולת קהלת קדושת.

[ה]דר עטרת· הוד תפארת[132] [אדונינו הז]קן הגדול [ה]ש[ר] · · · ל·
והמכובד סהל הידוע אביאלפצ̇ל תהא[133] נפשו נחויה· · · · · · · · · · · ·[134]
של צדיקים נתחייה·[135] תחת אשלי גן דתויה· בגן עדן שרויה·
מעץ החיים רוויה: מגמת מכתבי זה· מאיש עני ונבזה·
ההוסמך להיות מזה· טוביה עבדך הרזה· שעברו עליו צרות
כהלזה· ואין ספר לתקור בזה· ולא כדברי אשר אמר מה זה·[136]
ול[א כמ]נהג מי אני כי הביאותני עד זה·[137] נחקקו שתי [טו]רים
אלה אליך אדוני הזקן המ[כו]בד[138] שצ̇ להוד[יע] אודותיי·[139] [כי] ל[א]
באתי הנה בארץ מצרים בעבור [שא]בקש מן [הזקנים ד]בר
?? ?
(B/II) שאתכלכל[140] ואתפרנ[ס]· אבל באתי הנה בעבור דבר א[ח]ר[ים][141]

[132] The final ת is rather peculiar, yet the reading is beyond doubt. Gottheil-Worrell's apprehensions in regard to this as well as to the next faintly visible word are unfounded.

[133] This is Mann's correction of the first editors' rendering תחא. The ה is unmistakable.

[134] The word is completely faded. Mann's suggestion במחיצות is graphically impossible.

[135] Gottheil-Worrell have בגנת חיים, 'in the Garden of Life.' Mann rightly objects to it, because it deviates from the inner rhyme-scheme of the whole phrase. The epigraphy is also clearly against this reading. Mann, however, does not come forward with a suggestion of his own. There is no doubt that the word reads נתחייה. The difficulty lies in the sign immediately following the word צדיקים. It seems that the writer started penning the word דחויה after צדיקים. We can still recognize a very clear ד and the first two (or rather one and a half) strokes of a ח. Then he obviously changed his mind, crossed out the unfinished word and started writing a distinctly new word, נתחייה. (I am indebted for this reading to my wife.)

[136] Gottheil-Worrell missed altogether the biblical allusion in this as well as in the next verse. They must have read the passage ולא כִּדְבָרַי אשר אָמַר מה זה, for they translate it: "Nor is there anything like *my* words when *I* say 'What is this.'" It seems to me that Tobias alludes to Jud. 18 : 24: ויאמר (מיכה) את אלהי אשר עשיתי לקחתם ואת הכהן ותלכו ומה לי עוד ומַה זֶּה תאמרו אלי מה לך.

[137] Here the first editors failed to recognize a biblical quotation given in full. We have now an allusion to king David. Tobias invokes I Chron. 17 : 6 (and the same verse in II Sam. 7 : 18, with אנכי instead of אני). The ending עד זה replaced, for the sake of rhyme, the original עד הלם which appears in both biblical sources. Unfortunately, even these allusions fail to offer to the present-day reader a sufficient lead in this, perhaps intentional, vagueness of Tobias with reference to the objective of his visit to Egypt.

[138] Cf. the similar usage in B/I/18 as well as B/II/19, 25. Gottheil-Worrell have הנכבד.

[139] Mann's correction of the editors' אודות is both graphically and factually justified.

[140] This is Mann's correction of Gottheil-Worrell's שאתכרכר. See above, note 12 to the present essay, on the original contiguity of the lines and on the reason for Gottheil-Worrell's misreading.

[141] Mann's correction בעבור דְּבַר אֲדוֹנִי is in line with his stress on Tobias's employment by at-Tustarī as the main theme of our letter. Yet, leaving aside all the factual objections to this interpretation, even for graphical reasons this reading is untenable. Although, except for the initial letter, the whole last word in the line is badly faded, the unmistakable remnants of characters definitely exclude a ד immediately following the א. There is no mistaking in regard to a narrow two-legged letter occupying the second

וישבתי שנה תמימה במלאכת אדוני המפואר ולא ראי[תי] רווחה [במעשי] ידי· וגם לא עמדתי לפני אדם אחד שאב?[קש] ממנו מחיה· ולא בקשתי מן אדם וגם לא נתן? לי א[דם שום ד]בר מעולם] זולת [הדר] ······ [?אדוני] החל ············[142] במקום הזה· והאלהים יודע איך תיינו שלשת הנפ[שות] ...[143] השנה מכובד דותק המחיה ואמר לי אבי אלפרג [היבה] שׂ[צׂ] כי אדוני הזקן המיוקר חרה אפו בעבור כי שכנתי ביניכם וכאשר שמעתי דבריו אמרתי בלבי כי אולי הכבדתי [ע]ליהם כי כל יום ויום עומד[144] לפניהם ונקצר רוח אדוני ממני או [שמע בעבור שידו דופי[145] מ]יום שנכנסתי במקום ה[זה] וחר[ה] לו בשיכנותי ביניהם· ושמתי לבי שאלך אל ארצי ואל מולדתי ומשפחתי ומפיל תחינתי לפני אדוני הזקן השר המיוקר שיעשה שאלתי שבעבורה ירדתי אל המקום הזה כי אין הנה [מי שׂ]עשה[146] חסד עימי ולא שילם לי תלופו[147] זולתך כי תסדך נשאר עלי שלם ועוד הוספת ותוסי[ף] בזה הדבר ויהיה לך שכר בזה ובבא· והוא שתקת לע[בד]ך [ב]רו[ב] חכמתך כתב כי אפחד שלא ישיגני בדרך [כ]אשר השיגני בְּתָנֵּס[148] ולולי רחמי שדי ותסד אדוני הזקן המכובד הייתי [אמ]ות[149]

---

place (a ה or a ה), whereas a remnant of the upper horizontal bar of a ר (or a ד) is so distant from the א that it could have only been a third letter. It can also by no means be taken as the head of a ו (which is the third letter of Mann's אדוני), because it is too removed from what should have been taken as the residue of the letter's leg. In brief, the reading אַחֵר (or אֶחָד) is indisputable. Still, perhaps it may have constituted only part of the actual word, for the space which is still vacant after the three-letter אחר or אחד suffices for one broad and one narrow letter to be added, so as to warrant a reading בעבור דְּבַר אֲחֵרִים.

142 The whole line is almost completely illegible. Gottheil-Worrell reconstructed the first three words and some fragmentary letters at the end. My additional restorations unfortunately do not offer any illuminating clues.

143 Gottheil-Worrell's additional כל is graphically unjustified.

144 I.e., עומד (אני).

145 This half of the line is badly faded. The first editors correctly restored the two beginning words, but then read שירורותי, which of course did not make sense. Oscillating between a possibility of שְׁרִירוּתִי, meaning "stubborness," and of שֵׁירוּתִי, meaning "service," yet translating the passage according to the first solution, they still left the question mark to dominate both the text as well as the translation and notes. The factual implications that go into the reading suggested by me may be seen when recalling A/34-35 and my note thereto (n. 107).

146 Mann's correction שיעשה has no justification.

147 The Hebrew in the last section of the passage is not without difficulty. Gottheil-Worrell's translation of ולא שלם לי חלופו —to mean: "or (had anybody) requited me with good. Quite the contrary!"—seems to me unacceptable.

148 Vocalized in the original.

149 This is Mann's correct reading, replacing Gottheil-Worrell's faulty הייתי היום. The whole expression ולולי רחמי שדי ו. . . הייתי אמות —brings to mind 11. 20-21 of Letter I.

בבית הכלא ובימים ההם היה בידי ונתתי שוחד אבל [בא]לה הימים אין בידי מאומה ועל זה מפיל תחינתי לפני אדוני שיעשה עם עבדך חסד ולא יניתהו שיאבד כי ע[בד]ך יגדיל ויפאר שם אדוני שׂצׂ בכל מה שעשה עמי וע[ם כ]ל אדם בכל קהילות ארץ אדום הקרובות והרחוקות ואתקן שיני ותמישי[150] שיברכו לאדוני המכובד בבתי כנסיות· ומאת צורי המשאל שיסיר ממנו כל מחלה וכל גזרה רעה ככׄ לא תאונה וגׄ'[151]

[150] The first editors entirely misunderstood the passage and considered שיני וחמישי as denoting specific persons bearing the well-known Rabbinic academic ranks of שני בחבורה etc. The true meaning has been recognized by Mann, *Texts and Studies*, I, 374.

[151] Ps. 91 : 10.

TOWARD THE DAWN OF HISTORY

By Meir Ben-Horin

NOT THE USE of thought to accomplish purposes already given either in the mechanism of the body or in that of the existent state of society but the use of intelligence to liberate and to liberalize action, is the pragmatic lesson.[1]

It is our human intelligence and human courage which are on trial; it is incredible that men who have brought the technique of physical discovery, invention, and use to such a pitch of perfection will abdicate in the face of the infinitely more important human problem.[2]

THOUGHT VS. THE INEVITABLE

In the only summary he ever made of his conclusions,[3] Karl Marx, whom Professor Baron calls "indubitably the most influential revolutionary thinker of the modern era,"[4] made the following prediction:

In broad outline, the Asiatic, the ancient, the feudal, and the modern bourgeois modes of production can be indicated as progressive epochs in the economic system of society. Bourgeois productive relationships are the last antagonistic form of the social process of production. . . . but the productive forces developing within the womb of bourgeois society at the same time create the material conditions for the solution of this antagonism. With this social system, therefore, the pre-history of human society comes to a close.[5]

We in the mid-twentieth century do not subscribe to the curious anthropomorphism or vitalism inherent in the notion of productive forces creating conditions conducive to the emergence of nonantagonistic society. We regard as mythology the supposition that a pro-human, pro-democratic, pro-cooperative logic of a cosmic-historical dialectic,

[1] John Dewey, *Creative Intelligence* (New York, 1917), p. 63.
[2] John Dewey, *Philosophy and Civilization* (New York, 1939), p. 330.
[3] George H. Sabine, *A History of Political Theory* (New York, 1948), pp. 694 ff.
[4] Salo W. Baron, *Modern Nationalism and Religion* (New York, 1947), p. 2.
[5] Emile Burns, *A Handbook of Marxism* (New York, 1935), p. 373.

actualized in the class struggle, directs the movement of human experience towards eudaemonic fulfilment. We are critical of doctrines professing to discern patterns for conduct in extrahuman constellations of forces, natural or supernatural, and we remain on guard against ideologies of cis-experiential inevitabilities, economic, political, psychological, social.

Professor Childs says:

> Democracy is not nature's own unique mode of life. It is the product of a long and costly human struggle, and its life of freedom, of shared responsibility as well as its basic principle of government of, by, and for the people make demands on the individual that are ethically more, not less, exacting than the practices of authoritarian social and political systems. Nor is democracy inevitably fated to be the pattern of the future.[6]

Nor, for that matter, are theocracy, monarchy, the *Führerstaat*, the dictatorship of the proletariat, a South American junta, or Israel's clerico-socialist coalition; nor are peace, poverty, existence, coexistence, or nonexistence; nor, in Raymond Aron's analysis,[7] is there a predetermined historical necessity for atomic war between the United States and the USSR. As against existentialist cravings for "the freedom of Abraham *after* 'the Binding of Isaac,' his final trial . . . the freedom of man before God [where] theories, formulas, speculations, doctrines, dogmas and all 'isms' are silenced [and] issues and objects no longer matter,"[8] contrary to the neo-mystic's assertion that Truth may be achieved only through "unmitigated innate surprise" by "a mind unwarped by intellectual habit,"[9] mid-century Western man realizes that servitude, "the real passion of the twentieth century,"[10] is the result of failure of human choice-making, not of unalterable laws governing existence in space-time in the name of an inconceivably wondrous preexistent, time- and spaceless Being.

Ninety-five years after Marx's "Contribution to the Critique of Political Economy" with its prophecy of the end of prehistory, Marxism is an inadequate doctrine,

> for the reason that it makes the processes of history external to human choice and plans, and buries the person in society. Instead of understanding that the person is a higher emergent from the community, Marxism personifies the

[6] John L. Childs, *Education and Morals* (New York, 1950), p. 13.

[7] Raymond Aron, *The Century of Total War* (Garden City, New York, 1954), p. 165.

[8] Nahum N. Glatzer, *Franz Rosenzweig: His Life and Thought* (New York, 1953), p. xxxiv.

[9] Abraham J. Heschel, *Man Is Not Alone—A Philosophy of Religion* (New York, 1951), p. 58. For a critique of Heschel's position cf. Meir Ben-Horin, "Via Mystica," *JQR*, XLV (1955), 249-58, and "The Ineffable—Critical Notes on Neo-Mysticism," *JQR*, XLVI (1956), 321-54.

[10] Albert Camus, *The Rebel* (New York, 1954), p. 204.

community and endows its leaders alone with the true attributes of persons: this is in fact a regression to the theology of the Egyptian pharaohs, for whose personal enhancement a whole society worked and slaved.[11]

We know that the power that is reason and mind, the power that is the ability to effect both deliberate adjustment to and create modification of material conditions is, for social purposes, as real and as effectual as are these conditions themselves. In Schumpeter's words: "In a given situation, brain and nerves of the man at the helm are just as objective facts as are iron content of the country's ore and presence or absence of molybdenum or vanadium."[12] We are critical of the Marxian certainty that through the class struggle class-structured societies will of necessity be superseded by the classless society. For, if the Marxist denies the possibility of deliberate interference by human intelligence in the universal process, historical analysis merely points to an eternal continuation of the class struggle. In that case the classless society is a delusion. And if, on the other hand, he admits novel conditions to enter into the process, prediction of the outcome is impossible, and the classless society perhaps attains the status of a hope, not of a natural must.[13]

We of the generation which in its own lifetime witnessed World War I with its total of 65,038,810 mobilized forces and the destruction of nearly ten million soldiers plus ten million civilian casualties resulting from causes attributable directly or indirectly to the war;[14] we of the remnants of World War II with its total of over 90,000,000 mobilized forces and the destruction of some 35,000,000 military and civilian personnel;[15] we who must regard ourselves as the perpetrators, the victims, and the survivors of man's most sustained machomanic assault on his own life and reason—we cannot but return from the wars and the slaughter to regard person and reason as our supreme values. And as we look forward to the *possibility* of the obliteration of industrial civilization[16] which has

[11] Lewis Mumford, *The Conduct of Life* (New York, 1951), p. 225. Quotations used by permission of Harcourt, Brace & Company.

[12] Joseph A. Schumpeter, *Capitalism, Socialism, and Democracy* (New York, 1947), p. 399 n.

[13] Carl Becker, "The Marxian Philosophy of History," in his *Every Man His Own Historian* (New York, 1935), pp. 113-31.

[14] *Encyclopedia Americana* (1953), XXVIII, 650 ff.

[15] *Ibid.*, XXIX, 559 ff.

[16] Harrison Brown, Professor of Geochemistry at the California Institute of Technology, writes in *The Challenge of Man's Future—An Inquiry concerning the Condition of Man during the Years That Lie Ahead* (New York, 1954), pp. 222 f.: "As our dependence shifts to such resources as low-grade ores, rock, seawater, and the sun, the conversion of energy into useful work will require ever more intricate technical activity, which would be impossible in the absence of a variety of complex machines

brought longer life, greater personal security, and more material comforts than agrarian cultures, we have no choice but to rely on human intelligence and new and accumulated wisdom to stay clear of catastrophe and the return of "starvation, disease, and death on a scale difficult to comprehend."[17]

"In one way or the other, she [the Revolution] will surely come," wrote Ferdinand Lassalle, "and when, shutting out the din of the day, I become absorbed in the study of history, I hear her steps."[18] Ninety years after Lassalle, we do not hear the revolutionary motif in history but rather in the processes of thought.

THE PRACTICAL NECESSITY

Yet, having rejected the Marxian pseudo-immutabilities and determinisms, reflective humanity in the 1950's shares Marx's yearning for the dawn of history. It finds in him reinforcement for this yearning, much as it finds strength and support for it in the whole tradition of challenge to oppressive authority within Western religions, philosophies, politics, and sciences. As an "intellectual and ethical ferment,"[19] contemplating "not merely the abolition of legal and practical privilege but a reconstruction of the economic organization of society,"[20] Marxism has done its share in calling human intelligence into the arena of social affairs.

> There is a living kernel in the thought and ideas it failed to develop. As a program of scientific activity in behalf of socialist ideals, fortified by the lessons of experience, rearmed with deeper moral and psychological insights, and prepared to learn what it really means to be scientific, these ideas still constitute a promising social philosophy.[21]

The reduction and elimination of interhuman violence, the reconstruction of socioeconomic patterns along nonantagonistic lines, the development

---

and their products—all of which are the result of our intricate industrial civilization, and which would be impossible without it. Thus, if a machine civilization were to stop functioning as the result of some catastrophe, it is difficult to see how man would again be able to start along the path of industrialization with the resources that would then be available to him."

[17] *Ibid.*, p. 226. Cf. also Lewis Mumford, *In the Name of Sanity* (New York, 1954), pp. 10-33.

[18] Salo W. Baron, *Die politische Theorie Ferdinand Lasalle's* (Leipzig, 1923), p. 61.

[19] Sabine, *A History of Political Theory*, p. 715.

[20] *Ibid.*, p. 712.

[21] Sidney Hook, "What Is Living and Dead in Marxism," in his *Reason, Social Myths, and Democracy* (New York, 1940), p. 141.

of the world's backward areas, the reinterpretation of national sovereignty and independence in the light of Montagu's dictum that "interdependence . . . is the state of all living things,"[22] all these remain crucial problems in the second half of our century.

Democratic humanity stands

> committed to the achievement of certain great moral ends: the improvement of the lot of the ordinary man; the attainment of equality of opportunity and the elimination of exploitation of man by man; the abolition of social discrimination and the achievement of brotherhood among all races and nationalities; the removal of inequalities between the two sexes and the recognition of the right of women to unqualified enjoyment of economic, political, and cultural rights and opportunities; faith in and the full use of the resources of science, technology, and education for human progress; the elimination of poverty, insecurity, and ignorance from all elements of their populations; and the development of a free society in which men and women may individually and in association with one another devote themselves to creatively and socially useful activities.[23]

The two great wars in Europe and Asia, as a result of which America emerged as the great material power of the West, along with the two great counterrevolutions of Nazi and Communist mythology, as a consequence of which the New World replaced the Old as the world's spiritual arsenal of freedom, have tragically dramatized the potency of violence and authority to breed more ghastly forms of violence and authority. If America, history's greatest generator of democratic power, or, to paraphrase Marx, "the locomotive of democracy," is to move forward to more advanced forms of democratic organization and spirituality that will unite security and continuity and rising levels of material well-being with freedom of expression and inquiry and hypothesis; if it is to ascend the ladder of democratic fulfillment, it must recapture the calculated boldness of faith and works in which it was born. A new democratic maximalism must arise to meet the challenge of totalitarian mythocracy. A new democratic commitment is needed to build the imperatives of humanitarian rationality into the conditions of our existence.

In 1844 Louis Napoleon suggested in his book *Abolition of Poverty* "that just as the great achievement of Christianity had been to abolish slavery and the great mission of the Revolution of 1789 had been to abolish serfdom, so the great mission of the democratic revolution of the

[22] Ashley Montagu, ed., *The Meaning of Love* (New York, 1953), p. 11. Cf. also Bertrand Russell, *Human Society in Ethics and Politics* (New York, 1955), p. 220.

[23] John L. Childs and George S. Counts, *America, Russia, and the Communist Party in the Postwar World* (New York, 1943), pp. 90-91. Quotation used by permission of John Day Company, Inc.

nineteenth century was to abolish poverty."[24] A hundred and ten years later neither slavery nor serfdom nor poverty have been abolished; their abolition remains mission rather than achievement. While in 1949 Harold G. Moulton, a cautious and distinguished economist, suggested that a hundred years hence we in America should be able to "support a population double that of the present day on a plane of living eight times as high as that now prevailing," a study made under the auspices of the American Bar Association in 1951 concluded that at least thirty million Americans "cannot afford the minimum cost of necessary legal service" in order to obtain justice in the courts.[25] In England, Professor Alfred Marshall of Cambridge warned at the turn of the century that it was not unlikely that more than half of

> the best natural genius that is born into the country belongs to [the working classes], and of this a great part is fruitless for want of opportunity. There is no extravagance more prejudicial to the growth of national wealth than that wasteful negligence which allows genius that happens to be born of lowly parentage to expend itself in lowly work.[26]

Similarly, Princeton's famed zoologist, Edwin Grant Conklin, deplored the waste of talent in this striking passage:

> In all men the capacity for intellectual development is probably much greater than the actuality. The parable of the talents expresses a profound biological truth, men differ in hereditary endowments; one receives ten talents and another receives but one; but the used talent increases manyfold, the unused remains unchanged and underdeveloped. . . . [Herbert Spencer] Jennings [of Johns Hopkins University] has pointed out as one of the great tragedies of life the almost infinite slaughter of potential personalities in the form of germ cells which never develop. A more dreadful though less universal tragedy is the loss of real personalities who have all the native endowments of genius and leadership but who for lack of proper environmental stimuli have remained underdeveloped and unknown; the "mute, inglorious Miltons" of the world; the Caesars, Napoleons, Washingtons who might have been; the Newtons, Darwins, Pasteurs who were ready formed by nature but who never discovered themselves. One shudders to think how narrowly Newton escaped being an unknown farmer, or Faraday an obscure bookbinder, or Pasteur a provincial tanner.[27]

[24] Carl Becker, *Modern History* (New York, 1935), pp. 368 f.

[25] Quoted in George S. Counts, *Education and American Civilization* (New York, 1952), p. 194.

[26] Alfred Marshall, *Principles of Economics* (London, 1936), p. 212, quoted in Thad L. Hungate, *Financing the Future of Higher Education* (New York, 1946), p. 202.

[27] Edwin G. Conklin, *Heredity and Environment in the Development of Men* (Princeton, 1929), pp. 340 ff., quoted in Habib Amin Kurani, *Selecting the College Student in America* (New York, 1931), pp. 103-4.

Reluctant as we may be to concede the point, there is no escaping the conclusion that in 1920 Max Nordau justly admonished modern man that "the contrast between the perfection offered by technology and the insufficiencies with which the great majority must yet be content, accords to our material civilization a measure of cruelty altogether alien to ancient primitivism which subjected all to the same hardship."[28] The resolution of this contrast, threatening in the atomic age to atomize society itself, stands as the practical necessity of human survival in our time.

THE PRIVATE, THE PUBLIC, AND THE ABSOLUTE

Among the social developments seemingly furthering democratic humanity's "great moral ends" and the attainment of "the practical necessity of human survival" there stands out, because of its vast consequences and the controversy raging about them, the phenomenon which might be described as the eclipse of the private in the lengthening shadow of the public. Under the impact of continuing industrial revolutions culminating thus far in the harnessing of atomic energy to the service of ever widening areas of human needs, the *private* property of property and of profit increasingly turns into myth. Essentially the right to exclude other private—and public—interests, it is tantamount to the control of these interests.[29] Yet private property and private enterprise grounded therein grow in value through and by virtue of their public consequences, indeed, public consequences functioning to enhance the private *are* their value. But it is because of what one may be justified in calling the "public-within-the-public" nature of private enterprise in the present era of the corporate system—"its impact on the life of the community and of every individual is certain to be great; it may even determine a large part of the behavior of most men living under it"[30]—that there arises the public's concern and responsibility for the regulation of the consequences of private action affecting it. In this sense, private enterprise creates the public which "consists of all those who are affected by the indirect

[28] Max Nordau, "Das Wesen der Gesittung" (The Essence of Civilization), MS, p. 24. The MS is in the possession of Mme Maxa Nordau-Gruenblat, daughter of Max Nordau, in Paris. It has not been published in the original or in English. A Spanish translation (Madrid, 1930) is entitled *La Esencia de la Civilizacion.* Cf. Meir Ben-Horin, *Max Nordau, Philosopher of Human Solidarity* (New York, 1956), p. 141.

[29] Morris R. Cohen, *Law and the Social Order* (New York, 1933), p. 46.

[30] Adolf A. Berle, *The Modern Corporation and Private Property* (New York, 1933), p. 1.

consequences of transactions to such an extent that it is deemed necessary to have those consequences systematically cared for."[31] From this angle Schumpeter's thesis that "capitalism is being killed by its achievement"[32] is further substantiated in that its very success undermines the social institutions which protect it, and "'inevitably' creates conditions in which it will not be able to live and which strongly point to socialism as the heir apparent."[33] The capitalist process tends to destroy its matrix, the realm of the private in economy. Hence, the eclipse of the private is, ultimately, the eclipse of profit whose essence is indifference to public consequences other than those affecting profits. For, as long as the public possesses the power of self-assertion, it will, with increasing resolve, seek to render such indifference unprofitable. Thus, in time, the peculiarly private quality of acquisition and competition is subjected to basic modification by its own creature, the public.

Further analysis reveals that the self-destructive element in this "peculiarly private quality" is the drive toward the Absolute. This interpretation takes its clue from Werner Sombart's exposition under "Capitalism" in the *Encyclopedia of Social Sciences* which literally begs for further generalization. Discussing the spirit of the capitalist system under its three dominant ideas of *acquisition*, *competition*, and *rationality*, Sombart contrasts acquisition, the purpose of economic activity under capitalism, with earning a livelihood, the purpose of all precapitalistic systems in which "thought and action centered about the human being." He goes on to say that in capitalism

> there are no absolute limits to acquisition, and the system exercises a psychological compulsion to boundless extension. The fact that capitalistic enterprise has as its purpose a certain mode of utilizing a stock of goods signifies a complete divorce of the aims of capitalistic economy from the personality of the economic agent. The abstract, impersonal character of the aim indicates its limitlessness. . . . Profits, no matter how large, can never reach a level sufficiently high to satisfy the economic agent. The positive drive toward boundless acquisition is grounded in the conditions of management. . . .
>
> Acquisition therefore becomes unconditional, absolute. . . . Wherever acquisition is absolute the importance of everything else is predicated upon its serviceability to economic interests: a human being is regarded merely as labor power, nature as an instrument of production, life as one grand commercial transaction, heaven and earth as a large business concern in which everything that lives and moves is registered in a gigantic ledger in terms of its money value. Ideals oriented upon the value of human personality loosen their hold upon

[31] John Dewey, *The Public and Its Problems* (New York, 1927), pp. 15 f.
[32] Schumpeter, *Capitalism, Socialism, and Democracy*, p. xiv.
[33] *Ibid.*, p. 61.

man's mind; efforts for the increase of human welfare cease to have value. . . . *Fiat quaestus et pereat mundus.*

Those who, like the present writer, are wont to contrast the Absolute not simply with the relative or the indiscriminately transactive nature of all activity in nature but with the human or the compassionate and intelligent quality of distinctively human acts; those who identify the "absolute Absolute" with the inhuman rather than with the eternally valid Good, have little difficulty with Sombart's further analysis:

Acquisition which is quantitatively absolute degenerates eventually into unscrupulousness and ruthlessness. Business draws practical conclusions from the revolutionary supremacy of its ideals and seeks, without consideration for any conflicting interests, to clear all obstacles to the limitless and unqualified exercise of acquisition. The intensity of the acquisitive drive attains a point at which all moral and temperamental inhibitions disappear and all conflicting drives become inhibited.

Now applying to "the private" Morris R. Cohen's definition of property as the right to exclude others, and conjugating this definition with what was called the drive toward the Absolute, we arrive at what may be termed the post-capitalist and indeed the post-civilizational meaning of the private: the right to absolute exclusion of the public which is tantamount to the right to declare it superfluous or exterminable. In other words, the *terminus ad quem* of the absolute drive in the private is *the totalitarian state which actually exterminates ever new publics that it creates and declares "surplus."* The totalitarian state is *the private* elevated to the absolute power and exercising the right of exclusion from its total domain which embraces thought and life itself. As Hannah Arendt[34] has shown, the totalitarian state's distinctive institutions are those in which this absolute exclusion is put into practice: the slave labor camps and the extermination camps of the Nazi and the Soviet empires. This is the total eclipse of the private in the sense of the personal, the individual, and the human. It is an eclipse effected by the entrance of man into the shadow of the Absolute. It is the *via mystica* to the end of human history.

As the main generalization of the present paper it may now be stated that the consummate conjugation of the Absolute not merely with economics but also with religion and with science gives rise to the totalitarian abomination. Thus, in the embrace of the Absolute, love itself turns atrocity in the medieval Inquisition. For, as Professor Randall has it,

[34] Hannah Arendt, *The Origins of Totalitarianism* (New York, 1951).

Granted the presuppositions of the Church, that she was indeed the sole vehicle of a divinely revealed, and hence immutable, authoritative, and necessary truth, the expedience of the methods of the Inquisition may be questioned, but their logic and their morality are irrefutable. The most merciful love is then truly the extirpation of heresy root and branch, with fire and sword; and the blows fall upon the simple, pious, and evangelical love of the Waldensians and upon the destructive asceticism of the Albigensian Cathari alike. It is both the unforgivable sin and the greatest of tragedies that men should wreak intolerable wrong upon other men while earnestly and sincerely serving what they believe to be most high.[35]

Science itself, when free from the very antidote of the Absolute, erupts into monstrosity when chained to this diabolical power: it permits a Himmler to "process" to death millions of Jews and other "surplus" men and it makes possible atomic genocide and geocide.

In sum, the touch of the Absolute is the kiss of death to all human undertakings whatsoever and to the very thought of the divine. Taking account of recent history, Lord Acton's famous dictum, "all power corrupts and absolute power corrupts absolutely," calls for this addendum from the totalitarian age: *the Absolute powers all corruption and corrupts all power.*

The whole foregoing analysis now yields the following conclusion: The eclipse of the private is neither inevitable nor desirable. If democracy is to live, its disappearance behind the absolute curtain of the Absolute must be prevented. For democratic society is the association of a plethora of "privates," free to live and to pursue happiness not to the exclusion but to the *inclusion* of the public.

How can the private be disengaged from the Absolute?

Again a clue may be found in Sombart who, as indicated, mentioned as the third element in capitalism the power of rationality which implies long-range planning, adaptation of means to ends, precise calculation, use of scientific technology, and more effective organization of labor. Says Sombart in the aforementioned exposition:

While individual action under capitalism is informed by the ideal of highest rationality, the capitalistic system as a whole remains irrational, because the other dominant capitalistic idea, that of acquisition, of the unrestricted assertion by the individual of his power, leaves the regulation of the total economic process to the uncoordinated discretion of individual economic agents. From this coexistence of well nigh perfect rationality and of the greatest irrationality originate the numerous strains and stresses which are peculiarly characteristic of the economic system of capitalism.

[35] John Herman Randall, Jr., *The Making of the Modern Mind* (rev. ed., Boston, 1940), pp. 79-80. Quotation used by permission of Houghton Mifflin Company.

Clearly, to overcome these "strains and stresses" means to combat irrationality and to check the insane drive to the Absolute. It calls for the conversion of human energies into the dynamics of a broader rationality which embrace the "solidaritarian" unity of science-art and the love of man as end-in-himself. It calls for rededication to the religio-secular ideal of "social self-realization" or "this-worldly salvation."[36]

THE HUMAN PROBLEM

"All power corrupts"—except the power of thought and the power of love. Joined together, these powers constitute "human solidarity" which signifies the essential oneness of prospective, reconstructive intelligence and protective, experience-tested ethics. The social system reflecting the faith that the renewal of life and history may be achieved through the full activation of the mind-love core of man is democracy. The social system answering to the hope for renewal through a mystical embrace of the Absolute is totalitarianism, the degenerate offspring of authoritarian absolutism.

This *excludomanic* system institutionalizes a mysticism of unspeakable Awe and Terror designed to demonstrate that the Power is in fact absolute and not contaminated by what man is capable of experiencing without forfeiting his humanity. Assertions in Orwellian "Newspeak" to the contrary notwithstanding, the system repudiates faith in the spirit of man, in science, in education, and functions as the terrestrial manifestation of an otherworldly Immutable, Inscrutable, Inevitable, Ineffable, and Absolute.[37] In what Isaac Deutscher calls "the most strident bill of impeachment that any Socialist had ever drawn up against Lenin," Leon Trotsky's pamphlet entitled *Our Political Task*, the founder-to-be of the Red Army perhaps speaks the final word of condemnation. Comparing Lenin with Robespierre and his friends who had their metaphysical idea of Truth, their *Verité*, Trotsky observes that

> they could not trust that their *Verité* would win the hearts and the minds of the people. With morbid suspicion they looked round and saw enemies creeping from every crevice. They had to draw a sharp dividing line between themselves

[36] Ben-Horin, *Max Nordau, Philosopher of Human Solidarity*, chap. 3; Theodore Brameld, *Patterns of Educational Philosophy* (New York, 1950), pp. 480-506; Harold Schulweiss, "Mordecai M. Kaplan's Theory of Soterics," in Ira Eisenstein and Eugene Kohn, eds., *Mordecai M. Kaplan: An Evaluation* (New York, 1952), pp. 263-81.

[37] Cf. Meir Ben-Horin, "Communism and the Faith in Man," *The Reconstructionist*, Vol. XX, No. 1 (February 26, 1954), and "Martin Buber's 'Absolute Personality,'" *Judaism*, VI, No. 1 (Winter, 1957), 22-30.

and the rest of the world, and they drew it with the edge of the guillotine. . . . They spared no human hecatomb to build the pedestal for their Truth. . . . The counterpart to their absolute faith in a metaphysical idea was their absolute distrust of living people.[38]

To regard personality and intelligence as reflecting the image of the divine and to grasp the interdependence of the Truth and the Absolute and "the edge of the guillotine" is to arrive at the conclusion that what Dewey calls "the human problem" is a *human* problem, a problem, that is, to be solved not by authority destined forever to remain aloof to criticism, judgment, and public verification. The human problem is to be solved by cooperative intelligence. This means, first, that the notion of a spontaneous generation of freedom out of planlessness or of planning for exclusive private ends be relegated to the realm of superstitions. It implies, second, that intelligence must become the supreme instrument of social action, i.e., of the third major revolution in man's career: completing the revolution of language which established his superiority over a prehuman ancestry and climaxing the revolution of scientific method which assured his rule over nature as experienceable by him, the revolution of social intelligence will give man control over history. Finally, social *action* implies that intelligence is more than mere debate, "broad understanding," and endless framing of hypotheses alongside the stream of events. William James once complained that "the chronic fault of liberalism is its lack of speed and passion. Over and over again generalizations get into such a deadlock that a hole in the dam must be made somewhere,—then the flowing water will enlarge it. . . . Occasionally a leader with liberal ambitions has the *vis viva* of the rifle bullet."[39] More recently Max Eastman, speaking of an experimental scientific party, deplored the failure of liberals "to make the path of honest intelligence a path of consecration, of sacrifice, of heroic effort. We fail to make it grim."[40]

But in truth there is no intrinsic "softness" about intelligence as there is no inherent grimness or permanent detachment. In its forays into the Unknowns ranging from astrometry to microbiology, man's mind was held to its course by physical persistence, eager self-exposure to want, risk, danger, even death, and its path ascended to ever new conquests of formidable Everests—each step forward a new hazard, a broader horizon,

[38] Isaac Deutscher, *The Prophet Armed–Trotsky: 1879-1921* (New York–London, 1954), pp. 89-91.

[39] Quoted in Ralph B. Perry, *The Thought and Character of William James* (briefer vers., Cambridge, Massachusetts, 1948), p. 266.

[40] Max Eastman, *Stalin's Russia and the Crisis in Socialism* (New York, 1940), p. 266.

and the loneliness of the deeps and the summits. "Perhaps," says Mumford,[41]

> some of the spiritual authority that now adheres to science derives from the fact that the scientists have been the authentic saints of the modern age. From Copernicus to Pascal, from Faraday to Henry to Einstein, they have set an example of high spiritual devotion, untainted by the pomps and lusts of a wicked world.

Thought requires delay in the interest of prudent, goal-reaching action, yet in inaction it withers away. Thriving on freedom to probe the nature of nature and of man and to effect transformations of the environs in the interest of human solidarity, it will yet deny freedom to its denial. It concedes no a priori commitment other than to the protection of human life, to the freedom of competent inquiry, and to all-out opposition to atrocity. It is bound neither to "inevitable" violence nor to unconditional nonviolence; the logic of a situation may dictate the use of force. In *Liberalism and Social Action*—"a book which may very well be to the twentieth century what Marx and Engels's *Communist Manifesto* was to the nineteenth"[42]—John Dewey invites attention to the fact that "force, rather than intelligence, is built into the procedures of the existing social system, regularly as coercion, in times of crisis as overt violence."[43] He allows for the legitimacy of force

> when society through an authorized majority has entered upon the path of social experimentation leading to great social change, and a minority refuses by force to permit the method of intelligent action to go into effect. Then force may be intelligently employed to subdue the recalcitrant minority.[44]

Other instances presumably would be partisan action against totalitarian rule and police action against agents of totalitarian expansion, as, of course, free world military defense against totalitarian enslavement. Intelligence revolts against meeting atrocity with injustice. Yet it prepares to meet force with force.

For thought is not an opiate, neither of the kind that Marx attempted to banish nor of the kind that, after all, he built into his system.

Granted, "ideas are dangerous, but the man to whom they are least dangerous is the man of ideas. He is acquainted with ideas, and moves

[41] Mumford, *The Conduct of Life*, p. 202.
[42] Sidney Hook, *John Dewey, an Intellectual Portrait* (New York, 1939), p. 158.
[43] John Dewey, *Liberalism and Social Action* (New York, 1935), p. 63.
[44] *Ibid.*, p. 87.

among them like a liontamer. Ideas are dangerous, but the man to whom they are most dangerous is the man of no ideas."[45]

As Bertrand Russell impressively stated it,

> Men fear thought as they fear nothing else on earth—more than ruin, more even than death. Thought is subversive and revolutionary, destructive and terrible; thought is merciless to privilege, established institutions, and comfortable habits; thought is anarchic and lawless, indifferent to authority, careless of the well-tried wisdom of the ages. It sees man, a feeble speck, surrounded by unfathomable depths of silence; yet it bears itself proudly, as unmoved as if it were lord of the universe. Thought is great and swift and free, the light of the world, and the chief glory of man.[46]

The "human problem" is the application to "the Inevitable," to the "practical necessity," to the all-corruptive Absolute, and to our new human interdependence of this force which, born of nature, society, and history, may yet come to employ the prerationality of the first and the irrationality of the last to create solidaritarian culture.

TOWARD THE DAWN OF HISTORY

What, asks Professor Carleton S. Coon, prevents the peoples of the world from pooling their efforts in accordance with the law of the conservation of energy? Not, in his opinion, distance, time, or technology. Rather

> it is the retention by twentieth-century Atom Age men of the Neolithic point of view that says: you stay in your village and I will stay in mine. If your sheep eat our grass we will kill you, or we may kill you anyhow to get all the grass for our own sheep. Anyone who tries to make us change our ways is a witch and we will kill him. Keep out of our village.[47]

Although the Neolithic began three thousand years before writing, and five and a half thousand before the birth of Herodotus, the "father of history," Neolithic culture is much more than a subject of inquiry by prehistorians. Moving out of it may be the world's most difficult problem.[48]

[45] Gilbert K. Chesterton, *Heretics* (4th ed., New York, 1907), p. 297.

[46] Bertrand Russell, *Why Men Fight* (New York, 1916), pp. 178-79. This, essentially, is the same force of which Dostoyevsky writes in his *The Brothers Karamazov*: "Seeing the sins of men, one sometimes wonders whether one should react to them by force or by humble love. Always decide to fight them by humble love. If it is carried through, the whole world can be conquered. Loving humbleness is the most effective force, the most terrific, the most powerful, unequalled by any other force in the world."

[47] Carleton S. Coon, *The Story of Man* (New York, 1954), pp. 375-76. Quotations used by permission of Alfred A. Knopf, Inc.

[48] *Ibid.*, p. 123.

Neolithic reasoning, I submit, is twentieth-century insanity. By the same token, Neolithic faith is today's unfaith or idolatry. To follow through in the vein of Coon, it tells us across the ages: "My cow is bigger than your cow. My cow is bigger than any cow. My cow is the only Cow. My Cow is absolute Cow. My Cow is Absolute. Mine is the Absolute, and the Absolute is for me. I speak His language—there can be no other. Your cow is mere cow, your people are mere people, your tongue is mere tongue. I speak His language—so must you." Clearly, the heart of both Neolithic "reason" and Neolithic "faith" is absolutization—the removal from responsibility to living communities of informed men and women—of whatever under the sun and above reigns supreme in a human situation. It is the establishment of an authority beyond the "checks and balances" of free inquiry into conditions and of evaluation of consequences, beyond the reach of ordinary humans, alike beyond experience and experiment. But historically and logically, the authority of the Beyond inevitably means the authoritarianism of the few,[49] the armed clash of equally infallible "authorities," and, in our age, the extermination of the human race.

This holds true for Neolithic and for more recent "Neolithistic" absolutes. Their languages differ in sociopolitical imagery. Their intent is constant. To cite one latter-day example:

> Only transcendent faith that finds its absolute beyond the ideas, institutions, or allegiances of the world [can] meet the challenge of the demonic idolatry of Communism without falling into idolatry itself. To be genuinely democratic . . . democracy cannot refuse to recognize a majesty beyond its own, the majesty of the God who transcends all the relativities of the world and beside whom there is no other.[50]

The only unmistakable upshot of this effort is the projected subordination of democracy—government of, by, and for the people—to "the majesty." This categorical recommendation is proffered without clarification as to whether "transcending all the relativities" constituting the world is majestic or absenteeistic, democratically "recognizable" or undeterminable, divine or demonic. Yet, the process of transcending the infinity of *all* the world's relativities may be too infinitely laborious to be regal. Moreover, the success of this process of "disentanglement" would be the rise of further relativity vis-à-vis the world, an absolute relativity,

[49] Meir Ben-Horin, "Intelligence: The Guide to Freedom," *The Educational Forum*, XVIII (1954), 425-35.

[50] Will Herberg, "Communism, Democracy, and the Churches," *Commentary* (April, 1955), p. 392.

hence an absolute unreliability. For relativity is inescapable as long as the world exists. The "absolute Absolute" comes into being only as a result of the total disappearance of the universe. To posit the one is to posit the other. We thus come upon a "metatotalitarianism" which is "metatheologically" commensurate with the earthly totalitarianism of Atomic Age Neolithicism. Now facing us is the hopeless "intra-Neolithic" circularity of the attempt to meet "the challenge of the demonic idolatry of Communism" with the demonic idolatry of "meta-absolutism."

In the face of the new militancy of absolutism, we need to reaffirm "our faith in reason . . . ; it may lead us into error but nothing else can lead us ultimately in the right direction."[51] Organized religion itself, far from necessarily abetting mysticism's reliance upon the absolute, ought to

> help create that large-scale climate of opinion for the creation of a constructive world order. By turning inwardly and detecting ever new ways of human cooperation in the spiritual sphere they will also help devise means for a new human cooperation in the worldly sphere. By reforming themselves, they will help reform the world.[52]

The challenge of "demonic idolatry," Neolithic, totalitarian, and "metatotalitarian," must be met by the power of human reason joined to human love. And it is, to paraphrase Marx, when, in behalf of self-social values constituting the democratic faith, this militant power of intelligence is brought to bear upon the reorganization of commonly undesirable conditions that the prehistory of human community comes to a close.

It is when, in behalf of human salvation, men reverse "the drive toward the Absolute" and pool their energies to humanize their supreme loyalties and their living ideals that the earth will stand witness to the dawn of history.

[51] Lyman Bryson, *The Drive toward Reason* (New York, 1954), p. 119.
[52] Baron, *Modern Nationalism and Religion*, p. 271.

THE MESSIANIC SELF-CONSCIOUSNESS OF ABRAHAM ABULAFIA

A TENTATIVE EVALUATION

By Abraham Berger

PRACTICALLY ALL WE KNOW about Abraham Abulafia we learn from his own writings which, in contrast with those of other Kabbalists of his time, are rich in autobiographical notes and often show an anxiety for self-revelation. It would be difficult to find the proper place for Abulafia in a typology of Jewish Messianic personalities. Messianic personalities feel the weight of tradition to mean that their mission is to "fulfill what is written." Abulafia reinterpreted this mission in the light of his own ideas, and tradition often assumed a new form as it passed through the prism of his personality. It would be much more fruitful to compare him with Hellenistic mystagogues, Islamic Sufis, and Greek Orthodox Spirituals than with other Messianic pretenders in the Jewish tradition.

He was a man of personal humility in his relations with colleagues and pupils; yet, at the same time, he conveyed an overpowering sense of prophetic self-assurance. Eager for followers, he was disdainful of "fools" and the "mob." Self-styled a Messiah chosen by the Lord, but without any dreams of secular power; yearning for seclusion, yet fated always to wander; enthusiast and rationalist; an elegant stylist, whose most beautiful passages alternate with passages of sheer glossolalia; Antichrist by his own description, yet aspiring toward universal brotherhood—Abulafia was full of apparent paradoxes, and undoubtedly only a proper pathography of his personality could reveal the mainsprings of his behavior. What we are concerned with in this essay, however, is to gather a few of Abulafia's interpretations of himself as Messiah and possibly to analyze them to discover what kind of a messiah he thought himself to be.

Solomon Adret, his powerful adversary, calls him "that scoundrel Abraham who declared himself prophet and Messiah."[1] That Abulafia

[1] Solomon Adret, *Responsa* (Vienna, 1812), f. 71c-72a, No. 548:

did declare himself prophet and Messiah is clear from an examination of his works. Abulafia's conception of himself as the ultimate redeemer is a gradual development, springing directly and inevitably from his ever increasing consciousness of having been chosen as a prophet through a number of spiritual experiences dating back to his first prophetic call in the year 1271.[2] On various occasions, he declares that, like the great biblical prophets, his prophetic activity was compelled by a higher force,[3] overruling all his doubts;[4] this claim he extended even to his "literary" activity, such as his writing a commentary on Maimonides's *Guide for the Perplexed.*[5]

Professor Gershom Scholem, in his *Major Trends in Jewish Mysticism*, has masterfully analyzed Abulafia's theory of prophetic Kabbalah, in which prophecy is identified as a higher form of Kabbalism. As far as his own person is concerned, however, Abulafia goes further than that. A prophetic Kabbalist, if found worthy after much preparation, would become, during the period of his ecstasy, a "messiah of the Lord and an angel of God."[6] Abulafia even wrote manuals to help his followers in attaining this degree of ecstasy. He himself, however, reached for greater heights, for he claimed to be the Messiah as the highest prophet and the high priest. His claims to messiahship take on various forms: in his prophetic work *Sefer ha-Ot*, written in 1288, he sees himself as the pastor of the flock and the healer of the sick, the announcer of glad tidings and the stern preacher against those who despised his warnings.[7] In his commentary on the Pentateuch, which he wrote in the following year,

ואחד מהם היה אותו הנבל׳ שם רשעים ירקב׳ אותו אברהם ששם שמו נביא ומשיח בשסיליאה׳ ופתח בכזביו מבני ישראל.

[2] Cf. Gershom G. Scholem, *Major Trends in Jewish Mysticism* (Jerusalem, 1941), p. 125.

[3] וזאת ליהודה in Adolf Jellinek, *Auswahl Kabbalistischer Mystik* (Leipzig, 1853), p. 18:

בהגיעי אל השמות ובהתירי קשרי החותמות נגלה לי אדון הכל וגלה לי את סודו והודיעני עד קץ הגלות׳ . . . ואז הכריחני להתבאר בנבואה.

[4] מפתח השמות, Jewish Theological Seminary MS No. 843, f. 86a:

שבכל עת שאני נכנס בדרך זו׳ השפע גובר עלי ומגלה לי דרכי נפלאות תמים דעים שהם כבשונו של עולם ומצאני מספיקות רבות. . .

I wish to express my thanks to Rabbi Gerson D. Cohen, librarian of the Jewish Theological Seminary, for making available to me the wealth of the Seminary's manuscripts.

[5] Jewish Theological Seminary MS, Enelow Memorial Collection, No. 702, f. 22b:

ונשאתי ונתתי בלבי אם אעשה ואם אחדול ותבוא רוח ותעמידני על רגלי׳ ותקראני בשמי פעמים אברהם אברהם ואומר הנני׳ ויצא הקול ברעש גדול וילמדני באורח משפט. . .

[6] Cf. Gershom G. Scholem, כתבי יד הקבלה (Jerusalem, 1930), pp. 25 ff. (from Abulafia's חיי עולם הבא).

[7] *Sefer ha-Ot*, ed. by Adolf Jellinek in *Jubelschrift . . . Dr. H. Graetz* (Breslau, 1887), Hebrew section, pp. 65-85.

Abulafia sees himself as the Last Deliverer who is parallel with and successor to Moses, the First Deliverer.[8] Under obviously Christian influence, he also declares himself as priest and king of the order of Malkizedek. He writes: "I am priest on my wife's side, a Levite on my mother's side, and an Israelite on my father's side, and although this may be contrary to logic, it is not so for him who knows the 'mystery of Malkizedek, King of Salem, who brought forth bread and wine, and he was priest of God and most high'" (Gen. 14:18).[9]

Abulafia's identification of himself with his wife follows the analogy of Abraham and Sarah who were originally Abram and Sarai.[10] Abulafia adds the old gematria of Abraham and *Zelem Elohim* (the divine image). It is obvious that he is influenced by the various speculations about Adam, the perfect man who was originally androgynous, a state now approximated only by a close spiritual union of man and wife.

Despite the many influences of Christian ideas (and many more of them might be cited) in his Messianic self-interpretation, Abulafia saw himself as Antichrist.[11] He asserts his spiritual mastership over Jesus, the superiority of Sabbath over Friday.[12] Jesus' power, Abulafia insists, was based on the material Tree of Good and Evil, rather than on the spiritual Tree of Life. It is clear that he is identifying Jesus with the Church of the

[8] מפתח השמות, Jewish Theological Seminary MS No. 843, f. 48a:
והמעיין במה שנאמר בעניני המושיַע הראשון כראוי הוא לבדו יבין ממנו סוד המושיע האחרון הנזכר . . . וסימן האותיות השניות מצורפות בתיבות הנזכרות שעליהם חקוק ביה שמו (בראשית, יהודה, הבאים, שמר, מוצא, ואעידה) יעידו על סוד גדול והוא שסוד בי״ה שמו הוא משה הביא המשיח, ואברהם הוא נזכר באותיות השנית האלה . . .
ביה שמו is part of the massoretic tradition of the scribe. Cf., e.g., Ch. D. Ginzburg, *Massora*, II, 337.

[9] מפתח החכמה, Jewish Theological Seminary MS No. 843, f. 86a:
והכתו׳ אמ׳ עד עמוד כהן לאורים ותמים והסוד אצלי שאני כהן מצד אשתי ואני לוי מצד אמי ואני ישראל מצד אבי ז״ל ואע״פ שיש בזה שינוי מהסדר הראשון לפי מחשבת השכל, אין בו שינוי למי שיודע סוד מלכי צדק מלך שלם הביא לחם ויין והוא כהן לאל עליון.

[10] מפתח החכמה, Jewish Theological Seminary MS No. 843, f. 35a:
ואשר פדה את נפשי באברהם כל העולם שלו, . . . ובעדו כרת עמו בריתו . . . ובריתו שינוי התולדת להוסיף מכח הנקבות על כח הזכרות.

[11] מפתח השמות, Jewish Theological Seminary MS No. 843, f. 81b:
שעל כן נקרא המשיח אצל הנוצרים היונים אנדי כריסטוס כלומ׳ אדני האיש ההוא ברמז דבר האיש אדני הארץ אתנו קשות ועניינו שיעמוד כנגדו להודיע לכל שמה שאמ׳ לנוצרים שהוא אלוה ובן אלוה ואדם שזה היה שקר גמור שלא קבל כח מהשם המיוחד רק כל כחו תלוי . . . על עץ הדעת טוב ורע, ועניין המשיח תלוי על עץ החיים . . . וישו נתלה תלייה גופנית מפני שתלה עצמו באילן גופני והמשיח . . . יש לו כיום ח״י שנה על דבר רוחני [i.e., since his prophetic call in 1271] והוא השכל האלהי ונשארו לו מימי תלייתו שנתים ימים.

[12] מפתח השמות, Jewish Theological Seminary, MS No. 843, f. 80a: אבל חותם יום השביעי . . . הוא כח מלך המשיח (both = 453) וכו חותם יום הששי, ישו הנצרי (both = 671).

thirteenth century, the Church of arrogant prelates and proud scholastics.

The accident of Abulafia's birth in A.D. 1240, the year 5000 after the Creation, according to the Jewish system of reckoning, was also of great significance to him as a sign pointing to his mission.[13] He envisaged the final redemption as beginning in 1290—interpreting the Danielic year as referring to the Christian year A.D. 1290.[14] In this Abulafia differed from the other Jewish interpreters of his day, who usually counted the Danielic 1290 years from the date of the destruction of the Temple in A.D. 68. Obviously, Abulafia's certainty that redemption would come in his own lifetime,[15] together with his conviction that the birth of Christianity was a great spiritual catastrophe, made him select the earlier date.[16]

Although he was a strong opponent of Christianity, he insists, nevertheless, that the ultimate utopia is a universal recognition of the One Reality, when Judaism, Christianity, and Islam will all "serve the Lord with one consent" (Zeph. 3:9).[17] In his allegorical story about the precious pearl, claimed by all religions, but whose true ownership is still to be determined,[18] Abulafia adds: "The Lord will return the pearl to whom He chooses," and envisions a state of reality in which all mankind will look upon one another as parts of the same organism, just as a body

[13] Moritz Steinschneider, *Die hebräischen Handschriften der Hof- und Staatsbibliothek in Muenchen* (Munich, 1895), pp. 142.
ילדה . . . אשת הרב [שמואל]! הזקן לו לעת זקנותו במדינת קרססטה [סרקוסטה] אשר במדינת נגורא [ארגון] אחרי מלאת מספר ימי הגולה.

[14] מפתח השמות, Jewish Theological Seminary MS No. 843, f. 48a:
והכה ארץ בשבט פיו, סודו חנה זמן הגלות שסימנו ביד האומה הנוצרית שוה למנין מאמ דניאל אלף ומאתים ותשעים דהיינו סימן ארץ.
Cf. ס' הפליאה (Koretz, 1784), f. 53b (from Abulafia's *Sefer ha-Gan*):
ברא"ם אבר"ם, בני' אברך דיו, ר"ל מספר אברך דיו למספר הגלות, שמספר שנותיו היה ארכ"ב, אלף ומאתים ועשרים ושתים שנה, ויושלם בשנת החמשים, וישלימו הנוצרים שנת אלף ומאתים ותשעים.

[15] ספר החשק, Jewish Theological Seminary MS, Enelow Memorial Collection, No. 858, f. 13a ff.:
שאנחנו מובטחים בשם אשר הורנו על ידי זאת החכמה התוריית הקדושה שאנחנו בזמן הישועה.

[16] מפתח השמות, Jewish Theological Seminary MS No. 843, f. 68a:
עד אנה ינאצוני העם הזה . . . שרמז . . . קץ אחד מקצי הגלות שענין מספר אנה ה אלפים וחמשים והמבין יבין.

[17] מפתח החכמה, Jewish Theological Seminary MS No. 843, f. 68b:
להודיע ששלשתן בשם בימי הגוף [Judaism, Christianity, and Islam] עתידין לדעת את השם האחרון שנ' כי אז אהפוך אל עמים שפה ברורה לקרא כלם בשם יי' ולעבדו שכם אחד והסבה בידיעה זו היא רוב חכמת הגואל שנ' עליו הנה ישכיל עבדי ירום ונשא וגבה מאד

[18] Published by Moritz Steinschneider in *Hebräische Bibliographie* (Berlin, 1861), IV, 78-79, and from here reprinted in Israel Zinberg, *Geshikhte fun der yidischer literatur* (New York, 1943), IV, 472-73. Steinschneider suggests that this story may be the prototype of the tale of the three rings popularized by Boccaccio and Lessing.

has many organs functioning in harmony.[19] For, to Abulafia, the eventual achievement of the Messiah is no less than the absolute change of reality. The Messiah does not have to perform miracles, Abulafia proclaims, like those performed by Moses or Joshua, or Elijah and Elisha. Here Abulafia sounds like an echo of Maimonides, whom he held in reverence. Then comes the spiritual twist: the Messiah does not have to perform miracles in the sense understood by the masses of Jews and Gentiles, but he will do more—he will bring about a change of reality.[20]

What was Abulafia's call? Like other prophets, he cried for *teshuvah* 'a turning away'. He calls for a change in one's point of view. His scorn is directed against the learned and the rich who find proof that God is with them in the very fact that they are wealthy and honored and have large and prosperous offspring.[21] Abulafia feels that his Messianic task is to awaken those who are sleeping in the dusk of false ideas, in the materialist worship of Mammon and lust, and in the vainglory of learning, especially Talmudic learning,[22] and to lead them to the true light of Divine Reality in the contemplation of the Divine Name, which he sees as the true Paradise made available in this life.

His opposition to the hegemony of the aristocrats and the scholars in Jewish communal life eventually brought him into conflict with the

[19] אור השכל, Columbia University Library MS No. X893 Ab 92, f. 37ab:
ומפני שאין אנו היום באותה המדריגה שאנו מצפין לעלות עליה בכל יום, עדיין המחלוקת במקומה עומדת למי החמד' והאמת הלנו אם לצרינו, עד בא המכריע הדולה המרגלית מן הבור ויתנה לאשר יחפוץ לנו או להם, ואז יתברר האמת תכלית הבירור ותשיב החמדה לבעליה הראוי לירש אותה הנקראים בנים להשם, ותסור הקנאה והקטטה והמחלוקת והשנאה . . . ויראה כל איש ואיש, כל אחד ואחד מאישי המין כאלו הוא הוא מכרו וחבירו הוא הוא בעצמו, כמו שאדם רואה כל אבר מאבריו . . .
Steinschneider has ויתנה לנו instead of ויתנה לאשר יחפוץ, and he does not include the universalistic ending.

[20] מפתח השמות, Jewish Theological Seminary MS No. 843, f. 48a:
ויש מהם שישלחם השם לגאול עם יי' כמשה ומשיח וכבר נודע ענין יכולת משה על פי השם וגם נאמר על המשיח וברוח שפתיו ימית רשע וסודו י"צר ר"ע . . . ומופתי המשיח אין צורך להיותם כמופתי משה רבינו ע"ה ולא כמופתי אליהו ואלישע ע"ה . . . אבל גדולים מכלם, אך לא כפי מה שיחשבו ההמון יהודים וגוים, כי יש להם חדוש במציאות . . . והמעין במה שנאמר בעניני המשיח הראשון כראוי הוא לבדו יבין ממנו סוד המושיע האחרון הנזכר כי שניהם ביאתם בשם השם בהכרח.

[21] חיי הנפש, Jewish Theological Seminary MS, Enelow Memorial Collection, No. 385, f. 2b:
ולולי היות השם עמנו ומשגיח באמת בנו מאין היה לנו זה הטוב כולו והלא זהו הגמול המעולה אשר ייעד השם . . . על עבודתו ועל שמירת מצוותו כגון אריכת ימים בשיבה טובה והולדת בנים יבני בנים ולהיות בשררה וכבוד ועושר רב.

[22] חיי הנפש, Jewish Theological Seminary MS, Enelow Memorial Collection, No. 385, f. 2b:
והנה אנחנו רואים בעינינו רדיפת רוב חכמי תורתינו אחרי השררה והכבוד . . . ומרבים ממון ומבקשים המותרות והם רגעים להעשיר

rabbinical authorities. It is quite understandable that men like Adret saw a great danger to the Jewish community, especially to a Jewry in Diaspora, of a free expression of the prophetic spirit. The gift of prophecy, Adret insisted, can be attained only in the Holy Land, and the prophetic spirit would rest only on the wise, the strong, and the wealthy. Abulafia, in the overpowering sense of his own prophetic call, maintained that prophecy is possible not only *now*, but also right *here*, in the Diaspora. "The land on which the Shechinah always rests is the inner soul. Of it, it is said, 'The eyes of the Lord are always upon it from the beginning of the year until the end of the year'" (Deut. 11:12).[23] As for the wise, the rich, and the strong, they are meant, of course, in a figurative and spiritual sense.[24]

Abulafia makes no mention whatever of any political achievements of the Messiah. Even when he laments the miserable state of Jewry as compared with the power and might of the Nations, he finds comfort only in a future for a Jewry spiritually redeemed.[25] By removing the idea of Messiah from both the land of Israel and the political state, Abulafia runs counter to the Jewish tradition of his day, as expressed, for example, by Moses ben Naḥman, whom Abulafia places in the forefront of his spiritual mentors. When Abulafia went to Rome to face the Pope, he did not demand: "Let my people go," as Naḥmanides had foreseen,[26] but rather he went to see the leader of the Christian religion and to discuss Judaism with him.[27] By such spiritual deviations, Abulafia opened up curious religious possibilities, resembling in many respects the development of early Christianity in its separation from the parent faith, and the radical Sufis, who preached that the pilgrimage to Mecca may be undertaken in contemplation without leaving the physical confines of one's own room. In these radical nonnational ideas, Abulafia found few to follow him, and yet his influence was by no means negligible. His practical

[23] ספר החשק, Jewish Theological Seminary MS, Enelow Memorial Collection, No. 858, f. 32a:

וענין הארץ הוא . . . הפנימי אשר השכינה שם שורה תמיד ועליו נאמר . . . עיני ה׳ אלהים כה מראשית השנה עד אחרית השנה . . . ולפי דעת המאמינים כי זה בארץ ממש לבד׳ לית דינא אצלו והותרה לו הרצועה . . . וגם צריך שיכחיש שריית השכינה במצרים ובמדבר . . .

[24] מפתח השמות, Jewish Theological Seminary MS No. 843, f. 63b:

ואמ׳ אין הנבואה שורה אלא על חכם גבור ועשיר׳ והחכם הוא השלם במדותיו והגבור הוא הכובש את יצרו **והעשיר** הוא **השמח בחלקו.**

[25] מפתח החכמה, Jewish Theological Seminary MS 843, f. 17ab:

וזה היא **תקותינו** עוד היום שאנו בחשך הגלות ובערבות׳ והם באור העולם וביומו׳ ועוד יתהפך הדבר בצאתינו אנחנו מחשך הגלות הזה לאור העולם הבא לעתיד לבוא מערבי הגופניות אל בקרי הנפשיות ולילה כיום יאיר לנו.

[26] Cf. A. H. Silver, *A History of Messianic Speculation in Israel* (New York, 1927), p. 146.

[27] *MGWJ*, XXXVI (1887), 558.

Kabbalistic manuals were copied for generations by mystical aspirants, down to modern times. His attacks on the rich and the learned were taken over verbatim by the *Sefer Peliah* and possibly stood at the cradle of the *Raya Mehemna*—two works which had a tremendous influence on Kabbalistic movements down to our very day, and were especially influential in the Shabbethaian ideology.

THE CLOAKMAKERS' STRIKE OF 1910

By Hyman Berman

THE LADIES' GARMENT industry developed rapidly and chaotically after the Civil War. By the turn of the century it was one of the important New York industries, turning out an annual product valued at 160 million dollars, more than two thirds of which was attributable to the cloak, suit, and skirt branch of that industry. It was not until the twentieth century was well under way that the dress and waist branch began rivaling and eventually surpassing the cloak branch in importance.

The labor force of this expanding industry was recruited mainly from the ranks of the newly arrived immigrants who were largely inexperienced in the ways of the factory. This made it comparatively easy for the economically hard-pressed and marginal manufacturers to maintain and extend the sweating system at the expense of their equally hard-pressed workmen. Since competition was keen, for a comparatively small initial investment was needed in order to allow an aspiring manufacturer to become an actual producer, self-improvement in the industry was impossible. Therefore, only pressure applied by the labor force through organization and trade union activity could result in reforming the labor practices of the needle trades.

Failing attempts had been made during the nineteenth century to organize labor unions in the ladies' garment industry, and even after 1900, when the International Ladies' Garment Workers' Union was founded, constant bickering between locals, ideological conflicts among the members, and lack of understanding of the needs of the industry made organization of the labor force almost impossible. After 1905 some progress was made toward this end when an idealistic and revolutionary element migrated to the United States from Russia and began applying its talent to trade union activities.

During the first years after the establishment of the federation of ladies' garment union locals, the main activities of the affiliated local unions revolved around union label agitation and sporadic shop strikes. It was soon apparent that isolated shop strikes were ineffective as a means of organizing the labor force, for production in other shops made up for the loss of production in the one struck shop, and it was relatively easy for the boss of the struck shop to recruit enough "scab" labor from among the unskilled immigrants to continue operations. It slowly dawned on the labor leaders within the I.L.G.W.U. that only through a general strike, or a shutdown in an entire branch of the ladies' garment industry in one particular locality, could the trade be organized effectively. The first attempt to accomplish this was made in 1909 when the shirtwaist makers, predominantly young women workers, went out on strike. Despite enthusiasm and public support, the strike was a failure, since the leading waist manufacturers, organized in a trade association, refused to recognize the Union and within a year the hundreds of individual shop contracts between the Union and the manufacturers, which were entered into as a result of the general walkout, were scrapped. This practical failure was directly attributable to poor organization of and preparation for the strike which, in truth, was an "uprising."[1]

The success of the Shirtwaist Union in getting the bulk of the workers in that trade out in a general strike and the public sympathy which that strike aroused, however, caused the unionists in the cloak, suit, and skirt branch of the ladies' garment industry to intensify their efforts for a general strike in order finally to organize the trade. As early as the summer of 1908, when the cloak industry was extricating itself from the effects of the depression of 1907, it was clear to many of the Union leaders that seasonal shop strikes and seasonal unionism would not effectively organize the trade and bring order out of the chaos in this industry. By the beginning of 1910 many of the obstacles in the way of organization such as the dual unionism of the I.W.W. and the alienation of the Cutters' Union from the I.L.G.W.U. had been eliminated and only the adherence of the workers of the industry to the Union remained before a general strike could be proclaimed.

Throughout the year 1909 more and more workers were recruited into the various cloak and suit locals, thus creating living organisms out of empty shells. The major educational aim of the Union leaders was to show that shop strikes result in defeat and diffusion of the Union's strength and that only through a general strike when sufficient "scabs" to operate the industry would be lacking could the workers improve their economic position and their status in the industry. Except for shop strikes resulting

[1] For a detailed analysis of the above paragraphs see the author's doctoral dissertation, "Era of the Protocol; a Chapter in the History of the International Ladies-Garment Workers' Union, 1910-1916," chaps. 1-3 *passim* (Columbia University Library).

from employers' lockouts, there were practically no strikes in the cloak industry during 1909 and the early part of 1910.[2] To those in the Union who looked upon trade union activity as preliminary to socialist agitation, this peaceful period of preparation and organization was extremely distasteful. Failure to conduct militant strikes smacked of class collaboration, but despite the opposition of the socialists within the Joint Board was won over to this plan of peaceful preparation.[3]

The educational and agitational activities, coupled with the shot in the arm given the cloak locals by the shirtwaist general strike, began to bear fruit. The Cloak Operators' Union, Local 1, which had a membership of only two hundred in 1908, increased its membership to two thousand by June, 1910.[4] The Cloak Tailors' Union, Local 9, which had practically gone out of existence in 1908, had, as a result of the general strike agitation, not only successfully organized a large number of Jewish tailors by 1910 but also won the adherence of a few hundred Italian cloak tailors.[5] In December, 1909, the spirit of the unionized workers was clearly seen when in a referendum vote 90 percent of them agreed to contribute two dollars each toward the general strike fund.[6] From February to June, 1910, the trade was seething with anticipation of the expected proclamation of the general strike, and detailed preparations were executed.

Discontent within the trade served to underscore the words of the organizers and agitators, making their activities more meaningful and thus more fruitful. Although sweatshop conditions did not prevail throughout the industry, remnants of the long hours, low pay, and unsanitary conditions of the sweatshops remained in the mushrooming smaller contract shops of the East Side. The ease by which individuals with little capital could open shops in this trade and the constant influx of immigrant labor made the standardization of the industry almost impossible. The larger manufacturers, who had begun as small producers on Division Street, and had slowly, through cutthroat competition and the use of sweated labor, driven the giants of Broadway, mainly German and Irish manufacturers, out of business, were now being threatened with a

[2] Abraham Rosenberg, *Memoirs of the Cloakmakers and Their Unions* (New York, Cloak Operators' Union Local 1, 1920) (Yiddish), pp. 183-85; B. Hoffman (Zivion), *Fifty Years of Cloak Operators' Union*, 1886-1936 (New York, Cloak Operators' Union Local 117, 1936) (Yiddish), pp. 170-71.

[3] Report of Joint Board of Cloak, Skirt, and Pressers Unions of New York, *Proceedings of the Tenth Convention of the International Ladies Garment Workers' Union* (Boston, Mass., 1910), pp. 47-49.

[4] Report of Local 1, *ibid.*, pp. 51-52.

[5] Report of Local 9, *ibid.*, pp. 56-57.

[6] Report of President, *ibid.*, p. 17; Hoffman, *Fifty Years*, p. 169.

similar fate by the newer "moths of Division Street." Thus the working conditions were usually those that prevailed in the worst shops, and any desires which the more enlightened cloak manufacturers had of improving these conditions were strangled by the fear of competition. If one shop instituted electrically-driven machinery and charged the workers for the cost of electricity, many others were forced to follow suit. Quite a few of the contract or outside shops required their employees to provide their own tools and machines or charged the workers for the repair of the company machines.[7]

The evils resulting from the unstandardized, seasonal character of the industry, such as long hours during the busy season and virtual idleness during the nine remaining months of the year, the contracting system, both outside contracting and inside subcontracting, and the failure of wages in the industry to maintain an upward trend and thus to keep up with the rising price level, were the major abuses of which the workers complained.[8] To channel this discontent into constructive organizational efforts and prevent the dissipation of energy into disastrous shop strikes, the Cloak Joint Board hired organizers, held meetings, and began publishing a trilingual journal, the *New Post*.[9]

The manufacturers, too, were affected by the general-strike fever, and they tried to anticipate difficulty by producing their full line for the fall season during April and May, normally devoted only to producing cheaper styles for the jobbing trade. The Union leaders realized that this would improve the position of the employers financially, because of the lower rates paid for jobbing and in terms of a built-up inventory. Therefore they limited the amount of this production either by fomenting shop or building strikes or by pressure on the workers.[10]

The success of the Union in limiting the production of jobbing goods, the enthusiastic May Day parade, and the ever growing membership in the various cloak locals caused many of the workers to demand an immediate strike. When the responsible Union officials explained that

[7] Rosenberg, *Memoirs*, pp. 179-80; "Men Who Make Women's Clothing," *The Survey*, XXIV (August 13, 1910), 701-3.

[8] "The Cloakmakers' Strike," *The Outlook*, XCV (July 23, 1910), 596-97; Edith Wyatt, "The New York Cloak-Makers' Strike," *McClure's Magazine*, XXXVI (April, 1911), 708; "Reasons for a General Cloak Strike," *Jewish Daily Forward*, June 16, 1910, p. 4.

[9] Rosenberg, *Memoirs*, pp. 190-91. *The New Post* was originally a leaflet issued twice a week in the form of a newspaper, but after the cloak strike it became a full-fledged weekly newspaper. See Hoffman, *Fifty Years*, p. 171. The author in a thorough search has failed to find a complete file of this valuable source.

[10] Rosenberg, *Memoirs*, pp. 186-90; *Jewish Daily Forward*, June 24, 1910, p. 1.

strike preparations would be completed by the I.L.G.W.U. convention, and thus the strike would have to wait until that time, most rank-and-filers were satisfied, but a minority discontentedly accused the Union leaders of using the general strike agitation to gain members and money in order to keep their bureaucratic machine running and of having no intentions of calling a general strike.[11] The accusations did not dampen the spirit or diminish the activities of the many cloakmakers working assiduously for the general strike.

The majoı topic of discussion at the Tenth Convention of the International Ladies' Garment Workers' Union, which was held in Boston from June 6 to June 12, was the forthcoming cloak general strike. Each group of delegates from the cloak locals came to the convention with instructions to move for convention support of the proposed strike. So many resolutions regarding the cloak, suit, and skirt branch were introduced that Abraham Rosenberg, the President of the I.L.G.W.U., who was presiding at the convention, found it necessary during the first day of the proceedings to appoint a special committee to consider these resolutions.[12] The reports of President Rosenberg, Secretary-Treasurer John A. Dyche, and the delegates of the various cloak locals featured discussions of the general strike. On Friday, June 10, at the morning session, the special strike committee reported a resolution authorizing a general strike in the cloak trade. After John A. Dyche amended the resolution so as to give the General Executive Board of the I.L.G.W.U. more power in both calling and directing the strike, a five-hour debate developed. Those opposing Dyche's amendment wanted the direction of the strike to be in the hands of the Joint Board in line with the autonomous character of the I.L.G.W.U. John Dyche was interested in creating a more centralized control within the I.L.G.W.U. and his view prevailed, for the resolution was passed as amended by a convention vote of fifty-five to ten.[13]

The special strike committee recommended further that a tax of one dollar for male members and fifty cents for female members be levied in order to augment the strike fund. It also proposed that the newly elected General Executive Board be empowered to collect twenty-five and fifteen cents a week from men and women non-strikers respectively during the duration of the strike. The General Executive Board was instructed to

[11] Report of General Secretary-Treasurer, *Proceedings of Tenth Convention*, pp. 26-29; Rosenberg, *Memoirs*, p. 192; Hoffman, *Fifty Years*, p. 177; *Jewish Daily Forward*, May 2, 1910, p. 1.

[12] Report of Proceedings, *Proceedings of Tenth Convention*, p. 9.

[13] *Proceedings of Tenth Convention*, pp. 70-73.

draw up a list of grievances and demands to be presented to the manufacturers.[14] The convention approved the report of the strike committee but ruled that the strike fund assessment had to be approved by a membership referendum to be held no later than July 1.

The last action of the convention was to delegate Abraham Rosenberg and John Dyche to appear before the Executive Council of the A.F.L. to seek support for the cloak strike from the powerful Federation.[15] On June 20 the President and the Secretary of the I.L.G.W.U. appeared before the A.F.L. Executive Council in Washington and received a pledge of support for the strike which was immediately implemented by the Council's designation of its treasurer, John B. Lennon, to take an active part in the strike as a member of the General Strike Committee. President Gompers and Secretary Morrison also promised to participate in the giant mass meeting planned for June 28 at Madison Square Garden.[16]

Immediately after the convention, large-scale and detailed preparations were made by the General Executive Board and the Cloak Joint Board of New York for the general strike. The Union was convinced that the lack of organization caused the shirtwaist strike, despite the workers' enthusiasm and the public's support, to end without official union recognition by the larger manufacturers and was determined that this would be avoided in the cloak situation. A General Strike Committee consisting of five representatives of each of the nine locals belonging to the Joint Board was created and this committee was subdivided into nine subcommittees. Abraham Rosenberg, Sol Polakoff, and John Dyche acted as coordinators of the subcommittees and were given the task of deciding the exact time at which the strike would begin.[17]

The Strike Committee did not want the workers in the cloak industry to leave their jobs spontaneously without centralized direction and thus create the impression among the public of disorganization and chaos; therefore, it was agreed that a strike vote be taken on the second and third of July. In order to notify the cloakmakers dramatically of the strike vote and at the same time to present their case before the public, the Strike Committee also decided to hold a mass meeting on June 28 at Madison Square Garden. This was looked upon as a daring step by the rest of the

[14] *Ibid.*, p. 88.

[15] *Ibid.*, p. 95.

[16] *Jewish Daily Forward*, June 21, 1910, p. 1; Minutes, Executive Council, A.F.L., June 20, 1910.

[17] Hoffman, *Fifty Years*, pp. 179-80; *Jewish Daily Forward*, June 28, 1910, p. 5.

labor movement for this was the first time that one of the largest halls in New York City was hired for a labor meeting.[18]

Hordes of cloakmakers stormed the door of the Garden at five-thirty in the afternoon, even though the meeting was called for eight. The police reserves were quickly called out and at seven o'clock the doors of the auditorium were closed, for more than a capacity crowd of twenty thousand was jammed inside. Those who could not gain admittance to the hall quickly organized mass meetings outside. Inspector Walsh of the Police Department commented that this was one of the largest crowds he had ever seen in the Garden.[19]

Mingled between the musical strains of ragtime, operatic selections, and the "Marseillaise" were speeches by Abraham Rosenberg who presided, Frank Morrison, Hugh Frayne, Meyer London, Jacob Panken, Abraham Cahan, and Samuel Gompers. Rosenberg cautioned his listeners to conduct themselves in an orderly manner, participate in the secret strike vote, and leave the factories only when officially directed by a special edition of the *New Post*. The featured speaker, Gompers, blamed the cloakmakers themselves for what he called "miserable conditions" because they were seasonal unionists and hoped that they would be able to gain their demands without recourse to a strike. If they did not gain their demands peacefully then he hoped that they would all leave their work and not return until they gained a substantial victory. "This is more than a strike movement. It is an industrial revolution," he concluded to the cheers of the twenty thousand assembled cloakmakers.[20]

Five days later the polls were opened and at three places the Union members voted on the question of the general strike. It was apparent that most of the cloakmakers were in favor of the strike, but the magnitude of the vote surprised even the most optimistic Union officials when on July 4 the announced result showed that 18,771 were in favor of the strike and only 615 were against it.[21]

After deciding to call the strike on July 7 at two in the afternoon,

[18] Rosenberg, *Memoirs*, pp. 195-96; *Jewish Daily Forward*, June 28, 1910, p. 5.

[19] New York *Times*, June 20, 1910, p. 11. Edith Wyatt, "The New York Cloak-Makers' Strike," *McClure's Magazine*, XXXVI (April, 1911), 709. Although the author describes the Garden meeting, she declares incorrectly that the meeting took place on July 3.

[20] New York *Times*, June 30, 1910, p. 11; *Jewish Daily Forward*, June 30, 1910, p. 1; New York *World*, June 29, 1910, p. 16. The best summary of the proceedings of the Madison Square Garden meeting is to be found in the pages of the New York *Times*, although of the three accounts above cited it is the least sympathetic to the cause of the cloakmakers.

[21] *Jewish Daily Forward*, July 5, 1910, p. 1; Rosenberg, *Memoirs*, pp. 200-201.

Rosenberg, Dyche, and Polakoff called a meeting of the General Strike Committee for the evening of the sixth when all final preparations were made. The Hall Committee reported that it had hired a number of meeting places and read a list of the various halls at which the workers of designated shops would gather. The Relief Committee outlined a detailed and meticulous plan of relief payments which would have to be approved by both the shop chairman and the hall chairman before the needy striker would receive relief. The Press Committee arranged for the printing of the special edition of the *New Post* which was to appear in red the next afternoon and also prepared for the distribution of this novel strike call. The Settlement Committee reported that its headquarters would be at the Victoria Hotel at Fifth Avenue and Twenty-seventh Street and presented a proposed contract which those manufacturers desiring settlement would have to sign. Seeing that the groundwork was well laid, the Strike Committee adjourned, hearts pounding, waiting for the next day's actions.[22]

At seven the next morning, after the Strike Committee had officially proclaimed the strike for that afternoon, hundreds of messengers began distributing English, Yiddish, and Italian editions of the "Red Post," as the strike issue of the *New Post* was named, calling for a mass exodus from the factories at two that same afternoon. Abraham Cahan, editor of the *Jewish Daily Forward*, joined Rosenberg and Dyche at the time that the workers were to leave the factories, and this veteran of the Jewish labor movement was pleasantly shocked at the size of the outpouring. By two-thirty, Fifth Avenue, in the heart of the cloak district, and East Broadway, opposite the *Forward* building, were jammed with thousands of strikers. Traffic was halted by the mass of humanity and the newspapers agreed that New York had never before seen such a dramatic and sizable labor demonstration.[23] By the end of the week the reefer makers and raincoat workers as well as the Brownsville cloakmakers had joined the general strike, and there were anywheie fiom sixty to seventy-five thousand workingmen and women participating in the walkout.[24]

[22] Rosenberg, *Memoirs*, pp. 202-6; Hoffman, *Fifty Years*, pp. 182-85; *Jewish Daily Forward*, July 7, 1910, pp. 1 and 9.

[23] Rosenberg, *Memoirs*, pp. 207-9; New York *Times*, July 8, 1910, p. 1; New York *World*, July 8, 1910, p. 1.

[24] New York *Times*, July 12, 1910, p. 5; John Bruce McPherson, "The New York Cloakmakers' Strike," *Journal of Political Economy*, XIX, No. 3 (March, 1911), 154-55. The New York *Times* estimated on July 8 that 50,000 workmen were out on strike. Meyer London gavc an estimate of 60,000. With those workmen of allied trades, such as raincoats and reefers, joining the walkout, it is safe to estimate, as the

The confusion and chaos which had attended the first weeks of the shirtwaist strike were practically nonexistent in this strike because of the meticulous care which went into the preliminary preparations. The workers from the various shops were assigned their respective meeting halls; the picketing assignments were quietly and effectively made; and the union recruiting of the strikers did not bog down because of a shortage of secretarial assistance. The organizational structure, however, did not take into account those strikers who were unemployed before July 7, and no provisions were made to control these "orphans" as they were called. After much wrangling, and after the "orphans" threatened to scab if they were not accorded recognition, the Strike Committee arranged for hall and picket assignments for them. The Italian "orphans" were particularly troublesome, according to Abraham Rosenberg, for they opposed settlements with individual manufacturers on the ground that all left work together and, therefore, all should return to work together. In addition, the Relief Committee was never certain that it was not paying benefits to "banana peddlers" rather than to Italian cloakmakers. Although the Italian cloakmakers, who were assigned to shops, conducted themselves in every respect as militant trade unionists, the very existence of the Italian "orphans" led to an attempt to create a dual union during the height of the strike which was vigorously and violently put down.[25]

Although the strike came as no surprise to the cloak manufacturers, they were utterly unprepared to cope with the situation. The smaller contract shops and those independent shops having few machines and little invested capital could not afford a long-drawn-out conflict and their owners were the first to capitulate and sign the union contract. Five days after the strike began, Alexander Bloch of the Settlement Committee announced that sixty such manufacturers, employing close to five thousand workmen, had arranged for a settlement of the strike.[26] The larger manufacturers, exceedingly individualistic, hating and fearing interference in their businesses by either government, labor, or their own fellow cloak employers, were forced by the events of the first days of July, 1910, to organize themselves into a trade association. On the very day that the strike was called a number of cloak bosses met at the Broadway Central Hotel and drew up plans for a Cloak Association, and on July 11 at a

---

newspapers did during the month of August, that 75,000 were involved in the cloakmakers' strike.

[25] Rosenberg, *Memoirs*, pp. 210-15; Morris Winchevsky, "Report of Strike Fund Committee," *Jewish Daily Forward*, September 8, 1910, p. 5.

[26] New York *Times*, July 12, 1910, p. 5.

meeting of a few hundred manufacturers at the Hoffman House the Cloak, Suit and Skirt Manufacturers' Protective Association was organized with A. E. Lefcourt as Chairman, Max M. Schwarcz as Treasurer, Max Meyer of A. Beller and Co. as Secretary, and Julius Henry Cohen of the law firm of Cohen, Creevey, and Richter as Counsel.[27] Each member of the Protective Association was required to sign a pledge that he would adjust shop grievances with his employees with the aid of the Executive Committee of the Association, that he would seek to improve sanitary conditions in his factory, that he would not enter into any agreement with any organization, union or otherwise, which would involve the surrender of control and management of his factory or subfactories, that he would endeavor to preserve peace and join with other members to provide protection against physical violence to those ready and willing to work.[28] Even though this pledge seemed to close the door to union recognition, the members of the Protective Association were not the die-hards of the industry and were ready to eliminate the real grievances that existed, for they realized that in so doing they would probably eliminate the unscrupulous smaller manufacturers, who, through their exploitative methods, prevented a rationalized organization of the trade. These smaller manufacturers refused to join the Association, and when the announcement was made of the employers' group they issued a statement refusing to recognize the existence of the strike, claiming that the fixing of a minimum rate of wages would only benefit "the ambitionless, careless and incompetent workmen."[29]

Under cover of a letter dated July 5, 1910, signed by Alexander Bloch, the Settlement Committee sent to each manufacturer a proposed memorandum of agreement in which were embodied the demands of the Union. The contract, to remain in force for one year, was to be between the manufacturer and the Joint Board with the former engaging the latter "to perform all the tailoring, operating, pressing, finishing, cutting and button-hole making work required to be done by the Firm." It called for a forty-eight-hour work-week limitation, double time for overtime, and ten paid legal holidays, and it provided for a scale of minimum weekly wages for the "week workers" in the firm. The piece prices were to be set by the firm in consultation with a shop committee of employees. The

[27] *Ibid.*, July 8, 1910, p. 1; July 12, 1910, p. 5.

[28] "Pledge Signed by Each Member of Our Association," in *Cloakmakers' Strike Documents* (New York, Cloak, Suit and Skirt Manufacturers' Protective Association, n.d.), n.p.

[29] New York *Times*, July 12, 1910, p. 5; Edith Wyatt, "The New York Cloak-Makers' Strike," *McClure's Magazine*, XXXVI (April, 1911), 708-9.

proposed contract further required the elimination of subcontracting, allowed the employees to elect a shop delegate to act for them in dealing with the firm, eliminated home work, provided for arbitration of disputes without work stoppages, established regular weekly payment of wages and equal distribution of work, outlawed overtime during slack periods, and required the firm to furnish electrically-driven sewing machines and other accessories without charges to the employee. Outside contracting was allowed but the inside manufacturer was to be held responsible for the wages and conditions of his outside contractor. Only union members were to be employed and individual contracts and security payments by workers were to be eliminated.[30]

At first the larger manufacturers belonging to the Association ignored the receipt of the document and claimed in an appeal to the public, issued the same day that the Association was formally organized, that their employees had left work without complaint and without submitting any grievances.[31] A few days later the Association began attacking the proposed agreement on the grounds that the Union, through the shop delegate, would control the businesses of their members, and that agreements to limit employment to union members would constitute a conspiracy in violation of the Federal and State laws.[32] The newspapers of the city, with the New York *Times* in the forefront, attacked the proposed agreement as a reminder of the padrone system, with the Union acting as padrone forbidding recognition of individuality and sustaining incompetent workmen.[33]

The day after the entire cloak industry in New York was tied up, Michael J. Reagan, the Industrial Mediator of the New York State Board of Mediation and Arbitration, sent letters both to representatives of the employers and to the Union suggesting the appointment of a conference committee to mediate the strike. When after a week's time the State Board received no reply from the employers, although it did receive assurances from the Union that their representative would participate in any conferences arranged by the mediator, John Lundrigan, the chairman

[30] Alexander Bloch to Gentlemen, July 5, 1910, and enclosure Memorandum of Agreement reprinted in *Cloakmakers' Strike Documents*, n.p.; Julius Henry Cohen, *Law and Order in Industry* (New York, 1916), p. 14.

[31] "Cloak, Suit and Skirt Manufacturers' Protective Association to the Public," July 11, 1910, in *Cloakmakers' Strike Documents;* New York *Times*, July 12, 1910, p. 5.

[32] A. E. Lefcourt to John Lundrigan, July 18, 1910, in State of New York, Department of Labor, *Bulletin*, XII (September, 1910), 345-47.

[33] New York *Times*, July 16, 1910, p. 8.

of the State Board, instructed Mr. Reagan to press the issue and try to organize a mediation session before July 19.[34] This letter was sent by messenger to A. E. Lefcourt and a written reply was requested. Lefcourt, hiding behind the technicality that the Association was not founded until July 11, denied receipt of the earlier letter of July 8 and denied any official knowledge of the strikers' grievances. He suggested that the State Board of Mediation receive a written statement of grievances from the strikers and, although citing the Association pledge that no union agreement would be entered into, he reiterated the desire of the employers to adjust all legitimate grievances of their employees.[35]

As a result of the activities of mediator Reagan, a preliminary, informal conference was held on July 18 between members of the Association and members of the Strike Committee at which a tentative understanding was reached, subject to the approval of the executive boards of both organizations, that a committee of ten members from each side would meet in conference to work out a settlement of the dispute in the cloak and suit trade.[36] On the evening of the 18th the Executive Committee of the Association met and resolved that a conference be held provided that the representatives of the employees present a statement of grievances in writing to the employers' group and also agree to waive any demand for a closed shop. In a letter justifying the resolution, which was sent to John Lundrigan, the Association explained the reasons it had for not considering the Union's Memorandum of Agreement as a statement of grievances.[37] In order to expedite the mediation conference, Alexander Bloch replied for the Union with a list of grievances, even though he believed that the demand of such a list was uncalled for in light of the repeated demands of the workmen. As to the waiver of the closed shop demand, Bloch held that a waiver of any point by either side would limit and hinder the work of the conference and would thus put obstacles in the path of settlement of the labor dispute.[38]

Although the Executive Committee of the Association accepted the general list of grievances outlined by the Union's Settlement Committee as

[34] Michael J. Reagan to Alexander Bloch, July 8, 1910; Michael J. Reagan to A. E. Lefcourt, July 15, 1910. (All manuscript citations are from the Brandeis Collection, Law School Library, University of Louisville, except where otherwise noted.)

[35] A. E. Lefcourt to M. J. Reagan, July 15, 1910.

[36] Alexander Bloch to A. E. Lefcourt, July 18, 1910, enclosing Statement to the Press of Informal Conference dated July 18, 1910.

[37] A. E. Lefcourt to Alexander Bloch, July 18, 1910, enclosing Resolution of Executive Board; A. E. Lefcourt to John Lundrigan, July 18, 1910; New York *Times*, July 19, 1910, p. 2.

[38] Alexander Bloch to A. E. Lefcourt, July 19, 1910.

sufficient basis for beginning the conference, it categorically refused to enter into negotiations unless the Union would give a negative reply to three questions posed by the Association. Even though the Union denied any intentions of trying to interfere in the businesses of the cloak manufacturers and recognized that the continued employment of its members was predicated upon good business conditions, it refused to give negative replies to the questions whether the Union would demand recognition, whether the Union would demand exclusion of non-union labor from the cloak shops, and whether the Union would demand a signed contract from the Association.[39] In the absence of this demanded negative reply the Association refused to go along with a mediation conference and so notified the New York State Board of Mediation and Arbitration. John Lundrigan clearly foresaw these developments when a week before the breakup of preliminary negotiations he stated that there was little hope of an early settlement of the strike because of the question of union recognition. He put his finger on the issue when he said, "Without the Union the strikers do not see how they can enforce any concessions their employers might make." Even though many tradespeople had come to believe in the principle of collective bargaining, he saw a great complication in the cloak situation in the fact that the employers had gone on record so strongly against the Union.[40]

On July 21, the very day that the preliminary negotiations between the strikers and the Association were broken off, an active Boston social welfare worker, Meyer Bloomfield, acting on behalf of industrial peace and A. Lincoln Filene, was holding conferences between both sides looking for a resumption of negotiations in order to settle the strike.[41]

A. Lincoln Filene, a leading Boston merchant, who was interested in problems of social welfare and was a leading member of the Boston branch of the National Civic Federation, showed an immediate interest in the strike of the cloakmakers. Extremely interested in industrial peace with justice for both the manufacturer and the workingman, Filene had

[39] A. E. Lefcourt to Alexander Bloch and John B. Lennon, July 20, 1910; Alexander Bloch and John B. Lennon to A. E. Lefcourt, July 20, 1910; A. E. Lefcourt to Alexander Bloch and J. B. Lennon, July 21, 1910.

[40] A. E. Lefcourt to M. J. Reagan, July 21, 1910; New York *Times*, July 13, 1910, p. 3; John B. McPherson, "The New York Cloakmakers' Strike," *Journal of Political Economy*, XIX (March, 1911), 157-59; Edith Wyatt, "The New York Cloak-Makers' Strike," *McClure's Magazine*, XXXVI (April, 1911), 709.

[41] Memorandum of Conferences between Meyer Bloomfield and Principals to Cloak Strike, Thursday, July 21, 1910 (handwritten); for sketch of Meyer Bloomfield, see Donald Wilhelm, "Meyer Bloomfield," *The American Magazine*, LXXIII, No. 5 (March, 1912), 553-54, with photograph on p. 551.

sent a representative to New York to investigate conditions leading to the strike and to look into the possibilities of a peaceful settlement. On July 14, J. R. Simpson, the merchandise manager of Filene's, reported back to Lincoln Filene that the strikers' demands were justified but that he believed the Union had not yet demonstrated its capacity for self-government and its ability to support and enforce agreements. He recommended, therefore, that pressure be applied on the Union to give up its demands for a closed shop and for recognition if the manufacturers would agree to grant the workers' demands looking toward the elimination of the most glaring abuses in the industry. In a year or two, with maturity, the Union would be able to win recognition without a contest for they would be in an excellent position to organize the garment workers completely. If the manufacturers refused to clear their own house, then Simpson suggested that Filene "bring together 25 or so of the leading merchants of the country to get the manufacturers to do what is right."[42]

Meyer Bloomfield came to New York as a result of Simpson's suggestions and immediately contacted Bloch, Dyche, and Rosenberg, who showed great interest in a direct conference with the manufacturers but wanted the suggestion to come from a highly respected national figure. On the afternoon of July 21, Bloomfield contacted Lefcourt of the Association, who was pessimistic about the results of any unconditional conference with the Union but agreed to arrange a meeting of the Executive Committee to discuss the suggestions of the Boston gentleman. The next day Bloomfield had lunch with Julius Henry Cohen, the attorney for the Association, and afterwards met the members of the Executive Committee. The executive members reiterated that it was impossible to hold conferences without the Union's agreeing to certain conditions. It was finally agreed that if "a big man" acting for the Union would, together with Mr. Cohen, draw up conditions for a conference, then and only then could any progress be made. John Lennon and Dyche, acting unofficially for the Strike Committee of the Union, agreed to this suggestion, and when Bloomfield suggested that Louis D. Brandeis be invited secretly to draw up a "fair basis of negotiations" for the Union, Dyche and Lennon heartily agreed and suggested that Brandeis be invited to New York for a private talk.[43]

[42] Memorandum of Conversation between A. L. Filene and J. R. Simpson, July 14, 1910 (carbon typescript); J. B. McPherson, "The New York Cloakmakers' Strike," *Journal of Political Economy*, XIX (March, 1911), 160-61; Edith Wyatt, "The New York Cloak-Makers' Strike," *McClure's Magazine*, XXXVI (April, 1911), 710.

[43] Memorandum of Conferences between Meyer Bloomfield and Principals, July 21, 1910.

As soon as Bloomfield's memorandum reached Boston, A. Lincoln Filene contacted Brandeis and asked him to go to New York in order to help arrange a settlement in the cloak strike. Even though the Boston attorney had certain qualms regarding the possibilities of settlement of the strike and vowed that only with the withdrawl of the closed shop demand would he continue to act for the Union, Brandeis left for New York on July 23 taking a proposed agreement with him which made no provisions for a closed or open shop. When he began participating in the conferences with members of the Strike Committee, Brandeis quickly discarded his draft agreement which was too general to fit the detailed requirements of the peculiar industrial conditions of the cloak industry.[44]

Through the 23rd and 24th of July Brandeis conferred with members of the Strike Committee, endeavoring to get them to draw up a statement of grievances and to waive the closed shop demand, which were the conditions which the Association demanded before formal conferences could begin. On the latter day a majority of the Strike Committee, led by John Dyche and Alexander Bloch, submitted a document wherein were presented the major grievances of the strikers and suggestions for their elimination. The strike leaders hoped to create a permanent board of arbitration and demanded that "every employee who participated in the strike... be reinstated" in the event of a settlement. This document also authorized Brandeis to present their demands to the Association on behalf of the Union.[45]

When the Association balked at the demand for reinstatement of all strikers, Brandeis got the strike leaders to agree that the question should be one of the topics to be discussed at the formal conference. In transmitting all the demands of the Union to Julius Henry Cohen, Brandeis stated that the "[Union] officers understand fully that under this proposal the closed shop is not a subject which can be discussed at the conference." This was countersigned and approved by John A. Dyche.[46]

These actions by Dyche and the majority of the Strike Committee almost caused a split within the ranks of the Union which was averted only

[44] Notes of Telephone Conversation between A. Lincoln Filene and L. D. Brandeis, July 22, 1910; Proposed Labor Agreement with penciled notation in upper right-hand corner, "5 cop. taken by L.D.B. to N.Y. July 23, 1910."

[45] Original Proposal Submitted to Brandeis, undated and signed by ten members of the Strike Committee but not including Abraham Rosenberg; corrected copy of above, dated July 24, 1910, and signed by John A. Dyche and Louis D. Brandeis as attorney.

[46] L. D. Brandeis to J. H. Cohen, July 24, 1910; Statement on Reinstatement of Strikers signed by John A. Dyche.

by the last-minute intervention of Samuel Gompers. Abraham Rosenberg was indignant when on the 25th the newspapers carried the story of the conference preliminaries. He, together with the rest of the Strike Committee members who disagreed with the policy of the majority in waiving the closed shop demand, threatened to boycott the forthcoming conference between the Union and the Association. Only when Gompers hastily arranged a truce between the conservative and radical factions of the Strike Committee by adding Benjamin Schlesinger, a former I.L.G.W.U. President and then the Business Manager of the *Jewish Daily Forward*, to the Strike Committee in order to bolster the radical elements did Rosenberg agree to recognize the actions of the majority as legal.[47]

In the meantime the Manufacturers' Association had notified Brandeis that they had accepted the proposal for a conference with the hope "that the two organizations can together work out a constructive policy for the betterment of the industry."[48] On July 27 Julius Henry Cohen and Meyer London, acting for the Association and the Union respectively, wired Brandeis asking him to chair the settlement conference between the two groups which was to begin the next morning in the Metropolitan Life Building. Brandeis wired his acceptance and hopefully returned to New York.[49]

The next day the long-sought conference got under way. Each side was represented by ten men in addition to their respective attorneys, Cohen and London. The Union group consisted of some middle-aged intellectuals, young cloak workers, and militant old-time unionists. Among the manufacturers' representatives were some men of wide culture and learning who were prominent members of the Ethical Culture movement, a few who had risen from the East Side sweatshops, and one man who had been a union leader in the cloak strike which had tied up the New York market fourteen years earlier. As a group the men who sat around the table in a room in the Metropolitan Life Building were the best-informed persons then available regarding the complicated cloak industry.[50]

In order to facilitate quick settlement, Brandeis arranged the agenda of

[47] New York *Times*, July 26, 1910, p. 4; New York *Call*, July 26, 1910, p. 1; *Jewish Daily Forward*, July 26, 1910, p. 1; Rosenberg, *Memoirs*, pp. 223-24; Hoffman, *Fifty Years*, pp. 193-94.

[48] Julius Henry Cohen to Louis D. Brandeis, July 27, 1910.

[49] Meyer London and Julius Henry Cohen to L. D. Brandeis, July 27, 1910 (telegram); L. D. Brandeis to M. London and J. H. Cohen, July 27, 1910 (copy of telegram).

[50] Edith Wyatt, "The New York Cloak-Makers' Strike," *McClure's Magazine* XXXVI (April, 1911), pp. 710-11.

the conference, with the help of Cohen and London, in such a way that the least disputed items should appear first and the questions of implementation of the agreement or remedies, which could offer certain difficulties, should not be discussed until all problems in dispute were settled. The opening statements of the three lawyers were conciliatory and it seemed that a quick end to the strike was near.[51]

Through the first two days of the conference the proceedings went smoothly with the chairman, through his tactful use of conciliatory methods, getting both sides to agree to the elimination of the worst abuses in the industry. Where agreement could not be easily reached, as on the question of wages, arbitration was proposed. On the third day, however, harmony was shattered by the introduction of the question of remedies, which resulted in the discussion of the tabooed topic of the closed shop.[52]

Even though a semblance of harmony had been reached within the ranks of the Union representatives, the "radicals," led by Rosenberg, still felt that the majority had no right to waive the closed shop and tried several times unsuccessfully to discuss this question. On July 30, John Lennon raised the question of a union shop agreement. When Cohen objected to this as a violation of the agreement not to discuss the closed shop, Brandeis ruled that the discussion of a union shop was not prevented by the pre-conference arrangements. When the chairman ruled that London's proposal, that the group discuss the closed shop as a remedy if no other presented itself, was out of order, the Union representatives requested and received a recess to discuss the issues by themselves. In order to keep the conference in session, Brandeis used flattery, cajolery, and diplomacy.[53]

After the short recess, seeing that the conference was in danger of doundering on the issue of the closed shop, Brandeis introduced a plan which he hoped would avoid the evils of both the closed and open shop systems and retain the advantages of both. This was the preferential union shop or in the words of the chairman, "the manufacturer should, in the employment of labor hereafter, give the preference to union men, where the union men are equal in efficiency to any non-union applicants." This plan, it was thought, would avoid the creation of a labor monopoly

[51] *Minutes of Joint Conference between Ten Delegates of the Joint Board of the Cloak, Suit and Skirt Makers' Unions and Ten Delegates of the Cloak, Suit and Skirt Manufacturers' Protective Association*, July 28 to July 30, 1910, pp. 1-145 (Brandeis Collection).

[52] *Ibid.*, pp. 146-241.

[53] *Ibid.*, pp. 286-93.

by the union and at the same time present an opportunity to the unionists to organize the labor force.[54]

Even though their counsel, Julius Henry Cohen, did not believe that the plan would work, the manufacturers agreed to try the preferential shop. The Union representatives, this time led by Lennon, thought the concessions so minor that they wanted to terminate the conference. After Cohen accused the Union leaders of cowardice because they feared to face their militant membership with less than a closed shop, even though the leaders realized that the proposed agreement was the best one that they could negotiate, the chairman tried to avoid the imminent breakup of the conference by introducing less explosive topics than the closed-open shop. When discussions came back to the preferential shop, John Dyche gave the final Union verdict when he said, "I have no faith in it. . . . It is something too new. It cannot be done at this crisis."[55]

To avoid a complete rupture of negotiations, Brandeis suggested that the conference be adjourned and that Cohen and London together with the chairman meet and draw up an agreement incorporating the conference decisions as a basis for future negotiations. On August 1, Cohen sent Brandeis a written agreement which contained clauses regarding all the abuses discussed at the conference and provided for Joint Boards of Grievances, Arbitration and Sanitary Control. On the crucial question of the nature of union control, the proposed agreement contained a clause stating that the manufacturers were to announce their adherence to the principle of trade unionism, that the preferential union shop should prevail with the majority of employees belonging to the union and the manufacturers sympathetic to the organization of the workers. After Brandeis amended the preferential union shop clause to read "a shop in which union standards prevail and the union man is entitled to the preference," the agreement was sent to Meyer London, who without comment sent it on to the General Strike Committee.[56] When Rosenberg, Dyche, and Schlesinger all attacked the proposed agreement and the *Jewish Daily Forward* denounced the preferential shop as "the scab shop with honey," it was obvious to all that the conference had failed and that

[54] *Ibid.*, pp. 294-98.

[55] *Ibid.*, pp. 299-301, 308, 338.

[56] *Ibid.*, pp. 344-49; Julius Henry Cohen to L. D. Brandeis, August 1, 1910, enclosing Tentative Agreement; L. D. Brandeis to Julius Henry Cohen, August 1, 1910; Julius Henry Cohen to Meyer London, August 1, 1910, enclosing corrected Tentative Agreement.

an agreement could not be reached quickly.[57] The newspapers of New York, with the exception of the *Forward* and the *Call*, vigorously attacked the Union for not accepting what seemed to be a really constructive trade agreement. What these newspapers did not realize was that the suspicion and distrust engendered during the preceding two decades by the unscrupulous among the manufacturers could not be wiped away by a three-day conference. Many of the Union people were dissatisfied with the compromise on wages, other lost confidence in Brandeis when the Association announced that the Union's retaining of the Boston attorney was a tacit repudiation of the closed shop because of Brandeis's known antipathy to it, but the crucial consideration was the fear that since the determination of ability under the preferential plan would be the sole responsibility of the manufacturers, union men would be discriminated against and the open shop, with all its evils, would prevail.[58]

Although the conference failed, the peacemakers remained active. Brandeis returned to his summer vacation spot at South Yarmouth, Filene temporarily returned to Boston, but Meyer Bloomfield and Henry Moskowitz kept in daily contact with the developing situations in the cloak strike and informed both Brandeis and Filene of every new development. The Downtown Ethical Culture Center, which was headed by Henry Moskowitz, became the central headquarters for the peacemakers who hoped to exploit any opening in their endeavor to end the costly strike.[59]

In the meantime the strike continued in its accustomed manner with the Union attempting to sign up independent manufacturers and the Association exploring various legal methods of bringing the strike to an end on their terms.

[57] See statements of Union leaders in *Jewish Daily Forward*, July 30, 1910, p. 4; front page editorial of the *Forward* of August 3, 1910, told of the breakup of the conference and called the preferential union shop "a sugar coated poison pill," and an editorial appearing in the August 6, 1910, issue of the *Forward* claimed that the Brandeis preferential shop was a "scab shop with honey." Final Union rejection of the Tentative Agreement of August 1 was contained in a letter sent by Meyer London to Julius Henry Cohen and Louis D. Brandeis on August 3 and reprinted in the *Forward* on August 5.

[58] Press comments on the Union's rejection of the agreement seen in clippings mounted by Louis D. Brandeis in *Scrap Book on Garment Workers and Preferential Union Shop*, pp. 14-28; Meyer London to Julius Henry Cohen and Louis D. Brandeis, August 3, 1910; John B. McPherson, "The New York Cloakmakers' Strike," *Journal of Political Economy*, XIX (March, 1911), 179-80.

[59] J. Salwyn Schapiro, "Henry Moskowitz, Social Reformer in Politics," *The Outlook*, CII (October 26, 1912), 446-49. Hamilton Holt, "Henry Moskowitz: A Useful Citizen," *The Independent*, LXXVII (January 12, 1914), 66-67.

With every passing day more and more of the smaller manufacturers signed union contracts, and in order publicly to exploit this fact the General Executive Board arranged for marches and demonstrations of workers whenever they returned to work. This had a twofold effect upon the strikers for it bolstered their morale and it showed that the statements of settlement were not false.[60]

The strike fund which was collected before the beginning of hostilities was running low and it was necessary to replenish the supply of money in order to meet the normal expenses of the strike as well as the needs of the bulk of the strikers. At a meeting of representatives of the Workmen's Circle, the United Hebrew Trades, the Socialist Party, the Central Federated Union of New York, and the Forward Association it was decided to launch a concerted fund drive on behalf of the cloak strikers. The columns of the *Jewish Daily Forward* and the New York *Call* were opened to the fundraising committee and throughout the mouth of August these newspapers carried accounts of money collected. The cloakmakers who were working were not idle in this respect, for every working former striker donated from 15 to 25 percent of his wages to the strike fund. Morris Winchevsky, the noted Yiddish poet and journalist, who was in charge of the fund committee throughout the strike, reported that $246,403 was collected from various sources and that almost two thirds of that amount was distributed to the strikers in the form of weekly strike benefits.[61]

Even though the strike leaders, with the aid of the rest of organized labor, tried to maintain enthusiasm among the strikers and a favorable opinion among the public, the rejection of the Brandeis compromise regarding the union shop and the termination of the conference by the Union resulted in a wave of hostile comment from the press of the nation.[62] This shift in opinion by the press which reflected the general shift of public opinion gave the manufacturers and especially the Association a good opportunity to try to end the strike either through attracting dissident cloakmakers back to work or through applying for a sweeping injunction against the conduct of the strike by the Union.

[60] Rosenberg, *Memoirs*, pp. 219-21; *Jewish Daily Forward*, August 12, 1910, p. 4.

[61] Minutes, United Hebrew Trades, August 7, 1910 (YIVO); *Jewish Daily Forward*, August 3, 1910, p. 8; August 20, 1910, p. 1; New York *Times*, August 25, 1910, p. 2; Morris Winchevsky, "Report of Strike Fund Committee," *Jewish Daily Forward*, September 8, 1910, p. 5.

[62] For typical newspaper reaction see editorials in New York *Times*, August 2, 1910, p. 6; August 5, 1910, p. 8; *The Outlook*, XCV (August 20, 1910), 856.

On August 2, the same day that the General Executive Board of the Union was considering the Brandeis-Cohen compromise, rumors were circulated by responsible members of the Association that regardless of the outcome of the negotiations many manufacturers would attempt to resume production in order not to lose the entire fall season.[63] Three days later, after the rejection by the Union of the preferential shop compromise and the resultant shift in public sentiment against the strikers, these rumors were verified by an official statement issued by the Executive Committee of the Manufacturers' Association which claimed that workers were being recruited from Cleveland and Chicago. It was also announced that one hundred and ninety special policemen were hired by the manufacturers to protect the strikebreakers.[64] On Monday, August 8, attempts were made to open a number of struck cloak factories, but despite extraordinary efforts by the manufacturers, which included housing their newly recruited labor in hotels for their protection, no appreciable inroads were made in the effectiveness of the strike.[65]

The attempt to resume production in the face of almost absolute opposition by labor resulted in the first outbreaks of violence in the cloak strike. Several plants were invaded by the strikers, causing damage to the equipment and furnishings. Battles between the strikers and the special police broke out, with casualties on both sides. To the taunt that the manufacturers had hired strong-arm men as special policemen, the Association answered that the Union had hired some East Side gang members to dissuade strikers from returning to work. Stones and other missiles were freely thrown by strikers into scabbing shops and for the first time since the strike began mass arrests were made.[66]

The violence and arrests in the cloak strike caused the Acting Mayor, John Purroy Mitchel, to investigate the situation, and when this showed that neither side in the dispute had a monopoly on the use of illegal and violent methods he instructed the Police Department through the Police Commissioner, William F. Baker, to show no favoritism in the enforcement of the laws. To avoid the public controversy regarding police bias which characterized the earlier shirtwaist strike, Mitchel reminded Baker that the strikers had a right to organize and picket but did not have the right to force, intimidate, or threaten others to prevent them from

[63] New York *Times*, August 3, 1910, p. 12.

[64] *Ibid.*, August 6, 1910, p. 14; August 8, 1910, p. 14.

[65] *Ibid.*, August 9, 1910, p. 3; New York *World*, August 9, 1910, p. 5.

[66] New York *Times*, August 9, 1910; August 10, 1910, p. 20; Editorial, August 11, 1910, p. 6; *Jewish Daily Forward*, August 9, 1910, pp. 1 and 8.

working. This did not mean that strikers could not talk with strikebreakers. Only if intemperate or indecent language were used or violence threatened or perpetrated should the police interfere and arrest the wrongdoer. The Acting Mayor concluded that violators of the law, whether they be strikers or strikebreakers, should immediately be apprehended and brought to justice.[67] The next day, August 13, the Acting Mayor in another letter, this time to the city magistrates, cautioned them and their clerks to be tolerant and patient with the arrested strikers, especially with those who could not speak English fluently. He took this action in response to complaints he received regarding the inhuman treatment many arrested non-English-speaking people were receiving at the hands of the court clerks who were allowing their prejudices to color their behavior.[68]

Although Mitchel's letter writing was applauded by the strikers and Alexander Bloch publicly thanked the Mayor for this statesmanlike act, the employers were dissatisfied. Paul J. Bonwit, of Bonwit, Teller and Co., wrote the Mayor demanding police protection for his property and his loyal workmen and attacked Mitchel's order on the grounds that it reduced the Police Department to "an unmitigated farce."[69] The noise and complaints which the Association raised against Mitchel's order resulted in a Grand Jury investigation of the entire cloak strike. Immediately before the investigation, which began on August 24, Association spokesmen claimed that Mitchel's letter was an invitation to the strikers to indulge in acts of violence. Union spokesmen countered that pickets were still being arrested but that instead of taking orders from the manufacturers, the police, since the Mitchel order, had taken their instructions from police officials. Moreover, they insisted that "considering the number involved, the present strike is the quietest on record, and exaggerated statements by employers will not change the facts."[70]

In addition to the attempts to open their factories with non-union labor, the Association tried to defeat the Union through the use of the injunction. As soon as the negotiations broke off, Julius Henry Cohen, acting on behalf of Max M. Schwarcz, a leading cloak manufacturer and treasurer of the Association, applied for a sweeping permanent court order to

[67] John Purroy Mitchel to William F. Baker, August 12, 1910, in New York *Times*, August 13, 1910, p. 2.

[68] John Purroy Mitchel to Chief Magistrates McAdoo and Kempner, August 13, 1910, in New York *Times*, August 14, 1910, p. 2.

[69] New York *Times*, August 14, 1910, p. 2; Paul J. Bonwit to John P. Mitchel, August 13, 1910, in New York *Times*, August 17, 1910, p. 5.

[70] New York *Times*, August 25, 1910, p. 2.

restrain the strikers from picketing and the sympathetic newspapers from encouraging the strikers. After a quick hearing before Supreme Court Judge Irving Lehman on August 6, with Meyer London arguing on behalf of the Union against the injunction, a temporary limited injunction was granted to the petitioner restraining the Union and other interested persons from coercing any cloak employee to leave his work through the use of force, threat, fraud, or intimidation. The Union was also ordered to show cause why the injunction should not be made more sweeping and permanent, and Judge Lehman designated that the whole matter was to be argued before Judge Goff on the return date of the show cause order.[71]

In order to document and reinforce their contention that the strike was for the closed shop and consequently illegal, the Association, through Julius Henry Cohen and Max Meyer, tried to obtain the Union's authorization to Brandeis to act on its behalf and the letter in which John Dyche waived the closed shop as an issue for discussion at the first conference. Brandeis turned over the letters and telegrams which he received from Cohen and Meyer to Filene requesting that he, Bloomfield, and Moskowitz decide what should or should not be made available to the manufacturers. On August 8, A. L. Filene wrote Max Meyer that the papers he requested could be sent to him only if Meyer London agreed, for if Brandeis were to send the documents in question without the consent of the Union and its counsel then his neutrality would be open to question and his usefulness in any future negotiation would be handicapped. The next day, after the news of the Association's injunction attempt was made public, Filene wrote Brandeis that the requests of Meyer and Cohen should not be acceded to if the letters were to be used as evidence in an injunction proceeding. Brandeis agreed and Filene continued to insist that the documents or photostats of the documents could be turned over to the Association only with the consent of Meyer London.[72]

During the time that the hearings were being held for the permanent injunction before Judge Goff, Julius Cohen tried again to get the docu-

[71] *Ibid.*, August 7, 1910, p. 16; Supreme Court, New York County, Max M. Schwarcz v. I.L.G.W.U., pp. 1-6. (Reprinted pamphlet at New York Public Library.) To plead its case at the later hearings the Union engaged Judge Alton B. Parker. See New York *Times*, August 14, 1910, p. 2; *Jewish Daily Forward*, August 13, 1910, p. 1.

[72] Max Meyer to L. D. Brandeis, August 4, 1910 (telegram); Max Meyer to L. D. Brandeis, August 4, 1910; L. D. Brandeis to Staff, August 5, 1910; Brandeis, Dunbar, and Nutter to Meyer Bloomfield, August 8, 1910, enclosing cloak strike documents in their possession; A. L. Filene to Max Meyer, August 8, 1910; A. L. Filene to Louis D. Brandeis, August 9, 1910; Meyer Bloomfield to Henry Moskowitz, August 11, 1910; A. L. Filene to Henry Moskowitz, August 11, 1910.

ments from Brandeis without resort to a subpoena. He argued that many of the Union leaders were denying that they had waived the closed shop demand and that it was necessary to have the documents to convince the public and especially the strikers that these leaders were not telling the truth. Bloomfield and Filene agreed that the papers that Cohen wanted were papers which passed between Brandeis and the Union people in order to arrange a conference and that for Brandeis to turn over these papers to the manufacturers would place him in the position of betraying a trust.[73]

The theme which ran through the correspondence which passed between the peacemakers, Brandeis, Filene, Bloomfield, and Moskowitz, during the month of August was that their position of neutrality must not be disturbed. It was for this reason that Filene asked Moskowitz not to write an article for *The Outlook* on the cloak situation and that Moskowitz and Brandeis were cautioned not to make any public statements regarding the strike. Their refusal to accede to the manufacturers' requests for documents which passed between Brandeis and the Union leaders was the most important action in maintaining their neutral position and allowing them to continue to work behind the scenes for a settlement of the labor dispute.[74]

Henry Moskowitz and A. L. Filene were in New York through most of August but they kept their colleagues in Boston thoroughly informed of all the developments on the battle front. In a letter which Moskowitz sent to Bloomfield on August 12 he analyzed the situation for his Boston colleague and related the obstacles in the way of a peaceful settlement. On the one hand the "rabid" attitude of the *Forward* set the tone for the strikers in preventing compromise, and on the other hand the equally rabid attitude of Julius Henry Cohen prevented a statesmanlike approach by the manufacturers, Moskowitz wrote. Despite Cohen's tactless approach and his attempt to make "a lawyers scrap" out of the strike through injunction proceedings, Moskowitz related that he was able to "smell a schism" in the ranks of the Association with men like Reuben Sadofsky not fearing a closed shop and favoring union recognition and men like Max Meyer and Max Schwarcz fearing and opposing any official union recognition by the Association.[75]

In addition to keeping abreast of developing events in the strike, Filene

[73] Julius H. Cohen to Louis D. Brandeis, August 17, 1910; Memorandum of Telephone Conversation between A. Lincoln Filene and Meyer Bloomfield, August 19, 1910.

[74] A. L. Filene to Henry Moskowitz, August 11, 1910.

[75] Henry Moskowitz to Meyer Bloomfield, August 12, 1910.

and Moskowitz also tried to convince neutral citizens of standing in the Jewish community of New York to intervene on behalf of a peaceful settlement. At first they were inclined to press both Louis Miller, the editor of the Yiddish daily, the *Wahrheit*, and Joseph Barondess, a former cloak union leader, but in 1910 an active Zionist and member of the New York City Board of Education, into service as peacemakers, but when they discovered that both these individuals were *persona non grata* with the *Forward* people and that their intervention would only complicate matters by inciting internal squabbles and a newspaper war between the *Forward* and the *Wahrheit*, they gave up this plan.[76] Instead they were able to interest Louis Marshall, a leading constitutional lawyer, and Jacob H. Schiff, the New York banker, both prominent members of the Jewish community, in intervening as interested persons to get both sides to agree to private discussions looking toward a settlement of the already protracted struggle.[77]

The suffering which the strike had occasioned among the inhabitants of the East Side of New York, the number of unfortunates threatened with eviction from their flats because of nonpayment of rent, and the disruption of business in the Jewish community had already caused Marshall and Schiff to think of the consequences of further idleness of thousands of cloakmakers. It was, therefore, no difficult task for Filene and Moskowitz to convince the two Jewish leaders that they should attempt to bring about an honorable settlement.[78]

On August 22, after contacting Brandeis and receiving his statement regarding the preferential shop, Louis Marshall met separately with Union and manufacturer representatives. Even though Julius Henry Cohen repeated the Association's opposition to the recognition of the Union, going so far as to reject the preferential plan which the Association had accepted during the Brandeis conference, Marshall did not give up in despair. During the next few days Jacob Schiff and Joseph S. Marcus, President of the Public Bank on the East Side, were able to apply pressure to some recalcitrant members of the Association so that on the 25th Julius Henry Cohen agreed to participate in conversation with Meyer London and Louis Marshall. The meeting, held in the office of Louis Marshall, lasted far into the night, and agreements were quickly reached on those Union demands which had offered little difficulty during the

[76] Henry Moskowitz to Meyer Bloomfield, August 12, 1910.

[77] A. L. Filene to Louis Marshall, August 18, 1910 (copy sent to L. D. Brandeis).

[78] New York *Times*, August 20, 1910, p. 1; New York *World*, August 23, 1910, p. 7; August 26, 1910, p. 4.

previous Brandeis conference. The question of union recognition was again the stumbling block.[79]

Filene, who remained in close contact with Marshall in his peacemaking endeavors, formulated an agreement which he sent to Brandeis for his approval. The preferential clause was in the proposed agreement, as was the statement that the Union did not seek the "closed shop" but rather a "Union shop." Filene foresaw that the statement in the preferential clause, "non-union men of equal ability," would be unacceptable to the Union and requested Brandeis's suggestions. Brandeis telegraphed Filene that it might be wise to substitute another phrase for "non-union men" but that the provision regarding equal ability should remain. He also suggested that both sides submit the proposed agreement to a referendum vote. In the meantime, Benjamin Schlesinger suggested a different formulation of the preferential clause to Louis Marshall which avoided the use of both objectionable terms "non-union men" and "equal ability" but, because of Brandeis's objection, the original clause remained in the proposed agreement together with the compromise suggested by Schlesinger.[80]

It was the Filene proposals, based on the agreements reached at the earlier conferences as modified by Schlesinger and Brandeis, which Marshall was able to get Cohen and London to submit to their respective organizations as a result of the meetings held on August 25. The Executive Committee of the Protective Association agreed to accept the settlement but the Strike Committee was split on the issue. Many members of the Strike Committee, led by Alexander Bloch of the cutters, believed that despite the loss of the closed shop this was the best possible agreement which could be gotten. Abraham Rosenberg, on the other hand, led the faction which held that compromise on the closed shop issue meant defeat. They argued that the manufacturers could not hold out much longer and a refusal to settle at this time would lead to eventual victory. They were especially incensed at the provision which granted the manu-

[79] Meyer Bloomfield to A. L. Filene, August 21, 1910; New York *World*, August 23, 1910, p. 7; August 26, 1910, p. 4; New York *Times*, August 26, 1910, p. 16; Edith Wyatt, "The New York Cloak-Makers' Strike," *McClure's Magazine*, XXXVI (April, 1911), 712.

[80] A. L. Filene to Louis D. Brandeis, August 23, 1910, enclosing formulated agreement to be sent to Louis Marshall; Meyer Bloomfield to Louis D. Brandeis, Tuesday (no date given but internal evidence shows this to be August 23, 1910); Louis D. Brandeis to A. Lincoln Filene, n.d. (copy of telegram sent either on August 24 or 25, 1910); John B. McPherson, "The New York Cloakmakers' Strike," *Journal of Political Economy*, XIX (March, 1911), 184.

facturers the right to retain non-union men in their employ and remained hostile to the preferential clause of the agreement.[81]

The Strike Committee, because of its failure to agree, submitted the proposed settlement to the strikers for ratification without any recommendations to accept or reject. The *Jewish Daily Forward* printed the agreement with the suggestion that the strikers search their souls before accepting or rejecting the settlement. Louis E. Miller wrote an editorial in the *Wahrheit* recommending that the strikers accept the agreement. A number of New York newspapers trumpeted the end of the strike before any official action was taken.[82]

There was much confusion on the evening of August 26 when the strikers assembled at their meeting halls to discuss the proposed settlement. The majority of the strikers sided with the radical faction of the Strike Committee and looked upon anything less than the closed shop as a defeat. Many cloakmakers who were working in settled shops were against the proposed settlement because they felt that they would lose some of their gains if the Union settled with the Association for less advantageous terms than they had received. The false reports that a settlement had been reached caused many of the strikers to believe that they had been sold out, so that when the representatives of the Strike Committee came to the meeting halls to read and discuss the Marshall agreement, the cloakmakers were in an ugly mood. Respected strike leaders were hooted down, chased from the platform, and threatened with violence. John B. Lennon and Abe Mitchell, two influential members of the Strike Committee, had to flee for their lives from the Manhattan Lyceum; Alexander Bloch had to carry a revolver with him and could not walk the streets for the next few days without bodyguards.[83]

Having vociferously rejected the peace settlement, the howling majority adjourned from their halls to demonstrate their opposition in front of the *Forward* building. When, on the morning of the 27th, the strikers learned of the editorial in the *Wahrheit* urging them to ratify the Marshall agreement, they went to the building of that newspaper to show their discontent. As they neared the *Wahrheit* building someone threw a stone, breaking a window, and this was followed by a volley of stones. Someone shouted, "We made an open shop in the *Wahrheit*!" as police reinforce-

[81] Rosenberg, *Memoirs*, pp. 238-40; Hoffman, *Fifty Years*, pp. 201-3; New York *Times*, August 28, 1910, p. 3.

[82] *Jewish Daily Forward*, August 26, 1910, p. 1; *Wahrheit*, August 27, 1910, p. 1; New York *Evening Post*, August 26, 1910, p. 3.

[83] New York *Times*, August 28, 1910, p. 3; New York *World*, August 27, 1910, p. 5; August 28, 1910, p. 2.

ments arrived on the scene to control the situation. It was not until a number of *Wahrheit* employees had been injured and some strikers arrested that order was restored on East Broadway.[84]

The tumultuous protests against the proposed settlement continued throughout Saturday the 27th and culminated in a parade and demonstration of thousands of cloakmakers up Fifth Avenue. Even though they were dispersed by the police for lack of a permit, they reassembled and continued to demonstrate in the side streets and on the East Side. In the face of this determined opposition the entire strike leadership had no other alternative but to reject the proposed agreement in its entirety.[85]

In the midst of the tumult and demonstrations, Justice John W. Goff of the New York Supreme Court threw a bombshell when he announced his intention of granting the petition of Max Schwarcz for a permanent and sweeping injunction against the cloak strikers. On August 27 it became known that John Goff held the strike to be "a common law, civil conspiracy," for its primary purpose was not to better the conditions of the workmen but to deprive non-union men of their opportunity to work and to drive them from the industry. He held that although the unions "had not formally directed a systematic course of agression by criminal acts, the members of the unions acting in consort have connived at, condoned and morally supported such acts on the part of many of their members." He therefore found that the strikers were using illegal means to achieve illegal and immoral ends. In the light of these findings, John Goff prohibited the strikers from picketing or from interfering in any way with the normal operation of the cloak factories.[86]

The reaction of the participants to the injunction was immediate. Julius Henry Cohen and the members of the Association were jubilant, predicting that this decision, "the strongest one ever handed down in an American court against trade unionism," would break the back of the strike and result in an immediate victory for the manufacturers.[87] Henry Moskowitz and Lincoln Filene were shocked into silence by Goff's

[84] New York *Times*, August 28, 1910, p. 3; *Jewish Daily Forward*, August 28, 1910, p. 1; *Wahrheit*, August 28, 1910, p. 1; Rosenberg, *Memoirs*, pp. 241-42.

[85] New York *World*, August 28, 1910, p. 2; August 29, 1910, p. 5; New York *Times*, August 28, 1910, p. 3; August 29, 1910, p. 7; *Jewish Daily Forward*, August 29, 1910, p. 1; Rosenberg, *Memoirs*, pp. 242-43.

[86] New York *Times*, August 28, 1910, pp. 1 and 3; Supreme Court, County of New York, Max M. Schwarcz vs. I.L.G.W.U., 68 Misc. (N.Y.) 528 (534); J. B. McPherson, "The New York Cloakmakers' Strike," *Journal of Political Economy*, XIX (March, 1911), 182-83.

[87] Statement of Julius Henry Cohen in New York *Times*, August 28, 1910, p. 1, and in New York *World*, August 28, 1910, p. 2.

decision, which they previously predicted would be favorable to the unions.[88] Members of the Strike Committee were united by this decision and the conflict between Rosenberg and Bloch was forgotten when they issued a statement that the decision would be combated and appealed to the higher courts.[89] Samuel Gompers, speaking for the A.F.L., called the decision one which invaded constitutionally guaranteed rights and human liberty.[90] Even those newspapers which were unfriendly to the strikers because of the earlier rejection of the Brandeis compromise condemned Goff's actions as "a hard blow from the bench," "strange law and certainly very poor policy... which would seriously cripple defensive powers as legitimately belong to organized labor."[96]

Acting Mayor Mitchel was compelled to reexamine his previous order to the police to allow peaceful picketing, and after a conference with Judge Goff he wrote to Police Commissioner Baker on August 30 revoking his order of August 12. In so doing he stated that the Police Department was an administrative unit and must take its law from the courts and therefore must carry out the courts' mandate to prohibit peaceful picketing. In order to test the effectiveness of this new order, eighty-five Union members volunteered for picket duty and were quickly arrested and fined for contempt of court.[92]

While the Association was jubilant over the unexpected turn of events and the Union was preparing to fight and possibly even to defy the injunction, Filene was quietly working behind the scenes to get the Union officials to agree to the "protocol of peace," as the Brandeis compromise as drawn up by Louis Marshall was called. In a letter to Brandeis on August 31, Filene noted that if the *Forward* would only say the word or if Rosenberg would only have the courage to confront the militant strikers with the fact that by compromise alone would an honorable peace be achieved, the strike would end immediately.[93]

[88] Moskowitz and Filene's erroneous prediction is found in Henry Moskowitz to Meyer Bloomfield, August 12, 1910.

[89] New York *Times*, August 28, 1910, p. 3; August 29, 1910, p. 6; New York *World*, August 29, 1910, p. 5.

[90] New York *Times*, August 28, 1910, p. 3.

[91] Editorial, "A Startling Labor Decision," New York *Times*, August 28, 1910, p. 8; Editorial of New York *Evening Post*, as quoted by Edith Wyatt, "The New York Cloak-Makers' Strike," *McClure's Magazine*, XXXVI (April, 1911), 713; Editorial, "Enjoining a Strike," *The Outlook*, XCVI (September 10, 1910), 52.

[92] New York *Times*, August 30, 1910, p. 6; September 2, 1910, p. 5; John P. Mitchel to William F. Baker, August 30, 1910, in New York *Times*, August 31, 1910, p. 5; New York *World*, August 31, 1910, p. 3.

[93] A. Lincoln Filene to Louis D. Brandeis, August 31, 1910.

The incessant activities of Filene and Moskowitz, coupled with the injunction of Judge Goff, forced the General Executive Board of the I.L.G.W.U. to reevaluate its strike strategy and objectives. As a result of this reevaluation and in order to regain the right of peaceful picketing the Union officially dropped its demand for the closed shop. This decision was made known to the Acting Mayor when Meyer London, on September 1, wrote Mayor Mitchel that "hereafter each employer [will] be asked to maintain a union shop" rather than a closed shop. In general Meyer London was noting the desire of the Union to settle the strike on the basis of the protocol of peace. A copy of this letter was sent to the Association and Filene was able to get both sides represented by their respective attorneys to meet again on September 2 with Louis Marshall to draw up a settlement.[94]

By the afternoon of September 2, Cohen and London had agreed to the basic provisions of the settlement which, although based on the agreement reached a week before, had been improved through a clearer formulation of the terms "union shop" and "union standards." The preferential clause was rewritten to eliminate the objectionable terms "non-union men" and "equal ability" from the final agreement and the wage and hour questions were compromised, thus eliminating the necessity for arbitration on these issues. In other respects the protocol signed by Cohen and London was similar to the one rejected by the Union members on August 26.[95]

In order to avoid a recurrence of the riots of August 26 and 27 and in order to get approval of the protocol by the evening of September 2, the General Strike Committee decided that ratification of the agreement could be achieved by positive action of the shop chairmen of the striking cloakmakers. At six in the evening the representatives of the strikers, two hundred in number, met at the general strike headquarters and with a minumum of debate quickly ratified the strike agreement bringing the nine-week general strike of the cloakmakers to an honorable end.[96]

Jubilation was universal. The strike leaders and the *Forward* claimed a glorious victory, whereas Julius Henry Cohen, speaking for the manufacturers, declared that the protocol furnished "a great opportunity to

[94] Meyer London to John P. Mitchel, September 1, 1910, in New York *Times* September 2, 1910, p. 5.

[95] Compare Tentative Agreement of August 25 with Protocol of Peace of September 2 (official copies in Brandeis Collection).

[96] "The Outcome of the Cloakmakers' Strike," *The Outlook*, XCVI (September 17, 1910), 99-101; Hoffman, *Fifty Years*, pp. 207-8; Rosenberg, *Memoirs*, p. 245.

build up a strong working relation between the unions and the manufacturers."[97] The peacemakers were able to breathe easier for the first time in nine weeks and, more important, had come out of the situation without antagonizing either side. Cohen and London joined in thanking Brandeis, Marshall, Filene, and Moskowitz for their efforts on behalf of industrial peace with honor, and Filene wrote Brandeis congratulating him on the acceptance of the preferential shop principle, adding that both sides credited the Boston attorney with the successful compromise of the strike.[98]

When the news spread among the strikers in the meeting halls that the long strike had ended victoriously for them, they did not stop to examine the provisions of the settlement, but rather began a spontaneous celebration which continued far into the night. The joyful cloakmakers streamed from their meeting halls carrying their leaders on their shoulders and demonstrated their satisfaction by holding celebration meetings throughout the East Side. The streets near the *Forward* building on East Broadway became impassable when the strikers decided to serenade their leaders in front of that building. The celebrations continued into the Labor Day parade the following Monday. The floats and banners of the cloakmakers, who constituted the single largest group of paraders, equally condemned Judge Goff and praised their leaders and their own fortitude in achieving what they considered to be a decisive vitory.[99]

The cloakmakers' strike was probably the single most important strike in the entire history of the ladies' garment industry, for as a result of that strike the I.L.G.W.U. was permanently established as the effective bargaining agent in the industry. For the first time the Union was successful in negotiating an agreement with an Association of the larger manufacturers who controlled more than half of the cloak and suit industry. Of even greater importance, the cloakmakers' strike ushered in an era of cooperation between labor and management in the ladies' garment industry which is more remarkable if we consider that the ideological orientation of both the leadership and the membership of the Union was largely socialistic. In addition, many of the social inventions which came into being as a result of the strike, such as the preferential

[97] New York *Times*, September 3, 1910, p. 1; *Jewish Daily Forward*, September 3, 1910, p. 1.

[98] New York *Times*, September 3, 1910, p. 1; New York *World*, September 3, 1910, p. 3; A. L. Filene to Louis D. Brandeis, September 3, 1910.

[99] New York *Times*, September 6, 1910, p. 9; *Jewish Daily Forward*, September 4, 1910, p. 1; September 5, 1910, p. 1; September 6, 1910, p. 1.

shop, union and management coresponsibility for maintaining sanitary and health standards in the industry, and continuous arbitration and mediation through permanent boards of arbitration and grievances, made a profound impression upon the general public and were later modified and adopted by many unions and trade associations in the United States.

TRADITION AND INNOVATION

By Joseph L. Blau

NOT LEAST OF the elements of paradox that enter into the very nature of religion is the necessity that lies upon it, in its organized and institutionalized forms, to change while both seeming changeless and protesting its changelessness. For, it is clear, a religious organization maintains its hold over the hearts and minds of its adherents partly by its success in convincing them that they are following the way of their forefathers, that the sanctions of the past are theirs. And while there is no doubt some measure of truth in Jean Cocteau's aphorism that the past is valued only as a stick wherewith to beat the present, there is as much truth, if not more, in George Santayana's reasoned conclusion that an essential element in the complex we call religion is piety toward the sources of our being. Whatever name we may give to the ultimate source of our being, it is our parents and teachers who are the immediate source; more remotely, yet by no means ultimately, it is our ancestors and, generally, the past of our people that are the source of our being. The piety of which Santayana spoke need not at all times be directed toward ultimates, although if it were never directed toward ultimates it could scarcely be regarded as religious. Thus the injunction to "honor thy father and thy mother" is properly a religious injunction to the extent that it associates the more immediate sources of our being with its more remote and even its ultimate sources. Religion must, then, if it is to succeed in remaining a central influence in the lives of people, lay stress upon its roots in the past, its tradition, its heritage, its permanence and stability.

It is equally clear, however, that mere faithfulness to the past is not enough. For the life-problems that men look to their religions to solve or resolve are problems within the present. Whether or not we subscribe to one of the numerous theories of degeneration from a golden age or to one of the equally numerous theories of indefinite and inevitable progress, we must agree in one respect with the empirical investigator, historian, sociologist, or anthropologist; the present is not identical with the past. This is necessarily so, for man is an organic being and his cultural works derive from him an organic character; in an organism stagnation means death. As human cultures develop, human problems change. As human problems change, man's religions must adapt themselves to the changes or lose relevance, where loss of relevance entails loss of centrality, and loss of centrality implies loss of influence. The cultural changes that take place are manifold. Yet it seems to be no exaggeration to assert that in whatever aspect of a culture a change may begin, every aspect of that culture is ultimately and intimately affected by the change. Then whichever phase of life we are interested in chronicling will necessarily involve us in chronicling all phases of life. Any history, however limited in its scope, implies universal history. Religions, therefore, and religious history, since they are implicated in changing cultures, are themselves changing phenomena and records of change. The principle that we are exploring here is especially clear in those relatively simple historical situations where culture, nationality, ethnic group, economy, polity, and religion are different names that we apply to the same group, depending upon which aspect of its group life we are investigating. It is less clear, but no less applicable in more complex historical situations where a polity, for example, may comprehend parts of several ethnic groups, cultures, nationalities, or religions. As the complexities of human social organization multiply, a number of independent variables is added to the full complement of dependent variables with which a simpler situation presents the investigator. Interpretation of the situation becomes more difficult, but the principle of cultural change seems still to apply.

I take it, then, that religions must change with changing cultural situations if they are to be viable, and that they must, nevertheless, appear not to change if they are to be influential. They must seem to bring the wisdom of immemorial antiquity to bear upon the solution of present-day problems, yet not really to do so for the wisdom of antiquity is irrelevant to present-day situations except where it is so generalized as to be without content, to be vapid and inane. "Thou shalt not steal" is a fine general statement, but it does not in itself resolve the problem of a tempted person because it does not contain a definition of property, and this definition would be altogether different in different cultural situations. "Honor thy father and thy mother that thy days may be long" is a fine general principle; it is empty until the course of action involved in the word "honor" is specified. Such specification in terms of modern medical and psychological knowledge of geriatrics and gerontology might lead to a course of action diametrically opposed to the intent of the originator of the principle, that is, to the traditional wisdom.

For the sake of simplicity and convenience, I shall use the word "tradition" throughout the remainder of this paper to refer to the element of apparent permanence in religion and the word "innovation" to refer to the element of change. Although traditions are many and innovations many in the world history of religions, it is my thesis that these many specific cases repeat a few generic types of relationship between tradition and innovation. These paradigmatic relationships I hold to be discoverable within each of the major faiths of the world, limited neither by geography nor by the form of religious organization. In the context of this article, I shall illustrate these paradigms primarily out of the history of Judaism, but this limitation is accidental. In another context illustrations might be drawn from Hinduism, Buddhism, Islam, or Christianity. These paradigmatic relationships appear wherever a religion based upon tradition is a living force in the world today.

Although these typical relationships are always discoverable, and may, indeed, correspond to certain temperamental types among human beings, they stand out most clearly at critical epochs in the history of each religion. It is apparent that this must be so, for what we mean by a critical epoch is precisely one in which those who would apply the hallowed verities are confronted with a strikingly novel situation and, simultaneously, with the possibility that the verities are not applicable; that what experience has created and experience has hallowed, further experience may destroy. Critical epochs at which tradition must be retested for its value in a new situation have not been infrequent in the history of Judaism. It may be that the migratory life that historic circumstances imposed on the Jewish people has increased the frequency with which critical epochs of religious adjustment have recurred in Judaism. There was the major crisis precipitated by the destruction of the Temple and the consequent abolition of the priestly cultus. Another major crisis was caused by the shifting of the center of Judaism from the Holy Land to Babylonia. Later crises occurred when Southern Europe became the focus of Jewish creativity and the problem of coexistence with Christianity and Islam became paramount, and again when from Southern Europe the focus shifted to Central and Eastern Europe. A great crisis was caused by Jewish emancipation, which demanded the formulation of a new approach to coexistence. The adjustment of Judaism to American life and to the establishment of a national homeland may appear to future historians as aspects of the crisis of emancipation although to those who are living through them they seem to rank as major crises in their own right. It is from these critical epochs that we may best and most vividly illustrate the paradigmatic relationships of tradition and innovation.

The first two types of relationship that I would describe constitute equal and opposite dangers to the life of the religious group. They may be called "literalism" and "apostasy." Each is an extreme position. Literalism denies the present; apostasy denies the past. Literalism asserts the transcendent importance of tradition. It refuses to recognize the necessity for innovation in any way, shape, or form. What has been handed down to the literalist he insists upon transmitting without any alteration or adaptation whatsoever. Because of this insistence, the faith he holds no longer maintains its relevance to the life-situation in which he and his children exist. Literalism, carried to its ultimate point, is religious suicide. It is, however, rarely carried to that extreme. The Karaites, probably the most often-cited case of a literalist sect within Judaism, rejecting the whole corpus of rabbinic adaptations of Judaism and professing to return to a literal adherence to the biblical text, soon found it necessary to develop adaptations of their own in order to maintain the life of their group. Twentieth-century orthodoxy in America, a less frequently noted case of literalism, and a less obvious case, since it does not involve the attempt to maintain the ancient tradition but rather a relatively recent recension of that tradition, passes over into neo-orthodoxy, which recognizes the need for adaptation to current circumstances. No absolute literalism can maintain its viability; it is for this reason that I consider the assertion of an unqualified literalism as religious suicide. Apostasy is religious murder. It is the wanton rejection and, if it is carried to its ultimate point, the total destruction of tradition. Apostasy has never been carried to such an extreme in Judaism; had it been, there would be today no living Judaism. Even in times of enforced apostasy, many of the victims lived as crypto-Jews. Not compulsion and torture but, strangely, tolerance and emancipation in the nineteenth-century led to the largest wave of apostasy in Jewish life. Despite the fears of many observers, even this wave was made up of a large number of individual withdrawals from the Jewish tradition. At no time did the group apostasize, as, for example, a group of Frankists did in the eighteenth century. I have discussed literalism and apostasy here for the sake of completeness. It should be apparent that neither is a live option.

The other paradigms of which I shall speak all give some weight to both tradition and innovation and thereby escape the inevitable mortality of literalism and apostasy. They vary in the techniques that are proposed for reconciling the claims of tradition and innovation. Within its general pattern, each is capable of considerable variation in emphasis. I shall use the terms "rationalism," "allegorism," and "hermeneutics" to refer to the three major types under discussion.

Of all, rationalism most clearly evidences its character in its name. It is the attempt to use philosophic reason as a tool for the reshaping of tradition toward the needs of a new situation. Thus it is not a simon-pure rationality; some basic elements of the tradition are accepted as premises and not forced to stand trial at the bar of reason. The implications of these basic doctrines are, however, drawn by the operations of a rational logic, and much is made of the importance of logical consistency and systematic coherence in the drawing of inferences. Often the tradition on which this sort of rationalism is founded includes not only the religious heritage but also some philosophic system. Thus Maimonides, the chief of medieval Jewish rationalists, founded his system on both the Jewish tradition and that of the Arab Aristotelians. Maimonides asserted that these two divergent bases could not conflict; it is notable, however, that in order that there should be no conflict the philosopher had to interpret one system in terms of the other. In this case a balance was kept; sometimes he interpreted the language of the Jewish tradition in terms of the Aristotelianism that he knew and sometimes he interpreted the language of the Aristotelians in terms of the Jewish tradition. The balance was not always as well maintained by other writers. Gersonides, for example, held that there might be a conflict between faith and reason, that is, between Judaism and Aristotelianism, and that when there was such a conflict Judaism should invariably be interpreted in Aristotelian terms. It is, to my mind, significantly indicative of the importance of the non-Jewish cultural environment in determining how Jewish tradition shall be recast that the rationalistic impulse, so strong in Medieval Europe, had but one other major manifestation in Jewish life, in the post-Emancipation era of the nineteenth century. During this later rationalist renascence in Jewish thought there were those who, like Hermann Cohen, attempted a Kantian recension of Jewish tradition. Others followed Hegel and Schleiermacher. The primary impulse behind the early Reform movement in Judaism was rationalism; it is as a vestige of this original rationalism that even twentieth-century Reform retains a greater measure of systematic consistency than other branches of Judaism.

There are two chief dangers in the rationalist reinterpretation of religious tradition. The first, and perhaps least significant, is that the rational impulse is so strong and so attractive that it may swallow up the whole of religious life. Religion cannot be a matter of the head alone; the heart must be deeply involved. Religion is not exclusively a way of thinking, although thought and religion are not in opposition to each other. It is a way of living that expresses both a pattern of thought and an emotional response to that pattern. But thinking may often lead men to the suppression of their emotional responses, because emotion interferes with the process of thinking. Or, to say this another way, life demands immediate commitments while the object of thinking is to keep the maximum of openness as long as possible. There is then a possibility that rationalism may lead to the sanctification of reason and a consequent inability to take the decisive step of religious commitment. The second, and more important, of the dangers of rationalism is that it is difficult to limit the rational critique of traditional concepts to peripheral matters. Why, indeed, should not the central beliefs of traditional faith be subjected to the same searching analysis as more trivial matters? Why should the basic doctrines be exempt? Once the process of rational analysis is applied even to those principles of the faith that the milder rationalist has held in reserve it becomes evident that there is no "cosmic" doctrine of religion that can be proved without circularity. Maimonides held thirteen articles in reserve; the more thoroughgoing critique of Spinoza held back from nothing. Maimonides was, therefore, able to remain within the traditional faith, while Spinoza, though undeniably "God-intoxicated," could find no home in the religion of his fathers. Again, in nineteenth-century America, the most extreme rationalist among religious leaders of Jewish ancestry was Felix Adler; he too, like Spinoza, found that he could make no peace with the cosmic views of Judaism and, in following his reason, was led outside the faith. Rationalism, in sum, may be a useful method for reconciling tradition with the need for innovation but it involves the double danger of becoming itself a substitute for religion and of directing its critique against the very roots of tradition.

What I have called "allegorism," in some of its manifestations, for example in the Philonic reading of Jewish tradition, approximates closely to rationalism. In other manifestations, for example within the Kabbalistic tradition, allegorism is almost completely irrational. What unifies the diverse sorts of interpretation that I classify as allegorism is that they rest upon the assertion that the language of the tradition invariably asserts something different from what it appears to assert. The techniques that are used by allegorists for extracting the true meaning are various but the point of departure is the same. When a tradition is literary, as the Jewish tradition has been through most of its history, it is easy to understand the impulse out of which allegorism arises. For a written tradition is sacrosanct; it has passed beyond the state where textual emendations can be made with casual ease. Yet this traditional scripture contains, in addition to much that is noble, much that by later standards is trivial, undesirable, immoral, and erroneous. The temptation to discover some means of explaining away what we do not approve is hard to resist. Has not the Christian tradition explained one whole book of the Bible, the Song of Songs, as a prophetic allegory? A great many Jewish writers have tried to do the same, but usually with somewhat smaller segments of the scriptural text. Sometimes the allegorizing takes the form of poetic interpretation by analogy; Jehudah Halevi illustrates this technique well. Sometimes number symbolism is the device; Philo frequently uses number symbolism to derive his interpretations, and in the Kabbalistic literature *gematria*, a systematic form of number symbolism, proved most productive of novel interpretation. When the prevalent view was that there was significance in every aspect of the biblical text, the transposition of letters (Kabbalistic *tsiruf*) often brought out significance where none appeared on the literal surface of the text.

Though somewhat in eclipse, the method of allegorism cannot be said to be extinct today. It is not much used on the text of the Scriptures, save possibly in occasional sermons or rhetorical exercises. We can, however, find allegorism in Martin Buber's unhistoric and nonliteral readings of the traditions of Hassidism and in Leo Strauss's clever reinterpretations of Maimonides and Spinoza. Much of the writing of Abraham J. Heschel, too, seems to fall into the pattern of allegorism. In all these cases, allegorism has enriched current Jewish thought by adding new depth to its tradition. But allegorism is a two-edged weapon, precisely because it is so individual a technique. Whichever of its many methods we may use and on whatever text, another man may with equal validity and equal warrant use a different method on the same text, and thus arrive at a different interpretation. Thus allegorism does not lead to a science or to a philosophy but to a poetry of interpretation. When Christians, or Jewish converts to Christianity, used the methods of *gematria* and *tsiruf* to prove Christian doctrines out of the Hebrew Bible their interpretations were as justified as those of the Kabbalistic interpreters among the Jews. Once we accept the validity of allegorism as an interpretive technique we can draw no lines, except those of personal preference, between one interpretation and another.

We have, finally, to consider the paradigm that I have called "hermeneutics." The word means no more than "interpretation" and has a long history of use in religious and legal contexts. I use it here to mean "interpretation par excellence," interpretation based solely upon the objective construing of the text to be interpreted. Both rationalism and allegorism, as paradigms of interpretation, fall short of the ideal, rationalism, because it imports into interpretation a frame of reference that is external to the system under examination, allegorism because of its subjectivity. Hermeneutics, however, or interpretation narrowly conceived, remains at all times objective and public, and conducts its operations without introducing aids to interpretation *ab extra*. Any hermeneutic system, whether it be religious or legal, must follow a set of specific rules for the interpretation of words and statements. A particular interpretation may be challenged on the ground of failure properly to observe these rules. Like logical principles, hermeneutic rules guarantee validity, not truth; unlike logical principles, they are concerned with interpretation, not inference.

The use of hermeneutics, not always ingenuously though often ingeniously, has been the most characteristic method for adapting Judaism to changed cultural surroundings. The major stream of hermeneutic writing in Jewish history runs through the Mishnah and Midrash, the Talmud, the *responsa* literature of medieval and modern times, and the rabbinic commentaries on all the codes. Codification itself, though it has consituted one major enterprise within the rabbinic tradition, must be sharply distinguished from hermeneutics. The function of codification is purely taxonomic; it involves the classification and arrangement of interpretations but does not itself interpret. The form that is given to any codification may be suggestive for later hermeneutics and it may be based upon earlier hermeneutics, but it is not itself hermeneutics, any more than highway markers are driving. The rabbis have not only been masterly in their practice of hermeneutics; they have also been aware from early times of the need for a formalized system of rules. Shortly before the beginning of the Common Era, Hillel formulated seven basic rules (*middot*) for hermeneutics, and during the second century A.D. the school of R. Ishmael developed these into thirteen rules. For the purposes of legal interpretation within Judaism, the "thirteen exegetical principles by which the Law is expounded" remain basic, although for homiletic and hortatory purposes a far longer list of thirty-two principles is available. The latter system, ascribed to R. Eliezer, son of R. Jose the Galilean (c. A.D. 200), is known to us only in later recensions.

The bulk of accepted Jewish tradition, then, rests upon hermeneutics, and this method has, at times, proved to be a delicate and sensitive instrument for innovation that does not seem to be such. The interpretations codified in the Mishnah already take account of the changed conditions in Palestine after the destruction of the Temple. Differences between the *gemaras* of the Palestinian and Babylonian Talmuds are understandable in terms of social, economic, and political differences between life in Palestine and life in Babylonia. The *responsa* literature answers problems created by the conditions of life in various countries of the Diaspora. Rashi's commentaries on the Bible and, especially, the Talmud clearly reveal their European provenience and their medieval time. Into the nineteenth and the twentieth century, especially in Eastern Europe, hermeneutic techniques were the chief resource of Judaism for adapting tradition imperceptibly to the demands of innovation. There is, of course, a danger in relying on hermeneutics; it is the danger of over-caution, leading to an ultraconservative tendency to maintain the *status quo ante*. This is also true of legal hermeneutics. There is a general inclination among judges to construe the law as it has been construed by their predecessors, and thus much of legal hermeneutics resolves itself into the search for the precedent least out of tune with conditions at the time that decision is rendered, a rather negative approach. Thus it is that in many instances what in earlier times was a little-regarded minority opinion later becomes overwhelmingly the opinion of the judicial majority. The same negativity is characteristic of most religious hermeneutics in Judaism. The traditionary interpretation that serves as foundation for a decision adapting Jewish thought and practice to current conditions may come from an opinion that in its own time found no supporters. The possibility of utilizing opinions of this sort as precedents is all that stands between this tradition-oriented hermeneutics and a complete traditionalism. Its adaptations are unconscious and, as it were, unintentional reflections of the *Zeitgeist*.

There is, however, another possible way of using hermeneutic techniques that is probably hoary with antiquity but has been acknowledged in its use only of recent years. Again, although this variety of hermeneutics has had greater use in the legal discipline than in religious thought, it is usable religiously as well as juridically. This method consists in consciously determining, on other than hermeneutic grounds, what a satisfactory innovation would require and then using hermeneutics to justify these predetermined conclusions. The use of a technique of this sort allows of a far larger range of innovation while still retaining the strong appeal to tradition that is characteristic of hermeneutics. In recent Jewish thought, the Reconstructionist movement exemplifies well this type of self-conscious adaptation.

It is not my intention here to go beyond this description to an evaluation of the paradigms. An evaluation would do no more than to reveal the particular way of reconciling innovation with tradition that suits my temperamental proclivities. It is historically demonstrable that Judaism has met its major crises hitherto by the use of hermeneutics rather than allegorism or rationalism. To maintain that hermeneutics will continue to be the most effective technique for Jewish adaptation is to make assumptions about historical inference that would require more discussion than we can give them here. Professor Baron has insisted in his teaching that the Jewish life of any time and place is the resultant of the forces of Jewish tradition and the specific temporal and spatial environment. I have sought in this paper to specify and to delimit the typical processes by means of which this resultant may be derived.

FELIX LIBERTATÉ AND THE EMANCIPATION OF DUTCH JEWRY

By Herbert I. Bloom

IT IS WELL KNOWN that in medieval society groups of people settling in a given region were judged by their native law. In contrast to modern times, settlers were not tried by the laws of the land in which they settled but were judged by the laws of their own body or corporation; thus the Lombards, for example, were subject to their own laws. For this reason it was not unusual that the Jewish settlers were looked upon as a corporation and were often referred to as "the Jewish Nation" even as the Lombards are sometimes referred to as the Italian or the Lombardian Nation. Equality of rights in the modern sense was not known until after the emancipation. No one had equal rights. Each group or corporation occupied a special place in the society in which it functioned.

In the Middle Ages the Jew enjoyed a higher status than the serf who went along with the land,[1] as the Jew fulfilled a special function in the economy, that of payer of taxes and middleman, since he was among those with more movable property available. The Jewish Middle Ages lasted well into modern times, in Western Europe at least until the French Revolution, and in Eastern Europe until the twentieth century. In this study we will concern ourselves with the emancipation of the Jews in Holland, which will necessitate an examination of their pre-emancipation status in order to evaluate the emancipation itself.

The Jews came to Holland in groups toward the end of the sixteenth century although there had been individuals in small settlements in the Netherlands in earlier times. These had suffered the vicissitudes of moving from place to place because of hardships and expulsion. During the war between the Netherlands and Spain, Marranos had come to the country to escape the Inquisition. Jews had been welcomed in Amsterdam, for example, because of the economic benefits accruing from their

[1] Salo W. Baron, "Ghetto and Emancipation," Reprint from the June, 1928, issue of *The Menorah Journal*, pp. 1 ff.

settlement in the days of early capitalism. Much has been said about the rights of Jews in Holland. We will now examine their status.

When in 1556 Philip II succeeded his father Charles V on the throne of Spain, the beginning of Dutch liberation was imminent. Philip's cruelty and that of the Duke of Alba so oppressed his subjects that even Amsterdam, which for a long time remained loyal to the house of Hapsburg, finally revolted and enrolled in the ranks of William the Silent. In 1579 a treaty uniting the northern provinces of the Netherlands was ratified in Utrecht. This document was destined to be significant for the fate of the Jews in the Netherlands. Article XIII of the pact stated that no one was to be persecuted for religious reasons. Such a concept was revolutionary for its time and was the earnest of an era of relatively tolerant government. The United Provinces saw the advantage of the clause, since it permitted the settlement and trade of various religious groups within its borders.

The emergence of capitalism encouraged the settlement of people who could bring money to an area and foster international trade. Jews were particularly fitted for this process by their far-flung international contacts. A new order was gaining dominance in which the entrepreneur and the international trader were regarded as a definite asset. The medieval order was slowly breaking down before the forces of moneyed wealth. Mercantilism, or belief that gold resources were the essence of a nation's riches, was the economic theory of that day.

It must not be imagined that religious intolerance would find no place in the Netherlands. History was to prove that sect would fight sect and faction war against faction, but Article XIII of the Union of Utrecht made it possible for the United Provinces to offer an asylum to the persecuted Protestants throughout Europe and furnished a legal basis for the privileges and rights accorded the Jews during the existence of the United Provinces.[2]

As early as 1615, the states of Holland, in answer to a complaint lodged by factions in the Dutch Church that Jews had more freedom than they, appointed a committee to formulate regulations regarding the Jews. The most important of these was known as *Joden Reglement* (ruling concerning the Jews) propounded by the renowned philosopher and jurist, Hugo Grotius. The author's introduction pointed out that it was poor policy to permit Jewish settlement in spite of the old decrees without drawing up special regulations for them. He presented three of the most important questions: (1) Should Jews be tolerated in Holland? (2) should they be

[2] Herbert I. Bloom, *The Economic Activities of the Jews of Amsterdam in the Seventeenth and Eighteenth Centuries* (Williamsport, Pa., 1937), p. 4.

granted freedom of religion? and (3) what are the means of avoiding religious and political difficulties as a result of Jewish settlement? The first and second questions he answered in the affirmative. In answer to the third question, he presented a list of forty-nine regulations. Chief among these were the following: The Jews should have no distinguishing marks on their clothing and no more than three hundred Jewish families were to be accorded residence in Amsterdam. Jews were not to hold political or judicial office and were to act as notaries only for coreligionists. They were not to intermarry with "the daughters of the land."

Although the government of the country did not adopt these regulations as binding, they influenced the treatment of the Jews by the various municipalities. Grotius's suggestions may rightly be considered the first step in Jewish emancipation. The states of Holland declared that each city, within its domain, should have the right to allow or forbid Jewish settlement.[3] The autonomy of each area with reference to the treatment of Jews accounts for the difference in rights and privileges in different parts of the land. This condition, as we shall point out, is responsible for the many difficulties attendant upon the attainment of complete emancipation and equality of rights. Many occupations, especially those connected with the guilds, retail trade, and handicrafts, were forbidden to Jews. They were not even given the same privileges accorded other Dutch subjects who were not "burghers." In 1668 Christians who had sworn allegiance to Amsterdam were permitted to carry on crafts and trades controlled by the guilds, while Jews were not granted the same rights in spite of their protestations of fealty. As late as 1784, prejudice against them was too strong to concede tax exemption on Jewish religious institutions, although this was given to Catholics in that year and had previously been granted to Protestants in 1731 and 1737.[4]

In contrast to Amsterdam, where the Jews were permitted to settle, there were restrictions of various kinds in most cities, large and small, and especially in the bishoprics such as Maastricht, Deventer, and Utrecht. Although some Portuguese Jews settled in Utrecht after 1720, they soon left when their fortunes dwindled. A Jewish congregation was established there in 1789 upon the intervention of Prince William V. This was an exception to the general practice of the bishoprics, since we know that, as late as 1782, Jews were not permitted to stay overnight in Maastricht, Deventer, and Utrecht without special permission.[5]

[3] *Ibid.*, p. 19. [4] *Ibid.*, p. 31.

[5] Jac. Zwarts, "De Joodsche Gemeenten buiten Amsterdam," in H. Brugmans and A. Frank, *Geschiedenis der Joden in Nederland*, Part I (Amsterdam, 1940), pp. 450 ff.

The Marranos from the Iberian Peninsula, most of whom professed Judaism, were looked upon by the Dutch burghers as fighting a common cause with them against Spanish tyranny. Their contact with the Iberian Peninsula and their international trade were valuable. They were hardly the stereotype of a Jew which imagination and prejudice might have conjured up in the Calvinist mind. The Sephardim were worldly, conversant with European culture, and, in many cases, affluent. At the time of the influx of Ashkenazic Jews, most of whom were poor, the Sephardim took care of their less fortunate brethren.

The fortunes of Jewry in the Netherlands were, of course, inextricably linked with those of the country in general. When, due to wars and loss of international prestige, Holland yielded her place as the carrier of the world and had to bow to the trade hegemony of England, many Jews of prominence lost their fortunes, especially when a great number of them turned from trade to speculation, some even to wildcat ventures. Masses of poor Ashkenazic Jews had come to the country during the palmy days. Some had gained the status of brokers and middlemen, a few attained considerable wealth. When the bubble burst, there was not enough backlog to sustain the enormous philanthropic needs. The Sephardim had become effete and many sank into complete destitution, one of the reasons being that numbers of them lived on the income of the Dutch East India Company which stopped paying dividends. The Ashkenazim, unable to depend any longer upon their richer coreligionists, were more resilient, and although very poor, managed somehow to survive as peddlers, second-hand clothes dealers, and hucksters, with a few of them rising to prominence.

Restrictions had always been levied against the Jews but these restrictions seemed extremely severe in a period of decline. Sixteen years before emancipation in 1796, we hear that the Ashkenazic congregation had "3,540 poor families and single persons."[6] Despite widespread prejudice, Christians sometimes aided Jewish causes. During the severe winter of 1773-74 an unknown Christian contributed 3,000 guilders to the Jewish poor. A Christian society collected 507 guilders for their benefit. The city government allotted 6,000 guilders and later 2,500 more for their relief, stipulating that part of this money be allocated for the purchase of clothing, the presumption being that many Jews looked ragged and unsightly on the city streets.[7]

[6] J. M. Hillesum, "Uit de Geschiedenis der Joden in Amsterdam," *Elzevier's Geïllustreerd Maandblad*, LIV (August, 1917), 112.

[7] Bloom, *Economic Activities*, p. 217.

By today's standards the rights of the Dutch Jews before the emancipation were limited indeed. While there were no enforced ghettos, no distinguishing marks on Jewish clothing, no governmentally sanctioned persecution, and freedom of worship, a contemporary who fought for the emancipation in 1796 stated, "Jews are free to sing psalms publicly and are also free to starve."[8] So difficult was it for Jews to make a living that many of them eked out an existence in any way possible, often resorting to sharp practices. One of their defenders in the battle for emancipation countered the charge of Jewish unethical practices with the following:

If you deny thousands of people the opportunity to earn an honest living, if the few opportunities remaining open to them are not sufficient to feed thousands, when a whole multitude lives in the most desperate poverty and the most abject misery, you have caused this to thousands whose education you have impeded instead of helped. If there are then some among the wretched ones who are drained of their principles, driven by desperation, to quiet the helpless wail of suffering children, deceive you by stealing a piece of your bread, which nature presents as a reward of honest work, it was your injustice that did not permit them to make an honest living. Have you the right to condemn the whole people therefore, if an occasional instance of deceit occurs! [9]

In the seventeenth century opposition to Jews had been mainly on theological grounds. Just before the emancipation most of the tirades against Jews were based on the opinion that they were undesirable inhabitants of the country. We quote some instances. Baron de Bielfelt, cited by the city government of Den Bosch about 1769, says, in referring to the Jewish people: "A nation which is among the people what rabbits are among the quadrupeds, they multiply with an amazing fertility and they ruin the lands which they inhabit."[10] When, in 1777, Jacob Moses and Jozef van Lier from Maarsen applied for citizenship rights (*poortersrecht*) they were refused because of the protests of the guild of peddlers, who claimed that the Jews would compete with them unfairly and that those of the Jewish nation knew how to attract business in all kind of underhanded ways and in that way suppressed the commerce of the rest of the inhabitants. About the same time Jonas Samuel was denied the right to settle in Veghel since "Jews harm the area in which they settle because they multiply too much."[11]

[8] H. Italie, "De Emancipatie der Joden in 1796," *Amsterdamsch Jaarboekje voor 1897*, pp. 86 ff. quoting M. S. Asser.

[9] Sigmund Seeligmann, *De Emancipatie der Joden in Nederland* (Amsterdam, 1913), guoting Kantelaar in the National Assembly, August 23, 1796.

[10] Zwarts, "De Joodsche Gemeenten buiten Amsterdam," in Brugmans and Frank, *Geschiedenis der Joden in Nederland*, pp. 447 ff.

[11] *Ibid.*, p. 448.

On the educational side the Jews were excluded from regular schools and from at least two societies, "Felix Meritis," established in 1776, which sponsored concerts and lectures, and the "Maatschappy tot Nut van 't Algemeen" (Society for Community Welfare), established in 1784, which strove to improve teaching standards. Among the Sephardim the rudiments of secular education were included in the cultural structure. In some instances an elaborate background in the humanities was coupled with Hebrew learning. The Dutch authorities permitted freedom of the educational system in the Jewish schools. One of the great defects in training resulted from the fact that the rich Jews did not see to the improvement of the education of their poorer brethren.[12] The Ashkenazim brought scholars and teachers from Poland. Language was no barrier since they taught in Yiddish and were interested chiefly in Talmudic learning. Steinheim and other Jewish writers, in speaking of the "untidy guests" who descended on German-Jewish communities like "clouds of locusts," ignored a multitude of saintly and learned rabbis and teachers who, in the course of the seventeenth and eighteenth centuries, were the main bearers of Jewish culture in a civilization which, unrelieved by the forces of enlightenment, was being corroded by the acids of early capitalistic materialism.[13]

When the organization of the autonomous Jewish community seemed to have reached its apogee one can clearly discern in it incipient signs of disintegration and dissolution which augured badly for its survival in the stormy era of emancipation.[14] Such medieval vestiges as a special oath which degraded and humiliated Jews were still in use. In Amsterdam, though their marriages were registered civilly, Jews had to pay more than non-Jews and had to wait till all Christian marriages were recorded before they were served. All manner of humiliation was meted out to them by many Christians especially because of their dire poverty and their pro-Orange, that is, antirevolutionary, sentiments. Conditions such as these led to much Jewish self-abasement and moral degradation. Jews are described as being ragged and dirty and walking with bent head.[15] The Parnassim or Jewish leaders were said to countenance conditions such as

[12] J. Hartog, "De Joden in het eerste Jaar der Bataafsche Vrijheid," *De Gids*, XXXIX (January, 1875), 116, 152.

[13] Salo W. Baron, *The Jewish Community* (Philadelphia, 1942), II, 183 ff.

[14] *Ibid.*, II, 351.

[15] *De Denker* (1763-75); *Nederlandschen Spectator* (1749-60); *Hollandschen Spectator*, XI, 217.

contaminated women's ritual baths, and there were many other evidences of decay.[16]

From the foregoing it is plain to see that pre-emancipation Dutch Jewry was anything but free. While certain rights and privileges not accorded in other countries did obtain in the Netherlands, in order to arrive at a correct picture of Jewish conditions one must not be seduced by the all too prevalent impression that Dutch Jewry was well integrated into Dutch life. The majority of Jews, as has been pointed out, were still strangers belonging to a separate nation with a separate language, folkways, education, and function, not to speak of religion. The Jews were caught under the upper millstone of tyrannical rule by their Parnassim whose strictures were sanctioned by custom and government enforcement; for example, the Parnassim, with the help of the government, could imprison people and subject them to fourteen days' incarceration on bread and water for not complying with their demands that they buy meat from Jewish community slaughterhouses.[17] They exercised the ban and curtailed the rights even of the more liberal-minded among the Jews. The Parnassim were zealous of their power and feared that if they relaxed it the Jews would become backsliders. The absolutism of the Parnassim had reached the point where at least one rabbi promised in his contract that he would never oppose them.[18] They levied taxes, made assessments, doled out monies for the poor, regulated the order of synagogue procedures and honors, and in effect controlled the personal life of all members of the Jewish community.

The rise of the individual who would be free in his own right and contribute in his own right, not merely as a member of the community, was a result of growing capitalism and the breaking away from the medieval structures of society. The ideas of the French Revolution, which led to a changed status of the individual, were not unknown to the Jews. Little wonder then that the masses of the Jewish community and their leadership, lay and rabbinic, were very fearful of the new doctrines of liberty, equality, and fraternity. If the Jew in Holland were to become just another Dutch citizen, how far would he be loyal to the law and life of the Jewish community and the Jewish tradition? If the bonds of the ghetto were sundered, how could the Torah be binding on the Dutch Jew?

[16] D. L. Knappert, *Geschiedenis der Nederlandsche Hervormde Kerk* (n.p., 1911-12), II, 117 ff.

[17] Italie, "De Emancipatie der Joden in 1796," *Amsterdamsch Jaarboekje voor 1897* pp. 86 ff.

[18] Salo W. Baron, *A Social and Religious History of the Jews* (New York, 1937), II 207.

How could adherence to Jewish life be important? Surely there were instances enough among the more worldly and wealthy Jews of defection and "freethinking." There were honest questions as to how far the dream of Jewish liberation would really mean the acceptance of the Jew in the general life. Would the revolutionary thinking of the time really engender in the gentile population a love of the Jew as a brother? Was this a threat to Jewish survival? Was this a threat to the propagation and cultivation of Torah? All these fears and queries possessed the mind of the masses of Jewry. Would the breakdown of the community undermine the immemorial place of the Jew? Though he was deprived of rights and denied many areas of function, there was strength of sorts in communal solidarity and control. After all, a Jewish community could be represented to the government by its duly constituted spokesman. If this structure were to evaporate no one could speak officially and authoritatively for Dutch Jewry. Despite these fears and apprehensions, many of them justified, the forces of revolution and change were at work. There were a few Jews in the foreground of the battle for emancipation.

The revolution took place in the provinces of North and South Holland in January, 1795. With the help of the French, "the Patriots," under the banner of Liberty, Equality, and Fraternity, ended the rule of the House of Orange and created the "Batavian Republic." The revolution had been prepared for by the establishment of reading circles that seemed innocent enough. These circles propagated revolutionary ideas of "the rights of men and citizens." During the revolution they became known as societies. It was soon clear that their purpose had been to overthrow the government. On January 29, 1795, the Provisional Representation of the People of Holland proclaimed in essence: "All men are born with equal rights. These rights are freedom, equality, liberty, and safety. All are permitted freedom of speech and thought, of the press, and of assembly. There is to be no pressure upon man's service to God. He is free to worship, or to desist at will without let or hindrance. Because all are equal, all are eligible to all offices and services." The same proclamation was issued by the Estates-General in 1795. It was to apply to the entire country. The Jews had long been known to be pro-Orange. Their whole history in Holland had led them to this position. The House of Orange had always protected them. For example, Stadholder William V had allowed many, in spite of the law, to make an honest living through commerce and industry. Jews had not forgotten that during the uprising in 1787 the Patriots had opposed them. On the other hand, some hoped that the revolution would abolish restrictions and oppressive legislation.

They were hopeful because the revolution was aided by the French who had already emancipated French Jewry. It was expected that the revolution and consequent emancipation would free Jews from the power of the Parnassim and rabbis.[19]

Before the revolution, a Comité Revolutionair existed in Amsterdam and prepared the whole country for it. Its members precipitated the revolution in Amsterdam. The new municipal government consisted of those recommended by the Comité.

A group of prominent Jews, the elderly H. L. Bromet, Mozes Salomon Asser, eminent judicial scholar, Jacob Saportes, Dr. H. de H. Lemon, physician appointed by the Parnassim of the Ashkenazic Congregation to practice among the poor, Joachim van Embden, his son Jacob van Gelder, member of the citizens' cavalry, A. L. Hollander and his son Izak de Jonge Meijersz, David Friedrichsfeld, Juda Litwack, a successful scientist, and Carolus Asser, founded the Society Felix Libertaté in February, 1795. The first three mentioned constituted the directors with Dr. de Lemon as secretary. Their purpose was stated as follows: to educate one another and to know the true value of liberty and equality. Their true objective was to help the revolution and to prepare for the anticipated emancipation and equality of Jews. More revolutionary clubs were established with the most loosely conceived programs. The purpose of all of them was to further the new order. In the spirit of the new day, some gentiles, pleased with "the withdrawal of Jews from their isolation," joined the Society. On February 11, 1795, Felix Libertaté held its first meeting. Several directors of other societies, a secretary of the French commissariat, and some French officers were present. The president, H. L. Bromet, opened the meeting and gave the floor to M. S. Asser who delivered an address. He became the soul of the Society. In a lengthy discourse, outlining the purpose of the organization, he stressed his joy that Jews could assemble with non-Jews to work for the common good. He presented an historical review of the oppression and limitations of the Jews and said, "The light is breaking through." After two other addresses in the same vein, the meeting ended with the thrice-proclaimed, "Long live Liberty, Equality, and Fraternity." Many such meetings were held and attended by nonmembers and members of the best Christian families. A tree of liberty was planted by the government of Amsterdam on one occasion, and several members of Felix Libertaté were official

[19] Italie, "De Emancipatie der Joden in 1796," *Amsterdamsch Jaarboekje voor 1897*, pp. 86 ff.

representatives at the ceremony. There were two orphans of each religious group in the procession. Two from the Sephardic group and two from the Ashkenazic were included.

Felix Libertaté had the declaration of the "Rights of Man" translated into Judaeo-German. They requested that this proclamation be read in the synagogue. The Parnassim and rabbis on the other hand asked the Congregation to sign a petition stating that the reading of this document was contrary to Jewish law. Felix Libertaté, angered, asked the Comité Revolutionair to insist on the reading. The Comité agreed with Felix Libertaté and the Parnassim were asked to comply with its wishes. The Parnassim were prepared for this. They replied that they objected to curtailment of religious freedom. No such proclamation was read in the churches. On March 22, 1795, in the heat of the controversy, Felix Libertaté issued another proclamation outlining the advantages of the new order to rich and poor alike. This document was disrespectful to the Parnassim and was tantamount to a declaration of war between the two factions. The Parnassim appealed to the city government of Amsterdam which gave them permission to remove the petition from the synagogue doors and to invite representatives of Felix Libertaté to meet with the city officials and the Parnassim. This meeting yielded nothing to either party.

At the same time a heated dispute on the rights of Jews to serve in the city guard of Amsterdam was going on. Felix Libertaté wanted them to be admitted to duty. Two members of the city government inquired of the two chief rabbis, Mozes Saul of the Ashkenazic and Daniel Cohen d'Azevedo of the Sephardic Congregation, whether the law of Moses permitted Jews to bear arms on the Sabbath. The rabbis replied emphatically in the negative. Bromet had published a letter citing instances from history and the Talmud where the Jews were permitted to bear arms on the Sabbath and to violate other Jewish laws in time of emergency. The rabbis called Felix Libertaté's members atheists, whereupon Felix Libertaté pointed out that Rabbi Saul Levie, father of the present Rabbi Mozes Saul, in 1782 not only permitted Jewish sailors to fight on the Sabbath during the English war but even blessed them. The dispute continued. The municipality, in an effort to stop the argument, decided to curtail further petitions and refused to accept any unless signed by all members of the petitioning organizations. Meanwhile, the Jews were not permitted to serve in Amsterdam since it was thought too costly to outfit them. However, they did serve in other cities like Groningen, Leyden, Amersfoort, and The Hague (where a Jewish citizen, M. Ephraim, was made an officer); in fact, Jews in The Hague had been called to serve in the *Burgerwacht* (Citizen's Guard) since March, 1795.[20] Felix Libertaté continued to urge the authorities in Amsterdam to change their attitude. Unable to gain satisfaction from the city government, they appealed to the provincial authorities. The question remained under advisement. It was thought best to defer the whole matter until the expected National Assembly was convened.

After the revolution the number of people's societies or clubs was greatly increased. Fearful lest the multiplicity of organizations lead to political abuses and multiple voting, the city government of Amsterdam established neighborhood assemblies. Each burgher could only belong to the assembly in his own neighborhood. This reduced the number of clubs. There were sixty neighborhood assemblies in the city and five in the suburbs. Many well-meaning burghers who had not belonged to the clubs were now activated in the neighborhood groups. The meetings were held in schools, churches, and other public places. People were carried away by high-sounding revolutionary slogans but no one knew quite what the functions of the meetings were. Anti-Jewish feeling ran high among the masses. When the question of the Jewish right to vote was broached in Amsterdam, 14,000 Christian burghers in sixty neighborhood assemblies objected to Jewish membership in their gatherings. As we have pointed out, anti-Jewish feeling was no rarity before this struggle and it was not uprooted despite revolutionary sentiment. It was all well and good to proclaim "Liberty, Equality, and Fraternity," and to orate about the rights of "Man and Citizen," but what about Jews? They were undoubtedly human beings entitled to the "Rights of Man," but could they be citizens of the Batavian Republic? Were they Dutchmen? A number of periodicals, among others a paper called *De Domkop* or *Nationaal Volksboek* and *De Nederlandsche Overweeger* and *De Nederlandsche Echo* (about 1770), viciously attacked the Jews with such comments as "they [the Jews] wish to change from an oppressed people to a ruling folk." The tone and style of these periodicals was vulgar, slanderous, and abusive. Publications such as these helped to confirm the prejudices of the masses, who despite the revolutionary cries of equality and brotherhood had great difficulty effacing their age-long antipathy to Jews. These prejudices were repeated again and again. There were many

[20] H. Italie, "De Societeit Felix Libertate en wat zij voor de Emancipatie der Joden heeft gedaan," *Oud Holland*, 16th year, pp. 51 ff.; *N. Nederlandsche Jaarboeken*, 1795 p. 1575.

other expressions on the Jewish question which were not quite as vulgar and raucous but were still negative.[21]

Under the influence of writers like Moses Mendelssohn, Chr. W. Dohm, and others, some pro-Jewish sentiment was also expressed.[22] One of the most ardent champions of the Jews was a non-Jewish member of Felix Libertaté, Jan Christiaan Hespe. He raised his voice in indignation against the intolerant attitude of the people of Amsterdam. Among the most important of the Jewish leaders in the fight for suffrage were M. I. Asser and David Friedrichsfeld. Asser delivered many impassioned pleas and Friedrichsfeld published a German pamphlet championing the vote for Jews.[23]

Prejudice was so acute in Amsterdam that when a census was proposed, the question arose as to whether the Jews would be included. After some discussion it was decided that they had to be counted, but on special lists. The result showed that there were 20,335 Jews in Amsterdam in a total population of 217,000.[24]

The struggle for Jewish equality seemed to meet with little success.

[21] To cite a few instances: A pamphlet entitled "Memorial Dealing with Methods of Removing Dissatisfactions among the Citizenry of Amsterdam and Restoring Confidence in Their Provisional Representatives, Composed by a Fellow Citizen and Submitted to the City Government," March 30, 1795.

Another pamphlet states that Jews are not included among the burghers with good reason because "how can one trust to Jews offices which require integrity?"

A pamphlet, dated March 28, 1795, is entitled "Letter to the Jews by Jan Rechtuit [Straightforward]," pointing out that Jews are unfitted for the popular vote in the Netherlands.

Another pamphlet, "Brief Examination as to Whether a Jew Can Be Accepted as a Batavian Citizen, the Constitution [of the Batavian Republic] Being Based on the Natural Rights of Man and Citizen," concludes that the Jew is unacceptable as a citizen.

See Jacob da Silva Rosa, *Bibliographie der Literatur über die Emanzipation der Juden in Holland* (Frankfurt a. M., 1912), pp. 9 ff., # 37, p. 13, # 63. The author quotes from *De Verzamelaar*, p. 581, p. 14, # 69.

[22] Notably to be found in publications like *Nederlandschen Spectator* (1749-60), *De Denker* (1763-75), *De Republikein*, and the *Courier van Bataafsch Brabant;* Italie, "De Societeit Felix Libertate," *Oud Holland; Overdrachten*, II, 3 ff.

Some of the pro-Jewish pamphlets written by Christians are, for example: J. Krap Az.: "Jews Are Our Fellow Citizens, Dedicated and Submitted to the Assemblies of Representatives of the People of Holland" (Amsterdam, 1795). He states: "The sun of liberty must also illumine and dissipate the fog of ignorance. The attitude toward Jews is entirely unjustifiable."

An anonymous pamphlet: "The Case of the Netherland Jews Defended by a Friend of Truth and Justice" (Amsterdam, 1795).

See Seeligmann, *De Emancipatie der Joden in Nederland.*

[23] Dated December 14, 1795.

[24] Later figures indicate that there were 2,400 Sephardim and 21,000 Ashkenazim in Amsterdam at that time. Bloom, *Economic Activities*, pp. 203 ff.

A committee of Felix Libertaté headed by M. S. Asser, as usual, went to the citizens' societies in the more tolerant cities of Rotterdam, The Hague, Leyden, and Leidschendam to complain about the attitude of the Amsterdam neighborhood societies. Asser requested that Amsterdam be contacted about the situation, and, if this proved unsatisfactory, he urged that the societies from the other cities refuse cooperation. They complied with this request but were unsuccessful. The only satisfaction to Felix Libertaté was the sympathy expressed outside of Amsterdam. The addresses which Asser delivered in the various cities are of historical value since they summarize the history and condition of the Jews in Holland.

The assemblies of different cities were in constant correspondence. When those of the province of Utrecht decided to call a meeting of delegates in the city of Utrecht, in July, 1795, the call was misunderstood by some assemblies outside the province, who sent delegates believing that the meeting in Utrecht was national. Representatives of Felix Libertaté, among others, attended the meeting. After some discussion Utrecht decided that all the delegates outside the province could participate except Felix Libertaté. At this affront all representatives save those from Utrecht left with Felix Libertaté as a demonstration of friendship. Nothing came of the planned national meeting in Utrecht. Another meeting was proposed at The Hague, initiated by the assemblies of Leyden, Rotterdam, and The Hague, asking all assemblies and societies to send two or three delegates to The Hague on July 22 to plan a central meeting of all patriotic associations in the Batavian Republic. The planning meeting took place. Felix Libertaté was represented by Asser and Bromet. At this conclave there was no criticism of Felix Libertaté; in fact, Asser received a great many votes for the presidency. He accepted the chairmanship of the committee on organization of the central meeting. The central meeting was held in The Hague on August 24. Much to the amazement of Felix Libertaté, whose members had reason to be sure of their acceptance at the meeting, the tide had turned. Representatives of Gouda questioned the right of Felix Libertaté to a place in the meeting and inquired whether, as representatives of the "Jewish Nation," they should be present. Some representatives from other places were instructed to leave if Felix Libertaté were seated. Others, like those from Overyssel, pleaded for Felix Libertaté. Asser protested in a long memorial pointing out that one third of the membership of Felix Libertaté was Christian, whereupon the representatives from The Hague stated that all would accept Felix Libertaté if Amsterdam did. It is apparent that between the planning meeting and the gathering itself, Amsterdam had been at work undermining

Felix Libertaté's prestige when it realized the popularity of Asser at the organizational meeting. Asser and his friends left the gathering and expressed their sentiments in a brochure entitled "An Insult to the Rights of Man."

One of the main objections to giving Jews the right to vote was the belief that they conceived of the Messiah, for whom they waited, as a worldly king. This idea was repugnant to the "Patriots" and the "Revolution." Much was written on this subject.[25] On July 29, 1795, E. Shabracq addressed the meeting of Felix Libertaté, pointing out that in the former Jewish state there was no nobility or feudal right (*leenrecht*), and difference of opinion was tolerated. It was emphatically declared that Felix Libertaté did not regard the Messiah as a worldly king but as a redeemer. This widened the rift between Felix Libertaté and the rabbis and Parnassim.

To sum up, at the end of 1795 the immediate objectives of Felix Libertaté in Amsterdam were not accomplished. Jews of that city were not accepted in the guard. They had not achieved the right to vote. Felix Libertaté had estranged itself from many coreligionists and was deeply disappointed. However, the members cherished the conviction, borne out by history, that their aims would be achieved. The next year would witness the emancipation.

Before this could occur, in fact before the new order created by the revolution could function at all, local sovereignty of each hamlet, town, and city, not to speak of provinces, had to give way, both in theory and in fact, to centralized government.[26]

Earlier in this study we have shown that, as to the rights of Jews, each little area determined its own policy. This was true in almost all matters. Fragmentation of authority had to be mended. The credit for a broad outlook goes to the provisional representatives of the provinces of Holland who grasped the need and were ready to yield to the larger national good. In a meeting of the Estates-General on February 26, 1795, despite the opposition of the provinces of Zeeland and Friesland, they proposed the convocation of a National Assembly on March 1, 1796. The election of representatives for the National Assembly was carried out along the following lines: The country was divided into 126 districts of 15,000 inhabitants. Each district was subdivided into groups of 500 people. Each group of 500 chose one elector. Consequently each district

[25] For example, David Friedrichsfeld wrote "Republikanische Gesinnung und Juden Messias," April 9, 1795; he refers to Isaiah, chapters I and II.

[26] Jan Wagenaar, *Vaderlandsche Historie* (Amsterdam, 1749-89), LVIII, 13.

had 30 electors. Each group of 30 electors chose one of their number as representative, hence the National Assembly constituted 126 representatives. Jews along with other inhabitants were given the right to vote for electors in their respective districs. Many Christians abstained from voting, but still fewer Jews, percentage-wise, availed themselves of the opportunity, because of the division between members of Felix Libertaté and their sympathizers, and the large number of followers of the rabbis and Parnassim. The latter were still reluctant to yield to the new order, although they saw the futility of bucking the tide. Despite the comparatively small number of Jews voting, they obtained 12 electors. Asser received 14 out of the 16 electoral votes necessary to make him a representative. Had all Jews voted they would have had at least one and probably two representatives in the first National Assembly. Under the circumstances none were elected. The Assembly granted the right of petition to individual citizens, or groups of citizens, but not to societies, as they feared undue political pressure. The leading members of Felix Libertaté spoke for the Jews, although they could not represent the wishes of their own society. A document dated March 29 was addressed to the National Assembly and signed by H. L. Bromet, Izak de Jonge Meijersz, H. de H. Lemon, Carolus Asser, M. S. Asser, and Jacob Saportes, complaining that the revolution had not secured the expected freedoms for the Jews. The address expressed thanks to the Estates-General for giving Jews the right to vote and urged that the development of all other rights of full citizenship be permitted. Jews were allowed to vote but still excluded from many trades and crafts.

The National Assembly appointed a committee of seven to investigate matters presented by the petitioners. Two of the members of this committee, J. G. H. Hahn and Rutger Jan Schimmelpenninck, were known champions of the Jews. Their report was presented by Hahn on August 1 but did not come up for debate in the Assembly until August 22. Hahn pointed out that Jewish loyalty to the House of Orange was a result of the protection of the Jews by that dynasty. They would be even more loyal to the Batavian Republic if they were granted full citizenship. It would be a magnanimous act on the part of the Assembly to grant equal rights to the 50,000 Jews in the Netherlands. The debate lasted eight days. All the old arguments about the separate nationality of the Jew were voiced. The opponents further pointed out that Jews could not be full citizens unless they accepted the Constitution and abrogated their own laws. Some said that the masses of the Jews did not want citizenship. There was so much discussion pro and con that the issues were obscured. Schimmelpenninck finally proposed a decree proclaiming that no Jew, because he was a Jew, should be excluded from full citizenship if he desired it. The opposition tried to block the passage of the decree. Kantelaar, a pro-Jewish representative, proposed that the principle enunicated in the decree be accepted by the Assembly. His proposal was approved by the body and dealt the final blow to the opposition. It was agreed that Hahn's report be submitted to further editing. The opposition, though defeated, still tried to delay the end result. The final voting on the committee's revision took place September 2, 1796.

The National Assembly decreed: (1) No Jew should be denied any of the rights and privileges associated with the rights of Batavian citizenship; (2) a special missive should be circulated informing the respective provincial and municipal governments of this decree.[27] Amsterdam could no longer resist the will of the National Assembly. This decree applied to the entire country and abolished the old supremacy of the provincial and municipal governments.[28] Expressions of thanks were tendered the Assembly by groups of Jews. The equality of the Jews was incorporated into the National Constitution on April 23, 1798, and executed on May 4 of that year.

After the emancipation, Felix Libertaté had no *raison d'être* and was liquidated. Because of the estrangement of its members from the Jewish community, they formed a new congregation known as the "New Congregation Adath Jesurim," which lasted until 1807 when in the days of Louis Napoleon it was united with the old congregation.

As we have shown, there were no Jews in the first National Assembly, but by August 1, 1797, two Jews, Bromet and Dr. de Lemon, were chosen for the second Assembly and a year later Isaac da Costa Athias was seated as a member.

In 1798 the Batavian Republic became part of the French Empire. The Jews continued to integrate into the life of the country, although their social acceptance and absorption into the economic and professional life, was a long time in coming. Holland in 1805 became a kingdom, under Louis Napoleon, who was especially interested in the betterment of the Jewish lot. With the return of the House of Orange in 1813 few changes were made in Jewish life. Valuable revolutionary writings were destroyed

[27] See Appendix, Seeligmann, *De Emancipatie der Joden in Nederland.*

[28] In fact, by March 15, 1798, Amsterdam elected M. S. Asser a member of the court of justice, and on May 15 of that year Moses Moresco a member of the city government.

at that time, since many of the "Patriots" wished to obliterate the evidence of their anti-Orange sentiments. The Jews as a whole rejoiced at the return of the House of Orange.

The emancipation in Holland, as elsewhere, made an end of the existence of the old Jewish community. Vestiges of it still persisted until the Hitler debacle. But individual Dutch citizens who were Jews functioned in the national life.

The Jewish Middle Ages were over. The power of the community was broken; the force of custom and Jewish lore had lost much of its effect. There was no longer a "Jewish Nation" in the Netherlands. Dutch Jewry was now considered a religious body and regarded by the government as an aggregate of citizens belonging to the "Church." Many Jews became entirely assimilated, while others remained devotedly Orthodox. The parnas had little power in the life of the Jew, and the rabbi was counted among the clergy of the Netherlands. As individuals, Jews broadened their view of life, but the old question arises again: Was the emancipation in the Netherlands, though inevitable, a force for creative Jewish survival?

APPENDIX

Translation of "Special Missive Sent to the Respective Provincial and Municipal Governments by the National Assembly":

The National Assembly representing the people of the Netherlands to the highest constituted authorities:

Fellow Citizens!

As soon as the dawn of our most recent Revolution broke, the beginnings of liberty and equality, and the "Rights of Man and Citizen," were solemnly announced by the first representatives of the liberated people of the Netherlands. The people accepted these announcements as revelation. Little wonder! for they are based on nature, and their long suppression could not muffle nature's voice. They are incontrovertible truths that permit almost no debate, the most simple person immediately senses their force, and no one is shameless enough to oppose the noonday light of primary verities.

But since that time, sad experience has taught us in these matters how little people remain equal to their best selves, how often their words are belied by their actions, because of prejudice or personal gain. How prone many are, when actions are called for, to use their principles according to circumstances, either from ignorance or weakness; rather than to be loyal to their principles, they fit their principles into expediency.

It would not have been necessary for us to deliberate concerning the rights of that part of the inhabitants of the Netherlands, which professes the Jewish religion, had not some Jewish inhabitants submitted a petition, in which it appeared that some were in doubt as to whether the generally recognized principles also applied to them.

Such doubt would never have arisen in anyone's mind if the true nature of a "Citizens' Society," and the rights of all its members, had been properly considered in all its particulars and the fundamental principles maintained.

The decision which is the conclusion of our deliberations, which you receive herewith, is indeed no different, and could be no different, from the actualization of those principles whose execution the people of the Netherlands have entrusted to us, and upon which we have accepted our authority. It is no grant of privileges about which there is doubt or debate; it is merely a declaration that there are no reasons why rights should be denied to the Jewish inhabitants which can be enjoyed by every member of society if he possesses the qualities and subjects himself to the regulations which society requires of all its members.

The fabric of the Jewish religion can no more be an exception than that of any other church organization. That fabric can never be a task for the investigation of the lawmaker; he may not even inquire whether or not the Jewish law permits the Jew to become a citizen of the land wherein he dwells; he [the lawmaker] prescribes only duties and conditions. Whosoever subjects himself to these, and is not a citizen of another country, will, if he wishes it, be accepted as a member of the community of citizens. The question as to whether the acceptance of this membership is, or is not, at variance with his religious obligations is entirely a matter of his own conscience. We need no further develop this thought; your insight and your fidelity to the great foundations of our Revolution assure us that you are far above the prejudices, the doubts, and the self-seeking efforts of those who would exclude that portion of our fellow inhabitants from the blessings of their just rights. We expect, consequently, that you will defer to the justice of our accompanying decree, that you will further encourage the implementation of the principles upon which the decree rests, so that every Jew who wishes it may be granted these rights as far as this is possible before their inclusion in the Constitution.

It would be unreasonable that the Government, after having separated from the other church organizations, would have any negotiations with the Jewish congregations, which negotiations should have been severed at the same time that a new state of affairs was introduced into our country.

Therefore, if meanwhile privileges given by certain provincial and city governments to a Jewish congregation under the old order have not as yet been revoked, we urge that you declare to, and notify, the municipalities in the regions under your jurisdiction that these privileges be revoked as soon as possible.[29] It follows from the same principles herein enunciated that the municipalities be permitted complete freedom to maintain those regulations serviceable to them which do not interfere with individual rights.

We trust that this document is written in the spirit of your sentiments and no further word of urgency will be needed.

May you be herewith commended to God's Holy Protection.

[29] The old rights and privileges of Jewish communities had to be nullified under the new order since Jews as individual Batavian citizens, not as members of the Jewish communities, were to be granted rights [translator's note].

AMERICAN JEWRY—REFLECTIONS ON SOCIAL, COMMUNAL, AND SPIRITUAL TRENDS

By Samuel M. Blumenfield

THE CELEBRATION of three hundred years of Jewish settlement in the United States has brought in its wake a great variety of writings dealing with the history of American Jewry, its institutions, and its changing patterns. These works constitute an important contribution to an understanding of the history of the Jewish community on this continent. In this paper I shall attempt to sum up the salient features of American Jewry by limning some of its distinguishing characteristics and to present an estimate of its outlook for the future.

I

An important, perhaps decisive, phenomenon that confronts one in the attempt to analyze the nature of American Jewry is its relatively rapid numerical increase due mainly to immigration during the past decades. The community before us numbers more than 5,000,000 individuals living under one political and cultural system. To be sure, during the past century there has been a large population growth in many other countries, America among them; but the proportionate increase of the Jewish population of the United States is outstanding. It may be stated without fear of contradiction that no other Jewish community outside of Israel had grown in so spectacular a fashion in so short a period. The following figures are illustrative.

In 1654, twenty-four Jewish immigrants reached the shores of the New World. More than one hundred years later, in 1776, their number had grown to about 3,000; in 1840, despite a strong wave of German immigration, the Jews in the United States numbered only about 15,000, and constituted less than one tenth of one percent of the total population. With the passage of forty years, in 1880, the number had grown to 250,000; fifty years later, in 1930, it totaled 4,250,000—representing an increase of 1,700 percent. Thus American Jews, who in 1880 constituted only about one half of one percent of the total population, by 1930 had come to constitute between 2.5 and 3 percent—i.e., their proportion had increased nearly sixfold.

There is almost no analogy in Jewish history for so large a numerical concentration as that of the American Jewish community. (Russian Jewry, which was about 7,000,000 strong before World War I, was composed of various communities distributed through a number of lands under Czarist domination, such as Poland, Latvia, Lithuania, Estonia, Finland, etc.) This numerical strength is in itself a source of a sense of security and confidence that has enabled American Jewry to plan for itself and for other Jewries in a manner that communities more limited in number, such as those in Western Europe, have not been able to do.

Another factor contributing to the growth of the influence of American Jews is their concentration in large urban centers. It is estimated that some 43 percent of American Jews live in Greater New York, from 23 to 35 percent reside in other large cities, while only 21 percent are to be found distributed in smaller communities. Were it not for this urban concentration, the American Jewish community could not have been as active as it has been and achieved the status it now holds among a total population of more than 160,000,000.

It is worthy of note that at the beginning of the century Jewish community leaders were fearful of the consequences of the urban concentration of the Jewish population; they used many resources to induce Jewish immigrants to spread throughout the country. However, realities have shown that this very concentration has thus far affected favorably the molding of the social and cultural character of American Jewry.

Indeed, this very concentration has gained for the Jewish community that position of influence which every minority—ethnic, religious, or economic—needs to secure strength in a democratic system. It is a widely accepted notion that minority groups in the United States exercise at times greater influence than do majority groups. This is true only of minorities that are compact and well organized such as manufacturers' associations, professional guilds, unions, lobbies, etc. There is reason to believe then, that if the Jews in the United States had not been concentrated in large cities, they would not have achieved their present status and influence.

Another characteristic feature in the development of the Jewish community in the United States has been the proliferation of its various social and cultural institutions. Writers of American Jewish history usually divide the Jewish immigration into three major periods. The first, extending from the middle of the seventeenth century to the beginning of the nineteenth, consisted of a substantial number of Jews of Sephardic origin; the second period, covering the years 1825-80, was primarily one of immigration from German-speaking countries; and the third period, which began during the eighties of the past century and lasted to the twenties of the present century, was made up largely of Eastern European immigration. Since the twenties the proportion of native-born Jews has increased to the point where it now constitutes more than 75 percent of the Jews in the United States.

Each of the three designated streams of immigration came from a different political, economic, and cultural background. In the nature of things, this differentiation was conducive to social and congregational separatism, and, on occasion, even to mutual antagonism. It is well known that the first immigrants, who were of Sephardic origin, deprecated the German Jews, whom they considered "uncouth, narrow-minded and poor."[1] But once the German Jews had struck roots in American soil, they in their turn adopted the same attitude toward the growing number of new immigrants from Eastern Europe. True, they did not neglect the needs of their coreligionists, and established such institutions as hospitals, orphanages, and old age homes to meet their wants. Yet, there was a social barrier between the older and the newer immigrants. The Jews from East Europe, whom the German Jews invidiously labeled "Polacks," were discouraged from joining social organizations formed by German Jews (B'nai B'rith, for example) and therefore chose to form clubs and fraternal orders of their own. In historical retrospect, however, it can be said that this variety of social and cultural elements which have gone into the making of the American Jewish community was a blessing in disguise. The variety of backgrounds which the Jewish immigrant groups brought with them enlarged the horizon and enriched the content and form of Jewish life in the United States. In the course of time the members of the various Jewish immigrant groups merged in a "melting pot" of their own within the larger American "melting pot." As a result there emerged a Jewish type in which the pride and spirit of adventure that distinguished some of the early Sephardim were joined with the industriousness and practicality of the German Jews and the sensitivity and social idealism of many of the immigrants from Eastern Europe. Hence the ingenuity, vitality, and adaptability that are characteristic of present-day American Jews.

[1] Anita Lebeson, *Jewish Pioneers in America* (New York, 1931), p. 116.

No less drastic a transformation occurred in the economic fortunes of American Jewry. Within a generation or two, the Jewish immigrant economically surpassed the immigrants from other ethnic groups who arrived at the same time. The Jewish storekeeper and shopworker who had had to struggle to eke out a livelihood during the first years after his arrival eventually rose to occupy a relatively high rung on the American economic ladder. The following examples are illustrative.

In the 1930's, the Jews of Charleston (a community with a small number of immigrants) included: one physician, one dentist, several lawyers, two pharmacists, four teachers, and one rabbi. But by 1948 the same community numbered: eight physicians, seven dentists, eighteen lawyers, five pharmacists, nine teachers, eighteen engineers, seven social workers, four accountants, one orchestra leader, and four rabbis. And all these professionals in a community of fewer than 2,000 persons![2] In the large community of New York City, consisting of about 2,000,000 Jews and including a considerable number of workers and immigrants, a survey made in 1951 revealed that almost 12 percent of the Jewish families had annual incomes exceeding $10,000, as against 5 percent of the non-Jewish population in the same income bracket. Conversely, only 29 percent of the Jewish families earned less than $4,000 annually, as against 49 percent of the non-Jews.[3]

As late as the 1930's, Jewish sociologists tended to question the stability of the American Jewish economic situation.[4] Concern was expressed over the concentration of Jews in liberal professions and certain kinds of business pursuits. These critics feared that this occupational disproportion would inevitably place American Jews in the thick of cutthroat competition in the upper socioeconomic stratum, with all the dangers implicit in such economic warfare. The tragic experience of the Jews in Europe and the hardships experienced in the United States during the great depression of the 1930's led many Jewish community leaders and writers to urge American Jews to change their occupations and enter into new fields of economic endeavor. It is doubtful whether appeals for widening the area of economic pursuits have influenced the choice of American Jews, but it is evident that the tempo of technological progress and economic conditions during and following World War II have led to

[2] Charles Reznikoff and Uriah Z. Engleman, *The Jews of Charleston* (Philadelphia, 1950), pp. 263-64.

[3] Nathan Glazer, "Social Characteristics of American Jews, 1654-1954," *AJYB, 1955*, pp. 27-28.

[4] I. M. Rubinow, "The Economic and Industrial Status of American Jewry," National Conference of Jewish Social Service, *Proceedings* (May, 1932), pp. 28-37.

an expansion in the areas of occupation among American Jews. To be sure, the majority of American Jewry is located in urban middle-class commercial occupations; but there has been a manifest increase in the number of Jews gaining a foothold in branches of industry, the liberal professions, universities, and government offices in areas where previously they were not well represented. At the same time there has been a substantial transformation in American economic stratification. (During the period 1910-50, the proportion of Americans engaged in nonmanual, as distinct from manual, labor rose from 21 percent to 38 percent.)[5] There has been an expansion and increase in the area of communication: radio, television, and mass educational media generally have been made accessible to vast numbers of the American population. In the wake of this development has followed the leveling of many of the class barriers; powerful links have been forged joining city and village, industry and agriculture, science and labor. The net result has been that the economic status of the Jews in this country is no longer as conspicuously different from that of other groups of Americans as it was at the beginning of the century; the fears expressed during the twenties and thirties over the economic concentration of American Jewry have since lessened considerably.

The improvement of the economic situation of American Jewry has been accompanied by social changes. The dense settlement in urban Jewish "ghettos" has been succeeded by a spreading out into suburban areas and smaller places. This change in the Jewish residential pattern has led to a greater awareness of non-Jewish neighbors than had ever been the case in the larger metropolitan areas, with significant social and psychological consequences.

Contrary to expectations, the exodus from urban centers to outlying areas, far from proving a negative factor, has actually proved to be a positive influence on Jewish consciousness and activity. This has been particularly true of the synagogue and the Jewish school. In suburban areas the need to provide children with a Jewish education is felt and responded to much more sharply than in urban centers. (During the school year 1953-54, 28.3 percent of the Jewish children in New York City were enrolled in Jewish schools; the proportion in the suburbs was 59.4 percent.)[6] The European catastrophe and the rise of the State of Israel have certainly played an important part in the increased interest in Jewish

[5] A. J. Jaffee and C. D. Stewart, *Manpower Resources and Utilization* (New York, 1951), p. 190.

[6] Israel Chipkin, *J.E.C. Bulletin* (December, 1954).

education. The concern with non-Jewish neighbors may, however, have been one of the factors in favor of Jewish education in this suburban trend. The same concern may be the reason for the visible increase in the number of synagogues in recent years. Whatever the reasons, these developments give hope that the growing generation of native American Jews will come closer to their religious and cultural heritage.

This proximity to non-Jewish neighbors in the suburbs has also been important for another reason: it has helped to dispel to some degree age-old anti-Jewish prejudices based on ignorance in regard to Jewry and Judaism. Americans today, generally speaking, recognize the place of Judaism in the scheme of American civilization as of right rather than on sufferance. This change of attitude deserves special consideration, particularly in view of the fact that the Jewish population of the United States, constituting some 3.5 percent of the total population, is frequently allotted a religious representation as a third major religion.

This change did not take place overnight, or without considerable exertion. The Jews of the United States have been unremitting in their struggle to achieve and maintain equal religious and civic rights with other denominations—from the time of Asser Levy, who assumed leadership in this struggle soon after his arrival in America, to the current efforts in opposition to Christological holiday celebration in the public school system. American Jews have not sat idly by when they suspected their rights were being compromised or discriminated against; they have fought openly for the recognition that they knew to be their due. Thus, for example, they made presentations to invite a rabbi for an invocation at the opening session of the House of Representatives; as a consequence, Rabbi M. Raphall of New York was officially invited (in 1860) to lead the national legislature in prayer. On another occasion (in 1852) Rabbi Isaac Mayer Wise protested vigorously to the New York State Legislature because it had not included a Jewish representative in its roster of spiritual leaders. Rabbi Wise complained to the Speaker of the Assembly that this omission constituted an abridgment of religious equality. As a result of Wise's protest, he was not only invited to Albany but was also appointed as acting military chaplain. This led the leaders of the Christian denominations to overcome their earlier antagonism to Judaism and to recognize its claim to equality with all other religions.

A century ago, the governor of South Carolina issued a Thanksgiving Day proclamation couched in unmistakable Christian terms and refused to change this sectarian wording, despite the fact that it was called to his attention that it was offensive to the Jewish citizens of his state. The

Jews of South Carolina reacted by rejecting the proclamation; that year they refused to participate in the Thanksgiving Day celebration.[7]

Recognition from non-Jewish neighbors has not been American Judaism's sole accomplishment. There have been many changes for the better in the institutional phases of Jewish religious life: the formation of national federations of synagogue bodies; the organization of rabbinical associations, Orthodox, Conservative, and Reform; the founding of theological colleges and teacher training schools; and the substantial increase in the number of people previously indifferent to religious commitment who today are affiliated with synagogues and other religious institutions. These changes have their roots, to no small degree, in the new approach to religion—an approach embodied in the idea that a revision of concepts pertaining to some aspects of the faith and observance by no means implies a decline in, or denigration of, the value of religion itself.

There was a period in the history of American Judaism when change as such was associated with alienation from the Jewish heritage and established tradition. There was a widespread conviction that the first-generation immigrants alone had been capable of preserving Jewish cultural patterns; the second generation would drift away from the heritage of their fathers, the third would abandon the Jewish way of life, while the fourth would be completely assimilated. The same retrogression was also envisaged for the religious life; that is to say, whereas the first-generation immigrants actively practiced traditional Judaism, the second would accommodate itself to American mores leading to the Conservative synagogue, the third generation would move in the direction of Reform, and the fourth or fifth would be lost to the Jewish faith.

It may now be asserted that this cyclical theory of American Judaism has not proved adequate as a characterization of religious life. There has been a marked change in the attitude toward the complex of subjects associated with religion in American society, and antireligious rationalism is no longer either the exclusive or the dominant philosophy. The best testimony to this development is the fact that public education in the United States is once again wrestling with the problem of religion in a democratic school system, which less than fifty years ago was deemed to be no longer an issue. At the turn of the century it seemed that the constitutional separation of church and state had solved the problem of the school and religion once and for all. But, surprisingly, the very principle

[7] Morris U. Schappes, *Documentary History of the Jews in the United States* (New York, 1950), pp. 235-46.

of separation of church and state has come under sharp questioning. There is an appeal from many quarters for recognition of the right to public religious education, and a breach is threatened in the "high wall of separation" of church and state erected by the United States Supreme Court. The present trend suggests that the relation between religion and education in the United States is far from being settled; nor is the possibility of an American version of the European *Kulturkampf* entirely to be excluded.

Perceptible traces of the trend toward religion are also to be found in the Jewish camp. Religio-mystical views are infiltrating Jewish intellectual circles previously seemingly immune to such beliefs. The latter-day sentiment in favor of religious values and institutions among American Jews has been in no small degree influenced by a "reevaluation of religious values" in America at large. The first-generation immigrants, particularly those from Eastern Europe, came hastily to the conclusion that American society was basically materialistic and unsuitable soil for the propagation of religious ideas and practices. The very separation of church and state was, to many of them, prima facie evidence of indifference or even hostility to religion. However, as American Jews began to strike roots in the new civilization they discovered that despite the obviously pragmatic temper of the country, the social ideas of America were largely shaped by basic religious ideas and inspiration. They learned that the constitutional principle of separation did not flow from the French Revolution's tradition of opposition to religion; on the contrary, the principle of the separation of church and state as enunciated in the Constitution was an expression of religious freedom, of tolerance toward and even appreciation of the different religious streams in America. They came to realize that the American people as a whole was guided in its higher aspirations by religious teachings, many of its mores, as well as some laws, having their source in religious traditions and morality.

In different periods of history, human society seeks out sources of authority capable of furnishing its political and social life with moral sanctions and guidance. Thus, during the Middle Ages, the Universal Church provided an authority whose spiritual force was recognized in practically every phase of society. The French Revolution substituted for the Church the sanction of "the people" and their natural rights. The Communist system adopted the authority of the "proletariat"; and the Nazis that of "Blood and Soil."

Since its Puritan beginnings, American society has ever derived sanction and inspiration from religious teachings and practices. To quote a member of the United States Supreme Court: "To deny the existence of religious motivation [in American life] is to deny the inspiration and authority of the Constitution itself." No wonder then that in more recent years many spokesmen of the Jewish community, perceiving the trend toward religion in American society, have come to the conclusion that their own religious aspirations are in harmony and not in conflict with contemporary American attitudes.

The same potentiality for the free development of traditional Jewish interests and institutions is also available to American Jewry for Jewish education and culture. Jews have been devoted to learning for thousands of years; in the past the quest for knowledge primarily took the form of the study of the sacred writings. More recently, Jews have been avid for universal human knowledge. The fact that Jewish children have scored high in intelligence tests[8] may be explained by this passion for education among Jews. Whatever the explanation, the fact remains that a relatively high proportion of Jewish students, close to a quarter of a million, are attending American universities and colleges, a much greater proportion than that of the Jewish population to the total population. While the practice of discrimination in some institutions of higher learning, particularly in medical schools, is not yet a thing of the past, there have been signs pointing to a change for the better.

It is difficult to forecast the prospects for college-educated American Jews in terms of Jewish commitments. However, one need not be anxious about their leaving the Jewish fold as were European parents during the past century when their children flocked into the Gymnasiums and universities. It is common in this country nowadays to meet college-educated parents who themselves have no Jewish education, but who wish to make sure that their children learn about their people. I have elsewhere dwelt upon the prospects for Jewish education in this country.[9] At this point it may be worth while to mention one important development—the recent experimental efforts to determine the proper direction for American Jewish education. Summer camps, large-scale organizations for youth activities (with about one-half million members), all-day schools, synagogue centers, radio and television programs, and the like have offered many fine opportunities for new approaches to Jewish education. They may not present the solution to the problem of Jewish education, but they

[8] J. B. Maller, "A Study of Jewish Neighborhoods of New York," *JSSQ*, X (1934), 271-76; *Report of the Industrial Commission 1901*, XV, 478.

[9] *A Mid-Century of Jewish Education—Retrospect and Prospect* (American Association for Jewish Education, New York, 1950).

must be regarded as progressive steps in the right direction.

Thus far we have considered developments within the American Jewish community itself; however, it must be noted that activity in behalf of the Jewish people the world over holds a place of major importance in American Jewry. The contribution of American Jews to the philanthropic efforts on behalf of European and North American Jewry and to the upbuilding of the State of Israel is one of the brightest chapters in American Jewish history and in that of humanitarian enterprise in general.

In charitable endeavor and social service the Jews of the United States have been able to call upon a long tradition of philanthropy, together with a truly modern aptitude for social organization. As a result, Jewish social institutions in the United States have served as models for many American public and private social welfare and philanthropic institutions. These accomplishments account to some degree for the relatively low rate of criminality among Jews and the comparative stability of Jewish family life.[10]

II

So much for the virtues and strong points of this significant community within a community. The picture would be incomplete without examination of the other side of the coin: the failings and deficiencies of Jewry in this country; the organic feebleness of its institutional framework on the one hand, and the disorientation in its inner life on the other.

It is a source of wonder to those who are familiar with Jewish communal life in the United States that this important community, in the fullness of its vigor and humming with activity, should lack the organic over-all coordinating body commensurate with its aspirations and activities. While local and national philanthropic and congregational agencies are well organized and consolidated, the Jewish community as a whole is atomized and helplessly divided on any issue relating to its social and cultural well-being on a national scale. There are many individual organizations, but no organization; innumerable institutions, but not one that is recognized and can speak for all; freedom of opinion, expression, and action, but no democratic representation, either in internal or external affairs, appropriate for a community of five million souls living in a democratic country. True, in times of crisis or at the threat of persecution the

[10] J. B. Maller, "The Maladjusted Jewish Child," *JSSQ*, IX (1953), 285-95; X (1953), 157-62; Nathan Goldberg, "Jews in the Police Records of Los Angeles, 1933-47," *YIVO Annual of Jewish Social Science*, V (1950), 266-91; Thomas P. Monahan and William M. Kephart, "Divorce and Desertion by Religious and Mixed Religious Groups," *American Journal of Sociology* (1954), pp. 554-65.

fragments coalesce and join to take a stand against the common enemy; but even this temporary coalition, that springs up gourdlike overnight, holds together with great difficulty, for the lack of a regular, central, over-all coordinating organization. Once the "day of wrath" passes, each of the organizations returns to its jealously guarded independence, and "normalcy" sets in: a state of over-organized anarchy for all organizations, big and small alike.

The celebrated social philosopher Horace M. Kallen describes the situation as follows:

> Our Jewish scene presents a cut-throat competition between its manifold federated local organizations of interest, each asserting its own unique rightness, each tending to claim exclusive authority for itself on the ground that it alone possesses the sole doctrine and discipline which in its field of operations can be good for the Jews. Thus, whatever any other might be doing, each is disposed to reduplicate the other's works, to denounce the other's ways, and to declare itself entitled to total support for itself, whether as a denomination of Judaism, a Zionist party, an educational enterprise, a cultural endeavor, overseas service, or "defense." . . . [The new organizational formations] raised to a painful shrillness the disorder by disputation of the competing self-designated would-be spokesmen and benefactors of American Jewry.[11]

Why this communal "tohu vabohu"? To understand its source one must keep in mind the historic fact that the Jewish community in the United States is composed of various groups of diverse origins. It has inherited two modes of communal organization from overseas: the tradition of the Eastern European *Kehillah* which constituted an ethnic-cultural-religious structure; and the tradition of the Western European *Gemeinde*, a religious-congregational-philanthropic setup. In recent years there has been added the short-lived experiences of the post-World War I democratic communities in Eastern European countries and of the Vaad Leumi in Palestine. The American Jewish community, which, as constituted today, is in reality only some seventy-five years old (the bulk of immigration started in the eighties of the last century), has not had sufficient time in which to evolve a new, organic structure to meet its needs, which are different from those of the Jewish communities of both Western and Eastern Europe. Hence the competing drives: one, expressed in the founding of the American Jewish Congress and the calling of the American Jewish Conference, to include the entire community in an over-all organization after the pattern of Eastern and Central Europe; the other, to continue the West European pattern of quasi-ecclesiastic organization

[11] Horace M. Kallen, *Of Them Which Say They Are Jews* (New York, 1954), pp. 16, 19. Quotation used by permission of Bloch Publishing Company.

modeled after the Napoleonic Sanhedrin and Consistory. However, the American Jewish community both lacks the inner sense of mutual responsibility that prevailed in East European Jewish communities and is bereft of the external governmental influence that cemented West European Jewries. Hence, neither of the inherited patterns can serve the needs of the Jews of America.

The inner problems of American Jewry are even more difficult of solution. The situation can be summarized as one of cultural immaturity accompanied by spiritual instability.

Except for the fine old tradition of charity, still one of the hallmarks of American Jewry (though it too is fading, due to the organizational gulf separating donor and recipient), it would be hard to point to any spiritual value that is an integral part of Jewish consciousness in this country. Spiritual aridity and parochialism are to be noted in every area of American Jewish life—religion, education, and liaison with Israel.

For, despite the large number of imposing synagogue buildings being put up and the increase in the number of persons affiliated with these synagogues, there is no sign of a definite religious awakening. On the contrary: What is developing is a concept of religious life that requires nothing more than the payment of membership fees, like those paid to a fraternal order or clubhouse. This is true not only of Jews who call themselves Reform or Conservative but also of the majority of those who call themselves Orthodox but who feel free not to practice the teachings of their profession.

Indeed, one cannot escape the impression that the impelling motive for the increase in synagogue membership is not so much a personal need to associate oneself with the Jewish tradition as a concern with the old "Mah Yomru Hagoyim"—what will the Gentiles say?—if one did not do so. Such an approach to religious values may in the long run prove more harmful than beneficial to Judaism.

Bialik's words in another connection may be aptly applied to the religious situation of the Jews in the United States: "Behold a generation that is growing up in an atmosphere charged with phrase and popular refrains and fed on things that are mere breath and wind. A Judaism of convenience is being created.... Its yes and no are too uncertain."[12]

Elsewhere[13] I have commented on the great importance of the in-

[12] C. N. Bialik, "Halacha VeAgada," translated by Julius L. Siegel (New York, 1923).

[13] "The Present Status of Jewish Education in America," *Proceedings of the First American Zionist Assembly* (New York, 1954), pp. 98-106.

creasing number of children attending Jewish schools—as well as on the poverty of the education being doled out in these schools. Here I wish to dwell on the parents' attitude toward Jewish education, one that is certain to be the determining factor in the future of that education.

The most melancholy phenomenon of all is that in the United States Jewish education is regarded as something that is good for the other person, and not for oneself. Not long ago some parents would try to see to it that their children received a Jewish education out of filial piety; that is to say, to give the children's grandparents cause for gratification the grandchildren were urged to study Torah. But this loyalty to forebears has tended to disappear as an important motivation for Jewish education with the death of the grandparents themselves. Moreover, a progressive educational system that is child-centered has come into being. Jewish education, therefore, now calls upon parents to meet the spiritual and psychological needs of the children. But in either event, whether asked to sustain the grandparent or to sustain the child, Jewish education in the United States has not been self-sustaining. So long as the Jewish community that supports the Jewish schools has neither the understanding of the meaning of Torah nor the devotion to the ideal of a meaningful Jewish education—there is little reason to hope for or to expect an improvement in Jewish education in the future.

Similarly, there has been a loosening of the inner bonds linking most of American Jewry with Israel. The large financial contributions that American Jews have made to the building of Israel are well known. But their personal, human sense of closeness to Israel has greatly weakened; there is no longer the same appreciation there used to be of Israel's unique place in the Jewish consciousness and in the destiny of Jewry and Judaism. Only in the absence of a deeper comprehension of the meaning of Israel could the debate over dual loyalty have been waged in many Jewish quarters, particularly since the birth of the new state.

The question of Aliya or immigration to Israel has especially contributed to an uneasiness among Jews in the United States—including some Zionists. When, a few years ago, the question of Aliya was raised at the World Jewish Congress held in Basle, American Jewish leaders felt called upon to make public declarations of their wholehearted loyalty to America and American institutions. Apparently, despite all its impressive accomplishments, American Jewry still suffers from a sense of insecurity and inner instability. It is all the more amazing that such fears could prevail in a country whose history is informed with the spirit of mobility and pioneering. This spirit is not merely an historic memory in the United States;

it is expressed anew in our own day in the economic and social endeavor in behalf of underdeveloped and impoverished countries. Supreme Court Justice William O. Douglas, one of the great American liberals, in speaking of the aid proffered by America to such countries, has this to say:

> It could not be done by flying squadrons of experts, by high-pressured promotional efforts that we Americans know so well. It could be done only with patience and understanding of the villager and his problems. That would mean that the expert who went among them would have to become a member of the village community. He could not pay visits to the villages as an advisor; *he would have to live in the mud huts, eat the village fare, join the village festivities, come to know the psychology and superstitions of the people, and be one of them in language, in spirit, and in physical existence.*[14]

If young Americans can be asked to make a commitment of this kind on behalf of underdeveloped countries that are utterly alien to them in terms of culture, religion, and tradition, why cannot Jewish young people be asked to make similar commitments on behalf of Israel? Indeed, one who grasps fully the meaning of American values and ideals would be proud of every pioneer and emigrant from this country who is willing to help in the upbuilding of Israel—rather than to cringe from such pioneering emigration or to try to apologize for it. The emigrant would be regarded not only as participating in the building of a new country but also as an American ambassador of good will who is being loyal to the social promise of his native land. Witness the pride with which Americans speak of their missionaries rendering humanitarian services in primitive lands. Would such services be less spiritual in quality if motivated by a sense of kinship and a love for Judaism and Israel?

American Jewry's spiritual malaise has also contributed to the current weakening in moral fibre, followed by a lowering of the standards in communal and personal life. These are evidenced by the inordinate hunger for recognition for every service and contribution, small or large, as manifested by the thousands of banquets and innumerable testimonials without which it is almost impossible to achieve results even for the most worthy undertakings, be it for a hospital, a synagogue, a rabbinical school, or Israel.

Herzl once said: "The Jews who have so long been condemned to a state of civic dishonor have as a result developed an almost pathological hunger for honor."[15] If such a lowering in standards of values holds true

[14] William O. Douglas, *Beyond the High Himalayas* (New York, 1952), p. 314. Italics added. Quotation used by permission of Doubleday & Company, Inc.

[15] A. Bein, *Herzl V'Dreyfus* (Herzl and Dreyfus) (Youth Department of World Zionist Organization, Tel-Aviv, 1945).

ethical conduct and morality, what is there to expect from a generation now, when American Jews are not far removed from traditional sources of born or reared in an atmosphere of "mere breath and wind"? Beside the age-old tradition of humanitarianism and mutual responsibility which has helped mold Jewish life, Jewish immigrants carried with them memories of poverty and want of their younger days. These have kept their sympathies alert to everything that is liberal and sympathetic in human relations. But as the rising generation is becoming less familiar with poverty, and frequently ignorant of deprivation, perhaps the rabbinic adage, "Pay heed to the children of the poor, for from them shall issue forth Torah," may have to be changed to read: "Pay heed to the children of the wealthy, for from them may issue forth decay and corruption." Dr. Abba Hillel Silver has aptly described the new type of Jew, growing up without tradition or religious desciplines, as follows:

> What we should fear most is the rise of a generation of prosperous Jews who have no spiritual anchorage, or a generation of clever, restless Jews of quick ferment and high voltage, rooted in no religious training, reverent of no moral code, ignorant of all Jewish learning and held to social responsibility by no inner spiritual restraint, who will range and bluster all over the American scene from literature and art to politics and government and will commit their fellow Jews in the eyes of the American people. Such floating mines are a danger to any people, but especially to a minority people. Some of these mines are already exploding.[16]

These, then, are the achievements and failures, the positive accomplishments and the negative aspects that feature American Jewry after some three hundred years of its history. They almost balance each other: constructive and destructive forces, progress and retrogression, rise and decline, threat and promise. Small wonder that there is substantial division of opinion about the future of American Jewry. Optimists see the lights and speak in terms of new creative forces to be revealed in this country similar to those that were revealed in the Jewries of Babylonia and Spain in their golden age. Pessimists, on the other hand, see only signs of assimilation and disintegration, such as took place in Western Europe. Still others, considering realities, seek to evaluate the destiny of American Jewry not only in the light of experiences of the ancient past and the last century but also in the light of the revolutionary phenomenon of our own times: the rise of the State of Israel and the rebirth of Hebrew culture.

[16] Abba Hillel Silver, Address delivered Nov. 21, 1953, at the 22d General Assembly of the Council of Jewish Federations and Welfare Funds, Cleveland, Ohio.

These are new dimensions in Jewish history and should be given earnest attention in a consideration of the future of Jewry and Judaism in this country. Israel as a new and vital focus in the consciousness of modern Jewry, and Hebrew culture reborn as a compelling factor in the development of Judaism, present a new constellation and are bound to play a decisive positive role in the destinies of the largest Jewish community in the diaspora.

MORALITY AND RELIGION
IN THE THEOLOGY OF MAIMONIDES

By Ben Zion Bokser

CAN THERE BE a science of morals which is independent of the religious life? Can we, by the canons of reason and by the process of logical demonstration, formulate an absolute distinction between right and wrong? Moses Maimonides replied to these questions in the negative. Reason alone, he held, can offer no sure anchor to the moral code. The demands of morality can be grounded only in religion. Without religion our moral code becomes nothing but a set of conventional procedures, as uncertain as the shifting circumstances of popular taste, which is the only final authority of their being.

Maimonides states this position clearly in his *Treatise on Logic* (*Millot ha-Higayon*). He identifies four ways of knowing: sense perception, "as when we know that this is black, this is white, and this is hot"; the first postulates of reason, "as when we know that the whole is greater than the part, that two is an even number, and that things equal to the same thing equal each other"; conventions (*mefursomos*), "as when we know that uncovering the private parts is ugly, that compensating a benefactor generously is beautiful"; and traditions received from a person or persons known for their veracity.

The perceptions of the senses and the first postulates of reason, as well as the inferences drawn from them by logical demonstration—these enjoy universal assent. There is no difference among people possessing "normal senses and intuitions" as to their truthfulness. The ethical and moral norms, on the other hand, are enmeshed in the relativities of the human condition, "for there are propositions that have become known among one people and not among another; and whenever a precept is known among many peoples its acceptability is stronger." A like uncertainty prevails, of course, concerning the "truths" communicated by tradition. The general designation for the realm of morals that Maimonides employed here is *mefursomos* (Ibn Tibbon's translation of the Arabic

Al Mashurat employed by Maimonides) the generally agreed, or standards of behavior which derive their authority from common consent rather than from the demands of speculative reason.[1]

The position of Maimonides is reminiscent of the views of Aristotle: "The notions of nobleness and justice," Aristotle declared, "admit of variations and error to such a degree that they are supposed by some to exist conventionally only, and not in the nature of things." Aristotle did, of course, speak of the principles of morality and justice as a "natural law." But he appears to have regarded those principles as "natural" in the sense that they were inspired by a necessity flowing from the nature of man whom Aristotle defined as a "political animal," a creature, in other words, who must live his life within an organized society. The law which seeks to create a durable social order derives from a social impulse implanted in all men by nature so that they may "desire to live together." But these laws were not considered by Aristotle as a product of what he called demonstrative reasoning.[2]

We have a similar view in Plato: "Law," he declared, "could never, by determining what is noblest and most just for one and all, enjoin upon them that which is best; for the difference of men and of actions, and the fact that nothing, I may say, in human life is ever at rest forbid any science whatever to promulgate any simple rule for everything and for all time."[3]

Next to Aristotle himself, Maimonides considered the Islamic Farabi as the greatest authority in philosophy. Farabi's work included the effort to effect a conciliation between Aristotle and Plato. Farabi offers us a similar view as to the nature of the moral code. Philosophy, he taught, is essentially theoretical in character and its competence is the quest for the knowledge of beings as they really are. The problems of morals are outside its sphere. They have no anchor in speculative reason, and whatever knowledge we achieve in these realms is a contingent rather than an essential knowledge. The virtuous way of life or the realm of morals

[1] *Millot ha-Higayon*, chap. 8, edited and translated by I. Efros (New York, 1938), pp. 47 f. Cf. Leo Strauss, "Maimonides' Statement on Political Science," *PAAJR*, XXII (1953), 115 f.

[2] Aristotle, *Nicomachean Ethics*, I, 1. For the interpretation of Aristotle's doctrine of natural law, as applied to morals, see H. A. Wolfson, *Philo* (Cambridge, 1947), II, 175. Thomas Aquinas took Aristotle's characterization of law in the realm of morals as natural in the sense that the fundamental elements of justice are rooted in reason. Other Christian Aristotelians, Marsilius of Padua, for instance, interpreted the term "natural law" in this context as metaphoric, and Marsilius held that Aristotle looked upon such law as conventions. See the well-documented discussion on this subject by Leo Strauss, "The Law of Reason in the Kuzari," *PAAJR*, XIII, (1943), 47 f.

[3] Plato, *Statesman*, 294 B; see also Wolfson, *Philo*, II, 179.

belongs to the category of the practical arts and is a phase of politics rather than of philosophy.[4]

Maimonides wrote the *Millot ha-Higayon* when still a youth, but he never abandoned his conception of the relativity of moral and ethical truth, in so far as they depend solely on man-made canons of judgment. He asserts it again in his commentary on the Mishnah. Discussing the verse (Zech. 8:19) "And love ye the truth and peace," he suggests: "Know that truth applies only to the intellectual virtues, for these are truths which are not subject to variation . . . while peace refers to the moral virtues through which peace is established in the world." In the same context he continues with a definition of moral vices, such "as murder, theft, robbery, deception, the injury of the innocent, the return of evil for good, the disrespect to parents and the like." "These are," he declares, "practices widely known (*mefursomim*) among peoples as evil." Maimonides was aware that some of "our latter day wise men" looked upon the fundamental principles of morality as *sikliot*, or as grounded in reason, but he clearly dissociates himself from this opinion. He brands those entertaining this view as men afflicted with "the malady of the Kalam," the current school of religious apologists in Islam, for whose integrity and intellectual competence Maimonides had little respect.[5]

The same doctrine is followed in the *Mishne Torah*. It occurs, for example, in the discussion of the seven Noahide laws. These were the elements of basic religion and morality by which Adam, Noah, and other men of virtue ordered their lives prior to the Mosaic covenant. Included in this law were the prohibitions of murder, adultery, robbery, cruelty to animals (this was present in Noah's law, but not yet in Adam's), and the injunction to establish courts of justice. What was the source of these laws? How did Adam and Noah arrive at them? Maimonides admits that reason inclines toward these laws, but they could not have been established by reason. They were known and followed only because they were the subject of a special divine revelation which those men experienced, a revelation that was subsequently confirmed and given universal authority in the Mosaic law.

Maimonides, moreover, qualifies the traditional opinion as to the sufficiency of the Noahide law for men who live outside the Mosaic

[4] Leo Strauss, "Farabi's Plato," in *Louis Ginzberg Jubilee Volume* (New York, 1945), pp. 364 f.

[5] *Commentary on the Mishnah*, Eight Chapters, chaps. 4, 6. Saadia had taught that the principles of morals were demonstrable by reason. Cf. Saadia's *The Book of Beliefs and Opinions*, ed. by Samuel Rosenblatt (New Haven, 1948), Treatise III, chap. 2, pp. 141 f.

covenant: "Whoever adopts the seven laws [of the Noahide code] and is zealous in performing them is of the pious among the nations and is sure to have a part in the bliss of the hereafter, provided, however, that he adopts and performs them because they are ordained by the Holy One blessed be He in the Torah. . . . But if he performs them as a result of his own speculations . . . he is not of the pious among the nations, but of their wise men."[6] Why did Maimonides add this reservation which is unknown in the Talmud? It flows clearly from his conception that speculation is not an adequate anchor for the principles of morality, that the only sure source for its establishment is the imperative of a revealed religion.

The same doctrine is taught in the *Guide for the Perplexed.* It is the subject of the second chapter in the first part of the *Guide.* Having established that reason is God's greatest gift to man, that it is the divine image in him, Maimonides is confronted with the paradoxical situation that, according to the biblical story of Adam's fall, the "opening" of Adam's eyes, presumably an allusion to his enlightenment, came after he had eaten of the fruit of the tree of knowledge. This would suggest that Adam's disobedience led him to the state of reason. How could what was to have been a punitive act produce in man his greatest excellence?

Maimonides meets the issue by drawing a distinction between philosophical and moral truth. Before the fall, Adam was in possession of intellectual perfection in an unmarred state. He was able to pursue truth with his speculative reason. But because he was not plagued by sensual passions, he was without a concern for moral problems, where knowledge is uncertain and relative. This necessity to confront moral dilemmas, to deal with moral problems, to grope for the knowledge of good and evil, followed his disobedience.

> The intellect which God bestowed on man as his ultimate perfection was the one which was given to Adam *before* his disobedience. . . . By his intellect man distinguishes between truth and falsehood. This faculty existed in him to its fullest extent. The distinction between good and bad, however, is a matter of general agreement, not of intellectual activity. He possessed no faculty for dealing with the generally agreed in any manner and had no sense for it. When, however, he became disobedient, and turned toward the lusts of his imagination and the pleasures of his physical senses, then only was he punished by being deprived of his intellectual perception. . . . He thus acquired the sense for the generally agreed, and became absorbed in judging things as to their being good and bad.[7]

[6] *Mishne Torah*, Melakim 8 : 11, 9 : 1.

[7] *Guide*, Book I, chap. 2. I have used here the translation of Chaim Rabin, East

Maimonides believed that the divine law, which includes the principles of virtuous action, is in accordance with reason. Indeed, he believed that all the commandments of Scripture were capable of rational justification. "Every one of the six hundred and thirteen precepts," he declared, "serve to inculcate some truth, to remove some erroneous opinion, to establish proper relations in society, to diminish evil, to train in good manners, or to warn against bad habits." Yet if Scripture did not ordain these laws, we could not deduce them with any sense of certainty on the basis of speculation. The law of morals is, in other words, in accordance with reason, but not a product of reason; or as Maimonides put it: "The Law though not a product of nature is, nevertheless, not entirely foreign to nature."

Maimonides looked upon the law of the social order as "not entirely foreign to nature" because it corresponds to a natural need—the needs of social life. For Maimonides followed Aristotle in defining man in political terms, as a creature who by his very nature must live within the framework of society. And it is because man's social life reflects the shifting pressures of circumstances that the law by which he lives in society must necessarily be a mutable and uncertain law. As Maimonides put it in his well-known letter to Rabbi Hisdai ha-Levi: "The customs and opinion bearing on the physical life are by nature changeable, while the wisdom bearing on the life of the soul does not change with nature and is independent of it."[8]

What is the source of the conventional law, whose contents are the basis of the prevalent notions of right and wrong? Its popularity is only the outer token which tends to confirm it. How does it evolve, if not in the work of reason? It evolves, Maimonides argued, from the work of a faculty of the mind, other than reason, the faculty of the imagination

---

and West Library Edition, 1952. The Friedlander translation employs the term "apparent truths" instead of "the generally agreed." The Hebrew term used by Ibn Tibbon is *mefursomos.*

[8] *Guide*, Book III, chap. 31, Book II, chap. 40. The letter to R. Hisdai ha-Levi appears in a volume of letters by Maimonides, *Igrot u-teshubot l'Rabenu Moshe ben Maimon ha-Sefardi* (Warsaw, 1927). A similar distinction was made by Aristotle. See Wolfson, *Philo*, II, 177. Maimonides drew a distinction between the *mizvot*, the commandments which appear to us most reasonable, such as the laws governing social relations, and the *hukim*, ordinances of a ritual nature, such as the prohibition of eating certain foods, whose explanation is remote. But there must have been some cause for the establishment of each of the *hukim* as well, and if the cause seems remote, it is necessary to search harder for it. And the most plausible of scriptural laws is authoritative for us only because it is scripturally ordained, and it is therefore a divine imperative. Cf. *Commentary on Mishnah*, Eight Chapters, chap. 6.

which stirs some people to concern themselves with the problems of man and his relation to society.

The capacity to formulate laws for the government of society, the act of leading people in obedience to such laws, the will on the part of people to bend personal inclination for the common good—these are divinely ordained properties by which God has made provision for the creation and maintenance of a stable social order. Without such properties, society would perish in universal anarchy. But in so far as this law of the social order rests on man-made criteria of judgment, it is the work of imaginative construction, and its only ultimate support is the consent of the people.[9]

A man-made morality is, therefore, according to Maimonides, capable of error, and a state which is built on it may, in fact, prove a distortion of justice. The greatest source of error to which the state may fall prey is its encroachment upon the realm of belief. A man-made law must restrict itself to the realm of social action and stay away from beliefs and opinions which are the realm not of politics but of religion and philosophy.

Maimonides himself had experienced the invasion of the conscience by the secular state. When the Almohades conquered his native Cordoba, they put an end to the religious tolerance which had existed theretofore in Moslem Spain. They wrote their intolerances into a new law of citizenship. A person was given the alternative of conforming to the dominant religious group or leaving the country. Maimonides and his family, among others, took to flight, and it was not until many years later that he finally found a haven in Cairo, Egypt.

Maimonides counseled his people in some circumstances to resist the state, in the name of a higher morality than the law of the land. He sanctioned minor compromises—a nominal conformity if it did not call for too far-reaching an encroachment on one's inner life. Wherever possible, he advised his people to leave intolerant countries and migrate to freer climates. If that were impossible, a man might have to create an underground existence for himself and live his life in solitude. At times a man might have no alternative but to suffer martyrdom for the truth. As Maimonides generalized in his code:

> If he be in a country where the customs are evil and the inhabitants do not walk in the right way, he should go to a place where the inhabitants are righteous and conduct themselves in the way of good men. If however, the inhabitants of all the countries . . . conduct themselves in a way which is not good, as in our days, or if he be unable to go to a country where the customs are good . . . he should

[9] *Guide*, Book II, chaps. 37, 40.

lead a solitary life. And if his countrymen be so wicked and sinful that they do not allow him to dwell in that land unless he mingle with them and conform to their evil customs, he should repair to caves, thickets, and deserts rather than conform to the way of sinners.[10]

The realm of morals was for Maimonides a phase of practical philosophy. He also called it by a more familiar name—political science. He distinguished four categories in the general field of politics—the government of man himself, the government of the household, the government of the city, and the government of the large nation or nations. At least the first category, the act of cultivating personal virtue, is not usually looked upon as a branch of politics. But he placed it within the realm of politics because personal virtues such as calmness, courage, and temperance are prerequisites to a man's functioning in society. Only people who have attained virtuous character will know how to bend self-interest for the common welfare. It was this which Maimonides had in mind by the concept of self-government:

Self-government means the acquisition of worthy habits and the removal of unworthy ones, if already formed. By habit is meant those exercised characteristics that cling to the soul until they become habits which manifest themselves in actions. Philosophers describe habits as virtues and vices; and they call the worthy habits moral virtues, and they call the unworthy habits, moral vices. . . . The philosophers have numerous works dealing with virtues.[11]

Maimonides considered what the philosophers had to say on the subject of virtues. According to Aristotle, virtue is a middle point lying between two extremes, each of which, being an extreme, is a defect. Maimonides found ample support for this same theory of the golden mean in rabbinic literature. The Palestinian Talmud, for example, has this to say on the subject: "The Torah is compared to two paths, one of fire, the other of snow. Should a man turn to the former, he will be consumed by the fire, and if to the latter, he will perish from cold. What then should he do? He should walk in the middle way."[12] Maimonides invokes this principle as a guide to moral action.

The right way is the middle course in every one of the dispositions in man; it is that disposition which is equidistant between the two extremes, so that it is not nearer to the one than to the other. . . . How is this meant? He should not be passionate, nor easily irritated, nor like a corpse that is without feeling; but he should hold the mean between the two, not giving way to vexation except in

[10] *Guide*, Book II, chap. 40; *Mishne Torah*, Deot 6: 1; *Commentary on Mishnah*, Eight Chapters, chap. 4.

[11] *Millot ha-Higayon*, chap. 14.

[12] Hagigah II, 1, 77 a.

some serious matter where it is proper for him to be vexed, in order that a similar thing may not be repeated.

Maimonides applied this principle to a variety of specific moral situations and elaborated a table of virtues which may be seen in this geometric sense, as a mean between two extremes. Yet Maimonides was aware that the doctrine of the mean is not a sufficient anchor for moral action. For one thing, how can one determine the precise point which is the mean between the extremes? There are, moreover, varying dispositions in people, and we cannot expect a mathematical equality in their actions. Sometimes, too, a man ought to choose not the safe mean, but an extreme. Thus Maimonides warns:

> There are some dispositions in regard to which man is forbidden to adopt a middle course, but he should rather remove from one extreme to the other. This is the case with haughtiness of mind; because it is not the good way for a man to be merely meek, but to be of humble mind and exceedingly lowly of spirit. . . . Anger is likewise a most evil quality, and a man should keep aloof from it to the opposite extreme, and train himself not to be vexed even by a thing over which it would be legitimate to be irritated.

A man who becomes proficient in calculating the mean between extremes has attained practical wisdom. But there is a trait nobler than practical wisdom—the trait of saintliness which usually involves the affirmation of a moral extreme.

It is significant that Aristotle himself was aware that the doctrine of the mean is of but limited efficacy in moral guidance. "It is hard to be good," Aristotle declared,

> for surely hard it is in each instance to find the mean, just as to find the mean point or center of a circle is not what any man can do. . . . We ought also to take into consideration our own natural bias, which varies in each man's case, and will be ascertained from the pleasures and pains arising in us. Furthermore, we should force ourselves off in the contrary direction, because we shall find ourselves in the mean after we have removed ourselves far from the wrong side, exactly as we do in straightening bent timber.[13]

The morality of the golden mean, however, suffers from an additional drawback. It is without compulsion. For what can influence a person to choose the good when it is against his inclination? The mere knowledge of where virtue resides will be insufficient to overcome the swaying of our emotions when they point in another direction. Neither reason nor the mathematical balancing of virtues and vices can give us a sound anchor [illegible] moral imperatives. And then there remain the other categories of

…tle, *Nichomachean Ethics*, 1109a-b (II, 8).

morality, the government of the household, the city, the great nation or nations which depend upon laws. The fate of mankind hinges on the quality of these laws. Would it not have been tragic if only conventions were available to guide our moral conduct?[14]

Fortunately, now that the knowledge of biblical religion is widespread, Maimonides declared, we have an ample basis for a moral code, "for divine laws govern human conduct."[15] Maimonides looked upon morality as a derivative of religion. It begins with traditional religion as set forth in the literal interpretation of Scriptures. Its highest sanction on this level is the fear of God. It rises to a religion reinforced by metaphysical speculation and based on a philosophic interpretation of Scripture. On this level of being, its highest sanction is the love of God.

Maimonides surveyed the various categories of scriptural law and showed, on objective ground, their excellence. Scriptural law differs from a secular law in that it aims to give man two perfections, the perfection of his physical self, which includes ethics and morals, and the perfection that rises above the physical, the perfection of the intellect. The latter is accomplished in the Bible by means of correct opinions, stated categorically and without elaboration, concerning the basic elements of a religious creed. The elaboration of this creed, the fuller treatment of what we are to believe concerning God and His government of the universe, was left for a later effort, when a person attained intellectual maturity, an effort that was to be accomplished by speculative reason.

The contribution of the Torah to morality, on this level, consists in the specific provision of scriptural law, whose contents include an ethical element, specifying the personal virtues to be adopted, and the discipline of training by which this can be accomplished. They include, of course, also a body of laws to govern society. But equally important is the doctrine proclaimed in Scripture that "God is angry with those who disobey Him, for it leads us to the fear and dread of disobedience [to the will of God]."[16]

The retributive action of God expressed in rewards or punishments in consequence of transgressions or obedience to His will was a familiar theme in scriptural writings. Maimonides deepened it by his own con-

[14] *Mishne Torah*, Deot 1 : 4. *Commentary on Mishnah*, Eight Chapters, chap. 4.

[15] *Millot ha-Higayon*, chap. 14, and see Introduction by I. Efros, Section 5, p. 18. Cf. Strauss, "Maimonides' Statement on Political Science," *PAAJR*, XXII, 116-19.

[16] *Guide*, Book III, chap. 28. Cf. B. Z. Bokser, *The Legacy of Maimonides* (New York, 1950), pp. 50-56. Maimonides followed Aristotle in looking upon virtue as capable of attainment through a discipline rather than as an endowment of nature or as an object of pure study. See Wolfson, *Philo*, II, 196 ff.

ceptions. What is the most significant form of God's retributive action? It consists, as Scripture indicates, in the withdrawal or the granting of such commonly sought goods as health, prosperity, and peace. But it includes other forms as well. When a person has reached certain depths of sin, God may block his penitence in order to allow punishment to run its course. Callousness in a sinner, his hardening of the heart, as was the case with Pharaoh, is then itself an act of divine retribution.

The most serious form of punishment is the loss of the perfection of soul. That perfection is open to a person whose physical state is in a sound order. By virtue of God's punishment, this is denied him, and when this is denied he is blocked from pursuing his intellectual goals. He thus loses what is the highest reward of a soul perfected by the acquisition of truth—immortality. He suffers what the Bible calls *Karet*—a cutting off from his people.

The converse is similarly true—the highest reward of obedience to God's will is the opportunity to pursue intellectual perfection, with its peak attainment, the bliss of the hereafter, or the soul's immortality.[17]

Maimonides here applied his doctrine limiting immortality to those souls that had attained perfection through the realization of their intellectual potentialities, in the acquisition of truth concerning God, His existence, and His providence. And he based himself likewise on the doctrine that the perfection of the soul cannot occur except after the perfection of the body has been attained. The goods which figure in the traditional conception of retribution—health, prosperity, and peace—apply to the physical level of perfection. But they are of moment even for those who care deeply for the intellectual life, as preliminaries to it.[18]

The law establishing a sound social order was deemed by Maimonides as "imparting to its masters a knowledge of true happiness, showing them the way to obtain it, and a knowledge of true evil, showing them the way to avoid it." The happiness Maimonides refers to here must obviously be a happiness attendant on achieving life's first perfection—our physical or temporal existence "which cannot be in a perfect and good condition except by the cooperation of society." He followed closely here the parallel conception of Plato, as interpreted by Farabi. Philosophy, according to this view of Plato, "does supply the science of the beings and therewith man's highest perfection, but has to be supplemented by some-

[17] *Mishne Torah*, Teshubah 9 : 1; *Commentary on Mishnah*, Introduction to Helek, and Eight Chapters, chap. 8.

[18] *Guide*, Book I, chap. 70, Book III, chap. 27; *Mishne Torah*, Yesode ha-Torah 4:8,9.

thing else in order to produce happiness. That supplement is the right way of life which is the product of the royal art."[19]

Maimonides interpreted the biblical commandment to fear God (Deut. 6:13) in this sense, as a fear of God's punishments. To quote his definition in the *Sefer ha-Mitzvot*: "The fourth of the positive commandments of God is that we believe in His majesty, and fear Him, that we shall not be like the heretics who follow the wayward promptings of their hearts ... but we shall fear His punishments at all times. And this is what Scripture means in the verse, 'Fear the Lord thy God'" (Deut. 6:13).

The religion based on tradition and the literal interpretation of Scriptures and a piety base don the fear of God was, however, for Maimonides only a stage in a person's development. It was to be transcended as a person rose toward a higher maturing of his faculties. It is inadequate religiously because the simple affirmations of God's existence and His unity which we find in the literal text of Scripture do not give us an adequate conception of God. These truths require demonstration, which must move through the work of speculative reason, by a careful study of God's work, the order of nature.

It is inadequate morally because it is grounded in pragmatic motivations. It makes the performance of God's will a means to other ends. For a person who has risen high enough in his perfection, God can never be a means to other ends. He is the ultimate end. "Let not a man say," declared Maimonides,

> I will fulfill the commandments of the Torah, occupy myself with its wisdom, for the purpose of obtaining all the blessings which are written therein, or for the purpose of meriting the life of the world to come; and I will refrain from the transgressions against which the Torah utters a warning for the purpose of escaping the curses which are written therein, or for the purpose of not being cut off from the life of the world to come. It is not becoming to serve God in this manner. ... None serve the Lord in this manner except ignorant men, or women and children who are taught to serve Him from fear, until their mind is developed and they serve Him from love.

The encouragement of people to serve God out of fear is a tragic necessity born of the nature of man who "only does those actions which will either bring him advantage, or ward off loss. All other actions, he holds vain and worthless." Maimonides, therefore, generalized an all-inclusive principle of religious and moral pedagogy: "On teaching the service of God to children, women and the generally uneducated classes, one must

[19] *Millot ha-Higayon*, chap. 14; Strauss, "Farabi's Plato," in *Louis Ginzberg Jubilee Volume*, pp. 370, 386, 387.

base it on the fear of punishments and the expectation of rewards, until their understanding is stimulated and they attain more wisdom. Then one reveals to them this deeper principle by slow stages . . . and conditions them gradually to comprehend Him and to serve Him out of love."[20]

Maimonides was, of course, on solid rabbinic ground in this doctrine. A well-known Talmudic statement emanating from the school of Abba Areka or Rav (d. 247 C.E.) expresses a similar view: "A person should engage in the performance of the Torah and the commandments, even if not for their own sake, for he may finally come to perform them for their own sake."[21]

The contribution of the love of God to moral action is twofold. It serves as an incentive toward the performance of scriptural law, which has as one of its major objectives the perfection of our ethical and moral actions. But it serves, in addition, a deeper role. For the love of God stirs in men a yearning to imitate His ways in their actions. And the qualities of divine providence then become models which inspire like actions in people. A source of unfailing guidance is thus given us, competent to help us decide any new problem which may face us in our temporal existence.

The attributes of divine providence by which we are to model our lives may be summarized, according to Maimonides, in the terms *hesed* 'loving-kindness'; *zedakah* 'righteousness'; and *mishpat* 'judgment.' *Hesed* is pure charity; it is the exercise of kindness to those who have no claim on us or in a measure beyond what they have a claim for. *Zedakah* is a service to others in time of need, inspired not by any formal commitments but by a sense of moral obligation. *Mishpat* is an application of justice, and it manifests itself in mercy or punishment. To one who recognizes these virtues as the transcendent qualities of the universe, who can delineate their imprint in the rhythms of cosmic life, and sees them as the distinctive attributes of God's way with His creatures, they become ideals by which to govern one's own life.

These three attributes are only a condensation of the thirteen attributes God revealed to Moses when he had asked to know His ways. These attributes were cited, taught Maimonides, because

> they are required for the good government of a country; for the chief aim of man should be to make himself as far as possible, similar to God; that is to say, to make his acts similar to the acts of God, or as our sages expressed it in explaining the verse, "Ye shall be holy": He is gracious, so be you gracious; He is merciful, so be you also merciful.

[20] *Mishne Torah*, Teshubah 10: 1, 5; *Commentary on Mishnah*, Introduction to Helek.

[21] Sotah 22b.

And it was for this reason that Moses wanted to know God's ways. He was motivated by his need to govern the Israelites and for the government he wanted to have God's ways as a model to emulate.[22]

Maimonides invoked the principle of "the imitation of God" as a basis for many of his fine moral pronouncements, at times even modifying the basis of the classic law in the Talmud. The rule to help needy non-Jewish residents within a Jewish community is Talmudic, but there it is recommended for reasons of good public relations, being part "of the ways of peace," a reason of expediency in other words. Maimonides ignored the Talmudic motivation and grounded the law instead on the universality of God's mercy.[23]

Perhaps the most touching application of this principle appears in his treatment of the laws of slavery:

> The law permits subjecting a Canaanite slave to hard work. But though the law allows it, it is a mark of saintliness and of the ways of wisdom for a person to be merciful, and to pursue righteousness, and not impose upon him [the slave] a severe yoke, nor to oppress him. . . . And he is not to abuse him with the hand or with words. And he must avoid shouting or displaying anger to him, but speak to him gently and listen to his grievances. And thus it is written concerning the noble ways of Job (Job 31:13-15) in which he took pride: "Have I ever despised the cause of my man-servant or my maid-servant when they contended with me? Did not He who formed me in the womb form him also, and did not One fashion us in the womb?" . . . And thus it is said concerning the attributes of God which we are summoned to emulate: "His mercies are over all His works."[24]

How do the fear of God and the love of God arise in a person? The fear of God arises as a result of the performance of the divine commandments, and, in general, from meticulous attention to the traditional patterns of piety and the literal study of Scripture. It is this kind of piety which is fostered by the fear of God, and, in turn, this type of piety deepens the fear of God in the course of its exercise. The love of God is attained only through the recognition of the wisdom of God's creation, which becomes apparent through the study of science and philosophy, and through the philosophic study of Scripture. Speculative studies inspire this love, but

[22] *Guide*, Book I, chap. 54; Book III, chap. 53.

[23] Gittin 61a. In *Mishne Torah*, Mattenot Aniyim 7 : 7, Abodah Zarah 10 : 5, Abel 14 : 12, Maimonides gives us the standard law and he follows the Talmudic reasoning, basing it on "the ways of peace." In Melakim 10 : 12 he also repeats the Talmudic law, basing it on "the ways of peace," but he proceeds with a personal reaction in which he cites (Ps. 145 : 9): "The Lord is good to all and His mercies are over all His works."

[24] *Mishne Torah*, Abadim 9 : 8.

in turn the love of God inspires further study. Indeed, the command to love God is fulfilled only in the course of intellectual pursuits, in the realms of science and metaphysics. As Maimonides expressed it:

> Fear of God is inculcated when we act in accordance with the positive and negative precepts. But the truths which the Law teaches us—the knowledge of God's existence and unity—create in us love of God. . . . The two objects, love and fear of God, are acquired by two different means. The love is the result of the truths taught in the Law, including the true knowledge of the existence of God; whilst fear of God is produced by the practices prescribed in the Law.

Maimonides speaks of the knowledge which leads to God's love as "the truths which the Law teaches us." Obviously he cannot refer here to those truths which are apparent on the literal reading of the biblical text. Those who derive their truths from the literal text cannot possibly attain "the true knowledge of the existence of God."

In the famous simile coined by Maimonides to describe those who fail to enter the palace where the divine King is, he includes the adherents of a traditional piety rooted in the literal teachings of Scripture:

> Those who arrive at the palace, but go round about it are those who devote themselves exclusively to the study of the practical law; they believe traditionally in true principles of faith, and learn the practical worship of God, but are not trained in philosophical treatment of the principles of the Law, and do not endeavor to establish the truth of their faith by proof. . . .
>
> Only those who have succeeded in finding a proof for everything that can be proved, who have a true knowledge of God . . . they have reached the goal and are in the palace in which the King lives.

Maimonides distinguished two kinds of studies in the Torah, the study based on tradition, which aims at practice, at the knowledge of law and ritual, and the philosophical study. The latter he called "the knowledge of the Torah in accordance with the truth" (*hokmat ha-Torah al ha-emet*). The law which teaches us "a true knowledge of the existence of God" is the Law that has been studied philosophically, in accordance with "the truth," to use the Maimonidean term.

The love of God and the knowledge on which it is based cannot be attained without the work of reason. But neither is it attainable by reason alone. It rests on a twofold foundation, on reason as well as on revelation. The philosopher is not born a philosopher. Long before he attains the height of his intellectual powers he needs a faith to live by. He can find it only in Scripture, where he is offered the basic principles of knowledge concerning God in a kind of dogmatic affirmation. Thc rationalizations of these affirmations can wait for a later hour. But the basic knowledge which they offer is one of life's pressing necessities. The philosopher, being a citizen of the world before he becomes a philosopher, cannot do without them.

But even after he becomes a philosopher, he still needs the distinctive contribution which Scripture has to offer. There are powers of vision vouchsafed to the prophet in his moments of illumination which go beyond the powers of logical reasoning. The belief in a created universe, with its crucial implications concerning God's freedom to act outside the chain of natural causation, is a contribution of revelation. Reason stands helpless before this momentous question. Only the prophetic word, only Scripture, can proclaim this vital doctrine.

The philosophic content of religion moreover, according to Maimonides, was to be found in Scripture itself. It was to be found if one approached Scripture with the necessary skill of interpretation, looking for the hidden meaning of the text rather than its literal formulations. One of the great purposes of the *Guide for the Perplexed* was to offer such a key to what we may call a philosophic interpretation of the Bible, to save it from the errors of literalism.

The content of revealed religion itself as embodied in Scripture is an inspiration or a creation of God, and as such illustrates His providence, as do the phenomena of the natural order. Maimonides called attention to many striking parallels between the law as embodied in the phenomena of nature and the law of the Torah. Our quest for the knowledge of God's providence must, therefore, include a study of Scripture, in its deepest meaning.

The inclusion of the Torah among the wonders of God's creations whose study is to lead us to loving Him appears explicitly in the Maimonidean formulation of the third Positive Commandment in the *Sefer ha-Mitzvot.* The duty to love God, he explains, includes the call "to contemplate His commandments, and His utterances, and His works till we comprehend Him and feel utmost delight in our comprehension of Him, and this is the love concerning which we are obligated."

The two types of piety here recognized by Maimonides are in a certain sense sequentially related to each other. The simplest piety develops first in a man. In itself it is imperfect but it is a step toward the more perfect piety which arises later on.

The religious acts prescribed in the Law, as the various kinds of worship and the moral principles which benefit all people in their social intercourse with each other, do not constitute the ultimate aim of man, nor can they be compared to it, for they are but preparations leading to it.

And what is the ultimate aim of man? Maimonides is equally clear on this subject:

The perfection, in which man can truly glory, is attained by him when he has acquired—as far as this is possible by man—the knowledge of God, the knowledge of His providence, and the manner in which it influences His creatures in their production and continued existence. Having acquired this knowledge, he will then be determined always to seek loving-kindness, judgment, and righteousness, and thus to imitate the ways of God.[25]

Maimonides speaks occasionally of proficiency in moral principles as "wisdom." The prudent man who avoids all extremes, and orders his life by the golden mean, is a *hakam* 'wise man.' He likewise applies the term "wise men" to those who are skilled in the arts of government: "The wise men of the peoples of antiquity made rules and regulations, according to their various degrees of perfection, for the government of their subjects." We have already noted that Maimonides described non-Jews practicing the seven Noahide laws from purely rational considerations as "of their wise men." Only those who recognize these laws as resting on a divine revelation qualify for the designation *haside umos ha-olam* 'pious men among the nations.'

It is necessary to qualify the Maimonidean use of the term "wisdom" to cover proficiency in moral principles. The term *hokmah* 'wisdom' is for Maimonides a homonym. Its primary meaning is "the knowledge of those truths which lead to the knowledge of God." But it is also used, Maimonides indicated, to denote "knowledge of any workmanship"; "good moral principles"; and "cunning and subtlety." The designation of a knowledge of moral principles as "wisdom" is thus only a secondary use of the term. It is an inferior kind of wisdom. In its primary sense the term "wisdom" would not apply here. For the knowledge of morals is outside the scope of speculative reason, whose achievements alone lead to true wisdom.

A person who attains the highest knowledge of God is a *hakam* 'wise man' in the original and primary meaning of that term. But since the knowledge of God, in its fullest unfolding, draws a man to imitate God's actions, the higher "wisdom" therefore covers moral perfection as well. As Maimonides put it: "A *hakam* is a person who has attained perfection

[25] *Guide*, Introduction; Book I, chaps. 31-36, 65; Book III, chaps. 32, 34; Book III, chaps. 51, 54; *Sefer ha-Mitzvot*, Positive Commandment 3. The *Sefer ha-Mitzvot*, as a popular work, clothes his position in a more traditional form, in which the emphasis appears to fall on the study of Scripture, rather than of nature. But both realms of study are really included in his formula.

in both types of virtue [the intellectual and the moral] as is necessary."

Wisdom, in this sense, is not attainable by philosophy alone, for philosophy alone cannot tell us all that we need to know about God and the world and man's destiny within it. Nor is it attainable by mastering the simple faith of traditional religion. Wisdom is attainable only through a religion that has lifted its doctrines to full intellectual clarity and made them consistent with the demands of reason. In the words of Maimonides: "The knowledge of the Law (Torah) and the acquisition of true wisdom (*hokmah*) . . . are two different things; real wisdom demonstrates by proof what Scripture teaches us by way of tradition."[26]

Maimonides, we have noted, distinguishes two levels in man's response to God's existence, fear and love. But these emotions in turn are divisible into lower and higher levels. Fear exists on a higher level, as awe before the grandeur of God and the sense of insignificance which one feels in His presence. As such it is indistinguishable in quality from the love of God. Love, on the other hand, exists as well on a lower level, as a return for benefits received and benefits anticipated. Being pragmatic in its motivation, it is of the nature of the fear of God which has been branded as an inferior piety.

In the *Sefer ha-Mitzvot* which Maimonides wrote for the uneducated classes, he defined the fear of God, we have seen previously, as the fear of His punishments. In the *Mishne Torah* which he wrote for those who had attained a higher measure of intellectual and spiritual perfection, he demanded the higher fear. It is clear, too, from his discussion in this instance that on their highest levels fear and love are closely related. As he explains in the *Book of Knowledge*:

We are obligated to love and fear the exalted and awesome God, as it is written (Deut. 6:5), "And Thou shalt love the Lord thy God" and (Deut. 6:13) "Thou shalt fear thy God." And which is the right way of loving Him and fearing Him? At the time when one reflects on His works and His wonderful and stupendous creations, and from them perceives His wisdom which is incomparable and unbounded, he immediately loves, praises, glorifies and yearns with

[26] *Guide*, Book III, chap. 54; *Mishne Torah*, Deot 1: 4, Melakim 8: 11; *Millot ha-Higayon*, chap. 14; *Guide*, Book III, chap. 54; *Commentary on Mishnah* 5: 7. The printed editions of the *Mishne Torah* read *velo Mehakhomehem* instead of *ela mehakhomehem* in Melakim 8: 11. According to this, Maimonides would exclude those observing the Noahide laws because of rational considerations from the category of "wise men." While this reading is supported by the earliest editions (Rome, 1480; Soncino, 1490; Constantinople, 1509; Venice, 1550, 1574), three different recensions of *Mishne Torah* manuscripts, in possession of the Jewish Theological Seminary Library, E. N. Adler (Spanish), Schiff (Yemenite), Rabinowitz (Franco-German), read *ela mehakhomehem.* Responsum 117 of Rabbi Moses Alashkar (1466-1542) cites this passage of Maimonides and the reading here parallels that of the manuscripts.

an ardent longing to know the great God. . . . And when one reflects upon these very things he immediately recoils, is struck with fear and terror, and is overcome with the realization that he is a creature, insignificant, lowly and immature, standing with only slight and scanty knowledge. As David said (Ps. 8:4-5): "When I consider Thy heavens, the work of Thy fingers, what is man that Thou art mindful of him?"[27]

The fear of God, on its lowest level, was recognized by Maimonides as an independent category of piety, suitable as a preliminary stage in a person's intellectual growth. But the lower level of love is not considered by him at all. It is simply a phase of the lower fear. The element which both have in common is that they are self-centered and pragmatically motivated, and therefore of identical status. He expressed this opinion explicitly: "He who serves out of love engages in the study of the Torah and in the performance of the commandments and in the pursuits of wisdom for no ulterior considerations, not out of fear of evil that may befall nor because of the anticipation of benefits."[28]

In the Babylonian Talmud the lower levels of fear and love are both treated independently. In the well-known citation of the seven varieties of Pharisaism, the list concludes with "the Pharisee from love" and "the Pharisee from fear." The five preceding types of Pharisees are clearly objectionable. They are ostentatious, insincere, fanatical, and self-righteous. The Babylonian Talmud looks upon the last two types as also objectionable, which obviously suggests that the love here was understood to be an inferior love, a love of rewards, in other words.[29]

The same citation appears in the Palestinian Talmud, but here the order of the last two types of Pharisaism is reversed: fear precedes love. And the Palestinian Talmud proceeds to define love as the genuine love for God, such as was exemplified by the patriarch Abraham. The Palestinian text is clearly based on the sounder tradition, because it is not likely that the rabbis would offer us a list of various types of Pharisaism, all of them objectionable. They recognized the possibility that the Pharisaic ideal might be distorted, but the Pharisaic ideal itself was to them a lofty one. The Palestinian version is plausible because after listing types of spurious piety in Pharisaism, it moves to the final climax of listing a Pharisaism which is embodied in a genuine piety, beginning with fear, and ending with the most perfect, love.[30] Maimonides ignored the

[27] *Mishne Torah*, Yesode ha-Torah 2:1, 2. On the difference between the *Sefer ha-Mitzvot* and the *Mishne Torah*, see Bokser, *The Legacy of Maimonides*, p. 112, n. 6.

[28] *Mishne Torah*, Teshubah 10: 2.

[29] Sotah 22b.

'Berakot IX, 14b, bottom, and Sotah V, 20c, bottom.

Babylonian version of this citation and followed the tradition of the Palestinian Talmud.[31]

The quest for a criterion as well as a sanction for moral action has involved us in a discussion of some of the basic issues in the theology of Maimonides. For to Maimonides, moral philosophy is only a phase of a religious philosophy. And the ultimate source of our moral demands is in the will of God. The laws governing our relations to God must therefore be judged as also having a moral significance. In the words of Maimonides: "For these are called laws concerning man's relation to God, although in reality they lead to results which concern also his fellow-men; because these results become only apparent after a long series of intermediate links, and from a general point of view."[32] And to the extent that a man relates himself to God, all other assets of the spiritual life are given to him as well. Not the least of these is the answer to his need for moral guidance. No other source of guidance is available to a spiritually mature person.

[31] *Commentary on Mishnah*, Sotah 3 : 2.
[32] *Guide*, Book III, chap. 36.

AN AMERICAN JEW AT THE PARIS PEACE CONFERENCE OF 1919

EXCERPTS FROM THE DIARY OF OSCAR S. STRAUS

By Naomi W. Cohen

THE GREAT AND last generation of American Jewish *shtadlanim* was that of Jacob H. Schiff, Mayer Sulzberger, Oscar S. Straus, and Louis Marshall. Not until that generation passed on did American Jewry's concern for its coreligionists abroad become principally the depersonalized function of national Jewish organizations. A study of the Oscar Straus Papers[1] casts light on the aims and techniques of those stewards of the American Jewish community who, at the end of the nineteenth and beginning of the twentieth century, used their political, economic, and social influence to end persecution and discrimination.

The first reaction to crises on the part of the small group of prominent American Jews usually took the form of pressure upon the President, State Department, and American diplomats for official and unofficial remonstrances.[2] They also maintained direct contact with ranking European Jews, whose cooperation was sought in influencing their

[1] The Straus Papers in the Library of Congress were studied in connection with this writer's doctoral dissertation, "The Public Career of Oscar S. Straus" (Columbia University, 1955). Permission to publish these excerpts has been kindly granted by Mr. Roger W. Straus.

[2] The Straus Papers are especially illuminating on the pressure brought to bear on behalf of Russian Jewry during the 1890's and the first decade of the twentieth century. The administrations concerned were those of Presidents Harrison, Cleveland, and Theodore Roosevelt. Roosevelt and Secretary of State John Hay were also alerted in 1902 in the interests of Rumanian Jewry. To list the letters in the Straus Papers relating to this phase of American Jewish diplomacy would necessitate scores of entries. Parts of correspondence and incidents were published in: 51 Cong., 1 Sess., House Ex. Doc. No. 470; Oscar S. Straus, *Under Four Administrations* (Boston, 1922), pp. 106-8, 168-69, 171-73, 179-80; Tyler Dennett, *John Hay* (New York, 1933), pp. 396-99; Cyrus Adler, *Jacob H.Schiff* (2 vols., New York, 1929), II, 117-18, 120-21, 136-39, 153-54, 157-59; E. E. Morison, ed., *The Letters of Theodore Roosevelt* (8 vols., Cambridge, 1951-54), III, 508, 517, 518; V, 112-13, 207-8; Simon Wolf, *The Presidents I Have Known* (Washington, 1918), pp. 191-98, 202-8; Max J. Kohler and Simon Wolf "Jewish Disabilities in the Balkan States," *PAJHS*, XXIV (1916), 108-14.

respective governments.[3] When necessary, the American Jews organized relief committees for victims of persecutions and raised huge sums in their behalf.[4] Where feasible, they applied financial pressure on the anti-Jewish government[5] and aroused public opinion against the offender.[6] Singly or in very small groups, they worked discreetly and cautiously, because they feared the effects of mass agitation and public demonstrations on the part of Jews.[7] As a contemporary editorial pointed out, these individual leaders took it upon themselves to represent the Jewish people and to act for Jewish interests as they interpreted them; and this approach indicated the persistence of medieval practices in modern Jewish life.[8]

Among the *shtadlanim* of his generation, Oscar Straus held a unique position. Not only did he serve three times as American envoy to Turkey,[9] but he was also the first Jew to hold a cabinet post in the United States.[10] Known widely in American and European circles, he used his

[3] Baron Maurice de Hirsch was their key contact in Europe until his death in 1896 English Jews whose cooperation with the Americans is also revealed in the Straus Papers were Sir Julian Goldsmid, N. S. Joseph, F. D. Mocatta, Samuel Montagu, Lord Nathan Rothschild, Lucien Wolf, Sir Herbert Samuel.

[4] Especially noteworthy were the relief committees for the victims of the Kishinev (1903) and Odessa (1905) pogroms. Cyrus Adler, *I Have Considered the Days* (Philadelphia, 1945), p. 246; Adler, *Schiff*, II, 117, 133; *American Hebrew*, November 10, 1905, November 17, 1905, December 8, 1905. Relief and rehabilitation of those Russian Jews who immigrated to the United States were provided by the Baron de Hirsch Fund, organized in 1890 by the leaders of American Jewry; Samuel Joseph, *History of the Baron de Hirsch Fund* (n.p., 1935), chap. 1.

[5] Adler, *Schiff*, II, 122-28, 133, 140-43; Philip Cowen, *Memories of an American Jew* (New York, 1932), pp. 286-88; Straus to Samuel Montagu, April 9, 1906, April 11, 1906 (Straus Papers).

[6] One such project arose in 1891 when several Americans helped finance the trip to Russia by Harold Frederic, correspondent of the New York *Times*. Straus to Harold Frederic, June 30, 1891 (Straus Papers). Frederic's sympathetic articles on Russian Jewry were subsequently published as *The New Exodus* (New York, 1892). Oscar Straus personally endeavored to crush the long-standing myth of Russian friendship with the United States in newspaper and magazine articles. New York *Sun*, November 3, 1891; New York *Times*, May 20, 1903, February 14, 1904, February 25, 1904; "The United States and Russia: Their Historical Relations," *North American Review*, CLXXXI (August, 1905), 237-50. See also Thomas A. Bailey, *America Faces Russia* (Ithaca, 1950), pp. 126, 184, 192.

[7] Straus to Sir Julian Goldsmid, December 2, 1890; to Mayer Sulzberger, December 25, 1890; to Lucius N. Littauer [July 7, 1902] (Straus Papers).

[8] *American Hebrew*, August 18, 1905.

[9] 1887-89, under Grover Cleveland; 1898-99, under William McKinley; 1909-10, under William Howard Taft. Straus, *Under Four Administrations*, chaps. 3, 4, 6, 11.

[10] Secretary of Commerce and Labor under Theodore Roosevelt, 1906-9. Straus, *Under Four Administrations*, chaps. 9-10.

contacts repeatedly in behalf of Jewish rights. This vantage point, which led to numerous successes, helped convince Straus of the efficacy of American Jewish diplomacy conducted by the ranking few. In 1906, when plans were made for the organization of the American Jewish Committee, Straus opposed a broad democratization of the base of leadership, and he even objected to the restraints on individual pressure which membership on a small committee imposed.[11] Again, during World War I, he feared the organization of an American Jewish Congress, which he saw fraught with the evils of reckless and indiscriminate agitation.[12]

Though compromising in the end with the formation of the Congress,[13] Straus did not serve on any official Jewish delegation to the Peace Conference. He went to Paris as chairman of a committee to the League to Enforce Peace, an influential organization in the United States which had striven since its inception in 1915 to gain public approval for a league of nation.[14] While working at the Conference principally for the adoption of President Wilson's plan for a league of nations, Straus was drawn, nevertheless, into discussions concerning the questions of Zionism, Jewish nationalism, and anti-Jewish persecutions. The following excerpts from his diary are records of these discussions; they reflect Straus's approach and that of some of his contemporaries to current Jewish issues. The documents show, too, the pattern of the *shtadlan*, who, without organizational backing, joined with American and foreign Jewish leaders in weighing the merits of political Zionism and took it upon himself to oppose national Jewish rights to Secretary of State Robert Lansing. The most striking examples of unofficial diplomacy were the conversations about persecutions in Czechoslovakia and Poland, where Straus took a leading part in handling the incidents quietly, in small meetings, by the use of direct pressure.

Luncheon at the Crillion [*sic*] with Secretary of State Robert Lansing in his private suite.

Feb. 27: Lansing's secretary phoned me the day before, inviting me to

[11] *American Hebrew*, May 25, 1906; Straus to Mayer Sulzberger, May 24, 1906 (Straus Papers); Nathan Schachner, *The Price of Liberty* (New York, 1948), pp. 12-18, 24-26.

[12] *American Hebrew*, March 17, 1916, July 21, 1916, November 17, 1916.

[13] He served on the administrative committee which arranged for the Congress. *American Hebrew*, December 29, 1916.

[14] Ruhl J. Bartlett, *The League to Enforce Peace* (Chapel Hill, 1944), chaps. 3-4.

lunch with him today, which I did in his official suite at the Crillon.[15]

We had a very pleasant chat of about an hour and half. . . .

He did not seem to have been conversant or informed of the various stages of discussion regarding the articles of the covenant. I referred to the entire omission of the section respecting Civil and Religious Liberty which was contained in Article XIX of the tentative draft but which was finally omitted in the final draft because Japan desired the race question to be included. . . .[16]

I suggested this subject which was in fact a Bill of Rights should be incorporated in the treaty which would doubtless be made with each of the new nations fixing their territorial boundaries etc. by the League. He agreed with me it was wise to do this and to do it in just that way.[17]

He then spoke about the Zionist delegation which would appear before [him] that afternoon. Saying he was entirely openminded upon that subject. He was in favor of recognizing Jewish Nationality so that the Jews would not be troubled with dual allegiance. I told him while not a Zionist I had always been in favor of a free Palestine where all should have equal civil & political rights.[18] That I was opposed to dual nationality and to any nationality that might in any way cast a cloud upon my American nationality. He said of course it could have no reference to such men as I was, only to such Jews as resided in countries like Russia and Roumania. I said but it would not exist there but for proscription on account of race or creed or both, and with guaranteed freedom & equal rights in such lands there was no room or occasion for divided allegiances which had the same effect upon all oppressed peoples who had an historical past or nationality.

He favored my going to London to attend the League of Nations of the several nations. I told him about my bringing up the Civil and Religious Bill of Rights clause.[19] He also said he hoped I would remain in Paris until

[15] Lansing's diary for February 27, 1919, has but a brief reference to the discussion with Straus (Robert Lansing Papers, Library of Congress).

[16] See David Hunter Miller, *The Drafting of the Covenant* (2 vols., New York, 1928), I, 269; II, 323-25.

[17] This part of the discussion was reproduced by Straus in *Under Four Administrations*, pp. 412-13.

[18] Straus had expressed similar views in a letter to Max J. Kohler, November 9, 1918 (Max J. Kohler Collection, American Jewish Historical Society), and in a conversation with Herbert Samuel of England. Straus, *Under Four Administrations*, p. 399.

[19] At the meeting of the league of nations societies held in March, Straus submitted a religious liberty amendment to the covenant which was adopted by the delegates. Though President Wilson had originally favored such a clause, he later told Straus that he sought to achieve the same end by different means. Straus was satisfied when provisions for religious liberty were included in the treaties with the new nations.

the end of the Conference as I could be of great service. He thank[ed] me for the suggestions I had made etc.

Mrch 8th Mr Sokolow the well known British Zionist[20] called on me and we had a long chat. I told him about my talk with Weisman [*sic*] a few nights ago when he dined with me and his extreme views which played in[to] the hands of the antisemites instead of being an aid to the Zionists. He S did not agree with W. nor did he seem to have a high appreciation of him.[21]

Persecution of Jews threatened in Prague and in Czecho-Slovakia

Mrch 25. 4 P.M. A meeting was arranged at my apartment with the Premier Kramzh[22] and the Minister to France M. Benes[23] with our committee consisting of Judge Julian W. Mack, Felix Frankfurter, Aaron Aaronson [*sic*] the Agricultural expert of Palestine,[24] my young friend Louis [*sic*] Strauss,[25] the confidential Secretary of Hoover, and myself. The gentlemen all arrived except the Premier who as M. Benes explained was prevented because of an official committee meeting.

Louis Strauss had received two letters from Prague of the 16th inst from two of the Food Administration officials, both Jews, who reported that a press propaganda was carried on against Jews and that several attacks had been made, that 60 Jews were arrested in the Synagogue on Purim and they were about being expelled and sent to Pressburg the hot bed of the Bolshevists at present. I presented the matter to M. Benes, pointing out if pogroms occurred which the reports foreshadowed it would seriously prejudice his country and would alienate American sympathy and discontinue the food shipment. I told him of my coopera-

---

Straus to Wilson, March 24, 1919; Wilson to Straus, March 25, 1919 (Straus Papers); Straus, *Under Four Administrations*, pp. 414-17; *American Hebrew*, May 30, 1919.

[20] Nahum Sokolow was in Paris as a representative of the World Zionist Organization. He had met Straus first in 1887, when the latter was on his way to Constantinople. N. Sokolow, *Ishim* (Hebrew, 3 vols., Tel Aviv, 1935), I, 158-59.

[21] Chaim Weizmann had joined Sokolow in Paris to represent the Zionist Organization before the Council of Ten on February 27. Weizmann for his part considered Sokolow a perpetual compromiser. Chaim Weizmann, *Trial and Error* (2 vols., Philadelphia, 1949), I, 79, 85, 87, 243.

[22] Straus's spelling is unclear here. The Premier was Charles Kramar (or Kramarsh).

[23] Eduard Benes was the foreign minister of the new Czechoslovakian republic.

[24] Mack was president of the Zionist Organization of America and of the American Jewish Congress. He headed the delegation of the latter organization to Paris. Frankfurter served on the American Zionist delegation. Aaronsohn performed diplomatic missions for the Zionists after the war.

[25] Lewis L. Strauss.

tion with their President Prof Masaryk and the Mid-European Union[26] while in America; that I and others were attracted to Prof. M. because of his well known tolerance and liberal views, as it was remembered that Prof M. at great personal sacrifice had espoused the defence of Beilis [Hilsner?][27] in the notorious blood accusation persecution. Prof. Benes stated he was a disciple of Masaryk and always shared his social and political views. That his people had never persecuted the Jews, but he also appreciated that in these troubled times with the press propaganda referred to, pogroms might result. We pointed out that even a paper controlled by the Premier had articles against Jews and we read him abstracts from the letters referred to. M. Benes suggested he would at once telegraph President Masaryk and see that the anti-Semitic agitation is stopped—and he was sure President M. would take every precaution in accordance with his well known liberal and just policy. As this is precisely what we desired done, we expressed our satisfaction. Prof B. made a good impression upon us, as an upright and fair minded man, sincere in his desire to check any such agitation and thanked us for bringing the matter to his notice.[28]

Dinner with Baron Edmond de Rothschild

Mrch 29th Dined with Baron & Baroness Edmond de Rothschild at their beautiful residence, next to the British Embassy, 41 Faubourg St Honore, there were present Major James de Rothschild & his wife the elder son, Judge Julian Mack, Felix Frankfurter, Howard Gans, Bernard Flexner,[29] all ardent Zionists, and a daughter of the Baron & Baroness.

[26] The Mid-European Democratic Union was established through Masaryk's initiative in September, 1918, in the United States to provide information for the American public and guidance for its member nations. Paul Selver, *Masaryk* (London, 1940), pp. 284-85.

[27] In public statements and essays Masaryk had defended Hilsner, who in 1899 had been tried for the ritual murder of a Christian woman. Masaryk's stand had subjected him to criticism and attacks for several years. In 1913 Masaryk also spoke against the ritual murder charge preferred against Beilis. E. Rychnovsky, ed., *Thomas G. Masaryk and the Jews*, translated by Benjamin R. Epstein (New York, 1941), pp. 10-20, 149-51, 196-234, 253-57.

[28] Straus's account of the interview with Benes in *Under Four Administrations* (pp. 418-19) attributes to *Benes* the statement that pogroms would alienate American sympathy from Czechoslovakia and result in cutting off food shipments.

A few weeks later an official despatch from Prague quoted Masaryk as denying the reports of Jewish persecution. It also reported that a Jewish delegation from Prague went to Paris and explained the whole situation to Straus. *American Hebrew*, April 25, 1919. On further developments in Czechoslovakia and Masaryk's defense of the Jews see *AJYB*, XXI (1919-20), 241.

[29] Gans and Flexner were also members of the American Zionist delegation.

... The Baron is a thoroughly idealistic and fine type of a cultured gentleman. ... The Baron expressed himself as violently opposed to the extreme nationalist Zionists of the Weisman [*sic*] type, but entirely in accord with the moderates who seek a Palestine with equal rights under British protection. He said he was in hearty accord with that form of Zionism which is calculated to give greater protection for Jews outside as well as inside of Palestine. He called my attention why the Catholics and their press in France were opposed to President Wilson, because, he said, they were opposed to him a Protestant becoming the chief world peace make[r] a roll [*sic*] the Catholics claimed was the traditional prerogative of the Pope.

The son, Baron James, raised a Jewish brigade in Palestine from where he only returned two weeks ago.[30] He spoke in highest praise of General Allenby the conquerer of Palestine as a man of exceptional ability and learning combined with the qualities of an excellent officer.

The father spoke with pride of his son, who said did not like banking but devotes himself to Jewish matters. The Major said he was a Zionist. His advocacy combined with the prestige of his name and leading a part of the victorious forces, certainly is a most valuable asset for the cause. He impressed me very favorably as a man of poise and capacity. He is about 35, tall and strong in appearance with a manly and earnest face and manner.

Jewish Rights and Zionism

With a view of clarification and bringing together the American representatives of Zionism, and of Jewish rights and Mr. Lucien Wolf representing the British Jews, we had to dinner on Mrch 31. Lucien Wolf representing the Anglo-Jewish & other moderate groups, Judge Julian Mack, Louis Marshall, Cyrus Adler,[31] Aaron Aronson [*sic*] of Palestine, Prof Felix Frankfurter, Mr Charles A. Selden the Correspondent of the N.Y. Times and Mr. Louis [*sic*] Strauss of the Food Commission. There was a frank interchange of opinion and there did not seem to be any material difference between the Zionists and non Zionists re Palestine, all agreed to a free Palestine under the mandate of Great Britain was

[30] Cf. Vladimir Jabotinsky, *The Story of the Jewish Legion*, translated by Samuel Katz (New York, 1925), pp. 52, 114, 116.

[31] Louis Marshall was vice-president of the American Jewish Congress and a leading figure in the negotiations of the American delegation at Paris with European Jews. Though he was simultaneously the president of the American Jewish Committee, that organization appointed Cyrus Adler, chairman of the executive committee, as its special representative in Paris.

desirable with equal civil & political rights. It was agreed this did [not] preclude the formation of an industrial corporation composed of Jews for the purpose of acquiring lands now unoccupied or formerly held by the Sultan as as [*sic*] Crown lands, and preparing it by irrigation etc so as to make it suitable for colonization by Jewish immigrants. This did not preclude Arabs or others from seeking like concessions on similar terms for like purposes, however improbable it might be that other groups would seek or desire such concessions because of the fact that Palestine had no such historical and religious attraction for other groups for cultivation & colonization.

It seems to me the Zionists have made unnecessary opposition for themselves by emphasizing the vague terms of "Nationalism" and "National Homeland"—besides anticipating a distant future when Palestine instead of being as now 6/7th nonJewish, might become 9/10th Jewish or might in some distant future become entirely independent. Which contingencies would naturally alter the political status of Palestine and rightly so. The emphasizing what that status should or should not be at this time is not only unwise and highly impolite but raises dissension and bitter controversy among the Jews as well as creates opposition from Christians and Mohammedans. The extreme Zionists of the Weiseman [*sic*] & others of like type in America are responsible for this unfortunate condition which is calculated to create enmities, raise obstacles if not defeat the very purposes in view and prevent the concrete application of the very broad & liberal provisions under the Balfour Declaration. The Jewry of the World by this unwise course have been needlessly split wide & rancorously apart under the leadership of men who mistake their sectarian or group outlook for a national vision, predicated upon denying those rights, civil political and religious, to other groups in their new state, the denial of which has caused so much suffering and martyrdom for the Jews of the world for twenty centuries and more.[32]

Dr. Casimir Dluski one of the two Polish Delegates to the Conference Dines with us. April 8

I met Dluski recently at a reception given by Mr & Mrs Jean Finot the editor & proprietor of La Revieu [*sic*].[33] We had quite a talk about

[32] During the twenties Straus became more sympathetic to the idea of a national Jewish homeland in Palestine. *Augusta Chronicle*, March 14, 1921; *New Palestine*, October 5, 1932. The question of equal rights for all inhabitants had been disposed of to his satisfaction by the mandate. *American Hebrew*, April 30, 1920.

[33] *La Revue*.

Poland and the rights of the large Jewish population. He said he wanted to call on me and talk over the matter. He subsequently sent me several brochures written by Jews—doubtless with the purpose as appeared to me on reading them—to ingratiate themselves with the powers that be at the expense of the general welfare of their coreligionists.

He came to dine with me, Louis Marshall was also present also my young friend Lewis Strauss, who had several recent reports, the latest of Mrch 16th regarding Jewish oppression and anti-semitism in Poland.[34]

Dluski stated he had just left Paderewski, the Premier, recently arrived in Paris, who wanted to be cordially remembered and desired very much in the course of the next few days to meet and confer with me following our very pleasant conferences before his leaving New York.[35]

Dluski a physician by profession is the counterpart of his colleague Dmoski [*sic*] in the Peace Conference, and a much broader and fair minded man—not an avowed anti-semite like Dmoski, and who recognizes the necessity of giving the 3 or more million Jews their fullest religious and political rights.

I read to him abstracts from the report of H. N. Brailsford of Mrch 16th which the Food Commission had received from the British. It described the oppressive conditions of the Jews and their unjust treatment by Polish officials. These passages I read in English and Sarah[36] translated them in French. Dluski expressed his strong disapproval but said allowances must be made for the present war conditions in which Poland was in against some of the neighbors the Ukrainians and with Bolshevism. He said there had never before in Poland's long history been any pogroms, on the contrary he knew the Poles during the Russian dominations had at the risk of their lives shielded the Jews again and again. We then discussed the rights the Jews must have, Mr Marshall went fully into the subject

[34] The persecution of the Jews in Poland after the war is summarized in 66 Cong. 2 Sess., Sen. Doc. No. 177, *Mission of the United States to Poland* (Washington, 1920), pp. 4-12.

[35] On November 11, 1918, Marshall, Mack, Straus, and several others had met with Paderewski and Roman Dmowski in New York. The American Jews argued for the lifting of the anti-Jewish boycott, promising in return to urge Polish Jews in Poland and the United States to support the nationalist aspirations of the Poles. Marshall also submitted a draft of civil and religious rights to be incorporated into a constitution for new Poland. Straus Papers: Box 24, Random Notes, pp. 82-86. There is a striking similarity between Marshall's draft and the bill of rights drawn up by the American Jewish Congress in December, 1918. Oscar I. Janowsky, *The Jews and Minority Rights* (New York, 1933), pp. 266-67. On conferences of American Jews with Polish leaders see *Report of Proceedings of the American Jewish Congress*, December, 1918, pp. 27-30

[36] Mrs. Oscar S. Straus.

detailing his conferences with Dmoski in New York and the latter's attitude regarding the boycott which he D confessed with pride of having instituted. Dluski spoke disparaging[ly] of Dmoski whose views in this and in other regards neither he or Paderewski shared.

May 27th[37]

In the afternoon Dr Dluski the Polish peace delegate together with Lieberman a Jewish member of the Polish Diet called with the purpose of trying to explain if not justify the denial of Polish pogroms, evidently because of the publicity given by the great meeting in New York[38] the resolutions of which were cable[d] in extenso to Louis Marshall and by him presented to the President.[39] I heard them and gave them intimation of my views and the nature of our authentic information. I told them they had better see Mr Marshall whom Dluski had met previously at my apartment. D. left with me a statement regarding one of these pogroms. They stated they would be glad to confer with Marshall—so I arranged through Dr Cyrus Adler for the conference.

[37] Part of the following was reproduced by Straus in *Under Four Administrations*, p. 426.

[38] See New York *Times*, May 22, 1919.

[39] The interview with Wilson is described in Adler, *I Have Considered the Days*, pp. 312-16.

THE LAFAYETTE COMMITTEE FOR JEWISH EMANCIPATION

By Abraham G. Duker

FOLLOWING THE DEBACLE of the Polish Insurrection of 1830-31, some 30,000 participants in the revolt against Russia were forced to seek shelter in Central and Western Europe. These political émigrés have been identified in Polish history as Wielka Emigracja—the Great Emigration.[1] It profoundly influenced political and literary developments at home and abroad and is still viewed as the guide and mentor by all Polish factions and movements today. During their wanderings across the Germanies and their initial stay in France, the émigrés came face to face with westernized Jews who had attained positions of importance in the political life of France. In the process of reflection and deliberation on the causes of their defeat, some of the exiles arrived at the conviction that these could be traced, at least to some extent, to their failure to involve the Jews in the

[1] The material for this article was collected in the process of preparation of my doctoral dissertation at Columbia University under the direction of Professor Baron on the subject "The Polish 'Great Emigration' and the Jews: Studies in Political and Intellectual History." Some phases were discussed in my works: "The Polish Political Émigrés in the United States and the Jews 1833-1865," *PAJHS*, XXXIX, Part 2 (1949), 143-67; "Mickiewicz and the Jewish Problem," in *Adam Mickiewicz, Poet of Poland; a Symposium*, ed. by Manfred Kridl, with a foreword by Ernest J. Simmons (Columbia Slavic Studies, New York, 1951), pp. 108-25; "Joseph Berkowicz the Towianist," in *YIVO Bleter*, XXXV (1951), 165-74; "The Tarniks (Believers in the Coming of the Messiah in 1840)," in *The Joshua Starr Memorial Volume, Studies in History and Philology* (Jewish Social Studies Publications No. 5) (New York, 1953), pp. 191-201; "Polish Émigré Christian Socialists on the Jewish Problem," *Jewish Social Studies*, XV (1952), 317-42; "Leon Hollaenderski's Statement of Resignation. A Document of the Great Polish Emigration," *Jewish Social Studies*, XV (1953) 293-302; "Jewish Volunteers in the Ottoman-Polish Cossack Units during the Crimean War," *Jewish Social Studies*, XVI (1954), 203-18, 351-76; "Hollaenderski's Letter of Inquiry to Lelewel," *Studies in Bibliography and Booklore*, I (Cincinnati, 1954), 161-66; "The Polish Political Émigrés and the Jews in 1848," in *PAAJR*, XXIV (1955), 69-102.

For a terse summary of the problem of and literature on the Great Emigration, see my "Polish Émigré Christian Socialists," *Jewish Social Studies*, Vol. XV (1952). Important new publications are M. Kukiel's *Czartoryski and European Unity 1770-1861* (Princeton, 1955), and *Wiosna ludów* (The Spring of Nations) (5 vols., Warsaw, 1948-53).

insurrection. Among the earliest efforts to remedy the situation and to initiate a campaign among the Jews for the support of the Polish cause was the well-known "Appeal to the Israelite People" of October 3, 1832, commonly but erroneously identified as the "Lelewel Appeal."[2] Practical considerations of immediate urgency led to an effort to obtain the support of the Jews in the Near East, when the conservative Committee of the Polish Emigration[3] was about to dispatch a delegation to Egypt with an offer to furnish Polish experts and soldiers to Ibrahim Pasha's army.[4] Bartłomiej Beniowski,[5] the initiator of the Appeal of October 3, was also the person to suggest the possibilities of obtaining Jewish support in the Near East. In addition, his linguistic equipment evidently qualified him to become a member of the delegation.

In order to facilitate the contacts with the Jews in Egypt and Asia, Beniowski suggested the setting up of a "front" organization that turned out to be possibly the first interdenominational and even international body for the protection of Jewish rights in the world. This organization has gone down in Polish history as the "Lafayette Committee." In its own days it was called "The Philanthropic Society for the Acceleration of

[2] The full text of the Appeal will be found in Joachim Lelewel, *Polska, dzieje, i rzeczy jej* (Poland, Her History and Affairs), XX (Poznan, 1864), 117-31; in French, in E. Carmoly, "L'État des Israélites en Pologne," *Revue Orientale*, II (1842), 418-28, and in Leon Hollaenderski, *Les Israélites de Pologne* (Paris, 1846), pp. 117-31; in English, in Rev. H. A. Henry's translation of Hollaenderski's book, "The Origin of the Jews in Poland, Their History, etc." in *Jewish Chronicle* (July 14 and 21, 1865), p. 3. Originally Lelewel objected to the publication of the Appeal. Cf. Hollaenderski, *Les Israélites de Pologne*, p. 116, and Jean Czyński, "Les Israélites de la Pologne et l'Empereur de Russie. Xme lettre," *Archives Israélites*, VI (1845), 242. My larger work on Lelewel contains additional material on this subject. I also discovered in the Rapperswyl Archives (no. 1241) a shorter text of the Appeal, as yet unpublished, marked "Felix Wrotnowski's Project." On Lelewel, see my "Hollaenderski's Letter," as in note 1.

[3] This committee (Komitet Emigracji Polskiej) was the rival of the liberal-radical Polish National Committee (Komitet Narodowy Polski), headed by Joachim Lelewel, which was disbanded in December, 1832. In turn the Committee of the Polish Emigration was also disbanded in March, 1834, following a series of unsuccessful elections. Cf. Lewak in *Polska* (as in note 8), pp. 205-6.

[4] Cf. Adam George Bemis, *Un Mission Polonaise en Egypt* (2 vols., Cairo, 1938); and Adam Lewak, *Dzieje emigracji polskiej w Turcji* (History of the Polish Emigration in Turkey) (Warsaw, 1935), pp. 28 ff.

[5] Major Beniowski was a convert to the Catholic faith. He was a member of a group of Polish officers in the Russian army who had plotted to join the insurrectionists. Beniowski went over to the Poles in the thick of the battle. Cf. Mateusz Mieses, *Polacy chrześcijanie pochodzenia żydowskiego* (Christian Poles of Jewish Descent), I (Warsaw, 1938), 18-25. In the emigration Beniowski was a poverty-stricken radical. with a vivid interest in the cause of the Polish Jews.

Jewish Emancipation throughout the World."[6] Doubtless there were also other motives for setting up this Society or, as we will refer to it, the Lafayette Committee, such as the need for an additional outlet of anti-Russian propaganda and the genuine desire on the part of some of its founders who were liberals to promote Jewish equality. It has been maintained that the immediate incentive for its establishment was the aforesaid mission to the East. This is obvious from the testimony of Ludwik Orlicki,[7] who together with Colonel August Szulc and Major Beniowski constituted the delegation to Egypt. This is also confirmed by Adam Lewak, the outstanding Polish authority on the history of the Emigration.[8] This Society has received scant attention from historians, nor is there any mention of it in the standard works on Lafayette.[9]

[6] In its own days the organization was best known by this name. However, it has been called the Lafayette Committee in modern Polish sources, because of Lafayette's presidency or chairmanship.

[7] The pertinent passage in the original unpublished report of Ludwik Orlicki, "Polacy w Egipcie w 1833 i 1834" (The Poles in Egypt in 1833 and 1834), written in Paris, September 20, 1838, MS 1050, Mickiewicz Museum in Paris, reads as follows: "Major Beniowski, being of the opinion that the Jews might be of no small help in our activity, expected that he would be able to rally them to the movement in Asia, after assuming a certain dignity in order to be able to address them more effectively. For this purpose a Committee for the Emancipation of the Jews was organized under the leadership of General Lafayette. It had as its members Marchais, Cassin, J. Czyński, Major Beniowski, myself and others. However, it turned out later that this step was completely useless, because it is impossible to start anything with this nation because it will not become enlightened and will not abandon the Talmud."

Colonel Szulc served in the Egyptian army. Cf. Lubomir Gadon, *Emigracja polska* (The Polish Emigration), III (Kraków, 1902), 99. Andre Louis-Augustin Marchais (1800-1857) was a leading *carbonaro* and republican and founder of the society "Aide-toi, le ciel t'aidera." He was involved in revolutionary activities throughout Europe. Cf. *La Grande encyclopedie. Inventaire raisonne*, Paris, XXI, 993.

As for Cassin, the reference is most probably to Eugene Cassin (1796-1844), a philanthropist known in literary circles. Cf. Larousse, *Grande dictionnaire universelle du XIX siècle*, Paris, III, 510.

[8] Lewak based his statement exclusively on the Orlicki MS. He similarly attributed the mission's failure to the political indifference of the Eastern Jews. Cf. his "The Times of the Great Emigration," in *Polska, jej dzieje i kultura od czasów najdawniejszych do chwili obecnej* (Poland, Her History and Culture from the Earliest Times until the Present Moment), III (Warsaw, 1931), 211.

There is no mention of the Committee in Lewak's collection, *General M. R. Lafayette o Polsce; listy, mowy, dokumenty* (General M. R. Lafayette on Poland; Letters, Addresses, Documents) (Warsaw, 1934). Nor does Lewak allude to it in his introduction to *Katalog wystawy ku czci generała M. R. Lafayette'a 1834-1934* (Catalogue of the Exhibition in Honor of General M. R. Lafayette) (Warsaw, 1934).

[9] Louis Simon in his anonymous woik, *Die Juden in Russland* (Hamburg, 1844), p. 23, stated that "a society having as its purpose the obtaining of emancipation for the Jews in all the countries had been formed by influential Poles with Lafayette as its head. It had a brief existence and has failed to show any particular success." Henrich

Information in the authoritative histories of the Emigration is similarly scant.

Perhaps a detailed study of the French press and of the biographies and correspondence of the French persons involved would shed more light on this incident. Certainly the published sources are meager and cursory. The first mention in print of the existence of the Committee appears to have taken place in Czyński's *Question des Juifs Polonais*, whose author credits the Poles with the initiative for its establishment. Czyński explained that following the expulsion from Paris of the Committee's most influential members by Louis Philippe's government, it could be regarded

---

Hirsch Graetz reported in *Geschichte der Juden von den aeltesten Zeiten bis auf die Gegenwart*, XI (Leipzig, 1900), 437, "that a society was formed in Paris at whose head stood Lafayette, with the specific purpose of aiding the Israelites in Poland by all means." There is no mention of it in Simon Dubnow's *Weltgeschichte des jüdischen Volkes*, Vol. IX (Berlin, 1929). Zoza Szajkowski, "The Founding of the Paris 'Alliance,' 1860," *YIVO Bleter*, XXVIII (1941), 2, bases his brief description of the Committee on Antoni Ostrowski, *Pomysły o potrzebie reformy towarzyskiej w ogólności, a mianowiciej co do izraelitów w Polszcze*... (Thoughts on the Need of Social Reform in General, and Particularly Concerning the Israelites in Poland...) Paris, November 29, 1834. Palatine Ostrowski was a leading liberal aristocrat, wealthy landowner, and important officeholder, who had been interested in social reform and in "reforming" the Jews, whom he admitted to Tomaszów Mazowiecki, a city founded by him. During the insurrection he fought for the admission of the Jews to the National Guard and obtained permission to organize the special Jewish Guard of Warsaw, composed of Jews who refused to shave their beards. In the Emigration he was described as the "Polish Lafayette." His book was in its own times the most basic treatise on the Jewish problem in Poland. It was written under the impact of the establishement of the Lafayette Committee, and its first draft was a "memoir" for it. Cf. also W. G. [Włodzimierz Gadon], *Zbiór ustaw i obrzędów wymagających najrychleiszej reformy izraelitów osiadłych w prowincjach do Polski należących* (A Collection of Laws and Rites of Israelites Settled in the Provinces Belonging to Poland Requiring the Most Immediate Reform) (Paris, 1835), p. 51.

Gadon's work was similarly intended to serve as a source of information for the members of the Lafayette Committee. Its author was judge of the chief court of Wilno and a member of the Commission on Christian and Jewish hospitals in that city. He was also marshal in the County of Telz, boundary judge, and honorary inspector of schools.

Szajkowski accepts Ostrowski's version of the Committee's liquidation, according to which the major reason behind this step was the reluctance of the wealthy French Jews to undertake any action to defend their coreligionists in the countries where they were persecuted, because of their fear of bringing about increased persecution. No Jewish encyclopedia contains an entry on Lafayette. An examination of the writings of the standard literature about Lafayette failed to disclose any references to this activity or interest. There is rather scant information on the Lafayette Committee in S. Posener, *Adolphe Cremieux* (Paris, 1933), pp. 161-62. There is no mention thereof in the English translation of the same work, *Adolphe Cremieux, a Biography* (Philadelphia, 1940); see also note 8.

as dissolved.[10] Leon Hollaenderski, in turn, attributed the Committee's organization to Czyński's[11] efforts in the wake of the popularity which he enjoyed following the publication of the said brochure. Hollaenderski also attributed its demise to Czyński's radicalism and his expulsion.[12]

Letters from the Rapperswyl Collection in Warsaw, destroyed by the Nazis, help us to present a more realistic though still incomplete picture of the Lafayette Committee, its origin, sponsors, brief life, and mysterious demise. They verify that Beniowski was the father of the Committee, as it

[10] Jan Czyński, *Questions des Juifs Polonais* (Paris, November, 1833), pp. 21-22. Characteristically, all the references to the Committee were left out in the English translation of this work, *An Enquiry into the Political Conditions of the Polish Jews Considered in Relation to the General Interest of Europe in Which Are Delineated the Social State of Poland and the Causes Which Led to the Failure of the Last Revolution* (London, 1834). The work was translated by the émigré Albert Korytko, whose preface was dated June 4, 1834. This rare work is available at the Library of Hebrew Union College–Jewish Institute of Religion in Cincinnati.

[11] On Jan Czyński (1801-67), a radical and liberal of Frankist descent who retained his interest in Jewish life and was an outstanding fighter for Jewish emancipation, see my "Leon Hollaenderski's Statement of Resignation," *Jewish Social Studies*, XV (1953), 295, n. 7. Cf. also J. Danielewicz, "Jan Czyński and His Struggle for the Equality of the Jewish Population," *Biuletyn Żydowskiego Instytutu Historycznego* (Bulletin of the Jewish Historical Institute), Warsaw, No. 11-12 (July-December, 1954), pp. 96-108; and Krystyna Świerczewska, "Jan Czyński, a Political and Literary Figure and Publicist of the Times of the Great Emigration (1801-1867)," in *Towarzystwo Literackie im. Adama Mickiewicza. Oddział w Łodzi* (Literary Association Named after Adam Mickiewicz. Łódź Section), *Prace Polonistyczne* (Polonistic Works), Series VIII, 1950 (Wrocław-Łódź, 1951), pp. 111-36. I have collected a great deal of material on Czyński, mainly from the destroyed Rapperswyl Archives, and I hope to have the opportunity to prepare it for publication.

[12] To quote: "Here we must observe that M. Czyński committed a great fault; he mistook the question of the emancipation of the Israelites for a political question. Attributing all the evil to the aristocracy, he made common cause with the exclusive democrats. The cause which he defended was that of liberty of conscience, of justice and of humanity, and which should have been pleaded without any party spirit. The alliance of M. Czyński with the republican party had its effects. The government ordered him to quit France, and after his departure the committee presided over by General Lafayette was dissolved." *Les Israélites de Pologne*, p. 136; cited from English translation by Rev. H. A. Henry in the London *Jewish Chronicle*, July 23, 1865, p. 6. For bibliographical data, cf. my paper in *PAJHS*, XXXIX, Part 2 (1949), 159, n. 68.

Hollaenderski's information about the Society is not accurate. He attributed its establishment partly to the influence of Czyński's *Question*, which was published in 1833. It is reasonable to assume that Hollaenderski, who left Poland as late as 1841 (Rapperswyl [hereafter referred to as Rap.] MS 4; biography by Chodźko), had obtained this information directly from Czyński, who at that time did not care to reveal the Committee's true history. Hollaenderski could not have obtained this information from Lelewel as no question concerning it is included in the letter (Rap. MS 2365, Paris, July 22, 1844) addressed by him to the Polish leader in his search for information in the preparation of the cited work. (Cf. my article on it as in note 1.) Hollaenderski did not utilize the information in Ostrowski's *Pomysły* in his book.

was he who approached Lelewel early in 1833 with some plan for doing something for Jewish emancipation. To judge from the letters, Beniowski showed Lelewel a "sketch" or draft of some writing on this project. We may well presume that it was a plan for the Lafayette Committee. Lelewel in turn sought Czyński's advice and forwarded to him Beniowski's billet.[13] The archives fail to shed any light on the reaction of General Dwernicki,[14] the chief sponsor of the African delegation idea, to this particular project. Czyński, who played an important role in this connection, expressed doubt, in his letter to Lelewel of March 7, 1833, whether the scheme could be carried out on such short notice and retained some reservations concerning Beniowski's plan of organization. Nevertheless, he was aware of the project's potentialities, viewing them also from the angle of Polish-Jewish relations in the Emigration. He expressed his determination to be among "those persons who desire so important an object as the emancipation of the Jews from the burden of prejudice which oppresses them." He also gave Lelewel his promise that he would work honestly for this cause.[15] At the same time, Beniowski continued the work on the project while preparing for the journey.[16] By the middle of March,[17] Czyński was able to report to Lelewel, in a letter inviting him to become a member of the "directing committee," that "the idea of the emancipation . . . has

[13] Rap. MS 1265, Czyński to Lelewel, March 7, 1833. In a letter to Karol Edward Wodziński, on the same day, Lelewel mentioned that Beniowski was around to see him with a new project: "Ach! but good projects, were I in Paris, satisfaction would have been obtained from those of his and of Israel." Cf. Helena Więckowska, ed. *Listy emigracyjne Joachima Lelewela* (Joachim Lelewel's Émigré Letters) (3 vols., Kraków, 1948-52), I, 124. The reference to "Israel" most likely pertains to the Lafayette Committee. Interestingly, there is no record of Lelewel's letters to Czyński in Więckowska's collection. I have summarized a number of letters from Czyński to Lelewel pertaining to other émigré matters.

[14] General Józef Dwernicki (1779-1857), a leading insurrectionist commander and head of the National Committee of the Emigration, returned to Galicia in 1849.

[15] Rap. MS 1265. For the Polish text see Appendix, Item 1. Lelewel wrote to Zwierkowski from Tours, April 27, 1833, that Pułaski and Czyński became estranged because Czyński would not divulge the secrets of the Egyptian mission. Lelewel reported further that the secrets leaked out, that the Ministry of the Interior did not permit certain people to leave, and that "Szulc has terribly misled them and wasted a lot of time, perhaps all the preparations will have been in vain." Więckowska remarks that Szulc, who was sent by Dwernicki to Egypt, propagandized in favor of joining Mehmed Ali's army, expecting that a European war would break out, with Egypt, England, and France fighting Russia and Turkey. (*Listy emigracyjne*, I, 131, and n. 2.)

[16] Beniowski, in a letter to Chodźko, March 7, 1833, wrote that "the cause of the Jews, it seems, will get along well. It would be good if the citizen himself [Chodźko] were in Paris." Rap. MS 428.

[17] Rap. MS 1265, Letter of Czyński to Lelewel, March 17, 1833. Cf. Appendix, Item 2.

received more life and a wider field. The concern is not only with the Polish Jews but also with the Jews of the entire globe. Americans, Englishmen, Germans, almost all outstanding names will belong." He told Lelewel that Lafayette (whose interest in the Jewish "nation" was attested by Antoni Ostrowski)[18] had given his promise of assistance and expressed his willingness to address a letter to its prospective founders. The General, Czyński stated, refused to accept its presidency "because of his preoccupation and fear of a large correspondence." However, the honorary presidency would be offered to him. The projected committee was to consist of James Fenimore Cooper, Lemercier, Lasterie, Cremieux, Mauguin, Odillon Barrot, Lattyk,[19] Ostrowski, and others. News of the establishment of the Committee was to be released on Friday, March 22, 1833, following an organization meeting scheduled for Thursday. By that time the organization became known among the Polish patriots.[20]

Lelewel, as was to be expected, accepted the invitation. Czyński's organizational activities were continued with his usual energies and speed. He was able to report on April 7 that Antoni Ostrowski had enthusiastically espoused the cause and accepted membership. Czyński intended to publish this reply in the first issue of the Committee's planned bulletin, which was to be issued in French, German, and English, a project that was evidently never realized. Interest in the organization was also manifested in the inquiries concerning the Committee's activities received from many localities, particularly Alsace. A platform was to be adopted at

[18] To quote: "I had the opportunity to learn the nation Israel too has not been left out from his [Lafayette's] sympathetic attention." *Pomysły*, p. 3.

[19] On Cooper, see Robert E. Spiller, "James Fenimore Cooper and Lafayette: Friends of Polish Freedom," *American Literature*, VII (1935), 56-75. Among the members of the American Polish Committee in Paris were N. C. Barrabino, M. P. David, A. M. Nathan, and L. Hermann (Spiller, p. 65). Possibly some of these persons were Jews.

Comte Jean-Nepomucene Lemercier (1771-1840) was a well-known French playwright. Jean-Baptiste-Nicolas, Baron Lemercier (1789-1854) was a leading Bonapartist. Cf. *La Grande encyclopedie*, XXI, 1193. Charles-Philbert, Comte de Lasteyrie du Saillant (1759-1849) was a publicist, agronomist, and philanthropist. Cf. *La Grande encyclopedie*, Vol. XXI.

François Mauguin (1785-1849) was a celebrated lawyer and orator and a participant in the July Revolution. Cf. Larousse, X, 1356.

Camille-Hayacinth-Odillon Barrot (1791-1873) was a well-known orator and political figure. He was president of the society "Aide-toi, le ciel t'aidera." After 1848 he became a Bonapartist and was active in pro-Polish efforts during the Insurrection of 1863. Cf. Larousse, V, 507-8.

I could not identify Lattyk. Perhaps the reference is to Mathieu-François-Vincent Latil (1796-1890), a leading painter. Cf. Larousse, XXI, 4000.

[20] Cf. Ostrowski, *Pomysły*, p. 1.

a meeting to be held on April 13. Cremieux was expected to be "the body and the soul" of the movement.[21]

Soon, however, Czyński and his Polish co-workers faced serious difficulties. At a meeting held in the middle of April the more conservative members expressed their fear of the possible implications of Lafayette's proposed leadership, in the face of the increasing conservatism of Louis Phillippe's government. The General's presidency was, however, indispensable to the founders of the Committee, who counted on him to supply both the prestige and the "front" for the Society. The following letter of Czyński to Lelewel, dated April 23, 1833, is the only existing source of information about this disagreement.

> . . . At the last meeting of the society concerning the Jews, Adolphe Cremieux, after communicating with Rothschild, proposed the election of a president who would not have a strong political implication such as [that of] Lafayette. He held that more could be done in May when public opinion would be even calmer, or if the society would not have a political character. It was, therefore, decided to invite many more people of different political complexions, such as Tracy, Chateaubriand, many scholars, etc. (I do not expect that they have elected anyone who is suitable.) In such a case, this would be against our primary purposes, and I, in protest, would leave the society and would describe by what terms our first project was twisted. I believe that this will not be necessary.[22]

Indeed, the "primary purposes" mentioned in this communication could not have been merely the wish to help the Jews obtain emancipation. Nor could this desire account for either Czyński's emphasis on the need for speedy organization, his insistence on Lafayette's chairmanship, or his willingness to face a deep conflict with the Jewish members of the Committee about the tactics involved in the struggle for emancipation. Evidently, neither Rothschild[23] nor Cremieux had been aware of the true motives in the minds of the Polish founders. This disagreement was finally settled by a compromise. Lafayette was elected chairman or president and the membership of the Committee was expanded to include individuals of different political opinions.

Archival sources fail to reveal further details or even a general sketch of the activities of the Society. It seems that the organization was finally

[21] Cf. Appendix, Item 3.

[22] Cf. Appendix, Item 4.

Francois-Auguste, Vicomte de Chateaubriand (1768-1848) was the author of *The Genius of Christianity*. Antoine-Louis-Claude, Comte Destutt de Tracy (1754-1856) was a philosopher, psychologist, and Napoleonist. His son, Alexander-Cesar-Victor-Charles (1781-1864), was a Napoleonist and great liberal.

[23] James Jacob Mayer de Rothschild (1792-1868).

launched upon its brief public career at a meeting of the Société de la Civilisation, with an address by Antoni Ostrowski.[24] It is by the name of the Société de la Civilisation that Włodzimierz Gadon referred to the Committee in his work prepared for its guidance.[25]

In the meantime, however, Ibrahim made peace with the Sultan. Russian pressure in Istanbul forced the deportation of the Polish mission, which was ordered to leave Egypt in February, 1834. The Egyptians were willing to retain some of its members in their military service, but General Henryk Dembiński, Insurrectionist military leader, indignantly refused to accept the offer and left in June. Czyński and his associates evidently became more skeptical about the usefulness of the Committee's work for their group and more concerned with the prestige that it could bring to the rightist Emigration Committee. The wish to bring an end to the Lafayette Committee was evidently behind Czyński's statement of October or November, 1833,[26] regarding the Society's premature end.

Cremieux and Rothschild were not the only members who had been unaware of the Committee's true purposes or of this plan for liquidation. Ostrowski, while admitting that no progress had been made by the

[24] Société de la Civilisation, an early interdenominational group founded in 1829, had as its purpose the "support of the development of Civilization and the struggle against any obstacles in its way." It published the periodicals *Revue Sociale* and *Société de Civilisation.* It also conducted a "School of Philosophy," where lecturers of all faiths, including Jews, explained their views. Cf. Leon Płoszewski, in introduction to "Political Writings," in Adam Mickiewicz, *Dzieła wszystkie* (Complete Works, edition known as *Wydanie sejmowe—Sejm Edition*), VII (Warsaw, 1936), 351-54, on the basis of *Revue Sociale*, August, 1834; and Władyslaw Mickiewicz, *Żywot Adama Mickiewicza* (The Life of Adam Mickiewicz) (4 vols., Poznan, 1890-95), II, 249-52.

An appeal to the "civilized peoples" was issued by the Society on November 25, 1833. Included among the signatories was Prof. Michel Berr. Cf. [Binder], *Diplomatische Geschichte der polnischen Emigration*, von XXP, pp. 197-201. However, the appeal had no relation to the Lafayette Committee. The Society's call was for the contribution of Polish books for a projected library. It called forth the wrath of the Towarzystwo Pomocy Nauk (Society for the Aid of Learning), which was engaged in a similar project. Cf. Letter of Mickiewicz to Kajsiewicz, Paris, November, 1833, in *Dzieła Wszystkie*, ed. Reiter (Lwow), XI, 124. Cf. also Czyński, *Question*, p. 21.

[25] Gadon, *Zbiór ustaw*, p. vi. Evidently Gadon had been confused by the act of launching the Committee before a meeting of the Société de la Civilisation and thus combined the two bodies into one.

[26] Preface to *Question des Juifs Polonais.* The booklet was published in November, 1833. Interestingly, there are practically no references to the importance of cultivating the Jews of the Near East in the documents published by Bemis, *Un mission Polonaise en Egypt.* While General Dembiński's friend, the banker George Oppenheimer, mentioned in a letter to the General, August 21, 1833, that among the things that were worth knowing in Egypt was "the character of the situation of the Christians and Jews" (I, 242), there is no indication of any follow-up. Evidently, the Poles realized the difficulties of involving Egyptian Jews at an early stage.

Society in the past year, still considered himself a member of the Society at the time of the publication of *Pomysly*. The book was completed before April, 1834, and published in November, 1834.[27] As a matter of fact, this book was prepared by its author for the express purpose of furnishing guidance to the members of the Society on the problems of the Jews in Poland.[28] Likewise, Włodzimierz Gadon remained unaware of the decision to end the Society's existence while continuing to work on his booklet *Zbiór ustaw*. At the time of its appearance in 1835, the Committee had definitely ceased to exist. The anonymous publisher of Gadon's brochure, without knowing the true reasons behind both the Society's establishment and its liquidation, termed it "a fraud unparalleled in Poland." "Who would have believed," he remarked in his introduction, meanwhile confusing it with the Société de la Civilisation, "that books with the stamp of the Society donated by civilized people to the future library of Poland are already being sold on the street corners for a few pennies. What the poor tribe of Israel had lived to see."[29]

Another source testified to the demise of the Society early in 1835. It is the review of Ostrowski's *Pomysly* by Franciszek Wołowski (of Frankist descent) in the monarchist *Kronika Emigracji Polskiej*.[30] It constitutes the only reference to it in the contemporary émigré press. Wołowski might not have been aware of the Committee's true history. He considered it one of the "many non-dues paying organizations established for the personal gain of its leaders." In this particular case, Czyński, always the subject of attacks from Rightist quarters, bore the brunt of the accusations and was called to responsibility in insulting terms.

Czyński's excuse that the demise of the Committee was due to the expulsion of Polish leaders from Paris cannot be accepted as the sole reason for its liquidation.[31] Not all the Polish leaders were expelled. Furthermore, there were enough Jews and Frenchmen to carry on the work. No attempt was made to revive the organization after some of the expelled Polish democrats returned from their exile. But even during the leaders' absence from Paris, other émigré activities went on. More accept-

[27] The date of the publication of the work was November 29, 1834. It was in circulation in December. Even if sufficient time is allowed for the printing of such a lengthy book, it is clear that Czyński's verdict of the Society's demise went unheeded by its more "innocent" members.

[28] *Pomysly*, pp. 1-5.

[29] *Zbiór ustaw*, p. 6.

[30] *Kronika Emigracji Polskiej* (Chronicle of the Polish Emigration), II, No. 18 (February 2, 1835), 274-75.

[31] *Question*, p. 21.

able is the reason advanced by Ostrowski on the basis of conversation with French Jews, namely, that its Jewish members preferred to postpone the official release of the news of the Society's establishment to a more favorable date. This, he stated, was because "at present it will be considered by the despotic government as merely political propaganda and thus might make worse the situation of the Jews who are scattered throughout the world instead of aiding them."[32] But even this excuse does not explain the abandonment of the project by all, particularly by Beniowski and Czyński, its most devoted adherents. Czyński later stated that the Committee was dissolved because of Lafayette's death.[33] This was repeated by Cremieux's biographer Posener.[34]

It is possible that Lelewel and his associates, dissatisfied with Dwernicki's objections to the émigrés' overenthusiastic participation in the European revolutionary movements, did not care to continue with the Lafayette Committee. Such action was likely to bring prestige and contacts to the Committee of the Polish Emigration, which they refused to join. The failure of the mission to Africa can be viewed as a secondary cause of the Lafayette Committee's liquidation. At the same time, Dwernicki's Committee was less likely to be interested in gaining the support of the Jews because of its general *szlachta* character and mixed ideological composition. Perhaps the abandonment of the project might have been an indication of the beginnings of the doubt among the émigrés as to the prospects of immediate people's revolts in Europe, with a subsequent growing lack of interest in obtaining new allies, particularly among Jews, who were considered a doubtful element. Possibly the efforts invested in the Lafayette Committee, its slow development, and the cautious approach of some of the French Jews were other contributory reasons for the project's abandonment.

The Lafayette Committee was the forerunner of other similar organizations in which Czyński played a prominent part. There is evidence that Czyński had thought of reviving the Committee's activities in 1843. In fact, he had no doubt then that Cremieux would reorganize "the Committee which was dissolved by the death of General Lafayette . . . which had for its objective the acceleration of general Jewish emancipation."[35] In an editorial note following his sharp letter in defense of the Russian and

[32] *Pomysły*, p. 25.

[33] Letter vii in the *Archives Israélites* series; cited from (*First*) *Fruits of the West* (Kingston, Jamaica, 1844), p. 391.

[34] Posener, *Adolphe Cremieux*, I, 161.

[35] As in note 33.

Polish Jews, published in *Le Constitutionel,* Czyński was identified as "one of the members and founder of the Paris Committee presided over by General Lafayette having as its purpose to accelerate the emancipation of the Israelites in all the countries."[36] He was connected with the Comité Européen de Colonisation Israelite, established in 1844 for the purpose of settling East European and Italian Jews on the land.[37] In 1845, Czyński again proposed to Adolphe Cremieux the establishment of a similar organization, possibly the Comité Européen de l'Emancipation Israelite,[38] and idea realized, according to the biographer of this French statesman, "fifteen years later with the founding of the Alliance Israelite Universelle."[39] In 1848 Czyński briefly referred to the Lafayette Committee's establishment,[40] and in 1863 he was again instrumental in organizing the Alliance Polonaise de toutes les croyances religieuses.[41] Interestingly, the Committee for the Defense of the Rights of Jews in Central and Eastern Europe, affiliated with and headed by the same board as the Union for the Protection of the Human Person, claimed that "it was founded in 1832 by General Lafayette, was organized again in France in 1933."[42]

[36] *Le Constitutionel,* Supplement to No. 134, Paris, May 14, 1843, p. 7. To my friend Michael Schapiro, thanks for copying the article.

[37] Zoza Szajkowski, "New Materials about Altaras and His Colonization Plan," *YIVO Bleter,* XXI (1943), 49-50.

[38] Posener, *Adolphe Cremieux,* I, 161.

[39] *Ibid.*

[40] *Le Réveil d'Israél* (Paris, 1848), p. 150.

[41] My monograph on this organization on the basis of archival materials destroyed by the Nazis is still to be published.

[42] See back cover of *European Refugees and the Duty of the Democracies,* Series of Booklets in Memory of Jules Fribourg, published by the Union for the Protection of the Human Person by International Social and Economic Cooperation, Inc. (New York, 1946). Correspondence with the organization revealed that it had no new data on the Lafayette Committee. In a leaflet *Appel a l'opinion publique polonaise,* of the Comité pour la Defense des Droits des Israélites en Europe Centrale et Orientale, dated Paris, November 20, 1937, protesting against the treatment of the Jews in Poland and published in Paris in French and Polish, the reference is made that "over a hundred years ago the glorious Polish exiles in France, laying the foundations for the resurrection of the fatherland, have established a Committee whose aim it was to carry out the equality of law and obligations for the Jews and other citizens of Poland. The Honorary President of that Committee was General Lafayette. Its creators were Major Bieniawski [*sic*] [Benjawski in the French text] and I. [*sic*] Czynski, and Mickiewicz and Towianski supported it warmly." The appeal ends with the following: "From the depth of the soul, we who love and respect Poland, and are carrying forth the work of La Fayette, Czyński and Bieniawski in our Committee for the Defense of the Rights of the Jews in Central and Eastern Europe, call all those faithful to the ideals of the brotherhood of free peoples and free men to protest in the defense of the human dignity that was stepped on." (Polish text, pp. 3, 8.) Among the signatories of the appeal are dignitaries

APPENDIX

Item 1 Letter of Jan Czyński to Joachim Lelewel
Paris, March 7, 1833

Otrzymałem bilet obywatela pisany przez Bartłomieja Beniowskiego. Istotnie chcę należeć do liczby tych osób, co tak ważny przedmiot, jak jest emancypacja żydów z pod jarzmą gniotęcej ich opinji wyzwolić pragną—wiem ja jak jest silny przesąd moich współrodaków przeciw temu ludowi, wiem jakiej odwagi potrzeba do walczenia przeciwko temu wstrętowi, jaki ku nim powzięto, ale czuję zarazem, że prawda i sprawiedliwość skoro przemawiają do serc młodych, a w nich cała nadzieja—dlatego przyrzekam szczerze pracować w tym zawodzie. Beniowski nie przeczy, ze pierwszy szkic, którego niedostateczność aȝ nadto czuję, wziął i u obywatela zostawił—wątpie, żeby tak prędko jak Beniowski chce, projekt przyszedł do skutku.

Rapperswyl MS 1265

Item 2 Excerpts from Letter of Jan Czyński to Joachim Lelewel
Paris, March 17, 1833

. . . Myśl Emancypacyi, połowa Francuzów, przyjęta od nich chętnie nabrała więcej życia i rozleglejszego pola—już nie tylko o Polskich żydów, ale idzie o żydów całego globu. Amerykanie, Anglicy, Niemcy, wszystkie prawie znakomite imiona będą należeć—Lafaieit obiecał wsparcie i list do założycieli napisać— dla zatrudnień i z obawy korespondencyi licznych wymówił sie od Prezydentstwa wszelako prezedenctwa honorowa będzie mu ofiarowana: Cooper, Lemercier, Lasterie, Cremieux, Mauguin, Odillon Barrot, Lattyk, Ostrowski itp będą Komitet stanowić na ostatniej sessyi między innemi i ja wyznaczony zostałem na referenta do organizacyi. we czwartek Komitet będzie ustalony, a w piątek już o nim wiadomości.

Jeżeli obywatelu sobie życzysz bądź członkiem Komitetu dyrugującego racz mnie natychmiast napisać.

Rapperswyl MS 1265

Item 3 Excerpts from Letter of Jan Czyński to Joachim Lelewel
Paris, April 7, 1833

Jak tylko otrzymałem list od obywatela, w którym oświadczyłeś mi iź chętnie bierzesz udział w stowarzyszeniu mającem ludzkość na celu, tak zaraz napisałem do wojewody Ostrowskiego, ktory przysłał mi list obejmujący dwie stronnice w których opisuje swoją radość z zawiązania tego Towarzystwa. Jako General Gwardji daje świadectwo, że żydzi chcieli w wojsku służyc, ze w straży bezpieczeństwa dobrze się sprawowali, że i on wreszcie chcąc czynnie do tego Towarzystwa należeć, spodziewa się b. ważnych korzyści.

---

of all faiths. Among the inaccurate statements are the references to Mickiewicz's and Towianski's warm support of the Committee. There is no record of Mickiewicz's support, while Towianski arrived in Paris in 1841, years after the Committee's dissolution.

List ten przełżony na francuski, niemiecki, i angielski język będzie umieszczony w pierwszym biuletynie.

Z różnych okolic, a mianowicie z Alzacji i z Niemiec liczne nadeszły zgłoszenia z zapytaniem w jaki sposób Towarzystwo działać będzie: z tego powodu w przyszły piątek 12 kwietnia będzie sesja gdzie zasady dyskutowane i stanowczo przyjęte będą. Jeżeliby obywatel w tej mierze lub swoje uwagi, lub swój sposób widzenia lub wreszcie komplement chciał nadesłać, jago przyrzekam przeczytać i oddać to Akt lub do druku.

Tak stoi rzecz co do starozakonnych. Janowski[43] chcial gwałtem być w komitecie, czego nie można było dopuścić, dlatego, że on się nie dość ceni, a zanadto ciekawy i gadatliwy. Francuzi wymagają tego, co u nas nazywają punktem honoru, on byle czasem samej ciekawości dogodzić gotów sto osob pokłócić—w tym Towarzystwie znany obywatel Cremieux będzie duszą i ciałem.

Rapperswyl MS 1265

Item 4 Excerpt from Letter of Jan Czyński to Joachim Lelewel
Paris, April 23, 1833

Na ostatniem posiedzeniu Towarzystwa co do żydów Adolphe Crèmieux za porozumieniem się z Rothschildem wniósł, żeby wybrać Prezesa któryby nie miał tak mocnego charakteru politycznego jak Laffaied, utrzymując iź w Maju więcej będzie można zrobić, skoro opinja będzie jeszcze więcej blada, lub jeśli Towarzystwo nie będzie miało charakteru politycznego. Postanowiono więc zaprosić jeszcze wiele osób rozmaitej barwy politycznej jakoto Tracy, Chateaubriand, wielu uczonych itp. (nie spodziewam sie, że wybrano kogoś odpowiedniego), wtenczas to sprzeciwiłoby się naszemu pierwotnemu celowi i jabym protestując wystąpił z Towarzystwa i opisał bym jaką koleją pierwszy nasz pomysł skręcony został. Sądzę że tego nie będzie trzeba.

Rapperswyl MS 1265

[43] He was most likely the Democratic leader Jan Niepomucen Janowski. There is no mention of the Lafayette Committee in Jan Niepomucen Janowski, *Notatki Autobiograficzne 1803-1853* (Biographical Notes 1803-1853), ed. by Marjan Tyrowicz (Wroclaw, 1950).

THE BACKGROUND OF THE BERLIN HASKALAH

By Isaac Eisenstein-Barzilay

CLOSER ACQUAINTANCE with the pre-Mendelssohnian era shows the exaggeration of the role attributed to Moses Mendelssohn in the process of ushering in the age of Haskalah. Rather than the creator of a new period in Jewish history, he was one of its outstanding products, who lent it strength and impetus.

During his early *Lehrjahre* Berlin had already become a center of intellectual activity which attracted Jewish youths. At the time Mendelssohn was taking his first steps toward secular learning, Israel Zamosc of Poland had already attained profound mathematical knowledge; Aharon Gomperz was hard at work on his studies of mathematics, astronomy, and medicine and in close social contact with some of the French *philosophes* of the Prussian Academy for Science. Abraham Kisch of Prague, who was among Mendelssohn's early teachers in Berlin, obtained the doctorate from the medical faculty of the University of Halle in 1749.[1] To the pre-Mendelssohnian generation belonged Raphael Levi (born in 1705 at Weikersheim on the Tauber), who attracted the attention of Leibniz by his advanced knowledge of mathematics, French, and Latin.[2]

A younger contemporary of Mendelssohn was the tragic poet Ephraim Moses Kuh of Breslau (born 1731), who early departed from the traditional studies to devote himself to modern languages and literature. It is interesting to note that it was a Polish Jew, employed as a teacher in the Kuh family, who was largely responsible for the new tastes awakened in young Kuh. Before coming to Breslau, this Polish Maskil had lived in

[1] Ludwig Geiger, *Geschichte der Juden in Berlin* (Berlin, 1871), Book III, chaps. I, II. J. Eschelbacher, "Die Anfänge allgemeiner Bildung unter den deutschen Juden vor Mendelssohn," *Festschrift zum 70ten Geburtstage Martin Philippsons* (Leipzig, 1916), pp. 168-77. Guido Kisch, *Die Prager Universität und die Juden* (Maerisch-Ostrau, 1936), p. 26.

[2] J. Eschelbacher, "Die Anfänge... vor Mendelssohn," in *Festschrift... Martin Philippsons;* Max Erik, *Die Komedies fun der berliner Haskoleh* (Kiev, 1933), Introduction.

Berlin, but because his devotion to philosophy antagonized the orthodox leadership of the community, he had to leave that city.[3]

A most interesting case of an early and seemingly extreme Maskil was that of Isachar Falkensohn Behr, who came to Berlin from his native Zamosc in Poland in the sixties. Here he studied sciences and languages, and in a short time he attained such mastery of German that in 1771 his German poems were published under the title *Gedichte eines polnischen Juden*. "In them he sang of Doris and Phylis, Azlaja and Curonie; like Ramler he exalted the maidens, country life, and with him he also shared the enthusiasm for Frederick the Great and the Prussian ruling house."[4]

The Pursuit of Secular Learning among the Jews of Poland and Lithuania

During Mendelssohn's lifetime and generally independent of his influence, an awakened interest in secular learning became a pronounced characteristic of Jewish intellectual life not only in the West and in the Germanies but in Eastern Europe as well. A profound desire for mathematical and scientific knowledge gripped a number of Orthodox Jews of Poland and Lithuania.

An early example of these tendencies was Rabbi Shelomo Chelma who served in succession in the rabbinate of Chelm, Zamosc, and Lvov. His *Mirkeveth Mishneh*, a commentary on Maimonides's *Yad*, appeared in 1751;[5] in the introduction he states that while still a young man he became critical of the methods of the mystics and rabbis. He found them "devoid of clear and orderly knowledge ... and contemptuous of commonsense reasoning." To satisfy the "craving for wisdom," evoked in him by the reading of Maimonides, he began to study algebra, geometry, astronomy, logic, and even the art of poetry.[6]

Another pious Polish rabbi of the same period who yielded to the temptations of secular learning against his own explicitly stated better judgment was the otherwise little-known Rabbi Eliyahu of Pinchew. In the year 1765 he published in Berlin a book on algebra and geometry.[7]

[3] *Hinterlassene Gedichte von Ephraim Kuh*, 1st Bändchen (Zurich, 1792), "Biographie des jüdischen Gelehrten und Dichters Ephraim Moses Kuh," by Moses Hirschel, pp. 45-46.

[4] M. Kayserling, *Der Dichter Ephraim Kuh* (Berlin, 1864), Anhang, pp. 43-47.

[5] Shelomo ben Moshe Chelma, *Sefer Mirkeveth Mishneh 'al ha-Rambam* (Frankfort-on-the-Oder, 1751); cf. I. Zinberg, *Die Geschichte fun der Literatur bei Yidn*, Vol. V (New York, 1943), Book II, pp. 284-86.

[6] Shelomo Chelma, Introduction to *Sefer Mirkeveth Mishneh.*

[7] Eliyahu of Pinchew, *Melekheth Mahsheveth* (Berlin, 1765), cf. introductions to Parts I and II.

Another experience pointing up the trend to the diffusion of secular culture among the rabbis is that related by Shelemo Maimon in his autobiography. In the late sixties, when his keen mind was awakened by a desire for knowledge, he began a search for books on the sciences. He was fortunate, he tells us, to find that at some distance from his native village, in the house of the Oberrabbiner von S. (Stomm) there was quite a "sizable library" of German books. It turned out that, thirty years earlier, this rabbi had lived in Germany where he had acquired some German and "acquainted himself also with some of the sciences, with which he still occupied himself, though in a clandestine manner, at present."[8]

To a somewhat later part of the eighteenth century belong the numerous scientific books of the well-known Rabbi Baruch of Shklow, the disciple of the Gaon of Wilno,[9] the astronomical and mathematical studies of Rabbi Eliyahu ha-Cohen of Hechis,[10] the various books of Rabbi Jehudah Leib Margolioth in which he defended the study of natural sciences,[11] and finally the encyclopedic *Sefer ha-Berith* of Pinehas Eliyahu of Wilno.[12]

Indicative of this intensified desire for secular knowledge was also the relatively high number of Jewish youths from Poland and Lithuania who, beginning with the early thirties of the eighteenth century, attended various German universities and, above all, that of Frankfort-on-the-Oder.[13]

The Pursuit of Secular Learning among the Rabbis in the Germanies

This trend was not limited to Eastern Europe alone, but also found its counterpart among some rabbis in the Germanies. The following examples will substantiate this statement. Allegedly for the sake of a more

[8] *Solomon Maimons Lebensgeschichte*, ed. K. P. Moritz (Berlin, 1792), p. 144.

[9] Baruch of Shklow, *Sefer 'Ammudei Shamayim ve-Tifereth Adam* (Berlin, 1776-77); *Sefer Euclides* (The Hague, 1778); *Sefer Keneh Middah* (Prague, 1783). On the positive attitude of the Gaon to secular learning see mainly Rabbi Yisrael of Shklow, *Sefer Pe'ath Shulhan* (Safed, 1836), Author's Foreword.

[10] Eliyahu Cohen of Hechis, *Sefer Shevilei ha-Rake'a* (Prague, 1784).

[11] See mainly Jehudah Leib Margolioth, *Sefer Or 'Olam 'al Hokhmath ha-Teva'* (1st ed., 1782; Warsaw, 1842), Introduction; *Sefer Tal Oroth* (Frankfort-on-the-Oder, 1811), pp. 100, 102; *Beth Middoth* (Dehrenfurt, 1777).

[12] P. E. Hurwitz, *Sefer ha-Berith ha-Shalem* (1st ed., Brno, 1797; Warsaw, 1876). Worth mentioning in this context are also the scientific and linguistic attainments of Rabbi Mordekhai Aharon Guenzberg's father (born 1765), of whom he tells us in his autobiography, *Abiezer* (Wilno, 1863), p. 22.

[13] Louis Lewin, "Die jüdischen Studenten an der Universität Frankfort-an-der-Oder," *Jahrbuch der Jüdischen Literarischen Gesellschaft*, Vols. XIV, XV, XVI.

comprehensive and deeper understanding of Judaism, Jonathan Eibeschuetz declared legal not only the study of mathematics, physics, chemistry, botany, mineralogy, but also of music, drawing, and painting.[14] His contemporary opponent Jacob Zevi Emden boasted of his interest in all the sciences and the "affairs of the world." In his autobiography, he tells us that he acquired "perfect knowledge of the Dutch language ... and an ability to read and understand a great deal of Latin." He also had a keen interest in astronomy, physics, botany, medicine, statecraft, and history. "All these," he asserted, "my eyes have seen in their books. ... I am an expert in them ... and know everything."[15]

A great lover of secular learning was Rabbi Hirschel Lewin who served in succession as rabbi of London, Halberstadt, Mannheim, and Berlin. He read books on philosophy, mathematics, natural sciences, grammar, and Jewish history. He admired Mendelssohn, read his books, and gave his endorsement to the *Biur*.[16] Even more indicative of his proclivities for secular learning was the endorsement he gave to *'Ammudei Shamayim ve-Tifereth Adam* of Rabbi Baruch of Shklow. In it he wrote:

> During my early days, I approached for a while the gates of wisdom. I was like one who dips his finger in the ocean. ... Thier main proofs and demonstrations, however, ... especially those dealing with astronomy, remained, unfortunately, closed to me.

Indeed, he seems to have regretted deeply his failure to acquire a more profound knowledge of the sciences and blamed fate for having "tossed me around and kept me worried and preoccupied."[17]

Rabbi David Frankel, Mendelssohn's childhood teacher who later became rabbi of Berlin, was also a versifier who composed hymns in which he hailed the victories of Frederick II.[18]

Intense was the desire for secular knowledge and great the joy experienced at attaining it displayed by Rabbi David Friesenhausen of Fürth. Until the age of thirty, he tells us, he was completely absorbed in the study of the Talmud and its legal compendia. Various difficult passages

[14] Jonathan Eibeschuetz, *Ya'aroth Devash*, II (Karlsruhe, 1782), 44-45.

[15] Jacob Zevi Emden, *Megillath Sefer*, ed. D. Kahana (Warsaw, 1897), pp. 97-98.

[16] E. Landshut, *Toledoth Anshei ha-Shem u-Pe'ulatham be-'Adath Berlin 1671-1881* (Berlin, 1884), par. 11.

[17] It is interesting to note that even David Friedlaender, who had no great love for rabbis in general, praised highly Rabbi Hirschel Lewin. "He was," he wrote of him, "a German by birth. He knew well the Hebrew language and its grammar. He was even endowed with a sense for poetry. In his youth he composed hymns and read the *Moreh Nevukhim*." *Über die Verbesserung der Juden im Königreiche Polen* (Berlin, 1819), note to pp. 35-36.

[18] S. Bernfeld, *Dor Tahpukhoth* (Warsaw, 1914), Part I, p. 42.

which he came across in these books, as well as in Maimonides, and the direct contemplation of the phenomena of nature brought him to a sudden realization of his intellectual shortcomings. Henceforth, he could no longer suppress the strong desire for intellectual development and he delved into secular studies. Although the elucidation of these difficult passages, he assures us, was a sufficient reward for his many labors, he feels compelled openly to admit the deep inner satisfaction and happiness he derived from such studies.

No treasures can compare with it. . . . no words can express it adequately. . . . It is simply unbelievable. . . . only my innermost soul experiences it and is aware of it. . . . The only thing I can say is that if no human eye ever looked at God . . . one who knows the nature of heavens may well recognize Him. Through His wonderful awe-inspiring actions he may be looking at Him. Only by means of those sciences it becomes possible to contemplate His creation and thus see eye to eye the glory and magnificence of God.[19]

Some Characteristics of the Early Haskalah Trends

Haskalah, in the sense of constantly expanding intellectual horizons, thus became a pronounced feature in the life of wider sections of Jewry in East and West alike long before its official arrival. This also applies to some of its social and cultural aspects which manifested themselves in the life of the newly established communities of western and northern Germany as early as the end of the seventeenth and the first half of the eighteenth century.[20] In view of this, the Berlin Haskalah formed the end of a period rather than its beginning. This fact must be kept in mind, since it may help to explain, to some extent at least, the abruptness with which the Hebrew Haskalah in Germany came to an end.

On the other hand, caution should be observed in overstressing the intensity and scope of these pre-Haskalah tendencies, since it may lead to underestimating the revolutionary nature of the Berlin Haskalah. The early Haskalah tendencies in Poland, Lithuania, and among some of the rabbis in the Germanies were quite limited in scope and of an intellectual character only. Most of those early Maskilim were Orthodox Jews who

[19] David Friesenhausen, *Sefer Kelil Heshbon* (Berlin, 1796), Introduction.

[20] Cf. *The Memoirs of Glueckel von Hameln*, translated by Marvin Loewenthal (New York, 1931), *passim;* Zevi Hirsch Kaidanower, *Sefer Kav ha-Yashar* (Berditschew, 1825), chaps. XLIII, LXXXII, and *passim;* M. Hagiz, *Sefer Sefath Emeth* (Wilno, 1876), pp. 6, 27-28, 68, 88, 90; Jacob Zevi Emden, *'Ammudei Shamayim* (Altona, 1745), p. 38, and *Sha'arei Shamayim* (Altona, 1751), pp. 75, 78-79; D. Kahana, ed., *Megillath Sefer* [Emden's autobiography] (Warsaw, 1897), *passim;* H. J. D. Azulay (HIDA), *Sefer Ma'agal Tov ha-Shalem*, with introduction and notes by A. Freiman (Jerusalem, 1934), *passim:* Selma Stern, *The Court Jew* (Philadelphia, 1950), *passim.*

accepted Haskalah only phenomenologically, but completely rejected its religious, moral, and philosophical implications. They admired, to use their own terminology, "scientific reason," but opposed "philosophical" reason. They considered the new secular knowledge merely external and believed that it could be juxtaposed with the higher Jewish creeds and values without affecting them. Thus they embraced the new knowledge in a formalistic manner, but would not allow it to become a formative, educational force in Jewish life. As far as their ways of life, general outlook, hopes, and aspirations were concerned, they remained completely within the frame of traditional Jewry.[21]

The positive attitude of rabbinical Jewry to scientific learning, though no doubt reflecting the strong influence of the Enlightenment, was not in itself an exceptional phenomenon in Jewish intellectual history. Throughout the ages, Judaism was constantly absorbing various influences of the foreign cultures in the midst of which it dwelt. If, however, there was anything which distinguished the attitude of the eighteenth-century Orthodox Jews toward secular learning, it was not the result of a new *Weltanschauung* which they embraced but the consequence of the unique and revolutionary nature of scientific reasoning as such in the intellectual history of mankind. Indeed, had the new scientific methods been fully embraced by Orthodox Jewry, it would have led to many unforseen negative results in relation to the essentials of Judaism. Guided by its instinct for self-preservation, however, Orthodox Jewry never allowed itself to pursue the scientific principles and methods to their logical extreme. Never doubting the unquestionable "higher" truth of Judaism, their devotion to secular learning always remained qualified.[22] They drew a clear boundary line beyond which the inquisitive mind was not allowed to proceed.

It was this purely intellectual nature of the early conservative Haskalah, with its pronounced opposition to speculative reasoning and its utter lack of any sociopolitical ideals, which must be borne in mind to realize the wider scope and more revolutionary nature of the ideology of the Berlin Haskalah.

[21] On the nature of the early conservative Haskalah see mainly: Margolioth, *Tal Oroth* (Frankfort-on-the-Oder, 1811), Introduction, pp. 100, 102; *Beth Middoth*, pp. 17, 20-22; *'Asei 'Eden* (Frankfort-on-the-Oder, 1802), pp. 13-16, 18; *Or 'Olam*, Petihah; see also the introductions to the various books of Baruch of Shklow (see above, note 9), and Pinehas Eliyahu Hurwitz, *Sefer ha-Berith ha-Shalem* (Warsaw, 1876), pp. 212-13, 222.

[22] Cf. Eliyahu of Pinchew, *Sefer Melekheth Mahsheveth*, Introduction; see also the various books of Margolioth mentioned in note 21.

This, as mentioned, is also true with reference to the early social and cultural phenomena of Haskalah observed in the West and northwestern Germany. Certain characteristics of the growing Haskalah, in terms of a new attitude to life and the world, became noticeable there. Never, however, did they affect great numbers of Jews or did they crystallize into a social ideology. This was probably due to the relatively small size of the Jewish communities and the essentially unchanged attitude of the non-Jewish society toward them.

THE POLITICAL, ECONOMIC, AND CULTURAL BACKGROUND OF THE BERLIN HASKALAH

Königsberg, Breslau, and Berlin

Haskalah, as an organized movement with a distinct ideology, had first appeared in the border area of eastern Germany, in the Prussian cities of Königsberg, Breslau, Halberstadt, and, above all, Berlin. It was in these cities that a rising Jewish middle class, encouraged by the economic policies of the government which aimed to develop commerce and industry, began to emerge from the long Jewish cultural and social isolation. Around the middle of the eighteenth century the signs of Haskalah became evident in all these centers.

Thus, the three Friedlander brothers of Königsberg gave their children a secular education and assembled in their homes libraries of secular books and *objets d'art.*[23] Somewhat later, during the late sixties and early seventies, a number of Jewish youths assembled here to absorb the revolutionary ideas of Kant's critical philosophy which was still in the process of being defined.[24]

When Shelomo Maimon arrived here in the late seventies, on his way to Berlin, he was introduced to a group of Jewish students who were fully assimilated as to apparel, language, and ideas and to whom the rough-

[23] H. Jolowicz, *Geschichte der Juden in Königsberg* (Posen, 1867), p. 93. In his autobiography, Bendavid tells us about his father's library in Berlin in which there was a fine collection of Judaica side by side with the New Testament, the Koran, the works of Rousseau, Voltaire, and the contemporary German writers. Cf. Loewe, *Bildnisse berliner Gelehrten mit ihren Selbstbiographien*, 2d Sammlung (Berlin, 1806), quoted by Moritz Stern in "Jugendunterricht in der berliner jüdischen Gemeinde während des 18ten Jahrhunderts," *Jahrbuch der Jüdischen Literarischen Gesellschaft*, XIX, 45.

[24] Among his outstanding Jewish disciples were Marcus Herz (cf. Jolowicz, *Geschichte der Juden in Königsberg*, p. 93) and at a somewhat later period Bendavid and Euchel.

mannered and shabbily dressed Lithuanian *illuy* (genius) seemed ridiculous and repelling.[25]

Similar trends also became noticeable in Breslau. Thus, two brothers of the poet Ephraim Moses Kuh of Breslau had converted to Lutheranism[26] long before the much more publicized conversion of the two daughters of Moses, the rich Jewish banker of Berlin.[27] It was here, as well as in other parts of Silesia, that at the end of the century the ideals of the French Revolution found a much more fertile soil than in Berlin.[28] In Berlin, however, these tendencies gained even greater strength and a wider range of influence. This was due to a whole set of causes, external as well as internal, of both a general and local nature.

An outstanding feature in the background of the Haskalah movement was the amazing rise of Prussia within the Germanies during the seventeenth and eighteenth centuries. From a population of 750,000 in 1648 it rose to five million by 1786.[29] Parallel to the rise of Prussia was that of its capital. From a population of 6,000 in 1640 it grew to more than 140,000 by 1780.[30] Paralleling the growth of the city and despite the restrictive policies of the government, the Jewish community of Berlin continued to increase. The fifty families of 1670 grew to more than a hundred by 1700. By 1739 they numbered more than 262 taxpayers. By 1770 Berlin's Jewish population rose to close to four thousand, by far the largest community in the Germanies.[31]

The Rise of a Jewish Middle Class

Of great importance for the rising Haskalah was the social structure of the Berlin community, which as a result of the economic policies of the government became predominantly wealthy. By the year 1737 it counted only ten among its tolerated members who possessed a capital of less than 1,000 reichsthaler. The years 1728 to 1735 witnessed the beginning of Jewish participation in the rising industries of Prussia. Thus, in the year 1730, David Hirsch was granted monopoly rights for a period of twelve

[25] K. P. Moritz, ed. *Maimons Lebensgeschichte*, chap. XXI, pp. 261-63.

[26] E. Kuh, *Hinterlassene Gedichte*, p. 141.

[27] J. B. Koenig, *Annalen der Juden in den preussischen Staaten besonders in der Mark Brandenburg* (Berlin, 1790), pp. 319-25.

[28] A. Shaanan, *'Iyyunim be-Sifruth ha-Haskalah* (Rehavia, 1952), chap. IV.

[29] Cf. Sidney Bradshaw Fay, *The Rise of Brandenburg-Prussia to 1786* (The Berskhire Studies in European History, New York, 1937; 2d ed., 1950), p. 141.

[30] *Ibid.*, p. 49; see also Heinrich Silbergleit, *Die Bevölkerungs- und Berufsverhältnisse der Juden im deutschen Reich*, I (Berlin, 1930), 2, table 2.

[31] Cf. Max Erik, *Etyudn zu der Geschichte fun der Haskoleh* (Minsk, 1934), Book I, chap. I.

years to produce velvet in his workshop at Potsdam. Some years later (1748, 1752) permits were granted to Moses Ries, the son-in-law of Veitel Ephraim, and to Isaac Bernhard to establish workshops in Potsdam and Berlin for the production of silk.[32] Various other industries were also established by Jews during the fifties and sixties.[33] It was, however, mainly during the Seven Years War (1756-63) that some of the Berlin Jews accumulated larger capital sums. As a result of the war emergency they were drawn into the financial dealings of the greatly strained state treasury. "For the first time Jews were called upon to take part in actions of an historical scope, to help supply the urgently needed money for the long and costly war. They discharged their task in a very businesslike manner and also accumulated great wealth."[34] Isaac Moses, one of the three "mint entrepreneurs" left to his children a capital of 516,000 reichsthaler. Veitel Ephraim and Daniel Itzig, his partners, were undoubtedly much richer.

With the end of the war the government tried to channel the newly amassed Jewish capital into various industrial enterprises. Veitel Ephraim then founded a factory for the processing of gold and silver which in time became the greatest industrial undertaking of the capital. The metals it produced were not only supplied to the state but were also shipped abroad by its own transport facilities. Daniel Itzig bought the state iron foundry and tin plant of Sorge in the Harz. In 1772 he also took over the plant for the manufacture of English leather in Potsdam which had been established by the King a short time before.[35]

It was the growing importance of the Jews in the promotion of Prussian commerce and industry which forced the government, against its own strongly anti-Jewish attitude and policies, to grant the Jews certain liberties which were gradually to bring them out of their political and social isolation. Even during the rule of Frederick II, some of the outstanding Jewish merchants and manufacturers were put on a par with the Christian merchants and many restrictions, imposed on their traveling, settling, buying, and selling, were lifted.[36]

[32] J. Kulischer, "Ha-Yehudim ve-Ta'asiyyath ha-Meshi bi-Prussia ba-Me'ah ha-18," *He-'Avar* (Petrograd, 1918), No. II (Shevat, Nisan), pp. 108-28.

[33] Hugo Rachel, "Die Juden im berliner Wirtschaftsleben zur Zeit des Merkantilismus," *Zeitschrift für die Geschichte der Juden in Deutschland*, II (October, 1930), 3d Heft, 175-96.

[34] *Ibid.*, pp. 186-87.

[35] *Ibid.*, pp. 187, 189-90; see also Selma Stern, *The Court Jew*, chaps. V, VI.

[36] Rachel, "Die Juden im berliner Wirtschaftsleben," *Zeitschrift für die Geschichte der Juden in Deutschland*, II, 192; *Ha-Meassef*, Vol. III (Shevath and Ab, 1786); Ismar

It was this rising Jewish middle class, whose enrichment and contacts with the Christian nobility of the time only served to make it more conscious of its political degradation and social isolation, which became the moral as well as material mainstay of the first generation of Maskilim and their projects. It was also from among this class that the leaders of the struggle for Jewish emancipation came.

The Emergence of a Jewish Intellectual Elite

Closely connected with the emergence of a Jewish middle class and of no less importance to the cause of Haskalah was the rise of a Jewish intelligentsia in the capital, and the social contacts it established with its Christian counterpart. Indeed, it was this intelligentsia, more than any other social group, which helped to bring about a change in Christian-Jewish relations.

An important factor in this direction was the rise to fame of Moses Mendelssohn, whose home became a meeting place for the intellectuals and *Feingeister* of both creeds. In the late seventies the home of Marcus and Henriette Herz became a similar center of attraction for the new generation of youthful intellectual aspirants. Some of the wealthier and more educated Jews began at that time to frequent the popular theatrical performances. Henriette Herz tells us that once a year, while still a child, she was taken to the theater by her parents. Theatrical performances were also arranged from time to time in some of the private homes of the wealthy Jews. Thus at the age of nine, Henriette attended such a performance of *Richard III.*[37]

It was during this period that various reading circles, intellectual and aritistic groups, sprang up in the capital in which Jews and Christians freely mingled in an atmosphere of social equality. Many participants of these groups were animated by a curiosity for the latest in science, philosophy, and literature, and were greatly influenced by the humanitarian, cosmopolitan ideals of the Enlightenment. It was among these enlightened men and women, who formed a new class of an intellectual elite outside the various existing corporations of the state, that the notion of a civil society, supra-religious in nature, became popular, creating the theoretical frame for Jewish assimilation. For the first time the sons, and

---

Freund, *Die Emanzipation der Juden in Preussen*, 1st Band, Darstellung (Berlin, 1912), Part I, chap. III.

[37] *Henriette Herz, ihr Leben und ihre Erinnerungen*, ed. J. Fuerst (Berlin, 1858), pp. 94, 105-7, 110-11; see mainly chap. V, "Zur Geschichte der Gesellschaft und des Konversationstones in Berlin."

even more the daughters, of the rising Jewish middle class were exposed to the influences of the popular French language and literature and imbued with the spirit of religious indifference and cynicism.[38]

The Geographical Factor

The influence exerted on the rise of Haskalah and its development by the geographical factor, i.e., the proximity to Poland, the center of the great mass of Jewry, must not be overlooked. If the various factors described above formed the positive forces behind the Haskalah movement, it was the neighboring presence of the masses of Orthodox Jewry which constituted what may be called a negative force. These Jews were a living embodiment of social isolation, cultural backwardness, and perverse human existence. Their nearness served to bring to the attention of the Maskilim the gloomy historical realities of Jewry, and thus rendered their struggle real and meaningful.

It is worth recalling in this context that it was during the seventeenth and eighteenth centuries that the relation between Polish and German Jewries became closer. At the time Prussia started to emerge as a major power in European political life, Poland was steadily declining politically and economically. As a result of this decline, waves of poverty-stricken Jewish wanderers streamed to most of the Jewish communities in the Germanies.[39]

The annexations of parts of Pomerania and Silesia by Frederick II further increased the number of Jews in Prussian territory. By its population and economy Prussia was becoming a part of Eastern Europe rather than of the West. Most of the newly established industries depended heavily for their raw materials on the resources, and exported finished products to the markets, of Russia, Poland, and Hungary.[40]

The commercial ties between Prussia and Poland were strengthened during the rule of Frederick II, thus resulting in closer ties between their respective Jewries.

> Frederick wanted to make agrarian Poland the most important customer for Prussian manufactured goods and a source of the raw materials needed in Prussia, and since the main agents for trade in Poland were Jews, it was con-

[38] Fuerst, ed., *Henriette Herz*, pp. 123-31; D. Friedlaender, *Akten Stücke die Reform der jüdischen Kolonien in den preussischen Staaten betreffend* (Berlin, 1793), pp. 38-39, Bemerkung 2; Jakob Katz, *Die Entstehung der Judenassimilation in Deutschland und deren Ideologie* (Frankfurt a. M., 1935), pp. 23-46.

[39] Cf. Max Koehler, *Die Juden in Halberstadt und Umgebung bis zur Emanzipation* (Berlin, 1927), chap. IV, "Betteljuden."

[40] Kulischer, "Ha-Yehudim... ba-Me'ah ha-18," *He-'Avar*, No. II, pp. 118-20.

venient to make the Prussian Jews the intermediaries for the export of Prussian goods to Poland.[41]

Of much longer standing were the spiritual relations between theJewries of these two countries. Because of their high scholastic attainments, Polish Jews exerted a deep influence on German Jews. Since the seventeenth century most of the great rabbis in Germany had been Polish Jews or of Polish descent. Polish Jews also headed most of the *Yeshivoth* in the Germanies and filled most of the posts as private tutors (*Melammedim*). Around the early seventies of the eighteenth century the number of these *Melammedim* in Prussia alone exceeded five hundred.[42]

The Berlin Haskalah from this point of view constituted a rebellion of the richer and more secularized segments of German Jewry against the spiritual domination of Polish Jewry. It was, in substance, an asertion of their own maturity and spiritual independence.

Haskalah and Emancipation

The need to differentiate between the general spread of secularism among the Jews and the rise of an organized Haskalah movement has been pointed out. Mendelssohn had already made his contribution, and the new ideas of the time had long been felt among larger sections of the young generation, when the first attempts at an organized Haskalah took place. First among these was the founding of the *Freischule* in Berlin in 1778/9, which became in time one of the most effective means for the diffusion of the Haskalah ideals. Of greater influence, especially outside the Germanies, was the *Biur*, the first part of which was completed by Mendelssohn and some of the Maskilim during the early eighties, and, finally, the founding of the first Hebrew monthly, the *Meassef*, which ushered in a new era in the history of Hebrew literature.

These cultural activities, successively undertaken within a short period of time and constituting the collective expression of former individual attempts, where chiefly the result of the awakened hope for civil emancipation among the Jews of Prussia. It was during the late seventies and early eighties that the realization of these hopes seemed more feasible. Indications of the gradually changing Christian attitude could not escape the notice of the wealthier and more educated Jews and filled their hearts with a deep optimism.

The ever widening economic activities pursued by the rising Jewish

[41] Selma Stern, *The Court Jew*, pp. 148-49, and note 12 on p. 149.

[42] Moritz Stern, "Judendunterricht in der berliner jüdischen Gemeinde während des 18ten Jahrhunderts," *Jahrbuch der Jüdischen Literarischen Gesellschaft*, XIX, 39-68.

middle class, and the various liberties it succeeded in obtaining, the spiritual rapprochement between the emerging Christian and Jewish intellectual elite, the liberal voice of Lessing's *Juden* (1749) and his *Nathan der Weise* (1779), were all unmistakable manifestations of such a change. At the beginning of the eighties the realization of the aroused hopes of the Jews became even more feasible with the appearance of Dohm's *Über die bürgerliche Verbesserung der Juden.*[43] The Jewish problem, heretofore treated as merely an administrative matter, subject only to governmental regulation, Dohm's book brought out into the open as a public problem of general concern. For the first time in centuries common sense and human decency were applied to a problem which was pervaded with so much prejudice and superstition. Practically coinciding with Dohm's liberal appeal was the appearance of the *Toleranz-Patent* of the enlightened Joseph II. Though motivated by purely utilitarian reasons of state expediency and leaving many of the restrictions on Jews unchanged, the advance in ideas and approach which it manifested was nevertheless remarkable.[44]

It was in this atmosphere of a rising liberal public opinion that Mendelssohn returned to deal with the problems of Jewry and Judaism and made his two great contributions to the cause of the Haskalah and Jewish emancipation, the *Biur* and his *Jerusalem.* While through the *Biur* Mendelssohn's aim was to diffuse Haskalah, in the latter he made a powerful plea on behalf of Jewish emancipation in the name of tolerance and the secular concept of the state. The connection between the two, though perhaps unwarranted historically, was valid logically. That Mendelssohn, at least during the last period of his life, considered the diffusion of Haskalah conducive to Jewish emancipation may be gathered from one of his letters to Homberg in which Mendelssohn pointed out that there was but one path for Jews to follow, i.e., to acquire secular learning and create cultural values of general importance. Only such excellence would finally result in a new attitude toward the Jews.[45]

The direct connection between Haskalah and emancipation was most strongly exhibited in Wessely's *Words of Peace and Truth,*[46] which may best be defined as the manifesto of a Europe-oriented Jewry. Never before had a Jew, admitting complete devotion to the full scope of Jewish

[43] Cf. W. Dohm, *Über die bürgerliche Verbesserung der Juden* (Berlin, 1781), Vol. II (Berlin and Stettin, 1783).

[44] H. F. Pribram, *Urkunden und Akten zur Geschichte der Juden in Wien,* 1st Band (Vienna and Leipzig, 1918), "Toleranzpatent," pp. 440-43.

[45] Mendelssohn's *Gesammelte Schriften* (Leipzig, 1843-45), V, 680.

[46] Naphtali Herz Wessely, *Divrei Shalom ve-Emeth* (Berlin, 1781-82).

tradition, written with such enthusiasm of the material secular things of life and introduced a completely alien scale of values as the ideal to be pursued. It was this new positive attitude toward life and the world which permeated those pamphlets that so aroused the Orthodox.[47]

The awakened hopes for emancipation were also responsible to a great extent for the establishment of the *Meassef.* Among its projected aims were not only the study of the Bible and the revival of Hebrew, the dissemination of secular knowledge, and the development of a new taste for beauty, but also "the diffusion of information among the Hebrew readers in relation to the situation of the Jews at present . . . and the various benevolent plans kings and rulers were entertaining on their behalf."[48]

The fact that the *Meassefim* dealt little with the direct problem of emancipation must not be interpreted as a detachment from the immediate realities of their time, of which they were often accused.[49] To deal in Hebrew with a problem whose solution depended completely on governmental policies could not very well have yielded desired results. To the extent, however, that the Maskilim did consider the attainment of emancipation dependent on an inner reform of Jewry, the whole *Meassef* was no doubt permeated with that ideal. Their great absorption with the Bible, education, and morals, the many poems and essays they wrote on nature and in praise of the farmer and laborer, were all pervaded with the desire for an inner reform and rebirth of Jewry. The main aim of the Maskilim was to enlighten the Jews, imbue them with the consciousness of the new era, and bring them closer to the non-Jewish society, its manners, values, and ideals.

A final comment should be made on the communal nature of the Haskalah, which is best understood against the background of the unique status of the Jews in pre-emancipation Germany.

The Jews formed a closely knit community. In addition to their religious and cultural unity, the government imposed on them, for its own fiscal purposes, the principle of mutual responsibility which bound them

[47] L. Lewin, "Aus dem jüdischen Kulturkampf," *Jahrbuch der Jüdischen Literarischen Gesellschaft* (Frankfurt a. M., 1918), XII, 165-97.

[48] "Nahal ha-Besor," par. IV, *Ha-Meassef,* Vol. I (1784); "Toledoth ha-Zeman," *Ha-Meassef,* I (1784), 16.

[49] See M. Ehrenpreis, "Le'an?" *Ha-Shiloah,* I (1897), 499-503; Benzion Katz, "Toledoth Haskalath ha-Yehudim be-Russia," *Ha-Zeman* [quarterly] (1930), II, 21-33; J. L. Kantor, "Dor ha-Meassefim," *Sefer ha-Meassef* [supplementary to the *Osif*] (Warsaw, 1886), pp. 1-34.

still more closely.[50] When hopes for emancipation arose, their realization could naturally be envisaged only in the community frame. Had the first Maskilim anticipated the possibility of an individual emancipation independent of the Jewish community, the Haskalah movement would never have started. It was the *gegenseitige verbündlichkeit* (collective responsibility) which caused the Maskilim to campaign among the more conservative members of the community to prepare them for the anticipated emancipation. When, however, it became clear, in the first stage of the struggle, that the effort did not yield the desired results, the Maskilim resorted to a more individual approach,[51] and endeavored to drive home to the state authorities the concept of heterogeneity among the Jews, and that indeed "the difference between the enlightened and orthodox Jews is far greater than the one between Protestants and Catholics."[52] Thus Friedlaender and Wolfsohn, Bendavid, Homberg, and others repeatedly emphasized that the treatment of the Jews *in corpore* constituted a grave injustice to those who had done their utmost to deserve emancipation.[53] It is noticeable that parallel to the connection between the rise of Haskalah and the awakened hopes for emancipation ran another connection between the partial individual fulfillment of these hopes and the decline of the Haskalah in Germany.

[50] Friedlaender, *Akten Stücke die Reform der jüdischen Kolonien betreffend*, III, "Betrachtungen," 1st Betrachtung, "über die solidarische Verbindung der Juden."

[51] *Ibid.*, Appendix B, p. 50.

[52] Halle Wolfsohn, *Jeschurun oder unparteiische Beleuchtung der dem Judenthume neuerdings gemachten Vorwuerfe, in Briefen von Aaron Wolfsohn* (Breslau, 1804), pp. 116-17.

[53] L. Bendavid, *Etwas zur Charakteristik der Juden* (Leipzig, 1793), pp. 51-52.

ASPECTS OF THE JEWISH COMMUNAL CRISIS IN THE PERIOD OF THE NAZI REGIME IN GERMANY AUSTRIA AND CZECHOSLOVAKIA

By Philip Friedman

IN HIS PAPER "Aspects of the Jewish Communal Crisis in 1848,"[1] Professor Salo Baron thus epitomizes the effects of that crisis:

1. Decline in membership and in revenue of the Jewish communities
2. Undermining of communal control and weakening of communal authority
3. Growing indifference of several peripheral groups to the Jewish community, leading to aloofness, desertion, and even hostility
4. Democratization of communal leadership
5. Rapprochement between Jews and non-Jews, increased good will and fraternization leading to intermarriage and assimilation
6. Intensification of the issue of religious reform
7. Acceleration of free Jewish migratory movements
8. Reorganization and regeneration of Jewish communal life

Almost a hundred years later, under the Nazi regime, another communal crisis befell Jewish life. However, the effects of this crisis were different and opposite to those in the period of the "Spring of Nations."

The results of the communal crisis of the Nazi era were:

1. An increased membership in the Jewish community caused by an artificial, enforced concentration in the ghetto of all Jews, or rather all persons considered by the Nazis as "racial" Jews, converts included.
2. An immensely enhanced communal control and authority, endowed with the power to decide even over the life and death of the individual.
3. Instead of centrifugal tendencies, a strong centripetal trand was imposed from outside on the diffuse and previously scattered Jewish residents. Despite themselves, even totally estranged elements were prompted to active participation in the social and cultural life of the ghetto.
4. Instead of democratization, an entirely undemocratic setup of communal leadership was built up, leading in many cases to outright tyranny and dictatorship.

This essay is a part of a larger study on Jewish communal organization in the Axis-controlled European countries during the years 1933-45.

[1] Salo W. Baron, "Aspects of the Jewish Communal Crisis in 1848," *Jewish Social Studies*, XIV (1952), 99-144.

5. Instead of a rapprochement to the non-Jewish environment, Jewish life was developed on the basis of strict isolation from the outer world.
6. The issues in the community, instead of religious reform, were reduced to basic matters of primordial range: fight for mere survival, for food and shelter, and self-defense against cold, disease, sheer physical force, and brutality.
7. Instead of free migratory movements, the Jewish community was constantly threatened by forced deportation and expulsions on the one hand, and on the other, by forced or voluntary introduction of destitute expellees, deportees, and refugees into the crowded ghettos.
8. The finale was also entirely different and tragic: not regeneration and reorganization, but disintegration and extermination.

How the Jewish community tried to face these gloomy prospects of the most tragic crisis in its history, how Jewish groups and individuals tried to fight against these overwhelming odds, is a lesson to be studied and learned.

In this paper only some highlights of these developments may be traced. We have had to limit the scope of our research to a few areas of Central Europe, namely to Germany, the Protectorate Bohemia-Moravia, and Austria, where the Nazi regime began its attack on the status of the Jewish community even before the outbreak of World War II. The experience gathered by the Nazis in these areas seemingly became the pattern for their later policy in the occupied countries of Western and Eastern Europe, and also had some impact on the situation of the Jewish communities in the Axis and satellite countries.

The first community to be hit by the Nazi seizure of power was German Jewry. In 1933, the first year of the Nazi regime, there were 1,611 communities in Germany. By October, 1938, these had been reduced, by emigration and persecution, to 1,208.[2]

In the period of the Weimar Republic in some of the seventeen member republics of the Reich the Jewish communities were united into state associations (*Landesverband* or *Landesversammlung*). As late as 1928 a "Working Committee" of the "Jewish State Association in the German Empire" was established. Under the impact of the Nazi seizure of power and the "urgent needs of the situation," a permanent body, "The National Committee of Jewish German State Associations" (Reichsvertretung der jüdischen Landesverbände Deutschlands), was created in the summer in 1933. However, this body was succeeded in September, 1933, by the "National Committee of German Jews" (Reichsvertretung der deutschen

[2] Hilde Ottenheimer, "The Disappearance of Jewish Communities in Germany 1900-1938," *Jewish Social Studies*, III (1941), 189-206.

Juden), which was later renamed, under Nazi pressure, Reichsvertretung der Juden in Deutschland.

The Reichsvertretung was not a mere continuation of the former Committee of State Associations. It was based on a rather broader representation of various Jewish organizations such as, e.g., the Zionist organizations of Germany, the Orthodox Jewish organizations, the *Centralverein*, the Council of Jewish Women, the National Council of the Jewish youth organizations, the *Landesverbände*, and the larger Jewish communities.[3]

Curiously enough, the new Nazi rulers, who pelted the Jewish community with a veritable hailstorm of humiliating, restricting, and discriminatory decrees, did not concern themselves at first with this field of inner Jewish life. In his survey of Nazi anti-Jewish legislation[4] Bruno Blau listed no less than 132 anti-Jewish laws and decrees, between April, 1933, and March, 1938, until the first Nazi law concerning the Jewish communities was promulgated. The "Gesetz über die Reichsverhältnisse der jüdischen Kultusvereinigungen, vom 28, Maerz 1938" (*Reichsgesetzblatt*, Teil I, Seite 338) deprived the Jewish communities and associations of their positions as public bodies and their employees of the status of public employees. A second decree of March 29, 1938, denied the Jewish communities the privilege of property tax exemption.[5]

Neither the law of March 28, 1938, nor the supplement issued the next day defined the responsibilities and activities of the Jewish community. Nor did the law actually mention the *de facto* existence of the Reichsvertretung, which continued as before to operate as a central agency for Jewish welfare, religious, and cultural activities. However, *via facti*, new and onerous responsibilities were imposed upon the Jewish communal bodies and their organizational superstructure, the Reichsvertretung. At first the executive members of the Reichsvertretung[6] had a rather too optimistic vision of its legal and political possibilities.

[3] Jacob Marcus, *The Rise and Destiny of the German Jew* (Cincinnati, 1934), pp. 193-95, 197, 328. Hans Lamm, "Über die innere und äussere Entwicklung des deutschen Judentums in Dritten Reich" (Inaugural Dissertation, University of Erlangen, 1951; stencil copy in the library of YIVO, New York), pp. 98-101, 105.

[4] Bruno Blau, *Das Ausnahmerecht für die Juden in den europäischen Ländern, 1933-1945. I Teil. Deutschland* (New York, 1952), pp. 15-40.

[5] *Ibid.*, pp. 40-41.

[6] In a meeting on September 17, 1933, the following executive members of the Reichsvertretung had been elected: Rabbi Leo Baeck, President; Dr. Otto Hirsch, chairman; Dr. Siegfried Moses, vice chairman; Rabbi Dr. Hoffmann, Dr. Landsberger, Dr. Franz Meyer, Dr. Julius L. Seligsohn, Heinrich Stahl. Lamm, "Über die innere und äussere Entwicklung," pp. 99-100.

As early as the summer of 1933 the Reichsvertretung der jüdischen Landesverbände published a statement against "placing the blame for any system" on the Jews (the Nazis accused the Jews of supporting the democratic Weimar Republic, or the so-called *Systemzeit*). In the same statement the Reichsvertretung asked for "dignity, work, freedom," a free discussion on the "basis of justice, legality and honesty." In the summer of 1934 the Reichsvertretung intervened with the Reichsminister of Internal Affairs against the ritual slander campaign of the *Stürmer*. After the promulgation of the Nuremberg Racial Laws in 1935 the Reichsvertretung again protested and asked that an end be made to the defamation and economic boycott of the Jews.[7]

The next years of the Nazi regime extinguished this naive belief and prompted the Reichsvertretung to view its meagre hopes and abilities more realistically. The program of the Reichsvertretung was directed to meeting the desperate needs of the hour, to hastening Jewish emigration from Germany and to facilitating it by means of vocational training and assistance to emigrants, to supporting the increasing number of people ruined by the restrictions and persecutions, and to meeting the educational and religious needs of the Jewish population.[8] This program of activities is clearly reflected also in the budget of the Reichsvertretung for 1937, the last normal budgetary year before the vicissitudes of the year 1938. The requirements for 1937 amounted to 4,054,000 reichsmark. Significantly enough, the once-rich Jewish community in Germany was able to meet only one third of its own budget; only 1,591,000 reichsmark were drawn from internal income sources while 2,463,000 RM were contributed from abroad, chiefly by the American Joint Distribution Committee. Of this total 1,415,000 RM were spent on economic assistance, 1,150,000 on

[7] *Ibid.*, pp. 98, 105.

[8] In a message to the German Jews issued in November, 1936, the Reichsvertretung described its program in the following words: "Wohlfahrtspflege, Wirtschaftshilfe, Schul-und-Bildungswesen, Berufsumschichtung, Vorbereitung zur Auswanderung in alle Laender." Kurt Alexander, "Die Reichsvertretung der deutschen Juden," in *Festschrift zum 80 Geburtstag von Leo Baeck* (London, 1953), p. 79.

Before long the problem of emigration became the central issue. In July, 1938, the Reichsvertretung sent the managing director, Dr. Otto Hirsch, as its representative to the International Conference in Evian (on the border of Switzerland and France) dealing with the problem of refugee immigration. The negotiations of the Reichsvertretung also greatly contributed to effecting a considerable relaxation of the strict British anti-immigration policy, thus enabling many Jewish German refugees to emigrate to Great Britain after the events of November, 1938, in Germany. Kurt Alexander, "Die Reichsvertretung der deutschen Juden," in *Festschrift... Leo Baeck*, p. 83. M. Wischnitzer, "Jewish Emigration from Germany 1933-1938," *Jewish Social Studies*, II, No. 1 (1940), 23-44.

emigration, 719,000 on education, 447,000 for social welfare, and only minor sums on other communal needs and administration. The number of Jewish schools supported by the Reichsvertretung was 135 in 1935 and 160 in 1936. In 1936, 22,000 Jewish children received their education in these schools, 18,000 of them on the primary, 4,000 on the high school level.[9]

The leadership of German Jewry must have realized the fruitlessness of negotiations with the Nazi government about a tolerable status for Jewish life and protection of the rights of Jews. "I do not believe," writes a German Jewish leader,

> that the leaders of the Reichsvertretung could have cherished any illusions in the long run. They realized more clearly and quickly than the Jewish masses the impossibility of negotiating anything with this [Nazi] government. ... Of course, attempts were made to temper the impact of the onslaught against the Jews, and some results could have been achieved in several individual cases ... as, e.g., a comparatively undisturbed ... autonomy of the internal Jewish life, at least until 1938. They succeeded in getting permission for transfer of money, thus facilitating the emigration to Palestine, and in getting allowances for children who were sent abroad for education.[10]

As a result of legal restrictions and of persecution, Jewish emigration from Germany increased, several communities were dissolved, and the economic and moral strength of the remaining communities was seriously affected. This rapid disintegration cast a shadow, which was reflected in a note of resignation in the public statement of the Reichsvertretung. In its New Year's message to the German Jews in 1937 the Reichsvertretung stated: "The process of disintegration of German Jewry is going on. Many are now facing the problem of their emigration, and many others have to follow." Still more gloomy is the message issued on the eve of the Jewish High Holidays in 1938. There is sadness but no despair in this statement: "Heavier than in previous years has been the burden of [recent] events. Nobody in our midst has been spared. ... But we Jews are a kind of people who know where hope lies. Our perseverance

[9] On March 1, 1937, there were 167 Jewish schools in 144 communities in Germany, with 23,670 pupils. Of them 148 were elementary schools and 19 secondary and high schools. Lamm, "Über die innere und äussere Entwicklung," pp. 80-81.

[10] However, adds the writer quickly, as he explains this "autonomy," almost every meeting of the Reichsvertretung was watched by an official of the Gestapo and the leading officials had constantly to justify everything they undertook, large or small, to the Gestapo. Alexander, "Die Reichsvertretung der deutschen Juden," in *Festschrift... Leo Baeck*, pp. 78-79.

[endurance] is our force. We must keep alive in our hearts our faith, the fait of our Jewishness."[11]

Before long, events that followed this wistful New Year's message surpassed the most pessimistic forebodings. The assassination of von Rath in Paris by Jerakhmiel Grynszpan gave the Nazis a long-awaited opportunity to unleash a savage blow against the German Jews. During November, 1938, 191 Jewish synagogues were either burned or destroyed, about 7,500 Jewish shops were looted, about 20,000 Jews were arrested and tortured in jails and concentration camps, a collective fine of one billion RM was imposed on the German Jews, and a new series of anti-Jewish decrees was promulgated.[12]

In this new setup, which definitely marked the change of the Nazi cold war against the Jews into a hot war, an official rearrangement of the status of the Jewish central communal body was in order. As a matter of fact, the Reichsvertretung as a democratic representative body did not fit well into the fabric of the Nazi Reich. In the totalitarian state the *Führerprinzip* had to be applied to the Jewish community as well. By the "Tenth Decree supplementing the Reich Law on Citizenship" of July 4, 1939 (*Reichsgesetzblatt*, I, 1097 f.), a Reich Association (Reichsvereinigung) of Jews in Germany was organized with its main office in Berlin and local branches (communities) throughout the Reich. The chief function of the new Reichsvereinigung was defined as "to further emigration." Additional functions were: maintaining schools for Jewish children (all these schools being considered private schools), and furnishing relief for Jews. Membership in the Reichsvereinigung was compulsory for all "racial" Jews residing in the Reich, both German subjects and stateless, and optional for foreign Jews and Jews married to "Aryans." Contray to the constitutional statute of the Reichsvertretung, the laws and by-laws of the Reichsvereinigung provided no regulations about a General Assembly and the rights of the constituency to check the activities of the organization. The Executive Board therefore owed no responsibility to the members of the Reichsvereinigung.[13]

The institution of the Reichsvereinigung was considered by the Nazis as an important step toward the liquidation of German Jewry. No less than the official party organ, *Völkischer Beobachter*, found it appropriate to

[11] Lamm, "Über die innere und äussere Entwicklung," pp. 112, 116-17.

[12] Gerald Reitlinger, *The Final Solution* (New York, 1953), pp. 14-16.

[13] The text of the decree quoted in *The Black Book* (New York, 1946), pp. 508-9, and Blau, *Das Ausnahmerecht für die Juden*, pp. 71-74.

comment on this event on its front page on July 7, 1939, in the following words:

The tenth supplementary decree to the Reich Law on Citizens carries forward the solution of the Jewish question in a decisive manner. ... Its paragraphs have but one meaning and they do not allow the slightest doubt as to the national-socialist point of view, that the Jewish problem will be considered as a definitely solved question when there will be no more Jews in Germany. ... The most important thing is to get rid of them, all and sundry, and that as quickly as possible.[14]

The new Reichsvereinigung replaced, *eo ipso*, the former Reichsvertretung, whose assets were automatically transferred to it. The Executive Board of the Reich Association was partially drawn from the former executive members of the Reichsvertretung. Rabbi Leo Baeck was again appointed chairman. The other members were: Vice Chairman, Heinrich Stahl; Managing Executive Director Otto Hirsch,; members: Dr. Paul Eppstein, Moritz Henschel, Philip Kozower, Dr. Arthur Lilienthal, Dr. Julius L. Seligsohn.[15]

In the beginning of 1940 the Reichsvereinigung still had 142 primary and high Jewish schools under its supervision, as well as a number of vocational and preparatory courses. There were then more than 15,000 Jewish children under the age of 15 in Germany, and 300-400 teachers were employed in this educational system. The Reichsvereinigung also operated 90 homes for the aged, 26 children's houses, 14 Jewish hospitals, 16 residential homes for boys and girls, 6 homes for the sick and invalids, and 2 special homes. Early in 1942 the Jewish community in Berlin was still operating 17 soup kitchens for the poor.[16]

The Reichsvereinigung issued its official weekly *Jüdisches Nachrichtenblatt*, the only Jewish periodical left after the storm of 1938. The paper, named *Mitteilungsblatt* in 1941, and edited by Leo Kreindler, ceased publication in 1943. Contrary to the administrative practice in the Nazi-occupied countries, no Jewish police force was created simultaneously with the Reichsvereinigung. Only as late as December, 1942, was an auxiliary Jewish force (*Ordnertrupp*) established to help the Germans in

[14] *Völkischer Beobachter*, Süddeutsche Ausgabe. No. 188, as quoted in Hans Erich Fabian, "Die letzte Etappe," in *Festschrift... Leo Baeck*, p. 85.

[15] Lamm, "Über die innere und äussere Entwicklung," p. 125.

[16] American Jewish Committee, *The Jewish Communities of Nazi Occupied Europe*, prepared by the Research Institute on Peace and Post War Problems, July, 1944. *The Jews in Germany* (hereafter cited as *AJC Report*), pp. 30, 32, 40.

"cleaning up" (*Durchkaemmung*) Jewish homes for deportation.[17]

However, the positive tasks and responsibilities of the Reichsvereinigung were very limited and these were gradually reduced by the ever growing pressure of events. The Reichsvereinigung eventually served its German supervisors (the Reich Security Office—the central agency of the SS and police) as an instrument to control the Jewish population, to enforce emigration, and to exact the heavy taxes imposed upon the Jews (particularly the onerous emigration tax amounting to from 10 to 60 percent of total assets). In the final stage of Jewish history in Germany the Reichsvereinigung had the tragic task of actively cooperating in the liquidation of German Jewry and giving compulsory assistance to the anti-Jewish authorities—the historian of the Jewish community in Nazi Germany thus summarizes briefly the role of the Reichsvereinigung. However, it goes without saying that the majority of the leaders believed they could (by this policy) save not only their own lives but also some number of their coreligionists.[18]

[17] *AJC Report*, p. 24; Lamm, "Über die innere und äussere Entwicklung," pp 305-6; Reitlinger, *The Final Solution*, p. 160; *Hitler's Ten Year War on the Jews* (New York, 1943), p. 29.

[18] Lamm, "Über die innere und äussere Entwicklung," p. 120. Artur Eisenbach in his book, *Hitlerowska polityka eksterminacji Żydów* (Hitler's Policy of Exterminating the Jews) (Warsaw, 1953), p. 168, blames the Reichsvereinigung for being an "instrument of the Gestapo" and seeks to corroborate his statement by a quotation from the statistical report on the "Final Solution of the Jewish Problem in Europe" prepared by Inspector for Statistics in the Office of the Reichsführer SS, Mr. Korherr, on March 27, 1953 (mimeographed copy in the YIVO Archives). Eisenbach quotes Korherr's statement as follows: "This institution (die Reichsvereinigung der Juden in Deutschland) works under the control of the Reich Chief Security Office and for its purposes. Whatever was the initial doubtful attitude of the Jews [?] it seems that the *Reichsvereinigung* is doing an honest job."

However, as far as we could find out after a careful analysis of the Korherr document, Korherr was concerned with statistical aspects of the Jewish question only, and did not try to give any evaluation of the work and the policies of the Reichsvereinigung. Korherr made the above-mentioned statement while appraising the value of the statistical data collected by the Jewish autonomous bodies and only with reference to them. We quote the verbatim transcript of the statement in its original language: "Die folgenden Angaben über die Zahl and Entwicklung der Juden in Deutschland... sind... in der Hauptsache von der Reichsvereinigung der Juden in Deutschland und den Kultusgemeinden in Wien und Prag erstellt, die mit Zählungen, Zählkarten für die Bevölkerungsbewegung, Fortschreibung [?] und daneben mit Berechnungen und Schätzungen arbeiten. Diese jüdischen Dienststellen arbeiten unter der Kontrolle des Reichssicherheithauptamtes und für dessen Zweck.... Vom fraglichen Anfangsbestand der Juden abgesehen scheint die Reichsvereinigung der Juden in Deutschland zuverlässig zu arbeiten."

It seems that Eisenbach misunderstood and consequently misinterpreted Korherr's statement.

Both assumptions proved to be entirely wrong. Neither the hope of saving their own lives nor, at least, a part of their community was fulfilled. From a total of 318,200 persons classified as Jews according to the Nuremberg laws in 1939, only 31,807 were left in Germany by April 1, 1943. Of these only 14,000 were *Volljuden*; the rest were *Mischlinge* of various gradations.

By February, 1940, the first deportations to the "Lublin reserve" started. Later there followed transports to France (particularly to the Gurs concentration camp), to Lodz, Warsaw, Lublin, Riga, and Minsk, and to the concentration camps of Theresienstadt and Auschwitz. In all those places only a few thousand managed to survive and to return after the war.[19] Consequently, the area of activities of the Reichsvereinigung was increasingly narrowed. On June 20, 1942, the Reichsminister of Internal Affairs ordered the Reichsvereinigung to close all Jewish schools in Germany, "with regard to the recent development in the deportation of the Jews."[20]

The members of the Executive Board as well as the employees of the Reichsvereinigung shared the fate of their coreligionists. Their official capacity seems not only to have been powerless to protect them but, on the contrary, served to expose them to the Nazis. As early as December, 1940, Dr. Seligsohn was arrested, allegedly because he suggested the observance of a fast day on behalf of the deported Jews of Baden. After several months in jail he was sent to the Sachsenhausen concentration camp, where he died in 1942. Dr. Otto Hirsch, arrested in the spring of 1941, was sent to the Mauthausen concentration camp, where he was instantly killed. Dr. Conrad Cohn, head of the Relief Department, was arrested in the summer of 1941 and sent to Mauthausen, where he died. In June, 1942, a number of employees of the Reichsvereinigung, among them Dr. Arthur Lilienthal, Dr. Cora Berliner (head of the Emigration Department), Ilse Cohn, and Paula Fuerst (both of the Education Department), were deported somewhere to the East, probably to some place near Bialystok, and never came back. Heinrich Stahl (summer, 1942), Dr. Paul Eppstein (February, 1943), Moritz Henschel, Philip

---

In the meantime the Korherr report has been published, in abbreviated form, in Leon Poliakov and Josef Wulf, *Das Dritte Reich und die Juden. Dokumente Aufsätze* (Berlin-Grunewald, 1955), pp. 239-48.

[19] Bruno Blau, "The Last Days of German Jewry in the Third Reich," *YIVO Annual of Jewish Social Science*, VIII (1953), 197-98, 200; cf. also Bruno Blau, "Der Judenstern der Nazis," *Judaica*, IX, No. 1 (Zurich, 1953), 36, and Reitlinger, *The Final Solution*, pp. 42-43, 212-14.

[20] Blau, *Das Ausnahmerecht für die Juden*, p. 103.

Kozower, Martin Gerson, and Dr. Leo Baeck were deported to Theresienstadt. Of them all, only Henschel and Dr. Baeck survived the gruelling experience.[21]

On October 20, 1942, a large number of officials of the Jewish community in Berlin and of the Reichsvereinigung, according to some accounts about 600 persons, were designated for deportation. Some of them, however, failed to report, while others committed suicide. Enraged by this "lack of discipline," the Nazis arrested four leading officials of the Berlin Jewish community and four of the Reichsvereinigung and executed them on December 2.[22] Dr. Leo Baeck, the chairman of the Reichsvereinigung, was arrested five times and eventually deported to Theresienstadt on January 27, 1943. Dr. Max Wiener, a colleague of Dr. Baeck, observed of his work during the Nazi years: "No historian will ever be able to do justice to the fearlessness, outstanding humanity and dignity with which Baeck on many an occasion moderated and delayed measures of persecution. His efforts gained precious time during which many individuals were enabled to reach havens of refuge."[23] As a matter of

[21] Lamm, "Über die innere und äussere Entwicklung," pp. 127-29; *AJC Report*, p. 51; Fabian, "Die letzte Etappe," in *Festschrift... Leo Baeck*, pp. 90, 93. See also the biography of Otto Hirsch in *Allgemeine Wochenzeitung der Juden in Deutschland* (Düsseldorf, January 7, 1955), p. 8, "Portraet der Woche," by E. G. Lowenthal.

In an unpublished report of Mrs. Getrud Van Tijn, the representative of the American Joint Distribution Committee in the Netherlands, under the title "Contribution towards the History of the Jews in Holland from May 10, 1940 to June 1944," the writer described in the following words her impressions after a visit to the Reichsvereinigung in Berlin (p. 36): "The last time I was in Berlin in beginning of September 1939... I was appalled... Hirsch, Seligsohn and Brasch were in a concentration camp and Paul Eppstein, who was in charge, was so harassed that he was only a shadow of his former self." The extensive report of Mrs. Van Tijn (129 pp.) was submitted in stenciled copies to the Chairman of the AJDC in New York by J. L. Magnes, President of the Hebrew University, with an accompanying letter dated Jerusalem, November 23, 1944.

According to Else R. Behrend-Rosenfeld, *Ich stand nicht allein. Erlebnisse einer Jüdin in Deutschland 1933-1944* (Hamburg, 1945), it was not Seligsohn but Hirsch who was held responsible by the Nazis for the idea of a fast day in behalf of the deported Jews in Baden. She writes in her memoirs under the date of November 10, 1940 (pp. 106-7): "Die Reichsvereinigung hatte alle jüdischen Gemeinden in Deutschland im Gedenken an diesen furchtbaren neuen Schlag einen bestimmten Tag vorgeschlagen, an dem alle Gemeindeglieder fasten sollten. Dieser Anregung sind wir gern gefolgt. Doch teilte uns Herr Rat gestern zu unserem Schrecken mit, dass man den Ministerialrat Hirsch, den man als den Urheber dieser Anregung in der Reichsvereinigung ansah, verhaftet und ins Konzentrationslager gebracht habe. Eine solche Anregung sei als Sabotage der behördlichen Verfügung zu betrachten."

[22] Bruno Blau, "Der Geiselmord vom 2, December 1942," *Aufbau*, December 19, 1952; Lamm, "Über die innere und äussere Entwicklung," p. 305.

[23] Eric H. Boehm, ed., *We Survived* (New Haven, 1949), p. 283. About Rabbi Baeck's refusal to leave Germany in 1938 there is another interesting record by the Scottish Intelligence agent Sir Michael Bruce in his book *Tramp Royal* (London, 1954).

fact, during the Nazi period Dr. Baeck received many invitations to leave Germany, but turned them all down, including a call to the Rockdale Temple in Cincinnati, insisting that it was his duty to stay with the German Jewry to the end. Until 1939 he accompanied transports of Jewish children from Germany to England, but he always returned. It is only fair to quote Dr. Baeck's statement about the leaders of the Reichsvereinigung in his interview with Dr. E. Boehm: "The leaders of the National Association of German Jews applied themselves tirelessly and selflessly to their difficult tasks, often turning down opportunities for emigration because of their duty. . . . Persons in such exposed positions were of course arrested often and on the slightest pretext." About the sore problem of compulsory cooperation with the Germans in preparing the deportations, Baeck observed:

> I made it a principle to accept no appointments from the Nazis and to do nothing which might help them. But later, when the question arose, whether Jewish orderlies should help pick up Jews for deportation, I took the position that it would be better for them to do it, because they could at least be more gentle and helpful than the Gestapo and make the ordeal easier. It was scarcely in our power to oppose the order effectively.[24]

Sir Michael was sent by a group of British-Jewish leaders to Germany in the middle of November, 1938, to help in secret rescue operations. In a meeting with German-Jewish leaders in Berlin a suggestion was made to bring Rabbi Baeck for his safety's sake to Great Britain. To which Dr. Baeck replied: "I will go when I am the last Jew alive in Germany." And Wilfred Israel, the owner of the famous department store in Berlin, added: "I will go when the Rabbi goes" (Bruce, *Tramp Royal*, p. 242). There are almost no materials about the fate of the Jewish local community leaders. Noteworthy is the case of Dr. Eugene Isaac Neter, chairman of the Jewish community in Mannheim. As a partner of a mixed marriage, his wife being a pure "Aryan," he was eligible for exemption from deportation. But Dr. Neter decided to join his community when the deportation was decreed. He left his wife in Mannheim, however, because she was not strong enough to bear the hardships of the exile (Behrend-Rosenfeld, *Ich stand nicht allein*, p. 105). Miraculously he survived all the vicissitudes of deportation and concentration camp and lives now in Israel, in Kibbutz Dagania where he was interviewed by a German journalist (Gerhard Seger, "Von Damaskus bis Beersheba," *Aufbau*, March 18, 1955, pp. 19-20).

[24] Leo Baeck, "A People Stands before Its God," in Boehm, ed., *We Survived*, pp. 285, 288.

A Jewish community leader of Germany and survivor of the holocaust, Siegmund Weltlinger, in his personal narrative, *Hast Du es schon vergessen? Erlebnisbericht aus der Zeit der Verfolgung* (Frankfurt am Main, 1954), gives the following account of the tensions, dangers, and moral dilemmas involved in carrying on the activities of the Jewish community leadership under the Nazi regime (p. 22): "Es war durchaus keine einfache Sache, an verantwortlicher Stelle in der jüdischen Gemeinde tätig zu sein. Man schwebte stets in grosser Gefahr für sich und seine Familie und war ständigen Verhören, Drohungen und Erpressungen seitens der Gestapo ausgesetzt. Ausserdem versäumte man mit grosser Wahrscheinlichkeit jede Möglichkeit der Auswanderung.

Actually, by the spring of 1943 almost all leaders of the Reichsvereinigung and the Berlin Jewish community had already been arrested, deported, or executed, and only a small skeleton organization was left under Dr. Walter Lustig to take care of the survivors, Jews in mixed marriages and their children.[25] In practice, the activities of the Reichsvereinigung ceased early in March, 1943. On June 10, 1943, the assets of the Reichsvereinigung and of the affiliated Jewish communities and organizations were confiscated and transfered to the Office of the Oberfinanzpräsident Berlin-Brandenburg. The inventories made by the agency on this occasion showed an assessed property value of the Reichsvereinigung and its affiliated branches throughout the country of 144 million reichsmark and of the property of the Berlin Jewish community of over 22 and a half million reichsmark.[26]

The short-lived history of the Jewish community of Austria under the Nazi regime was one of rapid decline. When the Nazis marched into Vienna on March 12, 1938, there were approximately 185,000 Jews in

---

Vor allem aber legte man sich natürlich die Frage vor, ob es richtiger sei, mit der Gestapo zusammenzuarbeiten oder ganz einfach passive Resistenz zu üben, wenn nicht überhaupt die volle Verantwortung für die Durchführung vieler Massnahmen der Aufsichtsbehörde zu überlassen. In langen Gesprächen erörtete ich damals mit Dir Stahl das Für und Wider. Wir kamen beide zu der Überzeugung, dass es besser sei, bis zuletzt auszuharren und dass es vor allem für die jüdische Allgemeinheit von Nutzen sei, wenn die Durchführung der schwierigsten Anordnungen z.B. der Evakuierungen, von der Gemeinde selbst übernommen werde. Man konnte durch geschickte Verhandlungen manche Erleichterungen durchdrücken, konnte in dringenden Fällen Terminverlängerungen erlangen und hatte vor allem damals noch die Hoffnung, dass eines Tages das System zusammenbrechen werde und durch Aufschub viel gewonnen sei. Es war ein Wettlauf mit der Zeit, der leider von den Juden verloren wurde. Das konnte man damals aber noch nicht wissen, und es ist sehr leicht, heute zu sagen, dass alles ja doch nichts geholfen hätte. Dies ist bestimmt nicht richtig. Man denke nur an die kurze Zeit, als der berüchtigte Brunner aus Wien mit seinen Leuten auf eigene Faust die Juden von der Strasse oder aus Häusern wegschleppte, ohne dass irgendwelche Vorbereitungen noch getroffen werden konnten. Niemals aber sollte man vergessen, welchen persönlichen Opfermut das Verharren in der Leitung der Gemeinde bedeutete."

[25] Reitlinger, *The Final Solution*, p. 165; Lamm, "Über die innere und äussere Entwicklung," p. 130; H. E. Fabian, "Die letzte Etappe," in *Festschrift... Leo Baeck*, p. 93. According to Blau, "The Last Days of German Jewry," *YIVO Annual of Jewish Social Science*, VIII, 198, there were in Germany on September 1, 1944, 14, 574 Jews, both *Volljuden* and *Mischlinge*.

[26] Fabian, "Die letzte Etappe," in *Festschrift... Leo Baeck*, p. 92.

Lamm, "Über die innere und äussere Entwicklung," p. 15, quotes the results of a statistical inquiry made in 1944 by the Federation of Jews from Central Europe. According to this estimate the property of the Jewish communities and organizations amounted on November 9, 1938 (i.e., before the *Kristallnacht*) to 236 and a half million reichsmark. Lamm finds this estimate too low and estimates the worth of the Jewish communal assets in Germany in 1933 as minimally 300 million reichsmark.

Austria, 170,000 of them in Vienna, the rest in Graz, Linz, Mödling, Baden, Wiener-Neustadt, Krems, Innsbruck, and some towns in Burgenland. As early as March 26, 1938, Hermann Göring announced at a mass meeting that Vienna must be free of Jews within four years. Under terrible Nazi pressure, the exodus of the Jewish population was of necessity very rapid. Between March, 1938, and November, 1941, about 128,000 Jews left Austria. This emigration overlapped the compulsory deportations of Austrian Jews to the East which were started by the Nazis as early as October, 1939. Both movements contributed to a rapid depopulation. By December, 1939, only 55,000 Jews remained in Austria; in the first months of 1942, 30,000; at the end of that year, according to a Jewish source, 12,000 to 15,000, and according to Nazi official statistics, only 8,102. In June, 1944, no more than 1,000 Jews were reported.[27]

The Nazis, whose plans for a wholesale Jewish emigration from Austria were executed at such a formidable pace, did not bother to rearrange Jewish community life according to the patterns already developed in Germany. The community even retained its traditional name, Israelitische Kultusgemeinde, until December, 1942, when the religious Jewish community was dissolved and its functions transferred to a Council of Elders (Ältestenrat).[28] Since the smaller Jewish communities had practically

[27] *The Black Book* (New York, 1946), pp. 129-33; *Hitler's Ten Year War*, pp. 46-50; Wilhelm Krell, "La Communauté Culture Israelite de Vienne," in *Les Juifs en Europe (1939-1945)* (Paris, 1949), pp. 190-94. Korherr's report to the Reichsführer SS of March 23, 1943, p. 4, mentions only 8,102 Jews, and the same figure is repeated in Korherr's second report of April 19, 1943, p. 2.

[28] *Jüdisches Nachrichtenblatt*, Ausgabe Wien, No. 51, of December 18, 1942. In the issues of December 18 and December 25 (Nos. 51 and 52) of the *Jüdisches Nachrichtenblatt* two editorials appeared commenting on this important change. Both editorials pointed out in a wistful mood the great changes in the life of the Jewish community of Vienna since 1938: "In 1938 the community had to build up great relief activities for hundreds of thousands of people.... Every month about 10,000 emigrants, about 50,000 people in vocational training, about 38,000 patrons of people's kitchens, and about 3,000 children and aged persons in special homes had to be cared for.... The progressive reduction [of the community activities] followed the gradually diminishing number of Jews... and after the emigration [deportation] was completed it was not an easy job to rebuild [the organizational structure of the community] thoroughly.... It is a hard job to reduce [the community] in such a way that the still surviving small remnants should be able to become a harmonic entity capable of living.... The [new] Ältestenrat will look ahead to a hard task... particularly because for the first time a Jewish community is bound to embrace everybody who is a Jew according to his descent, while until now the Jewish faith alone used to be the basis of a Jewish communal bond." The Statute of the Ältestenrat (published in No. 51 of the *Jüdisches Nachrichtenblatt*) made it compulsory for every "racial Jew to belong to the Ältestenrat" (this name being used in the *Satzungen* not only for the Executive Board but for the entire body politic of the Jews). An earlier decree of March 25,

ceased to exist soon after the *Anschluss*, all Jewish communal life was concentrated in Vienna. Even after incorporation into the Reich, the Jewish community of Vienna was not affiliated with the Reich Association of German Jews. At that time the Jewish community council of Vienna was ruled by a Zionist majority with the well-known Zionist leaders Dr. Desider Friedman as chairman and *Oberbaurat* Robert Stricker as vice chairman.[29]

Soon after the Nazis entered Vienna they sent the chairman of the Jewish community and several of its members to the Dachau concentration camp, allegedly because the community council had failed to collect the subscription of 800,000 schilling demanded by the Nazis. Not until February, 1940, was Dr. Friedman released from the concentration camp and the amount of 800,000 remitted. From the beginning the new authorities required the Jewish community to cooperate actively in the "resettlement" of the Jews in the East. The lists of the persons eligible, the circular letters, the arrangements for the assembly points had to be prepared by the Jewish community. At that time the community itself employed about 350 persons and, in addition, about 25 in the Welfare Department. However, the number of the employees in the Welfare Department soon had to be increased to 100.[30] In 1942, between June and October, 13 transports of about 16,000 Viennese Jews were directed to Theresienstadt. Among the deported were the leaders of the Jewish community, Dr. D. Friedman, R. Stricker, Dr. Joseph Loewenherz, Managing Director of the community, and his deputy, Dr. Benjamin (Bernard) Murmelstein. Of these leaders only Dr. Loewenherz and Dr. Murmelstein survived.[31] In Vienna a skeleton staff of 180 persons was still operating, headed by Dr. Loewenherz, who, apparently, came back from Theresienstadt, Dr. Tuchman, and two other members of the former Executive Board, Dr. Ernst Felberg and Mr. Weiger. In March, 1943, Adolf Eichman wanted to deport this poor remnant as well but his order was rescinded through the intervention of the Deputy Commander of the Security Police in Vienna, Dr. Adolf Ebner, who asked that this

---

1942, retroactive to September 1, 1941, made secession from the Jewish community dependent on a special permit from the Minister of Internal Affairs (*Jüdisches Nachrichtenblatt*, Ausgabe Wien, No. 16, of April 17, 1942).

[29] Oskar Karbach, "The Liquidation of the Jewish Community of Vienna," *Jewish Social Studies*, II, No. 3 (1940), 255-78.

[30] *AJC Report* on Austria, pp. 27-28.

[31] *Ibid.*, p. 28; Zdenek Lederer, *Ghetto Theresienstadt* (London, 1953), pp. 249, 42-43.

group be spared in order to look after the interests of some 6,000 Jews in mixed marriages and their children.[32]

On March 15, 1939, the German troops crossed the Czechoslovak borders. The President of Czechoslovakia was forced to sign an agreement creating the so-called Protectorate of Bohemia and Moravia. Statistics compiled by the Nazis showed, as of March 15, 1939, 118,310 "racial" Jews in the Protectorate, among them 14,350 persons of "other than Jewish faith." Emigration continued in the first months after the invasion, reducing this number to 90,147 professing Jews by October 1, 1939.[33] The Jewish communities of Bohemia-Moravia were in a state of confusion and depression. They were immediately subjected to the supervision of the Gestapo, which means to a regime of terror and oppression. German policy toward the Jews was the same as in Austria: to promote Jewish emigration. For this purpose, the Central Office for Jewish Emigration (Zentralstelle für jüdische Auswanderung) was already in existence in Vienna in April, 1938; it was headed by a former Gestapo spy in Austria, Adolph Eichman. After the annexation of Czechoslovakia, Eichman, who had in the meantime been promoted to the rank of SS

[32] Reitlinger, *The Final Solution*, p. 165.

The last Jewish visitor to call on the Vienna Jewish community before the end of the Nazi regime probably was Dr. Rudolf (Rezso) Kasztner of the Jewish Relief and Rescue Committee (Vaad Ezra Ve-hatzala) in Budapest. Dr. Kasztner was in Vienna in January 4-15, 1945, and again on April 2, 1945. According to his information the head of the Ältestenrat was again Dr. Loewenherz, who was probably sent back from Theresienstadt. The Jewish administration was located in the old, now almost empty and derelict building of the former *Kultusgemeinde* in Seitenstaettengasse 4 where there were also short religious services on Saturdays. A kind of a small "synagogue" had also been established by the efforts of Dr. Tuchman, Chief of the Jewish Health Department, in an air raid shelter on 7, Malzgasse. Besides these two Jewish community officials Kasztner still found in Vienna the following Jewish personalities: the former Jewish *Kultusgemeinde* president and *Generalstabsartz*, now director of the Jewish hospital, Dr. Arnold Raschkes; Max Bienenstein, director of the Home for the Aged; and Dr. Mathias Reich, chief surgeon of the Jewish hospital.

Besides this group of Viennese Jews, Kasztner met in Vienna a large colony of Hungarian Jews who were deported to Austria in compliance with the agreement of July, 1944, between Adolf Eichman and the Jewish Rescue Committee of Budapest. Of these 17,500 to 18,000 Jews about 50 percent were brought to Vienna as factory hands and lived in special labor camps under SS supervision. Their only connection with the Jewish Ältestenrat in Vienna consisted in getting burial facilities for their dead in the Jewish cemetery and medical treatment for their sick in the Jewish hospital.

Dr. Rezso Kasztner, "Der Bericht des juedischen Rettungskomitees aus Budapest, 1942-1945" (n.p., n.d.), mimeographed and marked: *Vertraulich* (available in the YIVO Library, New York), pp. 49-50, 154-56, 171.

[33] Korherr's Report, p. 4; Peter Meyer, "Czechoslovakia," in *Jews in the Satellite Countries*, by Peter Meyer and others (Syracuse, 1953), pp. 60-61; Gerhard Jacoby, *Racial State* (New York, 1944), pp. 5-19.

captain, also established an office in Prague. The SS Captain (later General) Hans Günther, nicknamed "the smiling hangman," served as his second in command.[34]

The Prague office was later renamed "Zentralamt für die Regelung der Judenfrage in Böhmen and Mähren." By decree of March 5, 1940, of the Reich Protector for Bohemia and Moravia, the Central Office was granted supervisory power over all Jewish communities and all Jews in Bohemia-Moravia, including those of "non-Mosaic faith." The functions of the Jewish communities were described in this decree and several subsequent ordinances as follows: (1) to collect fees imposed upon Jews; (2) to provide relief for the poor Jews; (3) to collect statistical data about Jews; (4) to foster Jewish emigration; (5) to assemble persons for forced labor and for evacuation.[35] Thus, as in Germany and Austria, Nazi seizure of power brought radical changes in the basic structure and activities of the Jewish community. Dr. Wehle, one of the surviving leaders of the community, thus epitomized these changes:

> The Jewish religious community in Prague was transformed from a big denominational institution into a big autonomous body, with great powers and enlarged responsibilities in fields of activities entirely unexperienced until then; its competence was extended to so-called racial Jews and to the entire area of the Protectorate.[36]

The Germans centralized the Jewish communities by ordering several district communities (*Kreisgemeinden*) to supervise the work of the smaller communities in their respective areas.[37] The Jewish congregations of Greater Prague were united into one central community empowered to issue directives (*Weisungsrecht*) to other communities in the country.

[34] Reitlinger, *The Final Solution*, pp. 26, 153, 509; Lederer, *Ghetto Theresienstadt*, pp. 80-81.

[35] *Jüdisches Nachrichtenblatt-Zidovske listy*, Prague, of March 15, 1940, and of April 4, 1941; Jacoby, *Racial State*, pp. 233-34.

[36] Kurt Wehle, "Zidovska nabozenske obec za okupace a po osvobozeni CSR," in *Vestnik zidovske obce nabozenske v Praze* (hereafter cited as *Vestnik*), Prague, VII, No. 1 (September 1, 1945), 2-4. Dr. Wehle, a Zionist leader, at a congress held in Prague in September, 1945, was elected Secretary General of the Council of Jewish Religious Communities in Bohemia and Moravia and he kept this office till March, 1948, when he left Czechoslovakia. Meyer, *Jews in the Satellite Countries*, pp. 114, 121, 123.

[37] In an announcement of the "Jüdische Arbeitszentrale" in Prague, July, 1941, the following *Kreisgemeinden* are mentioned: Brno, Kladno, Hradec Kralove, Kolin, Pardubice, Plzen, Pisek, Protejov, Tabor, Trebic, Uherske Hradiste, and Praha. *Jüdisches Nachrichtenblatt-Zidovake listy*, Vol. III, No. 27, July 4, 1941. In the various issues of the *Jüdisches Nachrichtenblatt* of 1941 the following communities were still mentioned: Moravska Ostrava, Budejovice, Klattau, Bensov, Zlin, Milevsko, Ledec, Vodnanu, Luza, Olomouc, Pelhrinov, Trest, Litomysl, Lipnik, Dobruska.

Besides this, the registration services of all communities were concentrated in one Central Registration Office at the Prague community.[38] Gradually, with the progressive evacuation of provincial Jewry, the provincial communities disappeared, and the pitiful remnants were taken care of by the branches of the Prague community. Later on, the central community in Prague became, besides the Ältestenrat in Theresienstadt, the only representative body of the Jews in Bohemia-Moravia. In 1943 the name Jüdische Kulturgemeinde Prag was changed into Ältestenrat (Council of Elders), but its area of competence remained unaffected.[39] A list for December, 1941, shows the following departments of the Jewish religious community in Prague: for the provincial communities, for economics, finance, statistics, the Central Registration Office (*Zentralmatrik*), social welfare, emigration, hospitalization, the Chief Rabbinate,[40] education, judiciary, non-Mosaic Jews, housing, publishing of the *Jüdisches Nachrichtenblatt,* and so on.[41] But, as in all other Jewish communities under the Nazi regime, this apparently favorable image of teeming activities was a mere sham. Under constant pressure of German police terror, the community was called upon to cooperate with the Gestapo in matters of emigration, forced labor, deportation, registration of Jewish property, etc. The slightest sign of "lack of discipline" was severely punished. Thus, for example, in the fall of 1941, 1,000 Jews were ordered to report for "emigration" to the East. Only 500 reported. Günther's deputy in the Zentralstelle, Karl Rahm, regarded this as an act of sabotage on the part of the Jewish community leadership. Consequently he arrested the chiefs of the Emigration Department, Dr. Hanus Bonn and Dr. (Erich) Kafka, and sent them to the Mauthausen concentration camp. A fortnight later the Jewish community was advised that they both died in Mauthausen.[42]

[38] *Jüdisches Nachrichtenblatt-Zidovske listy*, Vol. III, No. 42, October 17, 1941. H. G. Adler in his recently published book, *Theresienstadt 1941-1945. Das Antlitz eines Zwangsgemeinschaft* (Tübingen, 1955), p. 683, sets March 15, 1940, as the date since when the provincial communities were put under the control of the Prague community.

[39] Wehle, "Zidovska" in *Vestnik* (September 1, 1945), p. 3; Meyer, *Jews in the Satellite Countries*, p. 113. The last *Judenältester* in Prague was the well-known Zionist Dr. Frantisek Friedman, who belonged, owing to his marriage with an English woman, to the privileged group of mixed marriages. Kasztner, "Der Bericht," p. 36. See also note below.

[40] The following members of the rabbinate are mentioned in *Jüdisches Nachrichtenblatt*, Vol. III, No. 38, September 19, 1941; Dr. Aladar Deutsch, Oberrabbiner, and the rabbis Dr. Otokar Kraus and Dr. Arpad Hirschberger.

[41] *Jüdisches Nachrichtenblatt*, Vol. III, No. 49, December 5, 1941.

[42] Karel Rahm Trial, in *Vestnik*, IX, Nos. 12 and 17 (1941), 168 and 253.

In this unequal fight the Jewish community leadership tried to use the tactics of delay and biding their time. Kurt Wehle summarized the bitter experience of this period in the following words:

> What could the Jewish community do confronted by the overwhelming enemy? It could only postpone, drag on, soften, sabotage, win concessions in little things, try to protect a part of its assets, such as the historical relics, the museum, etc. But the community could not prevent the Germans from reaching their main objective: the extermination of the Jews. This was the saddest chapter in the history of this ancient Jewish community and the saddest destiny was to serve as an instrument in enemy hands. . . . Until 1942 the main function of the community was relief and social welfare; after 1943 it was forced to cooperate in the liquidation.[43]

This policy of appeasement, of placating the enemy by partial sacrifices in order to save the rest, so characteristic of the Reichsvereinigung in Germany, was also considered the most feasible policy by the community leadership of Prague.

In the hour of mortal danger a kind of political truce came about between the two main camps, the assimilationist Czech Jews' party and the nationalistic Zionists. This bipartisan policy was symbolized by the joint leadership of Dr. Frantisek Weidman and Jakub Edelstein. Weidman, a leading personality in the group of the Czech-Jewish patriots, and secretary general of the Prague Jewish community before the outbreak of the war, had been involved in many heated political controversies with the Zionists in the 1930's. In October, 1939, he was appointed the responsible leader of the community by the German authorities.[44] His political opponent and, since the German occupation, close collaborator in communal affairs was Jakub Edelstein, scion of a Polish-Jewish hassidic family and a Socialist-Zionist.[45] The developments in the first two years of German occupation seemed to justify the appeasement policy. In October 17, 1939, 1,200 young Jews of Moravska-Ostrava and environment were mobilized and sent to occupied Poland in order to prepare a Jewish camp in the neighborhood of Nisko (in the district of Cracow on the river San). Plans for a large-scale deportation of Jews of Czecho-

---

The trial of Rahm, Gunther's deputy in Prague and later Commander of the Theresienstadt Ghetto, was reported in detail in *Vestnik* in twelve installments in 1947, in Nos. 10-26. The verdict of death was reported in *Vestnik*, X, No. 18 (April 30, 1948), 211.

[43] Wehle, "Zidovska," in *Vestnik*, VII (September 1, 1945), 3.

[44] Frantisek Fuchs, "Dr. Frantisek Weidman," *Vestnik*, VIII, No. 12 (October 28, 1946), 107; Lederer, *Ghetto Theresienstadt*, p. 157.

[45] Dr. E. Ornsteinova, "Vzpominka na Jakuba Edelsteina," *Vestnik*, VI, No. 3 (October 28, 1945), 19; Tresler, "Vzpominame velkeho muze a velkeho cloveka," *Vestnik*, VIII, No. 7 (July 10, 1946), 60 (with a black and white portrait of J. Edelstein).

slovakia and Austria to the Nisko area were under consideration. Several representatives of the Jewish communities of Prague and Vienna were brought to Nisko, among them Jakub Edelstein and Dr. B. Murmelstein, and were ordered to prepare a feasible project for this settlement. After submitting the project, they were sent home.[46] More transports were sent to Nisko from Vienna, Teschen, Bielsko, and Kattowitz, but none from Prague and other towns of Bohemia and Moravia. Beginning with September, 1939, there was talk in the Nazi press about the Lublin Reservation. In October, 1939, the first transports of Jews left for the Lublin Reservation from Vienna and from the Protectorate. But in 1940, while the transports of Jews from Austria and the incorporated Polish provinces to Lublin continued, the transports from the Protectorate were stopped for a number of months. Not until October, 1941, did the first five transports leave Prague for Lodz, while a further transport bound for Minsk in White Russia was suddenly stopped.[47]

There were several reasons for this German policy, but the biographers of Weidman and Edelstein give the credit for this development to the combined efforts of these two community leaders. According to these sources, Weidman and Edelstein succeeded in persuading the Germans of the usefulness of distributing the Jewish forced labor squads from

[46] The Nisko experiment, entirely abandoned by the Nazis after six months, was described in detail in the memoirs of J. Zehngut, "Nisko. Prubeh prvniho transporta zidu z protektoratu," *Vestnik*, Vol. XI (1949), Nos. 8, 9, 10, 11, 13, 26-27; T. Guttman, *Dokumentenwerke über die jüdische Geschichte in der Zeit des Nazismus*, Teil I (Jerusalem, 1943), pp. 62-66; Reitlinger, *The Final Solution*, pp. 43-44; Lederer, *Ghetto Theresienstadt*, pp. 203-4. Dr. Murmelstein later summarized his experience in the Nisko experiment in his "Geschichtlicher Überblick," p. 1, in the following words: "Es unterliegt keinem Zweifel, dass die Verfasser dieses Projektes die auf der Krim-Halbinsel bezw. in Birobidschan bestehenden jüd. Siedlungsgebiete vor Augen hatten, als sie an die Ausführung dieses Planes gingen. Selbstverständlich war jedoch hier kein Aufbauwille, sondern das Vernichtungsziel massgebend, und dementsprechend gestaltete sich die weitere Entwicklung. Die Durchführung war nämlich planlos unfähig und grausam zugleich; sie musste sich daher in vollen Sinne des Wortes—wenn auch über eine Reihe von Leichen—totlaufen. Der Plan scheiterte zum grossen Teil auch am Widerstand der Militarbeherden und der neu errichteten zivilen Verwaltung."

"Geschichtlicher Überblick" was an attempt at an impersonal historical account of ghetto Theresienstadt from its establishment to its termination in May, 1945. The "Überblick" was most likely written down immediately after the liberation, sometime in the summer or fall of 1945, and submitted soon thereafter to the Wiener Library in London. A copy, of 69 typewritten pages, was prepared by the courtesy of the Wiener Library for the YIVO archives in New York. This writer is very much indebted to the management of the Wiener Library for making this relevant source available to him.

[47] Philip Friedman, "The Lublin Reservation and the Madagascar Plan," *YIVO Annual of Jewish Social Science*, VIII (1953), 151-65; Lederer, *Ghetto Theresienstadt*, pp. 13, 204.

Bohemia-Moravia within the borders of the Protectorate.[48] This was considered an important achievement by the Jewish leadership. It proved also to be a remarkable advantage in the negotiations over the ghettoization of the Czech Jewry that soon followed. At a meeting of the Nazi top executives in Berlin on October 4, 1941, the establishment of ghettos in Bohemia-Moravia was decided upon.[49] The Jewish community in Prague was ordered to submit a plan to the Zentralstelle. Such a plan was submitted as early as October 9, 1941, and it envisaged the ghettoization of the 88,000 Jews of the Protectorate *within the borders* of Bohemia-Moravia. The initial German plan to build wooden barracks for the accommodation of all Czech Jews was soon abandoned after the memorandum of the Jewish community pointed out the extraordinary costs of building the necessary 1,300 barracks (at a cost of 125 million Czech *korons*) and the enormous amount of wood and other scarce material necessary for this purpose. Thus a plan emerged to accommodate the Jewish ghetto in one of the existing towns of the Protectorate. It was not easy to find such a refuge, since SS *Hauptsturmführer* Günther, in his letter of October 11, 1941, excluded a considerable number of towns. Eventually Theresienstadt, a garrison town with an old fortress and military barracks, was suggested to the Jewish communal leaders as the suitable place. The Jewish community tried to fight against this choice. In a memorandum of October 19, 1941, the Jewish community suggested the creation of three Jewish ghettos in the suburbs of Prague, Moravska-Ostrava, and Brno. The memo also pointed out that Theresienstadt (in Czech, Terezin) was already overcrowded. These objections were, however, not considered.

On November 10, 1941, the Germans ordered the Jewish community to send a group of pioneer workers (342 young men, most of them skilled craftsmen) to Theresienstadt, where they were scheduled to arrive on November 24 and immediately start work as *Aufbaukommando* No. 1 (AK1).[50] Thus the dangerous illusion of the so-called model ghetto, Theresienstadt, came into being. The pioneer group of AK1 was accompanied by several officials of the Prague community headed by Jakub Edelstein and engineer Otto Zucker, former head of the Palestine Office

[48] Fuchs, "Dr. Frantisek Weidman," *Vestnik*, Vol. VIII (October 28, 1946); Orensteinova, "Vzpominka... Edelsteina," *Vestnik*, Vol. VI (October 28, 1945).

[49] Frantisek Kraus, "K 4 Rijnu," *Vestnik*, XI, No. 38 (1949), 429.

[50] Dr. Rudolf Iltis, "Jak doslo k zalozeni terezinskeho ghetto," *Vestnik*, X, No. 48 (1948), 532; Mirko Tuma, *Ghetto nasich dnu* (Prague, 1946), pp. 14-16, speaks of 342 men; Lederer, *Ghetto Theresienstadt*, pp. 12-14. The negotiations and preparations which preceded the establishment of the camp-ghetto Theresienstadt are extensively described in Adler, *Theresienstadt*, pp. 16-36.

in Prague and chairman of the Jewish community in Brünn (Brno, in Moravia). On December 4 a second *Aufbaukommando* of 1,000 men arrived and the first Ältestenrat (Council of Elders) was appointed by the SS Inspector of the camp. Edelstein was nominated *Judenältester* and Zucker was appointed his deputy. They were made responsible for the construction of a ghetto where, according to German plans, 70,000 Jews were to be housed.[51]

The two leaders of the Ältestenrat were men of different type. While Edelstein liked the limelight, Zucker was retiring and modest. Both, however, were devoted to their work and looked upon it as a way to rescue the Czech Jews from deportation and annihilation. Edelstein was the "soul of the whole," "the father of everything." He invested a tremendous amount of energy, enthusiasm, and travail in the scheme of rebuilding the decrepit and dilapidated houses and barracks into a suitable housing project for many thousands. After all, the small garrison town which in 1940 was barely able to serve as living quarters for 3,500 soldiers and 3,700 civilians had to become the home of all Czech Jews and many others. Into Theresienstadt, from November, 1941, to May, 1945, were brought about 140,000 Jews from the Protectorate, Austria, Germany, Holland, Denmark, and Slovakia. Many stayed for only a few months until further deportation. The average Jewish population at any one time was between 35,000 and 40,000; the peak was reached in September, 1942, when the ghetto harbored 53,000 souls. There was not enough housing space, not enough building material to add new housing units; there was a dearth of food, of medical and sanitary supplies, of everything. The German SS administration, cruel and brutal, established a full set of regulations and restrictions which made the task of the Ältestenrat more miserable by its constant demand for forced labor, for victims of deportations, for "exemplary executions of undisciplined" persons, etc.

The old conflict between the Zionists and the assimilationists also had some bearing upon the social life of Theresienstadt. The Zionists were the most influential and active group in the ghetto and had a strong hold in

[51] Lederer, *Ghetto Theresienstadt*, pp. 15-20. The first Ältestenrat consisted of 13 members. The other members of the Council were: Dr. Rudolf Bergman, Leo Hass, Dr. Erich Munk, Erwin Elbert, Dr. Leo Janowitz, Dr. Egon Popper, Julius Gruenberger, Dr. Erich Klapp, Karel Schliesser, and Jiři Vogel (one name is missing). The former head of the Prague community, Dr. Weidman, never had any official position in Theresienstadt. He was nevertheless active in the social life of the ghetto and was known for several courageous public speeches on various occasions. He was deported to Auschwitz on October 28, 1944, and died there. Fuchs, "Dr. Frantisek Weidman," *Vestnik*, Vol. VIII (October 28, 1946); Lederer, *Ghetto Theresienstadt*, p. 157.

the Ältestenrat. On the other hand, the rank-and-file of the first transports were rather indifferent or even hostile to Zionist ideology. The non-Zionists interpreted the zeal of Edelstein and Zucker in building up and developing the ghetto as a device to transform the ghetto into a kind of preparatory training camp, *hakhshara*, for future immigration to Palestine.[52] Besides these two groups there were also others, such as the "racial" Jews, persons of Jewish descent but now members of the Catholic or other Christian churches, who had no feelings of solidarity, either by national or by religious bonds, to the ghetto population. For these, numbering about 9,000 souls in 1943, Theresienstadt was a forced commune, knitted together by sheer outside compulsion.[53] Another group in the ghetto, of rather little influence, were the Communists.

The young Elder of the Jews, Edelstein, was, according to several eyewitness accounts, a man with personality. He has been described by his ghetto fellow prisoners as of ready wit, a clever person, a bit of a demagogue, though a modest man, an able negotiator with the Germans, always ready to outwit them and to help his coreligionists. He was rather unpopular at the beginning but soon learned how to win the sympathies of the population. His brief experience in the camp of Nisko in 1939 stood him in good stead for his first steps in the administration of Theresienstadt. However, he again lost much of his popularity after the German delegated to the Ältestenrat the responsibility for selecting those to be deported to the East. An incident, however, showed that Edelstein had the stamina for leadership. In January and February, 1942, the German ghetto administration meted out a cruel punishment to nine Jews who had been arrested for having attempted to smuggle out letters to their relatives still at large. For this offense they had been sentenced to be hanged publicly, and the members and officials of the Council of the Elders had been ordered to watch the execution. Edelstein refused to attend and submitted his resignation which was not accepted by the SS command of the ghetto.[54]

[52] Tuma, *Ghetto nasich dnu*, p. 16; Lederer, *Ghetto Theresienstadt*, pp. 27, 41, 123-24, 132.

[53] Heinrich Liebrecht, "Therefore Will I Deliver Him," in Boehm, ed., *We Survived*, pp. 230 ff.; Lederer, *Ghetto Theresienstadt*, pp. 123-14. About the conflicts between the Zionists and assimilationists, as well as about the various nationalities and the converts in the camp see Adler, *Theresienstadt*, pp. 292-315.

[54] Tuma, *Ghetto nasich dnu*, pp. 32-33, 37; Liebrecht, "Therefore Will I Deliver Him," in Boehm, ed., *We Survived*, p. 230; Lederer, *Ghetto Theresienstadt*, pp. 41, 44; Orensteinova, "Vzpominka... Edelsteina," *Vestnik*, Vol. VI (October 28, 1945); Tresler, "Vzpominame velkeho muze a velkeho cloveka," *Vestnik*, Vol. VIII (July 10, 1946); Fuchs, "Dr. Frantisek Weidman," *Vestnik*, Vol. VIII (October 28, 1946).

The job of administering Theresienstadt was in some ways different from the activities carried on by the Jewish councils of Germany, Austria, and Prague. By an order of the SS of July 1, 1942, the entire non-Jewish population was evacuated from Theresienstadt. Here, therefore, there was concentrated an all-Jewish population, and a full-fledged territorial administration was commissioned to the Ältestenrat. The Ältestenrat had therefore to assume the full responsibilities of a normal city council in addition to its many special functions. The ghetto had its Building and Construction Department, which was particularly active after the Germans embarked upon their program of "embellishing" Theresienstadt after December, 1943.

The Technical Department, the Economic Department, the Department of Internal Administration (with a legal section, a housing section, a registry, a section for religious services, a postal service), the Labor Department, and the Health Department were also very active. A ghetto police, wearing special armlets and headgear, was established at the very beginning, and numbered approximately 200 until its reorganization in September, 1942, when its number was considerably increased.[55] To enlarge the self-deception of autonomy the Germans ordered the issue of a special currency for Theresienstadt by the Jewish Emission Bank (April, 1942). The notes of the bank, incidentally utterly worthless and never permitted to be circulated outside the ghetto, bore the effigy of Moses

---

Lederer, *Ghetto Theresienstadt*, pp. 20-22, does not mention Edelstein's resignation in January, 1942, but he tells of a second attempt of Edelstein to resign, on January 27, 1943, after the Ältestenrat had been reshuffled by order of SS General Adolf Eichman. However, this request was also refused by the Germans. Lederer, *Ghetto Theresienstadt*, pp. 42-43. A detailed description of this incidentic in Adler, *Theresienstadt*, pp. 83-86. The execution was carried out in installments: on January 10 two delinquents, on February 24 seven, were hanged.

[55] Lederer, *Ghetto Theresienstadt*, pp. 20, 59-60, 72. On December 31, 1943, the number of persons employed in the Police and Security Department was 964. Temporarily, also, the impression of great funds allegedly available for the "development" of Theresienstadt was created by the Nazis. However, as we can see from the following statement of a person as well informed as Dr. Murmelstein, a part of these funds was manipulated by various channels and excuses into the Reich treasury, while another part was frozen and had never been utilized for the benefit of the ghetto. To quote Murmelstein's Überblick," p. 6: "In den Jahren 1942 und 1943 wurde das Vermögen der aufgelösten jüdischen Körperschaften in Wien und Berlin ebenfalls nach Prag überwiesen, da in der Zwischenzeit Juden aus diesen beiden Zentren nach Theresienstadt gekommen waren, Kurz vor Auflösung des Ghettos war ein Betrag vor etwa 95 Millionen Reichsmark vorhanden, von welchem aber in April 1945 etwa die Hälfte zum Ankauf vom Reichschatzscheinen verwendet wurde, angeblich wegen der besseren Verzinsung."

holding the Tablets of the Law, and were signed by Jakub Edelstein.[56] The Nazis even issued postage stamps depicting a lovely landscape of

[56] Lederer, *Ghetto Theresienstadt*, pp. 62-63, 88. Photostats of Theresienstadt banknotes have been published in many books, e.g., in *The Black Book*, p. 291; Moshe Prager, *Hurban Israel be' Europa* (Eyn-Harod, 1948), illustrated annex (n.p.); K. E. Loret, "Paper Money Issued in the Concentration Camp of Theresienstadt," *The Numismatist*, IX (June, 1947), 422-23.

The Jewish community leadership was forced to cooperate with the Nazis in this deceptive farce. A characteristic episode happened in 1944. In spring, 1944, the Jewish Relief Committee of Budapest managed to send a sum of $10,000 for the relief of the Theresienstadt ghetto inmates. The money was sent to Dr. Frantisek Friedman in Prague who forwarded it to Theresienstadt. Afterwards the Jewish representative of the Jewish Relief Committee in Budapest, Dr. Kasztner, received two letters, one of May 24, 1944, from Dr. Friedman of Prague and another, of May 23, 1944, from Theresienstadt signed by Frantz Kahn, Dr. Paul Eppstein, Dr. Erich Oesterreicher, Dr. Erich Munk, Ing. Otto Zucker, and Gert Koerbel. In both letters the life in Theresienstadt was praised and depicted as a sheer idyll in a time when almost 70,000 Jews had been deported from Theresienstadt to the extermination camps in the East. The letter from Theresienstadt reads as follows:

"Lieber Chawer, . . . In Theresienstadt ist eine richtige jüdische Stadt entstanden, in der alle Arbeiten von Juden besorgt werden, von der Strassenreinigung angefangen bis zu einem modernen Gesundheitswesen mit einem grossen Stab von Pflegepersonal, von samtlichen technischen Arbeiten bis zur Verpflegung in den Gemeinschaftskuchen, von der eigenen Polizei und Feuerwehr bis zu einem besonderen Gerichts-Post-und Verkehrwesen, von einer Bank mit eigenem Siedlungsgeld und von Verkaufsladen für Lebensmittel, Kleidung und Hausrat bis zur Freizeitgestaltung, in deren Rahmen regelmässig Vorträge, Theateraufführungen und Konzerte stattfinden. Die Kinder, denen besondere Sorge gilt, sind in Kinder- und Jugendheimen, die nicht arbeitsfähigen Alten in Alters- und Siechenheimen unter ärztlicher Aufsicht und Pflege untergebracht. Die Arbeitfähigen sind vor allem für den inneren Diest eingesetzt. Aus allen Gebieten sind hervorragende Fachkräft zusammengekommen. Dies kommt nicht nur der hier zu leistenden Facharbeit auf technischem, hygienischem und administrativem Gebiete zugute, auch in der Freizeit hat sich dadurch ein reiches kulturelles Leben auf jüdischem und allgemeinem Gebiet entwickeln koenen. Eine Bibliothek mit nahezu 50,000 Bänden mit mehreren Lesezimmern, ein Kaffeehaus mit ständigen Musikdarbietungen dienen der Zerstreuung, insobesonders für die älteren Menschen. Zentralbad und Zentralwäscherei fördern die allgemeine Hygiene, auf die naturgemäss besonderer Wert gelegt wird. So kann man sich hier, wenn man die Äussere und innere Umstellung und Einordnung vollzogen hat, durchaus wohlfühlen. Eine Ansicht der Stadt ersehen Sie aus dem Briefkopf. . . ."

Dr. Friedman wrote in his letter: ". . . Alle arbeiten in ihren Fächern und haben sich auf ihren Gebieten hervorragend ausgebildet. Erich Munk ist Leiter des Gesundheitswesens in Theresienstadt. Erich Oesterreicher leitet dort den Arbeitseinsatz. Kahn betätigt sich in der Freizeitstaltung. Schuster widmet sich vor allem seiner kleinen Tochter. Die übrigen betätigen sich hauptsächlich in der Jugendfürsorge, die in Theresienstadt vorbildlich ist und Hervorragendes leistet. Sie haben ein reichhaltiges jüdisches Leben gestaltet, sind stolz auf ihre überaus reichhaltiges Bibliotek, ein grosses Theater mit Opernaufführungen, die täglichen Platzkonzerte, ein Kaffeehaus, Stadtkapelle und die täglichen Vorträge von sehr hohem Niveau. Dass die Gegend ausserst schön ist, durfte Euch bekannt sein, wozu man noch hinzufügen muss, dass besonders geschmackvolle Parkanlagen hergerichtet wurden. . . . Mit herzlichem Schalom Ihr Dr. Friedmann."

Theresienstadt.[57] They did everything to give the impression that Theresienstadt was a ghetto for privileged Jews, for protected prominent personages, and at the same time an *Altersghetto* for the aged. In addition to the Czech Jews, after June, 1942, many transports of German and Austrian Jews began to pour in; April, 1943, Jews from Holland; October, 1942, from Denmark; December, 1944, from Slovakia. While the transports from other countries never reached the dimensions of the Czech transports (73,608), the German and the Austrian Jews nevertheless were numerous enough (42,832 and 15,254 respectively) to influence the life of Theresienstadt.

The influx of so many new and heterogeneous elements with many leading Jewish personalities necessitated, of course, a reshuffling of the ghetto administration. In the period between October 1, 1942, and January 31, 1943, the Ältestenrat was reorganized three times. The first reorganization order of October, 1942, took notice of the population changes and introduced a number of German Jews into the Council. Edelstein was reappointed Elder and Heinrich Stahl, of the Reichsvereinigung der Juden in Deutschland, Deputy-Elder. Six of the former Czech members of the Ältestenrat were retained, and five new members, representatives of Austrian (Dr. Desider Friedman and Robert Stricker) and German Jews (Dr. Leopold Neuhaus of Frankfurt-am-Main, Karl Stahl, and Dr. Hermann Strauss) were added.

By order of SS General Eichman on January 27, 1943, this arrangement was, however, superseded by a more centralized body, the triumvirate consisting of Dr. Paul Eppstein (of the Reichsvereinigung), Dr. Loewenherz (of Vienna), and Jakub Edelstein. Eppstein was appointed head of the Board and this, according to Lederer, immediately caused Edelstein to resign his post. This resignation was not accepted, but a new reshuffling took place four days later. Instead of Dr. Loewenherz, Dr. Benjamin Murmelstein became a member of the Board of Three. These three leading officials had to run the ghetto with the help of the department chiefs (Ältestenrat), among whom important changes occurred as well. The various departments were reshuffled, and Austrian and German Jews

---

Facsimiles of both letters are reprinted in Kasztner, "Der Bericht," annex pp. 5-6. According to Adler, *Theresienstadt*, p. 121, the first banknotes were put into circulation as late as May, 1943.

[57] A facsimile of the stamp has been published in the catalogue of the Philatelic Exhibit, *A Century of Jewish History* (New York, 1950), prepared by Emil Weitz and sponsored by the American Section of the Jewish Agency, p. 15.

were given office there.[58] All these changes, however, were not ordered with the view of bringing more cooperation and harmony into the ghetto life. The Ältestenrat of the United Nations became instead rather a Council of Disunited Nations. The Germans incited the national groups against each other and the tension and competition were not diminished by the new arrangement.

As a matter of fact, the strains and intrigues that preceded the creation of the new trinational body were high enough to encourage an attempt at setting up a kind of a military dictatorship in the ghetto. In September, 1942, when the Ghetto Guard was reorganized, and elderly newcomer, Dr. Karl Loewenstein, was appointed commander of the police force. Loewenstein was a colorful personality; in World War I he had been a high-ranking German officer and, according to Lederer, aide-de-camp to the German Crown Prince. He came to Theresienstadt from Minsk, to which he had been deported from Germany. He had direct access to the German headquarters and this gave him a rather independent position toward the Ältestenrat. He organized the four hundred men of his guard along military lines, received special privileges for them, started to organize military parades with his men in the streets of Theresienstadt, and to interfere with the affairs of the Ältestenrat. His frequent clashes with the ghetto administration and his growing influence eventually led to his downfall. German authorities in Berlin were surprised to learn that a para-military formation had been organized in the ghetto. Simultaneously the Ältestenrat discovered some minor offenses in the conduct of the police commander. Loewenstein was put in prison and his special guard disbanded in September, 1943.[59]

[58] A photo of a staff meeting of the Ältestenrat, with Dr. Eppstein in the chair and about 16 other persons participating, has been published in *Vestnik*, IX, No. 12 (1947), 168. According to Dr. H. G. Adler (cf. note 59), "the *Ältestenrat* was of considerably less importance than the *Leitung* consisting of the *Judenältester* [and his two deputies—P.F.] with the staff of the *Zentralsekretariat* and his entourage." According to Sulamith Cholewa, "Di denishe yidn in Theresienstadt," *YIVO Bleter*, XXX, No. 2 (1947), 311, the Chief Rabbi of the Danish Jews, Dr. M. Friediger, was also a member of the Ältestenrat. The maximum number of members of the Ältestenrat was 27. A detailed description of the composition, the members, and the agenda of the Ältestenrat can be found in Adler, *Theresienstadt*, pp. 193-94, 248-54.

[59] Lederer, *Ghetto Theresienstadt*, pp. 60, 94. Another version of the Loewenstein episode is given by Dr. H. G. Adler, a Theresienstadt survivor who is now preparing a comprehensive psychological and sociological study on Theresienstadt. In a letter of December 10, 1954, to this writer Dr. Adler writes: "Dr. Loewenstein, an old German naval officer of half-Jewish origin, was installed as chief of the security department. Loewenstein's influence with the SS was relatively large, but the three internal camp leaders disliked his struggle against corruption and were frightened by his strong and stubborn personality which unfortunately was not understood by them.

In the meantime the triumvirate of the ghetto leadership was not getting along too well, anyhow. The head of the Ältestenrat, Dr. Eppstein, was considered by some of his fellow inmates "the weakest personage among these men. . . . He seemed to lack courage and merely complied with all orders from the [SS] Headquarters. . . . Not only was he disliked by most of the prisoners, but his prospects at the hands of the Germans were grim."[60] A former lecturer in sociology at the universities of Bonn and Heidelberg, Eppstein was a

lawyer, philospher, sociologist, piano virtuoso and poet, trying to appear as a socialist, a rather poor negotiator, and, in certain inexplicable instances, enormously ambitious. Among the German Jews he had the reputation of being a courageous and energetic man.[61] Why the SS men entrusted the leadership [of the Ghetto] to him is inexplicable. He was a wiseacre, wrapped in a strange pretense of sentimentality, an amateur of fantastic paintings, of Debussy and of atmospheric storms. . . . He did not like the Czechs but concealed his Germanism by [his] Zionism. . . . He was much more unpopular than his predecessor [Edelstein].[62]

In this originated a fight of all these four men and I must say that the role of the three leaders was at least imprudent and irresponsible. Loewenstein was eliminated late in summer 1943 by means which had a tremendously bad effect on the future of the camp."

Loewenstein's biography, his straight personality, and his sincere efforts to reform and improve some of the mismanagement in Theresienstadt were extensively described in Adler, *Theresienstadt*, pp. 135-36, and *passim* (see index). Karl Loewenstein published recently an interesting personal narrative: "Minsk. Im Lager der deutschen Juden," *Aus Politik und Zeitgeschichte*, Beilage zur Wochenzeitung *Das Parlament*, Vol. XXXXV, 56 (Bonn, November, 1956). This paper seems to be a fragment of a larger memoiristic work encompassing the author's experience in Minsk and Theresienstadt, in the years 1941-45 (see Adler, *Theresienstadt*, p. 723).

[60] Lederer, *Ghetto Theresienstadt*, pp. 43-44. Lederer's opinion in this respect concurs with the view of Dr. Adler who describes Eppstein as a "weak character, without conception" (in his letter of December 10, 1954).

[61] The same opinion, contradictory to Lederer's and Adler's evaluation, has been shared by another Theresienstadt survivor, the Catholic (former Protestant) German lawyer of Jewish descent, Heinrich Liebrecht: "Eppstein... was endowed with tremendous energy and was always fair and honest." Liebrecht, "Therefore Will I Deliver Him," in Boehm, ed., *We Survived*, p. 230.

[62] Tuma, *Ghetto nasich dnu*, pp. 32-33.

The moral climate of the Lilliputian ghetto empire, its dictatorial elite, and the personality of its leader, Dr. Eppstein, changed and twisted by the dictatorial powers commissioned to him, have been pointedly analyzed by Emil Utitz in his book, *Psychologie des Lebens im Konzentrationslager Theresienstadt* (Vienna, 1948). Dr. Utitz, formerly professor of philosophy and psychology at the universities of Halle a. d. Saale and Prague, spent more than three years in ghetto Theresienstadt and made the following observations (pp. 68-69):

"Im Wahne der Gefangenen wurde das Lager eben zu einer Art Zwergstaat, in dem sich reaktionäre Strömungen mit fortschrittlichen in seltsamster Weise vermengten.... So entwickelte sich tatsachlich—besonders im Jahre 1944—eine skurrile Art eines

Before long Eppstein's first deputy and former Elder of the Jews, Edelstein, became the victim of Nazi suspicion. In November, 1943, he was arrested, together with some of his closest co-workers, and indicted for having aided and abetted the escape of fifty-five ghetto inhabitants who evaded a transport destined for Auschwitz. In December Edelstein with his family was sent to Auschwitz and was shot there, on Himmler's order, in June, 1944.[63]

The next to be liquidated was Eppstein. After February-March, 1944, when the Austrian SS Colonel Karel Rahm (until then in Prague) took over the command of the camp, Eppstein's position was undermined.

---

karikaturistischen Serenissimusstaates. Der Judenälteste umgab sich mit einem ganzen Hof. Es war kaum möglich zu ihm vorzudringen. Die Gewährung einer kurzen Audienz erschien eine besondere Vergünstigung. Seine orakelnden Worte sollten in ihrer Dunkelheit unerschöpflichen Tiefsinn bekunden. Ansprachen ans Volk waren festliche Anlässe. Feierlichkeiten waren überhaupt sehr beliebt. Zwar gab es keine Denkmäler zu enthüllen, dafür aber Eroffnungen von Anstalten und dgl. mehr, wobei es weniger auf den praktischen Inhalt ankam, als auf die formale Fassade. Kunst und Wissenschaft wurden huldvollst gepflegt. Es gab sogar eine Art Hoftheater, an dem die höchsten Herrschaften Gefallen fanden. Ihre Anwesentheit galt als ehrende Auszeichnung, ihr Lob als unsichtbarer Lorbeerkranz. Um den Serenissimus drängten sich ehrgeizige und ränkelspinnende Maitressen. Er war selbstverständlich unbeliebt, nur ein kleiner Teil lakaienhaft beflissener Günstlinge huldrigte ihm; ihnen lächelten denn die Strahlen seines Wohlwollens, ihnen gegenüber milderte sich die herrscherliche Strenge.

"Dabei handelte es sich um einen begabten kultivierten Akademiker, wissenschaftlich vorzüglish ausgebildet, künstlerisch selbst tätig und verständnissvoll. Die Verhältnisse waren stärker als er. Eitelkeit, Ehrgeiz, beginnender Grössenwahn zerbrachen ihn. Und das Ende: die SS-Leitung — und er war stolz darauf, dass er sich auf ihre Behandlung so gut verstand — verhaftete ihn, verschleppte ihn und brachte ihn um."

[63] Utitz, *Psychologie... Theresienstadt*, p. 37; Lederer, *Ghetto Theresienstadt*, pp. 102-3; Orensteinova, "Vzpominka... Edelsteina," *Vestnik*, Vol. VI (October 28, 1945). After Edelstein's arrest, up to his deportation in September, 1944, Otto Zucker represented the Czech Jews in the *Leitung*.

An interesting sidelight on Edelstein's personality has been added in the report of Mrs. Van Tijn, "Contribution towards the History of the Jews in Holland," pp. 34-35: "In March 1941 we received a visit of two Jews from Prague—Edelstein and Friedman—who told us that they had been delegated to visit us by the "Centralstelle für Jüdische Auswanderung" in Prague which was dealing with the whole Jewish problem in Czecho-Slovakia. They told us that a similar S.S. office would be opened in Amsterdam, that the emigration forms which were to be used in Holland would be modelled on those in use in Czecho-Slovakia and that their orders were to make us acquainted with the contents of these questionnaires as well as with the general procedure.... Any feelings of misgivings I might have had against Edelstein and Friedman—Jews visiting us at the orders of the Gestapo—soon gave place to a feeling of appreciation, particularly for Edelstein. I do not know what estimation Czecho-Slovakian Jewry has of him and his activities but I can only say that when he initiated me into this new work he mainly taught me how to obstruct and delay.... Whereas my dealings with Edelstein and Friedman concerned mainly the future emigration of Jews, they had many talks with Prof. Cohen in his capacity as President of the "J.R." [Joodsche Raad], warning

Rahm disliked the Germans (the *Grossdeutschen*) with the peculiar hatred of a stalwart *Österreicher*, and a German Jew was a rather easy target for his feelings. One day, soon after Rahm's arrival, Eppstein returned from his usual visit to the SS Headquarters with a black eye. This was the beginning of the end. In September, 1944, Eppstein was ordered to Headquarters where he was humiliated and killed. A few days later a purge of the German and Czech members and officials of the Ältestenrat began. All those who had been friends of Edelstein, Zucker (deported in September, 1944), and Eppstein were sent to the East.[64]

During those trying months when the stars of Edelstein and Eppstein kept fading, the star of Dr. Murmelstein, Eppstein's second in command, steadily rose. Soon after Eppstein's arrest the Council of Elders was disbanded and all executive power transferred to Dr. Murmelstein. Before World War II Benjamin Murmelstein had served as rabbi in one of Vienna's suburbs. He was a lecturer at the Jewish Theological Seminary and, according to Lederer and Tuma, also at the University of Vienna. He was the author of several popular books and pamphlets on Jewish

---

him as to the task which lay ahead of him. In Czecho-Slovakia the notorious Eichman was in charge of handling the Jewish question and he, a close associate of Himmler and at the same time a good connoisseur of the Jewish question, was a particularly vicious specimen of the S.S. Although it was probable that those who would be put in charge in Holland might not be quite as bad, still Edelstein did not seem to have many illusions on this subject. I think it was he who told Prof. Cohen that he would probably be made the mouthpiece of such dreadful news concerning the Jews that he would become hated and despised by his own people. This was said at a time, it must be remembered, when actual deportation had not taken place."

The report of Mrs. Van Tijn has been recently supplemented by another contemporaneous document, the diary of Menahem Pinkhof, a leader of the Jewish Haloutz underground in Holland, published in *Yediot bet lohamey ha-getaot*, Bulletin of the Ghetto Fighters House, No. 1 (13), Haifa, January, 1956. Pinkhof writes in his diary (p. 18): "Edelstein, at that time head of the Judenrat in Theresienstadt, visited Holland in the beginning of 1941, in order to give consultation on the organization of the Judenrat. Beside this assignment he made a short visit to our Institute [the Halutzim farm] in Lundstrecht. In the serene rural atmosphere of our farm, with only two or three of our *haverim* [closest friends] attending the meeting, he expressed his absolutely pessimistic views as to the fate of the European Jewry, if the war will not end soon, 'and there is no hope for it.'"

More about Edelstein's arrest and his death in Auschwitz is in Adler, *Theresienstadt*, pp. 155-56 and 730.

[64] Rahm Trial, *Vestnik*, IX (1947), 168-69; Lederer, *Ghetto Theresienstadt*, pp. 148-55; *Ghetto nasich dnu*, pp. 43-46. It is worth while to add here the explanation given by Dr. Adler: "Eppstein felt himself almost as the emperor of the camp, though not in Rumkowski's [dictator of the ghetto of Lodz—P.F.] fashion, and, in consequence, he made disastrous mistakes. This was the true reason for his imprisonment under a flimsy pretext in the early autumn of 1944 and of his execution a few days later."

history and the Talmud.[65] In 1937 he became a member of the executive board of the *Kultusgemeinde* in Vienna and remained on the Board during the Nazi occupation as well. He was deported, on January 19, 1943, to Theresienstadt and in the same month appointed second deputy to Eppstein. After Edelstein's fall he actually became the most influential member of the Ältestenrat. In the beginning of December, 1943, the Germans entrusted the important assignment of taking charge of the "embellishment" program to Murmelstein. Visits by international committees were expected in Theresienstadt, and the Nazis wanted to show off with a perfect Potemkin façade of a "model ghetto." This assignment seemed to be Murmelstein's main contribution to the administrative activities of the Ältestenrat until the arrest of Eppstein. At first, there were no great changes after Murmelstein's appointment. The deportations from Theresienstadt continued under his administration for a full month (from September 28 to October 28), reaching a very high number, and then suddenly stopped.

In all, 86,934 people were deported to the East from Theresienstadt. Thirty-five transports of 44,000 people in 1942, 8 transports of 12,000 in 1943 until Edelstein's arrest (November, 1943), 10 transports of 12,500 until Eppstein's arrest, 11 transports of 18,500 during Murmelstein's administration.[66] Of course, no conclusions about the diplomatic efficiency of the Ältestenrat could be drawn from these figures. Various reasons, entirely beyond the influence of the Jewish communal leadership, had a great deal to do with the German decisions on deportations. In the last months of 1944 the strategic situation of Germany and the shortcomings of the transportation system substantially hampered the implementation of the deportation program.

In general, Murmelstein continued the policy of political expediency pursued by his predecessors. Lederer believes that this was the only possible policy, since any attempt at open defiance would have entailed the liquidation of the ghetto, and considers Murmelstein's policy as particularly clever. According to him Murmelstein was

> an extraordinary man. . . . Besides being a man of scholarly attainments and great organizing abilities he was also extremely ambitious. Though highly

[65] E.g., in 1935 Murmelstein published a polemic booklet, *Einige Fragen an Prof. P. Severin Grill, Verfasser der theologischen Studie: Der Talmud und Schulchan Aruch.* Eingeleitet von Oberrabiner Dr. David Feuchtwang. Hg. von der Union der Österreichischen Juden. Probably one of his last prewar publications was his *Geschichte der Juden: Des Volkes Weltwandern* (Vienna, 1938), 408 pp.

[66] These figures are based on statistics published in Lederer, *Ghetto Theresienstadt*, pp. 205-51.

strung he knew how to conceal and control his emotions. . . . It is certainly more than a mere coincidence that his favorite characters were Herod the Idumaean and Flavius Josephus. . . . It appears that he saw himself as another Flavius Josephus who, undeterred by the vociferous contempt of his people, worked for its salvation.[67]

A somewhat dissident view has been given by another fellow inmate of Theresienstadt, Mirko Tuma:

A man weighing no less than 100 kg (220 pounds), with an enormous head, a sunken nose, small eyes and puffed up lips. He used to tell everybody around him that the Righteous God (in whom he had no personal faith at all) called upon him to sacrifice himself for the sake of the persecuted Jews and, if necessary, to dishonor his own reputation in order to protect them.[68]

There were, however, also other, entirely different opinions.

After the deportations of October, 1944, the Germans embarked upon a policy of stabilization. No more transports were sent out from Theresienstadt. On the other hand, some transports (more than 8,000 persons) kept on arriving in Theresienstadt from Germany, Prague, Vienna, and Slovakia until April, 1945. Two transports left Theresienstadt for freedom: in February, 1945, a transport of 1,200 left for Switzerland, and in April several hundred (about 350) Danish Jews were "repatriated" to their country. Of course, the Jewish leadership in Theresienstadt had no influence whatsoever on these two acts of unusual Nazi generosity which were caused by the international situation and the endeavor of the German henchmen to create extenuating "alibis" for themselves.

In those last months of "stabilization," from November, 1944, until the liberation in May, 1945, the Ältestenrat was reorganized. To Murmelstein, who remained chief of the administration, four other executives were added representing the four main nationalities of Theresienstadt: Rabbi Leo Baeck for the German Jews; Dr. Albert Meissner, a former member of the Austrian Parliament and Minister of Justice (1920-29) and Social Welfare (1934) in Czechoslovakia; Dr. Edward Maurice Meijers, a famous Dutch lawyer, substitute councilor at the High Court of Justice in The Hague, and professor of Civil and International Law at the University of Leyden; and *Hofrat* Heinrich Klang, an

[67] *Ibid.*, pp. 58, 159, 167.

[68] Tuma, *Ghetto nasich dnu*, pp. 43-44. Dr. Adler draws the following short but sharp silhouette of Dr. Murmelstein: "Among all the internal leaders he was the most intelligent and cautious, but also the coldest and most unscrupulous, fighting mainly for his personal survival. His behavior against the inmates was far from human and in his fits he did not even restrain from beating people."

authority in civil law and university professor in Vienna.[69] A few days after the departure of the Germans, early in May, 1945, Dr. Murmelstein resigned and Theresienstadt was run by the Council of Four. On May 12, 1945, Jiři Vogel, a Czech Jew and member of the first Ältestenrat, was appointed head of the community by a general consent of representatives of all groups of the former prisoners.

As in other liberated countries, heated discussions about the role of the *Judenrat* and its alleged or real collaboration with the Germans immediately began. In October, 1945, the Jewish community of Prague established a Court of Honor (civic court, *Ehrengericht*) to investigate charges and complaints against the former executives and employees of the Jewish community administration during the Nazi regime.[70] Murmelstein, the only surviving leading executive of the Theresienstadt ghetto, was arraigned by Czechoslovak authorities and freed.[71] He was again arraigned in Rome by a Civic Court of the Organization of the Jewish Displaced Persons in Italy in August, 1948, but the case was dismissed.[72] On the other hand, the staunch defenders of the Ältestenrat and its policy of expediency pointed to the fact that Theresienstadt was the only ghetto with almost 19,000 survivors (17,320 on the day of liberation in Theresienstadt, the rest rescued via Switzerland and Denmark during the early months of 1945). However, it still remains to be decided how much credit for this can be given to the efforts of the Ältestenrat and how much was merely the result of the international developments and of the internal controversies among the Nazis. Final judgment cannot be passed now, and perhaps can never be passed, on this very complicated question.

[69] Lederer, *Ghetto Theresienstadt*, p. 191; *Ghetto nasich dnu*, p. 48; Baeck, "A People Stands before Its God," in Boehm, ed., *We Survived*, pp. 292, 296; *Festschrift... Leo Baeck*, p. 97; cf. also the moving post-mortem about H. Klang by Guido Kisch in his review of *Österreichische Rechts-und-Staatswissenschaft in Selbstdarstellungen*, in *Historia Judaica*, XVI, Part 2 (October, 1954), 134-35. The last to visit the camp before its liberation was Dr. Kasztner of the Jewish Rescue Committee of Budapest. He was in Theresienstadt on April 16, 1945, and had a talk with Dr. Murmelstein, then still chief of the administration, and with Dr. Leo Baeck. Kasztner, "Der Bericht," pp. 178-80.

[70] *Vestnik*, II, No. 2 (October 28, 1945), 15.

[71] Lederer, *Ghetto Theresienstadt*, p. 166, n. 2. Among other unpublished sources, Lederer also utilized for his book the "Geschichtlicher Überblick" by B. Murmelstein. *Ghetto Theresienstadt*, p. 267; cf. above, note 46.

[72] Report on the trial published in *Baderekh*, Rome (September 3, 1948), p. 3.

JEWISH IMMIGRANTS IN LONDON IN THE 1880's

By Lloyd P. Gartner

ALTHOUGH MILLIONS OF persons migrated from and through England in the nineteenth century, comparatively few emigrants from the Continent settled there permanently. British ports throve on transmigrants, whether Irishmen who crossed to Liverpool to set sail for America, or emigrants from the Continent who arrived at Grimsby and traversed England in order to board an Atlantic emigrant ship on the other coast. Among the relatively few who did stay in England for any length of time, some remained just long enough to earn the necessary few pounds to enable them to exchange the Old World for the New. In the swirl of departing natives and of foreign migrants passing through, those who settled permanently in England comprised a very small fraction. Their reasons for settling in England were various—intention to return home soon, lack of money to venture on, or quite accidental factors. There is also the more striking case of political exiles who took refuge in England to await better times for their several causes.

The Jews are conspicuous enough among the thousands of emigrants who remained to constitute one of the principal Continental groups which settled in England. They were mostly from Central and Eastern Europe, but the proportion and number from Eastern Europe increased greatly as the century drew to its close.[1] From the viewpoint of the total number of Jews who migrated in the nineteenth century, these early migrants are not important. Viewed as a chapter in the history of Jewish settlement in England, they merely continued the flow of immigration which has been a pervasive feature of Anglo-Jewish history ever since Resettlement times. By the end of the 1860's, internal conditions in Eastern Europe were reaching a stage which released a torrent of Jewish emigration with few parallels in Jewish or general history.

[1] Cecil Roth, *A History of the Jews in England* (2d ed., Oxford, 1949), pp. 225 ff., 265 ff.; M. D. George, *London Life in the XVIIIth Century* (2d ed., London, 1930), pp. 126-30.

Most of the Russian and Polish Jews who arrived in England before the late 1870's were single young men. Many of them left their homes for the brighter prospects of distant lands, and more particularly for the purpose of avoiding the severities of Russian conscription.[2] Some were hardly more than vagabonds who moved from town to town on the Continent and were finally unloaded upon England by their respective communities, especially by port cities like Hamburg and Königsberg.[3] Three major misfortunes in Eastern Europe at the close of the 1860's slowly forced this picture to change and foreshadowed events which were to come: the commencement of Rumanian persecutions, the famine in northeastern Russia in 1869-70, and the border expulsions in the same years.[4] By that time, not only railroads but also ample maritime transportation was available, providing augmented facilities and lower fares for those inclined to try a new land. The new land was, however, seldom England. Those who did come usually had the intention of returning home, or of going on farther.

THE JEWISH COMMUNITY AND IMMIGRATION

The events of 1881-82 in Russia, despite all of their emotional shock, did not fundamentally alter the movement of Jewish population, although they created an atmosphere of panic in East European Jewry and stirred Western Jewish communities to political and philanthropic action. Vigorous measures were undertaken in relief of pogrom victims, and efforts were made to modify the Russian government's anti-Semitic policy. The negative intention of these exertions was to prevent substantial numbers of Jews from migrating westward.[5] From the 1880's onward, international Jewish migration was conclusively regarded as an international Jewish concern, and each Jewish community had some body to deal with migrating Jews and, where possible, to encourage them to move on else-

[2] J. G. Eccarius, *Der Kampf des Grossen und des Kleinen Kapitals oder Die Schneiderei in London* (Leipzig, 1876), p. 25.

[3] Board of Guardians for the Relief of the Jewish Poor, *Minutes*, June 6, 1872 , March 25, 1873.

[4] *HaMaggid*, Vol. XIV, Nos. 13, 14 (March 30, April 6, 1870).

[5] "In fact, it is a serious feature of the present movement that a very large accession to the mass of the foreign poor in London will result." *Jewish Chronicle* (cited hereafter as *JC*), March 31, 1882. "After the movement of English feeling in favor of Russian Jews, there is no doubt that the first "city of refuge' to which our persecuted brethren will flee is England. Already we see the beginnings of such an Exodus." *JC*, March 17, 1882. Cf. also *JC*, August 20, 1880, March 3, 10, 1882, March 19, 1886.

where.[6] The Russo-Jewish Committee in London, supported by the Mansion House Fund, anxiously strove either to repatriate refugees or to send them on to America.[7] Yet the committees proposed and the migrants disposed. In spite of native English Jewry's efforts and desires to the contrary, thousands of Russian and Polish Jews settled in London, in addition to smaller numbers in the provinces, especially in Manchester and Leeds.

The Jewish community of England of which the immigrants became members, while varied in its origins and continually replenished by immigration, achieved a cohesive organization by a long organic growth. Its principal institutions in the nineteenth century stemmed from the Ashkenazic Great Synagogue, its officials and auxiliaries, of the eighteenth century. This institution in the East End was regarded as the parent of all Ashkenazic synagogues in London (and even in England and early nineteenth-century America), which loyally regarded themselves as but its branches and subsidiaries. The Great Synagogue's rabbi was the religious head of Ashkenazic Jewry in London and then in the provinces and, in early years, America. From this developed Victorian England's Chief Rabbinate, which towered over a thoroughly subordinate Jewish ministry. The entire system was written into the United Synagogue Act of 1870, which established an organic union, both spiritual and financial, of the chief London synagogues. The political representation of the Jews was through the Board of Deputies of British Jews, elected through synagogal constituencies, and familiar to all Jewry through the humanitarian labors of its President, Sir Moses Montefiore. The principal welfare agency of London Jewry, the Board of Guardians for the Relief of the Jewish Poor, originated in 1859 as an amalgamation of the charities of the larger synagogues and received a large part of its budget from the United Synagogue. This substantial charity advanced beyond the contemporary philosophy embodied in the English Poor Law by supplying its clients with "self-help" in such forms as business loans, apprenticeships, and sanitary knowledge. Its main beneficiaries, however, were always foreign Jews who required the necessities of life during their frequent periods of adversity.

[6] Z. Szajkowski, "Emigration to America or Reconstruction in Europe," *PAJHS*, XLII (December, 1952), 157-86 *passim.* Mark Wischnitzer, *To Dwell in Safety* (Philadelphia, 1949), pp. 37-66.

[7] Report of meeting of Guardians to discuss relations with the Mansion House Fund, *JC*, March 3, 1882. For final report of the Mansion House Fund, cf. *JC*, October 27, 1882.

Not all was as smooth as appeared on the surface. The Reform movement had caused a painful schism whose marks were still evident years later. The poorer classes, mostly made up of immigrants, remained outside the communal organism in small synagogues and societies. The Jewish communal system established in London, however, maintained the flexibility and possessed the means and prestige necessary ultimately to "digest" newer elements. The group which ruled this community of some 40,000 Jews in 1880 was a highly cohesive and intermarried group of wealthy merchants and a few manufacturers, with financiers at the top. Names like Rothschild (practically the Royal Family of the Jewish community), Montagu, Mocatta, Goldsmid, Louis Cohen and his sons, Samuel, and some few others were an interlocking directorate of the Jewish community. The repose and inclusiveness of the Jewry which they governed was to be jarred and then strained by the masses of East European Jews who settled in England.

The immigrants' ports of arrival in England were usually either Grimsby or Tilbury. Grimsby arrivals sometimes settled down in the provinces, and occasionally moved to London, but for the most part they shuttled across the Midlands by special trains to launch their Atlantic crossing from Liverpool. Arrivals at Tilbury, but a short distance down the Thames from the heart of London, presented more of a problem to native Jewry, for Tilbury was a terminal port, and a larger proportion of those who debarked there was cast directly upon the streets of the East End within a few short hours. For fear of appearing to encourage immigration, native Jewry turned a blind eye to the unsavory conditions at the dockside, and in the decade of the 1880's it made no attempt to shield the arriving Jews from the waterfront's abundant number of cheats and malefactors.[8]

The efforts which were made to establish an effective protection for arriving immigrants are a microcosm of various attitudes to immigration. Native Jewry, represented in charitable works by its Board of Guardians, kept hands off the problem. It enforced its early rule, which required six months' residence to acquire eligibility for its benefits.[9] Assistance for refugee immigrants, particularly if they desired to go on or to return, was extended by the Russo-Jewish Committee in limited amounts to those

[8] For a specimen description of an arriving emigrant boat, cf. Charles Booth, ed., *Life and Labour of the People*, Volume I: *East London* (London, 1889), pp. 580-83.

[9] Board of Guardians, *Minutes*, August 31, 1859. The rule was evidently relaxed during the emergency of 1881-82. Cf. remarks of President Lionel L. Cohen to Annual Meeting, in *JC*, March 17, 1882. Nor was its enforcement always stringent; *JC*, November 17, 1885. Cf. also *Die Tsukunft*, Vol. I, No. 35 (March 20, 1885); *JC*, July 20, 1883.

who could qualify under the loose term "refugee." Practical immigrant aid came from a different quarter and by odd means. It came to light during 1884 that Simon Cohen, a pious baker known to his contemporaries and to later folklore as "Simha Becker," had established a sort of shelter in Back Church Lane, a stone's throw from the central intersection of the East End. It seems that he merely kept up a crude refuge for the homeless or jobless, where they could pray, study sacred literature, sleep somehow, and, after a fashion, be fed. Immigrants were also accommodated by this austere hospitality. This transmigration of an East European charitable practice aroused no sympathy among native Jewish philanthropists, whose ideas in such matters were largely controlled by Poor Law philosophy. They succeeded instead in having "Simha Becker's" refuge shut down for more-than-sufficient sanitary reasons, in the face of some East End protests.

A new and better-supported institution arose to take its place in the following year. This was the Poor Jews' Temporary Shelter, which had the substantial support of several native Jews who were more sympathetic with immigrants—Hermann Landau, a stockbroker who had come from Poland in the 1860's, Samuel Montagu, Ellis Franklin, and Bernard Birnbaum. The new Shelter confined itself to immigrant aid alone, and allowed nobody to remain over fourteen days. Not only did it give no dole, but it declared, in accord with the best contemporary charitable thought, that payment would be required of all those who could afford it. Having thus sought to allay any anxiety that the Shelter would make England appear over-hospitable to prospective immigrants, and having organized it on necessarily stern lines, the sponsors turned to the Jewish Board of Guardians in an effort to reach a mutual accommodation. The Guardians' widely esteemed President, Lionel L. Cohen, drew up a proposed agreement with the Shelter's representatives and appealed to his Board to accept it. This they declined to do, and for some years matters proceeded in a state of mutual nonrecognition.[10]

[10] On the foundation of the Shelter, cf. *JC*, March 27, April 3, May 15, May 29, June 5, June 19, June 26, July 3, September 11, October 9, October 16, October 23, October 30, November 13, 1885, April 16, 1886. The proposed agreement between the Shelter and the Guardians stipulated: 1) no cash relief to be provided; 2) no workshop to be opened by the Shelter in order to make work; 3) only single males to be admitted; 4) 14-day limit with no reentry permitted; 5) persons who did not secure employment upon leaving the Shelter would be turned over to the Guardians for repatriation; 6) the Shelter might conduct its own appeal for funds, since it reached classes not reached by the Guardians; 7) the Guardians must approve changes in the Shelter's rules; 8) three representatives were to sit on each other's committees. Opposition to this agreement claimed that any Shelter would precipitate a flood of

IMMIGRANT DEMOGRAPHY

The following figures, showing the rising tide of Jewish immigration, furnish the background which makes Jewish communal policies and tensions assume a significant dimension:[11]

	Population of England and Wales	*Aliens in England*	*Population of London*	*European Aliens in London*
1871	22,712,266	100,638	3,254,260	51,084
1881	25,974,439	118,031	3,816,483	55,136
1891	29,002,529	198,113	4,211,743	87,443

	Russians and Poles in England	*Russians and Poles in London*
1871	9,569	5,294
1881	14,468	8,709
1891	45,074	26,742

While the number and proportion of aliens was thus rising in general, the increased number and proportion of Russians and Poles is particularly significant, and the more so when one removes from the total of aliens the large number of foreign seamen who happened to be in British ports at

---

pauper immigration. *JC*, October 9, 1885. Board of Guardians, *Minute Letter Book*, p. 192, January 9, 1888; House of Commons, *Report... on Emigration and Immigration (Foreigners), 27 July 1888*, pp. 106-23 (esp. Min. 2157), 137-39, 146-47, 312-13; House of Commons, *Report... 8 August 1889*, pp. 80-81, 92; Board of Trade, *Reports on the Volume and Effects of Recent Immigration from Eastern Europe to the United Kingdom* (C. 7406), 1894, pp. 29-35; Royal Commission on Alien Immigration, *Minutes of Evidence* (Cd. 1742), 1903, Min. 16,271; V. D. Lipman, *A Social History of the Jews in England, 1850-1950* (London, 1954), pp. 92-93 (lacks evidence for the "Rothschild subsidy").

[11] *Census of England and Wales, 1871*, Vol. II (C. 676-1), Table 3, pp. 5-6; Vol. III (C. 872), Table XXIII, p. li, Table 15, pp. 25-26; *Census... 1881*, Vol. II (C. 3563), Table 3, pp. 5-6; Vol. III (C. 3722), Table 9, p. xxiv, Table 10, p. xxv, Table 13, p. 22, Table 13A, pp. 23-25. *Census... 1891*, Vol. II (C. 6948-1), Table I, p. v, Table 2, pp. 11-12; Vol. III (C. 7058), Table 10, pp. 20-21. Statistics of Jewish immigration are insuperably difficult. The fundamental assumption must be the equation of "Russians and Poles" with Jews, with the exception of a very few non-Jewish Russians and Poles, especially in Scotland and Manchester. (House of Commons, *Report... 8 August 1899*, pp. 63-69 [Testimony of James Keir Hardie]; Royal Commission, *Minutes of Evidence*, [Cd. 1742], Min. 21,111-21,117, 21,192-21,194, 21,740-1, 22,035-22,120.) However, the rest is all Jewish. An indeterminate proportion of German, Austro-Hungarian, and Rumanian immigration is also Jewish. The best contemporary guides through the maze of confused and uncertain immigration figures of the 1880's are Board of Trade, *Reports* (C. 7406), 1894, pp. 1-23; H. Llewellyn Smith, "Influx of Population," in Booth, ed., *Life and Labour*, esp. pp. 543-54; Joseph Jacobs, *Statistics of Jewish Population in London, 1873-1893* (London, 1894).

census time. Withal, these figures are still rather slight for England as a whole, although they become rather perceptible in London. The number of Russians and Poles in London becomes conspicuous when the district of Stepney is examined:[12]

	Population of Stepney	*Aliens in Stepney*	*Russians and Poles in Stepney*
1871	275,567	14,030	3,435
1881	282,676	15,998	6,682
1891	285,225	32,374	22,029

Thus, over four fifths of the Russians and Poles in London were concentrated in one area of the metropolis. Further statistical analysis, not here attempted, as well as much contemporary testimony, will show, moreover, that the Jewish concentration in the East End was confined to a sharply limited section, in which many streets were inhabited by Russian and Polish Jews alone.[13]

The native Jewish community in England, which did not need to concern itself too much with an average annual increase of 490 Russian and Polish Jews in the 1870's, had to have serious regard for the average annual increase when it rose to 3,061 in the 1880's. For Stepney alone, the average annual increases were 325 and 1,535 in the two decades, respectively. Furthermore, these increases scarcely reflect the much greater number of Russian and Polish Jews who stayed briefly, nor do they even intimate the immigrants' English-born offspring, who were subjects of the Crown although they lived within the Jewish immigrant community.

For an immigrant group, and particularly one many of whose members were enroute to or from the Old World or the New, the ratio of the sexes is surprisingly close to even. In contrast to the overwhelmingly male composition of most of the Continental groups which settled in England during these years, we observe a high percentage of females, as in the following specimen from the Whitechapel census registration district:

[12] By "Stepney" before 1888 is meant the Registration Districts of Whitechapel, Mile End Old Town, St. George's in the East, and Stepney proper. Cf. Board of Trade, *Reports* (C. 7406), 1894, pp. 151-53.

[13] The basic movement is eastward, northeastward, and southeastward from the historic Jewish core at the eastern border of the City of London. The best representation is graphic; cf. the frontispiece map in C. Russell and H. S. Lewis, *The Jew in London* (London, 1901), reprinted in *The Jewish Encyclopedia*, *s.v.* London, and in Lipman, *A Social History of the Jews in England*, between pp. 94 and 95; it is best used in conjunction with Booth, ed., *Life and Labour*, end paper.

RUSSIANS AND POLES

	Male	Female	Percentage of Females
1871	1,694	1,218	41.8
1881	2,768	2,435	46.9
1891	7,257	6,281	46.4

The age distribution among arriving immigrants follows the curve usual in migrating groups, with the great preponderance falling between 15 and 40 years of age.

The relatively high proportion of females certainly suggests considerable family migration, although families did not necessarily migrate together. It seems to have been a common practice for the husband to arrive in England first, and then to send for his wife and children. A further step might take the husband on to America, leaving wife and children behind, to be supported by remittances, other members of the family, and by communal charity, until he could again send for them. Such piecemeal movement was necessary because few could pay for the entire voyage of a whole family at one time. However, long and unhealthy separations were not uncommon, and the London Jewish charities tried to prevent the whole practice by means of exhortation and by refusing all aid to such "deserted wives," thereby requiring them to enter the public workhouse if they desired relief. This severe policy seems to have been invoked only occasionally, as an object lesson to discourage the practice or to show that official Jewish charity would not assume responsibility in these cases.[14]

MAKING A LIVING

At all events, the immigrant had to support himself practically from the day he arrived, besides saving what he could in order to move himself or his family elsewhere. We have an inkling of the vocational background which he brought with him from a later segment of 9,047 lodgers at the Poor Jews' Temporary Shelter (in five years falling between 1895-96 and 1907-8) who described themselves as "following a calling."[15] By assimilating such overlapping terms as "dealer," "merchant," and "traveler" under the heading of petty trade, and by doing likewise for other vocational

[14] B. Spiers, *Divrei Dvash* (Hebrew *Honied Words*) (London, 1901), pp. 35-36.

[15] Poor Jews' Temporary Shelter, *Annual Report*, 1895-96, 1899-1900, 1901-2, 1903-4, 1907-8.

descriptions, we find 2,599 (29 percent) to be in clothing trades, 2,054 (23 percent) in petty trade, 977 (9 percent) in boot- and shoemaking, 719 (7 percent) as carpenters, and 205 (2 percent) in agriculture. The remaining 2,493, or nearly 30 percent, were spread among a great variety of small trades, including butchers, bakers, printers, coopers, barbers, furriers, jewelers, coachmen, locksmiths, cigar makers, painters, descending numerically to one acrobat. Although the number of persons without fixed vocations is not clearly indicated, there does seem to be a rough validity to the rest of the reckoning.

The trades which these Jewish immigrants followed display several common characteristics. Thus, they usually stood in a transitional position between handicraft and factory systems of production, so that the manufacturing process was actually divided between factory and workshop, machine and hand labor. Jewish labor in England clove to the workshop; in fact, when industries like tobacco, walking sticks and canes, and boots and shoes converted largely to factory production, the Jews tended to slip out of them. The Jewish immigrants' trades were also possessed of qualities which peculiarly suited the Jewish workers' backgrounds, social milieu, and aspirations. For example, the manufacturing process still required many of the steps to be done by hand. Some skilled handiwork, such as pattern cutting in cloth or leather, could be done only by hand, while at the foot of the ladder, other work like blackening shoes could be done better by cheap labor than by any machine yet invented. A skilled, slow-working, well-paid English craftsman could make a complete pair of shoes or a suit of clothes, but rare was the immigrant who could do it. Hence a second necessary characteristic of Jewish immigrant trades—extensive subdivison of labor. A skilled clicker (leather cutter) or clothing machinist (sewing-machine operator) had his assistants who did the less skilled part of the work for him. Thus, an intricate wage scale was developed, with wide gradations corresponding to a worker's skill and output. The immigrant trades were also rapidly expanding and highly seasonal, and had to depend upon a large reserve supply of pliant Jewish and female labor to perform slightly skilled work for long, cramped, and tedious hours. The Jewish worker was willing to forego the better hours, working conditions, and regularity of employment of an English factory in order to work among his own people, frequently in the employ of an old townsman or a relative. In view of the welter of individual workshops and the relatively small amount of capital required to become an entrepreneur, the Jewish immigrant workman also had his opportunity to become an independent businessman, whatever the risk.

On the other hand, direct entrance into general retail trade was not as easy in London and the provinces as in America. No part of England was remote from the network of retail trade, and no economically virgin area remained where an enterprising peddler could profitably dispose of his wares and start up the ladder to a store of his own. Within the cities, costermongering on the streets was a venerable craft, which extended no welcome to fresh competition from Jews. Petticoat Lane, London's historic street market in the Jewish section of the East End, became inhabited with Jewish dealers.[16] In fine, petty trade among Jewish immigrants in London was necessarily confined to trafficking for the most part in the needs of their fellow Jewish immigrants.

It was the complex and kaleidoscopically shifting clothing trades which proverbially were the livelihood of Russian and Polish Jewish immigrants, even more so in London than in America. Although the extent to which Jews created the cheap ready-made clothing industry is uncertain, there is no doubt concerning their significant role in its establishment and expansion, well before large numbers of East European Jews worked in that branch of the trade.[17]

The following table will show the relative position of immigrant Jews in the London tailoring trade:[18]

	NUMBER OF TAILORS IN LONDON			NUMBER OF RUSSIAN AND POLISH TAILORS IN LONDON		
	Male	*Female*	*Total*	*Male*	*Female*	*Total*
1871	23,516	14,780	38,296	1,128	161	1,289
1881	22,744	18,477	41,221	2,728	536	3,264
1891	27,474	24,872	52,346	4,431	1,296	5,727

[16] Cf. *JC*, May 13, 1880.

[17] Cf. Eccarius, *Der Kampf... in London;* (E. Moses and Son), *The Growth of an Important Branch of British Industry* (London, 1860); A. E. Sayous, "Les travailleurs de l'aiguille dans l'East End vers le milieu du XIXe siècle," *Revue d'Economie politique*, XIII (October-November, 1899), 861-77; Sayous, "L'immigration en Angleterre," *La Grande Revue*, Année 4, I, (1900), 229-44; Beatrice Potter, "Tailoring," in Booth, ed., *Life and Labour*, pp. 209-40; D. L. Munby, *Industry and Planning in Stepney* (Oxford, 1951), pp. 51-63; (John Burnett), *Report to the Board of Trade on the Sweating System at the East End of London, 17 February 1888;* House of Lords, *Select Committee on the Sweating System*, 5 vols., 1888-90.

[18] *Census of England and Wales, 1871*, Vol. III (C. 872), Table 11, p. 16, Table 12, p. 20, Table 18, p. 39. *Census... 1881*, Vol. III (C. 3722), Table 10, p. 16, Table 13, p. xxxiv; *Census... 1891*, Vol. III (C. 7058), Table 7, pp. 14-15, Table 14, pp. xlvi-xlvii; Board of Trade, *Reports* (C. 7406), 1894, p. 154. The figure of Jewish tailors for 1891 includes only East London and Hackney, although this probably constituted a great majority of the Jewish immigrant tailors.

It may be estimated from available figures for smaller areas within the East End in 1891 that about half of the East European Jews in London of working age were tailors of some sort. However, the labor of the Jewish tailor was not diffused throughout the trade at the varied steps in the making of a garment, nor in the several systems by which it was produced. It was concentrated in distinct branches of the industry and normally in Jewish shops, i.e., small workshops whose owner and all or nearly all male workers were Jews, with some Christian women and Jewish girls. Before a Jewish workshop commenced its operations upon a garment, the cloth had usually been patterned and cut—ready-made or bespoke (made to order)—upon the premises of a West End merchant clothier, by a skilled English or perhaps German tailor. If it were the best bespoke, it was probably completed at the clothier's by workers who were paid at the union rate of the Amalgamated Society of Tailors. If not, it was becoming the rapidly increasing practice to dispatch it to the Jewish workshop, where it was completed by division of labor—sewing, pressing, and minor finishing, like buttonholes, pockets, and basting, each done by separate workers. This division of labor became so intimately associated with Jewish work that some contemporaries thought it a Jewish invention, a distinct discovery by some species of Jewish economic genius.[19] Actually, division of labor reached back much earlier in the century, when it was called the slop system and was used for the cheapest sort of shoddy clothing and for uniforms.[20] The novelty was the application of the slop system to the manufacture of ready-made and even bespoke clothing, when it became more widely known as the "sweating system."

Under the division of labor in the sweating system, an intricate wage scale was developed, corresponding quite minutely to the worker's skill. It could range from 5/ or 6/ a week for an unskilled, toiling "greener" to 30/ and sometimes more for the master machinist. He was followed by the master presser, at 20/ to 25/ a week, and by the basters, fellers, and buttonholers far behind, whose earnings seldom exceeded 13/ or 14/ a week. These last were usually Christian and Jewish girls and women, as well as "greeners" aspiring to work their way into the higher brackets.[21]

[19] Thus Beatrice Potter, in Booth, ed., *Life and Labour*, p. 213: "an industrial discovery made by the organizers of Jewish and female labour."

[20] On the sweating system in uniforms, cf. testimony of William John Crampton, House of Lords, *Select Committee on the Sweating System*, Vol. I, 1888, Min. 10,478-10,557, esp. 10,517.

[21] For union wages, cf. Board of Trade, *Sixth Annual Report of the Chief Labour Correspondent on Trade Unions* (C. 7436), pp. 100-101. Immigrant Jewish tailors' wages are given in many places, but are often contradictory. The most reliable estimates

It was the "greener's" fond hope to copy what his own employer had probably once done—become a master worker, then recruit his own hands and open a shop with himself as entrepreneur and head worker. Then he had to besiege City merchants to give out some of their work to him.

Critical abuses overlaid the whole system. The price of labor could be forced down all too easily, because the merchant clothier or his agent, who picked and chose among importunate workshops, could easily be arbitrary about the price he would pay. If workmen of the highest skill in the workshop had to be well paid, there was always a dependable flow of unskilled or slightly skilled labor who could be paid the very lowest wages. Wages as stated were not bad for workmen with some skill; in fact they generally equaled the "log" of the Amalgamated Society of Tailors. The real evil lay in another direction. Weeks of driven labor alternated with weeks of hungry idleness, for garment making was a seasonal trade. Even in the busy season, hours were

> often as much as 16 . . . per day, with the usual hour for dinner and the imaginary half hour for tea deducted. In some cases the hours are shorter than these, but in others the men work 18 hours minus meal times. The average of the trade is not less than 14 hours actual work per day. . . . Overtime is not in any sense recognized, and no matter how many hours may be worked, it all counts in the day's work. But this [busy] season lasts only for three months out of the twelve, and during the other nine months the workers do not average more than half-time. Not only is the slack season the worst for the workers in the important matter of earnings, but strange as it may appear, many of them are also then most cruelly victimised as to the hours they are called upon to work. The sweater so arranges matters that all the work to be done must be got out on the three last days of the week. Thus he will send for his hands, or so many of them as he may require, to start on Thursday morning, and tells them he has received a certain quantity of work which must be out by the Friday night or the Saturday morning. Work will then commence at 7 o'clock in the morning of Thursday and go on right through the night and up to 4 o'clock on the Friday afternoon. If there is a special pressure of work, real or imaginary, it will be carried on to 6 or 7 o'clock in the evening. For this spell of 33 to 36 hours the men will receive two days' pay. If they are called upon to work fractions of a day, eight hours is a half-day and four hours is a quarter-day.[22]

Nor was this the full measure of the abuses. The greatest notoriety was attained by the sweatshops' physical conditions.

---

are those of Beatrice Potter in Booth, ed., *Life and Labour*, pp. 221-25, based upon 901 Jewish workshops; House of Lords, *Select Committee on the Sweating System*, Vol. II, 1889, pp. 584-88; Burnett, *Report to the Board of Trade . . . 1888*, pp. 11-17.

[22] Burnett, *Report to the Board of Trade . . . 1888*, p. 9.

The smaller sweaters . . . use part of their dwelling accommodation, and in the vast majority of cases work is carried on under conditions in the highest degree filthy and unsanitary. In small rooms not more than 9 or 10 feet square, heated by a coke fire for the pressers [*sic*] irons, and at night lighted by flaring gas jets, six, eight, ten, and even a dozen workers may be crowded.[23]

These conditions, lineal descendants of the story in Thomas Hood's "The Song of the Shirt," came to be bathed in public indignation in the mid-eighties, especially after the publication of the account in *The Lancet*, organ of the British Medical Association.[24] Although the conditions described were hardly new, these matters came to notice before the Victorian public during a decade when the social conditions of the "outcast classes" were fixed in the public gaze as never before, and when the customary formulae of economic individualism no longer commanded automatic acceptance. In spite of considerable clamor, very little could be done by the public authorities. All of the conditions, however shocking the details, were subject to state regulation only where the labor of women or minor children was involved. Furthermore, nearly the entire burden of inspection in the East End lay upon the shoulders of one man, J. B. Lakeman. This anonymous hero was supposed to enforce the Factories and Workshops Act in the estimated 2,000 workshops of all descriptions in the East End, including entire factories, and to prosecute violators before local magistrates. He complained that when he did enter a workshop-dwelling after the legal hours of work, the women workers would frustrate his mission by pretending to be members of the family or social visitors! As a result, most violators seem to have been prosecuted on account of Sunday work. "It is strange that complaints do not reach us from these people as from Gentile workers," Lakeman wondered, and thought that the reason lay in the Jews' willingness to work at any price.[25] Some of his typical notes upon Jewish sweatshop pestholes suggest his experiences: "Closet stench abominable, without water, not ventilated. No trap to drain."[26] Of another workshop-dwelling: "Workroom dirty; fowls all over the place; dustbin foul and uncovered. W. C. offensive.

[23] *Ibid.*, p. 7.

[24] A. Smith, "A Polish Colony of Jewish Labourers," *The Lancet*, March 5, 1884, reprinted in *JC*, May 9, 1884; D. F. Schloss, "The Sweating System," *Fortnightly Review*, N.S., XLVII (April 1, 1890), 532-55. For a more intimate view of the human consequences of sweating, cf. Isaac Stone, *Eine kurtse lebens beshreibung fun a Londoner Shneider* (English title: *An Historical Sketch of a London Tailor*). "Published by the Jewish Tailor Workers' Society" (London, 1884). A possibly unique copy is in the possession of YIVO.

[25] *Report of H. M. Chief Inspector of Factories and Workshops* (C. 2825), 1881, p. 17.

[26] *Report of H. M. Chief Inspector of Factories and Workshops* (C. 4369), 1885, p. 35.

Workroom dirty."[27] After years of daily rounds from one sweatshop to the next, Lakeman still found it "surprising how people can live under such conditions."[28]

Sweatshop economics and their human consequences did not prevail only in the making of clothing. During the 1880's nearly as many East European Jewish immigrants were employed in the making of boots and shoes as in the making of garments. As in the latter trade, the Jewish share in boots and shoes was also principally in ready-made footwear, which many small Jewish entrepreneur-workers took to their shops in order to complete a process which had begun on the premises of the merchant shoemaker.[29] Just as the Jewish workshop in the garment trade had taken already cut fabric to be fashioned into an article of clothing, so did the Jewish boot and shoe workshop take the cut leather and make a shoe of it. The workshop-dwelling of a skilled bootmaker had long been typical in the boot and shoe trade, where members of the craftsman's family and perhaps one or two journeymen were kept busy. Jewish entrepreneur-workers expanded the workshop, took in ready-made work, and developed a division of labor.

The inner structure of the boot and shoe workshops was the same as the clothing workshop; however, the two industries were moving in different directions. The boot and shoe industry did not halt at a workshop stage, but entered upon full-scale factory production of boots and shoes, especially in the provinces. The Jews found that their stakes were in a declining system of production within the industry, and it was only their appallingly sweated labor which kept them in a position to compete at all. The small entrepreneur was ultimately hardly any better off than his workers, as the Jewish shoe workers' union recognized by inviting him into its ranks. The hopelessness of the competition with factory production was recognized, both by the slowly declining number of Russian and Polish Jews who found jobs in the trade, and by the successful strike for the elimination of outdoor workshops in 1890, which at least temporarily forced all work in the trade to be done on the merchant shoemaker's premises or in factories. That the London portion of the boot and shoe industry lagged behind the provinces in conversion to factory production is partially attributable to the fresh labor power which Jewish immigration

[27] *Ibid.*, p. 36.

[28] *Report of H. M. Chief Inspector of Factories and Workshops* (C. 4702), 1886, p. 16.

[29] "Alien Immigration in Relation to the Boot and Shoe Trade," in Board of Trade, *Reports* (C. 7406) 1894, pp. 67-94; David F. Schloss, "Boot Making," in Booth, ed., *Life and Labour*, pp. 241-308.

poured into the workshop system, enabling it to combat, albeit unsuccessfully and at high human cost, the final hegemony of factory production. Its workshop conditions were as bad as in the clothing trade, when not worse. Cellar and underground workshops were quite common, and the failure of state inspection in them was as complete as in the clothing workshops. Shoemaker's pallor and stained hands from blacking shoes were occupational labels, like the tailor's stoop.[30]

These were the principal livelihoods of East European Jews in London in the 1880's. Much smaller numbers worked at cigar and cigarette making, cabinetmaking, and other crafts. Hardly any of them entered the great English manufacturing industries or transportation and maritime occupations.

GLIMPSES WITHIN THE IMMIGRANT QUARTER

While he could do little to alter the conditions of life in a strange land, the most conspiciuous reaction of the Jewish immigrant to his lot was a spectacular flaming rebellion, mostly on paper. In London of the 1880's the Jewish labor and socialist movement came into the world, and in these early years it was militantly revolutionary.[31] The genesis of Jewish socialism, led by Aaron Lieberman, had taken place in the summer of 1876, but it vanished without leaving any trace until it was revived in 1884. Everything happened nearly at once in that year. The *Polish Yidel*, the first Yiddish socialist newspaper, began to appear weekly; the International Workingmen's Educational Club opened its doors; the first socialist tracts in Yiddish were published; Jewish trade unions commenced an uninterrupted history. In all of these facets London was the pioneer both for Russia and America, because of its fortuitous combination of civil liberties, nearness to Continental intellectual currents, and the existence of a substantial and reasonably distinct Jewish proletariat.

Intellectual development and sectarian disputes aside, the history of Jewish socialism in its early years is fundamentally the story of efforts made by a small circle of dedicated revolutionary enthusiasts to organize labor unions among Jewish workers for the principal purpose of instilling

[30] *JC*, August 14, 1891; *Die Tsukunft*, Vol. I, Nos. 16, 17, 18 (November 7, 14, 21, 1884); *Arbeiter Freind*, Vol. XI, No. 14 (January 10, 1896); Vol. II, No. 36 (October 7, 1887); Vol. III, No. 8 (February 24, 1888).

[31] Cf. E. Tcherikover's accounts in E. Tcherikover, ed., *History of the Jewish Labor Movement in the United States* (2 vols., New York, 1943), pp. 76-135, and "The Beginnings of Jewish Socialism" (Yiddish), *YIVO Historishe Shriftn* (Vilna, 1929), columns 469-532.

revolutionary convictions among them, while the members whom they succeeded in recruiting were mainly concerned with improving their immediate lot through conventional trade union action. A strike, therefore, had quite different significance to the humble worker and to the fervid agitator. The latter welcomed it as a sign of maturing revolutionary consciousness and advised workers not to dabble overmuch in melioristic aims—precisely what the workers did want![32] No firm labor union came into being in any of the major Jewish trades, partly because the revolutionary idealists' view of the utility of trade unions was not conducive to their growth, but mostly because of the instability of the immigrants' trades and their rapidly shifting labor supply. The unions were in a constant state of fission and amalgamation, and few workingmen would give their sweated pennies to any union unless they could soon see tangible results from their investment. The union mushroomed during a strike but usually collapsed soon after, regardless of the outcome—failure exacted its usual penalty of dissolution, while success was equally disastrous, since the workers saw no point in continuing to support a union once it had achieved its aims.[33]

The great clothing strike of 1889, that *annus mirabilis* in English labor history, clearly reflects the essential shortcomings of the early Jewish labor movement.[34] It originated as a spontaneous walkout in two or three firms, and to the surprise of all, perhaps 10,000 workers had left their jobs in a few days. The revolutionists, dazzled by what they thought was a revolutionary spirit aroused by their exertions, jumped to the forefront. However, a notably unrevolutionary series of aims, directed at prominent abuses in the sweating system, was all that was asked:

WE DEMAND:

1. That the hours be reduced to 12 with an interval of one hour for dinner and half-hour for tea.
2. All meals to be had off the premises.
3. Government contractors to pay wages at trade union rates.

[32] For example, "every worker's organization is good and useful... trade unionism does not lead the workers directly to a goal, because it betters their lot very, very little for a very insignificant period and it is only good so far as it opens the worker's eyes and shows him that he must strive for something else." *Arbeiter Freind*, Vol. II, No. 24 (April 22, 1887).

[33] Georg Halpern, *Die Jüdische Arbeiter in London* (Berlin, 1903), lists 38 Jewish trade unions in 1902; none of them had an uninterrupted history of more than seven or eight years; see pp. 66-68.

[34] The main source for the "Great Strike" is the *Arbeiter Freind* for the six weeks commencing with August 30, 1889. Cf. *JC*, September 13 and October 4, 1889. The strike poster was made available to me in London by kind permission of its owner, Mr. A. R. Rollin. A series of these posters is now in YIVO.

4. Government contractors and sweaters not to give work home at night after working hours.

The strike dragged on for six to seven weeks, with individual workshops coming to terms one by one. Daily rallies were held in the East End and in Victoria Park in nearby Hackney to keep up spirits, and to prevent a split between strikers and their socialist leadership, which the employers and the Jewish communal interceders were anxious to cause. Yet when the triumphant end came and the demand for the curtailment of hours was won, no enforcement machinery remained. Within a matter of weeks after the great strike, the trade drifted back to the old conditions, and the stirring movement seemed to have been little more than a lengthy mass demonstration.[35] This remarkable affair is a glaring proof of the disorganized state of both the Jewish labor movement and the clothing industry.

For the greater part of the Jewish immigrants, any reaction they had to the transformations and perplexities of their lives was less a revolt against their injustices than a determination to cling to as many of the old ways as they could. If in their livelihoods and physical conditions of life they had to put up with what they encountered, at least in their religious life and in the education of their children they were determined to exercise some degree of control. In view of the Sabbath morning open-air labor market,[36] and the great disparity between synagogue seats and the actual size of the immigrant population as well as other factors, it cannot be maintained that the entire immigrant body was thoroughly observant. On the other hand, the Judaism of the small towns of Eastern Europe was the Judaism which was familiar and one to which an undoubtedly large proportion faithfully adhered.

Mutual incomprehensibility existed between the highly centralized, thoroughly Anglicized religious organization of native English Jewry and the immigrants' congeries of perhaps as many as 50 little synagogues in the East End, many of them bearing the names of their members' home towns. Although native Jewry would have liked to bring them into the official community, it was unable to come to grips with real conditions. The highly unrealistic idea of a "colossal" synagogue to replace the independent petty congregations was aired from time to time. A more practical scheme was Sir Samuel Montagu's combination of the immigrant

[35] *Arbeiter Freind*, Vol. IV, No. 44 (November 1, 1889); No. 45 (November 8, 1889).

[36] (Aaron Lieberman), "The Jews in London" (Hebrew), *HaEmet*, No. 3 (1877), pp. 43-46; *Ivri Anokhi*, Vol. IX, No. 21 (February 12, 1875); *Polish Yidel*, Vol. I, No. 9 (September 19, 1884), No. 10 (September 26, 1884).

synagogues into the Federation of Synagogues in 1887, under his benevolent despotism, although the organization was distrusted as potentially schismatic and a surrender to immigrant backwardness.[37] Of the native community's few means of cummunicating with the immigrant masses, a favored one was the Saturday afternoon Yiddish sermons by a communal preacher in the historic Great Synagogue. There they were warned against the allurements of the missionaries who abounded in the East End: "Some men and women say they only go there seldom, in order to eat, drink and get some money and so forth, but . . . even by 'seldom' they are committing a weighty transgression"[38] The Jewish socialists, with their vigorous antireligious propaganda, were hardly more desirable in the preacher's eyes: "There are some people who do not perform God's commandments and also turn their backs on the laws of the land, who cause a number of evils to the Jewish community and particularly to Judaism . . . all that this evil sect desires is to be free of all restraint."[39] Against budding movements of high Orthodox secession from the body of the community, he pleaded: "Who knows what will be the outcome of this split? Without doubt the split will cause many breaches in matters of Torah and piety."[40] Such efforts showed what some of the native Jewish community's hopes were — reasonable piety, Anglicization, communal union under native Jewish leadership, and abstention from radical movements.

While little enough could be done to change the adults, hopes were focused upon their children. The native Jewish community had established and long supported a network of Jewish voluntary schools before state education entered the field. The Jews' Free School in Spitalfields towered physically and numerically over all others; its 2,800 children in 1882 and 3,400 in 1886 made it the largest elementary school in England.[41] Although it combined both general and Jewish studies, the native community uttered complaints that "our poor" lack confidence in the "religious instruction imparted by intelligent Englishmen."[42] The same was presumably true for the other Jewish schools supported by the community with state subsidies after 1870, where Jewish instruction was also made part of the curriculum. An immigrant voice praised these schools, but

[37] Lipman, *A Social History of the Jews in England*, pp. 120-23, 127-31.

[38] Spiers, *Divrei Dvash*, p. 12.

[39] *Ibid.*, p. 19.

[40] *Ibid.*, p. 46.

[41] Jacobs, *Statistics of Jewish Population in London*, n. p.

[42] *JC*, January 30, 1880.

declared that their "main purpose is to make Englishmen of the Jews."[43] Judaization was a more personal matter to the immigrants, for a large proportion of their sons went to *hedarim* (one-room schoolhouses), in disregard of whatever Jewish training had been given the children during the school day. Estimates of the number existing in the Jewish quarter were varied, but all lamented their presence.[44] Better-organized Talmud Torahs came some years later, generally led by modernist circles within the immigrant community.

During the 1880's, the basis of the East European immigrant community in London was thus laid. Its essential characteristics—economic, demographic, cultural—were firmly outlined. The following twenty-five years were to enlarge the scope of the picture and vigilantly publicize the problems it presented, but they did not alter its lines.

[43] D. Steinhart in *Die Tsukunft*, Vol. II, No. 50 (June 25, 1886).

[44] A Guardians inspector found and described 23 *hedarim*. Board of Guardians, *Executive Minutes*, December 4, 1884. Their sanitary condition was not found to be unduly unsatisfactory. Letter, D. F. Schloss, Hon. Sec., Guardians Sanitary Comm., to L. L. Alexander, Hon. Sec., Guardians, *Minute Letter Book*, p. 111, December 5, 1884. Perhaps 45 percent of the boys in the Jews' Free School attended a *heder*. *JC*, February 13, 1885. A later report estimates "considerably more than 200 *Chedarim* in the East End" with over 2,000 boys in attendance. *JC*, April 10, 1891.

DOES THE JEWISH PAST HAVE A FUTURE?

By Sholome Michael Gelber

IT WAS DIFFICULT for the Hebrew slaves in Pharaoh's Egypt to make bricks without straw. However, it would have been utterly impossible for them to have created their religious civilization without a sense of history. For the way the Jewish people has chosen to see things in historic terms has become an indispensable element in Jewish cultural life.

Perhaps one of the most distinguishing features of Jewish civilization is this preoccupation with the past. The Jews, indeed, have always had an uncommonly deep concern with precedent and a feeling that the common memory of Jewish experience is of major importance. History is so fundamental to Judaism, in fact, that its absence might probably have destroyed its very survival; or at least rendered it something of a very different quality from what we know to be Jewish.

Many other peoples, even peoples as ancient as the Chinese, seldom looked at life historically. Leading Indian religions, moreover, have always been indifferent to history, stressing, instead, kinds of mysticism or rituals and formulae based on magic. Furthermore, a historic view of things might never even have occurred to some of the pagan peoples of Europe who found in the mysteries of Nature a fascination and a fear upon which they arranged their lives.

Perhaps the Jews were not unique in stressing history but they were persistent in expressing most things they put their hands to in terms of what had gone on before. They did this to what they inherited and borrowed from other peoples.

The Spring festival, for instance, which others celebrated in honor of the birth of new life, is a case in point. For they chose to call this naturalistic rite the Passover, and infused it with a different meaning than everyone else. They told of their liberation from Egyptian bondage at this season and therein gave social significance to what was once a festival to Mother Nature; they toasted the virtue of Freedom in place of the wonders of Springtime.

They did the same thing to the winter's ancient celebration and transformed the religious meaning of this time of the year from the naturalistic to the historic. They spoke of the Maccabean victory over the tyrant Antiochus Epiphanes as an appropriate thought for the winter and recalled the triumph of a civil right over an oppressive dictator. What came to them as a sort of Yuletide was transformed into the moral lesson, Channukah. And so right on down the line. All the festivals, from the Sabbath to Purim, from Pentecost to the New Year, acquired social meaning and said something about man's relationship to man, rather than man's relationship to Nature.

This transformation of the holidays was no mere coincidence. It was a conscious rebellion against naturalism in religion and the primitive rites that go with the worship of Nature. The biblical story of the sacrifice of Isaac articulates the Jewish position along these lines. It is a dramatized editorial which advances the case against the sacrificing of human life in order to flatter the deity. It seems to say that there was a time when child sacrifice was an acceptable form of worship to which even Abraham adhered. The times changed, however, and the deity no longer approved of infanticide; for human life is the most sacred of all things and must not be destroyed, especially in prayer.

The indignation of Samuel in being called from the dead by the witch of En-dor at the request of King Saul is another indication of the Jewish movement away from the magic of a Nature-minded world. Witchcraft was forbidden by Jews even if it worked. Not because it did not work, for indeed the witch of En-dor, according to the legend, actually resurrected the ghost of Samuel. Of course it may be assumed that the author never believed for a moment that witchcraft is effective, but he gave the lady from En-dor the benefit of the doubt in order to communicate to the readers and the listeners of the story without their interrupting him by saying, "I knew of a witch who actually could work miracles." Naturalism is declared by this story to be an out-and-out evil, even if gullible people choose to believe in it and even derive benefit from it.

This rebellion against naturalism was really a plea for History. The revolt against Nature-festivals and magic rites was an argument calling upon the Jews of antiquity to see life in the context of society. But society is of this world, not of the great beyond. Therefore the Jewish concern for History was not simply the view of the antiquarian or the attitude of a museum curator; it was a burning interest in current events. The affairs of the day should be judged, they said, in the perspective of the past.

It was here that the early Hebrews found themselves in discord with the ancient Egyptians. For the latter it may be said that the theme of their life was death. In death, in its preparation, in mummies and pyramids, dirges and masses, they found the secret of the universe. But the Hebrew Psalmist answered them with songs which declared the very opposite to be true, when he said, "I shall not die, but live," or, "The heavens, the heavens are the Lord's but the earth hath He given to man," or, "The dead shall not praise Thee, only the living, the living shall praise Thee."

In a later era, the Jews even strengthened their single-minded stress on the preeminence of life whan it was decided that the concept of a world to come is voluntary and, therefore, a good Jew can either believe or disbelieve in it, without guilt of heresy. The requirement to fear God, however, is obligatory; and the requirements that men should do justice and love mercy, should love their neighbors and should care for the widow and the orphan, were rigid rules that countenanced no backsliding. For Judaism, with its stress on History, was a religion of this world and a faith in ethical values that would lead to social harmony.

Although the Judaeo-Christian tradition is a common denominator which contains a social and an historic attitude relevant to life in this world, the two strains which comprise it differ on the fundamental position of eschatology. The emphasis, even in modern Christianity, is on salvation in the world to come. The very symbol of that faith is a cross. This ancient instrument of death is an appropriate sign of the faith, since it teaches that its founder had to die in order to save the souls of men. In Judaism the symbols of the faith are the Torah which are rules for life in this world, and its Ten Commandments which are the core of its social laws. Even the Mogen David, the shield of David, is precisely an instrument of protection against death. It is actually a means of survival, a bar against extinction and a projection of the will to live.

These Christian and Jewish symbols indicate a divergence in attitude which, indeed, is as real as the thinking of the two groups themselves. In the Western world, Judaism is still the most articulate and consistent believer in the primacy of history, the preeminence of society, and the superiority of moral emphasis upon conditions on this planet.

That History will triumph one day over Nature is a further conviction of Jewish civilization. For of what value is a goal to so practical-minded a people as the Jews if it is unattainable? History, with its implications of social welfare and harmony for the peoples of the world, had to be elevated, therefore, to the status of a sure winner if the principle of its paramountcy was to be acceptable. Isaiah's vision that the lion shall lie down with the lamb and a young child shall lead them, or Amos' prediction—"Behold the days cometh sayeth the Lord, when the ploughman shall overtake the reaper and the treader of grapes him that soweth seed and the mountains shall drop sweet wines and all the hills shall melt. And I will bring again the captivity of my people of Israel, and they shall build the waste cities, and inhabit them; and they shall plant vineyards and drink the wine thereof; they shall also make gardens and eat the fruit of them"—are the expressions of faith in the victory of History over Nature. Confidence in this ultimate good has become basic to Judaism and has colored its entire configuration. This has been true, at least until the present day. The question is, where do we go from here? Does the past have any future in Jewish thought and practice?

Until a few decades ago most Jews were observant and the historic practices, the old teachings, and the traditional forms were widely followed Today, when Jews conform less to the requirements of tradition than most of their grandparents did, they still retain many of their historic customs. They go to synagogues on the New Year and on the Day of Atonement. They have circumcision ceremonies for their sons and bar-mitzvah celebrations for their adolescent boys. They say Kaddish and *Yahrzeit* prayers and attend *Yizkor* services after the death of parents. They work for the rebuilding of the State of Israel and contribute to the United Jewish Appeal. Some contemporary Jews retain more, and others conserve less, of the symbols and mores of the culture, but a large number observe at least some of the ways which time and use have made important.

It would be fair to question, however, how much of even these less numerous historic practices proceed from conviction about living as Jews or from affection for things Jewish. Does a present-day Jew say Kaddish when his parent dies because he believes in the sanctification of God's name, because he believes in the ultimate goodness of creation during the months of his greatest loss, when he has been deprived of one who is the very source of his life? Or do the Jews of our generation continue to go through the motions of at least part of the historic ways for other reasons, some of them even un-Jewish?

Do they adhere to ceremonies and customs for *superstitious reasons*, for instance, which are the negation of the faith and contrary to the spirit of Jewish history? Or do they continue to participate in the pattern of historic forms because it is simply a *cultural lag*, and they are either too lazy or too unthinking or even too cowardly to extricate themselves from the well-rooted configuration of religious things to do? Or do they save a piece of tradition for reasons of *nostalgia* which are sentimental and affectionate in quality, resembling more the emotions of attachment to a pet, a homestead, or a family retainer than an identification with a well-reasoned way of life founded upon ethical ideas? Or do they practice Judaism in whatever degree they desire because they are really tribalists, wanting to belong to a group of their own, irrespective of its merits or beliefs?

It is well-nigh impossible to assess why Jews behave as they do in their Jewish practices. All of these factors, nostalgia and tribalism and superstition and cultural lags, may play their parts. The interesting aspect of the situation at this point, however, is that a historic view of things, a conviction about Judaism, and an affirmative belief in the values of Jewish religious civilization still play somewhat of a role and also influence, in a certain measure, the rising generation. If their observance has been severely pruned in our time, it has still not been felled.

A case could be made for the urgency of Jewish influence as an ethical force in the Western world. Certainly our age is suffering from a kind of spiritual malnutrition that is bringing us close to moral starvation in many aspects of our personal and group lives. The brutality of the Nazis and their friends, the rise of Fascism, and the cruel excesses of the Communist menace have all been nurtured in powerfully religious states. After hundreds of years of church influence, why have European religions been so ineffective when dictators have crushed the innocent and pilloried the weak? Is it not as though Central and Eastern Europe had never heard of the Sermon on the Mount? Where is the confidence in benevolence and goodwill upon which the Prince of Peace established his following? Some of the very countries which have accepted his leadership for centuries have turned most conspicuously, and some are still turning, to totalitarianism, to war, and to concentration camps. Possibly the religious institutions of Germany, Italy, and Russia have been so lavish with their guarantees for salvation in the world to come that they have disregarded this world, which is also part of God's creation. Wickedness has been rife in our time because many really disbelieve in religion, for this place.

Why? Because we are unschooled in the canons of virtue and goodness.

The moral force of Judaism, however, with its strong historic view of things and its reasonable social attitudes, is something the world requires as much as the cure for cancer and the solution to vascular diseases. For Judaism is a leaven which elevates man by its stand for decency in society. Historic Judaism has often played a part just as an influence on other religions and on other cultures.

It has had a humanizing effect on man quite without an evangelistic hoop-la or high-pressure missionizing zeal. Its effectiveness has often proceeded from its example. Can a decent example of historic Judaism be recreated? Can it be done? Surely it is needed!

There are four categories of modern Jewish life which attempt in their own ways to re-create historic Judaism.

First, there are the rabbis of the Neo-Orthodox, Conservative, and Reformed movements. The work of these religious leaders cannot be summed up fairly and accurately with generalizations, nor can a reasonable blanket statement be made that is entirely applicable to each member of the profession. Preponderant tendencies in the calling, however, are apparent and may be noted with impartiality. The rabbis of these three groups have, by and large, abandoned their traditional roles as men of learning, as respected teachers, and as thinkers.

They depend, instead, on oratory which is, at best, a more ephemeral influence than many other techniques of communication. They teach less and less of the moral law and attend more and more meetings where the moral law seldom gets a look in. They talk little about ethical monotheism, although they generously give large portions of their time to visiting the sick and attending to the bereaved. They are pastors, more than traditional rabbis. They are, therefore, coming closer to the calling of St. Gregory the Great, whose prime concern was "On Pastoral Care," and further from the spirit of the Jewish daily prayer which, on listing the virtues of life, concludes that "study of Torah is equal to them all put together." The rabbis of our day of the Neo-Orthodox, Conservative, and Reformed schools are becoming like social directors. A growing number of them try to attend functions galore and attempt to make people feel wanted by friendly handshakes, warm greetings, and convivial questions about the wife and children. An enlarging minority of rabbis discharge their responsibilities in the manner of functionaries at a summer hotel. Not that there is anything wrong with oratory, pastoral care, meeting-attendenace, and a healthy slap on the back. A debilitating tendency of the rabbinate proceeds from the pre-occupation of rabbis with these less fundamental functions, at the expense of thinking, teaching, and studying. And the result is that more and more sensitive members of Jewish communities in the Western world, even though they may belong to synagogues, fail to take their rabbis seriously, and are far from influenced by them along religious or cultural lines.

Secondly, the synagogues are often something quite separate and apart from the rabbis. For temples and synagogues are largely controlled by their *Baal Ha Bathim* or lay leaders. Here again it is difficult to say may things that are applicable to all these institutions, but reasonably easy to say a few things that are pertinent to their trends.

Their services are boring, and most people stay away for that simple reason. Legions of religiously-minded Jews would frequent the services more regularly if there were only a quality of interest to them. But the modern services of all the three major Jewish groupings are tuneless and unenthusiastic. By comparison with old-fashioned Eastern European Orthodox Judaism or Christian Episcopalianism or the eastern spirit of the Spanish and Portuguese *Minhag*, they are flavorless and flat.

The newer style Orthodox services lack *Kavanah* on the one hand and esthetic attraction on the other. The modern English prayers of the Conservative and Reformed liturgy are, for the most part, quite devoid of taste and are written with less craftmanship than such a delicate task requires. Their subject matter is often jumbled, a single prayer dealing, sometimes, with six or seven topics, in tones of saccharine sentimentality.

The ritual is very short on movement in all three groups of services, and the trend has been to diminish the possibilities of ritual even more by copying the architecture of Christian churches which relegates the congregation to the status of an audience. The functionaries are removed to a platform separated from the people. The historic synagogue was less concerned with revenue from seat-holders and could enjoy the esthetic satisfaction of affording a fair measure of space to the service. The *bimah* was in the center, the ark in front; the members sat around. It was congenial to see the face of another member sitting opposite and to feel reasonably close to the center of what was going on. The new synagogues and temples are so arranged that the only available point near by on which a worshipper's eye can focus easily is the neck of the congregant in front.

The dryness of services is making the synagogue a very flimsy force in establishing a connection between current Jewry and the colorful experiences of its antecedents.

Thirdly, the Jewish schools comprise a category which attempts to continue the substance of historic Judaism by teaching its essentials in modern terms. The strictly Orthodox schools are an anomaly which may or may not persist, but the nonfundamentalist academies are the ones that are most significant to these observations because, it is felt, perhaps even unjustifiably, that the largest numbers of Jews will continue, as time goes on, to abandon Orthodoxy for the more experimental expressions of the faith. Since the concern here is for the future, then, it is the non-Orthodox schools which must be looked at as links in the chain of historic Judaism.

If, as Ben Sirah said, "the fruits of a tree betray the husbandry thereof," then it is the children who grow up in the Sunday Schools and Talmud Torahs, etc., that are the best test of the effectiveness of these institutions. If a knowledge of Jewish culture is any gauge of their Jewish schooling, then most of the pupils are not very well husbanded. The children of the rising generation who go to Jewish schools even for years come out of them in droves knowing very little about what Isaiah had to say, only bits and pieces about what Rabbi Akiba did, and a smattering of what Jews think about the major problems of human existence. Nor is the nurturing of an intelligent loyalty to Judaism accomplished by the educational institutions. Affection for things Jewish and convictions about Judaism are insufficiently strengthened in the hearts and minds of the young by the educators of our day.

It would be possible to go "scientific" at this point and demand a definition of what is meant by standards of sufficiency and insist that controlled experiments be conducted with the Sunday School or Talmud Torah children to test whether the consequences of their work are as inadequate as is here maintained. It is perhaps just such "scientific" and technique-ridden thinking which has had an adverse effect on present-day teaching. There is still something to be said for common sense, and it is plain to see as one travels from community to community in America and meets the Jews over the years that the young are profoundly ignorant of Judaism and that the teachers are not able to do much about it. What with all the "highly trained" executives in the field and the plethora of memoranda they have been writing to each other over the decades, there is still not a single first-class book in English introducing historic Judaism to students. Perhaps the poetry, the romance, the imagination, and the sparkle of the tradition go badly with methodology and the mystique of current pedagogical abracadabra. Perhaps the educators need a little more of the actual inspiration of storytellers and less of the motivation of an aspiring Pd. D. preparing exhaustive studies on *how* a story should be told. Perhaps they need to do, rather than tell how it should be done. Be that as it may, if a vital and a high enthusiasm for Jewish values and an appreciation of the historic view are required by present-day Jewry, it will have to look elsewhere than to the professionals in Jewish education. For try as they may, their schools are just not reaching the hearts of the people.

The fourth category is a large one which embraces all the organizations in Jewish life, from Y.M.H.A.'s to hospitals, from free loan societies to old folks' homes, from U.J.A. to child welfare agencies. At the outset let it be said that in the over-all picture these organizations are a remarkable accomplishment. The efficiency of so many of their operations in a variety of centers is of such a high order that the Jewish communities are constantly receiving commendations from other sources. No one doubts that Jews do a good job in fund raising, in caring for the sick and indigent, in group work, in caring for old people, etc., etc.

The question is, how effective are the social agencies in articulating a distinctly Jewish position and in advancing the attitude of historic Judaism? The fact is that although Jewish organizations are housed by Jews, they are often not only secular in quality, but sometimes even un-Jewish in attitude. The U.J.A. is a case in point. To collect more money the fund-raisers often resort to flattery, to materialism, to adulation of the rich, to shaming a fellow man in public, and to character assassination, all of which are repugnant to Jewish ethics and even can be said to violate Jewish law. Yet the fund-raisers say that it is only by employing such coarse techniques that adequate monies have been collected to meet the crises of our time. It is, then, the old question of ends and means, and in the process of working it out, the U.J.A., which saves Jewish lives in some places, is killing the very spirit of compassion and respect for the dignity of the individual very close to home.

Nor are the Jewish hospitals, which give succor and care to the weary, havens of Judaism. They do a good medical job, but so do the Roman Catholic hospitals and the Protestant rest homes. There can, of course, be little that is distinctly Jewish about a place which tries to bring physical health to patients. Hospitals do not exist to articulate a religious or a denominational or a philosophic position. But when the participants in the organization of hospitals display attitudes and exhibit ways of doing things which are radical deviations from the requirements of Jewish social behavior and even contrary to the leitmotif of the Torah, then something is wrong. The envy that exists among doctors, for instance, or the conflicting ambitions between department heads, and the disregard for other people on the part of, let us say, some honor-seeking board member are but a few of the well-known failings in decency that obtain in hospitals. The hospitals, in some cases, are arenas of conflicting egos, and they are, therefore, dismal places for us to search for moral enlightenment. They are dark spots to find an example of the Jewish conscience, even though they do good work on a physical level.

The power politics and the honor seeking which permeate scores of Jewish organizations is a frightening and a melancholy thing. The lust for honors is making shallow fools of many of the politicians and ward heelers in Jewish life. And the main casualty is the spirit of Judaism. What is needed, perhaps, is an Anti-Kovod League to bring the egos of the North American Jewish community down a peg.

If the world requires the humanizing influence of historic Judaism, then, the future of the Jewish past will have to be planned more painstakingly than it is at present. Neither the rabbinate, the synagogues and temples, the schools, nor the organizations are presently equipped to discharge their historic responsibilities satisfactorily.

There is no cause for despondency, however, and no reason for a feeling that inevitability will destroy historic Judaism. Things may appear shadowed, but the wisdom of the Greek proverb is applicable: "The stars only shine when the world grows very dark." The social attitudes of Judaism, the rebellion against naturalism, the opposition to exclusive otherworldliness, the faith in the eventual triumph of History over Nature are all manifestations of the will to live.

Never in the story of peoples has a group emerged from a holocaust as the Jews of our generation have done, with such an overwhelming affirmation of faith in life. They crawled and dragged themselves out of Belsen or Auschwitz, only skeleton-sized, bereft of their families, robbed of their treasure, stripped of their youth, deprived of six million of their own, and said to the world, even as their teacher Moses had taught them thousands of years before, "I am that which I am," and I choose life. The overpowering and indomitable will to live of the contemporary Jew is best measured by his brave creative works in fashioning the third Jewish commonwealth in Israel, against staggering odds. It is the arch example of the triumph of History over Nature. The Jewish twentieth century is a tale of the rise of Misery, which is followed by Misery's own subjugation at the hand of the Jews themselves. It is a story so noble that it must mean the elevation of mankind by at least one more rung in Jacob's ladder. From the gas chambers and crematoria to the Negev and Galilee, from slavery to freedom, the record of contemporary Israel spells the victory of a will to live.

A people with such inner fortitude and vision will scarcely lose its tradition and its sense of history because the rabbis and synagogues and schools and organizations are weak. The chances are that such a vigorous group will learn to cope with these problems more subtle than Nazism and these challenges less dramatic than forging an independent state. It will be done perhaps, without the same zeal, but with a similar competence in dealing with practicalities.

If the rabbinate is less effective than it might be, one reason is that much of the talent and the energy of Jewry has gone into making good businessmen and skilled technicians and adept professionals. The same goes for the field of education. The preoccupations of our time, generally, have been economic, often directed toward power seeking; and people of ability have given their capacities to making a place for themselves in the sun. The stress has been on tangible things. And the Jews have participated in the fashion. That is why the things that were said above, about Jewish organizations and religious institutions and schools, are really just as applicable to the Christian and nonsecular institutions of our culture.

But since Judaism with its sense of history has something of extraordinary merit to offer, it cannot afford to wait with the rest of the world until the *Geist* improves.

Does the Jewish past have a future? It could have, a bright one. It probably will. The Jews themselves have shown that they are made of good stuff. The obvious example of Israel is one indication of the high quality of the people. But the younger generation of North American Jews is another. For they are generous, responsible, and communally-minded. On many levels they show that they have a better sense of values than their parents. They are further away from the first push to emancipation and are more relaxed about the things that used to make their elders anxious. Let it be said to their credit that many North American Jews are groping for a Judaism that will give them an intelligible and attractive connection with Jewish history. They talk a great deal with their friends about ways to establish rapport with the tradition of Jewish civilization. They often say that they are concerned about their children's Jewish education and many even complain and are often disgusted with the pedestrian quality of what rabbis and educators have to offer. Why? Because they seemingly want the past to be part of them. Such people make it possible to hope for a better future in the structure of American Jewish life.

Hope is sometimes a partner of wishful thinking. If new instrumentalities to advance historic Judaism are to be made, and others are to be remade, to suit the needs of the day, then what is more needed than thoughts, however desirable, are practical suggestions and workable plans of an experimental nature. Even if such ideas should fail to capture popular approval, the mere effort to develop them might encourage other ideas which could, in turn, prove to be successful. Experimentation is the stuff of which progress is made.

For instance, it might be suitable to adopt, by means of a campaign of encouragement, example, and public education, a new kind of social discipline for the Sabbath. In the place of the restrictions which are "more honored in the breach than in the observance," it might become the contrived fashion to entertain guests at home on Friday evening, and make of the Sabbath eve a universally accepted party night, or social time. Celebrations and festive meals and the inviting of guests might give those who never observe the Sabbath at present some good feelings about it. Sabbath should give a rhythm to time by becoming a day in the week which is regularly special and delightful. Its contrast with the other days could lend a dramatic quality to events. And people at all times, but especially in this age of anxiety, need the benefits of rhythm and contrast, particularly between work and ordered rest.

Since Judaism is a historic culture it is appropriate that one of its most fundamental forms should be in terms of sanctifying Time, which is exactly what the Sabbath does.

The fact that the Sabbath is becoming atrophied by disuse in the lives of most contemporary Conservative and Reformed Jews is an offense against Time. It is more the pity because the use and abuse of Time is a major factor in each of our lives. There are great psychological advantages to revering it, to setting aside a piece of it for fun and goodwill and leisure and relaxation in this workaday world of ours. The historic advantages are also of large dimensions, for the Sabbath, being well rooted in Judaism, can always be a popular expression of identification with the moral tradition of the faith.

The chances of our returning to an orthodox observance of the Sabbath are remote, because so many of us just do not believe in the authority of its legal structure and do not enjoy the nature of its practices in our kind of a world. But the idea of Sabbath is good. We would be well advised, therefore, to try to adjust Sabbath observance so that it can become meaningful in our kind of world. Not just easy, but meaningful and relevant.

If many of the rabbis and teachers do not measure up to their jobs, that too is a shortcoming about which much can be done. There is a great deal of ability in Jewry. There is talent galore in many fields and apparently enough people with a combination of those particular capacities that go to make effective rabbis, teachers, and administrators. The problem is to engage the interest of competent young students and encourage them to enter the Jewish professions. Already, the material rewards are satisfactory in many of the callings, and they are improving continually in others. There is, however, no sustained and efficient effort by the seminaries and other schools for professional training to sound out the youth, to seek for what is needed, and to make creative that aspect of Jewish life which has to do with personnel. When the search for, and training of, personnel becomes creative and organized on a wide base, however, the chances are that the form and quality of the entire community will enjoy benefits. If we could muster our human resources, and channel them effectively, it would be possible to make our schools and synagogues and general organizations more vital and more relevant to the needs of the people.

Just because the rabbi has not enough time to be a pastor is no reason why pastoral work should not be done. A compassionate and considerate people like the Jews will not ignore the delightful obligations of visiting the sick and comforting the bereaved and offering the hand of friendship to the traveler. Why, indeed, these worth-while assignments should ever have become major functions of the rabbis is curious. For they are really the duties of each and every member of the community.

Just as the Jews have dispensed, since the days of the Temple, with the practice of employing a single goat to carry away all their sins, so should they also prohibit the tendency to furnish the rabbis with a monopoly on most of the community's deeds and acts of personal righteousness. What is needed, perhaps, is public ownership of the means of virtue!

Everybody should be a pastor. The man who belongs to a synagogue or temple is expected to pay his dues. Possibly these should be measured in denominations of responsibilities, as well as money. The member in good standing of any synagogue or temple should be required to make a weekly call on someone who needs a friendly visit. The practice of serving each other systematically will benefit the visitor as well as the visited. For Judaism, which preaches *G'miluth Chasadim*, should practice it, not simply employ rabbis or functionaries to practice it for the people. When the storekeeper, or the builder, or the clock manufacturer, or the lawyer feels obliged to leave his business in order to bring good cheer and sympathy to a widow, an orphan, a cripple, or a patient, then the real concept of Jewish pastoral care is being practiced. For Kol Yisroel "*all* Israelites are responsible, one for the other," the dictum says.

Meetings of budget committees and organizational boards are no substitute for pastoral calls. The Jew who sits on committees discharges one sort of very important responsibility, which has certain kinds of personal and social consequences. The Jew who combines this duty with the tenderer task of meeting and sharing with and helping his fellows is fulfilling another kind of function. For when people are in painful or difficult circumstances, and someone tries, by means of himself, not by his money or by his office or by his power or by his postition or by his resolution, but by the use of the direct contact of his personality, to improve their lot, he is really improving his own character and adding stature to his experience.

If we could popularize pastoral care we would be fashioning a mighty link between the social tradition of Judaism and ourselves. It is, moreover, a workable thing to try to do. Universal pastoral care can far outstrip preaching and talking and propagandizing in its effectiveness. For when anyone, even the tired businessman, actively does something he is likely, because he is taking the initiative, to be more influenced by its implications than he is by listening or reading. And if such doing is influential enough it will, in turn, encourage a more sensitive ear and a more observing eye. A compassionate community which taxes a measure of each and every member's time for pastoral work will tend to be eventually more concerned with ethical ideas, with a historic view of things, and with the making of a better today in the perspective of what went on in the world yesterday.

It would be possible to advance further suggestions; to make a plea for a particular kind of experimentation in the form and content of religious services; to argue for a Sunday School system which is stripped of its present wide variety of subjects, in place of one simple effective technique, and that is pure Haggadah—storytelling; to present a case for a subsidized theater of plays on Jewish themes; to advance programs which could put the summer camps to better use as places for moral training; and to suggest more innovations and plans and experiments along these lines.

The principle of the day should be to use our imaginations and our efforts to find new idioms of Jewish expression. The creative continuity of Judaism is desperately needed by Western civilization. The world requires a historic view of things. The Jews, moreover, are abundantly capable of invigorating Jewish cultural life in order to play a part as a humanizing force in our topsy-turvy world. The key is effort. And the motto of our experiments which can provide the Jewish past with a significant future might well be the words of Rabbi Tarphon, who used to say, "It is not thy duty to complete the work. But neither art thou free to desist from it."

AN AMERICAN ANTI-SEMITE IN THE NINETEENTH CENTURY

By Leonard A. Greenberg and Harold J. Jonas

DESPITE DISAGREEMENT in emphasis, most historians recognize the period from 1865 to 1900 as an era of vast changes—political, economic, cultural, social—affecting, indeed, every aspect of American life. Much of the record is sordid, giving evidence of violence and corruption in business and government alike. The dominant theme in this historical symphony is constructed on chords of business, labor, the farmer, the Indian, with major variations alternating between prosperity and depression in ever increasing tempo.

One fact emerges above all: this was an era which developed tremendous social and political pressures. In the midst of apparent prosperity, unemployment and depression were nonetheless quite real. The year 1894 was "the blackest" since 1865. "No depression so serious was to occur again until after 1929."[1] Feeding voraciously on the spoils of war, mere business became monopoly. Its appetite whetted, monopoly spawned "trusts." Such "captains of industry" as Vanderbilt, Rockefeller, Carnegie, and Morgan dominated the period by their daring ventures in railroad, oil, steel, and finance generally. It was the day par excellence of the "merchant prince" in American life.[2]

But as their separate interests clashed, labor and industry met in head-on conflict. Strikes for improved working conditions brought retaliation

[1] Dwight L. Dumond, Edward E. Dale, and Edgar B. Wesley, *History of the United States* (Boston, 1948), p. 496.

[2] Cf. Oliver P. Chitwood, Frank L. Owsley, and H. C. Nixon, *The United States from Colony to World Power* (New York, 1950), p. 538. The temper of the times is vividly illustrated in a contemporary *Puck* cartoon (January 23, 1889, reproduced in Dumond, Dale, and Wesley, *History of the United States*, p. 510) by Keppler, showing the "U. S. Senate"; grouped behind the senators, in formidable array, are paunchy representatives of the trusts—paper, bag, coal, tin, sugar, iron, copper, steel beam, nail, and others. Above, a plaque boldly proclaims: "A Senate of the monopolists, by the monopolists, and for the monopolists."

and bitterness in return. In this economic warfare, the lockout, blacklist, and injunction, commonly used instruments of management, were often bolstered by state militia and Federal troops. The conflict became daily more serious. In 1886 alone, some 340,000 workingmen participated in demands for the eight-hour day. Six years later, with conditions hardly improved, hundreds of "Pinkertons" were imported into the bitter Homestead steel strike. Methods which they used—rifle, dynamite, cannon, blazing oil, and natural gas—were not calculated to improve poor men's humors.

As the century drew to a close, a dramatic movement of protest crystallized in the person of "General" Jacob S. Coxey. As he led his army of unemployed from Ohio, they were joined en route by marchers from Los Angeles, San Francisco, Seattle, and Chicago. In Washington the authorities ordered their arrest for walking on the lawn, a tactic which offered no solution for the rapidly deteriorating conditions which brought the marchers together in the first place.[3]

This was America in the 1880's and 1890's—outwardly calm and contented, inwardly boiling with volcanic fury. Even then, apparently unrelated forces were in operation which would be instrumental in bringing millions of new settlers to these shores from Europe and Asia—immigrants from Russia, Poland, Austria-Hungary, Italy, and the Mediterranean. A vast proportion were Jews, who, like their predecessors, cherished the notion of exchanging pogrom and persecution for freedom and equality. Disillusionment came soon. Many discovered in the New World only wasted years of sweatshop existence. To all, discrimination, prejudice, and anti-Semitism were, alas, still important factors to contend with.

Within the space of two years, 1888 and 1889, there appeared in New York City three books in particular which peddled a vicious brand of anti-Semitism, compounded of ancient lies and contemporary jingoism. Though published anonymously, *The Original Mr. Jacobs*,[4] *The American*

[3] Cf. Arthur M. Schlesinger, *The Rise of Modern America, 1865-1951* (4th ed., New York, 1951), p. 154.

[4] *The Original Mr. Jacobs: A Startling Exposé.* New York, The Minerva Publishing Co. 10 West 23d Street. Corner of Fifth Avenue. Press of J. J. Little & Co., Astor Place, N.Y. Copyright 1888. vi + 308 pp. (Hereafter referred to as *OMJ.*) Cf. *A Catalog of Books Represented by Library of Congress Printed Cards.* Issued to July 31, 1942. Vol. CXLVIII, 1945. Pp. 301-2. (Hereafter referred to as *LC.*) Like many of Timayenis's other publications, this book contains neither publication date nor author. However, *LC*, Vol. CXLVIII, attributes authorship to Timayenis, as do other sources.

Jew,[5] and *Judas Iscariot*[6] were written by one and the same person, Telemachus T. Timayenis, self-styled teacher and professor, linguist, publisher, editor, and businessman; controversial figure in Boston's Greek community; onetime "confidant" of John D. Rockefeller; anti-Semite; and, incongruously enough, an immigrant of Greek ancestry.

THE MAN: TELEMACHUS T. TIMAYENIS

Telemachus Thomas Timayenis (1853-1918) was born to Thomas T. Timayenis, a high school teacher, in Smyrna, Turkey.[7] At the age of 16 or 17, he came to the United States,[8] living in Springfield, Mass., New York City, Boston, Lowell, and Tewksbury, Mass., where he died in 1918, an inmate of a state institution.[9] On July 31, Timayenis was buried in Tewksbury Centre Cemetery, the "town cemetery," thus bringing an eventful life to a close in a most uneventful manner.[10]

In the United States, T. T. Timayenis taught French and the classics at Springfield Collegiate Institute, and at one time was a carpet importer in Springfield with his brother Demosthenes.[11] Moving to New York about

[5] *The American Jew: An Exposé of His Career.* Profusely illustrated. New York, The Minerva Publishing Co. 1888. 1st ed. v + 219 pp., inlc. front. 3 pl. (Hereafter referred to as *AJ.*) Cf. *LC*, CXLVIII, 301-2.

[6] *Judas Iscariot: An Old Type in a New Form.* New York, Press of the Minerva Publishing Co. Copyright 1889. v + 292 pp. (Hereafter referred to as *JI.*) Cf. *LC*, CXLVIII, 301-2.

[7] Cf. *LC*, CXLVIII, 301. John Foster Kirk, *A Supplement to Allibone's Critical Dictionary of English Literature and British and American Authors...* (Vol. II, Philadelphia, 1891): "Timayenis, Telemachus T., a native of Greece, resident in America." In *JI*, Timayenis described himself as "a Greek by birth and education." Smyrna, at this period, was in reality under the rule of the Turkish Empire. Possibly hoping to bring distinction on himself, Timayenis described his father at one point as follows: "Prof. Thomas Timayenis, one of the illustrious litterateurs of the modern Greek nation... for years... connected with the Evangelical College of Smyrna." (New York *World*, 1888[?]; undated photostat.) Occasionally Timayenis used the alternate spelling, Telemaque, although most references favor the Greek form, Telemachus. For much of the biographical data on Timayenis's life, the authors are grateful to a number of individuals, including Dr. Lee Friedman; Dorothy Mozley, reference assistant, City Library Association, Springfield, Mass.; Mildred C. O'Connor, Boston Public Library.

[8] *JI*, p. iv: "I arrived in America about twenty years ago, with $15 in my pocket and by dint of hard work and perseverance, unaided, I created the position that I occupy today in the literary world." This would place his arrival in the United States about 1869, when he was about 16 or 17 years of age.

[9] Timayenis was admitted to the state institution June 29, 1918; he died July 29 from arteriosclerosis. Cf. letter, Mildred O'Connor to Harold J. Jonas, January 28, 1955.

[10] Letter, Mildred O'Connor to Harold J. Jonas, January 28, 1955.

[11] Springfield (Mass.) *City Directory*, 1876-77, 1877-78, 1878-79. There is no entry for 1879-80.

1879-80, he taught children of well-to-do families at his own institution, the New York School of Languages.[12] At 10 West 23d Street he established the Minerva Publishing Company, producing, in the space of seven or eight years, a variety of books and pamphlets.

Later, in Boston, he became successively cigarette manufacturer, Greek consul, editor and publisher, and, in his declining years, "when he was sick most of the time and unable to make a living, his brother took pity on him and sent him to live in a boarding house in Lowell, paying his expenses, and where he died."[13]

Often a center of controversy, Timayenis in 1888 was accused of embezzling Minerva Company funds. In the ensuing court hearing, it was reported that he had, on several occasions, threatened various individuals with a revolver, although there is no report of his having fired it.[14] The *World* reporter covering the case described the defendant as "swarthy, full-bearded and fiery looking, [he] is the author of 'The Original Mr. Jacobs' and other works."[15]

In full-page spread in the Boston *Sunday Herald* (September 29, 1907), Timayenis wrote a by-line story entitled "Rockefeller: A Confession by His Secret Service Man." He described an earlier relationship with Rockefeller which involved communicating confidential information to the elder financier, in return for which he was duly compensated. With some breast-beating, Timayenis also described his remorse at having to resort to such unethical tactics while at the same time justifying his course of action.[16] Some time later, Timayenis was again in the news, following

[12] *JI*, p. iv; *Sunday Herald*, Boston, September 29, 1907, Magazine and Women's Section, pp. 1-2.

[13] Statement of unidentified contemporary of Timayenis, quoted in letter, Mildred O'Connor to Harold J. Jonas, January 28, 1955.

[14] In a wonderfully refreshing tongue-in-cheek style, a New York (*World*?) reporter covered the case. One of the articles (January 4, 1889) was headlined: "TIMAYENIS DIDN'T SHOOT. In Fact His Manner Betrayed Nothing of the Fire-Eater. Still, Mr. Dickson Pictures the Author of "The Original Mr. Jacobs' as a Bloodthirsty Flourisher of Revolvers, Who Repeatedly Threatened to 'Fill Him Full of Lead'—All Hands in Court."

[15] See note 14.

[16] The full-page spread featured photos of Timayenis and Rockefeller side by side, with the subhead explaining: "Greek Who, as Tutor in Wealthy New York Families and Friend of the Powerful, Picked up Crumbs of Important Information for Oil King, Pictures Him as Man of Fears, Lover of Public Approbation and Prodigy in Money-Making." Timayenis describes how Rockefeller, finding no further use for his services, ignores him and eventually dispenses with him completely. Cf. letter, Allan Nevins to Harold J. Jonas, November 18, 1954: "JDR Jr. told me that Timayenis got into some kind of trouble... and I got the distinct impression that it was rather serious trouble, which convinced JDR Jr. that he was a man without character or principle. It is certain that JDR Jr. came to regard him as a fraud."

sensational (and apparently unfounded) charges which he had leveled against the Greek chargé d'affaires at Washington. On September 14, 1911, the Boston *Herald* reported an "indignation meeting," of "about 1000 members of the Greek community," which expressed indignation at Timayenis's statements, accused him of misrepresenting the Greek community, and finally stigmatized him "as a traitor to Greek interests in this country."[17]

While still a young man, Timayenis completed his first known book, *The Modern Greek*.[18] Thereafter, he wrote or edited fourteen additional works, ranging from the scholarly to the sensational. *A History of Greece*,[19] *Greece in the Times of Homer*,[20] and *A History of the Art of*

[17] Cf. Boston *Herald*, September 9, 1911 ("Boston Editor Attacks Consul—T. T. Timayenis Complains to Washington about L. Caftanzoglu's Attitude"); September 10, 1911 ("Declare Consul Charges False—Greek Societies of Boston Are Indignant Over Attack by T. T. Timayenis"); September 14, 1911 ("Timayenis Declared to Be Working for Personal Ends Against Compatriots").

[18] *The Modern Greek: Its Pronunciation and Relations to Ancient Greek, with an Appendix on the Rules of Accentuation*... By T. T. Timayenis... New York, D. Appleton & Co. 1877. xii + 216 pp. Cf. *LC*, CXLVIII, 301-2. Apparently the same work, but in a different edition, is *Language of the Greeks, with Appendix on the Rules of Accentuation*. $1.50. Springfield Collegiate Institute, Springfield, Mass. [1878].

[19] *A History of Greece from the Earliest Time to the Present*. With maps and illustrations. New York, D. Appleton & Co. 1881. 2 vols. Another edition appeared in 1883. Cf. *LC*, CXLVIII, 301-2. The Cooperative Publication Society (New York and London, copyright 1880) published still another edition, in the "World's Best Histories" series. The 1883 edition is "respectfully dedicated to Rev. Dr. J. H. Vincent, President of the Chautauqua Literary and Scientific Club, as a token of admiration for his well-directed efforts for the promotion of popular education" (p. iii). "...this work [is] undertaken at the request of my esteemed friend Dr. J. H. Vincent... [and] my warmest thanks [go] to my friend and associate in the New York School of Languages, Professor Henry C. Miller" (pp. v, vi). Kirk, *A Supplement to Allibone's Critical Dictionary*, Vol. II, quotes the *Nation* (XXXII, 339) as follows: "It has a peculiar animation and directness which make its narrative uncommonly attractive.... When the author leaves the field of narration he is less fortunate. The chapters upon religion, constitution, etc., are rather lacking in insight and in appreciation of the results of recent scholarship."

[20] *Greece in the Times of Homer: An Account of the Life, Customs, and Habits of the Greeks during the Homeric Period*. New York, D. Appleton & Co., 1885. xi + 302 pp. Cf. *LC*, CXLVIII, 301-2.

The American Hebrew (1888), referring sarcastically to Timayenis as "the literary heir of Homer," hinted strongly at plagiarism: "Did not Tim demonstrate in his 'History of Greece in the Times of Homer' that he was endowed with a singular gift of ascertaining what is good in the historical works of other writers and of appre— (we came near saying appropriating) appreciating their value when pieced together for the purpose of making a book?" (XXXVII, No. 7 [December 21, 1888], 126.) Interestingly enough, *Greece in the Times of Homer* was dedicated to John D. Rockefeller.

Magic[21] were followed by *A Disputed Inheritance*,[22] *His Last Passion*,[23] *Contes Tirés de Shakespeare*,[24] and *Hervor, the Gaul*.[25] Until shortly before his death, Timayenis edited the *Eastern and Western Review*, a monthly magazine published in Boston.[26] Of particular interest to this paper, however, are the three anti-Semitic publications issued by Timayenis under the aegis of his own Minerva Publishing Company in New York.

THE ORIGINAL MR. JACOBS

The Original Mr. Jacobs was published early in 1888.[26] This "startling exposé," issued anonymously, contained a number of violent anti-Semitic canards, many of ancient and time-worn vintage.

An account of "life, customs and habits of the Jews" was followed by vicious generalizations about alleged Jewish "characteristics," including a discourse on physical indications by which one can recognize individual Jews.[28] The remainder of *The Original Mr. Jacobs* was concerned with

[21] *A History of the Art of Magic, Containing Anecdotes, Explanation of Tricks, and a Sketch of the Life of Alexander Herrmann.* New York, Press of J. J. Little & Co. 1887. 135 pp., front., illus. At least two other editions are known: [1888], "60th thousand," 25¢ paper-bound; [1901], slightly enlarged, issued as, *A History of the Art of Magic... and a Sketch of the Life of the Three Herrmanns, Carl, Alexander and Leon*, "rewritten by W. E. Goemann, Dec. 15, 1901" ("70th thousand"). Both editions bore the Minerva Publishing Co. imprint. Cf. *LC*, CXLVIII, 301-2; Bowker, *The American Catalogue, 1884-90*, p. 521.

[22] ...*A Disputed Inheritance*. A thrilling story of love, mystery and intrigue. By the author of "The Original Mr. Jacobs." New York, M. J. Ivers & Co. c.1888. 315 pp. (Issued as "American series, No. 2.") Cf. *LC*, CXLVIII, 301-2.

[23] ...*His Last Passion;* a sensational and realistic story of English modern life, by Martius [pseud.]; ed. by the author of "Unsatisfied." New York, The Minerva Publishing Co. 1891. viii + 246 pp. (Issued as "Minerva series, No. 41".)

[24] *Contes tirés de Shakespeare; d'apres l'Anglais de C. & M. Lamb.* Scribner, $1. [1902?] Cf. Marion E. Potter, *The United States Catalog. Books in Print 1902* (2d ed., Minneapolis, 1903), p. 1916.

[25] *Hervor, the Gaul;* a drama in five acts. Boston, The National Press. [c. 1908.] 72 pp. Cf. *LC*, CXLVIII, 301-2; *The United States Catalog* (1912) p. 2539; *The American Catalog, 1908-1910* (New York, 1911), p. 1379.

[26] Timayenis was editor from 1907, when it was established, until June, 1916; it ceased publication, December, 1916. Cf. letter, Lee M. Friedman to Harold J. Jonas, October 28, 1954.

[27] See above, note 4. Cf. also Harold J. Jonas, "Anti-Semitica Americana," *Contemporary Jewish Record* (October, 1941), pp. 564-71; Leonard A. Greenberg, "Some American Anti-Semitic Publications of the Late 19th Century," *PAJHS*, XXXVII (1947), 421-25.

[28] *OMJ*, chap. 1, pp. 1-55. Cf. p. 21: "Having indicated the principal traits common to all Jews, let us now examine more closely the race and the species. The principal signs by which the Jews can be recognized are the following: The famous hooked nose, the restless eyes, the close-set teeth, the elongated ears, the square nails (instead of

evidence of "degeneration of the Jews," with individual chapters covering "The Jews' Hatred for the Christians"; "The Jews, the Rulers of our Epoch"; "The German Jews"; "The Commune"; "Baron Hirsch—the Upper Class of Jews"; "The Jews' Hatred of Children."[29]

"The Jew" as portrayed by Timayenis is guilty of innumerable sins, shortcomings, vices, and crimes:

> The Jew is a born trafficker, a born liar, full of cunning and intrigue. The Aryan [by contrast] is enthusiastic, heroic, chivalrous, frank and confident. The Jew sees nothing beyond the present. The Aryan is the child of Heaven, constantly preoccupied with superior aspirations. The one lives in the real, the other in the ideal.
>
> The Jew is mercenary by instinct. He has the bent for everything pertaining to business, for everything that gives him the opportunity to cheat his fellow men. The Aryan is agriculturist, poet, and, above all, a soldier. War is his element. He goes merrily to face danger, and he despises death.
>
> The Jew has no creative faculty. On the other hand, the Aryan invents. Not one invention was made by a Jew. ... The Aryan organizes, creates, while the Jew derives all the resulting advantages, which he naturally keeps for himself. ... However perspicacious the intelligence of the Jew may appear, it is in reality limited. He has neither the faculty to foresee events, nor of looking beyond his hooked nose; nor the gift of understanding delicate shades of thought and character.[30]

Combining many accusations, *The Original Mr. Jacobs* accuses Jews of being nihilists, free-thinkers, liberals; of possessing great wealth; of "cornering" the liquor trade; in general, of being dishonest in business.[31] Furthermore, these Jews have only hate and contempt for the Christian.[32]

Bolstered by historical "documentation," Timayenis parades the hoary ritual murder allegation and revives the ancient *foetor Judaicus* canard:

> It is a matter of fact that the Jew is ill-smelling. This smell exists even among the richest, a *fetor judaica* [*sic*], which indicates the race and assists them to recognize one another. The most charming Jewesses, notwithstanding the

---

being tapered in the shape of an almond), the flat foot, the round knees, the soft hand, almost melting with the hypocrisy of the traitor. Often they have one arm longer than the other. Lavater observes: 'Physical degradation closely follows upon moral degradation. This is strongly remarked among the Jews, who, of all races of men, are the most depraved.'" Timayenis elsewhere dwells on the "hooked nose" concept, too.

[29] *OMJ*, pp. 56-308.

[30] *Ibid.*, pp. 6-8.

[31] *Ibid.*, pp. 7, 56, 85 (footnote), 236, 295, and *passim.*

[32] *Ibid.*, pp. 63, 296, 307: "At times a smile full of meaning illumines these bloodless visages at the thought of some joke played upon a Christian. The fox, in fact, is the allegorical beast of the Jew. The *Meschabot Schualim* [*sic*], or *The Fables of the Fox*, is the first book put into the hands of the young Jew. Later in life he finishes his training by exercising every manner of deceit and theft upon the Aryan.... Workingmen, as

perfumes they use, justify the words of Martial: "Qui bene olet male olet." This fact has been a hundred times verified. All Jews are ill-smelling, "puent," said Victor Hugo.[33]

What was the source for *The Original Mr. Jacobs*, compounded as it was of lies, insinuations, and innuendoes, and cunningly directed toward the baser instincts of sensationalism and morbidity?

To *La France Juive* of Edward Drumont [Timayenis wrote], a duodecimo in two volumes, containing together more than one thousand pages, the author gratefully acknowledges his obligations for assistance derived in the preparation of this book. *La France Juive*, however, is not a safe guide for the average reader. Every statement of Drumont has been carefully analyzed, examined, and fully verified before it was accepted by the author for publication in this volume. . . . it must be confessed that the French writer is too often carried away by his prejudices, while his attacks on Americans, and on Free-Masons, and on Protestantism are not only unwarranted, but puerile and spiteful in the extreme.[34]

The "obligations for assistance" modestly mentioned by Timayenis were,

---

soon as you study the manoeuvres of the Jew, you will declare him a criminal. His work among you is revolution and disorder. . . . The Jew is a false brother. . . . The hatred of the Jew for the Gentile is a historic fact which the Jew writers themselves are unable to deny. Formerly they bought Gentile prisoners from the Romans solely to torment them and to put them to death. . . . From the beginning to the end of this book, what has the reader seen? Nothing but the hatred of the Jew for the Gentile."

[33] *Ibid.*, pp. 241-308; 46. "While affirming the persistency of hatred among the Jews, it may not be amiss to speak somewhat fully of their bloody sacrifices, accusations a thousand times proven, and against which the Jews always defend themselves with the impudence that characterizes them" (p. 242). A full recital of "ritual murder" accusations begins with A.D. 1071 (Blois) and ends with 1670, with this statement for present conditions: "Similar crimes to this day are committed in the Orient" (pp. 242-44). Literary and historical allusions include: Chaucer's *Canterbury Tales* (in particular, the *Prioress's Tale*, wherein "we are introduced to a horrible crime committed by 'the cursed Jew,' who seized a small boy 'young and tender was of age,' held him fast, cut his throat, and threw him into a pit"); the Damascus affair ("we will mention the murder of Father Thomas in Damascus, in 1840, the details of which are well known"); the Tisza-Eszler case (incorrectly described as "the affair of Tisza Elzlar") (pp. 242, 244, 252). For thirteenth- and sixteenth-century references to *foetor Judaicus*, cf. Jacob R. Marcus, *The Jew in the Medieval World: A Source Book, 315-1791* (Cincinnati, 1938), pp. 143, 166.

[34] *OMJ*, preface, p. v. Cf. Edouard [Adolphe] Drumont, *La France Juive: Essai d'histoire contemporaine* (Paris, C. Marpon & E. Flammarion, 1886?), 2 vols., 20th ed. Drumont (1844-1917) is regarded as having been a spokesman of French anti-Semitism under the Third Republic. *La France Juive* was "the second best seller of the 19th century, having gone through more than one hundred editions, besides many translations in several languages." *Universal Jewish Encyclopedia*, III, 603. Cf. also *Jewish Encyclopedia*. Through his subsequent writings, and his own newspaper, *La Libre parole* (1892), Drumont exercised considerable anti-Semitic influence on the Dreyfus case and in France generally.

indeed, heavier than he dared to admit, for a cursory examination of the English and French texts reveals that whole sentences were lifted from *La France Juive*, unedited and unacknowledged, let alone "analyzed, examined and fully verified." The quotation which referred to differences between Aryan and Jew[35] appeared in the French version as follows:

> Le Sémite, est mercantile, cupide, intrigant, subtil, rusé; l'Aryen est enthousiaste, héroique, chevaleresque, désentéressé, franc, confiant jusqu'à la naiveté. Le Sémite est un terrien ne voyant guère rien au-delà de la vie présente; l'Aryen est un fils du ciel sans cesse préoccupé d'aspirations supérieures; l'un vit dans la réalité, l'autre dans l'idéal.[36]

Even misspellings were transferred *in toto*: "Il [le Juif] semble alors tout plongé dans la Kabbale, absorbé dans la lecture du *Zohar* ou du *Sepher Zetzirah*" (*La France Juive*) — "He seems to have plunged into the dreams of tradition, to have been absorbed in the study of the *Zohar* or of Sepher Zetzirah" (*The Original Mr. Jacobs*).[37]

Not content with presenting "facts," *The Original Mr. Jacobs* also projected specific action: prohibiting additional Jewish immigration, boycotting Jewish candidates, and publishing a further exposé of prominent Jews in America.[38] "We have in this book," Timayenis wrote,

> pictured the Jew as he is, has been, and always will be. Who the prominent Jews in America are, what they have tried to do, what they have succeeded in doing, and what they may yet do, will be told, together with their antecedents,

disposed; that when they quit Europe for America, they leave their prejudice behind, and try to adopt our American ideas. The Jew never rids himself of his venom. A serpent is a serpent, whether in the old world or in the new."

[35] See above, p. 271.

[36] Drumont, *La France Juive*, p. 9; cf. *OMJ*, p. 6. Cf. the following: Drumont, p. 20, *OMJ*, p. 10; Drumont, p. 24, *OMJ*, p. 64; Drumont, p. 31, *OMJ*, p. 19; Drumont, pp. 464-65, *OMJ*, p. 293.

[37] Drumont, *La France Juive*, p. 189; *OMJ*, p. 78. Cf. also Drumont, p. 403 (*OMJ*, p. 256 quoting from Dr. Justus's *Judens spiegel:* 'Les livres théologiques des Juifs se partegent en deux catégories, à savoir Peschath et Kabala. A la première classe appartiennent le Talmud et le Schulchan. Or, d'après le Schulchan Aruch, *ce n'est pas un péché si un Juif tue un chrétien.* (Loi 50 et 81.) Dans le Talmud publié a Amsterdam en 1646, *il est ordonné aux Juifs d'exterminer les disciples du Nazaréen.* (Sanhedrin Pireck X, Cheleck et Aboda, Sarah *Prieck I.*)'"

[38] *OMJ*, pp. 307-8: "Let the reader consider the havoc that the Jew has wrought in France, and let him ask himself if he is willing to have the Jew accomplish the same in America. It is the duty of all, irrespective of faith or nationality, of all who live in America, of all who have the good of America at heart, to combine and to resist Jewish encroachment. Let stringent laws be passed, forbidding Jews to enter the country. Let all her voters, irrespective of party, be imbued with one thought: Not to permit a candidate known to have one drop of Jewish blood in his veins to be nominated, much less to be elected to any political office, even the lowest. Nothing could be more absurd than the opinion one sometimes hears expressed, that the Jews among us are peacefully

one and all, in a fearless way, in a forthcoming book entitled, *The American Jew*.[39]

THE AMERICAN JEW

The American Jew proved a most fitting sequel to *The Original Mr. Jacobs*.[40] No longer so dependent on *La France Juive*, Timayenis now concentrated on the American milieu.

"The Jew" is no longer merely "an enemy of mankind"; he is now accused of a number of newer, and more specific, sins. He is responsible for the "crime of incendiarism";[41] he deals purposely in putrid foods;[42] he is "loud, vulgar, and intrusive";[43] "the Jews, as a race, are undoubtedly the dirtiest people on the face of the earth";[44] next to his "lust for money," the strongest "passion" in the Jew is licentiousness;[45] because they "literally drip disease and filth with every step they take," the Jews are, of course, responsible for all the plagues and epidemics on the face of the earth;[46] they are scoundrels and a "race of parasites."[47]

While Timayenis the journalist frequently resorted to sensationalism,

[39] *Ibid.*, p. 308; this is the concluding sentence.

[40] See above, note 5. A copy in the Hebrew Union College reads: "First edition, 30,000 copies. . . . Price 50 cents." A New York Public Library copy, a later edition, reads: "Minerva Library. Issued Quarterly. No. 2." According to Timayenis's statement, it appeared "less than three months" after *OMJ* (*AJ*, p. iii).

[41] "This crime of incendiarism, previous to the advent of the Jews, was with us, comparatively speaking, unknown. The Jews mulcted the insurance-companies of vast sums of money before the companies became aware of the fraud practised upon them. It is a matter of record, that many of the leading insurance-companies of today hesitate, and often refuse, to insure the stock of any one having a Jewish countenance or a Jewish name" (*AJ*, p. 7). Cf. *Sunday Dispatch*, Philadelphia, April 21, 1867, reprinted as item 147 in Morris U. Schappes, *A Documentary History of the Jews in the United States, 1654-1875* (New York, 1950).

[42] *AJ*, p. 14. Cf. illustration, opp. p. 16: "Storing the stale fish over night."

[43] *Ibid.*, p. 24. Typical of much of Timayenis's coarseness is the following: "As for the fat Jewesses, as they waddle across the hotel veranda, their gross paunches quivering, and their coarse, pudgy fingers covered with diamonds, they are objects offensive to the sight, blotches on the summer landscape, veritable eyesores. They, in their way, are quite as objectionable as the men" (pp. 24-25).

[44] *Ibid.*, pp. 26-27.

[45] *Ibid.*, p. 81.

[46] *Ibid.*, p. 90. With typical "objectivity," Timayenis points out that "it has been demonstrated" that "all" epidemics that occur in various parts of the world from time to time "spring from the Jew, who literally drip disease and filth with every step they take" (p. 190). The accusation of responsibility for plagues, epidemics, and disease was, by this time, already over 500 years old, having been invoked in 1348-49 on the occasion of the Black Death throughout Europe. Cf. Salo W. Baron, *A Social and Religious History of the Jews* (New York, 1937), II, 29; III, 106.

[47] *AJ*, pp. 205, 213.

often using crude and base language, Timayenis the scholar tried to impart an air of scientific detachment which would lend suitable weight to his words. Thus, every chapter begins by quoting some ancient "authority" or alleged source of Jewish literature. Lavater, Eisenmenger, Napoleon, the Talmud, Lacretelle, and Shakespeare are all used in this way, with additional reference as well to *The Original Mr. Jacobs*.[48]

An innovation in *The American Jew* was the significant use of illustrations. Timayenis had obviously learned the value of caricature and cartoon, the visual portrayal of that near-obscenity which he tried so hard to effect. Captions on typically anti-Semitic illustrations were made to read: "on the summer-hotel veranda"; "storing the stale fish over night"; "how we may know him"; "the Jew immigrant," who was replete with hooked nose, beard, "stove-pipe" hat, pack under arm, and sly look in the eye, as he emerged from a building labeled "Castle Garden."[49] Initial letters of each chapter were generally woven into some obscene or vicious cartoon which described the chapter contents. Chapter XII, "The Jew in His Relation to the Law," showed "the Jew" garbed in long gown, bearded, wearing a skullcap, and craftily eyeing an unevenly balanced scale which he holds in his left hand; the right hand, held behind his back, grasps a curved dagger, ready for use.[50]

The individual who executed these vicious caricatures was Valerian Gribayédoff, "a talented Russian artist in New York."[51] Under Joseph Pulitzer's direction on the New York *World* he had been drawing a regular cartoon feature which became "the first series of political cartoons even appearing in an American newspaper."[52] Obviously talented, Gribayédoff nonetheless created some of the most shocking examples of anti-Semitic art in the pages of Timayenis's *The American Jew*.

Timayenis's anti-Semitism was now becoming more direct through use of illustration, appeal to near-obscenity, strong reliance on historical and literary "authorities," frequent references to the *magnum opus*, *The Original Mr. Jacobs*, and, above all, outright appeal to deep prejudices.

In addition to insistent demands for specific action—such as boy-

[48] *Ibid.*, pp. 31, 134, 196. On the cover and title page appears the following: "Foul deeds will rise, Though earth o'rewhelm them, to men's eyes" (*Hamlet*, I, ii, 257).

[49] *AJ*, title page; opp. pp. 8, 16, 26.

[50] *Ibid.*, p. 134.

[51] Joseph Pulitzer, quoted in James Wyman Barrett, *Joseph Pulitzer and His World* (New York, 1941), p. 81.

[52] Arthur M. Schlesinger, *The Rise of the City* (New York, 1933; 3d printing, 1940), pp. 187-98. Pulitzer bought the *World* from Gould in 1883; the cartoon series started the following year, with Walt McDougall and Gribayédoff alternating.

cotting the Jews, driving them from political life, curtailing immigration, and, eventually, expelling them from the country[53]—*The American Jew* projected a publication which would be dedicated solely to fulfilling these various anti-Semitic programs.

We have been requested [wrote Timayenis] by many prominent men in literary, financial, and commercial circles to establish a monthly publication, to be called "The Anti-Semite." We have been assured of ample support in this venture. . . . The periodical we propose to establish, will give a faithful account of the deceits, crimes, and fraudulent transactions of the Jew, in all channels of business. It will be published . . . at one dollar per year. Efficient correspondents throughout the United States will watch the Jew, and will keep us informed of all his deeds, or rather, misdeeds, which will be fearlessly recorded in "The Anti-Semite."[54]

By means of this publication, "efforts will not be spread in urging the passage of laws that will afford some protection to the commercial community, and to society in general, from the Jew."[55] Timayenis never carried out his grandiose scheme, although he did make one additional contribution to anti-Semitic literature in American life.

JUDAS ISCARIOT

Judas Iscariot: *An Old Type in a New Form* was Timayenis's last known anti-Jewish tract.[56] No longer in need of Drumont and other European prototypes, Timayenis became more proficient in style and more adept in the technique of defamation. Of course, the old canards were still present,

[53] *AJ*, pp. 167, 192, 218-19. The following is a clear formulation of the expulsion theme: ". . . but one sentiment should animate the American people, and this should find expression in the one curt but emphatic cry, 'The Jew must go'" Let there be no angry denunciation, no unseemly haste, no injustice, but calm, deliberate, and firm resolve. . . . Give them time to convert all their wealth into gold and bills, and let them go whither they list. To Europe if the European people will still consent to be preyed on by them, and, if not, to their own country where they are assured of protection by the Turkish Empire. . . . from Maine to Louisiana, from New York to the Golden Horn, let the American people rise as one man, and assert in deep tones of calm unwavering resolve, 'We want no parasitic race among us: THE JEW MUST GO!'' On this note, *AJ* concludes.

[54] *Ibid.*, p. iv. It is significant to observe that the terms "anti-Semite" and "anti-Semitism" were then of recent coinage. "The term first appears in Germany toward the close of the financial panic which grew out of the wild speculation following the Franco-Prussian war (1870-71)" (*Universal Jewish Encyclopedia*, I, 341). The word "anti-Semitism" was probably first used by Wilhelm Marr in 1879, the same year in which he founded the Anti-Semitic League.

[55] *AJ*, p. iv.

[56] See above, note 6.

frequently quoted from the two earlier works.[57] While still largely sensational, *Judas Iscariot* tried to project, more than ever, that scientific detachment so characteristic of the impartial "scholar."

A number of new features now appeared in *Judas Iscariot*: (a) increasingly correct use of Hebrew and, to a lesser degree, Yiddish;[58] (b) delineation of an entirely new category of Jews, *Judaisants*, "those who act like the Jews, those affiliated to the Jew system";[59] (c) development of the concept that anti-Semitism is, in fact, caused by and due to Jews themselves;[60] (d) prediction of America as the leading anti-Semitic country, coupled, however, with the ingenuous admission that there is a "wide open" field for anti-Semitic agitation in the United States;[61]

[57] Following the last page of text, *The Original Mr. Jacobs*, allegedly in its "50th edition," is described as "powerful, original, exasperating"; *The Sacramento Bee* is quoted as describing *The American Jew* as "a more bitter attack on the Hebrews of the country than a volume issued some time since under the heading "The Original Mr. Jacobs.'" Cf. *JI*, pp. iii-v, for typical chapter headings: "Anti-Semitism in America"; "Mixed Marriages"; "Usury"; "Monopoly—The Rothschilds"; "The Jew in the Liquor Business"; "The Jew Is a Liar"; "The Jew Is a Thief"; "The World's Verdict."

[58] Cf. *JI*, p. 47 (*matzes; sholet; Shmah, Yisroel Adonoy Elokhekho Adonoy echad; bes keneses*); p. 49 (*Kehalim*); p. 50 (*Orelim; Avodeh elilim; mishpotim; notsrim*); p. 76 ("The Hungarian name for the Jews, *Zsidó*, is a derivative of the Hebrew *Hezid*, meaning 'to lie'; so that *Zsidó* or *Hazudó*, a liar, accurately and faithfully depicts the Jew"). Timayenis elsewhere states that he has "studied the law... under the guidance of a prominent old rabbi" (*JI*, p. 90). In elaboration, he points out "that there is not a single word in my quotations that I have not myself examined thoroughly. My G'moro quotations are taken from the Bavli; the Mishnas from Bavli and a new Krotoschin edition. I specify the place from which every quotation is taken, and guarantee the genuineness of each and every one. As I have been careful to avoid even the most trifling mistake, and have made these quotations in no spirit of malice or unfairness, I shall not take notice of incompetent critics" (*JI*, pp. 223-24). Cf. also *JI*, p. 287.

[59] "I will even add, that the *Judaisants*, or those who act like the Jews, those affiliated to the Jew system, are even more grasping, more rapacious... than the Jews" (*JI*, p. 21). Cf. *JI*, pp. 22-26, for a detailed description of the "oil-king," a tremendously wealthy financier, "a pillar of the Baptists [who] plans his campaign of money for the day—a cruel and exterminating campaign, that has driven many men to suicide, wrecked entire families, and hurled others into an untimely grave." People like this have "created amidst us a class of men arrogant, cruel, distant, cold, aristocratic, ignorant, but purse-laden, such as the 'oil-king;' a class which, for want of a better name, we will call *Judaisants*." The description here presented is a thinly-disguised portrait of Rockefeller; cf. also *AJ*, pp. 125-28, for a similarly uncomplimentary description of "The Petroleum King."

[60] "Anti-Semitism is a foreign plant inasmuch as the Jews who pour in from abroad bring along with them their abominable character, which invariably excites hatred; and thus they, the Jews, give rise to anti-Semitism" (*JI*, p. 54).

[61] "...the field for anti-Semitism is not only wide open, but it is hungry for the seed, swallowing hundreds of thousands of our anti-Semitic books.... I can safely say that America bids fair to become the leading anti-Semitic country; and, as we are a practical nation, it may safely be said that, while the European nations will speculate about

(e) disavowal of personal hatred for Jews as individuals;[62] (f) insistence that Jews are not workers;[63] and, finally (g), a startling project to "lay out a part of the Territory of New Mexico—most resembling Palestine—and establish there an independent Judea, similar to the reservations of our Indians, and call it a Jewish reservation . . . a Talmudic theocracy, a new Jerusalem, where they can quietly await the arrival of the Messiah."[64] Like Timayenis's projected anti-Semitic publication, the New Mexico theocracy was never realized.

Judas Iscariot further discussed the value of the *Anti-Jew*, previously called "The Anti-Semite," and originally broached in *The American Jew*. No longer content with hinting at economic advantages which anti-Semitism would provide—in itself hardly a novel thought, since Europe's medieval emperors hit on the same idea at least six centuries earlier[65]—*Judas Iscariot* now spelled out the economic benefits:

The *Anti-Jew* will reach communities and countries where no other American publication can have access. If you are a manufacturer of iron-ware, tools, machinery, farming implements, or an importer from any country, you can reach eastern countries in Europe where American competition is highly desirable. Our magazine will be an important help to you. Send us your advertisement before you send it to Jews or Jewish slaves.[66]

'civilized measures' looking toward the solution of the Semitic question, America will meet the issue promptly and land the Jews where they least expect; and the Jewish question will be solved practically, radically, and quickly" (*JI*, pp. 55-56).

[62] "I would not say all this if it were not from earnest conviction and positive knowledge of the facts [that Jews are perjurers, hypocrites, etc.] . I feel no animosity, I have no personal hatred against individual Jews; but I know the race" (*JI*, p. 191).

[63] Timayenis expressed this thought in a variety of ways in all three books. Cf. *JI*, p. 202: "Imagine a Jew, with his thin, long fingers, shaped for theft, with his shaky, crooked legs and his flat feet, handling a plow or spade!" Also: "Think of a Jew, pick-axe on his shoulder or a wheel-barrow in his hands, working in the mines! Picture to yourself a Jew bustling around a blast-furnace, working in a powder-mill, blasting rocks, building stone walls, roofing a ten-story building, driving trucks, unloading ships, whaling in ice-covered boats, sawing ice on the rivers, dressing lumber, floating rafts, lassoing horses, branding wild bulls on the ranches, serving as a seaman on a man-of-war or a torpedo boat! Just think of it!" (*JI*, pp. 202-3).

[64] *JI*, p. 292. Since New Mexico was not admitted to the Union until 1912, twenty-three years later, it represented, at this time, one of the farthest outposts of American society.

[65] Cf. James Westfall Thompson and Edgar Nathaniel Johnson, *An Introduction to Medieval Europe, 300-1500* (New York, 1937), p. 855, for reference to Edward I's economic gains derived from expulsion of Jews from England (1290); cf. also S. W. Baron, *A Social and Religious History of the Jews*, II, 37-38. "I need encouragement and support," wrote Timayenis (*JI*, p. 290; cf. *AJ*, p. iv); "I shall feel thankful to all my readers if they will write me after reading this book, stating that they are willing to support the *Anti-Jew*. It will enable me to survey the field of operation."

[66] *JI*, p. 290.

Possibly this was the motivation for Timayenis's anti-Semitism: financial and economic reward. In this respect he was not alone. However, his contribution to *anti-Semitica Americana*, such as it was, lay not in his three tracts, but also in his efforts to make anti-Semitism, as a movement, acceptable and respected to the American public. "The camp of the anti-Semites," he wrote, "is recruited from the most enlightened elements of our modern society, and, in fact, from the class of men who are and always have been partly the creators of modern civilization, partly its leaders."[67]

MINERVA PUBLISHING COMPANY

Minerva Publishing Company, publisher of all three volumes, was founded in 1888 for the purpose of "making, purchasing, printing and selling ... plates, drawings, books, papers and pamphlets."[68] Corporate trustees included Timayenis, his wife, Betsy d'Andria Timayenis, Emma Dickson, and her husband, James B. Dickson, "the theatrical manager."[69] Capital stock was subscribed in the amount of ten thousand dollars.[70] In 1924 the corporation was dissolved by proclamation of the governor of New York for nonpayment of taxes.[71]

During its effective period, 1888-96, Minerva is known to have published nine items: *The Queen of Beauty*; *A Peep at Our Cousins*; *A History of the Art of Magic*; *The Preachers*; *...His Last Passion*; *A Modern Don Juan*; in addition to the three anti-Jewish tracts.[72] *An Atheist Monk* and

[67] *Ibid.*, p. 48.

[68] Certificate of incorporation, Minerva Publishing Company, filed November 22, 1888. Cf. *Publisher's Weekly*, October 6, 1888, for full-page advertisement notifying the trade of *The Original Mr. Jacobs*, "one of the best selling books in the market today."

[69] Certificate of incorporation, Minerva Publishing Company. Timayenis used the signature "Telemaque" on this document. For reference to Dickson, cf. the (New York) *World* (?), January 4, 1889, "Timayenis Didn't Shoot."

[70] The certificate of incorporation provided for "four hundred shares of twenty-five dollars ($25.00) each."

[71] April 2, 1924 (Division of corporations of the State of New York).

[72] *The Queen of Beauty*, "original, Powerful, and dealing with contemporaneous personages and events"; *A Peep at Our Cousins*, "by a maid of honor" (author identified as George Hastings; cf. photostat, New York *World*, December—, 1888 [?]); *A History of the Art of Magic...*, "60th thousand" [1888]; *The Preachers*, by a Monk (Minerva series, No. 25, July, 1890); *...His Last Passion*, a sensational and realistic story of English modern life, by Martius, ed. by the author of "Unsatisfied" (15th thousand, Minerva series, No. 41, 1891); *A Modern Don Juan*, "a powerful, realistic novel," "an instantaneous success... the great romantic novel... deals with well-known Contemporaneous Persons and Events in American Life"; see above, notes 4-6.

Dr. Phillips, "a story of Jewish society,"[73] may also have been published during this period.[74] Most of Minerva's publications were released anonymously or pseudonymously. For the most part, they fell into three categories: anti-Semitic, anticlerical, belletristic.[75] One notable exception, *A History of the Art of Magic*, appears to have been a reprint of another publisher.[76]

Despite apparent financial difficulties at the outset,[77] there were many indications that Minerva's work was of technically good quality. Length of volumes, bindings, use of line-drawings and colored inks all suggest that a skilled printing establishment had produced the books.

In locating on 23d Street near Fifth Avenue, Timayenis selected a neighborhood which attracted many social and political "greats" of the era. Twenty-third Street at that time was known as the "great white way." Down the block was Koster and Bial's, theatrical mecca for performer and audience alike, while near by were such famous locales as the Fifth Avenue Hotel, the Flat Iron Building, and Delmonico's.

Despite favorable indications of technical skill and location, however, Minerva Publishing Company never quite fulfilled the promise represented by its prototype—Minerva, Greek goddess of wisdom. For it can be fairly well established, in the absence of further reports, that Timayenis's publishing firm was the first in American history devoting itself even partially to anti-Semitic literature. Perhaps fuller records will one day be available to establish additional facts about this phase of Timayenis's life.

TIMAYENIS AND MINERVA

INFLUENCE AND SIGNIFICANCE

Judging from sample notices, *The Original Mr. Jacobs* evoked mixed reactions. John Davis, "editor, Junction City [Kansas] *Tribune*, on June

[73] Cf. *JI*, advertising matter: "In Preparation: *An Atheist Monk*.... *The first edition* of this original and powerful book *will be 60,000 copies*. Orders now booking"; "*Dr. Phillips*. A Powerful, Realistic Novel. A Story of Jewish Society. It was written in a fearless manner.... more than 60,000 copies have already been sold."

[74] By 1896, Minerva was thought to be "now out of business" (*The American Catalogue, 1890-1895* [New York, 1896], p. xxiv); however, a revised edition of *A History of the Art of Magic*..., "rewritten by W. E. Goemann, Dec. 15, 1901," still carried the Minerva imprint. See above, note 22.

[75] Anti-Semitic: *OMJ*, *AJ*, *JI The Preachers* (some unfavorable references), and possibly *Dr. Phillips*. Anticlerical: *The Preachers*, *A History of the Art of Magic* (in part). Belletristic: *A Modern Don Juan*.

[76] The earlier edition was issued in New York, "Press of J. J. Little & Co., 1887."

[77] See above, p. 268.

14, 1888, wrote that he "was much impressed with the usefulness" of *The Original Mr. Jacobs.* "Through your kindness," he continued, "I received a copy.... Since then I have bought about eight copies for my friends, at various points in my travels, and they are all interested."[78] Editor Davis urged "every public teacher, every statesman, and every intelligent citizen [to] make the acquaintance of this 'Original Mr. Jacobs.'"[79]

However, the Cleveland *Plain Dealer* described it "as a specimen of blind, brutal bigotry."[80] The *Saturday Evening Post,* while identifying it as "a terrible diatribe upon the Jewish nation," nonetheless agreed "that in its historical, political, and social details, it is of intense interest."[81] "A fearful book, indeed," was the New York *Dramatic News* summary.[82]

In 1889 Miss Johanna von Bohne wrote an unusual counterreply: *Jew and Gentile: A Commentary on "The Original Mr. Jacobs" and "The American Jew."*[83] Identifying herself as "a lady of good family, belonging to the Protestant faith," Miss von Bohne declared that she was "not afraid to reveal my name and antecedents," an obvious dig at Timayenis's penchant for anonymity.[84] In wisely observing that expulsion of Jews, as demanded by Timayenis, would reap rich financial benefits to their persecutors, Miss von Bohne went on to recommend outlawing of anti-

[78] *AJ,* end papers. Davis also went on: "I am continually inquiring for the book in the bookstores; and where not found, I tell the bookseller to send for it. I have found it here [Junction City, Kansas], and in Clay Centre, Kan.; at Clark's bookstore in Cincinnati Union Depot "The Original Mr. Jacobs' is *not permitted to be sold*! The bookseller had a supply, and was selling them, was forbidden to sell, and returned the supply. That was the story told me; and I considered it a good joke,—a joke that will readily re-act on the monopolies. I hope you are making big sales. I am now anxious to see the next book, 'The American Jew.' Will it be ready soon? I hope it will show the agency of the Jew in some of our American wars and swindles."

[79] *AJ,* end papers. Excerpts were also included from the *Saturday Evening Post* (Phila., Pa.); *Evening Standard* (New Bedford, Mass.); *Plain Dealer* (Cleveland, O.); *Dramatic News* (New York, N.Y.); *Union* (Manchester, N.H.?); and *Times* (Kansas City, Kan.).

[80] *AJ,* end papers. The *Plain Dealer* also recommended: "The bigots who preach this crusade against Jews should join the other bigots who preach a similar crusade against Catholics, and troop off to Alaska together, where their blood might become cooler, or they could turn around and hate each other as fiercely as they now hate the descendants of Abraham, and the spiritual children of the Pope."

[81] *AJ,* end papers. "It is an American book reproducing and teaching the 'Jew-hate' which of late years has been so strong in Europe, notably France and Germany" (*Saturday Evening Post*).

[82] *AJ,* end papers.

[83] Johanna von Bohne, *Jew and Gentile: A Commentary on "The Original Mr. Jacobs" and "The American Jew"* (New York, 1889; The Judge Publishing Co., Potter Building, 38 Park Row), 30 pp., price 15 cents.

[84] *Ibid.,* preface.

Semitic literature. "I hold," she wrote, "that all indecent publications (anonymous or otherwise) ought to be suppressed by law, on the same principle that indecent pictures are prevented from circulation."[85]

According to Timayenis's flamboyant statements, his anti-Jewish books were greeted by general efforts to boycott his productions, while threats were supposedly made on his life and calumnies published about him in the "Jewish press."[86] Stripped of excess verbiage, though, it becomes evident that both *The Original Mr. Jacobs* and *The American Jew* did cause a stir among Jewish readers.

Following the embezzlement incident, when Timayenis had been "lodged in the Tombs,"[87] *The American Hebrew* wept crocodile tears over his fate:

> My tears, alas! are flowing fast
> And overrun a pail.
> Timmy's in the watch house
> Timmy's in the jail.
>
> *Unprinted Ballad*[88]

In a wonderfully sarcastic vein, the editor continued:

> Telemaque Tombs Timayenis in jail! What must the shades of Sophocles, Euripedes [*sic*], and Aeschylus think of that country which imprisons on a charge of grand larceny the one upon whom their mantle has fallen! . . . How erratic it was to accuse the Hellene Telemaque of being a Jew hater? He did not hate the Jews. All things else having failed, he sought to make money out of blackguarding the Jews. Drumont succeeded, why not Timayenis?[89]

Well might *The American Hebrew* take notice, for within the space of one year, Telemachus T. Timayenis accomplished the following significant projects: (a) founded an anti-Semitic publishing firm; (b) introduced Drumont to America via *The Original Mr. Jacobs*; (c) proposed what appears to be the first anti-Jewish magazine in the United States; (d) projected an American "ghetto";[90] (e) perpetuated a series of vicious anti-Semitic canards in American life.

[85] *Ibid.*, p. 9.

[86] Cf. *AJ*, pp. iii, 195. ("Neither threats of boycott nor their mutterings of personal danger have any weight with us. We are ready to lay down even life for a principle"), and end-papers; *JI*, pp. iv-v ("Some time ago I was accused of embezzling the funds of the Minerva Publishing Company—a company which I founded myself, and with my own money and brains. I was arrested, and for a time the Jewish press published the vilest calumnies against me"); p. 289 ("I defy the whole Jewdom"); and *passim*.

[87] *The American Hebrew*, XXXVII, No. 7 (December 21, 1888), "T.T.T.", p. 126.

[88] *Ibid.*

[89] *Ibid.*

[90] Timayenis used the phrase "Jewish reservation." Though not discussed previously, it should be noted that Timayenis's prejudiced ideas extended to other ethnic

Carlo Gardini, one-time American consular agent in Bologna, visited the United States during the 1880's. Writing of his experiences, he later commented:

> That which ... made me open my eyes wide with surprise was the assertion of my companion about the Jews. These people, he said, would not be admitted to the best Saratoga hotels, not even were they the Rothschilds in person. In the land of democracy, where freedom of laws and of religion reach their apogee, I would have thought such restrictions fantastic. However, these were the facts, and one must come to believe that anti-Semitism has roots so deep and so strong in America that it will be impossible to extirpate them.[91]

Whatever else he may have accomplished, T. T. Timayenis contributed, quite definitely, toward the growth of that kind of anti-Semitism which Gardini described in his travels.

---

groups as well, including the American Indian, the Negro, and the Chinese. Cf. *AJ*, p. 190 ("...the Jews are a filthy race,—more filthy than the Chinese"); p. 205 ("The industrial aptitudes of the Jews are perhaps on a slightly higher plane than those of the Red Indian..."); p. 208 ("We refuse citizenship, and with good reason, to the Chinese..."); *OMJ*, p. 286 ("...the apathy of a Turk, the cruelty of a Zulu, the cunning of a Greek, the changeableness of a Frenchman, the stability of a German, the insincerity of an Armenian... the treachery of an Indian..."); *JI*, p. 59 ("...equality can be sanctioned only so far as it is economically, financially, and socially practicable; only in so far as it is consistent with national well-being. Let us, therefore, not talk about equality of races, creeds, and colors, as embodied in our lofty principles—theoretically. We must make allowance for cold, hard, practical facts."); p. 65 (Chinese and Negroes are considered as "dangerous," "abominable," not "assimilable"). This aspect of Timayenis's prejudice appeared most sharply in *JI*. In view of his acknowledgment of Carlyle's influence (in the preface, *JI*, p. iii, he wrote that Carlyle's writing "first suggested to me... writing the present book"), cf. J. Salwyn Schapiro, "Thomas Carlyle, Prophet of Fascism," *Journal of Modern History*, XVII (June, 1945), 97-115, for an admirable analysis of Carlyle's antidemocratic sentiments and his "overmastering belief in the doctrine of inequality among men."

[91] Carlo Gardini, *Gli Stati Uniti* (1891), quoted in Oscar Handlin, *This Was America* (Cambridge, 1949), p. 349.

FLIGHT FROM THE SLUMS

By Hyman B. Grinstein

A MAJORITY of the Jews in the United States, in the last one hundred years, were domiciled in the slum areas of the large cities. Prior to this period these cities had not developed run-down districts to any great extent. Accordingly, before 1850, the Jews seem to have been little influenced by the crowded conditions, even though they often lived near or within the poorer sections. The problem arises only after the mid-nineteenth century, when on the one hand the cities began to spawn run-down neighborhoods on a large scale, and when on the other hand the stepped-up migration of Jews brought to this country many impoverished people, who, unable to live in better sections, were obliged of necessity to make their homes in the slums.[1]

The ethical and moral standards of the Jews have been traditionally of a high character. While an occasional thief or a person of a loose moral nature might have been found in the old Jewish community in Europe, antisocial individuals in general were extremely rare. The Jews brought this high moral sense with them to this country. In the entire history of the Jews in Colonial times as well as during the early national period, say until 1865, there were only a few cases of arrests of Jews for crimes

This paper was delivered in New York on December 30, 1954, at a joint session of the American Historical Association and the American Jewish Historical Society.

[1] General references to Jews and the slums are: for New York, Philadelphia, and Chicago, Charles S. Bernheimer, *The Russian Jew in the United States* (Philadelphia, 1905); House of Representatives, *Report of the Committee on Manufactures on the Sweating System;* for Chicago, Phillip P. Bregstone, *Chicago and Its Jews* (Chicago, 1933); Louis Wirth, *The Ghetto* (Chicago, 1928); for New York, Jacob A. Riis, *How the Other Half Lives* (New York, 1900); Hutchins Hapgood, *The Spirit of the Ghetto* (New York, 1909); Samuel Ornitz, *Haunch, Paunch and Jowl* (New York, 1923); *Jewish Messenger*, Vol. XXX, No. 22 (New York, 1871); *American Israelite*, Vol. XVI, No. 42 (Cincinnati, 1870); *Menorah*, VII (New York, 1889), 215 ff.; Michael Gold, *Jews without Money* (New York, 1935); for Boston and Chelsea, see Mary Antin, *The Promised Land* (Boston, 1942); for Indianapolis, see *Hamelitz*, Vol. XX, No. 77 (1884); for Syracuse, see *Hatzofeh Beeretz Hahadashah*, Vol. I, No. 3 (New York, 1871).

against property. Indeed, there is no record of the conviction of a Jew of a major crime against a person in the first two hundred years of Jewish experience in the United States. One of the first Jews to be convicted of murder in the state of New York was Pesach Rubinstein, who in 1874 was charged with killing his cousin Sarah Alexander. Even this case, when its proceedings are carefully considered, appears to have been a trumped-up affair in which the chief of police of Brooklyn was over-anxious to convict and the jury desirous of rendering a hasty verdict.[2]

After the 1870's, however, the Jews begin to produce their share of criminals, seemingly to a lesser extent, however, than other minority groups. The existence of crime, for example, on the East Side of New York became glaringly apparent when in 1908 the Police Commissioner of New York City made the exaggerated and unfounded charge that half of the criminal element of the city was Jewish. The reply of authoritative Jewish bodies denied this assertion but admitted nevertheless the existence of crime among the Jews.[3]

It may be of interest to seek to determine the probable causes of criminality among the Jews of the United States. There is much to the contention that, on the face of things, it would appear that the crowded areas of the cities were largely responsible for the rise of crime among the Jews.[4] Other factors, of course, must be considered as well. Thus, for example, the "machine" and the political groupings of the large cities undoubtedly, for reasons best known to themselves, encouraged criminal elements to flourish. Some immigrants, ignorant of the loftier ideals of the American way of life, may have thought that this criminality was the proper manner of living in America and often were led to this attitude by the actions of a corrupt police force and other corrupt officials.[5]

[2] Hyman B. Grinstein, *The Rise of the Jewish Community of New York* (Philadelphia, 1945), p. 259; *Jewish Messenger*, VIII, 141. The first American Jew to commit murder was Dr. Moses Lowenberg, who killed a patient over nonpayment of fees. This case appears to have been a matter of temporary insanity. Cf. *Israelite*, VIII (1861), 182; *Jewish Messenger*, XIII (1863), 171. Another case, probably of an innocent person, was that of Bennet Scop who was accused of killing Jacob Goodman, a fellow peddler, in Ohio in 1870. Cf. *Israelite*, Vol. XVII, No. 7 (1870).

[3] Harry Sackler, "The Kehillah of New York," in *Jewish Communal Register* (New York, 1918); Norman Bentwich, *For Zion's Sake* (Philadelphia, 1954) p. 77; for crime among Jews see Bernheimer, *The Russian Jew in the United States*, pp. 344, 356 ff., 362 ff.

[4] Jacob A. Riis, *Children of the Poor* (New York, 1892), p. 78.

[5] David Blaustein, "The People of the East Side," in *University Settlement Studies*, I, No. 2, p. 78; Jacob Riis, *The Battle with the Slums* (New York, 1902), pp. 68 ff.; Hillel Rogoff, *Meyer London* (New York, 1930), p. 9; Ornitz, *Haunch, Paunch and Jowl*, pp. 207 ff.; Bernheimer, *The Russian Jew in the United States*, pp. 36, 39.

Another factor might have been the Jewish home in the slum area which was divided against itself and the tension between parent and child which was widespread.[6]

Juvenile delinquency indeed was a plague in the crowded sections of the cities. Children virtually lived in the streets. Parks and playgrounds were provided rather late in the nineteenth century, and there was no real attempt to provide space for play and recreation until the twentieth century. After a day in school and an afternoon dodging traffic while playing in the streets, many Jewish children came home often to find that their time and effort were needed to help their mothers complete work on piles of garments which they brought home from a clothing manufacturer. As soon as this chore was completed the child ran down to the streets to become subject to its baneful influences. In many cases children had no time to play at all for they were sent out after school to peddle in the streets to augment the family income.[7]

The home generally was not a sheltering haven for the child. The front room, which in many flats was the only room that had air and light, was usually reserved for boarders, single or married men who were waiting for their families or relatives to migrate from Europe. The kitchen or sometimes even the front room itself was a sweatshop. The crowded bedroom without windows was a stifling place, especially in the summertime. No wonder then that so many children took themselves off at every opportunity to frequent the streets and the alleys.[8]

Two schools for pickpockets existed on the lower East Side of New York. A claim is advanced, however, that most of the "students" of these schools ultimately became respectable citizens. Our own informant, who personally knew many of the criminally-minded people on the East Side, maintains that only a small percentage of those who were delinquent in their youth continued their antisocial behavior into adulthood. Many of them ultimately fled from the slums and in flight shed their evil ways.

[6] Blaustein, "The People of the East Side," in *University Settlement Studies*, Vol. I, No. 2; Morris Cohen, *A Dreamer's Journey* (New York, 1949), pp. 98-99.

[7] Riis, *The Children of the Poor*, pp. 36 ff., 78; Morris Rosenfeld, "In Shop und in der Heim," in *Schriften* (New York, 1908); Ornitz, *Haunch, Paunch and Jowl*, pp. 35 ff.; Z. Libin, "*Brief fun die Catskills*," in *Gesamelte Verk* (New York, 1915); Jacob Gordin, "Ohn a Heim," in *Dramen* (New York, 1911); Bernheimer, *The Russian Jew in the United States*, pp. 55, 75, 93, 358-59; Jo Davidson, *Between Sittings* (New York, 1951), pp. 5 ff.; Cohen, *A Dreamer's Journey*, p. 75; *Jewish Messenger*, Vol. XXVI, No. 23.

[8] Hapgood, *The Spirit of the Ghetto*, pp. 24 ff.; Jacob Gordin, "Kreitzer Sonato" and "Ohn a Heim," in *Dramen;* Riis, *The Children of the Poor;* Antin, *The Promised Land*, p. 270; Nathan Kushin, *Memoirs of a New American* (New York, 1949), p. 59; Cohen, *A Dreamer's Journey*, p. 99.

Perhaps the deeply rooted moral concepts of Judaism were able to come to the fore once the environment of the slums had been left behind.[9]

The question of immorality among the Jews in the slum areas presents quite a problem. There are no statistics or adequate information on a matter which is generally in the "hush-hush" category. Jacob A. Riis made a statement in 1894 concerning the lower East Side in New York which is shocking. "If it is true," he said, "of the Jew who through eighteen centuries of oppression and tyranny preserved intact in him the patriarchal home idea . . . that in a single generation in New York's tenements—always the filthiest and darkest and most crowded to be found anywhere—he breaks down; that his daughters become immoral and his sons thieves to an alarming degree—then what share in it had this tenement that does ever and everywhere violence to the home ideal?"[10]

Louise Ware in her biography of Jacob A. Riis admits that on occasion Riis would exaggerate in order to emphasize a point. One must also consider the fact that this statement was made during the depression of 1893 when some workers on the East Side were led to commit suicide because they had no food for their families and when others fought in the streets over a stale piece of bread.[11] Still it cannot be denied that for a long time Allen Street was a "red-light district" and that immorality existed in other cities as well.[12] Here too our informant tells us that many of those who inhabited the notorious Allen Street thoroughfare became respectable people when they moved to better sections of the city.[13]

Run-down areas adjacent to each other, in which various ethnic groups lived, brought about in many instances both bad feeling among the groups and close social ties. It is a most remarkable phenomenon that, whereas Irish and German gangs often attacked East European Jews on the lower East Side, there was nevertheless some friendliness especially among the Irish and the Jews who lived on the fringes of these slum areas. These close social ties led occasionally to intermarriage between individuals from these groups.[14]

The Jews of the Chinatown area in New York were "tough" individuals.[15]

[9] Interview with X. For a decline in crime among the Jews in more recent times, see, e.g., Nathan Goldberg, "Jews in the Police Records of Los Angeles," in *YIVO Annual of Jewish Social Science* (New York, 1950).

[10] Louise Ware, *Jacob A. Riis* (New York, 1938), p. 104. For immorality see also Bernheimer, *The Russian Jew in the United States*, pp. 346-47, 357.

[11] A. S. Sachs, *Die Geschichte fun Arbeiter Ring* (New York, 1925), pp. 99-100.

[12] Ornitz, *Haunch, Paunch and Jowl*, pp. 56 f.; Hapgood, *Spirit of the Ghetto*.

[13] Interview with X.

[14] Interview with Moe Aronson.

[15] *Scribners*, XV (1894), 459.

They were rarely attacked by Irish or Italians living in the neighborhood and when attacked they replied in kind. Thus on one occasion when a gang attacked the Chinatown Jews, the bearded patriarchs ran into a Jewish bakery on Bayard Street, imbedded their fists in freshly baked pumpernickel loaves, and thus equipped with superior boxing gloves they ran out to meet their adversaries. Needless to say the Gentiles were surprised and the Jews were the victors.[16] The older Jews of the East Side of New York and in other cities, however, were not known for their ability to defend themselves. As a result Jewish gangs of young people developed to protect the older generation. In some cases these gangs, originally organized for self-defense, continued to operate with other and less worthy goals.[17]

II

Of particular interest to us, as we view the beginnings of East European life in this country, is the strong desire of the migrants to rise out of the slum area and to move into better sections. Even the old German and Polish Jews sought to escape from the run-down neighborhoods as these developed in the large cities. But before the Jew could move out of the ghetto he had to rise economically.

The German and the Polish Jews were the first to move out of the East Side of New York to an "uptown" area. Some East European Jews followed them and virtually turned their backs on their own brethren whom they left behind in the old quarter. Kasriel Sarahson, publisher of the *Tageblatt*, termed these Jews *yahudim*, parvenus who attempted to "pass" as German Jews.[18] Other East European Jews refused to leave the slums even when they could afford to do so. Their synagogues and *Hebras* and perhaps their occupations and business enterprises forced them to remain in the ghetto. To satisfy the needs of these people, some Jews erected newer tenements within the slum area to accommodate their richer coreligionists.[19] In some instances whole sections were rebuilt

[16] Interview with Moe Aronson.

[17] Bernard Horwich, *My First Eighty Years* (Chicago, 1939), pp. 130, 135-37; Eliakim Zunzer, *Ale Verk*, I, 261 ff., 266; Z. Libin, "Der Eibiger Id," in *Gesamelte Verk;* J. D. Eisenstein, *Otzar Zichronotai* (New York, 1929), p. 79; Jacob Gordin, "Lacht Noch," in *Erzehlungen* (New York, 1908).

[18] Gordin, "Ohn a Heim" and "Auf Die Berg," in *Dramen;* Morris Rosenfeld, "Der Kalvarier Datsch," in *Schriften.*

[19] Tenement buildings of a better type were erected in New York's ghetto, for example, by Moe Aronson's father and by Harry Fischel, among others. The author is indebted to Mr. Lee M. Friedman for calling his attention to this inner development within the Jewish section.

within the ghettos. But most of the second-generation and certainly all of the third-generation East Europeans fled from the slum areas and abandoned even the better housing which their fathers attempted to provide for them. Often, the better sections to which they repaired in turn became run-down, and a new trek was initiated to newer sections and better neighborhoods. The history of the Jews in the United States may be plotted, even in the earlier periods, as one of constant escape from one section to another, especially in the larger cities of the country.

This constant moving about obviously brought desirable and undesirable results. While it is true that many Jews began to shed the evil concomitants of slum life as they moved into better neighborhoods, the Jewish community as such lost heavily. Buildings were sold or even given away to other ethnic groups. But what is of even greater importance is that the community had to rebuild itself every thirty or forty years and in some cases even every twenty years, and in the process it lost a great deal of the experience developed in the old ghetto. Thus in New York City, for example, when Harlem was abandoned in the late 1920's several institutions of great importance went by the wayside never to be resurrected. The Uptown Talmud Torah, a giant in Jewish religious educational effort, was lost in the change and with it went the experience that this school had developed over a long period of time.

The Jewish community itself underwent great transformation as older ghettos were abandoned and newer ones developed. Synagogue membership in many cases was completely revamped. Thus, for example, when the Ohab Zedek Congregation on the lower East Side moved to Harlem at the turn of the century its membership continued Hungarian. But, when it moved once again in the 1920's to the West Side, it found that its membership was no longer homogeneous and that non-Hungarians had enrolled as communicants. The sons and daughters of the original members now lived dispersed in many sections of greater New York and they could not possibly retain their active membership even if they desired to do so. Thus the Jewish community as such underwent revolutionary changes as the Jew moved from section to section.

III

Still all was not as dark as has been delineated. There was a brighter side to the life in the ghetto. Once having fled from the ghetto the Jews developed coteries in the newer sections based on cultural interests, on economic or social standing. But in the old slum area there was a greater feeling of the equality of all men. The stoop in front of the New York tenement house was a great leveler. Here old and young met of an evening, especially on hot nights when the temperature within the flats was unbearable. Here the old social gradations brought to this country from Europe disappeared in the misery which was the lot of all. Here and in the cafés and social clubs, lasting friendships were made; and people became vitally interested in each other. In these social gatherings discussion could be heard on all topics of the day.[20]

Out of these social gatherings and sidewalk forums came a deepening interest in the welfare of minority groups. These discussions brought about the effort to create unions for labor and the inspiration to lead these unions to great heights. If the I.L.G.W.U. and the Amalgamated are great instruments today for the welfare of labor it should not be forgotten that their members and their leaders as well originally lived in the slums.

The Jews came to this country with a deep feeling for the underprivileged, the poor, and the downtrodden. Centuries of living in the European ghettos as disfranchised people had induced them to view with sympathy the life of the poor and the wretched. The slum area only intensified this feeling and stimulated a desire to create a better life for all minority groups whether Jewish or Gentile. The fact that Jews were interested, for example, in social security and in the New Deal is an indication that their mode of life in the past one hundred years had the effect of molding in them a personality attuned to the sufferings of the unemployed, the aged, and the poor.

The rise of Yiddish and Hebrew literature within the confines of the ghetto is an astonishing result of life in the slums. One would hardly expect that men who bent over their machines during a long and arduous day in the sweatshop, whose nights were only brief periods of troubled rest in a twenty-four-hour period of toil, could find within themselves the spirit of song and concentrated thought and the desire to place on paper creative efforts of a high order. And yet the flowering of Yiddish literature took place in the slum areas, especially those of New York City, and it was often promoted by individuals who toiled in the sweatshops. Indeed, Rosenfeld sang of the machine and the workingman, while Gordin, Kobrin, Libin, and other initiated a revolution in the Yiddish theater

[20] The intellectuals gathered in cafés on the East Side of New York to discuss current events, but the mass of the people was restricted to the stoop in front of the tenements. Cf. Hapgood, *Spirit of the Ghetto*, p. 90. For the leveling influence of the slums, see Z. Libin, "Bitere Shpass," in *Gesamelte Verk*.

with their plays of merit. Short story writers came forward to depict life as they saw it and newspapermen wrote endlessly for an eager mass of readers.[21]

Not all of Yiddish literature was of a high quality. There was *shund* and a cheap vaudeville in the theater and in the music hall, and the *roman* in the pamphlet and the newspaper—vulgar creations which whetted the appetites of those who tried to forget the misery of the slums.[22] But the more intelligent demanded the better play and the short story of a finer quality. At one time the claim was made that often when the legitimate English stage had nothing of importance to offer, the Yiddish stage drew even non-Jews to its better productions.[23]

Out of the slums, within the last one hundred years, came an ever-increasing number of professional people, men of learning and stature. Louis Waldman, labor attorney, in describing the East Side evening school which he and many other Jews attended for an education, said: "A list of graduates of my class, if it were compiled, would constitute a minor Who's Who in art, business and the professions of New York today."[24] It was here in the midst of the filth and the suffering of the ghetto that the evening schools were filled to capacity and here that parents made superhuman sacrifices to send their sons on to higher education.[25]

In an earlier age the old German and Polish Jew rarely thought it advisable to persuade his son to enter the professions or to study in higher schools of learning. The immigrant of an older generation thought that

[21] Leon Kobrin, *Erineringen* (New York, 1926); Hapgood, *Spirit of the Ghetto;* Elijah Shulman, *Geschichte fun der Yiddisher Literature in America* (New York, 1943); Antin, *The Promised Land*, p. 258.

[22] Paul Klapper, "The Yiddish Music Hall," in *University Settlement Studies*, Vol. II, No. 4; B. Gorin, *Geschichte fun Idischen Teater* (New York, 1929), pp. 73 ff., 203 ff.

[23] Cf. Kobrin, *Erineringen*, I, 42 ff.

[24] Louis Waldman, *Labor Lawyer* (New York, 1944), p. 31.

[25] The citations in the sources in regard to culture among the Jews are too numerous to mention. A few are: Bregstone, *Chicago and Its Jews;* Williams Walling, "What the People of the East Side Do," in *University Settlement Studies*, Vol. I, No. 2; U. S. Senate Committee, *Report of the Committee of the Senate upon the Relations between Labor and Capital* (Washington, 1885), p. 96; C. Davidson, *Out of Endless Yearnings* (New York, 1946), pp. 24 ff.; Frank Weitenkampf, *Manhattan Kaleidoscope* (New York, 1947), p. 213; New York *Herald*, December 22, 1907; Charles Bernheimer, "Jewish Immigration," in *University Settlement Studies*, Vol. II, No. 3; Sachs, *Die Geschichte fun Arbeiter Ring*, p. 82; Hapgood, *Spirit of the Ghetto*, p. 36; Bernheimer, *The Russian Jew in the United States*, p. 38; Cohen, *A Dreamer's Journey*, pp. 85, 94 ff., 111; Benjamin L. Gordon, *Between Two Worlds* (New York, 1952), p. 143 ff.; Antin, *The Promised Land*, pp. 198 ff., 352 ff., 337 ff. For the increase in the number of Jews in colleges, especially in New York City, see *Jewish Messenger*, XII, 27; XV, 3, 158, 198.

an elementary schooling was sufficient and invariably took his son out of school at the age of thirteen or fourteen to help in conducting the business in which the family engaged. True, in the latter part of the nineteenth century when the glamor of conducting a clothing manufacturing plant or a retail store had worn off, there was a trend to send sons on to higher education. But even when he could afford to do so, the immigrant prior to 1860 cut short his son's education and often frowned on any tendency to develop latent ability in art or in cultural areas. Music, since it entailed little or no formal schooling, was an exception to this general pattern and hardly a home existed without its piano or its musical instrument.[26]

But the immigrant after the Civil War valued higher education from the very beginning, and he made every effort to educate his child. It is quite possible that the system of evening schools in the large cities enabled the son and daughter of the immigrant to achieve aims to which an earlier generation could not aspire. For indeed even the latter-day immigrant took his son out of school at an early age. But now with evening schools and preparatory and free schools available, the son managed to educate himself and to enter the professions. Perhaps it was the deeply ingrained respect for learning which the East European Jew brought to this country that was responsible for the wide interest in higher education. Morris Raphael Cohen felt that the intellectual capacity of the Jew was retarded in Europe and that it suddenly found release on the American scene. "It was as if a great dam had broken and the force of water accumulated over many years had been let loose."[27] Whatever the reason, the results were of great importance to the Jewish group and to America. For if it is true that Jews are prominent in the theater, in music, in art, in law, and in medicine, and if it is true that some 25 percent of the top scientists in this country are Jews, it is also true that this phenomenon may be explained in part at least by the desire of those who fled from the ghetto and even of those who remained in it to reach out to finer things.

IV

Flight from the slums meant very often flight from Jewish tradition and religious practice as well. It is true, of course, that the history of religious laxity among American Jews is at least two hundred years old.[28] Yet

[26] *Hebrew Leader*, Vol. XIII, No. 15; *Jewish Messenger*, Vol. XXII, No. 2, No. 19; *American Israelite*, Vol. XIV, No. 20.

[27] Cohen, *A Dreamer's Journey*, p. 95.

[28] See Hyman B. Grinstein, "The American Synagogue and Laxity of Religious

this development in which many sons and daughters of East European Jews fled from the ghetto and either divorced themselves completely from Jewish tradition or joined the Reform movement bespeaks an attempt to bury the past. True, much of Jewish educational effort in the ghetto was pitifully inadequate and negative in its results. The *siddur melamed* and the *heder* brought to the fore unlearned and uncouth teachers who were rarely respected by their students, and whose influence upon the rising generation was not one to be remembered and cherished. Then again there was much conflict between parents and children in the ghetto over the matter of religion and religious observance. This conflict was never resolved.[29]

But over and above these influences and problems was the glorified position of the so-called German group. All over the country the older settlers created a coterie geared to a new type of religion, that of Reform Judaism. The East European Jew and his descendants were well aware of the existence of this upper coterie; the German Jew was cognizant of the existence of thousands of East Europeans in the slums.[30]

The cleavage that existed between the older German and Polish settlers and the East Europeans worked to create two distinct groupings. On the one hand, the older settlers drew in on themselves soon after the Civil War and tried to dissociate themselves from their poorer and more recently arrived brethren. On the other hand, this cleavage tended to make the East European Jew consider his own group as un-Americanized and to imitate the German Jew as the status figure in the community at large. A cartoon published in 1881 and drawn by F. Opper, himself a Jew, depicts a German Jew, already well established, standing in front of his store. Passing by on the sidewalk is a Russian Jew, a peddler clothed in ancient and torn garb with flowing beard and earlocks. The German Jew speaks to the reader and says: "I was once like him. But that was long ago. Today I am a different person, today I am a different Jew."[31]

In other words, the existence of a ghetto and a slum area made the German Jew himself draw away from the East European and from the practices and ideologies which he represented, so as to dissociate himself from every possible identification with this so-called nonmodern person.

Observance" (typescript, Columbia University Library).

[29] Ornitz, *Haunch, Paunch and Jowl*, pp. 31, 62 f.; Hapgood, *Spirit of the Ghetto*, pp. 23 ff.; Cohen, *A Dreamer's Journey*, pp. 98 ff.

[30] *Jewish Messenger*, Vol. XL, No. 17 (1876).

[31] *Puck*, XI, 178. The statement given here is a paraphrasing of a jingle which appears beneath the cartoon.

Of course he helped the East European Jew and dispensed charity to him. But beyond that he would not go. The East European Jew, on the other hand, began to reconsider his ways, and often he and his children were motivated to divest themselves of their past so as to be acceptable to their German brothers.

The reform of Jewish religious practice or its complete abandonment was always a matter primarily of social adjustment.[32] Very few people understood the theories of Reform spun by David Einhorn or Samuel Hirsch. Change in ritual was always first and foremost a means of becoming a "different" Jew, one seemingly more acceptable to the Gentile neighbor. In 1871 the *Jewish Times*, a Reform journal in New York, spoke quite bluntly concerning the reasons for the success of the Reform movement. When money is made, the Jews want to mingle with Gentiles, to eat at their tables, and to have Gentiles visit their synagogues. "It would not do to exhibit the old medieval locality with its musty unintelligible service." A more recent study claims that in Boston the "impetus for reform came from a handful of German-born merchants. These merchants, of Orthodox background, were successful men who aspired to the manners and outlook of native Bostonians. They wanted to acquire the Boston speech, the Boston dress, the Boston religion: they wanted to be like unto others."[33] During the slum era the problem was thus further intensified when the German, withdrawing from identification with his brethren in the ghetto, went to great lengths to abandon the practice of his ancestors, and the East European Jew took the very same steps in an attempt to adjust himself socially to both the German Jew and the Gentile neighbor. True, the problem described here appears to be one of the emotions rather than one of pure reason. But then the person who refuses to identify himself with his poor brethren or who flees from the ghetto or who throws off mores centuries old is largely beset with emotional problems.

Radicalism among the Jews at the end of the nineteenth century likewise might be attributed in part at least to the slums. While it is true that some socialist and anarchist leaders of the late nineteenth century came from abroad, other leaders and their followers were bred in the slums. The fact that almost all of the biographical and autobiographical material of these leaders describes conditions in the slums is in itself an indication

[32] Grinstein, *The Rise of the Jewish Community of New York*, pp. 368 ff.

[33] *Jewish Times*, III, 24; Arthur Mann, *Growth and Achievement: Temple Israel, 1854-1954* (Boston, 1954), pp. 45-46.

that these people were largely influenced to preach a change in society because of the life they saw or experienced in the shabby sections of the large cities.[34]

V

The experience of the Jew in the slums thus presents a mixed picture of both light and shadows. While, on the one hand, the rise of crime, juvenile delinquency, immorality, and gang warfare can be largely attributed to the run-down neighborhoods; on the other hand, a deepened social sense, a greater feeling of the equality of all men, and a flowering of Yiddish literature were also to some extent the products of the slums. While, in one way, the flight from the ghetto brought a constant reorganization of the Jewish community both in the organizational sense and in the pattern of practice and observance; in another, it afforded men and women the opportunity to lead new lives in an ever changing and better environment.

But above all the results of living in the run-down neighborhoods stand the great intellectual achievements of those who fled or who attempted to flee from the ghetto. For indeed mankind may little remember the struggles, the poverty, the disease of the slums, after the slum areas shall have disappeared from the face of our land. But it cannot but long remember the contributions in various fields of human endeavor which the dwellers of the dilapidated tenements made.

Essentially the immigrant Jew in every period was a common man. The upper classes in Jewish society whether in Germany, in Poland, in Rumania, in Austria, or in Russia rarely ventured forth to migrate to a new land. They had no reason to do so. It was the common folk, the unlearned and the humble, who came here. Still, although these immigrants were from the lower classes, they were, nevertheless, intelligent people. The Jews in the last one thousand years at least engaged in an inbreeding of intellectual and upper classes. Many members of the so-called lower classes constantly moved into and became members of the upper class by virtue of their learning. Thus in time, with movement up and down among the classes, an intelligent group was evolved even in the lower echelons of society. Had these Jews remained in Europe it is extremely doubtful that they would ever have attained for themselves, their children, or their grandchildren those conditions necessary for

[34] Cf., e.g., Rogoff, *Meyer London;* Gold, *Jews without Money;* Cohen, *A Dreamer's Journey*, pp. 72 ff.

achievement in fields of culture, scholarship, and learning. It is even doubtful that they, their children, or their grandchildren could have remained alive in a hate-ridden Europe. America afforded the Jew both the peace of mind necessary for achievement and the possibility of rising on the social and economic ladder. If the slum experience gave the Jew that urge and drive to create out of himself something that he could not have achieved in Europe, then the slum experience with all its faults, with all its misery, and with all its difficulties was a boon both for the Jew and for this our beloved land.[35]

[35] This essay is in the nature of a prolegomenon to the subject. Some topics such as health and tenement laws have not been treated. Dr. Bertram W. Korn also called the attention of the author to the need for a wider study of the slum area which would include all of the ethnic groupings and would contrast the effect of slums on them and would point out differences and similarities in remaining or in fleeing from these run-down neighborhoods. Generally speaking, the student of American Jewish history is not equipped to make such a study. He is too much preoccupied with the Jewish group and other groups are not within his ken. On the other hand, it seems that American historians generally have not devoted too much attention to this subject. Although they devote space to a descriptive discussion of the slums, they have not delved into the relationship between these slums and the effort on the part of the ethnic groups to free themselves from their influence. Nor have they devoted much attention to the connection between the slum and such aspects of life as fellowship, democracy, and the cultural advance of society. Perhaps a cooperative venture should be undertaken by American historians and specialists in the history of various ethnic groups to study these aspects of slum life in relation to the general advance of American civilization.

WELLHAUSEN'S INTERPRETATION OF ISRAEL'S RELIGIOUS HISTORY

A REAPPRAISAL OF HIS RULING IDEAS

By Herbert F. Hahn

THE HISTORY of Bible criticism in the nineteenth century was largely the story of the application to biblical literature of the same methods of literary and historical criticism as had been worked out in the study of other ancient literatures. Dominating this story was the name of Julius Wellhausen, whose *Prolegomena to the History of Israel* was the most cogent presentation of the arguments for the literary and historical conclusions toward which the criticism of the century had been tending. He provided the scientific basis for the theory of documents which was widely accepted by contemporary scholars as explaining the origin and composition of the Pentateuch. In general outline, this theory is still the common property of scholarship in the field of biblical literature.

But Wellhausen also worked out a circumstantial history of the development of Israel's religion which no longer enjoys a consensus of acceptance, although it paralleled and depended upon his history of the documents. Wellhausen described an evolutionary development proceeding through three distinct stages. The stage of primitive worship, exemplified by the popular religion of the early Israelites, was characterized by ritual practices of a simple and spontaneous nature. It was succeeded by the stage of ethical consciousness expressed in prophetic religion, which attempted certain reforms in ritual practice. The final stage was the elaborate ceremonial type of religion prescribed in the Levitical legislation. The general implication of this history, viz., that the most characteristic features of Israel's religion were late developments growing out of an evolutionary process from lower to higher forms, has been challenged since Wellhausen's day by the majority of scholars in the field of biblical religion.

The chief objection to the evolutionary interpretation of Israel's religious history has been that it seemed to deny the continuous existence of a basic core of belief and practice giving unity and consistency to the whole history of the religion. Wellhausen and his followers described a diversity of religious belief and practice which not only made each successive stage quite different from its predecessor but also introduced a colorful variety into each stage. The trend of recent criticism has been in the opposite direction. Without denying the fact of diversity in the long and complicated history, scholars now emphasize the uniformity of a continuing tradition in the midst of the diversity. They consider Wellhausen's interpretation as having missed the essential point of the religious history he attempted to describe. His researches had illuminated certain aspects of the history never before clearly apprehended, but these aspects were secondary to the central core of religious tradition. Because Wellhausen failed to emphasize the continuity of fundamentals in Israel's religion, his interpretation is suspected of giving an essentially false picture of the course of religious development.

It has become fashionable to discredit Wellhausen's reconstruction by saying that it was influenced by Hegelian principles of interpretation. The charge seems plausible in the light of Wellhausen's statement that he had learned "most and best" from Wilhelm Vatke, who was demonstrably an Hegelian.[1] It may be worth while to examine this charge, as a means of reassessing the nature and the significance of the ruling ideas which influenced Wellhausen's interpretation.

On the surface, the interpretation of Israel's religious history which Wellhausen derived from his study of the biblical documents bore the marks of the Hegelian dialectic. As Vatke had done, he divided the history into three significant periods, and his description of the characteristics of each period corresponded closely to that of Vatke. But Wellhausen made no slavish imitation of the latter's dialectical scheme. Vatke had found the key to the interpretation of Israel's history in the Hegelian principle that an historical development is the result of a synthesis of two antithetical situations. Vatke started with the *thesis* that the early religion of Israel had been characterized by a simple, ceremonial type of worship similar to that portrayed in the patriarchal narratives (which, according to the critics, really reflected the conditions of the early monarchical period); the *antithesis* to this stage of religion he found in the prophetic denunciation of ceremonial worship; and the climax of the religious development, he concluded, was reached in the *synthesis* between the prophetic emphasis on spiritual worship and the purified ceremonial elaborated by postexilic Judaism. For Wellhausen,

[1] See, e.g., Johannes Pedersen, "Die Auffassung vom Alten Testament," *ZAW*, XLIX (1931), 170-74.

however, the significant contrast was not that between the early religion and prophetic religion but that between the former and postexilic Judaism. He regarded the early religion of Israel as a "natural" religion in which worship grew out of life, the rituals being conducted at local shrines in intimate connection with the activities of the people.[2] Postexilic Judaism, on the other hand, he found artifical because of its preoccupation with minute regulation of the ritual forms of worship. As he saw it, Judaism separated religion from life, depriving worship of its natural spontaneity by reducing it to a set of prescribed religious exercises.[3] This contrast between the natural religion of the early period and the prescriptive religion of the later period Wellhausen felt so strongly that, for him, postexilic Judaism rather than prophetic religion was the antithesis of the early religion of Israel. While Judaism could be interpreted as the synthesis of a purified ritualistic worhsip with the prophetic principle of ethical monotheism, the legalistic emphasis by which the synthesis had been effected was, to Wellhausen's way of thinking, an uncreative antithesis to the natural, spontaneous character of worship in the early period.

Clearly, Wellhausen's exposition did not fit the Hegelian dialectic. He did not describe a progressive development which reached its climax in the synthesis of previously existing antithetical elements. Prophetic religion he regarded not so much as an antithesis to the early forms of ritual worship as a creative step forward which emphasized the universal significance of a principle—the principle of moral law—which had already been implicit in the early religion of Israel. The legalism of postexilic Judaism, on the other hand, he regarded as a stage of degeneration from the high type of religion represented by prophetic teaching. It was not simply an Hegelian antithesis to the early religion of Israel, to be taken up at some later time into a higher synthesis; it was a permanently irretrievable decline from the original vitality of Israel's religion.[4]

Thus, it was not Hegelian dialectic that vitiated Wellhausen's interpretation of Israel's religious history. A more legitimate ground for criticism lies in the antinomian tendency of his description of postexilic Judaism. Wellhausen did not adequately appreciate the role of the Law in the history of the Jewish people. As Israel Abrahams once pointed out, the Law was not a stage of degeneration from Prophecy but, equally

[2] See *Israelitische und jüdische Geschichte* (3d ed., Berlin, 1897), chap. II.
[3] See *ibid.*, pp. 131-32.
[4] See *ibid.*, chap. XIII.

with Prophecy, a factor in religious development; its purpose, too, had been to moralize the whole life of the people.[5] Wellhausen had failed to consider whether a hearty devotion to the ceremonial law was really incompatible with spiritual vitality. To his way of thinking, the substitution of the principle of conformity to prescribed religious exercises for the religious individualism which had once flourished free of institutional restrictions meant that the postexilic system was merely the stereotyped shell of a former reality.[6] This interpretation was not determined by the Hegelian dialectic; it was a personal judgment.

Can we lay a finger on the source of Wellhausen's attitude? Certainly he was not motivated by an animus toward Judaism. Rather, his negative attitude toward the formalized worship of the postexilic period was an inversion of his positive appreciation of the spiritual values inherent in the earlier stage. The impressive feature, to Wellhausen, of the world of the early Israelites was its freshness and naturalness. It contrasted significantly with the rigidity of communal life under the Levitical constitution. In ancient Israel, the social system was a human and moral, not an artificial, institutional order. It was indigenous, growing naturally out of the relations between men associated in common endeavors. Rights and duties were not derived from external institutions which had a validity and compulsive force of their own. They were personal, and their observance sprang from an inner urge, a respect for the integrity of the social pattern. Each individual was responsible for the success of the whole. He did not merely conform, but took an active part in making the moral order effective. In doing so, he acted with a free initiative, not according to an external norm.[7] Moreover, the social order was characterized by the complete absence of a distinction between the secular and the religious. Religion was the very essence of life, and the ritual of worship was an expression of life, not a thing set apart in its own sphere.[8]

Here, if anywhere in Wellhausen's system, is Hegelian doctrine. Wellhausen's description of the world of ancient Israel as a genuinely integrated world could be taken as an example of Hegel's principle of true universals. The idea that only *that* society is really vital and human in which individuals find their true being in their relationships to each

[5] Israel Abrahams, "Jewish Interpretation of the Old Testament," in *The People and the Book*, ed. by Arthur S. Peake (Oxford, 1925), p. 406.

[6] See his *Abriss der Geschichte Israels und Juda's* ("Skizzen und Vorarbeiten," No. 1 [Berlin, 1884]), pp. 97-98.

[7] *Israelitische und jüdische Geschichte*, p. 24; *Prolegomena zur Geschichte Israels* (Berlin, 1883), p. 437.

[8] See *Prolegomena*, p. 80.

other and to the organic whole illustrates Hegel's definition of a true universal. A true universal was the organic union of an absolute idea with the particular facts, which are not merely examples of it but are embraced in it and exist only in relation to it and to one another.

But pointing out the analogy between Wellhausen's exposition and Hegel's definition is not equivalent to saying that one was derived from the other. In other respects, Wellhausen's view of Israelite antiquity does not fit the Hegelian philosophy. Hegel described ultimate reality as in a continuous process of becoming. A true universal was forever realizing itself in ever higher forms, approaching closer at each step to the absolute idea of itself. Wellhausen saw no progress toward complete realization in the history of Israel's religion. For him, the most genuinely integrated form of the religion had existed at the beginning, and what came after was a degeneration which (in his own words) "denatured and rendered lifeless" the old forms of ritual worship.[9]

His feeling in the matter seems to have sprung from an ideological bias of his own—from a conviction that a "primitive" social order was of more historical significance than a complex, institutionalized system. Such a conviction ran counter to the teaching of Hegel, for whom the most highly developed religious system and the most institutionalized political system were the climax of historical development. It was characteristic of Wellhausen, however, to regard the original form of a people's social and religious organization as the one which provided the real basis for evaluating its contribution to history. In each of the three areas of historical investigation to which he devoted himself during the course of his career—the ancient Israelites, the primitive Arabs, and early Christianity—Wellhausen gave his most sympathetic interest to the earliest period, the period in which the socioreligious system existed in its original form.[10] To him the original was the genuine. Thus, while Hegel interpreted the history of human culture in terms of progressive development, Wellhausen tended to emphasize the eternally valid nature of the natural, primitive forms of human society. Wellhausen was not a good Hegelian in his evolutionary doctrine. Whereas the Hegelian idea of development implied continuous progress, Wellhausen put a primary valuation on the initial stage in socioreligious development as the only genuinely significant stage.

[9] *Ibid.*, p. 185.

[10] See the full discussion in F. Boschwitz, *Julius Wellhausen: Motive und Massstäbe seiner Geschichtsschreibung* (Marburg, 1938). The writer is indebted to Professor Baron for the opportunity to study this monograph, from which a number of ideas for this article have been drawn.

This intellectual bias of Wellhausen in favor of the original social order reflected Romantic rather than Hegelian thought. The belief that early institutions had been superior to modern institutions was frequently expressed in the historical writings of the early nineteenth century. It represented a certain dissatisfaction with contemporary industrial civilization and the desire to return to a less complex, more natural type of social organization. This predilection for the natural and primitive had been generated by Rousseau's conception of the ideal "state of nature" at the beginning of human history. Itself an unconscious adaptation of the conception of a "golden age" in the past, Rousseau's conception was the germ from which the Romantic interpretation of history had grown.[11] Wellhausen's viewpoint derived most of its substance, however, from Johann Gottfried Herder, the Romantic philosopher-historian of the human spirit. Aware of the richness and variety of human life and recognizing the importance of emotional experience in the life of humanity, Herder studied history with eager attention to the spiritual factors in human culture. All his researches into the origins of poetry and religion were at the same time a search for the human "soul" in history: the spirit which gave rise to great poetry and religious feeling. In the poetry of Israel, for example, Herder found expressed a deep feeling for the vital reality of life. The sense of well-being and happiness reflected there he took to be the natural result of a "genuine" form of human life. Just so did Wellhausen find in the organic union of social and religious factors in the life of early Israel the spiritual integration and self-sufficiency which for him represented the genuine society. His notion that the ideal society was one that had not yet become tangible in fixed, institutional form but was an association of free individuals guided by the unwritten laws of the natural order was a Romantic notion akin to Herder's.

The wide disparity between Wellhausen's view of early Israel's socio-religious system and the probable historical reality reflects the degree to which his interpretation was influenced by these ideological overtones. The charge of Hegelianism cannot be sustained against him, but it is only fair to say that his work was not "scientific." It obviously differed significantly from the historiography of the so-called scientific historians of his day. The latter limited their work to the accumulation and classification of critically ascertained facts; they believed that the task of the historian was not to judge the past but only to report what had actually

[11] See Benedetto Croce, *History: Its Theory and Practice*, translated by Douglas Ainslie (London, 1921), chap. VI: "Historiography of Romanticism."

happened.[12] Wellhausen, however, wrote from the conviction that the most important task of the historian was interpretation. He concerned himself not only with the empirical data but with general conceptions that would illuminate the significance of the data. Wellhausen as historian embodied both the erudite scholar and the thinker. His history of Israel's religion, therefore, was not so much a scientific study as a philosophical view of that history.

Nevertheless, in the combination of critical method for ascertaining the facts of history with exposition of an interpretation conceived to be implicit in the facts lies the chief interest of Wellhausen's work. Quite apart from the question of the accuracy of the interpretation, the intention to seek the larger meaning of the facts is the significant element in Wellhausen's methodology. It explains the wide popularity of his work in his day and contains the clue to its partial rejection in the present day.

Wellhausen was not content, as the scientific historians often were, to treat the sources as ends in themselves; that is, he was not content merely to accept the surface data presented by the sources. It was his conviction that the documents were the products of a whole intellectual or spiritual culture, and that the historian must go below the surface to grasp this larger whole. He must endeavor to live and think again the life and thought of which the documents were written expressions. In this respect, Wellhausen was again following the lead of Johann Gottfried Herder, who had believed that the processes of history could not be fully understood without entering sympathetically into the ways of thinking and feeling of humanity in the past. Herder had described the life of various nations, peoples, and cultural groups in such a way as to show how each had fulfilled the destiny of man by attaining a unified spiritual life in the special way determined by its own circumstances. Wellhausen attempted to do the same for Israel.

But the attempt to go beyond what the documents said in order to comprehend the spiritual physiognomy of early Israel raised the question of proper method. How did one determine the content of a thought-world not explicitly described in the sources? Wellhausen found his answer in the thesis of Wilhelm von Humboldt that all aspects of life in a particular epoch, including literary expression, were influenced or determined by the dominant conceptions of the age.[13] Wellhausen was

[12] See Eduard Fueter, *Geschichte der neueren Historiographie* (3d ed., Munich, 1938), pp. 461-66.

[13] See Otto Kittel, *Wilhelm von Humboldts geschichtliche Weltanschauung* (Leipzig, 1901).

convinced that the conceptions which were explicit in the biblical writings were the dominant conceptions of the age in which the authors lived, not those of the ages which they wrote about. He must therefore identify and discount the points of view which dominated the written accounts of early Israel's history, in order to uncover the original content of ideas which, for him, constituted the genuine thought-world of early Israel.[14] To separate the original background of ideas from the interpretations of the later authors, editors, or compilers, Wellhausen had recourse to the method of "tendency criticism" initiated by Ferdinand Christian Baur earlier in the century. Since each author had his "tendency," an unconscious bias which inevitably reflected the dominant conceptions of his own age, an analysis of the leading ideas which seemed to have guided the author's interpretation of historical tradition would have the way for getting at the underlying tradition itself.[15] Once the assumptions which had generated the points of view adopted by the writers were made clear, the original tradition could be rescued from the interpretations overlaid upon it.

What Wellhausen's method amounted to, essentially, was an attempt to restore the original historical tradition, freed of interpretations which obscured or even distorted it, to its rightful place as the genuine history. He believed that the didactic theology of the biblical documents, which found a causal relationship between the misfortunes of the people and their sin in deserting the Law, was no part of the original tradition. It was not the "natural" history of the people but a theological interpretation of history springing from the dominant conceptions of the postexilic age. Wellhausen was convinced that it presented a conception of Israelite antiquity which was unrelated to the actual experience of the early Israelites. He was certain that the "natural" history of their experience was primary and the "religious" version of their history secondary. Hence he wanted to translate the tradition back into its "profane" form. His purpose in separating the original, natural history from later theological accretions was not simply to restore the past as it had actually been, in the interests of scientific method, but mainly to gain an insight into a socioreligious system which to him was a significant reality.

It was Wellhausen's emphasis on the natural history as the genuine history of early Israel, in preference to the official history which reinterpreted national life in theological terms, that gave his work its appeal to

[14] See *Prolegomena*, pp. 390-91.

[15] The whole second section of the *Prolegomena* is devoted to such an analysis.

his contemporaries. For his own generation Wellhausen summed up better than any other Bible scholar the point of view which seemed appropriate in the intellectual atmosphere of the day. It was a time when a secular and humanistic interpretation of history was popular, even in a field such as the biblical, which had previously been dominated by theological points of view. Before the nineteenth century scholars had not conceived the possibility of any approach to biblical interpretation other than a theological one. The Bible was a religious literature, expressing a providential view of history which alone gave it significance and value, and scholars took its theology seriously. But Wellhausen and his generation reacted against the theological interpretation of the Bible. They insisted that the theology of the Bible was an accretion to the original historical tradition, and that the proper business of the historian was to recover the original tradition. To a generation trained in the scientific, objective method of historical research this approach to the study of the Bible had great appeal.

It is, however, the very same aspect of Wellhausen's work which has led to a rejection of his reconstruction of Israel's religious history. A new generation of scholars has grown up which does not share his ruling ideas. Bible scholars now regard the religious message or messages of the Bible as of primary importance, with the result that theology has once more become of paramount concern. The methodology of Wellhausen, which set aside the theological assumptions of the authors as secondary, is regarded as a faulty one. However interesting it may have been to gain an insight into the character of early Israel's religious culture, it is the theological interpretation of Israel's religious experience by the authors, who attempted to set it in the framework of a comprehensive world-view, that gives the biblical writings their ultimate significance. The emphasis has shifted, therefore, from the historical study of Israel's religious experience to the theological interpretation of its universal meaning.[16]

There is, however, one aspect of Wellhausen's work which need not be rejected out of hand. Though he set aside the theological assumptions of the biblical authors in making his interpretation of Israel's religious history, he tried first of all to analyze (by the method of "tendency criticism") what these theological assumptions were. It was important to his method to understand the theology of the sacred writings in their own terms. He objected to the practice of reading into the documents of the Old Testament certain doctrinal interpretations drawn from the New

[16] See James D. Smart, "The Death and Rebirth of Old Testament Theology," *Journal of Religion*, XXIII (1943), 1-11, 125-36.

Testament. It is still the proper task of the theological scholar to seek to understand the religious thought to which the ancient authors themselves gave expression, and to describe the basic viewpoints from which *they* interpreted historical events and the spiritual experience of their people.[17] Subjective judgment arising from the religious interest of the exegete cannot be permitted to influence the exposition of these basic viewpoints.

[17] See Millar Burrows, "The Task of Biblical Theology," *Journal of Bible and Religion*, XIV (1946), 13-15.

THE CONSERVATIVE RABBINATE

A SOCIOLOGICAL STUDY

By Arthur Hertzberg

THE CHANGING NATURE of the role and function of the rabbi in America,[1] his own changing beliefs and practices,[2] and the considerable rise, in recent years, in the status and economic reward of the rabbinate as profession[3] have all occasioned considerable discussion. Despite some scholarly and much impressionistic writing on the subject, we still do not really know the answer to the question: Who are the rabbis? There exists, for example, a widespread belief that one group, the Orthodox, has been producing the rabbis for the several denominations into which the American synagogue is divided. This impression, like most others about the rabbinate, is based on no measurable scientific fact. No study exists of the social and economic background of the rabbinate, its nearness to or distance from European origins, its level of Jewish education, and the religious and cultural quality of the homes from which the Jewish clergy come.

This essay is based on an inquiry devoted primarily to the Conservative rabbinate, though some all-too-inadequate information about the Reform group, chiefly for comparative purposes, is to be found in the footnotes. It is based on a questionnaire that was answered anonymously in the spring of 1943 by a random 45 (those who took the trouble to reply) of

[1] See Marshall Sklare, *Conservative Judaism* (Glencoe, Illinois, 1955), chap. 6; Jerome E. Carlin and Saul H. Mendlovitz, "The Rabbi: A Sociological Study of a Religious Specialist" (an unpublished M.A. thesis at the University of Chicago, 1951); and Horace Kallen, *Judaism at Bay* (New York, 1932), pp. 202-20. The files of the various popular and semipopular journals of Jewish discussion, such as the *Reconstructionist*, *Judaism*, *Commentary*, and *Jewish Spectator*, abound in articles discussing the role of the rabbi.

[2] The only extended study, in book form, of the beliefs of the rabbinate is a Columbia Teachers College doctoral dissertation: Joseph Zeitlin, *Disciples of the Wise* (New York, 1945). See also, most recently, Eliezer Whartman, "Attitudes of American Rabbis on Zionism and Israel," *Jewish Social Studies*, XVII (1955), 121-32.

[3] Evidence for this assertion is to be found, in part, below in this paper. See also Walter Duckat, *Opportunities in Jewish Religious Vocations* (New York, 1952).

the 78 students then enrolled in the Rabbinical School of the Jewish Theological Seminary (JTS). The same questionnaire was filled out in the spring of 1955 for all 118 of the students then in the Rabbinical School of the Seminary. In the later study the information was provided in some cases directly by the students and, for the rest, by members of the staff of the Seminary. Several questions, chiefly those relating to family incomes, could not be dealt with adequately in this way. The 1955 study is therefore less complete in its picture of each student, but, in compensation, it provides full coverage of the entire student body.

It should be noted that the 45 respondents in the year 1943 are now all in their middle to late thirties and therefore have ahead of them an average of at least thirty years in the active rabbinate. The 118 respondents in the more recent group have an average of forty or more years of active rabbinic career in their futures (disregarding the quite small minority who will, if past experience is any guide, leave the rabbinate for ancillary or other professions). This means that the present study is based on 163 respondents as over against a present total membership in the Rabbinical Assembly, the rabbinical organization of the Conservative movement, of some 600.[4] To put it another way, once the 118 now at school have graduated (by 1960) the Conservative rabbinate will number something over 700. This study deals, therefore, with 20-25 percent of the Conservative rabbinate as a whole and with that part of the body which has the longest future ahead of it.

FAMILY BACKGROUND

In attempting to fix the family background of the students the following kind of information was obtained:

1. Synagogue identification of parents
2. Birthplace of parents
3. The ritual observances of the parents, with particular reference to observance of the Sabbath and of kashrut
4. The language spoken at home
5. The occupation of the father
6. The average income of the father for the five years prior to the date when the questionnaire was filled out. On this last point direct information is available only for the 1943 studies of the Seminary and the Jewish Institute of Religion (JIR).

The synagogue identification of the parents of the Seminary students has

[4] See appendix to the *Proceedings of the Rabbinical Assembly of America*, Vol. XVIII (1954), and *AJYB*, LVI (1955), 232.

undergone a significant change between 1943 and 1955. In 1943 four out of every five families were identified as Orthodox and the remainder were Conservative (35 Orthodox, over against 9 Conservative). In 1955 the picture is radically different. Though the Orthodox group still furnishes a bare majority, almost half of the present group come from homes which are identified as Conservative. The figures for the 1955 study are 59 Orthodox, 57 Conservative, 1 Reform, and 1 unknown. In sum, therefore, the Conservative movement, which was in 1943 largely dependent upon the Orthodox group for its rabbinic candidates, is at present producing almost half of its own rabbis.

In part this change is no doubt due to the rapid growth in the last fifteen years of the number of congregations and individual families formally associated with the Conservative movement.[5] The economic rewards of the rabbinic career in the Conservative group have at least doubled, dollar-wise, and have therefore risen substantially in real income in the twelve years that intervene between the 1943 inquiry and the more recent investigation.[6] Less tangible factors, such as a rise in status of the rabbinate in the last ten years, have been of some importance. Perhaps the most significant cause, however, has been a conscious decision by the leadership of the Seminary to recruit rabbinic candidates as much as possible from within the ranks of the movement.[7] In 1946 the Leadership Training Fellowship, a nation-wide network of advanced study circles for adolescents, was established. Its announced larger purpose was to prepare a cadre of learned laymen and of well-versed candidates for all the Jewish professions. Certainly the hope that out of its ranks rabbinic students would materialize for the JTS was, and is, ever present. Significantly, 24 of the 118 individuals covered by the 1955 study were members

[5] A mimeographed statement, dated January 1, 1955, which was circulated as part of a packet of material on behalf of the joint fund-raising campaign of the central bodies of the Conservative movement, conveys the following information: the number of congregations formally affiliated with the United Synagogue of America has risen from 260 in 1945-46 to 446 in 1953-54. The National Women's League, the organization of synagogue sisterhoods, has risen from 372 affiliates to 600 in the same period. *AJYB*, LVI (1955), 231, gives the number of congregations affiliated with the United Synagogue at the beginning of 1953-54 as 486 and the sisterhoods in the Women's League, as of January 1, 1954, as 570.

[6] See note 3.

[7] There was a discussion about finding young people for the Jewish professions in a formal session at the Rabbinal Assembly (RA) Convention in 1944 (see *RA Proceedings*, VIII [1941-44], 248-60) and a further discussion about "The Rabbi in Education" at the 1946 convention, at which the initial efforts of the Leadership Training Fellowship were discussed by Rabbi Moshe Davis (*RA Proceedings*, X [1946], 180-83). See also Sklare, *Conservative Judaism*, pp. 197-98.

in their teens of such a Leadership Training Fellowship group (4 of the 24 were, however, from Orthodox homes).

This desire of the Seminary to produce a rabbinate from the resources of its own movement continues unabated. At its 1955 graduation exercises six Conservative synagogues, which were the home congregations of some of the 25 graduating rabbis of that year, were singled out for special honors. It can, therefore, be assumed with considerable assurance that the Conservative movement has about reached a turning point and that in the future the majority of its rabbis will be coming from Conservative homes. This change, barely begun in 1943, was in 1955 at the halfway mark. Its consequences, so far, for the background of the rabbinic candidates is worth analysis.[8]

In the last twelve years a significant shift has taken place in the birthplaces of the parents, in the direction tending away from the immigrant origins of the family.

Table 1. Birthplaces of Parents

	JTS 1943		JTS 1955	
	Number	*Percent*	*Number*	*Percent*
Both foreign-born	29	64	73	62
One foreign-born	12	27	20	16
Both American-born	3	7	23	20
No information	1	2	2	2
Total	45	100	118	100

In all cases but two, those families in which one parent was foreign-born represented a foreign-born father. In effect, therefore, 9 out of 10 in 1943 and 8 out of 10 in 1955 of the families of students of the Seminary were headed by immigrants. Taking all parents, male and female, into account, the figure for the Seminary rises from 20.5 percent American-

[8] Our information on the Reform group is based on a random 21 who replied to the questionnaire out of a student body of twice that number at the Jewish Institute of Religion in the spring of 1943. In that year the Institute was still an independent, nondenominational school, but the vast majority of its graduates were entering the Reform rabbinate. In the 1943 study of the JIR student body, out of the 21 who replied, 10 were from Orthodox homes, 8 were from Conservative ones, the parents of one were Reform, and two were from agnostic or unaffiliated families. Even more than their contemporaries at JTS, the JIR group was almost totally unrepresentative of the denomination it was to serve, but perhaps the more interesting parallelism is the almost exact likeness to that which the JTS student body was to become, in family synagogue identification, a dozen years later.

born in 1943 to 28.5 percent in 1955.[9] The Seminary figures represent what might have been expected, an increase in the course of twelve years of about one tenth in the American rootedness of the students' families, but one needs to go beneath the surface of these percentages.

The question of birthplaces of the parents of the Seminary students becomes all the more revealing when the two studies are subdivided according to the synagogue allegiances of the families.

Table 2. Birthplaces of Parents by Synagogue Allegiance

	1943				1955			
	ORTHODOX		CONSERVATIVE		ORTHODOX		CONSERVATIVE	
	Number	*Percent*	*Number*	*Percent*	*Number*	*Percent*	*Number*	*Percent*
Both foreign-born	26	72	3	33	47	80	24	42
One foreign-born	6	17	6	67	9	15	11	20
Both American-born	3	8	0	0	2	3	21	36
No information	1	3	0	0	1	2	1	2
Total	36	100	9	100	59	100	57	100

The 9 of Conservative background in 1943 is too small a figure to admit of significant statistical analysis, though it is interesting that the group of families with one American-born parent is here a strong majority. What is significant is that the Orthodox group in 1955 is even closer to its immigrant origins in *all* categories than its predecessors in 1943 and is certainly markedly atypical of the present-day American Jewish community as a whole. It is the Conservative half of the 1955 group which shows pronounced changes: disregarding sex, almost half the parents, 53, are now American-born, over against 59 foreign-born. The rabbinic candidates from the pews of the denomination itself are beginning to take on a second-generation cast. They are startingly more indigenous than both their predecessors in 1943 and the other half of the Seminary's present student body.

Where do these various parent belong, compared to the general demographic profile of American Jewry? Our studies provide no precise figures for the ages of the parents but, remembering that JTS students are on the average in their early to mid-twenties, it is reasonable to assume that their parents would all fall in the age groups over forty. These

[9] Birthplace of Parents—JIR 1943: both foreign-born, 17—81 percent; one foreign-born, 4—19 percent; both American-born, 0—0 percent; no information, 0—0 percent. Total, 21—100 percent.

various middle-aged parents, as classified in Table 2, show the following percentages of native birth: JTS Orthodox 1943—17 percent; JTS Conservative 1943—33 percent; JTS Orthodox 1955—11 percent; JTS Conservative 1955—47 percent.[10]

In a methodologically doubtful study of Chicago Jewry in 1930 the figure for those to be between 43 and 67 years of age in 1943 (disregarding immigration and other changes in the interim) is 24 percent. A study of Pittsburgh in 1938, which gives no data as to the distribution by age of native- and foreign-born, supplies the information that 7 out of 10 Jewish family heads of all ages were foreign-born. The figure was undoubtedly higher for the middle-aged parents, perhaps approaching the proportion of 9 out of 10 for JTS 1943. There is more specific information for three communities, Trenton, Passaic, and Norwich, which in their general characteristics appear quite typical of American Jewry as a whole at the time of the studies (1937 for the first two and 1938 for the third). In the 45-64 age bracket Trenton had 17 percent native-born, Passaic had 8 percent, and Norwich showed 14 percent. In New York itself a study of Jewish youth between 16 and 24, done in 1935, revealed that 83 percent came from families in which both parents were foreign-born and 8 percent had one foreign-born parent.[11] These percentages look very much like the 17 percent native-born parents of JTS Orthodox 1943, but it must be remembered that the New York ratios had changed in the years between 1935 and 1943 and that those in the 45-64 bracket in 1937 in Trenton and Passaic and in 1938 in Norwich were from 50 to 70 in 1943. By that time there were large groups of younger middle-aged parents in those communities, by then from 40 to 50, who were respectively 46 percent, 40 percent, and 40 percent native-born. JTS Orthodox was already, if these communities are a fair sample, somewhat more immigrant than the rest of its generation.

This is startlingly true in the case of JTS Orthodox 1955. More recent community studies of the 1940's and 1950's provide us with little precise information on nativity. We can perhaps proceed best by using the figures for Trenton, Passaic, and Norwich, with allowance for

[10] For the sake of brevity and clarity we shall use JTS Orthodox 1955 throughout this study to refer to the families identified as Orthodox in synagogue allegiance and JTS Conservative 1955 to refer to the Conservative families.

[11] The figures in this paragraph are, with one exception, based on tables in *Jewish Population Studies*, Sophia Robison, ed. (New York, 1943). The references are as follows: Chicago, p. 132; Trenton, p. 17; Passaic, p. 26; and Norwich, p. 74. The percentages for New York are from Nettie Pauline McGill, "Some Characteristics of Jewish Youth in New York," *JSSQ*, XIV (1937), 253.

the estimated 250,000 new immigrants in the last two decades. Those from 25 to 54 in these three communities in the 1930's, who by 1955 were from 42 to 71, showed the following incidence of native-born: Trenton—54 percent; Passaic—60 percent; and Norwich—52 percent. Even allowing for recent immigration, it is obvious that JTS Orthodox 1955 is a throwback to a vanished pattern and now comes from a very narrow base. It is JTS Conservative, with its 33 percent native-born parents in 1943 and, more significantly, 47 percent native-born parents in 1955, which is, allowing for immigration in the intervening years, today almost precisely demographically typical.

Table 3. Ritual Observances of Parents of JTS Students

	1943				1955			
	ORTHODOX		CONSERVATIVE		ORTHODOX		CONSERVATIVE	
	Number	*Percent*	*Number*	*Percent*	*Number*	*Percent*	*Number*	*Percent*
Sabbath-observant	31	86	7	78	51	86	39	68
Not Sabbath-observant	3	8	1	11	2	4	6	11
Partial	1	3	1	11	1	2	0	0
No report	1	3	0	0	5	8	12	21
Total	36	100	9	100	59	100	57	100
Kosher at home	36	100	8	89	56	95	41	70
"Partially kosher" at home	0	0	1	11	0	0	0	0
No report	0	0	0	0	3	5	16	30
Total	36	100	9	100	59	100	57	100
Kosher outside the home	34	94	8	89	17	29	13	23
Probably kosher outside the home [a]	0	0	0	0	35	59	20	35
Not kosher outside the home	2	6	1	11	3	5	2	3
No report [a]	0	0	0	0	4	7	22	39
Total	36	100	9	100	59	100	57	100

[a] In the 1955 replies 81 of 116 questionnaires had no information about kashrut outside the home. It seemed reasonable, however, to assume that those families which were listed as Sabbath-observing and kosher in the home were almost certainly observing kashrut outside the home. They are, therefore, listed in the second category. All of the others for whom there is no report are so listed in the above table.

It seems important in estimating the home background of a rabbi, especially one who will be serving within a traditionalist movement, to know something of the nature of ritual observance within his family. The Seminary, in fact, has always required personal observance of Sabbath and kashrut of its entering students.[12] Our information in the 1955 replies is not entirely adequate, but it does lend itself to the conclusion that the parents of the present student body are somewhat less observant than those of twelve years ago.

In every category, with the unlikely exception of kashrut outside the home, families of JTS Orthodox 1955 parallel Orthodox predecessors, then the vast majority, of 1943. It is the JTS Conservative 1955 that shows measurable changes. We are sure of the Sabbath observance of only seven out of ten and know definitely that one out of ten, the same as the over-all average in 1943, was not Sabbath-observant. It is a fair presumption, however, that a substantial number, perhaps even all, of the 21 percent (12 out of 57) for whom we have no information preferred not to be on record with an answer that they assumed would be embarrassing.

With respect to kashrut, too, we must very likely make the same assumption. No one represented in the 1955 study put himself on record as coming from a home that did not observe the dietary laws, but here, too, one guesses a preference for saying nothing among some, at least, of the three out of ten who never answered the question. Kashrut outside the home is even more difficult to discuss with any certainty. We can assume such observance with considerable confidence for only six out of ten (the number of "definites" and "probables") or, at most, seven out of ten (the number of definite Sabbath observers) of the JTS Conservative 1955 parents.

On the other hand, those parents identified with Conservative congregations are certainly quite unrepresentative of the general level of ritual observance to be found in the denomination as a whole. In a recent survey of board members of Conservative synagogues throughout the country it was established, by sampling techniques, that 37 percent kept strictly kosher, 27 percent kept partially kosher (e.g., no separate dishes), and 36 percent were not kosher at all in their homes.[13] With respect to Sabbath, it is common knowledge that no denominational group in American Jewry has a laity which shows, in cross-section, seven out of

[12] See *Register* of the Jewish Theological Seminary, 1953-54, p. 23.

[13] Emil Lehman, "National Survey on Synagogue Leadership" (United Synagogue of America, mimeographed; New York, 1954), p. 15.

ten Sabbath-observing homes. The homes of the rabbinic students at JTS from Conservative backgrounds are therefore primarily from the relatively small "right wing" of the laity of the movement.[14]

Our information on the language spoken at home is far from adequate for the 1955 inquiry at JTS.

Table 4. Language Spoken at Home

	1943		1955	
	Orthodox	*Conservative*	*Orthodox*	*Conservative*
English exclusively	7	6	2	16
English and Yiddish	19	3	13	6
Yiddish exclusively	9	0	7	0
Hebrew	1	0	2	0
Some Hebrew	0	0	0	0
Not given	0	0	35	35
Total	36	9	59	57

With regard to language, as above on other matters, the figures for the Orthodox homes in 1943 and 1955 look quite alike, and one would guess that the distribution would not change much if we knew the facts on the 35 for whom we have no report. It is also probably a fair presumption, from the definite figures we do have for the Conservative families in both years, that English is the exclusive language in two thirds to three quarters of the homes. If this reasoning is valid, it means that Yiddish is disappearing from the early background and becoming at least a semiforeign language to most of the "Conservative" segment and perhaps a quarter of the "Orthodox" segment of the Conservative rabbinate of the near future.[15]

Perhaps the most marked changes in the last twelve years occur in respect to parental occupation. As is well known, these years have represented a time of tremendous occupational redistribution for the American Jewish population as a whole and of substantial rise in economic and social class.[16] Certainly such a phenomenon is indicated by the

[14] A few comparative figures from the JIR study in 1943 are worth recording: 9 homes were Sabbath-observing, 9 were not, and 3 were partially so; 19 homes were kosher and 2 were not; 15 parents observed kashrut outside the home and 6 did not—a situation of measurably less observance, perhaps 20 percent, than the parents of JTS Conservative 1955.

[15] The comparative figures on language spoken at home for the JIR in 1943 are: English exclusively, 8; English and Yiddish, 12; Yiddish, 1. This is somewhere between the two halves of the JTS group in 1955, but closer to the Orthodox group, for a majority have grown up hearing Yiddish spoken at home.

[16] This is the most studied question in American Jewish sociology. The most recent

occupations of the parents of rabbinic students, comparing the two parts of this study.

Table 5. Occupation of Fathers

	1943		1955	
	Orthodox	*Conservative*	*Orthodox*	*Conservative*
Clergy:				
Rabbis	5	1	5	5
Cantors	1	0	0	1
Hebrew teachers	2	1	2	1
Shamassim and Shochetim	3	0	1	0
Professionals	1	1	6	7
Manufacturers	2	2	1	5
Businessmen	8	1	14	20
Clerks and kindred workers	2	2	4	9
Manual workers	9	0	14	5
Peddlers	2	1	0	0
No report, retired, or deceased	1	0	12	4
Total	36	9	59	57

The differences between 1943 and 1955 are striking. In 1943 the clergy provided 13 of the 44 rabbinic candidates, exactly 30 percent, and of these 13 only 2 came from the Conservative group. The 15 children of clergy found in the 1955 study are only 15 percent of the total (100) for whom we have information on parental occupations, and they now divide almost evenly, 8 from the Orthodox and 7 from the Conservative. It is fairly evident that, in so far as the clergy is concerned, the Conservative is in the process of replacing the Orthodox in the parentage of that segment of the JTS student body. The Seminary is arriving at the point quite usual in Protestant theological seminaries, and in American professional schools as a whole, of having a marked representation of the children of alumni in its student body.[17] For the children of Orthodox clergy in 1943

general statement is Nathan Glazer, "Social Characteristics of American Jews, 1654-1954" in *AJYB*, Vol. LVI (1955). See also Sophia Robison, ed., *Jewish Population Studies, passim*, for the basic information available for the late 1930's, and the summary, as of 1940, in Nathan Reich's essay "Economic Trends in American Jewry," in *The American Jew: A Composite Portrait*, Oscar Janowsky, ed. (New York, 1942). For a summary and analysis of more recent data from the late 1940's and early 1950's see the articles by Ben B. Seligman in *AJYB* for 1950, 1951, and 1953 and the essay "Economic Status and Occupational Structure" by Eli E. Cohen in *AJYB*, Vol. LI (1950). The studies in the 1930's for the most part provide no data on occupational rank, but those which are available can, with caution, be used as a qualified sample of the whole.

[17] See Ernest Havemann and Patricia Salter West, *They Went to College* (New York, 1952), pp. 14 and 214-16, for evidence as to tendency of alumni to send their children to their own undergraduate alma mater. Data as to Protestant theological seminaries is from a sampling by the author of confidential files at one such representative school.

and before, enrollment at the JTS betokened not only intellectual and spiritual change but also considerable economic and social mobility. In a sense, Schechter's unhappiness at this notion to the contrary notwithstanding, the Seminary was performing the function that Warburg, Schiff, and its Reform benefactors clearly desired, that of "Americanizing" the rabbinate of the East Europeans.[18] The rising number of children of alumni and the marked drop of children of clergy in the total body in 1955 are both evidently part of a new pattern, the profile of a denomination becoming rooted in the American scene and supplying itself, as other denominations do, from a cross-section of its resources, both clerical and lay.

If we exclude the children of clergy from our calculations, because they are obviously a special case as candidates for the rabbinate, comparison of the occupations of the children of the laity will sustain the thesis of "normalization" of the origins of the Conservative rabbinate. Of the 24 lay parents of the Orthodox group in 1943, 13 (2 clerks, 9 manual workers, and 2 peddlers) were at the lowest end of the scale of economic pursuits. Despite all the economic restratification of American Jewry in the last twelve years, in the 1955 study 18 of the 39 lay parents in the JTS Orthodox 1955 group are still to be found in the three lowest categories in Table 5. Businessmen, among Orthodox parents, represent exactly one third in 1943 (8 of 24) and a little more than a third (14 of 39) in 1955. The only marked difference is a rise in the professional category, from 1 to 6 in twelve years, a change to be explained in part as the only measurable influence of a dozen years of occupational restratification and in part by the fact that the professionals represented in all categories of Table 5 are primarily teachers, accountants, etc., i.e., the lower income professionals.

The occupational profile changes markedly in the JTS Conservative 1955 group. Disregarding the 7 clergy and the 4 for whom there is no report, we know the occupations of 46 parents from the Conservative laity. For the first time the middle and upper-middle class pursuits of the professions, manufacturing, and business are an overwhelming majority, 32 out of 46. Even the 14 in the lower status groups show a reversal of the situation in the Orthodox groups of 1943 and 1955: the higher status white-collar workers are now a much larger group (9) than the manual workers (5). To summarize this discussion in percentages: excluding the children of clergy, the Orthodox parents in 1943 were 46 percent in the definitely middle-class pursuits; the figure is 57 percent (4

[18] Sklare, *Conservative Judaism*, pp. 193-94.

out of 7) for Conservative parents in 1943. In 1955 it is 59 percent for the Orthodox and 70 percent for the Conservative.[19]

How representative of the economic structure of American Jewry as a whole are the stratifications shown above? This question is complicated by the fact that the 1943 group of all backgrounds at the Seminary, as will be developed later in this study, was overwhelmingly from the large Jewish centers and, in its majority, from New York City, whereas the 1955 study of the Seminary shows a much wider dispersal throughout the country, especially in the half of Conservative background. A study of Jewish youth in New York conducted in 1935 showed that almost half of their fathers were manual workers, one third were owners, managers, and officials in business, one tenth were clerks, and 4 percent were professionals.[20] In the same year in Detroit a comparable study showed that almost half the fathers were in the business group and about 40 percent were manual workers.[21] These figures look not too far different from the picture of the JTS student body in the 1943 study, but it must be noted that the JTS students in this group are slightly more middle-class than the total community. Only 9 of a total of 44 parents in 1943 were manual workers.[22]

[19] The figures for 20 replies from JIR are as follows: clergy, 4; professionals, 1; businessmen, 5; white collar, 4; manual workers, 6. There were therefore 10 in the middle class and 10 below, with not so large a manual workers' group. On this point too, taking into account that the year was 1943, the parents of the JIR group were already at least parallel to and probably somewhat beyond the parents of JTS Orthodox 1955 and on the way to the status of the JTS Conservative 1955 parents.

[20] Here are some figures outside New York for the economic distribution of male workers, by socioeconomic class, in the 1930's: Buffalo (1938) showed 14.3 percent professionals; 32.2 percent proprietors, managers, and officials; 24 percent clerks; and 27.5 percent manual workers. Detroit (1935), for all male workers, had a few more clerks and kindred workers (31.5 percent), 37.3 percent proprietors, etc., and 39.9 percent manual workers (*Patterns of Jewish Occupational Distribution in the United States and Canada*, Report Number 6, Jewish Occupational Council, New York, 1940). To summarize, these communities show an average of around 35 percent in the middle-class pursuits, a figure which parallels the one for New York. The parents of JTS Orthodox 1943, the lowest status group, show 47 percent in those brackets, a definitely higher status.

[21] See Nettie Pauline McGill, "Some Characteristics of Jewish Youth in New York," *JSSQ*, XIV (1937), 255, and S. J. Faumann, "Occupational Selection among Detroit Jews," *Jewish Social Studies*, XIV (1952), 17-50. See also Reich, "Economic Trends in American Jewry," in Janowsky, ed., *The American Jew*, p. 170, where the same tale, that children of Jewish skilled workers neither desire nor actually do follow their parents into the laboring class, is told in terms of a study of Jewish youth in Baltimore in 1940.

[22] In 1938 a study of the members of *Landsmanshaften* showed the following economic stratification: 75 percent were workers and white-collar employees, 15 percent were small tradesmen, and 10 percent were managers, professionals, and

As for the 1955 stratification, the sum conclusion of the many community studies between 1948 and 1953, which represented a fair sampling of the American Jewish community outside New York, showed an average of about 60 percent in the definitely middle-class categories of the professions and proprietors, managers, and officials.[23] A sampling of New York and surroundings done twice, in 1948 and again in 1951, when adjusted to apply only to males, seems to add up roughly to this: 15 percent to 20 percent in the professions; 30 percent proprietors, managers, and officials; 20-25 percent clerical and sales; and 20-25 percent manual workers.[24] The "Orthodox" half of the JTS student body in 1955 conforms pretty well to this New York pattern, except for being a little low in the clerical and sales category, but the "Conservative" half looks very much like the rest of American Jewry. Analyzed another way, the demographic studies of the 1930's, especially those of New York and the larger centers, showed a primarily immigrant pattern of occupational distribution. It is quite in keeping with the facts that the parents in 1943 were found to be largely in conformity with that pattern. The more recent studies, especially those outside New York, are now of a labor force primarily American-born and it is therefore not surprising that the JTS Conservative 1955 parents should show 89 percent in nonmanual occupations.

Nonetheless it can be shown that this last most middle-class group of Seminary students is from lower echelons than that segment of the laity which is at the helm of congregational affairs. The survey in 1954 of synagogue boards in the Conservative movement came up with the

---

government workers (*Entsiklopediah Ivrit*, VII, 254). Since the *Landsmanshaften* at that time were almost entirely immigrant in composition, i.e., the same kind of people represented among the parents of JTS Orthodox 1943, this is further evidence for our assumption that these parents are somewhat higher in the socioeconomic scale than a cross-section of their generation.

[23] Seligman, in *AJYB*, LI (1950), 28; LII (1951), 12; LIV (1953), 14. Newark, where both the city and the suburbs were studied in 1948, shows 35 percent in middle-class parents in the city and 51 percent in the suburbs. Allowing for the fact that those figures are based on all workers and are therefore lower than they would be for males alone, they would seem to provide evidence that the fathers of JTS Orthodox 1955 are somewhat more middle-class than the big-city average. The fathers of JTS Conservative 1955 fit rather well the suburban, smaller community economic profile, or, in other words, are quite typical of the economic pursuits of those areas in which Conservative Judaism is strongest (Sklare, *Conservative Judaism*, p. 66). See also the sample study of religious denominations by the Federal Council of Churches of Christ in 1945-46 (Cohen, "Economic Status and Occupational Structure," *AJYB*, LI, 64).

[24] Glazer, "Social Characteristics of American Jews," *AJYB*, LVI, 27, and notes *ad. loc.*

following occupational analysis; 30 percent in the professions; 50 percent in the proprietor, manager, and official categories; 9 percent in the white-collar group; and 1 percent manual workers.[25] Expressed in percentages for the 46 lay parents in JTS Conservative 1955, the breakdown is as follows: 15 percent in the professions; 54 percent proprietors, managers, and officials; 20 percent white collar; and 11 percent manual workers. The JTS students from Conservative homes are coming from the pews of the congregations, but the supply is sparsest from the front pews and grows correspondingly heavier as one moves farther back. There is still a measurable class difference between the parents of even these most middle-class future rabbis and the boards with which they will deal in their future careers.

It is difficult to proceed further with the economic analysis of the families of the 1955 group because, as we noted at the beginning of this essay, we lack precise figures as to the annual average income of the parents for the five years preceding the date of the questionnaire. We do have 43 replies out of 45 concerning the annual average income of their parents for the 1943 group.

Table 6. Economic Background of JTS Students

(available only for 1943 group)

Annually	*Number*	*Percent*
Less than $1,500	7	16
$1,500–$2,000	15	35
$2,000–$3,000	12	28
$3,000–$4,000	4	9
$4,000–$5,000	4	9
$5,000–$7,500	0	0
$7,500–$10,000	0	0
Above $10,000	1	3
Total	43	100

It is quite striking in Table 6 that 34 of the 43 who replied came from homes under the $3,000 a year level in the late 1930's and early 1940's. It is to be noted that in the first half of the 1940's the average initial salary for a graduate of the Seminary was in the neighborhood of $3,000 per annum.[26] It seems then that four out of five of the students at the Seminary were, upon graduation, pretty well assured of beginning their

[25] Lehman, "National Survey on Synagogue Leadership," p. 3.

[26] The author, being himself a graduate of JTS in 1943, can attest to this figure.

professional careers at a higher level than what then seemed to be the terminal income of their parents.[27]

As for the 1955 group at the Seminary, we can only, in the absence of precise information, draw some perhaps not too fanciful inferences from the facts we do know. It will be recalled that the JTS Orthodox 1955 was paralleled by the demographic and occupational distribution of Jews in New York City. We find, in a study done in 1951, that 12 percent of the Jewish households in the city had incomes of more than $10,000 and 29 percent were below the $4,000 mark.[28] It would be unreasonable to assume, in the light of what is generally known about the denominational proclivities of Jewish families in the upper income brackets, that the 12 percent at the very top are represented as strongly in the Orthodox group as elsewhere. The most reasonable guess should perhaps proceed by using the 29 percent below the $4,000 mark as a basing point and adding 5 percent to each subsequent category. An estimated income scale for the parents of JTS Orthodox 1955 would then be:

	Percent
Less than $4,000	29
$4,000–$6,000	33
$6,000–$8,000	14
$8,000–$10,000	14
Above $10,000	8

Since the average beginning income today of a Seminary graduate is in the $6,000–$7,000 range, this projection would mean that the parents in the 1955 Orthodox group are assumed to be about 70 percent below that income level, a rise of 10 percent vis-à-vis the 1943 situation. This is perhaps not too inaccurate an estimate.

As for the JTS Conservative 1955 parents, oblique information bearing on their economic position is equally meager. For what so few replies may be worth as a guide, the 7 Conservative parents reporting in 1943 were of somewhat higher estate than the rest of the group. None was earning less than $1,500, only one was earning less than $2,000, four were in the $2,000–$3,000 bracket, and 2 were in the $3,000–$5,000 group. The bottom and the top were both unrepresented in a group solidly in the middle.[29]

[27] In the JIR group in 1943 this seems just as true. The parents of 5 were earning less than $1,500, 6 were in the next bracket, and 7 in the one above that. Nineteen out of twenty-one were thus below the $ 3,000 per annum salary figure.

[28] Glazer, "Social Characteristics of American Jews," *AJYB*, LVI, 28.

[29] In general, the middle classes and above are most wary of providing answers to questions about wealth. Glazer tells us that in the 1951 survey of income levels in

Aside from the recent samplings of New York City and suburbs referred to above, information on average annual income is available in only one recent study, that of Los Angeles in 1950.[30] Estimating from the distribution of income among the various economic pursuits as given in these two studies we arrive at the following figures for the parents of JTS Conservative 1955:

	Percent
Less than $4,000	24
$4,000–$8,000	48
$8,000 and over	28

This leads to the conclusion that perhaps half, or possibly a bit less than half, of the parents of this group were earning annually less than $6,500–$7,000, the probable beginning salary of these rabbinic students upon graduation. For the first time, it is likely that as much as one fifth of these candidates for the rabbinate will not ever earn more, or even as much, as their parents at the peak of economic productivity.

These estimates for the JTS Conservative 1955 parents may seem too low when compared with the income distribution of board members of Conservative synagogues. In this group 54 percent had an annual income of over $10,000, 26 percent earned from $6,000 to $10,000, and only 13 percent were earning less than $6,000.[31] As we have maintained above, however, there is evidence in the occupational distribution of the parents of the JTS Conservative 1955 that they are not from the top social and economic brackets of their congregations, the group from which board members are primarily recruited. Our guess for the income distribution of the JTS Conservative 1955 parents may well be low, but not so low as these figures for the board members would indicate.

On the balance it seems evident that there is now a really substantial group of candidates for the rabbinate at the Seminary, especially from those families identified with the Conservative movement, for whom

---

New York City 15 percent of the Jewish households refused to answer as compared to 10 percent of the non-Jewish ones. Seligman in discussing the income figures for Los Angeles (see note 30) speaks of great difficulty in obtaining the information. Is it perhaps evidence of middle-class background that in the 1943 study of JTS the only two who did not answer the question about income were both from among the small group of nine from Conservative background and that our difficulty in getting most of the JTS 1955 student body to answer the questionnaire directly was largely in their reluctance to provide data as to family income?

[30] Seligman, in *AJYB*, LIV (1953), 19.

[31] Lehman, "National Survey on Synagogue Leadership," p. 5.

entering the clergy is not a marked socioeconomic step forward. In this, too, there is a sign of normalization and greater similarity to the upper social echelon denominations in Protestantism.[32]

THE STUDENTS

In the questionnaire on which this study is based considerable information was requested about the rabbinic candidates themselves. Though not a single subjective question was asked, an attempt was made by indirection, through inquiries about their major subjects at college, training toward other fields before entering rabbinical school, and the like, to shed some light on the motivation of their decisions to become rabbis. The results were unsatisfactory and inconclusive. We are, therefore, left with four kinds of information about these two groups of Conservative rabbis-to-be:

1. Places of birth
2. Cities in which they spent their formative years
3. Colleges they attended
4. Their preliminary Jewish education

The figures for the birthplaces of the Seminary student body prove that the students themselves are markedly closer to immigrant origins than the rest of their generation.

Table 7. Birthplaces of JTS Students

	1943		1955	
	Orthodox	*Conservative*	*Orthodox*	*Conservative*
United States and Canada	26	8	48	55
Foreign countries	10	1	11	2
Total	36	9	59	57

Only three of the eleven foreign-born in 1943 came to the United States after adolescence, as over against ten out of the thirteen in 1955. The explanation is no doubt to be found in the stoppage of immigration in the 1920's and early 1930's followed by an estimated influx of about 250,000 Jews after the beginning of the Hitler era.[33] It should be noted that, even as early as 1937, .6 percent was the highest figure for the

[32] The sampling of confidential files, alluded to above, of one Protestant theological seminary showed a comparable situation among students from the Presbyterian denomination.

[33] Glazer, "Social Characteristics of American Jews," *AJYB*, LVI, 34.

number of foreign-born among the age group from fifteen to twenty-four in three fairly representative communities (Trenton, Passaic, and Norwich).[34] If we knew the facts for the entire American Jewish community today, the figure would undoubtedly be lower. Only the JTS Conservative 1955, with its 2 foreign-born out of 57, looks anything like as far from Ellis Island as the whole of that age group.[35]

Analysis of the geographical distribution of these groups of rabbinic candidates (the information requested was the community in which each spent his adolescence) provides further evidence that the Conservative rabbinate is well on the way toward becoming more representative of its congregations. We have data for 44 of the 45 respondents in 1943 and for 110 out of 118 in 1955:

Table 8. Geographical Distribution of JTS Students in Adolescence

	1943		1955	
	Number	*Percent*	*Number*	*Percent*
New York	23	52	40	36
Cities with more than 50,000 Jews	14	32	34	31
Cities with 50,000–20,000 Jews	3	7	8	7
Cities with less than 20,000 Jews	1	2	18	16
Foreign	3	7	10	9
Total	44	100	110	99

In three of the five categories the percentage distribution is almost exactly the same in 1943 and in 1955. The changes are a decrease of 16 percent in students from New York City, and a really striking increase in the number of candidates for the Conservative rabbinate from the smallest Jewish communities, a ninefold increase from 2 percent to 18 percent.

This kind of redistribution, which, as we shall soon show, is based on the increased rootedness of the JTS students in the Conservative movement, was already being foreshadowed in 1943 by the 9 students from Conservative homes then at the Seminary: 3 were from New York, 4 from cities of over 50,000 Jews, and 2 were from Jewish communities of 50,000–20,000. By 1955 the breakdown, by family synagogue allegiances, is as follows (we have data for 54 in each group):

[34] Robison, ed., *Jewish Population Studies*, pp. 17, 26, and 74.

[35] In the JIR in 1943, two out of twenty-one were foreign-born, a situation between the two halves of JTS 1955.

Table 9. Geographical Distribution of JTS 1955 as Adolescents by Synagogue Allegiance of Family

	ORTHODOX		CONSERVATIVE	
	Number	*Percent*	*Number*	*Percent*
New York City	25	46	15	28
Cities with more than 50,000 Jews	14	26	19	35
Cities with 50,000–20,000 Jews	2	4	5	9
Cities with less than 20,000 Jews	4	7	14	26
Foreign	9	17	1	2
Total	54	100	54	100

The JTS Orthodox 1955, compared to the same group in 1943, shows a decrease in students from New York City and the other large communities, some increase in students from the smallest communities, and a substantial increase, referred to above, in students who received their preliminary education abroad. Despite the changes, this half of the 1955 group is not very much different from its predecessors in 1943. In both cases nine out of ten received their earliest Jewish impressions either abroad or in the very largest communities in this country. They are the products of the most intensive Jewish life available today outside of Israel.

We find, once again, that it is the JTS Conservative 1955 that is a new kind of group. New York furnishes only a little more than one in four of the "Conservatives," not really any more than the smallest Jewish communities, which together provide 26 percent. It seems obvious that the explanation for this radically changed distribution is to be found in the demography of the Conservative movement. We have no statistics as to the distribution, by size of the Jewish community, of the incidence of Conservative congregations and their affiliated families. It is, however, common knowledge that the relative importance of the movement is strongest in the smaller towns. New York City, with almost half of the entire Jewish population of the country, has at present no more than 75 members of the Rabbinical Assembly actively serving in pulpits. The largest Jewish communities, the next category, employ something over 100 of the members of the Rabbinical Assembly. The rest, roughly two thirds of those actively in the pulpit, are in towns with less than 50,000 Jews.[36] Even a cursory reading of the most recent published list of congregations which belong to the United Synagogue will substantiate

[36] See geographical distribution of the members of the Rabbinical Assembly as given in the *Proceedings*, Vol. XVIII (1954), Appendix II.

these figures.[37] Even if we assume that the one third or so of the synagogues in the largest centers have about two thirds of the total membership in the movement, it is still true that much of the numerical strength of Conservative Judaism and most of its rabbinic manpower (the people who largely motivate and train young people in their synagogues to enter the rabbinate) are in the smaller towns.[38]

Before we pass on to the analysis of the preliminary Jewish education of these rabbis and rabbis-to-be, a word needs to be said about their college and university background. Certain interesting differences do occur between 1943 and 1955. Yeshiva College alumni led the list by far with 27 of all the students at the Seminary in 1955 (of whom 6 were from Conservative homes), thus representing almost one in four of the entire body and one in three of the JTS Orthodox 1955. In the 1943 group Yeshiva College provided 8 of the 44 for whom there is a report, i.e., less than one fifth of the whole group, and about one fourth of those from Orthodox homes. The New York City colleges were the alma maters of more than one third (16) of the 1943 group and of one fourth (27) of the 1955 students. The "ivy colleges" and other top-ranking privately endowed universities are equally prominent in both years: one quarter of the students in each (11 in 1943 and 28 in 1955) are alumni of such schools, but the geographical distribution is, as was to be expected, wider in the latter year. Only 4 out of 44 in 1943 attended college elsewhere than on the Eastern seaboard (those 4 were from the Midwest), whereas 23 out of 118 are alumni of Midwestern and Far Western schools in the 1955 group.[39]

We turn now to a concluding consideration of the preliminary formal Jewish knowledge that the various rabbis-to-be brought with them to the Seminary. Because of the wide variety of standards and hours of attendance in Jewish schools we have had to make some fairly arbitrary assignments of numerical values in order to treat the available information statistically. The tables to be presented below are based on the following assumptions: we regarded a year spent in a parochial school, a five-day-a-

[37] See *United Synagogue Calendar-Diary, 5715 (1954-1955)*, appendix, the listing of affiliated organizations.

[38] JIR 1943 shows 9 out of 21 from New York City, 9 more from cities of more than 50,000 Jews, and 3 from smaller towns, i.e., a distribution which looks rather like JTS Orthodox 1955 on the beginning of the way toward JTS Conservative 1955.

[39] JIR 1943 showed the following distribution of college background: 10, almost half, from the city colleges of New York; 2 from Yeshiva College; 5 others from Eastern schools and 4 from the Midwest; in sum, a not much wider distribution than JTS 1943, but with an understandably much smaller number from Yeshiva College.

week Hebrew school, or a Hebrew high school as one full year of schooling. A year at a three-day-a-week Hebrew school was counted as two thirds and a year of private tutoring (there were relatively few cases of this last) was treated as one half of a full year. Sunday School attendance was counted as one quarter for each year. Years spent at Hebrew colleges were counted as one each.

On such weighted figures Table 10 gives us the preliminary Jewish education, on average, of the students in each of the two groups.

Table 10. Pre-Seminary Jewish Education of JTS Students

	Preliminary	*Teachers' College*
1943 (45 responses)	9.5 years	2.5 years
1955 (115 responses)	7.8 years	2.6 years

In the over-all picture the average Seminary student in 1955 has had one tenth of a year more Hebrew college training than the earlier generation, a difference hardly great enough to be significant. It is, however, striking that the 1943 group had an average 9.5 years of intensive Jewish education in its preliminary background as over against the 1955 group with more than a year and a half less, a decline of almost one fifth.

This inquiry into the preliminary education becomes more revealing still when divided in terms of those from Orthodox families over against those from Conservative families in each of the two years.

Table 11. Preliminary Education of JTS Students

	Orthodox Families	*Conservative Families*
1943	10.0 years	7.7 years
1955	9.4 years	6.1 years

The JTS Conservative 1943 consisted of only nine people and the 7.7 figure is therefore based on too small a number to be of importance, but the figure for 1955, based on almost half of the present Seminary student body, is statistically significant. Even if we use unweighted figures for JTS Conservative 1955 (based on the knowledge that many, if not most, Conservative congregations, and certainly almost all such synagogues in the smaller towns, are providing only three-day-a-week Hebrew schools,[40] and we therefore regard attendance in such a school

[40] Louis Katzoff, *Issues in Jewish Education* (New York, 1949), p. 45. This book, which is subtitled "a study of the philosophy of the Conservative congregational school," is the only full-length study of the subject in existence. Katzoff speaks of the two-afternoons-a-week Hebrew school as so much the overwhelming pattern of the

as the equivalent of a full year of Hebrew school education) we still arrive at 7.3 years of any kind of formal Jewish training as the average for those of Conservative background in the present student body.

In Hebrew teachers' college background, too, there is a distinction between JTS Orthodox 1955 and their Conservative counterparts. Of the 59 in the former group, 43 completed a full four-year course at such a school, 2 attended for 3 years each, 2 had 2 years each, and 3 appear to have had equivalent training in European schools. The JTS Conservative 1955 shows one with 5 years at a Hebrew teachers' college, 24 who completed a full course of 4 years, 5 with 3 years of attendance, 4 with 2 years, and one with one year. On the other hand, our figures do not really show the effects of the new pre-theological department instituted by the Seminary within the last decade and quite obviously aimed at enriching the background of candidates for its rabbinical school from Conservative homes. Much of that work has been done during the summers and quite a number have spent time in Israel in recent years learning Hebrew quite intensively.[41]

We must therefore conclude that in 1943 the amount of formal Jewish education which the individual students brought with them to the Rabbinical School was substantially higher than that of the present group.[42] The

---

more intensive Conservative Jewish education as to shrug aside all other forms. Since the time of his study (1945-46) there has been some progress toward intensification. Uriah Z. Engelman, in *AJYB*, LII (1951), 103, shows 13.6 percent of all enrollees in the kindergarten and elementary division of Conservative congregational schools as attending more than three days a week (including Sunday). How much of this percentage reflects congregational kindergartens, as over against the older group, is not stated. See also Sklare, *Conservative Judaism*, pp. 145-58.

[41] It needs to be added that the Rabbinical School at the Seminary has increasingly in the last decade or so required of many of its students that they remain for five or even six years of study before being ordained, in place of the minimal four-year course.

[42] The Jewish parochial school plays a constant role in providing candidates for the rabbinate at JTS. In 1943 something over one third (17 out of 45) had attended parochial elementary schools for an average of 6.3 years. This represented almost half the JTS Orthodox 1943, for only one of the JTS Conservative 1943 had attended a parochial school. In addition, 9 completed parochial high schools, representing more than one fourth of 32 who had been to a Hebrew high school. In 1955, 40 of 115 respondents show the same average, 6.3 years, of attendance at a parochial school and again represent more than one third of the whole. Exactly one third, 24 of the 72, of those who went to a Hebrew high school attended a parochial school. The one significant difference is that JTS Orthodox 1955, like its 1943 predecessors, shows half (29 of 59) with parochial elementary backgrounds, but now almost one fifth of JTS Conservative 1955 (11 out of 57) have attended parochial school. In his article on Jewish education in Janowsky, ed., *The American Jew*, p. 71, Isaac B. Berkson estimated that in 1940 the parochial school affected no more than 2 percent of all Jewish children receiving some kind of Jewish education, though almost 10 percent of the Hebrew

over-all decline appears to be approximately 15 percent in terms of hours devoted over the years, prior to entering the Rabbinical School, to Jewish training.[43]

CONCLUSIONS

All of the facts and trends discussed in this essay seem to point to one central conclusion: a new kind of Conservative rabbi, a product of the denomination itself, has now made his appearance, and the future almost certainly belongs to him. As yet those of Orthodox background are quite clearly an overwhelming majority in the Rabbinical Assembly and a bare majority in the Seminary student body, but the trend is in the other direction. Whatever substantial changes we have been able to discern in this study were not related to the passage of a dozen years between 1943 and 1955. Quite the contrary, the physiognomy of the Orthodox-origin groups in each of these two years remained remarkably stable. The dynamics of the situation under analysis has been almost entirely the change in denominational allegiance of the families of these rabbis-to-be.

We are able, from the facts in hand, to present a fairly rounded description of the "older," Orthodox-origin type of Conservative rabbi. He is a first-generation American, if not himself foreign-born. Spiritually and culturally his immediate roots are in that segment of East European Jewry which transplanted to American soil the most intense ritual observance, "Yiddishkeit" (including the Yiddish language), and Jewish education. Though only a small minority of this group have themselves had experience of the European yeshiva (or its equivalent in a few places in America), their Jewish education is almost as intensive as could be conceivable for individuals who have undergone the whole range, including college, of secular education. Most come from families whose socioeconomic level is, at the very highest, lower middle class, or from

---

school child population at any one time were in parochial schools. He quoted the Jewish Education Survey of 1936 as giving a figure of 4,500 in such schools in New York City in 1936, as compared to a weekday school enrollment there in 1941 of 45,000-50,000. Engelman, in *AJYB*, LII (1951), 98, estimates that 15.3 percent in 1949 and 16.1 percent in 1950 of all students in weekday schools in the United States attended parochial schools. As a supplier of students for the Conservative rabbinate, parochial schools are obviously the single most productive source.

[43] JIR 1943, where the replies to the questions on preliminary Jewish education were written down rather haphazardly, shows, on the most generous estimate, an average of 7.1 years of Hebrew school and around 2 years of Hebrew teachers' college, i.e., at maximum an average preliminary Jewish education about on the level of JTS Conservative 1955.

the homes of Orthodox clergy, so that their entrance into the Conservative rabbinate is, in their case, part of the general trend of their generation toward mobility upward. Though many, if not a majority, are spending their careers in suburban or smaller Jewish communities, they themselves mostly began in the tight-packed immigrant East Side of New York and the largest northeastern cities. If the decision to enter the Seminary and become a Conservative rabbi was not, for all the men of this type, a matter of serious spiritual crisis (as it undoubtedly was for some), they are nonetheless rabbinic personalities themselves in process, or at the end of a process, of considerable refashioning of their own individuality.

The "newer" type, from Conservative homes, is not yet quite as clearly defined. American-born himself, he is not yet entirely second generation, though in a clear majority of the families at least one of the parents is American-born. He is from the most traditionally observant segment of Conservative Judaism, but nonetheless for a substantial number the decision to enter the rabbinate has represented an acceptance upon themselves of greater burdens of the Law than they have seen their parents bearing. Yiddish and the culture of the East of Europe is more and more a memory, something they are reading about, rather than a living tradition they experienced pretty much at firsthand at home. Though their entrance into the rabbinate still represents for some a measure of social mobility, it is no longer overwhelmingly so. The element of spiritual crisis is now, in so far as it exists, of different quality: not the problem of breaking with one's Orthodox past but rather the question of feeling called to the rabbinate as one's vocation.

These newer rabbis owe their formal Jewish education primarily to the Conservative movement. They are for the most part products of its congregational schools, of its youth groups, and of the Seminary's various new preparatory courses. The future Jewish education of this type of Conservative rabbi is primarily dependent on whatever level of educational achievement Conservative Judaism as a whole will attain. The emerging new type of Conservative rabbi is of the denomination and at home within it. The future of the Conservative pulpit is now clearly in the pews of the congregations.

THE JEWISH ASSOCIATION IN AMERICA

By Isaac Levitats

AS PART OF MY STUDY of the Jewish community in Russia, 1772-1844, I examined many minute books of Hevrahs (such as Hevra Kaddisha, Shas, etc.) and became aware of the important role these associations played in catering to Jewish group needs. What has become of these societies in America? Thus far history has hardly explored this aspect of Jewish society. Many general histories do not even mention the subject. While considerable information can be culled from some local histories, there are practically no monographs on any one organization.

In this essay an attempt is made to sketch the development of the following societies: Hevra Kaddisha, congregation, Landsmanshaft, lodge, benevolent and study association. My study of Jewish school boards is available as a doctoral dissertation at the School of Education, Syracuse University. Other societies, such as fraternities, sororities, social clubs, Zionist groups, and others, were omitted for lack of space. It appears that associational activities embrace almost the entire gamut of Jewish group life and offer a key to a better understanding of our past and to more informed and intelligent social planning for the future. The interpretations presented are far from definitive; they are more in the nature of a hypothesis to be tested by further research.

HISTORY OF THE HEVRAH

The antecedents of the Hevrah date back to the talmudic period in Babylonia. The Hevra Kaddisha probably already existed at that time, although Jewish social needs were largely cared for by the community as a whole; we do not, therefore, find any other type of association in that period. The Hevrah flourished in Spain in the thirteenth century and continued to develop until the expulsion. There were societies for burial, sick-care, charity, and other communal needs. From Spain the Hevrah was transplanted to Italy and from there to Prague (1564) and to Central and Eastern Europe. The spiritual implications of sickness and burial, ritualized by the Kabbalists in sixteenth-century Palestine, deepened the religious meaning of association. These societies were patterned after the Christian religious guilds.

The main distinguishing characteristics of the Hevrah were its lay management (there was no sacramental distinction between laity and clergy in Jewish life) and its autonomy (it resisted federation with other local associations or with regional, national, or international agencies). The Hevrah submitted to control and supervision by the local Kahal only. This decentralization of authority in each town or village in Jewish community organization and social life helped to give fortresslike strength to each local group.

The Hevrah defied the corroding influences of time and space. In Poland and Russia it further pulverized Jewish community life, but under coordination by each local community it gave an excellent account of itself in carrying out the purposes of cohesive, purposeful group living. When the Russian government abolished the Kahal in 1844, the elusive Hevrah not only continued virile and strong; it took over some of the functions of the Kahal and maintained Jewish community life in its traditional ways. It nurtured the synagogue and the religious conventicle, sustained child and adult study, provided social welfare, and harnessed the burial function for constructive community purposes.

THE HEVRAH IN AMERICA

Contrary to the popular assumption that Jewish community life must dissolve under conditions of Emancipation, the Hevrah not only survived in America, but it experienced unparalleled growth. Freedom of association afforded the Hevrah a new lease on life. It was restricted neither by the American government nor by the Kahal. The individual in the association was now offered unlimited opportunities for status and prestige, for learning democracy, and for crisis stabilization through mutual aid. Such groups spread throughout America.

While the small number of Jews in the Sephardic period prevented specialization, and associational life was centered in the synagogue, the deep-rooted traditions of German and Russian Jewries brought forth a plethora of associations. The following types of associations were formed approximately in this order: burial society, Minyan, congregation, benevolent society, school association, lodge, institution, social and cultural group, Landsmanshaft, Zionist and social organization, family circle, cousins and memorial club.

The rugged individualism of the association caused it to resist local coordination and to preserve its independence. To this day each organization—synagogue, Landsmanshaft, Hevra Kaddisha, school, congregational study group, and mutual aid association—prefers to go it alone. While isolation remains the cardinal characteristic of the Hevrah, great strides have been made in the direction of coordination and federation and on the local level. Fund raising and social welfare are now largely communalized. Coordination in other spheres proceeded slowly. The "Y" and Center gathered in much of the leisuretime activities. Bureaus of Jewish Education were started in 1910 in New York. Civic-protective work in some cities achieved community status. A few localities have community councils to coordinate all communal activities. The distinction between the membership association, which is the subject of the present study, and the communal agency (Welfare Fund, Bureau, Center) must be kept clearly in mind. The national organizations, most of which serve a particular type of local membership association, are also in a category by themselves.

JEWISH SOCIAL NEEDS

The original social needs of American Jews were those of immigrants. After centuries of an inbred existence, when each district or townlet had its own religious ritual and dialect, the Jewish masses were thrown together with their own and with the teeming millions of other nationalities. Though Jews all, they were different in so many ways that only among *Landsleit* would one find kindred and understanding souls. The economy of plenty was yet but a legend; many years of privation and hard labor had to pass before the immigrant achieved some sort of economic security. The elements of new-found freedom, diversity, equality of opportunity, *Shtetl* loyalty, and expanding economy were decisive in the evolving pattern of Jewish social needs.

1. *Prayer Service and Burial.* It required but one corpse to create a need for a Jewish cemetery; ten adult male Jews were needed for a Minyan. Which came first? More often it was the cemetery that came first; in many cases it was the congregation. In most settlements it took but a few years for a Minyan to be assembled. The first nucleus of common group living was thus started in the congregation. The congregation has remained the most lasting form of Jewish group living in America.

2. *Mutual Aid.* Each new arrival was in need of some sort of assistance

by his fellow Jews to get started in the new country. A free loan, medical and spiritual care in cases of illness, and endowments for widows offered a substantial sense of security.

At first the recent arrivals had their own troubles and wanted to take care of each other. Only after they got on their feet did they expand their activities to include charity.

3. *Religious Benefits.* One of the main benefits derived from an association in Europe was intercessional, that is, the members of the association interceded by prayer or study for the soul of their fellow member in the case of sickness or death. The need for intercession was very real for the Orthodox Jew of those days and persists to this day in attenuated form.

4. *Social.* The need for companionship and fellowship was present from the start. Who else would listen to the tribulations of adaptation to a new and strange environment; who could help maintain contact with the relatives and friends in the old country and engage in nostalgic reminiscences of the good old days of an integrated existence; who could best join in sipping tea or breaking bread if not someone who hailed from the same cultural and social milieu?

It took time before these primary groups crystallized into formal associations. At first all recreational activities centered around the synagogue or the mutual aid society. Then social forms developed which provided an outlet for these leisuretime needs: the club, the lodge, the Landsmanshaft—exclusive groups with secret rituals and special regalia, all lending prestige and security behind closed doors.

5. *Education and Culture.* For a long period the Jewish education of children was left to the individual parent. Then either one of the existing associations—the synagogue, the mutual aid society—or a special school association began providing school facilities.

Adult education and literary and artistic pursuits had to wait until the immigrant had laid his hands on a few dollars and felt economically secure. Then cultural groups evolved.

6. *Occupational.* The industrial revolution and socialist ideologies produced the need for labor unions. Special Jewish occupations produced such guilds as those of butchers, tailors, etc.

7. *Civic Protection.* The complex task of protecting the Jewish group against anti-Semitism in a period of anti-Jewish onslaughts at home and abroad had to be left to the communal and national agencies.

A human being requires the satisfaction of many needs at any one period. While most burial societies served specialized needs, other associations served the many needs of the whole person. For that reason it is often difficult to distinguish between a congregation, a Landsmanshaft, a benevolent association, or a social group. This insight largely eliminates the questions as to which association came first or which was most important.

THE HEVRA KADDISHA

In Europe there was only one cemetery in a community, only one Hevra Kaddisha; monopoly of the mortuary service made it possible to use the proceeds for the maintenance of Jewish institutions. In a sense, the dead imparted life to the community. The most illuminating insight into this life-giving quality of the Hevra Kaddisha can be gained from an examination of the experience of our neighboring South and Central American Jewish communities. Here the Hevra Kaddisha was transplanted by the European immigrants in undiminished power. Only one such society was organized in each locality. It became synonymous with community or Kahal, and to this day Jewish institutions are maintained largely from the revenue of the Hevra Kaddisha.

In the United States each new synagogue, benevolent society, or lodge, each tiny Landsmanshaft secured its own cemetery. These associations have a secure source of revenue which helps maintain them. An oligarchy often controls these associations and gives little heed to the religious and social needs of the community. This is the penalty paid by American Jewry for its lack of a sense of community.

There are, however, some exceptions to this rule. Many communities organized special societies for burial of the poor. Some of these societies gradually amassed coniderable wealth, because they also served the well-to-do. An example of such a society which uses its revenue for community building is the Chesed Shel Emeth Society in St. Louis, Missouri, founded in 1888. To this day the society maintains a large number of local and overseas Orthodox agencies.

San Francisco, California, is another example of community control of burial being made into a powerful force for the good of the entire community. The Jews of that city own a funeral parlor, the Sinai Memorial Chapel. At the end of 1954 the foresight of an earlier generation yielded a profit of $50,000 which was distributed among sixty local organizations.

The mortuary industry has become highly commercialized in America. The spirit of free enterprise has placed burial in the hands of individuals; the community benefits but little.

THE CONGREGATION

The synagogue is the oldest and most universal Jewish institution. Its centrality in Jewish community life has been taken as an axiom by most students of Jewish life. Wasn't his religion the distinctive characteristic of the Jew? Wasn't the synagogue the only communal structure in many communities? However, if we view the congregation as a membership association, as a group of people, a better understanding of the role of the synagogue emerges.

A majority of scholars point out that in the Sephardic period the synagogue was coextensive with community; all communal activities then emanated from the synagogue. But during the German and Russian periods the synagogue lost its hold on Jewish life; all other associations operated outside its fold. They consider this development a reversal of Jewish history; some would like to restore centrality to the synagogue.

The fallacy of this view lies in a misreading of Jewish history. Not the synagogue, but the community, the Kahal, was the central agency. The Kahal controlled the synagogue. In fact, in addition to a communal Beth Hakneseth and Beth Hamidrash there were associational conventicles and private places of worship. The community house of worship was central only to the extent that it acted as an arm of the Kahal. In America the absence of a Kahal created a vacuum which some of the associations sought to fill. For a while, in the Sephardic period, when the number of Jews was very small, autocratic government the rule, and associational specialization not yet a necessity, the synagogue exercised strong social control.

As soon as the population increased and ethnic, ritualistic, economic, and other divisions created a variegated community, a proliferation of independent societies ensued. In general, then, Jewish historic experience in America has made the congregation one of the many associations catering to Jewish needs. It has remained so to this day. Only by taking its rightful place in the associational life of the community can the synagogue fulfill its mission. When all organizations learn to operate as an organic whole serving the manifold needs of the individual Jew in a purposeful manner will a *modus operandi* be achieved.

Those who still believe that the congregation came first and remained "a centripetal force in Jewish community life" should look at and study the record.

The Jewish Burial Ground Society in Chicago was formed in 1845 and only a year later KAM congregation followed; the very next year an independent Hebrew Benevolent Society came into being. Then, in 1861, a Chevra Kadisha u-Bikur Cholim, which existed for a number of years, added religious services to its activities. In New York the Great Synagogue developed from a Hevrah which originated in 1852. In Keokuk, Iowa, a charity society changed in 1855 to a congregation. In Philadelphia, too, many benevolent societies developed prior to and independently of congregations, beginning in 1801 with the Female Association for Relief of Women and Children in Reduced Circumstances. The first association of Russian Jews in Philadelphia was a Chevra Bikur Cholim, followed by similar associations and finally by congregations. Like evidence can be adduced from almost every Jewish community where the Hevrah fathered the synagogue. That is why there were so many congregations called Hevra Mishna Ugmoro (Chicago), Bikur Cholim (New York), Tillem (Psalms) and Chayteem (Tailors, in Rochester), and so on. Reform temples were very frequently preceded by Reform *Vereine*. Certainly the host of Landsmanshaft synagogues in the Russian period were mutual aid associations first, and only secondarily congregations. Their congregational activities were listed in their constitutions alongside of sick, burial, and death benefits. The benevolent, social, literary, labor, and lodge associations not only competed with the synagogue; they sought wider, extra-synagogal horizons. They took an interest in the non-Jewish society about them and sought to emphasize communal versus narrow and divisive religious interests.

True, many charitable and communal activities still issue from the synagogue. In recent years the synagogue has sought to recapture some of its former activities. The Free Synagogue in New York placed emphasis on social service to the extent of spending more than half of its budget on this work. The Society for the Advancement of Judaism advocated the idea of a synagogue center to cater to recreational needs. But by and large the realities of Jewish community life restrict the synagogue to its specialized functions of worship and education.

THE BENEVOLENT ASSOCIATION

"The Jewish civilization certainly stands alone during the pre-Christian era in upholding the cause of the poor and in regarding their condition as brought on not by themselves but by the evils of the social order" (*Intelligent Philanthropy*, by Faris, Laune, and Todd, p. 64). Prophetic insistence on social justice and the minority status of the Jew among the nations always made him care for his own. Charity was a recognized community responsibility. In the ghetto community with its wide gap between rich and poor, pauperism was as common as charity.

In the egalitarian American society, where there were no native Jewish poor, charity largely assumed the form of mutual aid. Today's poor immigrants might be tomorrow's rich benefactors. The great majority of the population, therefore, preferred to belong to societies where rising fortunes could be shared and crises stabilized by reliance upon one another. Even where eleemosynary societies existed, the immigrant first sought to exhaust the mutual-benefit resources of his own group before resorting to public charity.

Historically charity was dispensed by the community or by associations controlled by it. The synagogue, where one could find the town population at festive or mournful occasions, was the center for charity collections in boxes, or for more ostentatious contributions. Crowds could also be reached at funerals, weddings, or other celebrations.

In the Sephardic period the synagogue dispensed charity before the creation of specialized societies. In the German period the benevolent association, while often in close contact with the synagogue, more frequently completely divorced itself from it. Thereafter these mutual aid and charitable associations multiplied rapidly until they outnumbered all other societies put together. Their heyday came in the Russian period with the rise of the Landsmanshaften. While in Europe, due to the disfranchised status of women, there were hardly any separate women's charitable associations, here female associations multiplied to the extent that they soon outnumbered the men's groups.

There was much work to be done. At first temporary aid was extended to the immigrant, the transient, the local poor, sick, or the departed who needed burial. It was constructive assistance that made possible rapid economic adjustment. In the decades prior to 1880, when immigration was not overwhelmingly heavy, attention could be given to the building of institutions: hospitals, orphan homes, homes for the aged, lying-in dispensaries, and sheltering homes. The vast stream of immigrants that poured in incessantly after that time overtaxed the existing charities, and for a while the non-Jewish community had to help in some measure. But very soon the mutual aid association, the Landsmanshaft, took over the major share of cushioning the first steps of adjustment.

For many decades the small group carried the brunt of social welfare. Simultaneously, however, a movement for federation took root. Just as the benevolent association was the first to be emancipated from the synagogue, so it was the first to merge with other associations for common action. The United Hebrew Beneficial Society in Philadelphia originated as carly as 1822. The United Hebrew Relief Association in Chicago was organized in 1859 by nine groups. The first federation of local charities became a reality in Boston in 1895, followed by the Associated Jewish Charities in Chicago in 1900 and by many others. The increased demands upon the American community for overseas needs gave rise in 1925 to the first Jewish Welfare Fund in Oakland, California. Although most of the early benevolent societies are now defunct, some of them have experienced amazing longevity. In Charleston there is an association that originated in the first half of the nineteenth century.

It is generally recognized that the Jews pioneered in the elevation of social service standards and served as an example for the non-Jewish community. Once Protestant social welfare was freed of ecclesiastical control, there ensued a rapid influx of professionally trained workers and a modernization of methods. The rise of community chests during World War I, which were joined by Jews for their welfare and recreational needs, caused a further mutual influence. The higher standards of relief among Jews permeated also to the non-Jewish field. Councils of Social Agencies were especially instrumental in bringing a rapprochement between Christians and Jews.

THE LANDSMANSHAFT

Throughout Jewish history immigrants have exhibited an unusual solidarity with their brethren who hailed from the same country. In the Russian period in America the Home Town, the *Shtetl*, became the strongest cohesive force. Landsmanshaften were formed wherever there was a sufficient number of immigrants from the same townlet.

The fact that no other ethnic group exhibited such a tendency in America is rather startling. The other ethnic groups retained a loyalty to church and state; these loyalties caused the creation in America of organizations patterned after European religious and political institutions. The Italians, for example, have brought over their local church organizations, named after patron saints. The Ukrainians, Serbs, and Croats have associations that are composed of nationals of an entire region or country. The Jews, however, had no such binding forces; their traditions of self-government included only those of Kahal and Hevrah. These were transplanted to these shores. Jews from the same locality even tended to settle in the same streets and to engage in the same occupations.

Ethnic division appeared as early as the latter part of the so-called

Sephardic period. The Portuguese, English, Dutch, Bavarian, Bohemian, and German Jews tended to establish their own synagogues, benevolent associations, and literary societies. After the mass immigration of the 1880's Jewish group life became highly fragmented. There is the story of the Jews of Drohichin, a village near the town of Chomsk, who began frequenting the Minyan of Jews from the latter town. Several months later they found the doors shut in their faces and were forced to form their own association.

The WPA study of New York Landsmanshaften (1938) contained information on 290 Anshes—that is, synagogue Landsmanshaften—715 societies, 287 ladies' auxiliaries, 71 ladies' aid, 164 Workmen's Circle branches, 76 family circles (these date back to 1887), 145 societies named after persons, 39 relief committees, 25 "patronates" engaged in redeeming political prisoners in Europe, and a host of other groups. Altogether they estimated that there were some 3,000 Landsmanshaften in New York. Of these a Dutch society was the oldest, dating back to 1859, followed by the Anshes, the first of which originated in 1862. Most of the Landsmanshaften were formed in the first decade of the twentieth century.

Most of these organizations exist today. In 1951 the United Jewish Appeal in New York worked with 2,000 Landsmanshaften and 1,000 ladies' societies with a total membership of 400,000. In fact, the total number of small "folks" groups in New York, including congregations, is set as high as 7,000. Among these are trade and neighborhood associations—such as the New York Jewelers Benevolent Association, the Manhattan Lodge, the Theatrical Square Club, the East Side Mineral Water Dealers, and the East Bronx Society. In Baltimore and other cities there are Hebrew butchers' and similar associations. Some of the larger European communities have created here many specialized associations, such as the Bialystok Anshe Chesed, Achim Tovim, Ahavas Achim, Bikur Holim, Home for the Aged, and their ladies' auxiliaries and young people's groups.

In 1953 a total of 431 Folks Organizations cooperated with the Chicago Combined Jewish Appeal. The total number of Landsmanshaften in America may be estimated at between five and six thousand.

Each Landsmanshaft has a constitution. These are very much alike, with minor deviations. They provide that the name shall not be changed, nor shall the association be dissolved so long as there are seven members. The objectives shall be burial, distress, sick and death benefits, as well as the maintenance of Jewish identity and moral uprightness. There shall be three types of meetings: regular—once in two weeks, general—once in three months, and special. Officers and committee chairmen shall be elected for a term of six months. New members shall be Jews between the ages of 18 to 21 and 35 to 45 who are of good moral character, have not intermarried, pass a medical examination, and are admitted by the membership in a secret ballot where three black balls disqualify a candidate.

The following fees shall be charged: a registration fee to accompany an application for membership; an inititation fee that shall vary with the age of the newcomer; membership dues to be paid quarterly; a cemetery and doctor's fee; and payment for synagogue seat, if the society has its own place of worship for the High Holy Days.

The society shall pay the following benefits after the first six months: (1) sick benefit up to a maximum amount for each year; committees shall visit a sick member and, if necessary, shall keep a night vigil; (2) death benefit—free burial, a hearse and two carriages for the funeral, a Minyan in the mourner's home during *Shiva*, and an endowment to the bereaved family consisting of a specified assessment on all the members; (3) financial assistance—outright donations to poor members, free loans, and, if possible, funds for old age, disability, unemployment, and strikes.

Fines shall be imposed for failure to visit the sick, to attend a funeral or committee meeting, to observe the rules, or to settle lawsuits without prior resort to the conciliation efforts of the society. Membership shall be forfeited for failure to pay dues, false medical claims, conversion, polygamy, or moral turpitude.

While originally charity was specifically excluded, the Landsmanshaften gradually engaged in extending aid to institutions in their home towns, bought United States savings bonds in World Wars I and II, gave relief to sufferers of the two wars, and assisted Hias, the JDC, the UJA, and other national Jewish funds.

Despite the dissolution of many Landsmanshaften in recent decades, they are still going strong. They did not go bankrupt, as did some lodges, because of the assessment feature of their insurance. Ownership of cemeteries served as a major source of income. Recent refugees have tended to join the Workmen's Circle, the Farband, or new associations of "Katzetlers" (inmates of concentration camps).

For a long time isolation was the very essence of the Landsmanshaft. But gradually they joined workers' orders, Rumanian, Polish, Lithuanian, and other national federations, and finally councils of organizations or folk's divisions within local welfare funds.

Little educational or cultural work was done, with the exception of those that had synagogues to which were attached study groups or Talmud Torahs, and the labor orders which opened schools that served as centers for adult social and cultural activities.

A most interesting phenomenon are the new Landsmanshaften in Los Angeles and Miami consisting of migrants from other American communities. The benefits are mostly social. Similar societies have also been formed in Israel as a result of the Ingathering of the Exiles. Loyalty to a geographic locality of origin still remains a strong Jewish trait.

LODGES OF FRATERNAL ORDERS

The first major departure of the Hevrah from its habitual resistance to central control was the fraternal order. It originated locally partly as a reaction against religious parochialism and in favor of a community spirit. It largely imitated the non-Jewish fraternal orders where some of the founders of Jewish lodges were initiated into the secret ritual of exclusive, prestige-giving orders. It flourished when the mutual aid associations found it profitable to belong to a larger whole, where numbers made for greater security of investment. Finally, it saw its greatest expansion at the turn of the twentieth century when commercial insurance was on the decline.

Lodges started out as mutual benefit associations which were subordinated to a supreme governing and legislative body. The lodges that originated in the German period gradually included in their program Americanization of immigrants and participation in the civic life of the non-Jewish community. Along with the literary, social, and recreational associations, the lodge was the bridge between the Jewish and the general community. In its later stages it was natural for the lodge to turn its attention to a large extent to nonsectarian and civic-protective activities.

The Independent Order B'nai B'rith started in 1843. Its mutual aid and insurance features were abolished in 1900 and secrecy was done away with in 1920. The United Order True Sisters (1848) has continued to claim nonsectarianism, though 95 percent of its membership is Jewish. The Free Sons of Israel (1849) consisted of a poorer element. Brith Abraham (1859) was launched by Hungarian Jews; when the Independent Order of the same name broke away from it (1887), it attracted the large masses of East European newcomers and became the largest order with a membership of over 200,000. Six more orders were started in the 1890's, fourteen in the following two decades, and only two between 1930-47. Regional orders were also organized such as Western Star, Progressive Order of the West, etc. Most of these vanished in short order. The high point of Jewish fraternalism was reached in 1913 when the total membership exceeded half a million. In addition to Jewish orders, the general orders, which were largely tolerant, always attracted the wealthy Jew. Soon many lodges of the Masons, Elks, Knights of Pythias, Odd Fellows, and others became exclusively Jewish and have persisted in fairly large numbers to this day.

A special place among the orders is occupied by the workers' lodges which combined benefits with socialism. The Workmen's Circle (1900) substituted socialism for the synagogue. The Jewish National Workers Alliance (1910) combined Zionism with socialism. The International Workers Order (IWO—1930, later JPFO—Jewish Peoples Fraternal Order) attracted the left-wing proletariat. These orders advanced the Yiddish language and culture. Alone among the orders they established schools which became centers for adult education and socialization. The cultural and social aspects of their work give them a unique place among the mutual aid associations; it also explains their greater viability.

The growing popularity of commercial insurance in the last three or four decades has eliminated many orders altogether and has caused others to change their functions. B'nai B'rith, for example, has shifted its emphasis to anti-defamation activities, civic work, philanthropy, and overseas aid.

Like the Landsmanshaft, the lodge easily competed with commercial sick benefit insurance. Its sick visiting committees reduced the cost of claim administration; many members never asked for the benefits that were rightfully due them. Not so with life insurance. The original post-mortem assessment system assured solvency, since the lodge promised to pay in endowments only what it collected from its membership. This worked well so long as a majority of the members were comparatively young. With increasing average age, however, endowments had to decrease for lack of an influx of young blood. The younger generation turned to commercial insurance that was based on actuarial calculations. The low cost of fraternal insurancc did not last long.

Another reason for vanishing fraternalism is the changing leisuretime activity pattern of most Americans. The amusement and recreation afforded by the lodge have been supplanted by the automobile, the movie, radio, and television. The two basic needs supplied by the lodge—insurance and fellowship—have gradually become commercialized.

STUDY ASSOCIATIONS

In the ghetto community adult study societies clustered about the syna gogue. The study of Halacha and Aggadah was widespread. The more learned joined Mishna, Talmud, or Shulhan Arukh classes; the less scholarly listened to expositions of Ain Yaakov, Midrash, Hayyei Adam, and other moralistic texts. The Hasidim tuned their ears to the Rabbi's discourses. The followers of Musar dwelt on ethical Judaism. Gifted Maggidim had eager listeners on a Sabbath afternoon.

We know of no record of adult studies in the Sephardic period. The early immigrants were generally uneducated; few scholars braved the hardships of life in a new country. The first record we have for New York is the Hebrew Literary and Religious Library Association that was started at Shearith Israel in 1841. Hebrew and customs were taught. In 1846 Rabbi Max Lilienthal formed a Hevra Shas. Rabbi Ash, some years later, lectured on the Talmud at his Beth Hamidrash.

Literary societies spread throughout the country in the second half of the nineteenth century. These were patterned after similar German societies, of which some Jews were members. Their programs consisted of music, lectures, debating, recitations, and dramatic presentations, as well as social and fund-raising affairs. The content was general literature; a minority also discussed Jewish topics. The Young Men's Hebrew Associations, which were started a century ago, followed the secular and social programs of the literary societies.

The East European immigrants also established literary groups; these were conducted in Yiddish or Hebrew and gave priority to Jewish topics. Education societies, self-educational clubs, and workingmen's education clubs prospered. Some of these turned later into schools for the propagation of socialist ideas.

The masses were almost wholly absorbed in the struggle for existence. Yet we find a good many study groups, particularly at the synagogues. These transplanted old traditions on the new soil. The Hevra Mishna Ugmoro at the Mariampol Synagogue in Chicago in 1894 studied one chapter of the Mishna and a page of the Talmud before and after the evening service. At the Kalvaria synagogue in Chicago a Hevra Torah engaged a teacher for religious subjects. Congregation Bnai Abraham, established in Philadelphia in 1882, had many study societies including Ain Yaakov, Mikra, Thilim, etc. They covered the entire Talmud three times; it took seven years each time. To this day such Hevrahs are to be found in most of the larger Orthodox and Conservative synagogues.

There is less formalism in maintaining a *Pinkas* or in the election of officers, but the feasts and some intercessional benefits are still kept up. Some communities still have a Hevra Shas where every member undertakes to cover a certain portion of a tractate; corporate completion of the entire Talmud is celebrated at a banquet. The recent refugees have set up islands of study and meditation in the more Orthodox sections of the large cities. In Brooklyn there is a Hevra Shas consisting almost exclusively of common laborers; the teacher is one of their own. At the Shomre Emunah in Borough Park some eighty businessmen and professionals meet regularly for a study of the Talmud. A similar group of Dutch Jews meet at Moriah in Manhattan under the leadership of Rabbi Soloweichik. The Hevra Shas at the Queens Jewish Center offers courses in Maimonides, the Talmud, and other sacred books. In addition to a "daily page" of the Talmud there is also an attempt by Rabbi S. T. Stern of Kansas City, Missouri, to launch a "daily Halacha" consisting of ten paragraphs a day from the Shulhan Arukh. These Orthodox groups carry on their work without fanfare or publicity; little of their activities reaches the public eye.

The Socialist, Zionist, Hebraist, and Yiddishist movements also caused the formation of many study, cultural, and literary groups. They met for a discussion of contemporary Jewish problems and sought to develop modes of social action.

In recent years many national agencies for the promotion of adult education have sprung into action. Temples and synagogues, Zionist, community relations, educational, and recreational roof organizations have provided a steady stream of program aids and publications to their local chapters. The peak of adult interest in education was reached about 1948, followed by a considerable decline. Television and prosperity have brought apathy and unconcern with social or Jewish issues. Valiant efforts are being made to organize "retreats"; such are the laymen's institutes of the National Academy for Adult Jewish Studies of the United Synagogue of America and the "Wildacre institutes" of B'nai B'rith. Limited interest is evinced in the adult study programs of Centers, synagogues, and temples. In the Orthodox and Conservative synagogues only Jewish subjects are taught, such as Hebrew Bible, history, the Talmud, customs, and ceremonies. The Reform temples, in addition to some Jewish subjects, also include a large number of secular topics.

However, the environmental forces of a materialistic and anti-intellectualistic civilization set at naught the idealistic plans and programs of the leaders.

CONCLUSION

The associations here reviewed have experienced considerable change in structure and function in the course of the centuries. Yet all of them are still here and the formation of new types of groups goes on apace. School boards alone have a total membership of some 30,000 men and women. The other associations have memberships that run into the hundreds of thousands. The grand total must amount to three or four times the Jewish population of America because of the considerable number of "joiners" who belong to several groups. (A tally of memberships in national organizations alone for a recent year, based on the American Jewish Year Book, yielded over ten million.) The extent of totally unaffiliated Jews is not known. Their number is negligible in the smaller cities and considerable in the impersonal metropolitan centers. Mirrored in this incessant activity is an irresistible need to stick together, to live in social groups. Jewish community life cannot be understood without a full realization of the importance of these small cells for the propagation of a virile group life, for the perpetuation of Jewish existence in freedom and voluntarism.

All signs point to a continued proliferation of the species called Hevrah. Suburbanization removes the Jew from the metropolitan jungle into a more closely knit—because smaller—community. Community as such has become too large and complex for comfort or intimate familiarity. The tendency now is toward participation in organizational and institutional activities instead of the town meeting. There is the added fact that the immigrant patterns of social behavior developed on an ecological basis—in a ghetto where community was coterminous with a limited city area. Now geography alone need not be depended on for group associations.

Generally the sociology of American Jewry is still in its swaddling clothes. Associational activities have hardly been treated. There is, therefore, a great need for a series of monographs on the history and present status of each of the multitude of organizations which dot the Jewish landscape. What a windfall for doctoral dissertations! National and local agencies could do much to get started—if they would but realize the importance of research for communal planning.

The first step in gathering information should be to launch a nationwide search for organizational materials and the establishment of local, regional, or national archives. At present there is not the slightest appreciation of the value of constitutions, minute books, program materials, and other documents that emanate from the various associations. People feel that since they have no literary value, they may be discarded. There is as yet no sense for Jewish sociology as a science or a community discipline.

What lessons for social action emerge from our presentation?

It is important to keep in mind that the major characteristics of the Hevrah in America—isolation, mutual aid, *Shtetl* loyalty—were conditioned by the immigrant nature of Jewish society. We are now in a transition period between immigrant and native patterns. Social groups with millennial traditions cling to their old ways with unusual tenacity. The transition period will therefore last at least several decades. Social scientists and social workers must reckon with both the old and the new forces operating in Jewish life.

It seems to us that in addition to the specific theoretical and practical ideas enunciated in the earlier sections of this study there are two main conclusions.

1. The order of the day is the community approach. The major divisive tendencies brought over from Europe are foreign to the native American Jew. He tends rather to coordination, common action, and efficiency. The associations will therefore gradually have to yield a certain portion of their sovereignty to the larger community. This must be achieved by voluntary action on the part of the association and must be the result of an educational process. The associations will gradually learn that life has become too interdependent and will work for constructive goals.

2. The communal, coordinating agencies, on the other hand, must learn to understand and respect the historic conditions that gave rise to the association. Once such understanding is achieved, the community workers will be able better to deal with the membership association. Mutual respect will create modes of cooperation. The principle of the autonomy of constituent groups within larger bodies will safeguard their just rights. Nor can integration be foisted or superimposed upon the small group. Again it must be the culmination of an educational process.

In short, the slogan should be "unity in diversity." Federate—yes, but safeguard the rights of the association, because it is the mainstay of our group life.

ON MARRIAGE IN ALALAKH

By Isaac Mendelsohn

ANCIENT ALALAKH, modern Tell Atshanah, in the plain of Antioch, was excavated by Sir Leonard Woolley from 1937 to 1949[1] and the cuneiform texts found there have recently been published by D. J. Wiseman.[2] The texts (about 460 tablets), dating from the eighteenth and fifteenth centuries B.C., deal with the economic, social, and political life in the kingdom of Alalakh which at that time was inhabited by a mixed population consisting of Hurrians and Canaanites. This is the first time that we have come into possession of a large body of legal and business documents from that region[3] and the light they shed on various aspects of Syrian society in the first half of the second millennium is of truly inestimable value. The purpose of this paper is to discuss, on the basis of five fifteenth-century documents, one socioeconomic aspect of life in Alalakh, namely, marriage.

Marriage in Alalakh was, as in any other part of the Ancient Near East, a civil affair based on a written contract and concluded in the presence of witnesses. The legal term *riksātum* = *riksu* 'bond, contract,' employed in Babylonia, Assyria, and Nuzi for marriage contract, is not found in the five fifteenth-century marriage contracts.[4] Instead, the following expressions are used: *a-na É.GI.A-šu iš-al-šu* (No. 17:4) 'he asked him (the father, for the hand of his daughter) as his bride';[5] *a-na DAM-šu*

[1] See Sir Leonard Woolley, *A Forgotten Kingdom* (Baltimore, 1953).

[2] D. J. Wiseman, *The Alalakh Tablets* (Occasional Publications of the British Institute of Archaeology at Ankara, No. 2, London, 1953). Additional texts were published later by the same author in *Journal of Cuneiform Studies*, VIII (1954), 1-30.

[3] This paper was written before the appearance of J. Nougayrol's *Le Palais Royal d'Ugarit*, Vol. III (Paris, 1955), containing Akkadian legal and business documents from Ugarit.

[4] Nos. 17, 91-94.

[5] For a similar phrase in the Elephantine papyri of the fifth century B.C., cf. E. G. Kraeling, *The Brooklyn Museum Aramaic Papyri* (London, 1953), No. 7:3. אנה אתית על ביתך ושאלת מנך לנשן יהוישמע שמה אחתך לאנתו 'I have come to thy house and asked of thee the woman Yehoyishma by name, thy sister, for marriage.'

i-ḫu-u[*z*] (No. 91:4) 'he took (her) for his wife'; and *a-na É.GI.A-šu il-qì-šu*[6] (No. 93:4) 'he took her for his bride.'

Before the marriage was consummated, the bridegroom presented to his future father-in-law a *tirḫatu*, usually translated "a bride-price." The *tirḫatu* (written NÍG.SAL.ÚS.SÁ) is mentioned in Nos. 92 and 93, but is not mentioned in Nos. 17 and 91.[7] One may, therefore, venture the opinion that, as in Babylonia and Assyria, the *tirḫatu* payment did not constitute an essential element in the Alalakhian marriage transaction; the validity of the marriage contract did not depend on the *tirḫatu* payment.[8] Normally, the *tirḫatu* in the Ancient Near East was paid to and retained by the bride's father. This does not seem to have been the custom in fifteenth century Alalakh. There, if my interpretation of the difficult text No. 92 is correct, the *tirḫatu* was still paid to the girl's father, but retained by the bride. Text No. 92 is a marriage contract concluded between Irihalpa and Naidu. Lines 6-14 stipulate what is to happen in the event the marriage breaks up either because of the fault of the husband or that of the wife, and lines 15-20a set forth the conditions of succession of Irihalpa's sons born by Naidu and another wife of his.[9] Lines 6-14 read:

(6) *šum-ma* [1]*SAL na-i-du* [1]*i-ri-ḫal-pa i-z*[*i-i*]*r-ši*[10] (7) *ù uk-ta-na-aš-ši-id-šu NIG.SAL.ÚS.SÁ* (8) *ša su-ḫa-ar-ti ik-la mi-nu-um-me mi-im-šu* (9) *ša É a-*[*bi*]*-ši wa-ad-du-ši i-li-qì ù i-pá-ṭar* (10) *šum-ma SAL su-ḫa-ar-ti i-na ap-pí-šu* (11) *i-ša-ad-da-ad-ši NIG.SAL.ÚS.SÁ* (12) *ú-ta-ar mi-im-mu-ši ša É a-bi-ši* (13) *ša ú-še-er-ri-bu wa-ad-du-ši* (14) *i-li-qì ù i-pá-aṭ-ṭar*[11]

(6) If Naidu hates Irihalpa (7) and she continuously harasses him, the *tirḫatu* (8) of the young girl [i.e., Naidu's] he [Irihalpa] shall retain, but whatever (9) was apportioned to her in her father's house [i.e., her dowry], she shall take and depart; (10-11) if. (however), he [Irihalpa] "leads her by the nose" [i.e., mistreats her], the *tirḫatu* (12) he [Irihalpa] shall return (to Naidu's father),

[6] Compare the Ugaritic and Hebrew *lqḥ* 'to take (a wife).'

[7] The left part of No. 94 is illegible; a *tirḫatu* may or may not have been mentioned there.

[8] For the interpretation of the Babylonian *tirḫatu* and its Ugaritic and biblical counterpart the *môhar*, cf. Millar Burrows, *The Basis of Israelite Marriage* (American Oriental Series, Vol. XV, New Haven, 1938); for the latest discussion of the Babylonian *tirḫatu*, cf. E. Szlechter, "L'affranchissement en droit suméro-akkadien," *Archives d'Histoire du Droit Oriental et Revue Internationale des Droits de l'Antiquité*, I (1952), 136-44.

[9] Lines 1-5 and 20b-24 are partly abraded.

[10] Written *ši* instead of *šu;* cf. No. 94:19 where the text has *i-zi-ir-šu ù i-zi-bu-šu* 'if she hates him and leaves him.'

[11] For the transliteration and translation of lines 15-20a see below.

and whatever from her father's house (13) she brought with her as her portion [i.e., her dowry], (14) she shall take and depart.

If the interpretation of these lines is correct, the husband is in the possession of the *tirḫatu* which he had, originally, paid to his wife's father as her "bride-price." How did it turn up in his hand? The only plausible explanation would be to assume that the *tirḫatu* was handed over to Naidu by her father as a gift, in addition to her dowry, and she in turn gave it back to her husband for investment in his business though retaining legal title to it. The situation then is as follows: if Naidu hates her husband and leaves him, she forfeits the *tirḫatu* as penalty for breach of contract; if, on the other hand, Irihalpa mistreats his wife and by so doing forces her to leave, he forfeits the *tirḫatu* (to which he would be entitled if his wife left him without cause), as a penalty for breach of contract on his part.

If the retention of the *tirḫatu* by the bride in this case is to be taken as the norm, the Alalakhian marriage in the fifteenth century had already passed the stage of being an outright purchase marriage. Since the Alalakhian population at this period was partly Hurrian, it should cause no surprise to find that a similar development of the *tirḫatu* took place in the Hurrian colony at Nuzi. In one Nuzi marriage contract we find that the *tirḫatu*, which amounted to 40 shekels of silver, was divided into two equal parts; one part was kept by the girl's owner and the other one was tied into the bride's "girdle" as her dowry.[12]

In Babylonia and Assyria it was customary for the bridegroom to send gifts to his future father-in-law. These "betrothal gifts" are called in the Hammurabi Code *biblum* (pars. 159-161), and in the Middle Assyrian Laws *biblu* and *zubullu* (pars. 30-31). The same practice prevailed also in Palestine as is evident from the narratives in Genesis 24 and 34. In the first case Eliezer bestowed in the name of Isaac *migdānôt* 'choice presents,' on Rebekah's brother Laban and on her mother Milcah.[13] In the second case, Shechem was willing to present to Jacob and his sons a *mattān* 'a voluntary gift,' over and above the *môhar* 'the bride-price,' if only they would give him Dinah for a wife. That this usage was known in Alalakh is shown by text No. 17:5-6. Here, a certain

[12] R. H. Pfeiffer and E. A. Speiser, *One Hundred New Selected Nuzi Tablets*, No. 55:10:15 (*Annual of the American Schools of Oriental Research*, Vol. XVI [1936]); see also E. A. Speiser, "New Kirkuk Documents Relating to Family Laws," *Annual of the American Schools of Oriental Research*, Vol. X (1928-29), No. 26.

[13] The active part played by Laban in giving his sister into marriage suggests that Bethuel, Rebekah's father, was dead and hence the "betrothal gifts" were presented to the bride's nearest kin, in this case to her brother and mother.

Shatuwa asked Apra for the hand of his daughter "and in accordance with the custom of the city of Halab he [Shatuwa] brought him [Apra] a *nidnu* [a betrothal gift]" (*ù ki-ma pa-ra-aṣ* (*al*)*ḫa-la-ab*(*KI*) *ni-id-na i-za-ab-bil-šu.*[14] The term *nudunnu*(*m*) is used in both the Hammurabi Code (pars. 171-172) and in the Middle Assyrian Laws (pars. 27, 32) for gifts presented by the husband to his wife; and in the Neo-Babylonian period it connotes the dowry given to a daughter by her parents.[15] The Alalakhian *nidnu* must have had a different meaning, since it is clearly stated in the text that it was given by the bridegroom to his future father-in-law. The Alalakhian *nidnu* must, therefore, be a synonym of the Canaanite *mattān*[16] 'betrothal gift.'

It was common practice for wealthy fathers to give a dowry to their daughters. In Babylonia and Assyria the dowry is called *šeriktum* = *širku,*[17] in Nuzi *mulugu,*[18] in Ugarit *ṯlḫ* and *mlg,*[19] and in the Old Testament *šillûḥîm.*[20] The dowry was the woman's private property and her husband had no legal title to it. It was given to her by her father as a kind of insurance to fall back upon if widowed or divorced. A dowry, though not referred to by a technical term, is mentioned in text No. 92 cited above. If Naidu leaves her husband, whether of her own free will or forced to do so by her husband's misbehavior, she takes with her "whatever had been apportioned to her in her father's house," i.e., her dowry.

The Alalakhian family was polygamous in character and organization.[21] A man could marry as many wives as he was financially able to maintain, unless a specific clause in the marriage contract denied him the right to do so. The highly interesting but involved text No. 91

[14] The phrase "in accordance with the custom of the city of Halab" refers, most probably, to the content or value of the gift, and not to the practice itself.

[15] Cf. G. R. Driver and J. C. Miles, *The Babylonian Laws* (Oxford, 1952), I, 265-71, and *The Assyrian Laws* (Oxford, 1935), pp. 198-205.

[16] See also the Ugaritic *mtn* 'gift.'

[17] Hammurabi Code, pars. 176-184; Middle Assyrian Laws, par. 29 in Driver and Miles, *The Assyrian Laws.*

[18] Speiser, "New Kirkuk Documents Relating to Family Laws," *Annual of the American Schools of Oriental Research,* Vol. X (1928-29), Nos. 31:17, 32:5, etc.

[19] Cf. C. H. Gordon, *Ugaritic Handbook* (Rome, 1947), Text No. 77:47.

[20] I Kings 9:16; Micah 1:14; see also Gen. 16:1-6; 24:59, 61; 29:24, 29; 30:3-9; Josh. 15:19; I Sam. 25:42.

[21] For polygamy in Ugarit cf. A. van Selms, *Marriage and Family Life in Ugaritic Literature* (London, 1954), pp. 19 f.; J. Obermann, *Ugaritic Mythology* (New Haven, 1948), pp. 30 f. In biblical Palestine a man was free to marry as many wives as his wealth allowed him. The Deuteronomic law 21:15 takes it as a matter of fact that the normal well-to-do family consists of two wives.

contains a declaration by Akap-tahe[22] (who seemed to have several wives) that if either of the two women A and Z give birth to a son he will not take a third wife, but if neither of them gives birth, he will marry a third wife. The clause reads:

(24) *ša SAL a-kap-kí-a-š*[*e ù*] (25) ¹*SAL zi-li-ip-na-nu-a* (26) *i-ba-aš-ši i-na bi-ri-*[*ši-na*] (27) *ša ú-la-dú* (28) *DAM-tam ša-lu-uš-ta la* [*iḫ-ḫa-az*] (29) *šum-ma ki-la-li-ši-na-ma la*[23] [*ullada*] (30) *ù DAM-tam ša-lu-uš-ta* (31) *i-iḫ-ḫa-az di-nu LU*[*GAL*]

(24-27) If either one, be it Akapkiashe or Zilip-Nanua, gives birth (to a son), (28) he will not take a third wife, (29) but if both of them do not give birth, (30) a third wife he may take. Judgment of the king.

The fragmentary text No. 93:7-8 carries a provision stating that if the woman does not give birth to a son within the period of seven years, the husband may take a second wife. The text reads: *šum-ma MU 7.KAM ú-ul ù-l* [*i-id*] [*ù DA*]*M-tam ša-na-am i-li-q*[*i*] 'if she fails to give birth in seven years, he may take a second wife.' The damaged text No. 94:9-10[24] contains a similar provision: ... *MU 7.KAM* ... *DAM-tam ša-na-am* ... '... seven years ... a second wife ....' The stipulation restricting the husband from marrying a second wife was probably inserted in all marriage contracts of well-to-do brides where the girl's father was in a position to impose such a pledge on his future son-in-law. The reason underlying it was, of course, to safeguard the status of the woman in the household and spare her the humiliation of sharing her husband with a rival wife.[25]

Similar restrictions against marrying a second wife are found in many marriage contracts from Nuzi. To cite only a few examples: the husband cannot take a second wife;[26] the husband may marry a concubine only if his wife fails to bear children;[27] the husband may take another wife if his first wife does not bear a son;[28] the husband agrees not to take a second wife or a concubine as long as his present wife lives.[29] And finally there is the case of a certain Wullu who was adopted as a son by

[22] Wiseman reads Akap-Dagan.

[23] Text has *šu*.

[24] Text in *Journal of Cuneiform Studies*, VIII (1954), 7.

[25] Cf. I Sam. 1:6.

[26] Pfeiffer and Speiser, *One Hundred New Selected Nuzi Tablets*, No. 55:29-30 (*Annual of the American Schools of Oriental Research*, Vol. XVI [1936]).

[27] Speiser, "New Kirkuk Documents Relating to Family Laws," *Annual of the American Schools of Oriental Research*, Vol. X (1928-29), No. 2:17-21.

[28] *Ibid.*, No. 26:18-23.

[29] C. H. Gordon, "Nuzi Tablets Relating to Women," *Analecta Orientalia*, Vol. XII (1935), No. 25:8-9.

one Nashwa and simultaneously married his adopter's daughter. A clause in this adoption-marriage transaction states that "if Wullu takes another wife, he shall vacate the lands and houses of Nashwa."[30] Wullu may take a second wife only at the penalty of losing his inheritance as the adopted son of his father-in-law.

A biblical parallel to such agreements in marriage contracts may be seen in the case of Jacob. After having conceded Jacob's right to depart with his wives, children, and property, Laban made Jacob swear that he would not take other wives besides Leah and Rachel: "If you ill-treat my daughters, or if you take wives besides my daughters, although no man is with us, remember, God is witness between you and me."[31] As long as Jacob was attached to Laban's household there was no possibility for him to marry more wives, but in Canaan, far from his father-in-law's presence, there was no legal hindrance in his way, hence the solemn oath that he would not do so.

Paragraph 142 of the Hammurabi Code[32] states that if a newly married woman who is not at fault "hates" (*i-zi-ir*) her husband, she may take her dowry and return to her father's house. A clause in two of our documents shows that a similar privilege was accorded to Alalakhian women. Text No. 92:6-9, already cited above, provides that if Naidu "hates" (*i-zi-ir*) her husband Irihalpa, she may take her dowry and leave. Lines 17-19 of the fragmentary text No. 93[33] read: *šum-ma* ... [1]*SAL bi-it-ta-ma-al-ki* [*i*]*-zi-ir-šu ù i-zi-bu-šu* 'if Bitta-malki hates him [her husband] and leaves him."

According to the evidence supplied in text No. 92 an Alalakhian father could disregard the rule of primogeniture and appoint a younger son to the status of a "first-born." Lines 15-20a of the marriage contract of Irihalpa and Naidu read:[34]

(15) *šum-ma SAL na-i-du NU A.TU DUMU.SAL ŠEŠ-šu* (16) [1]*i-wa-aš-šu-ra i-na-an-din* (17) *šum-ma x-x-x*[35] [1]*i-ri-ḫal-pa* (18) *a-na pa-ni-im-šu A.TU ù EGIR-šu* (19) [1]*SAL na-i-du A.TU TUR.RA na-i-du-ma* (20) *rab-bu-ti*

(15) If Naidu does not give birth to a son, the daughter of his brother, (16) Iwashshura, shall be given (him as a wife); (17) if x x x (another wife) of Irihalpa

[30] C. J. Gadd, "Tablets from Kirkuk," *Revue d'Assyriologie et d'Archéologie Orientale*, Vol. XXII (1926), No. 51:20-24.

[31] Gen. 31:50.

[32] For the interpretation of this paragraph cf. Koschaker, *Zeitschrift für Assyriologie*, XXXV (1924), 199-212, and Driver and Miles, *The Babylonian Laws*, I, 298-303.

[33] Text in *Journal of Cuneiform Studies*, VII (1954), 7.

[34] Lines 6-14 of this document have already been discussed above.

[35] Text partly abraded.

(18) gives birth to a son first and afterwards (19) Naidu gives birth to a son, the son of Naidu alone (20) shall be the first-born.[36]

As in the cases of the disposition of the *tirḫatu* and the stipulations concerning marriage of a second wife, the Nuzi documents present parallels also to the right of a father to disregard the rule of primogeniture. In one document a father declares that he had first annulled his "relationship" with his son but later restored him into sonship and appointed him as the elder son, with the right to a double share of the inheritance.[37] In a marriage contract the condition is laid down that the husband may take another wife, but the sons of the first wife, whether born before or after the second wife gives birth to sons, shall be the only heirs.[38] The same attitude seems to have prevailed in Ugarit. After the death of Baal, El called on his consort Asherah to select one of her sons to be made king—any one whom she favored.[39] In another instance El promised Keret that his wife would bear him seven sons and seven daughters and added: "to the youngest one (of the daughters) will I give the birthright" (*ṣǵrthn abkrn*).[40]

It is in the light of this Hurro-Canaanite legal background that allowed a father to pass over his eldest son and award the birthright to a younger son that the Deuteronomic legislation concerning primogeniture (Deut. 21:15-17) stands out in marked relief. Opposing the arbitrary power of the father to order the manner of succession to his estate,[41] the law decrees that:

If a man has two wives, the one loved and the other disliked, and they have borne him children, both the loved and the disliked, and if the first-born son is hers that is disliked, then on the day when he assigns his possessions as an inheritance to his sons, he may not treat the son of the loved as the first-born in preference to the son of the disliked, who is the first-born, but he shall acknowledge the first-born, the son of the disliked, by giving him a double portion of all that he has, for he is the first issue of his strength; the right of the first-born is his.[42]

[36] I am indebted to Prof. A. Leo Oppenheim for the elucidation of these lines.

[37] Speiser, "New Kirkuk Documents Relating to Family Laws," *Annual of the American Schools of Oriental Research*, Vol. X (1928-29), No. 8.

[38] Gadd, "Tablets from Kirkuk," *Revue d'Assyriologie et d'Archéologie Orientale*, Vol. XXIII (1926), No. 12.

[39] Gordon, *Ugaritic Handbook*, Text 49:1, 16-18.

[40] *Ibid.*, Text 128:iii, 16.

[41] Cf. the cases of Esau and Jacob (Gen. chaps. 25, 27); of Manasseh and Ephraim (Gen. 48:13-20); and the appointment of Solomon to succeed to the kingship (I Kings chap. 1).

[42] See also Gen. 49:3.

DOCTOR SAMUEL JOHNSON'S GRAMMAR AND HEBREW PSALTER

By Isidore S. Meyer

TO FACILITATE the teaching of Hebrew in British Colonial America, three instructors of that language in this country were responsible for the publication of Hebrew grammars written in English. Instead of using the customary Hebrew-Latin textbooks, Judah Monis[1] and Stephen Sewall[2]

In the preparation of this paper I wish to express my thanks to Mr. Milton Halsey Thomas, Curator of Columbiana, Columbia University, for making available to me material relating to Samuel Johnson, including Johnson's Hebrew Psalter and unpublished manuscript material; Mr. Roland Baughman, Head of Special Collections at Columbia University Library, for the use of published and unpublished material in the Johnson Collection; and Professor Jacob R. Marcus for permission to publish an unpublished letter of Dr. Samuel Johnson to Stephen Sewall.

[1] Monis was the author of דקדוק לשון עברית: *Dickdook Leshon Gnebreet, a Grammar of the Hebrew Tongue, Being an Essay to Bring the Hebrew Grammar into English to Facilitate the Instruction of All Who Are Desirous of Acquiring a Clear Idea of This Primitive Tongue by Their Own Studies; ...And Published More Especially for the Use of the Students of Harvard, at Cambridge in New-England...* (Boston, 1735); see A. S. W. Rosenbach, "An American Jewish Bibliography," *PAJHS*, No. 30 (1926), p. 35, item 28. For a brief biographical account of Monis see the *Dictionary of American Biography* [cited hereafter as DAB], X, 86. By 1715-16, Monis was in friendly correspondence with the intellectual leaders of New England. See *Sibley's Harvard Graduates: Vol. VII. 1722-1725: Biographical Sketches of Those Who Attended Harvard College in the Classes 1722-1725:* with bibliographical and other notes by Clifford K. Shipton (Boston, 1945), pp. 639-46, particularly p. 640.

[2] Stephen Sewall (1734-1804), Hebraist and classicist, compiled a grammar entitled *An Hebrew Grammar Collected Chiefly from Those of Mr. Israel Lyons, Teacher of Hebrew in the University of Cambridge; and the Rev. Richard Grey, D. D., Rector of Heaton, in Northamptonshire. To Which Is Subjoined a Praxis Taken from the Sacred Classics, and Containing a Specimen of the Whole Hebrew Language: with a Sketch of the Hebrew Poetry, Retrieved by Bishop Hare* (Boston, 1735). The Hebrew type used in its printing was destroyed by fire in January, 1764. Rosenbach, "An American Jewish Bibliography," *PAJHS*, No. 30, lists this edition, p. 54, item no. 43, and reproduces the title page of same on p. 55. He records three other editions, respectively, p. 121, item no. 126 (1802); p. 127, item no. 136 (1806), and p. 149, item no. 165 (1812). On Sewall, see *DAB*, XVI, 612. In 1764 he became the first incumbent of the newly established Hancock professorship of Hebrew and other Oriental languages. He held this post for twenty years.

at Harvard[3] and Doctor Samuel Johnson,[4] upon his retirement as President of King's College, pioneered on these shores by authoring Hebrew grammars. Johnson's motivation, as stated in the opening sentence of the preface to the second edition of his grammar, is that he was "greatly desirous to promote the study of Hebrew in America," and for that reason he had drawn up his "short English and Hebrew grammer together." His long-range objective, also, was to establish a professorship of Hebrew in English Colonial America.[5]

Hebrew had been a favorite study of Johnson's throughout his life. His interest in the subject had first been stimulated by his finding a book of his grandfather's which contained some Hebrew words which no one could explain further than to inform him that it was the language used by Moses and the Prophets and in which the Old Testament was written.[6] This increased his curiosity. During his college days at Saybrook, Connecticut, he covered most of the Greek Testament and a portion of

[3] On the early study of Hebrew at Harvard, see Isidore S. Meyer, "Hebrew at Harvard (1636-1760)," *PAJHS*, No. 35 (1939), 145-70.

[4] Johnson's work bears the title: *An English and Hebrew Grammar, Being the First Short Rudiments of Those Two Languages, Taught Together. To Which Is Added, A Synopsis of All the Parts of Learning* (*Grammatica est Janitrix Sapientiae*). By Samuel Johnson, D. D. Late President of King's-College in New York; now Rector of Christ's Church, at Stratford, New England. London: Printed for W. Faden, near Shoe-Lane, Fleet Street. MDCCLXVII [Price One Shilling].

The second edition of this grammar was printed in 1771 in London, "corrected and amended," by the same publisher. It was reprinted in 1776 in London by B. Law. For Johnson's biography, see *Samuel Johnson, President of King's College: His Career and Writings*, ed. by Herbert and Carol Schneider with a Foreword by Nicholas Murray Butler (4 vols., New York, 1929), Vol. I, "Autobiography and Letters"; Vol. II, "The Philosopher"; Vol. III, "The Churchman"; and Vol. IV, "Founding of King's College." See also *DAB*, X, 118-19; E. Edwards Beardsley, *Life and Correspondence of Samuel Johnson, D. D.: Missionary of the Church of England and Connecticut, and First President of King's College, New York* (Boston and New York, 1887); Thomas Bradbury Chandler, *The Life of Samuel Johnson, D. D.* (New York and London, 1824); *Biographical Sketches of the Graduates of Yale College with Annals of the College History, October, 1701*–May, *1745*, ed. by Franklin Bowditch Dexter, I (New York, 1885), 115-17, 123-28; *Extracts from the Itineraries and Other Miscellanies of Ezra Stiles, LL.D., 1755-1794 with a Selection of His Correspondence*, ed. by Franklin Bowditch Dexter (New Haven, 1916), pp. 222-23; Samuel Johnson, *Some Historical Remarks Concerning the Collegiate School in New Haven Now Yale College* (New Haven, 1933); John B. Pine, "Samuel Johnson, D. D., First President of King's College," *Columbia University Quarterly*, I, No. 1 (December, 1898), 1-12; I, No. 2 (March, 1899), 122-34; Adam Leroy Jones, *Early American Philosophers* (New York, 1898), pp. 22-45.

[5] See *infra*, note 29.

[6] On Johnson's early interest, see his autobiography in Schneider, *Samuel Johnson*, I, 3 ff.

the Hebrew Psalter.[7] His tutor there was Joseph Noyes, but in his leisure he continued his Hebrew studies. In later years his philosophical and theological readings induced him to renew his interest in that language and to refresh and improve his knowledge of it.[8] At King's College he taught "Hebrew to such as would learn it." The instruction was primarily intended for those preparing for the ministry.[9]

[7] Beardsley, *Life... of Samuel Johnson*, pp. 4-5; Dexter, *Biographical Sketches of the Graduates of Yale College*, I, 116; Pine, "Samuel Johnson, D. D.," *Columbia University Quarterly*, I, No. 1 (December, 1898), 2.

[8] Johnson was drawn into the antiscientific movement of the Hutchinsonians in their controversy with the Deists and Newtonian physics. See Theodore Hornberger, "Samuel Johnson of Yale and King's College; a Note on the Relation of Science and Religion in Provincial America," *New England Quarterly*, VIII (1935), 378-97. The Hutchinsonians were the followers of John Hutchinson (1674-1737), who taught that the Bible contained the elements not only of true religion but also of rational philosophy and that Hebrew must be taught without vowel points, his interpretations being based on fanciful symbolism. Among the books in Johnson's library were Hutchinson's *Philosophical and Theological Works*. See "List of Books from the Libraries of Samuel Johnson, S. T. D., First President of King's College and William Samuel Johnson, First President of Columbia College," Johnson Collection, in Special Collections, Columbia University Library. Cf. Schneider, *Samuel Johnson*, II, 19-20, in his evaluation of Johnson's endeavor "to make the study of nature subservient to religion," and Norton Garfinkle, "Science and Religion in England: The Critical Response to the Work of Erasmus Darwin," *Journal of the History of Ideas*, XI, No. 3 (June, 1955), 376-88, who states that before 1790, "orthodox opinion then assumed that science and religion were complementary, not contradictory, that scientific investigations would confirm the literal truth of the sacred writings." Hutchinson attacked the scientists in his *Moses' Principia* (1724). Parkhurst's emphasis on the consonantal Hebrew text, and George Horne's opposition to Kennicott's endeavor for collating the Hebrew MSS were due to Hutchinson's views on the study of Hebrew without vowel points. Horne believed that Hutchinson had excelled Newton in his understanding of the physical causes moving the world. See the *Encyclopedia of Religion and Ethics*, VI (1914), 889. According to Leslie Stephen, *English Thought in the Eighteenth Century* (London, 1876), I, 391, "By getting rid of the points, it was somehow possible to make the Hebrew Scriptures mean a great deal, which had occurred to nobody before the days of Hutchinson." He classed Hutchinson (p. 389) among "the whimsical writers, in whom a lawless fancy supplies the place of sound reasoning." Julius Bate (1711-71) and John Parkhurst, both Cambridge men, were Hutchinsonians and authors of Hebrew dictionaries. Johnson, although critical of Hutchinson's obscure language and his strictures of Sir Isaac Newton, was impressed by his work (Schneider, *Samuel Johnson*, I, 30-31). In a letter dated June 25, 1767, to Dr. Robert Lowth, Johnson condemned the extremism in which the Hutchinsonian disputes were carried on (Schneider, *Samuel Johnson*, I, 409-10).

Earlier, on November 4, 1760, Thomas Secker, Archbishop of Canterbury, had written to Johnson concerning Horne, whom we have mentioned above, and stated that he "is, I believe, a good man, but deeply tinctured with Mr. Hutchinson's notion of philosophy and Hebrew, both of which I take to be groundless, notwithstanding a superficial attempt to prove a seeming agreement between the former and Sir Isaac Newton, whom Mr. Hutchinson held to be an atheist." Johnson's Hebrew grammar is without points and follows the Hutchinsonian system.

[9] See "Laws and Orders of the College of New York, adopted June 3, 1755," Schneider, *Samuel Johnson*, IV, 225-29.

During his presidency of King's College Johnson prepared a paper which he desired to be read by the Governors of that College at the next meeting after his death or dismission from the College in which he earnestly recommended to them

> to countenance and encourage the study of Hebrew which I taught to as many as would, as being the mother of all languages and eloquence as well as the fountain of all knowledge and true wisdom, that they may be able to read with understanding these most venerable monuments of the antiquity of man; the Hebrew-scriptures. ... This is now become a fashionable study, and even a gentleman's accomplishment, but is indispensably necessary for all such as are designed to be teaching Christianity.[10]

On March 1, 1763, at a meeting of the Board of Trustees of the College, a plan of education was presented by order of the same Board of November 16, 1762, in the formulation of which the influence of Doctor Johnson's recommendations may be discerned.[11] Among the books listed for study during the fourth year at the College are Hebrew grammar and the Hebrew Bible. At the same meeting Doctor Johnson's resignation was tendered, and at the meeting of the Board on the next day it was accepted with thanks for his faithful service.[12]

Johnson retired to Stratford, Connecticut, and it was here that he began the instruction in Hebrew of his grandson, Billy, the son of William Samuel Johnson.[13] Doctor Johnson affectionately referred to his grandson

[10] Schneider, *Samuel Johnson*, IV, 115-16.

[11] *Columbia University, Early Minutes of the Trustees, Volume One: 1755-1770*, under date of March 1, 1763.

[12] *Ibid.*, March 2, 1763, Cf. Pine, "Samuel Johnson, D. D.," *Columbia University Quarterly*, I, No. 1 (December, 1898), 21-22.

[13] A short biographical account of his grandson, Billy, whose full name was Samuel William Johnson (1761-1846), is found in Dexter, ed., *Biographical Sketches of the Graduates of Yale College... July, 1778–June, 1792*, IV (New York, 1907), 118. He was graduated from Yale in 1779, became a lawyer, and served as a Representative in the General Assembly of Connecticut and as a Judge. The elder Samuel Johnson presented a copy of the psalter-prayer book, which he published, to his six-year-old grandson which bears the latter's inscription, "Sa. William Johnson, his Book, 1767." See Milton Halsey Thomas, "The Reverend Samuel Johnson's *Collection of Prayers* (1759)," Bibliographical Society of America, *Papers*, XLVIII (1954), 416-21, particularly p. 419.

For data on Samuel Johnson's oldest son, William Samuel Johnson (1727-1819), statesman and jurist, see Dexter, ed., *Biographical Sketches of the Graduates of Yale College*, I, 762-64, and *DAB*, X, 131-34. He was graduated from Yale College in 1744 and served as a delegate to the Constitutional Convention in 1787; was a member of the Connecticut Assembly 1787-89, and United States Senator from Connecticut until 1791. From 1787 until 1800 he served as President of Columbia College. In his manuscript "Catalogue of books read from year to year," Special Collections, Columbia University Library, we learn that in 1730, at the age of four, he had read *The Primer* and at the age of five, *The Psalter* and *Catechism*. For genealogical data on the Johnson in his letters to Billy's father, who had gone to England, and reported to him on the grandson's progress in his studies.[14] In the process of teaching Billy, he felt the necessity of preparing his grammar, *English and Hebrew Taught Together*; and it was during William Samuel Johnson's sojourn in England that the elder Johnson negotiated through him to see the grammar through the press of W. Faden in London. Johnson's manuscript of his grammar was brought to England by Mr. S. Giles, a New York schoolmaster, who went there to take Orders in the Protestant Episcopal Church; but, unhappily, on his return the ship was stranded at Cape Henlopen, and Giles and twenty-eight others perished in the waves. A transcript of the manuscript from which the first edition of Johnson's grammar was printed by Faden in 1767 was presented to the author by Giles. The transcript is dated 1765.[15] A second edition, corrected and amended, appeared in London in 1771. Johnson died the following year and the second edition was republished in that city in 1776, four years after his death.

JUDAH MONIS'S HEBREW LETTER TO SAMUEL JOHNSON

About two decades before Judah Monis published his own grammar, in a letter published here for the first time, Monis recognized Johnson's familiarity with Hebrew shortly after the latter's graduation from Yale College by corresponding with him in Hebrew. Johnson then resided in Guilford, Connecticut. Above the address Monis wrote in cursive Hebrew script:

הגבר והוקם על יברכהו ממעל: והעושה שלום
במרומיו הוא ישפוך עליו שלומיו הבחור התורני המשכיל ונבון
כבוד שמואל גֿואנשון החונה בעיר גילפֿורד נר״ו

which freely translated reads:

The excellent gentleman, may he be blessed from above: and He who makes peace in his High places, may He pour forth upon you His [blessings of] peace.

---

family, see Milton Halsey Thomas, "The Bible Record of William Samuel Johnson, D. C. L. (Oxon.) L. L. D., and His Descendants," *New York Genealogical and Biographical Record* (July, 1939) [reprint]. Cf. George C. Groce, Jr., *William Samuel Johnson: A. Maker of the Constitution* (New York, 1937).

[14] On March 12, 1767, Samuel Johnson wrote to his son that Billy "has perfectly learned both his Greek and Hebrew letters," Schneider, *Samuel Johnson*, I, 394, and in subsequent letters sent from Stratford, Conn., to the father in England, Samuel Johnson reported on Billy's progress.

[15] Johnson Collection in Special Collections, Columbia University Library.

The scholarly, intelligent, and discerning youth, the honorable Samuel Johnson who resides in the town of Guilford, may the All-Merciful guard and save him.[16]

The text of Monis's letter is written in square Hebrew characters with vowel points, followed by a brief explanation in English why he writes in Hebrew. We reproduce here the Hebrew text, minus the vowel points, followed by a free translation:

ליד אהובי: האיש נודע בשערים שמו: הבחור הנחמד: המשכיל ונבון: כבוד שמואל ג̄ואנשון נר״ו:

תמה תמהתי מכבודך על ששמעתי איך עברת בתוך עיר ישיבתי
ובבתי [sic!] לא באתה [sic!] כאשר נדרת לבא יום הסכמת [sic!]
של רבי שמואל קוק ובבתו [sic!] [לא באת] וכבר ידעת מה שכתב
שלמה בספר קהלת טוב שלא תדור משתדור ולא תשלם וידוע תדע
שבימי לא עלה במחשבתי שתלמיד חכם כמותך לא תהיה תוכו
כברו ואם כן בתשובתך הת[מ]תה ידוע אדע שמניעתך לא בא
בשבילך אלא מן הטעמים שכבודך רוצא [sic!] להטעים:
ותלמידי הבחור י[ו]סף אוהב הוא לקת צדך ומליצתו לא
ישר בעיני עד שכבודך תשב לי כדין וכהלכה ואם ככה את
עושה [לי] להשמיעני רוח שפתותיך שושנים אז ידע ידעת[י]
שכבודך רוצ[ה] אהבתי ומכלל אין אתה שומע לאו וחיית
ורבית ובכן אין עוד מילה בלשוני רק אשאר בתפילה לאל
חי ואין שנית ברוך הוא וברוך שמו לעד ולעולמי עולמים
שישלת רוחה בככה והצלחה בכל מעשה ידך בתכמה אמיתיית
ולשיעת [sic!] נפשיית היום יום ו׳ וביום י״ט
לחודש אדר שנת חמשת אלפים ארבע מאות ושישה ושבעים
לבריאת העולם וכנגד יום ב׳ לחודש מארצו שנת אלף
שבעה מאות וט״ו:
נאום צעיר דמן חברייה
יהודה מוניש

To the hand of my friend: the man whose name is known in the gates, the pleasant young man, the intelligent and discerning, honorable Samuel Johnson, may the All-Merciful guard and save him:

I was surely astonished by your honor when I heard how you had been in the city in which I reside and that you did not come to my home as you had promised to come on the day of the ordination of the Reverend Samuel Cooke,[17] [nor did you come] to his home. And you surely know what Solomon wrote in the *Book of Ecclesiastes*, "Better it is that thou shouldst not vow, than that thou

[16] Johnson Collection, Columbia University Library. In the margin, Johnson wrote in square Hebrew characters שלום לי מעם יהוה האלהים [Peace is with me from the Lord, God].

[17] In Dexter, ed., *Biographical Sketches of Graduates of Yale College*, I, 28-33, we learn that Samuel Cooke was a member of the Class of 1705 at Yale and his ordination is said to have taken place on February 14, 1715/16 (p. 29).

shouldst vow and not pay."[18] And you surely know that in [all] my days there never entered into my mind that a scholar like you would not be sincere and therefore in your truthful answer I will surely know that your being prevented [from coming] was not due to you but for reasons that your honor wishes to explain. And my pupil the young man Joseph, who is [your] friend, took your side but his defense is not right in my eyes until your honor will suitably and properly answer me. And if thus you do to let me hear from the spirit of your lilied lips,[19] then will I surely know that your honor desires my friendship; and if not, we derive by implication the negative. And may you live and prosper. And so I have nothing else to say except that I will remain with a prayer to the living God and there is no other, blessed be He and blessed be His name forever and unto all eternity, that He shall send you comfort, blessing, and prosperity in all the work of your hands with true wisdom and spiritual salvation. [Dated] this day, Friday, the 19th day of the month Adar, in the year 5476 Anno Mundi, corresponding to the 2d day of the month, March, 1715.
Thus saith the lowliest of the fellowship

Judah Monis

The explanatory postscript, to which we have referred above, is to be found directly below the Hebrew text of the letter.

Sr For Want Inglish Words, & for Want Knowledge in the Greek & Latin Tongue, & to Express my Selfe, & for be Satisfy you Take particular Pleasure in the Hebrew Tongue, I did it in לשון הקודש [the Holy Tongue] Therefore, I do Desire of you to Take it in a friendship way, and please to Answer me in the same. No More onley Ramine in the Meane While, You m^t humble s^t.

Judah Monis[20]

JOHNSON'S HEBREW PSALTER

The first King's College commencement took place on June 21, 1758.[21] The order of holding the commencement, the procedure of admitting candidates to the degrees of Bachelor and Master of Arts, and the

[18] Ecclesiastes 5:4.

[19] Cf. Song of Songs, 5:13 b.

[20] Written at the bottom of the letter in Johnson's hand is the inscription! ועד אמן ברוך אל יהוה לעולם and the Greek translation of the same [Blessed is God, the Lord, forever and ever. Amen. Stratford ye 2nd of Mch 1715/6]. About the time this letter was written, Monis was in New York City, for he had taken the oath of abjuration "upon the true faith of a Christian" shortly before, on February 28, 1715, and was listed as being "of New York, merchant," on the official document recording same, now at the New-York Historical Society Library. Cf. "The Oath of Abjuration, 1715-1716," *New York Historical Quarterly*, II, No. 2 (July, 1919), 35-40.

[21] On King's College first commencement, see Milton Halsey Thomas, "King's College Commencement in the Newspapers," *Columbia University Quarterly*, XXII, No. 2 (June, 1930), 226-27, who reprints the account given in the *New York Mercury*, June 26, 1758, No. 306. See also the *New York Gazette or the Weekly Post-Boy*, June 26, 1758, No. 805, and Schneider, *Samuel Johnson*, IV, 246, 280-81.

formula used have been fully described elsewhere.[22] In the ceremony, we are informed, a little book, a Psalter or Testament, was used. Shortly before Columbia University's Bicentennial was celebrated, the University came into possession of the Hebrew Psalter used by Dr. Johnson in conferring the academic degrees on King's College's earliest graduates. The Psalter was edited by William Robertson of Cambridge, England, and was published in London in 1685. The text is in Hebrew and also contains the Hebrew text of the *Book of Lamentations*. On the last flyleaf facing the inside cover, one finds the following inscription:

> Samuelis Johnson liber, quo in Gradibus
> Academiciis conferendis, uti solet An. Dom. 1758.

[22] Schneider, *Samuel Johnson*, IV, 273-80; the "Formula ad. Gradus Admittendi" is given there on p. 277. The title of the Psalter used by Dr. Samuel Johnson at the commencement exercises reads as follows:

ספר תהלים
הוגה בעיון נמרץ בנקודות ובטעמים׃
עם הקרי והכתיב ואותיות גדולות
וקטנות על פי המסרה וגו׳

Sepher Tehillim
i.e.
Liber Psalmorum
Curâ speciali Editus, cum Punctis Voca-
calibus & Accentualibus; ut &, cum
notis Keri & Kethib, & literis majuscu-
lis & minusculis, secundum ipsas notas
Masorethicas, &c.
Item,
איכה *vel* ,ספר קינות
Sepher Kinoth,
i.e. *Liber*
Lamentationum Jeremiae,
qui scil. (à prima libelli voce,) dici-
tur Echah, tam cum, quàm sine Punctis
& Accentibus, Editus,
à Gulielmo Robertson, A. M.
C A N T A B R I G I A E,
Typis Johan. Hayes, Typographi Academici,
Prostant, verò, venales, Londini, ad in-
signe Bibliorum, in vico, vulgò vocato,
Ludgate-Hill, 1685.

This is followed by the Latin formula used in bestowing the respective degrees, referred to above. The Psalter was already in Johnson's possession in the year 1717. On other blank leaves of this small tome there are inscribed other passages in Latin, Greek, and Hebrew. There is an attempt made by Johnson to reword Psalm 117 so as to establish rhythm in the two verses that make it up as well as an endeavor to write two lines of Hebrew in metric form:

אם נעשה מעשנו כרצון יה אלינו׃
גם הוא יעשה לנו טובה כרצוננו׃

["If we will perform our task as the Lord desires of us,
He also will do good unto us in accordance with our desire."]

Or:

אם נעשה נתנו מצות אלהינו׃
הוא יעשה לנו כל מחמודנו׃

["If we will perform the commandment of our God,
He will fulfill for us all of our desire."]

Judging from another inscription written herein, Johnson also used this Psalter in teaching Hebrew to others, for in it he outlines the order in which biblical Hebrew texts should be studied before the entire text of the Hebrew Scriptures is attempted. He writes: "Let the first Chapters of Genesis and these select Psalms be first well studied with the English translation." Then follows the order in which the Psalms should be studied,[23] until all of them shall have been read. This order of study is virtually identical with the instructions given elsewhere to his grandson, Billy, for whom he had first written his *English and Hebrew Taught Together*, in which he counseled the young son of William Samuel Johnson as follows:

When I am gone you must read these over & over from time to time, to keep fresh in your memory which I have taught you. The Lord's prayer—The Creed—The Ten Commandments, The 3 first Chapters of Genesis and then these Psalms.

This latter manuscript bears the date February 19, 1771. He passed away in 1772.

Johnson's affection for the Psalms can best be appreciated by reading his "Sermon on the Beauty of Holiness in the Worship of the Church of

[23] Samuel Johnson manuscripts in the Columbiana Collection (courtesy of Mr. Milton Halsey Thomas).

England," published in New York City in 1761.[24] He considered the Psalms admirable compositions that had stood the test of time; he emphasized that King David was one of the greatest patterns of true devotion that ever lived and that those who "know the original, are very sensible that no translation can come up to the noble simplicity and grandeur of the original language." On one of the blank pages of his Hebrew Psalter he writes: "See the verses with a line against them in Psalms 103. 36. 73 & 16 these taken together in the order as here set down constitute one excellent Divine Song." The translation of the twenty verses selected by Johnson follows:

1. [A Psalm] of David:
   Bless the Lord, O my soul;
   And all that is within me, bless His holy name.
2. Bless the Lord, O my soul
   And forget not all His benefits:
3. Who forgiveth all thine iniquity;
   Who healeth all thy diseases;
4. Who redeemeth thy life from the pit;
   Who encompasseth thee with lovingkindness and tender mercies;
5. Who satisfieth thine old age with good things;
   So that thy youth is renewed like the eagle. [Ps. 103:1-5.]

6. Thy lovingkindness, O Lord, is in the heavens;
   Thy faithfulness reacheth unto the skies.
7. Thy righteousness is like the mighty mountains;
   Thy judgments are like the great deep;
   Man and beast thou preservest, O Lord.
8. How precious is Thy lovingkindness, O God!
   And the children of men take refuge in the shadow of Thy wings.
9. They are abundantly satisfied with the fatness of Thy house
   And Thou makest them drink of the river of Thy pleasures.
10. For with Thee is the fountain of life;
   In Thy light do we see light.
11. O continue Thy lovingkindness to the upright in heart. [Ps. 36:6-11.]

12. Nevertheless, I am continually with Thee;
   Thou holdest my right hand.
13. Thou wilt guide me with Thy counsel,
   And afterward receive me with glory.
14. Whom have I in heaven but Thee?
   And beside Thee I desire none upon earth.
15. My flesh and my heart failed;

[24] Schneider, *Samuel Johnson*, III, 515 ff.; see in particular pp. 518-19 and p. 526, where Johnson states: "the Psalms are a most copious storehouse of devotion, consisting of an endless and most beautiful variety."

But God is the rock of my heart and my portion forever. [Ps. 73:23-26.]
16. I will bless the Lord, who hath given me counsel;
Yea, in the night seasons my reins instruct me.
17. I have set the Lord always before me;
Surely He is at my right hand, I shall not be moved.
18. Therefore my heart is glad, and my glory rejoiceth;
My flesh also dwelleth in safety;
19. For thou wilt not abandon my soul to the nether-world;
Neither wilt Thou suffer Thy godly one to see the pit.
20. Thou makest me to know the path of life;
In Thy presence is fulness of joy,
In Thy right hand bliss for evermore. [Ps. 16:7-11.]

In his Hebrew Psalter, then, Johnson found twenty verses to fashion a Divine Song, and on Columbia's seal today, a fragment of that song still remains, albeit in Latin translation: *In lumine Tuo videbimus lumen* (Ps. 36:10b).

Moreover, the mastery of the Psalms in Hebrew could not only provide inspiration, but it could at the same time serve a more prosaic purpose—one could simultaneously learn 1,184 Hebrew roots of a grand total of 1,867 pure Hebrew roots found in the Hebrew text of the Bible. In an earlier edition of the Psalms Johannes Leusden has placed an asterisk before 564 verses in Psalms which contained the aforementioned number of roots and which constituted approximately two thirds of all those contained in the Hebrew text of the Bible.[25] Leusden had added a list of references to 546 other biblical verses, arranged according to book, chapter, and verse, in which the balance of 683 roots could be easily found. This list is also appended to Robertson's 1685 edition of *Sepher Tehillim* as well as the system of indicating by asterisks those verses in the Psalter containing the 1,184 roots. It is not to be wondered at that Johnson wrote in his copy of the Robertson edition of the Psalter, after having enumerated the order in which the Psalms were to be studied, that these were to be gone over and "over again with all the rest & then to begin the Bible & read through."

[25] The use of the Psalter as a textbook is emphasized by Johnson in a letter to John Parkhurst on November 1, 1771, where he writes: "I am extremely desirous, good Sir, that you would publish a Hebrew Psalter, with an English translation, side by side with some necessary emendations, as a means for my purpose of promoting these studies in this country, to which it would be very subservient. I am indeed sensible that the historical books are easiest for beginners, and I would wish them to begin with Genesis, but the Psalms are so precious a volume that I would wish soon to go over them, or at least some of the easiest and most instructive of them." (Schneider, *Samuel Johnson*, I, 481).

THE JOHNSON-SEWALL CORRESPONDENCE

The Psalter, as we have indicated, served alongside the Hebrew grammar as the basic textbook of elementary Hebrew studies. The various Hebrew grammars written in England and in America during the Colonial period were prepared in order to simplify instruction in the Holy Tongue. Johnson had found time in his leisure, upon his retirement as President of King's College, to prepare his Hebrew grammar. He sent copies to Dr. Richard Lowth, Bishop of Oxford, and author of *De Sacra Poesi Hebraeorum Praelectiones* (Göttingen, 1758), to Naphtali Daggett[26] at Yale, and to Stephen Sewall at Harvard, among others, and endeavored to elicit from them their views about this pioneer labor of love. He had begun the preface to his first edition with these remarks:

> I have drawn up this short English and Hebrew Grammar together, because those Languages appear to me to be the simplest and easiest, and (as to the Grammatical Structure of them) the most like one another of any that I know, and also from a Persuasion, that as soon as a Lad has learned to spell and read English well, it is much the best to begin a learned education with the Hebrew.[27]

It was after his correspondence here and abroad that, four years later, in the preface to the slightly corrected second edition he broadened his scope. The grammar was not only to serve his young grandson, but as we have indicated above, its author was desirous of promoting the study of Hebrew in America. It is not our intention here to quote *in extenso* from the full correspondence of Johnson relating to this subject. We wish merely to indicate at this point Johnson's awareness of what was being done in the mother country and in the colonies in the field of Hebrew learning, and his efforts to promote the study of Hebrew and to improve his grammatical writing by enlisting the support and criticism of those who could best advise him.

In a letter from London, dated May 3, 1768, Lowth acknowledged the receipt of Johnson's grammar and stated that he had read it with much satisfaction and added:

> It is as clear and full as anything I have met with in so small a compass. I am glad that the study of Hebrew hath made a beginning, and some kind of progress in North America; and I doubt not, that having been so well introduced and still enjoying some patronage and assistance, it will continue to increase, and, in time, flourish.[28]

[26] *DAB*, V, 28.

[27] The 1767 edition.

[28] Chandler, *Life of Samuel Johnson*, pp. 202-3. In Johnson's Library, we find listed Benjamin Kennicott, *The State of the Collation of the Hebrew Manuscripts of the Old*

In the same letter Lowth told Johnson of a great and important literary undertaking and sent him "some copies of Dr. Kennicott's last Annual Account of the Collation of Hebrew MSS. of the Old Testament; to which I have added a few copies of a pamphlet very lately published by the same author," explaining the undertaking and requesting Johnson to "dispose of these among your friends, as you please." In subsequent letters to Johnson, Lowth kept him informed of the progress of Kennicott's work.

Although the Thomas Hancock Professorship in Hebrew and other Oriental languages had been established at Harvard College several years before, Johnson tried to enlist Lowth's support in having a Hebrew professorship established (was he unaware of what was going on at Harvard?); and on May 16, 1771, Lowth wrote among other things:

I wish it were as much in my power as, were there an opportunity, it would certainly be my inclination, to promote your useful proposal of establishing a Hebrew Professorship in North America. We must leave to God's good providence this and many other improvements in that country, and I doubt not of their being in due time accomplished.[29]

From his correspondence with this leading British Hebrew scholar we discern how serious Johnson was about establishing the study of Hebrew on a sound collegiate basis.

As for American teachers, Naphtali Daggett of Yale had written earlier on February 4, 1768, as follows:

I have had the Pleasure of perusing your Hebrew-English Grammar which I conceive to be a very ingenious useful Introduction to those Languages. As to the Hebrew Part, I cannot pretend to be a competent Judge; but so far as my little Knowledge of that Language reaches I cannot discover any Defect in your Gram[r] I return you hearty thanks for your Goodness in presenting us with one of them.[30]

From Harvard came the acknowledgment of Stephen Sewall, who in 1764 had become the first incumbent of the newly established Hancock Professorship to which we have referred above. The text of this communication follows:[31]

Testament (London, 1768), "List of Books from the Libraries of Drs. Samuel Johnson... and William Samuel Johnson, presented to Columbia University... October, 1914," Special Collections, Columbia University Library.

[29] See Chandler, *Life of Samuel Johnson*, p. 206, and Schneider, *Samuel Johnson*, I, 478. For other letters from Lowth to Johnson, relating to Hebrew studies, and the work of Dr. Benjamin Kennicott, see Chandler, *Life of Samuel Johnson*, pp. 202-5.

[30] Johnson Collection, in Special Collections, Columbia University Library.

[31] Johnson Collection, in Special Collections, Columbia University Library.

Cambridge, 28th December 1767

Rev^{d} & Hon^{d} Sir,

I take it very kindly that you have been pleased to present to our Library, through my hands your "English & Hebrew Grammar."—I received it today just as I was going to College to read a lecture on the Chaldee language; so that I have had opportunity yet only to give it a very cursory reading.—I shall take the freedom to peruse it more carefully, before I deliver it to the Librarian.—I am sincerely obliged to every gentleman who favors me with intelligence & advice, respecting oriental literatures; as I am much engaged in promoting that most useful branch of learning.

I was taught the rudiments of Hebrew by Mr Monis. But as he understood but very little of Grammar, I must confess, while I attended his instruction, & studied his grammar only, I never could discover any "form or comeliness" in the language.—Since that I have formed very different conceptions of it.

Mr Parkhurst's Lexicon[32] came into my hands pretty soon after it was published. I liked it so much as to recommend to my pupils; but the price discouraged most from purchasing it. Since that one Mr Pike of London has published a Lexicon,[33] improved, I think, upon Parkhurst's plan. It is comprised in one small 8v^{o} volume, containing, however, all the *Hebrew* words, primitive & derivative, of the Old Testament, explained in all their senses as fully as is done by Buxtorf & other lexicographers. Besides the *imperfect* or anomalous verbs, with their derivatives, are disposed in such a manner, that a learner may more readily find them, than in any lexicon I ever saw before. I have strongly recommended to my pupils, who are now pretty generally furnished with it. It was published last year.

I have endeavored to procure every grammar of reputation I could hear of—Shikhard's;[34] the Westminster Compendium; Doctor Bennett's; Doctor Grey's; that of Mr. Lyons's teacher of Hebrew at Cambridge G. B.[35] Doctor Gregory Sharpe's letters on the same subject &c. &c.—In pronunciation I have conformed to a Pamphlet intitled "The true and ancient manner of reading Hebrew." By John Robertson M.D.[36]

[32] *A Hebrew and English Lexicon without Points* (London, 1762). For list of other editions, see Cecil Roth, *Magna Bibliotheca Anglo-Judaica* (London, 1937), pp. 366 and 368.

[33] *A Compendious Hebrew Lexicon, Adapted to the English Language, and Composed upon a New Commodious Plan; to which Is Annexed a Brief Account of the Construction and Rationale of the Hebrew Tongue.* By Samuel Pike, London. Printed for the author and sold by E. and C. Dilly, 1766. It was prepared "to greatly facilitate the learning of Hebrew" and to aid the student "in investigating the root" (p. 7).

[34] Wilhelmus Schickard, *Horologium Hebraeum*... (London, 1639). For the listing of other authors and titles of Hebrew grammars and dictionaries published in England, see Roth, *Magna Bibliotheca Anglo-Judaica*, pp. 361 ff.

[35] G. B. refers to Great Britain, to distinguish Cambridge, England, from Cambridge in Massachusetts.

[36] We have examined *The True and Antient Manner of Reading Hebrew without Points and the Whole Art of Hebrew Versification Deduced from It Both Laid Down in so Plain a Way as to Be Easily Learned in a Few Days* ([2d ed.], London, 1757). The first edition was published in 1747.

In this the Masoretic points are excluded, & the power of the letters determined from principles, to me quite satisfactory.

You will pardon, Sir, this long letter from an unknown hand. A sympathy of passion for the advancement of oriental literature (so essential-necessary to illustrate the Sacred oracles) which you are pleased to express, has drawn it from my pen.

I am,
Revd Sir
with good respect,
your obedient
humble Servant
Stephen Sewall

P.S. Mr Wigglesworth presents his duty.
Mr President & Mr Winthrop[37] I have not had the opportunity to see. They are both well.
I have never seen Parkhurst's "Easyest Introduction," &c.

Doctor Johnson.[38]

A little over two months later, Johnson replied[39] to this letter as follows:

Stratford Mar. 1. 1768

Dear S^r

(So I write from the Sympathy you speak of) I am very glad Cambridge is in so good a way for improving in the Oriental learning, under the Instruction of a Gentleman so enterprizing & likely to make much proficiency. I hope these things will soon bring us nearer together, & I doubt not but we shall all be one in the approaching millennium: to which the late great attention given in all the Learned World, to the Study of the Hebrew Scriptures, seem, to be leading on.–

Mr Parkhurst's is doubtless the best lexicon to study the Holy Scriptures with. However I am glad of Pike's Abridgment, & have sent for one for my little Grandson. Mr Pike has an excellent knack at Abridging. You have doubtless seen his *Philosophia Sacra*, which is a pretty summary of Mr Hutchinson's Scripture Philosophy.[40] So is Mr Spearman's *Inquiry after Philosophy & Theology*, (indeed better), which Mr William Jones, author of The Catholic Doctrine of the Trinity, late of Oxford, has confirmed by many Experiments, in his *First Principles of Natural Philosophy*. The System of Attraction & Vacuum seem falling before them I wish I could know your good M^r professor Winthrop's Opinion of these Books.[41]

I have seen the Grammar you mention, except G. B.[42] unless by this you

[37] John Winthrop (1714-79), astronomer, physicist, mathematician. He was America's first astronomer and Newtonian disciple according to the *DAB*, XX, 414-16.

[38] This name appears at the bottom of the letter.

[39] American Jewish Archives (courtesy of Prof. Jacob R. Marcus).

[40] Concerning the Hutchinsonians and their philosophy, see *supra*, note 8.

[41] On July 24, 1769, Sewall informed Johnson that "Mr. Professor Winthrop, Sir,

mean Julius Bate. I have also seen your's which is a good Summary of the Masoritical Way. But I believe you are now convinced it is much best to disregard the points. Dr Robertson's Book is one of the finest pieces of criticism I have ever seen: but as to the power of ט, פ & ת, I confess the Septuagint rather prevails with me: however the matter is not much.

That *Easiest Introduction* is not Parkhursts. It is only an easy praxis for young beginners.—Pray tell me what you think of Mr Parkhurst's Opinion, which was also mine, of the great Expediency of beginning a learned Education with the Hebrew, & whether you think any Grammar, published by his Advice, may be of any good use to that purpose or what Improvement you think may be made upon it for young beginners? I find no manner of difficulty in teaching Hebrew to my little pupil, who is but 6½ years old. My hearty complemts to Mr President, & to Messrs the Professors,—I am Sr

Yr respectful Friend
& very humble servt
Sa. Johnson

By my distance from the press my Gramr is defaced by many faults: Some I mended & I have since observed more, wh I desire you to mend.

p. 18. 1. 18. for ז r. ן.
p. 32. 1. 25. after future, insert as.
p. 37. 1. 17. read Infinitive
p. 40. 1. 3. for נ r. ו.
p. 47. 1. 11. for ד r. ך probably there are more.
I wish I had recollected you have types.[43]

From this hitherto unpublished correspondence and from Johnson's inscriptions in his Hebrew Psalter we learn of his solicitude not only for providing sound Hebrew instruction for his grandson but also of his efforts toward maintaining cultural ties with those who participated in furthering and encouraging Hebraic studies in this country. His grandson, Samuel William Johnson, then, would not be faced with the dilemma that had confronted Johnson himself when his interest was first aroused as to the meaning of the Hebrew words in the book owned by Billy's great-grandfather. We should be reminded, at the beginning of Columbia University's third century, that in a southern New England community an American educator, churchman, and philosopher, through a modest pioneering contribution, helped lay the foundation of Hebraic studies in America.

---

is a firm believer in the Newtonian system. It cannot therefore be supposed he would entertain a very high opinion of a scheme so opposite to that as the Hutchinsonian is" (Schneider, *Samuel Johnson*, I, 457).

[42] As explained *supra*, note 35, Sewall was referring to Great Britain and not to Julius Bate, author of *Hebrew Grammar: Formed on the Usage of the Words by the Inspired Writers*. . . (London, 1751).

[43] All these corrections were made in the second edition of 1771.

TYPES OF LECTURES IN THE BABYLONIAN ACADEMIES

By Samuel K. Mirsky

THE LECTURES GIVEN in the Babylonian academies were of various types. First, there were daily lectures on specific topics, intended for the students only. At the conclusion of the lecture, an assistant remained with the students to be *mesayem metibta de yoma lerabannan,* to clarify obscure points and answer any question the students had on the day's lecture. This type of lecture was called *metibta.* A description of this kind of lecture and particularly of the role of the assistant, as delivered in the Palestinian Academy of the third century, is clearly given in Baba Qama 117a.

That the same kinds of lectures were delivered in the Babylonian academies of the fourth century, which were modeled after their Palestinian prototypes, is indicated by the conversation between Rab Papa and Abaye in Berakhot 20a.[1] Since the term *metibta* is usually used in the Talmud in the sense of "an academy," Rashi, in his explanation on the above-mentioned passage, finds the passage confusing and is at a loss to explain it. Nathan of Rome, however, in his *Arukh*[2] correctly defines the term *metibta* in this passage, as meaning "topic." The word *metibta,* derived from the root "j't'v" (to sit), acquired two meanings, one "academy" and the other "session." Thus the statement made by Rab Papa to Abaye in the above-mentioned conversation becomes clear. What he is saying is: In the years of Rab Judah, the founder of the academy of Pumbedita, instruction was limited to the order of the Mishnah which deals with civil and criminal law, while in our time we give lectures in our sessions on the entire Mishnah including the last tractate, *Ukatzin,* upon which we hold *teleisar metibtin,* i.e., thirteen lectures or sessions.

Similarly the term *seyuma,* referring to the function of the assistant as

[1] Also quoted in Taanit 24a and Sanhedrin 106b.

[2] *Arukh, s.v.* j't'v.

mesayem metibta de yoma lerabannan, is used in connection with a lecture held by Raba at the Babylonian Academy.[3] Rashi attempts to relate this term to *pirqa* or *kalla*, but none of his explanations is fully satisfactory. But the phrase "thus said Raba," used repeatedly in this passage, which recalls the exact phrase repeated by the *mesayem metibta de yoma* in Baba Qama 117a, clearly indicates that the reference here is to a *metibta de yoma* (a daily session), and not to *pirqa* or *kalla*.

The second type of lecture given in the Babylonian academies was known as *pirqa*. Lectures of this type were delivered in the synagogue of the academy on the Sabbath, and intended for both the students and the general public. For these lectures, too, the Palestinian academies served as models.[4] The lectures were delivered after the completion of the reading of the weekly portion which followed the *shaharit* service. Although the lectures were given primarily to draw people from neighboring synagogues to worship in the synagogue of the academy, attendance at these lectures was mandatory upon the students. In this connection the incident concerning R. Avia in the Talmud is very illuminating.

Rab Avia grew weak and did not attend to *pirqa* of Rab Joseph. On the morrow when he came [to the academy] Abaye wanted to ease the mind of Rab Joseph [so that he should not be angry with Rab Avia for not attending the *pirqa*] and asked, "Rab Avia [in the presence of Rab Joseph] why did you not come to *pirqa*?" To which Rab Avia answered, "My heart grew faint and I couldn't [attend]." He [Abaye] said to him, "Why did you not taste [eat] something and come?" He answered him, "Are you not of the opinion of Rab Huna who said one is forbidden from eating anything until after he prays the Musaf?"[5]

The custom of delivering lectures on the Sabbath "in order to teach and instruct Israel what is forbidden and what is allowed"[6] was of ancient origin.

Since these lectures were intended for the general public as well as for the students, they could not be pure halakhic discourses, and were therefore blends of halakhic and aggadic material. At the Jabneh Academy we find that it was customary to deliver such a discourse on Sabbath, and that this was one of the duties which fell to the head of the academy.[7] Professor Louis Ginzberg, puzzled by this fact, exclaimed,

[3] Baba Batra 22a.

[4] Berakhot 28a; Hagigah 3a. The synagogue as a part of the academy can be traced back to Jerusalem, in the days before the Jabneh Academy was founded, Pesahim 26a; cf. Tosefta Sanhedrin 7; *Pal. Tal.* Sanhedrin 1.4; *Bab. Tal.* Sanhedrin 88b.

[5] Berakhot 28b.

[6] *Midrash Abkhir*, quoted in *Yalkut Shimeoni*. Cf. *Targum Jonathan*, Judges V, 2; Sotah 49a; Rashi on Mishnah Sabbath 16:1, *Bab. Tal.* Sabbath 115a.

[7] Berakhot 28a; Hagigah 3a.

"Could they not find a greater distinction for the head of the Academy than that he used to lecture before the people's assemblies."[8] This bemusement was aroused in him by the fact that the Talmud Yerushalmi[9] mentions the raising of R. Elazar Ben Asariah to the position of *Ab bet din* and does not mention his right of delivering public sermons, apparently because the latter function was not considered sufficiently characteristic of the office. However, he ignored his own remark, "Can it be that the author of this beraita [in Yerushalmi] overlooked what is stated in so many places: Whose Sabbath this was,"[10] which implies that delivering such lectures was considered one of the privileges of the head of the academy.

It stands to reason that it was not always the head of the academy himself who delivered these sermons. However, the right to delegate another to deliver such lectures at the synagogue of the academy or at any other place designated by the head of the academy was always one of the privileges of the office. Thus even the Geonim of Baghdad, who considered themselves the heirs of the geonic tradition of Babylonia, issued appointments which carried with them the privilege "to expound the Torah in public, and fix *pirqey* and to have a *meturgeman* [interpreter] stand before him, and to precede his *derasha* with the formula: 'Hear ye, what his opinion is'; and followed the sermon with the Sanctification of the Name."[11]

Asaf has already called attention to the similarity between this formula and the statement found in the epistle of R. Sherira Gaon in which the Gaon related the controversy that sprang up between David and Daniel when R. Joseph and R. Abraham served as heads of the Academy: "Then arose the *sheliha dezebura* [equivalent to the *meturgeman*] and announced: Hear ye: what the opinion of the heads of the academy is."[12]

He also indicated the similarity between the above-mentioned formula and the fragment found in the Genizah which reads, "Hear ye, what his opinion is and submit to what he says."[13]

I would add to this that the last part of this statement, "and submit to what he says," suggests that an *halakha* pronounced at a public lecture

[8] Louis Ginzberg, *Perushim on Yerushalmi* (New York, 1941), III, 194.

[9] *Yer. Berakhot* 4:5.

[10] Ginzberg, *Perushim on Yerushalmi*, III, 207. The reference to the "so many places" are: *Tos.* Sotah, VII, 9; *Mekhilta*, Bo. 16; *Abot de R. Nathan*, 18.

[11] S. Asaf, "Letters of R. Samuel Ben Ali," *Tarbiz*, I, 102 ff.

[12] *Epistle of R. Sherira Gaon*, ed. Lewin, p. 111.

[13] S. Asaf, *Ginze Kedem*, No. 4, p. 63.

was legally binding. In view of the legal force enjoyed by *halakhot* pronounced at a *pirqa*, the main feature of the *pirqa*, which would otherwise defy explanation, becomes perfectly clear.

The following two features of the *pirqa* have never been sufficiently understood. Every lecture opens with a question, hence the name *sheelta*, and the phrase *shoalin ve dorshin*.[14] The question often asked and never satisfactorily answered is: why did the *pirqa* always follow this peculiar form and what is its origin? The second feature, which seems to be essential to the *pirqa* and which derives from the first, is the necessary presence of an *amora* (*meturgeman*) stationed beside the lecturer.[15]

The institution of *pirqa*, as I have stated, can be traced back not only to the Academy of Jabneh, but even to that institution upon which the Academy of Jabneh was patterned, the High Court known as the *Bet Din ha-Gadol*, and the synagogue attached to it.[16] The function of this High Court was primarily to expound and interpret laws when requested to do so by representatives of the lower courts. These requests were directed to the High Court in the form of a question.[17] It was the question form which made the reply authentic and binding, for it thus became a directive for practical conduct. The place where the public lecturer sat came to be regarded as a reflection of the place from which authentic instruction went forth to Israel; just as the one sat at the side of the altar, so did the other. Thus it was said: "A master who sits and lectures in public, is considered by Scripture, as if he offered up sacrificial blood and fat upon the altar."[18]

In consequence of this, the public lecture was given the form of the old authoritative instruction. Moreover, the practice of limiting the number of questions to three, which was adopted at Jabneh in keeping with the pattern of the Sanhedrin,[19] prevailed at the public lectures as well. Thus we find that, on the occasion of R. Levi b. Sisi's inaugural public lecture, he was presented with three questions.[20] Even more striking is the fact that the book *Wehishir*, composed on the model of

[14] Pesahim 6a; Megillah 29b.

[15] Gittin 43a; "Rabba son of Rab Huna caused an amora to stand by him and discoursed as follows..." Statements of this kind are found in countless places in the Talmud.

[16] See above, note 4.

[17] *Bab. Tal.* Sanhedrin 88b; *Pal. Tal.* 1:4; Tosefta Sanhedrin, chap. 7; cf. Gen. Rabba 70, and Tanhuma, Bamidbar, sec. *Hukkat*, par. 21.

[18] Abot de R. Nathan 4a.

[19] Tosefta Sanhedrin, VII, 7.

[20] *Pal. Tal.* Yebamot 12:6; Gen. Rabba 81; cf. Tanhuma, sec. *Zav* 5.

the *Sheeltot*, precedes each sermon on the portion of the week by three halakhic questions.[21]

From all of the above, it is abundantly clear that theoretically the privilege of delivering the public lecture, the *pirqa*, belonged to the Nasi in Palestine and the Exilarch in Babylonia. In practice, however, they usually delegated one of the officers of the Academy to deliver, or to arrange for others to deliver, the lecture. The official title of the officers so delegated was *Ḥakham*. Under the presidency of Rabban Simeon B. Gamliel, toward the end of the second century R. Meir was the *Ḥakham*,[22] and in this light we readily understand the phrase, "when R. Meir used to hold his *pirqa*."[23] And this perhaps is the meaning of the statement made by R. Judah in his will that his son Simeon be the *Ḥakham*.[24]

In view of the above we can also understand the precise meaning of a technical term, *Ḥakham methib pirqey*, which otherwise could only be vaguely understood. The Mishnah in Erubin 3:6 states: "A man can set a conditional *erub* and say . . . if the Hakham comes from the East, my *erub* is intended towards the East [so that I can walk beyond the limit of the two thousand cubits and attend his lecture on the Sabbath], and if he comes from the West my *erub* is intended towards the West." On this the Talmud raised the question that R. Isaac stated that the condition is made in reverse, i.e., if the *Ḥakham* comes from the East my *erub* is to the West (the intention being to have a pretext for being legally forbidden to attend the lecture). To which the Talmud replies: "This is no contradiction. The one case refers to a *methib pirqey* and the other to a *makre shemaa*."[25] From the above, we can deduce that the institution of *pirqa* was taken over by the Babylonian Jews from Palestine, and that the person who arranged and delivered the *pirqa* was given the title *Ḥakham*.

In Babylonia, where the academies developed in a more systematic and lasting manner, the institution of *pirqa* also had a more systematic development and a longer duration. They were also more insistent on the attendance of the students and members of the academies at these lectures.

In comparison to the daily sessions of the academy, which were called *metibtin* or *metibata*, attendance at the *pirqey* placed no hardship on the students. While in the former, questions and refutations were encouraged,

[21] *Wehishir* (Leipzig, 1873). It is to be deplored that in editing this book Freimann did not underscore the three introductory questions to each lecture, and generally failed to compare this book and the *Sheeltot* from the point of view of form.

[22] Horayot 13b.

[23] Sanhedrin 31b.

[24] Ketubot 103b.

[25] Erubin 36b; cf. *Pal. Tal. ad. loc.;* see also *Arukh s.v.* Perek (2).

and the heads of the academy were satisfied only with active and critical participation in the day's studies, in the *pirqey*, on the other hand, questions by the students and their active participation in the lecture were actually discouraged. To picture the kind of participation which was demanded of the students in the *metibta* it will be sufficient to quote the known remark of R. Johanan to R. Elazar his student:

"Are you as the son of Lakisha?" he complained: when I stated a law the son of Lakisha used to raise twenty-four objections, to which I gave twenty-four answers, which consequently led to a fuller comprehension of the law; whilst you say, "A Baraita has been taught which supports you!" Do I not know myself that my dicta are right?[26]

The difference between the *metibta* and the public lecture can be seen in the following statement: R. Jannai had a certain disciple who at the daily lectures raised critical points but refrained from raising any critical points at the public lectures of the Festival Sabbaths. R. Jannai applied to him the text: "And to him who ordereth his way I will show the salvation of God."[27]

Equally illuminating in this connection is the comment made by Raba concerning his student Raba b. Liwai who suffered a mishap, "This is [his punishment] for raising questions at the *pirqey*."[28]

There is a passage in Ketubot which has caused great difficulty to all commentators and translators. The passage reads:

What is meant by *ṭayyalim*? Raba replied, "Beney Pirqey."[29] Said Abaye to him, "Those of whom it is written (Psalm 127:2) 'It is vain for you that ye rise early and sit up late, ye that eat of the bread of toil; so He giveth unto those who chase their sleep away'; which R. Isaac explains as referring to the wives of the scholars who chase the sleep from their eyes in this world and achieve thereby the life of the world to come, and yet you say that (*ṭayyalim*) are Beney Pirqey?"[30]

The term *Beney Pirqey*, and thus the entire passage, caused difficulty to all commentators. Rashi, and following him the Tosafists more clearly and elaborately, were forced to resort to a strange etymological explanation to give meaning to the word *ṭayyalim* in this context. The Tosafists stated that the word *ṭayyalim* is derived from the Aramiac word *ṭula*, which means "shade," and explained the term as referring to

[26] Baba Mezia 84a.
[27] Moed Katan 5a.
[28] Pesahim 110a.
[29] See the Soncino translation which renders this phrase "day students" and thus completely distorts the passage and makes it incomprehensible.
[30] Ketubot 62a.

students who live at home.[31] This explanation is unsatisfactory both etymologically, for *ṭayyalim* is a Hebrew word meaning "those who walk at leisure," and contextually. In view of what we have so far established, the meaning of the text becomes clear. *Beney Pirqey* is a technical term, meaning those who attend only the public lectures, used in contradistinction to the *Beney Metibata*, who were full students and attended the daily lectures at the academy. Raba's meaning, therefore, was to compare *ṭayyalim*, idlers, to the *Beney Pirqey*, who were not required to prepare or actively participate in the academy sessions.

Characteristically enough, it was this very feature of the *pirqa* which did not please the students of the *metibta.* They found little profit in attending the *pirqey*, for the halakhic part of the discourse dealt only with such *halakhot* as had already been threshed out in the *metibta* and were presented in a simple form. Consequently it was the aggadic part of the discourse which engaged their interest. This also helps explain the meaning of the known but hardly understood passage in Hagiga: "R. Johanan b. Beroka and R. Eleazer Hisma went to pay their respects to R. Joshua at Pekīn. Said he to them: What was the Aggadah[32] today."[33]

The halakhic part did not interest him for it would add nothing to his knowledge. He therefore asks: What was the Aggadah in to-day's lecture?

For the public, on the other hand, the halakhic discourse, as simple as it was, was usually above their heads, and so for them, too, the aggadic element was the most interesting.[34] The general public was drawn to these lectures, and whether they understood them or not, would run to hear them, as the statement "the reward of the *pirqa* comes from the running to it"[35] implies. For the students and the members of the academy, however, who could not actively participate, by questions and refutation, in the discourse, the attraction was not so great. For them disciplinary measures made attendance mandatory.

Some scholars of Nizunia absented themselves from the Pirqa of Rab Hisda.[36] Thereupon he instructed Rab Hamnuna: "Suspend them." He went and said to

[31] Ketubot 62a; *s.v.* Ṭayyalim.

[32] See the Soncino translation which renders this word as "new teaching." This is incorrect. In this instance aggada is used in its technical sense, as can be seen by their reply which refers only to aggadic part of the discourse.

[33] Hagiga 3a.

[34] See Sota 49a: "On what is the world at large based... on the 'May His great Name be blessed' [which is uttered at the conclusion of] the Aggada." Rashi *ad. loc.* explains that this refers to the prayer pronounced at the conclusion of the aggadic part of the public lecture on the Sabbath.

[35] Berakhot 6a.

[36] Here, too, the Soncino translation mistranslates "session" for the term *pirqa*, and all its implications are not properly understood and appreciated.

them, "Why did you not attend the Pirqa?" They said to him, "Why should we attend? When we ask him something, he doesn't answer us."[37]

Another fact that made the students reluctant to attend the *pirqey* was that they could not, out of respect for the lecturer, leave in the middle of the discourses which at times were rather lengthy. Concerning Rab Huna's *pirqey*, Rab Aha b. Jacob stated: "We were a group of sixty scholars and all became impotent as a result of the long *pirqey*[38] of Rab Huna," and the names of many scholars who suffered thus are given.[39] For this reason, as well as to indicate that their attendance was not dictated by the need of learning something, the practice developed among some rabbis of not occupying their regular places in the academy, but of finding seats at the rear of the hall during the *pirqa*. With this in mind, another term which otherwise cannot be clearly understood is explained.

The Talmud frequently makes use of the term *shilhey pirqey*, for instance, "Rabbah and Rab Joseph were once sitting *beshilhey pirqey* of Rab Sheshet."[40] The Soncino translation renders the phrase "the end of a discourse of R. Sheshet's session,"[41] and bases the translation on the comment of Kaplan in the *Redaction of the Babylonian Talmud*. "The phrase *shilhey depirqey* seems rather to be a technical term denoting a special session at the end of a series of Talmud lectures."[42] Kaplan apparently based himself upon Rashi's comment on this phrase "after he concluded the *derasha*."[43] However, Kaplan confused *shilhey depirqey* with *seyuma demetibta*, which I have explained elsewhere.[44] These are two completely separate and distinct concepts. The *seyuma* refers to the halakhic discourse in the *metibta* and has nothing to do with the *pirqa*, which was a public lecture.

[37] The translation of the Soncino "he cannot answer," implying that Rab Hisda did not know the answer to their question, is incorrect, for immediately afterwards Rab Hisda answered the question put to Rab Hamnuna by the students. It is generally inconceivable that the students should have said of Rab Hisda, the head of the academy, that "he cannot answer" our questions. Their complaints were more probably directed at the fact that questions were not permitted at the *pirqey*.

[38] Here the Soncino translation renders *pirqey* by still another word, "discourse." This is obviously incorrect, for the word *pirqey* is consistently and repeatedly used in the text and refers solely to the public lectures.

[39] Yebamoth 64b.

[40] Erubin 65b.

[41] Here *pirqa* is translated by both words, "session" and "discourse," which is indicative of the apparent uncertainty in the mind of the translator of the exact meaning of the term.

[42] Julius Kaplan, *The Redaction of the Babylonian Talmud* (New York, 1933), p. 257.

[43] Erubin 65b. But Rashi specifically uses the word *derasha* which means a public lecture and not a session in the sense of *metibta*.

[44] See above.

The true meaning of the phrase *shilhey depirqey* seems to me to be indicated by what I have pointed out above. It has to do with place and not with time. *Shilhey depirqey* was the term used by the Talmud in referring to the practice of seating oneself at the rear of the hall during the *pirqa* and has nothing to do with the conclusion of the discourse. That this is the true meaning of the phrase can be seen in a passage in Baba Mezia 64a:

Rab Kahana said: I was sitting *beshilhey pirqa* of Rab and heard him repeatedly mention "gourds, gourds," but did not know what he said. After Rab arose I asked them [the students] what was that "gourds, gourds" that Rab said? They answered me, "This did Rab say: If a man gives money to a gardner for gourds, etc."[45]

From the context it becomes evident that Rab Kahana's difficulty in understanding Rab's discourse sprang from the fact that he was sitting at a distance from Rab and could only hear snatches of what was said. Kaplan's explanation of *shilhey depirqey* as referring to "a special session at the end of a series of Talmud lectures"[46] not only fails to give a satisfactory explanation of this passage but forces him to give a tortuous interpretation of the entire concept:

Apart from attributing to R. Kahana—surely undeservedly—the character of a tardy student, the common explanation of this quotation fails to bring out a plausible story. It will be noticed that the statement of Rab is very brief. The word [*kari*] is repeated in it only once, and if R. Kahana heard this word twice, he must have heard the full statement. The explanation also fails to account for the plural form of [*pirqey*].[47]

It is true that "the common explanation of this quotation fails to bring out a plausible story," but it is just as true that Kaplan's own explanation fails to make the story any more plausible, for two reasons. In the first place, he reads into the passage something that is not found in it and is not called for, "a special session at the end of a series of Talmudic lectures." In the second place, he confuses two separate and distinct matters—the *siyuma*, which applies only to a *metibta*, and the *shilhey pirqey*, which clearly refers to a public lecture.

The only explanation, it seems to me, which allows a clear and correct understanding of the passage is the explanation we have given—*shilhey pirqey* is the term used to designate the practice of scholars, who considered themselves colleagues rather than students of the lecturer, and were

[45] Baba Mezia 64a.
[46] Kaplan, *The Redaction of the Babylonian Talmud*, p. 257.
[47] *Ibid.*, p. 254.

fond of sitting at the rear of the hall during the *pirqey*. The statement made concerning Rab Kahana, that he was one of the two who "needed the teaching of Rab, the reasoning of Rab they did not need,"[48] is further proof that our explanation is a true one. Rab Kahana was one of those who did not need to hear the public, and consequently popularized, lectures of Rab. He attended them only out of respect for Rab, but seated himself *beshilhey pirqey*, at the rear of the lecture hall, to indicate that he came to pay his respects, not to learn. From still another source is the soundness of our explanation affirmed. In categorizing the different types of students who attended lectures, *Abot de R. Nathan* describes one type as "he who removes himself and sits at a distance (from the lecturer) so that people shall say, that one does not need (the reasoning) of the Hakham (lecturer)."[49] Here, there can be no doubt that the reference is to a practice, common among some scholars, of choosing seats at the rear of the hall. Another point buttressing this explanation of *shilhey pirqey* is that it explains still another difficulty which puzzled the proponents of different explanations—the plural form of the word *pirqey*. Their difficulty springs from their explanation of the passage as relating to a single specific incident, which makes the plural form incongruous. If, however, the term *shilhey pirqey* is a technical designation for a common practice, the plural form is perfectly natural and correct.

That there was still another reason for this practice of some scholars of sitting at the rear of the hall is indicated by Rab Joseph's statement: "I was sitting at a *pirqa* and fell asleep."[50]

The institution of *pirqa* underwent a more widespread and intensive development, both in frequency and in duration, in Babylonia, than it did in the land of Israel. There were two prime factors in this development. First, the *pirqa* in Babylonia was grafted onto a well-established earlier Babylonian institution, and, secondly, the political situation which forced the abrogation of the *pirqa* in the land of Israel did not affect Babylonia.

Long before the establishment of academies in Babylonia, the institute of *sidra*, as is well known, was in existence.[51] Though a clear definition of *sidra* is not found, there can hardly be any doubt that it refers to a place where lectures were given on the *sidra*, the section of the Torah designated

[48] Sanhedrin 36b.

[49] *Abot de R. Nathan*, chap. 40 (Schechter ed., version 1, p. 126).

[50] Sabbath 56b.

[51] *Iggeret R. Scherira Gaon*, ed. Lewin, pp. 78, 80 (and Talmudic sources Yoma 22a, Hulin 137b. cited there).

as a weekly portion to be read in the synagogue.[52] With the establishment of the academy in Sura (ca. 242),[53] the institution of *sidra* was transformed, in the synagogue of the academy, into a *pirqa*, modeled after the *pirqa* of the Palestinian academies, while in the other synagogues the institution of *sidra* continued as in the past.

In criticizing Eppenstein[54] for having failed to understand this entire institution when he said that *reshey pirqey* "denotes scholars who worked through a chapter of a Talmudic tractate as against *Reshey Hasedarim* who mastered a whole section of the Talmud,"[55] Jacob Mann was undoubtedly justified. When, however, he declared that *pirqey* were occasional assemblies convened by the heads of the schools or the Exilarchs[56] he laid himself open to the same charge. *Pirqey* were lectures delivered regularly on each and every Sabbath and holiday, and those designated by the head of the academy to serve as the lecturers were called the *reshey pirqey*.

As I have indicated above,[57] this was one of the functions of the Nasi in Palestine and the Exilarch in Babylonia, because these public lectures represented authoritative halakhic teachings transmitted to the public, and consequently they required the official impress of the heads of the community. The Nasi in Palestine, who had less temporal power than the Exilarch in Babylonia, and whose office, in consequence, was primarily one of spiritual leadership, as is indicated by his designation as "lawgiver," opposed to the designation "sceptre" applied to the Exilarch,[58] would more often deliver the *pirqa* himself, though he, too, delegated this right to a *Ḥakham*, who served as the authorized deliverer or arranger of these lectures.[59] The Exilarch, on the other hand, who attained office by

[52] See my Hebrew article "Lesidrey Hayeshibot be-Babbel bi-tekufat ha-Amoraim," *Horeb*, III (1936), 109-24.

[53] *Iggeret R. Scherira Gaon*, pp. 78,80. In 530 Sel. Era, which is equivalent to 219 C.E. when Rab returned to Babylonia from Palestine for the first time. He then served as *meturgeman* to R. Shila, *Resh Sidra*, and returned again to Palestine in the hope of receiving full ordination, in which he did not succeed. Finally he returned to Babylonia and established the academy at Sura, which brings us to approximately 242 C.E. The date given by most historians for the founding of the academy, 219, is based on the statement of R. Sherira which refers to Rab's descent to Babylonia, but this can hardly be accepted, since a number of years elapsed from the first descent of Rab to the establishment of the academy in Sura.

[54] Eppenstein, *Beitraege z. Gesch. u. Literatur im Gaon. Zeitalter* (Berlin, 1913), pp. 18-19.

[55] Jacob Mann, *Texts and Studies* (Cincinnati, 1931), I, 198.

[56] *Ibid.*, I, 196.

[57] See above, p. 379.

[58] Sanhedrin 5a.

[59] See above, p. 379.

virtue of birth rather than on the strength of scholarship, retained the official right of pronouncing authoritative halakhic teachings only through the sanction of the scholars of the academy. In practice, however, he redelegated this power to the scholars themselves.

Only by comprehending this position of the Exilarch in regard to the *pirqa* can we grasp the full import of the phrase *ḥakhamim dibbruhu* used repeatedly and consistently by the author of the chronicle *Seder Olam Zuta*. J. N. Epstein, in his article "Philologisch-historische Miszellen,"[60] marks the difficulty raised by this phrase. He rejects the explanation of Krauss that the phrase originally meant "to allow someone to speak," and accepts the opinion put forth with strong reservations by Lazarus, that the phrase refers to the lecture delivered by the Exilarch at his election. The main difficulty hinges upon the question: Is the term used when one of higher rank introduces one of lower rank, or vice versa? But in the light of what I have said this phrase loses all its troublesome difficulties.

The authority of the Exilarch to pronounce authoritative halakhic decisions in public was derived from the scholars, and he in turn delegated this power to the scholars of the academy. At an annual assembly on a specific Sabbath he would personally delegate this power to the heads of the academy. This illuminates the significance of the report of Nathan ha-Babli describing such an annual assembly under the name of *rigla de-Resh Galuta*.

Nathan ha-Babli describes this event, as is known, in great detail.[61] This celebration began on Thursday and lasted through the Sabbath. Rab Sherira Gaon also discusses the *rigla de-Resh Galuta* and says: "And since the *rigla de-Resh Galuta* was instituted in Mata Mehasia, the heads of Pumbedita had to go there on Sabbath Lekh Lekha, for this was the Sabbath of Resh Galuta."[62]

Thus we see that Sabbath "Lekh Lekha" was designated as the Sabbath on which this celebration took place. That this was the case is reaffirmed by the lecture which discusses the importance of the Oral Law, and especially of the role played by the two Babylonian academies, found in *Tanhuma* at the end of section Noah. This lecture bears all the earmarks of having actually been delivered as it is recorded, at such an

[60] J. N. Epstein, "Philologisch-historische Miszellen," *Monatschrift* (1919), pp. 253-59.

[61] *Nathan haBabli's Report*, ed. Neubauer, II, 84; Ibn Virga, *Shebet Jehuda*, No. 42, ed. Mosad Bialik (Jerusalem, 1947), pp. 115-17.

[62] *Iggeret*, ed. Lewin, p. 81.

assembly. Although found in section Noah, Louis Ginzberg has correctly pointed out that this lecture was misplaced and properly belongs in Lekh Lekha.[63] This conjecture he later substantiated by the discovery of the fragment of *Tanhuma*, section Lekh Lekha, which contains a similar lecture.[64] Why this event, which served as a kind of reception in honor of the Exilarch, was celebrated on this particular Sabbath, however, has never been adequately explained.

At first glance the name *rigla* implies some connection between this event and *regel*, in this case the Festival of Tabernacles. One might perhaps be tempted to identify this event with the one mentioned in the Talmud: "Rab Hisda and Rabba bar Rab Huna, when they came on the *Shabbata de-rigla*, etc.,"[65] on which Rashi comments that they came to listen to the lecture and to pay honor to the Exilarch. There is, however, no basis for such an assumption, for the context of this particular passage indicates that it took place during the festival of Sukkot, whereas the Sabbath of Lekh Lekha, the Sabbath of the Exilarch, occurs three weeks after Sukkot.

Others have been otherwise tempted. On the basis of a geonic responsum[66] some have tried to connect the custom of fasts, known as BeHaB (after the days of the week, Monday, Thursday, and Monday, which follow the festival on which they were observed), with the *Shabbata de-rigla*, which began, as reported by Nathan ha-Babli, on a Thursday.[67] This supposition is extremely far-fetched. In the first place, these fasts were observed after every holiday, not only after the Festival of Tabernacles. In the second place, when the geonim were queried as to the origin of this custom of fasting on BeHaB, they replied that they did not know; that undoubtedly the author of *Halakhot* [*Gedolot*][68] found the custom to be so, but the people as a whole did not accept it.[69] In the third place, the two sources from which we derive our entire knowledge of this *Shabbata de-rigla*, R. Sherira Gaon and Nathan ha-Babli, do not mention any connection between the Sabbath of the Exilarch and the fasts. In this case, at least, the proof *ex silentio* does carry weight.

In the absence of any tenable theory to explain the connection between

[63] Ginzberg, *Geonica* (New York, 1909), I, 5, n. 1.

[64] *Ginzey Schechter* (New York, 1928), I, 18.

[65] Sukkah 26a.

[66] *Geonic Responsa, Hemda Genuzah*, 4 (2).

[67] See S. Krauss's article in *Livre d'hommage Dr. Samuel Poznanski* (Warsaw, 1927), p. 134.

[68] Cf. *Halakhot Gedolot*, Venice ed. p. 40a.

[69] *Ha-Eshkol*, 11, 3; ed. Z. B. Auerbach (Halberstadt, 1867), p. 9.

the Sabbath of the Exilarch and the Sabbath of Lekh Lekha, I put forth the following hypothesis.

The well-known passage in the book *Tanna de-Be-Eliyahu* quoted in the Babylonian Talmud[70] divides world history into three periods, two thousand years of chaos (Pre-Torah), two thousand years of Torah, and two thousand years of the Days of the Messiah. The Talmud then proceeds to clarify the meaning of the phrase "two thousand years of Torah," and to establish the two points in history when these two thousand years began and ended. They conclude that they began in the fifty-second year of Abraham's life, concerning which the Bible states "and the souls which they [Abraham and Sarah] had made in Haran,"[71] and ended one hundred and seventy-two years after the destruction of the Second Temple.[72] What particular event took place one hundred and seventy-two years after the destruction of the Temple is not recorded. This date, however, corresponds to the date of the establishment of the academy at Sura by Rab.[73]

In the light of the foregoing we can perhaps arrive at an understanding of the establishment of Sabbath of Lekh Lekha as the Exilarch's Sabbath. The verse in Genesis 12:5 quoted above occurs in the weekly reading assigned for Lekh Lekha. When a suitable Sabbath was to be selected on which to renew the delegation of authority for the *pirqey*, they found the Sabbath of Lekh Lekha, containing the verse which marked the beginning of the two thousand years of Torah, most fitting and proper. The two thousand years of Torah refer not to a particular event, but to the process of reducing the entire Torah to writing, a process which included not only the reduction to writing of the Law of Moses, the Written Law, but also the *Deuterosis*, the Oral Law, which was reduced to writing by R. Judah ha-Nasi.[74] Considering that the beginning of the process, in the days of Abraham, took place in the land which they

[70] Abodah Zarah, 9a. The author and place of origin of the *Tanna de-Be-Eliyahu* is still a moot question; see the introduction of M. Ish-Shalom to his edition of the book, and the article by V. Aptowitzer in *Jewish Studies in Honor of Kohut* (New York, 1925), which gives a bibliography of the works dealing with this problem. On the basis of internal evidence I believe that the theory giving a Babylonian origin for this work is the correct one. Cf. M. Margoliuth, *Sefer Asaf* (Jerusalem, 1953), pp. 370-90.

[71] Genesis, 12:5.

[72] See Rashi, Abodah Zarah 9a, *s.v.* Ko maeinet.

[73] See above, note 53.

[74] The statement: "From the days of Moses to Rabbi [R. Judah ha-Nasi] we do not find scholarship and office combined in one person" (Sanhedrin 36a) tends also to equate the type and quality of their work. And the further statement made there by Rab Ada Bar Ahaba, "and I say further, that from the days of Rabbi to Rab Ashi

called Babylonia, and that the end of the process, which coincided with the establishment of the Babylonian Academy by their own Aba Arikha who brought with him the Mishnah of Judah ha-Nasi, they felt that that Sabbath was the most appropriate for the celebration of what in modern terms might possibly be called a "charter day."

This theory which I am putting forth may perhaps seem to be too fortuitous to be true, but fortunately the lectures delivered on these occasions which have come down to us seem to bear me out. The lecture found in *Tanhuma* deals precisely with the topic mentioned above, the unity of Oral and Written Law which is implied in the phrase "two thousand years of Torah," and the guiding hand of Providence in establishing the academies for the continuation of that process. What is more, the first *Sheelta* for Lekh Lekha deals with this very same topic,[75] and the introductory lecture of the *Halakhot Gedolot* also deals with the same topic.[76]

From all of this it becomes clear that the description given by Nathan ha-Babli of the lecture held on the *Shabbata de-rigla*, which agrees with the standard form of all the lectures in the book *Sheeltot*, has nothing to do with the installation of an Exilarch. These were annual events celebrated on the Sabbath of Lekh Lekha, and certainly the Exilarch was not reinstalled every year. The lecture described was simply the *pirqa* delivered on the Sabbath of Lekh Lekha either by the Exilarch himself, or by the head of the academy in his presence.[77] In the amoraic period this ceremony was not as yet fixed. Whenever the Exilarch happened to be present, he delivered the lecture, as is found in Yoma: "The Exilarch happened to come to Hagrunia, to the school of Rab Nathan, Raffrim and all the scholars came to the *pirqa*; Rabbina did not come."[78] Similarly it is recorded that "Rab Hisda introduced Rabbana Ukba and he lectured."[79] In the Geonic period, however, the ceremony

[who began to edit the Babylonian Talmud] we do not find scholarship and office combined in one person," conveys the thought that the process of writing the Torah was still continuing.

75 See N. Z. Berlin, *Haamek Sheoloh, ad. loc.*

76 See Lewin, "Derasha beshbah haTorah," *Sinai* (1940), pp. 178-220.

77 Neubauer, *Nathan haBabli's Report*, II, 84: "And the Exilarch begins the lecture on the portion of the day, or he gives permission to the head of the academy of Sura to begin to lecture," etc.

78 Yoma 78a.

79 Beza 29a. According to the version of Rab Zemah Gaon, quoted by Epstein, "Philologisch-historische Miszellen," *Monatschrift* (1919), it should read "Rabbana Ukba the son of the Exilarch," but Rabbana, "our Master," seems to imply the Exilarch himself.

became fixed and traditional. The difference between the Amoraic and the Geonic periods seems to lie in the fact that during the former period the center of authoritative instruction was still located in the Land of Israel and not in Babylonia, whereas in the latter period the Babylonian Academy had become the center. Consequently, during the earlier period the tradition was not yet established. In the Geonic period, however, an annual assembly was held (on the Sabbath of Lekh Lekha) during which a symbolic ceremonial in which the power to transmit authoritative instruction to the public at large (*pirqey*) was enacted. This assembly became known as the *rigla de-Resh Galuta*. The name *rigla de-Resh Galuta* served to underscore the distinct character of this assembly, in contradistinction to the *rigla*, in an ordinary sense, that is, the festival on which the Exilarch or anyone else could deliver a lecture.

The word *rigla* by itself, without any descriptive qualification, means "festival," but by extension it came to stand as the name of the lecture held at a festival. Gradually the term broadened and was applied to any lecture delivered at an extraordinary public assembly, for example, a lecture held at an anniversary assembly called to commemorate the passing of a great man.

> All those *rigley* held by Amoraim were days which were set out of respect for a great man who died on that day, and from year to year, when that day arrived scholars from the surrounding areas gathered to visit his grave together with the other people, and to convene a scholarly convocation.[80]

In the same manner, the annual convocation called to pay honor to the Exilarch and to receive from him the power of authoritative public teaching for the entire year, though it had nothing to do with the festival, was identified as a *rigla*, the *rigla* of the Exilarch.

It seems to me, moreover, that the term *ḥakhamim dibruhu*, used by the chronicle of *Seder Olam Zuta*, was a technical term applied to these *rigley* of the Exilarch implying that the *ḥakhamim* introduced the Exilarch as their head. This is not to say that the scholars recognized the Exilarch as their superior in scholarship. On the contrary, they proclaimed his temporal ascendancy only in order to give sanction to the authorization given them by him. It is in this light that the statement of Nathan ha-Babli, that at the reading of the Torah the Exilarch was called first, but the heads of the academy were not called after him, assumes significance. It was done to show that though the Exilarch was called to the Torah

[80] Yebamot 122a, Rashi, *s.v.* telatha rigley, based on geonic responsa. Cf. Kiddushin 13a, "when Rab Assi passed away the rabbis gathered to compile the teachings they had heard from him"; see also the glosseries of Z. H. Chayes to Nedarim 23a.

first as the head of the people, he was not considered the superior of the scholars. Lacking this context, the statement of Nathan ha-Babli would have no meaning and would be irrelevant to his description of the *rigla de-Resh Galuta*, but with this context the source of the authority of the Geonim is clearly delineated.

It was from these assemblies that the Geonim drew their power and authority. For the very essence of the Geonic authority, as stated by R. Sherira Gaon, was "to establish *Pirqey* and to set *metibata*,"[81] and it was at these annual gatherings with their ceremonials that this right and duty was annually reaffirmed. And thus on every subsequent Sabbath and holiday during the year, the *pirqey* were delivered by designated scholars of the academy, who were given the title of *reshey pirqey*.

In the well-known Novella 146 of the Justinian Code, in which these lectures on the Sabbath and holidays, the *pirqey*, were forbidden, the *archiperiketai* are explicitly mentioned.[82] It has been fairly well established that the name Deuterosis, also mentioned in this Novella, refers to the Mishnah,[83] and that the prohibition issued in the year 553 was directed at those lectures in which the explanation of the Mishnaic texts played an important role.

The lectures took one of two forms, *yelammedenu* or *sheelta*. These two forms I discussed at length elsewhere; suffice it here to say that this prohibition cut short the development of the *pirqey* in Palestine, upon which the Babylonian *pirqey* were modeled, and in the other countries under Byzantine rule, while in Babylonia the *pirqey* continued to exist and develop.

The lectures given in the Babylonian academies, those delivered as study-lectures to the students—*metibata*—and the more popular lectures delivered at public assemblies—*pirqey*—were, so to speak, dismantled, reassembled under proper topic headings, and incorporated in appropriate places in the Babylonian Talmud. Pronouncements originally formulated as part of the *pirqey* are introduced in the Talmud by the technical term *derash*, and countless numbers of such sayings stud the pages of the Talmud. The discourses under the name *metibata* are introduced either by *Tenan Hatam*, or *Itmar*, or *Ibaya lehu*, depending on the point of issue

[81] *Iggeret*, ed. Lewin, p. 99; "And there were years of persecution and trouble at the end of the Persian rule and they *couldn't establish Pirqey and set* metibata and 'midbar' [introduce or conduct] the customary Geonic way."

[82] See discussion on this Novella in discourse VII, at the end of Vol. III of Graetz, *History of the Jews* (in Hebrew); Zunz, *Gottesdienstliche Vorträge der Juden*, chap. 20, n. 133; Mann, *Texts and Studies*, I, 195-99.

[83] Eppenstein, *Beiträge*, p. 26, n. 4; and references listed in n. 82 above.

of the particular discourse. The *pirqey* themselves, however, the public lectures recorded as they were delivered, were apparently lost. The question arises: What happened to these *pirqey*; where can they be found? The answer, I believe, is: In the Book of *Sheeltot*. The Book of *Sheeltot* is a book of *pirqey*.

After the redaction of the Babylonian Talmud the material of the *pirqey* remained in the archives of the Babylonian academies, with a wealth of other material. It was from these archives that the minor tractates of the Talmud, edited by the Geonim but dating back to the amoraic or even tannaitic period in origin, were rescued. And it was from these archives that the material of the *pirqey* was gathered and transmitted, with or without editing, from master to student.

I further believe that the book *Metibot*, of which fragments only have been uncovered, contained the outlines of study-lectures (*metibata*) delivered at the academies during the amoraic and Geonic periods. B. M. Lewin, one of the most distinguished scholars of the Geonic literature, gathered together quotations of terse decisions of law cited in early rabbinic literature in the name of the book of *Metibot*, and issued them, together with the fragments uncovered in the Geniza, under the name *Metibot*.[84] Upon examination, however, it becomes obvious that these two bodies of material are not at all similar. While the former are merely quotations brought in the name of *Metibot*, the fragments of the book itself contain complete outlines of study-lectures delivered at the academies. A comparison between these lecture-outlines and their corresponding discourses in the Talmud will show that there is a direct relation between the outline and the final form of the material as found in the Talmud. The outlines *per se*, if not viewed against the background supplied by the full Talmudic discourse, lack coherence. They partake of the nature of all outline-notes, which are of value to the lecturer but not to the reader. Apparently, therefore, we have in these fragments the original material and form which the lecturer used to shape his discourse in *metibata*, hence the very name *Metibot*. Unfortunately, the fragments do not give us sufficient material upon which to base a definitive judgment, and I therefore put this forward only as an hypothesis.

However, that the *Sheeltot* are a compilation of *pirqey*—public lectures delivered at the academies—there can be no doubt. It seems that after the redaction of the Talmud a book like *Metibot*, containing lecture-outlines of the *metibata*, lost its value. A book like the *Sheeltot*, containing

[84] B. M. Lewin, *The Book Metibot and the Book Hefez* (Jerusalem, 1933).

lecture outlines of the *pirqey* on the other hand, did not lose its value. Although most of the material contained in it had been incorporated and scattered throughout the Talmud, the institution of *pirqey* continued through the Geonic period, and therefore such a book served a practical purpose and filled a need.

Apparently another book, containing lectures similar to the type found in the *Sheeltot*, and which in fact bears the very name *Pirqey*, has come down to us, albeit in a very fragmentary form. When the first fragment of this book was discovered by Solomon Schechter he called it "Halochot in the Order of the Weekly Readings," and called attention to its similarity to the *Sheeltot*.[85] He also recognized that a different fragment published previously by Harkavy was in reality part of the same book.[86] Subsequently Louis Ginzberg published still another fragment of this book, though its true name was still unknown,[87] and Jacob Mann published two more fragments of the same book and recognized that his two fragments and the one published by Ginzberg were all part of the selfsame book.[88] Still later Ginzberg published another fragment which he entitled "Three Responsa of Pirqey Ben Baboi," and reprinted all of the other fragments of the book, to which he prefaced an important evaluation of all the then-published fragments.[89] Despite Schechter's original discernment of the nature of this book as a book of lectures similar to the *Sheeltot*, there was still great uncertainty of the nature of the book. Lewin later published another fragment,[90] which is a direct continuation of the fragment Ginzberg published under the title "A Medrash Similar to Those of Tanhuma Parsha Lekh Lekho," and identified it as a fragment of *Pirqey Ben Baboi*. Contrary to Ginzberg's opinion, Lewin believed that it was a fragment of another book. Lewin was but one step from concluding that *Pirqoi Ben Baboi* was a compilation of the same type as *Sheeltot*, for this lecture on the portion Lekh Lekha deals with the same topic, praise of the Oral Law, as does the first *Sheelta* on Lekh Lekha, and yet he failed to draw this conclusion. Epstein went so far as to suggest that Pirqoi was not the title of the work, but was the first name of its author Ben Baboi,[91] a suggestion which was accepted as fact by

[85] S. Schechter, *Jubilee Book for David Z. Hoffman*, p. 262.
[86] A. A. Harkavy, "Hadoshim gam Yeshanim," *Hagoren*, IV, 71-74.
[87] S. Ginzberg, *Geonica*, II, 50-53.
[88] J. Mann, in *REJ*, LXX, 129 ff.
[89] L. Ginzberg, *Ginzey Schechter*, II, 140 ff. and 504 ff.
[90] B. M. Lewin, "Miseridey haGenizah," *Tarbiz*, II, 396 ff.
[91] J. N. Epstein, in *Tarbiz*, IV, 411.

Aptowitzer.[92] Mann, however, expressed serious doubts of the acceptability of this suggestion.[93] The truth seems to me, with all deference to the distinguished scholar, J. N. Epstein, to have been approached by Schechter in his decision made when the first fragment of this book was discovered, even before its name was known, that we have before us fragments of a book containing the *pirqey* of Ben Baboi, a student of Raba, who in turn was a student of R. Jehudai Gaon.

Sheelta de kalla is a phrase common in Geonic literature. Yet in truth it is an extremely vague and amorphous term, beclouded by doubts and wrapped in uncertainty. We are not sure if the wording is correct, and granted the wording, its meaning is still obscure. Further to confound the issue, two additional terms, *Kalla Zutrati* and *Kalla Rabati*, both in connection with *sheelta*, keep cropping up.

In *Halakhot Gedolot* it is stated, "these are the expositions given by Mar Rab Haninai, head of the academy, in a *sheelta de Kalla*."[94] The reading in both editions of the *Halakhot Gedolot* is corrupt, and three variants of the key phrase are found. One reads *sheelta de Kallakh*,"[95] another *sheelta de Kallah*,[96] and a third *sheelta de Ballakh*.[97] Halevi, in an attempt to preserve both readings of the Venice edition, suggests reading *Kalla Lekh*, which would mean the *kalla* of the Sabbath of Lekh Lekha, and which, according to him, would correspond to the *Kalla Rabbati* mentioned by R. Sherira Gaon in his *Iggeret* which seems to correspond to *rigla de-Resh Galuta*.[98] Sassoon, on the other hand, suggests that the statement of the *Iggeret* itself should be read *Babla*: "The readings of the two versions in *Iggeret*, p. 111, are not satisfactory. I take the right reading to be *Babla Rabbati*, a name used for Baghdad."[99]

In a different place the *Halakhot Gedolot* lists questions put to Mar Rab Haninai Gaon in a *Kalla Rabbati*.[100] The very same material is quoted

[92] Aptowitzer, *Jahresbericht de Israel-Theol. Lehranstalt in Wien* (1933), p. 32.
[93] J. Mann, in *Tarbiz*, IV, 78-79.
[94] *Halakhot Gedolot*, *Hilkhot Bekhorot*, Venice ed., p. 138 (4); Berlin ed., p. 594.
[95] *Halakhot Gedolot*, Venice ed.
[96] *Halakhot Gedolot*, Venice ed., given as another version.
[97] *Halakhot Gedolot*, Berlin ed.
[98] Halevi, *Dorot Harishonim*, III, 95.
[99] David S. Sassoon, *A History of the Jews in Baghdad* (Letchworth, 1949), p. 10, n. 1.
[100] *Halakhot Gedolot*, *Hilkhot Gittin*, Venice ed., p. 78 (3); Berlin ed., p. 325. In the Geonic Responsa *Shaarey Zedek* the reading is "Rab Haninai Gaon put these questions in a *Kalla Rabbati*" (p. 71, par. 6); so too in the book *Ittur*, *Shlishut*, Lemberg ed. (1860), p. 16 (4). Cf. *Geonic Responsa*, ed. Harkavy, No. 312, and *Or Zarua*, Vol. I, par. 724.

in the Geonic Responsa as having taken place in the month of *kalla*,[101] which seems to indicate that the two are identical.

This confusing tangle makes it apparent that if we are to understand the significance of the term *Sheelta de kalla*, we must trace the development of the institute of *kalla*.

I will not enter into a discussion of the etymology of the name *kalla*, concerning which so much has been written. The listing of some sources dealing with this question should suffice for this study. S. Krauss, in three articles,[102] suggests the word *klallim* as the source of the name; B. Halper puts forth the word *kula* as the source;[103] and J. N. Epstein maintains that *kalla* is identical with *dara* (i.e., row).[104] Our prime interest, however, is not in the name, but in the form and nature of this institution.

The origin of the institution of *kalla* is traceable to the economic circumstances of the students in the Babylonian academies which caused the division of the academic year into two "semesters," one ending in Elul and the other in Adar. It was to this that Raba referred when he told his students: "I beg of you, during the days of Nisan and Tishrey do not appear before me so that you shall not need to worry for your maintenance the entire year."[105] But an even more fundamental motivation in the establishment of the *kalla* was the desire to pattern the Babylonian Academy on the Palestinian model. It was this desire that led to the designation of the last month in each term as the *yarhey kalla*, at which all of the scholars who had already left the walls of the academy would gather to hold conferences on a specific tractate, previously assigned.

In the Palestinian academies, from Jabneh to Tiberias, scholars would gather in daily session to discuss those very topics, one after the other, which became the basis for each tractate of the Mishnah. At the conclusion of their discussions they would call for decision, by vote, on each matter, and it was in this manner that the *setam* (anonymous) Mishnah was formed, and the Mishnah, as a whole, was edited. So in Babylonia, scholars would gather for daily sessions during the last month of each semester to discuss a tractate of the Mishnah, comment on it, and arrive at a decision by vote. In this manner the anonymous *gemara*, and the

[101] *Geonic Responsa*, ed. Harkavy, No. 312.

[102] Samuel Krauss, *Hashiloah*, XVIII, 65 ff.; *Livre d'hommage Dr. Samuel Poznanski*, pp. 142 ff.; *Sefer Hajobel, J. N. Epstein* (1950), pp. 125 ff.

[103] B. Halper, in *JQR* (1914), pp. 546 ff.

[104] J. N. Epstein, in *JQR* (1921), pp. 546 ff.

[105] Berakhot 35b.

Babylonian Talmud as a whole, was created. The tractate studied on a particular month was called *mesekhta* (tractate) *de-kalla.*[106]

The difference between the lectures given at a *metibata de yoma*, outlined above, and the lectures given at the *kalla* is indicated by a passage in the Talmud. The former could be given on topics picked at random, while the latter could deal only with the assigned tractate, which all were required to know and prepare beforehand.

The scholars said to Raba: "You, master, are loaned to us." . . . he exclaimed: "On the contrary, you are loaned to me. For I can change you over from one tractate to another, whilst you cannot." But neither was entirely correct. He was lent to them during the Kallah days, whilst they were loaned to him for the rest of the year.[107]

During the months of *kalla* the academy took on its full glory and splendor[108] and most closely resembled its Palestinian prototype. In view of all this, which is quite clear, one may indeed wonder how the uncertainty and vagueness concerning the term *resh kalla* developed. The reason for this vagueness is traceable to the confusion which developed over a passage in Baba Batra:

Rab Nahman b. Isaac was the *resh kalla.*[109] Every day before entering *kalla* he would run through his discourse with Rab Adda b. Abba, and then he would go to *kalla.* One day Rab Papa and Rab Huna the son of Rab Joshua detained Rab Adda b. Abba because they had not been present at the *siyuma.* They said to him: "This matter of the tithing of cattle, how did Raba discuss it?" He said to them: "Thus siad Raba and, thus said Raba."[110]

Rashi explains *resh kalla* as "one who lectures in public on Sabbaths." Halevi, a traditional historian who ordinarily accepts Rashi's interpretation as definitive, is moved to demur in this case:

Were it not for the words of his holiness,[111] I would say that in its simple meaning, this passage does not deal at all either with the ordinary instruction in

[106] Besides the explicit description of the *masekhet kalla* during Geonic times given by Nathan ha-Babli, allusions to it are found in the Talmud itself, which indicates that this was the practice in Amoraic times as well. See the discussion of the minimum requirements for a scholar, in Taanit 15b, according to the explanation of R. Hananel; contrary to the explanation of Rashi, R. Hananel's explanation is undoubtedly the correct one as he drew his information directly from the Babylonian Geonim.

[107] Baba Mezia 97a.

[108] Berakhot 17b.

[109] The Soncino translates this term "the regular preacher (on Sabbaths)." This reading is in reality the interpretation of Rashi which has caused so much confusion. It is hard to understand why the translator did not use the term *resh kalla* instead of reading into the text a comment by Rashi as if it were the text itself, without so indicating.

[110] Baba Batra 22a.

[111] An indication of his high reverence for Rashi.

a metibta. . . . and the words "every day before entering Kalla" indicate that the reference is only to daily lectures and the regular order of study.[112]

In his demurrer, however, he is brought to an even more difficult explanation than Rashi, for he assigns to the *resh kalla* the function of summarizing and explaining to the students the discussions held at the daily sessions, while the passage in Baba Batra talks only of the *yoma de-kalla,* which obviously refers only to the two months of *kalla* and not to the sessions of the rest of the year.

The explanation of the term *resh kalla* seems to me to be very clear, and there is no need for assigning to Rashi an error in so obvious and simple a matter. The first question which arises is, what brought Rashi to connect the *resh kalla* with the Sabbath, when it is clear in the text that the reference is to a daily lecture? To understand this we must keep in mind the two categories into which the lectures were divided, those given during the regular semester, and those given during the special months of *kalla.* Within each of these categories there was a further division of the lectures into two kinds. There were, first, the daily lectures, called *metibata,* which were intended primarily for the regular students of the academy and which could deal with any chosen topic. Besides these, there were the lectures delivered on Sabbaths and holidays, called *pirqey,* which were intended primarily for the general public and dealt with topics found in the reading for that particular week.

The same division applied to the lectures given on *kalla.* Daily lectures, intended for the scholars who had gathered for the *kalla* and the students of the academy, were given, except that they dealt with the Mishnah of the assigned tractate. On the Sabbaths the regular *pirqey* were held, except that in keeping with the special character of the *kalla,* they were accompanied with greater pomp and ceremony. These last were known as the *sheelta de kalla.*

The lectures on the assigned Mishnah were delivered in formal sessions, with the scholars occupying fixed seats, and were presided over by the head of the academy:

And they would gather and come from all the places in the month of *kalla,* which was the month of Elul in the days of the summer, and Adar in the days of winter; and each one of the students . . . [seven rows seating seventy people as in the Sanhedrin].[113]

The division of the first row into seven *reshey kalley* and three others,

[112] Halevi, *Dorot Harishonim,* III, 224.
[113] Report of Nathan haBabli, see *Iggeret,* ed. Lewin, p. 94, n. 4.

equal to them in rank but not in office, can be understood in the light of the arrangement of the Palestinian Academy. There, the first seats were occupied by the seven members of the cabinet who decided the intercollation, and three others.[114] These daily *kalla* lectures were presided over by the head of the academy and not the *reshey kalley*, for the *reshey kalley* occupied the seats in the first row and consequently could not preside over the lectures.

The lectures on the Sabbaths of the month of *kalla*, on the other hand, were presided over by the *reshy kalley*. It is, therefore, clear why Rashi defined *resh kalla* as one who lectures in public on the Sabbath. Indeed, Rashi found it necessary to make this comment because of the very fact that it was possible to misunderstand the passage in the Talmud and assume that the *reshey kalley* presided over the daily *kalla* sessions, which was not so.

The text cited above, concerning Rab Nahman b. Isaac, the *resh kalla*, is, therefore, to be understood in the following manner. The phrase "every day before entering *kalla*" refers not to a daily lecture but to every day on which Rab Nahman b. Isaac was to lecture, that is, on the Sabbath. Rab Papa and Rab Huna the son of Joshua asked Rab Adda b. Abba what Raba had said "because they had not been present at the *siyuma*" for the reason that only those topics which had been discussed and clarified at the daily lectures were presented at the public lectures.[115] They therefore wanted to know what had been discussed at the *siyuma* in order to better understand the lecture which Rab Nahman b. Isaac was going to deliver at the *pirqa*.

In like manner we can understand another passage in which Rashi, consistent with his method, makes a similar comment in order to avoid a possible misinterpretation, and which Halevi again misunderstood, attributing to Rashi an error which is not his.

"Rab Nahman said: we do not serve a summons not to those who gather for *kalla* on *Kalla*, and not to those who gather for *rigla* on *rigla*." On the phrase "those who gather for *kalla* on *Kalla*," Rashi says, "Those who come to hear the lecture every Sabbath, we do not summon him to come on Monday [during which the courts sat] for he will refrain from coming to *kalla*."[116] On Rashi's comment Halevi again says: "We cannot

[114] Sanhedrin 10b; see *Tosafot*, *s.v.* shibah, quoting a passage in the Palestinian Talmud which sheds light on the interrelation, in the structural form between the Sanhedrin and the academy.

[115] These topics seemed to be designated by a technical term, *hilkhot zibur*. See Sabbath 139a.

[116] Baba Qama 113a.

understand the words of his holiness. It seems clear that the reference is here to those who come and gather on the months of *kalla* from all the places."[117]

Once again Halevi misunderstood Rashi. Obviously Rashi was aware of the fact that *kalla* was the time during which scholars gathered. But Rashi was not referring to the scholars, who are hardly the type who have to be summoned to court, but to those who came to *kalla* to hear the Sabbath *kalla* Lecture which was intended for the general public. And it was these people who were not to be discouraged from attending the *kalla*.

It is true that a *pirqa* was held on every Sabbath of the year, but the *pirqey* held on the Sabbaths of the months of *kalla* were outstanding events. Because of the great gathering of scholars, not only local inhabitants attended them, but people from all the country gathered to hear the *pirqa* lecture.[118]

Apparently the greater splendor of the public lectures held on the Sabbaths of the months of *kalla* overshadowed the lectures given on the Sabbaths of the rest of the year, and, in consequence, the latter were no longer referred to as *pirqa* but as *kalla zutrati*—the lesser *kalla*—and the former were called *kalla rabbati*—the greater *kalla*. Thus, too, those who presided over the yearly Sabbath lectures were no longer called *reshey pirqey* but *reshey kalley zutrey*, the heads of the lesser *kalla*, in contrast to those who presided over the Sabbath lectures during the months of *kalla*, who were called simply *reshey kalley*. That this is what happened is proven conclusively by the fact that the very *sheelta* which *Halakhot Gedolot*[119] records as having been delivered at *kalla rabbati* is reported as having been delivered on the month of *kalla* by R. Samuel b. Hofni.[120] The identification of *kalla zutrati* with *pirqey* is also proven by the *sheelta* which is numbered in the printed edition as No. 165:

Rab Hiya b. Abin said: I am of the *reshey kalley zutrey* of Rab Huna,[121] and six hundred scholars would come to him; and when the scholars arose from the academy of Rab Huna and shook out their clothes, there arose such a dust that

[117] Halevi, *Dorot Harishonim*, III, 224.

[118] Halevi, not discerning the difference between the two, asked (*Dorot Harishonim*, III, 224), since the people who attented the *pirqa* were local inhabitants, why did Rab Nahman ask: "Was it for your purposes that I gathered ye people together." But obviously Rab Nahman was not addressing the scholars who gathered to participate in the daily sessions, but those who had gathered for the Sabbath lecture, and these were not only the local inhabitants.

[119] *Halakhot Gedolot*, Venice ed., p. 78 (3); Berlin ed., p. 325.

[120] *Geonic Responsa*, ed. Harkavy, No. 312.

[121] The parallel passage in the printed edition of the Babylonian Talmud does not

it covered the light of day; then they would say in the West [Palestine], the Academy of Rab Huna has arisen.

From the context of this *sheelta* it is clear that the *kalley zutrey* refer to the *pirqey* of Rab Huna, the lectures delivered on an ordinary Sabbath of the year, for this statement of Rab Hiya b. Abin is immediately preceded by a description of the *Pirqey de Rab Huna*.[122]

The title *reshey pirqey* was superseded by the title *reshey kalley*, with the additional descriptive word *zutrey* omitted. The function of the *resh kalla* was to lecture on the Sabbath, and when the head of the academy delivered the lectures himself, the *resh kalla* served as his assistant. This parallels the practice of the *pirqa* on the Sabbath of Lekh Lekha, the Sabbath of the Exilarch; ordinarily, the head of the academy delivered the lecture, but when the Exilarch himself lectured, the Gaon served as his *meturgeman*. Consequently, the *reshey kalley* were always present at the Sabbath lectures, whereas the head of the academy did not always appear. This also clarifies something which puzzled some scholars. In the order of dignitaries blessed in the prayer *Yekum Purqan*, the *reshey kalley* precede the Exilarch and the heads of the academies, an apparent breach of the order in rank, which calls for an explanation.[123] In the light of the above, the reason for this order becomes understandable. Since the *reshey kalley* were always present, they were named first in the blessings, and after them the others, who were not present, were named in accordance with their rank, namely the Exilarch and the heads of the academies. This is still the practice today when offering the prayers of blessing; those who are present are always mentioned before those who are absent, regardless of their respective ranks.

The well-known account of the death of Rabba b. Nahmani reads:

Rabba b. Nahmani by cause of persecution died. They informed against him to the government. They said: There is one man among the Jews who causes twelve thousand people of Israel to evade the Carga of the king: one month during the summer, and one month during the winter.[124]

---

contain the words *me-reshey kalley zutrey;* in examining various MSS of the *Sheeltot* I found that in some the phrase reads *me-reshey zutrey*. The absence of the word *kalley* is apparently the copyists' omission.

122 The two statements, the description of Rab Huna's *pirqey* and the statement of Rab Hiya b. Abin, which come together in the *Sheeltot*, are separated and found in two different tractates in the Babylonian Talmud, the first in Yebomot 64b, and the second in Ketubot 106a.

123 S. Krauss, in *Jubilee Book J. N. Epstein*, p. 131, offers the strange explanation that this refers to the *darshanim* in Palestine. See also the remark by the editors who call attention to the fact that this question, why the *reshey kalley* come first, and his answer, were already given by Rappaport.

124 Baba Mezia 86a.

In commenting on the manner of evasion Rashi says:

> They gather to him in the months of Nisan and Tishrey to hear the lectures of Passover and the Holiday [Sukkot]; and when the agents of the king seek to collect the head tax for each month they are not found in their homes.

All modern scholars, including the traditionalist Halevi,[125] have charged Rashi with committing the obvious error of mistaking the months of Nisan and Tishrey for the months of *kalla*, Elul and Adar. R. Yoel Sirkes, in his glosses on the text, calls attention to the comment of R. Samuel b. Meir in Baba Batra 157b where the months of *kalla* are mistakenly given as Nisan and Tishrey. It is true that R. Samuel b. Meir, commenting on a passage, which is also found in the *Iggeret* of R. Sherira Gaon,[126] dealing with the two cycles of Rab Ashi in which all the tractates of the Mishnah were discussed, obviously the months of *kalla*, did fall into error. But Rashi, who in so many places throughout the Talmud mentions Elul and Adar as the two months of *kalla*, is to my way of thinking not at all guilty of an error in this instance.

At the conclusion of each of the two months of *kalla*, the academy was not suddenly deserted. The many scholars who had gathered for the *kalla* lectures returned each to his own home, and the regular students, who had to find means of maintaining themselves, as we have already noted, turned to their respective occupations, but a different kind of student filled the academy. In the two months following the months of *kalla*, the academy was turned into what might be called a People's University. The general public flocked to the academy during the months of Nisan and Tishrey to hear lectures on the laws of the holidays. Rashi felt that those who informed on Rabba b. Nahmani were not attacking the venerable institute of *kalla*, but were aiming at the custom of giving lectures to the public, in the months following *kalla*, on the laws of the holidays. He therefore identified the two months as Nisan, during which Passover is celebrated, and Tishrey, during which the High Holy Days and Sukkot are celebrated. That this is truly Rashi's meaning and that, furthermore, he is justified in his comment is borne out by the passage which we have already noted above. Rab Nahman abjured the giving of summonses to those who gathered for the *kalla* on *Kalla*, and those who gathered for the *rigla* on *rigla*.[127] He was obviously referring to two separate institutions, *kalla* and *rigla*, which were conducted one after the other.

[125] Halevi, *Dorot Harishonim*, III, 224.

[126] *Iggeret*, ed. Lewin, p. 93.

[127] Baba Qama 113a.

On the phrase *berigla*, used by Rab Nahman, Rashi says, "they came to hear the laws of the *regel*, thirty days prior to the *regel*."[128] It was to this custom of holding lectures on the laws of the holidays that Rashi was referring.

We have, then, evidence for still another category of lectures held at the academy, lectures on the holidays, called *rigley*. There were thus four types of lectures in the Babylonian Academy: 1) *metibata*, 2) *pirqey*, 3) *kalley*, and 4) *rigley*. These are the four rivers which fell later into the sea of the Babylonian Talmud, so that they can now hardly be recognized. Only through tracing them to their origin can we understand the nature of the Talmud.

[128] The phrase "thirty days" is not to be taken literally. The expression is based on the statement, "They inquire and discuss the laws of Passover thirty days prior to Passover' (Pesahim 6a; see *Tur Orah Haim*, No. 429).

A FUNCTIONAL APPROACH TO THE HALACHAH

By Emanuel Rackman

PHILOSOPHERS EXPLORE the Halachic literature of Judaism for its ethical and moral insights. Theologians try to glean from its premises the core of a Jewish creed. Historians examine it for the facts it reveals about the social, economic, and political past of the Jewish people, and jurists analyze its dialectic for unique conceptions of property and obligation. However, many an anomaly which baffles students of the Halachah can best be understood by a functional approach, by asking not what the law is but rather what it did, or what is was expected to do.

Even if the substantive and procedural rules of the Halachah were never more than elements of a speculative discipline instead of an operative legal order, it behooves us to study it functionally, because its norms were meant to be applied and not to remain merely theoretical. One will arrive at distorted conceptions if one ignores this basic premise. For the Halachah is more than a system of rules and values; it projects a legal order and must be viewed within the framework of the legal order it projects.

It is the purpose of this essay to demonstrate, by a number of examples, how this functional approach can help to rationalize unusual Halachic rules. The propriety, for example, of indulging in self-help for the protection of one's legal rights is discussed in the Babylonian Talmud.[1] One may indulge in self-help if economic loss is threatened by another.[2] Even the destruction of another's life or the maiming of his limb is permitted when that other is presently menacing the life of a third human being, not alone the life of the person availing himself of self-help.[3] One may not, however, inflict bodily harm upon another in the course of righting wrongs already committed.[4] Yet in the event of an accidental homicide, Jewish

[1] Unless otherwise indicated, all references herein are to the Babylonian Talmud.
[2] Baba Qama 27b.
[3] Sanhedrin 73a.
[4] Makkot 12a; Maimonides, *Mishne Torah*, Hilkot Rozeah, I, 5.

law permitted the next of kin of the victim to pursue the killer unto death unless the latter sought asylum in one of the designated cities of refuge. One cannot rationalize this exception by blithely assuming that Jewish law indulged in human weakness and tolerated the vendetta. Such a rationalization is neither consistent with Jewish ethics nor with the Halachah's violent opposition to lynch law. Since Jewish ethics insists that only he who murders with malice and premeditation shall be executed, it would seem that the Halachah recklessly endangers the life of the man who kills accidentally. Furthermore, if Jewish law tolerated the hot temper of the blood avenger, as did many systems of primitive law, why was not the same consideration tendered hot-tempered husbands with regard to their adulterous wives, or irate fathers with regard to their daughters' rapists or seducers? Third, Jewish law made it almost impossible to execute even the malicious murderer by outlawing circumstantial evidence in capital cases. How can one reconcile this almost insane regard for the safety of the accused with the wanton abandonment of the accidental killer to the wrath of the murdered man's next of kin? What is more, one authority even makes it a religious obligation (*Mitzvah*) for the next of kin to pursue the killer.[5] This authority certainly did not hold that the Halachah was merely indulging human weakness when it permitted self-help for the purpose of vengeance.

The entire subject assumes an altogether different character when one approaches the problem from a lawyer's point of view—the functional approach. One then begins by asking how Jewish criminal justice was expected to operate. What were its provisions for the apprehension of criminals, the investigation of their offenses, their prosecution, and their punishment? The available sources indicate that the Talmudic scholars assumed that when a murder had been committed, the murderer, whether he killed wittingly or unwittingly, would flee to a city of refuge.[6] If he did not, he would have incurred the risk of being killed by the blood avenger. It would be the threat of the blood avenger that would make the law *self-enforcing*. That threat would solve the problem of crime detection. In the city of refuge the muderer could find peace. He could there confess his crime and thereafter be returned in safety to the site of the crime for trial, although in the trial his confession would be of no consequence whatever. After trial he might be acquitted altogether and restored to his home; or he might be found guilty of homicide by negligence so that he would be returned under safe escort to the city of refuge,

[5] Makkot 11b.

[6] Makkot 9b.

there to atone for his sin; or he might be executed for wilful murder—which was rare, if not impossible. In the final analysis, however, there would be little or no reliance upon a police force or district attorney. The threat of the blood avenger would take their place. It would be he who would set in motion the machinery of crime detection and punishment.

This would be the enforcement pattern in the event of murder. And that the law so intended can be gleaned from the fact that an almost similar system was used to stimulate the return of stolen property. Jewish law distinguished between *Gezelah* and *Genevah*.[7] The former was theft by one who revealed his identity when committing his crime. When apprehended he was expected to make simple restitution. When, however, one stole without revealing his identity to his victim, he had committed the crime of *Genevah*, which might result in a severer penalty—not alone the return of the theft but in addition the payment of an equal sum or triple or quadruple that sum. The Talmud gives ethical reasons why the latter type of thief was punished more severely—he feared man but not God. Even the circumstances for triple and quadruple payments (commonly known as "four and five," including the principal amount of the theft) are assumed to have ethical implications. Commentators, however, overlook the fact that by providing a penalty for the thief who conceals his identity while none is provided for the more brazen criminal, the law is expediting its own enforcement. For any man who commits an act which is subject to a penalty (a *qnas*), as distinguished from simple restitution, can confess to his crime and thereby be relieved of the penalty. He will be thus relieved even if witnesses subsequently establish his identity and prove the crime, so that his confession was not needed.[8] Nonetheless, his confession relieves him of the possibility of paying more than the gain derived from his crime. In effect, this was a bonus to the thief for his contribution to the detection of his own crime.

One may ask whether Jewish law was not indulging in the frivolous when it invited all who were subject to penalty to confess and be relieved of their penalties. Jewish law, however, provided a safeguard. The confession, to be effective, must at least obligate the criminal to some detriment to which he would not be subject without his confession. Otherwise, the subsequent appearance of witnesses might cause penalties to be imposed. To avoid the dire consequences of their testimony, the thief, for example, must at least incur the obligation of making restitution. In one

[7] Baba Qama 79b.
[8] Baba Qama 14b and 74b.

case the detriment might even be to brand his ox as a goring animal, which might later increase his liability in tort.[9] Thus one finds here another instance of the law's concern with its own enforcement and the rationale for an anomalous rule providing a milder penalty for the thief who brazenly leaves a calling card than for the sneak who fears detection.

Another illustration is the use of the oath in civil suits. That the Halachah sanctioned the use of the oath as a form of proof has been cited as an instance of trial by ordeal in Jewish law. Again a functional approach to the Halachah is revealing. The oath was not regarded as a form of proof. If a plaintiff could not sustain his claim because he had but one witness and not the two required by the Torah, or if the defendant had made admissions which gave rise to suspicions, then the defendant was given an opportunity to clear himself by oath from the suspicions arising from his own admissions or from the testimony of the solitary witness. Thus, said the Talmud, all oaths required by the Bible are oaths to be administered not for the purpose of establishing claims but rather for the purpose of clearing the defendant of obligations alleged but not adequately proved.[10] Yet, what was the technique used to guard against perjury? Again the law provided for its own enforcement. Let a man be a proven perjurer, then in any lawsuit in which he might be obligated to take an oath, he would be denied credibility and his adversary—usually the plaintiff—would be privileged to take the oath in lieu of proof.[11] The plaintiff would then recover the amount that he pleaded as due. Thus anyone who would be reckless with oaths would make life intolerable for himself. He would place himself at the mercy of unscrupulous claimants who with proof adequate only to place upon him the burden of an oath find themselves prevailing in their causes by taking oaths themselves, since their victim has been precluded from clearing himself. In effect they acquire this privilege as a powerful weapon against him. This was the essence of the conception of the oath—a means of clearing oneself. The sanction to prevent its abuse was not in the form of criminal penalties, which could almost never be imposed, but rather in the form of a rule of procedure which materially altered substantive rights. That rule was enough of a deterrent to insure the integrity of the man who swore.

It was not unusual in Jewish law to resort to this type of sanction. For

[9] See *Hagoot ha-Gra* on the Rosh, *Baba Qama* I, 20; and Ezekiel Landau, *Nodah Biyehudah*, 2d ed., Even ha-Ezer, Responsum 23.

[10] Shevuot 44b.

[11] Shevuot 44b.

example, a woman who had meager proof of her husband's death might be permitted to remarry. However, if her husband did appear after her remarriage, she suffered a disability exceeding that of the woman who had two competent witnesses to establish her husband's death and who subsequently remarried, only to be chagrined thereafter by the reappearance of her first husband. In the latter case, the woman could return to her first husband. In the former, she could live with neither the first husband nor the second. By imposing this penalty the law sought to insure the fact that she would exercise great caution before acting upon the assumption that her husband was dead. The law eased the burden of her proof in the first instance because it dealt so harshly with her in the event that she was proven to have acted recklessly with respect to her remarriage.[12] The same rationale applied to oaths. One could clear oneself easily, but woe unto him who accomplished it with perjury!

The functional approach to the Halachah is even more revealing with regard to the most famous of the so-called biblical ordeals—the ordeal of the *Sotah*. Let a husband suspect his wife of infidelity; let him warn her in the presence of witnesses that he does not want her associating with the alleged paramour; and let there be witnesses that she violated his wishes—then though the husband could not kill her, he could bring her to the priest who would give her a potion to drink. The results would establish whether she had committed adultery or had been merely indiscreet. On its face this appears to be as unequivocal an instance of trial by ordeal as can be found anywhere. However, the functional approach applicable to our understanding of oaths in Jewish law is equally enlightening here.

The Talmud related the law of oaths to the law of *Sotah*[13] because the *Sotah*—the suspected wife—must take an oath as to what she and her paramour did. Yet, since the Talmud establishes as a major premise that oaths are only for the purpose of clearing a defendant, how can the oath be used to demonstrate the guilt of the woman with or without the potion? The Talmud admits that the failure of the potion to prove guilt is no proof of innocence, for if witnesses to guilt appear after the accused has drunk the waters they are believed.[14] The more realistic purpose of the so-called ordeal, according to the tenor of the Talmudic discussion, is to clear the wife of her jealous husband's suspicions. The law denied him the right of self-help; the Halachah gave him no pretense for vengeance

12 Yevamot 88a.
13 Qidushin 27b.
14 Sotah 6a.

in the name of a "higher law." If the circumstances, however, were suspicious, he could go to the priest who would urge the wife to confess her sin if she was guilty. No punishment would follow other than her divorce and the forfeiture of her property rights. If, however, she was innocent she had naught to fear from the drink. God had permitted His Holy Name to be inscribed on parchment which was placed in water, though He knew that His Name would thus be erased by the liquid. Yet he lent His Name to this abuse that He might be a party to the restoration of marital tranquillity. Therefore, if innocent, the wife was cleared and restored to her now-assuaged spouse. This was the law in operation—not in fact, for the law fell into disuse early in Jewish history—but the law as the Talmud visualized it in operation.

The utterly paradoxical view of the Pharisees with regard to the impeachment of witnesses also becomes more intelligible in the light of the functional approach. If two or more witnesses accused a person of murder and the latter was convicted and executed, the witnesses, when subsequently impeached, were not punished. If, however, they were impeached between the court's sentence and the execution, they must pay the penalty which they sought to mete out to their victim. The Sadducees justly complained that this was unreasonable.[15] Furthermore, one of the Talmudic scholars suggested that there was no reason why the impeaching witnesses should be more trustworthy than those impeached.[16]

The punishment of false witnesses with the same punishment which they sought to impose upon the accused is found in the code of Hammurabi. The rabbis, however, interpreted the biblical equivalent as a limitation, for in the final analysis why should the impeaching witnesses be more trustworthy than the impeached? The Oral Law understood *Hazamah* to mean the impeachment of the witnesses without any reference whatever to the accused murderer or to the victim. *Hazamah* meant the impeachment of the witnesses by reference to their being elsewhere on the date of the alleged murder. In effect, therefore, the impeaching witnesses were launching an independent suit for perjury against the witnesses in the murder action and in such an independent suit the newly accused must bring proof other than their own word. This is the Maimonidean view.[17] But Maimonides does not explain why the punishment of the accused in this new perjury action must be guided by the timing in the murder action that preceded it, so that if the accused in that action

[15] Makkot 5a.
[16] Sanhedrin 27a, and Baba Qama 72b.
[17] Maimonides, *Mishne Torah*, Hilkot Edut, XVIII, 2, 3.

has already been executed, the perjury action must be discontinued.

Yet, from a functional point of view the rule makes sense. Law frequently involves a balancing of interests—sometimes its own. For the proper operation of any legal system it is necessary that witnesses tell the truth and that there be sanctions against perjury. It is also necessary that witnesses should not be deterred from coming forth to testify. To subject witnesses to an unrelenting threat that they may be impeached at any subsequent time would only deter them from testifying in the first instance. Yet to relieve them of all punishment for false testimony would be equally unthinkable. Therefore, the institution of *Hazamah* becomes the lever. The witness is subjected to the threat of a perjury suit but only for the briefest possible interval—between sentence and execution—and only under very limited circumstances—in fact, the most limited conceivable: *testimony about themselves alone with regard to which they ought to be in the best position to defend themselves and obtain proof of their innocence.* A sanction against perjury is established but not one so severe that men will evade their biblical obligation to bear witness when they have knowledge of relevant facts. And so important was this sanction that if witnesses so testified that their testimony was not capable of being impeached by the method of *Hazamah*—e.g., they did not remember dates or places—then their testimony was rejected altogether. If they could not specify dates and places, how could impeaching witnesses prove that they were not at the scene of the crime but elsewhere!

It thus becomes apparent that to understand the rationale of many Halachic rules requires that the Halachah be regarded as a system of law projected for a legal order, and not as a detached body of rules each of which exemplifies no more than an ethical or moral principle. The study of any law—and the Halachah is no exception—requires a functional approach. Otherwise, one misses the very life of the law—its relation to purpose, including the purpose of its own enforcement.

SOME ATTITUDES OF NINETEENTH-CENTURY REFORM LAYMEN

By Stuart E. Rosenberg

THE LAY PROPONENTS of radical Reform in nineteenth-century American Judaism were religious pioneers without a theological program. To be sure, they espoused certain rabbinical platforms and enunciated certain principles of progress. Nevertheless, seen in retrospect, their viewpoints were essentially pragmatic. Facing the new political situation created by their American nationality and citizenship, they had to improvise a new series of responses, as members of a separatist religious community. In this circumstance, it is not hard to understand why one cannot expect them to have been consistent with their own "theories," or, indeed, to have been theoretical at all.

In fact, one basic objection they raised to the traditional Judaism of their forefathers was its theoretical rather than its practical nature. They were children of the new America, fashioned into activists and experimenters by the conditioning of the environment. In the nature of things, classical Reform in America came to be the work of the layman, rather than the result of carefully weighed and neatly polished dialectics of rabbinical scholars. The latter were primarily the weather-vanes of new Jewish society in America. They tended to follow the wants rather than to establish the needs of their people. In a real sense the scholars were the adherents and followers of those whom they claimed as their disciples.[1]

In a way this had to be so. The problem of adjusting their outlook to the American scene was the problem of the Jewish citizen who lived in a paradoxical community. On one hand, he resided for the first time in a democratic community, in which there was official separation of church from state. How then could he justify social separatism, or indeed any separatism beyond the scope of ritual and theology? Yet he understood

[1] This was true of Reform in Prussia in the last decades of the eighteenth century and until the middle of the nineteenth century. It was also true of the first attempts at Reform in Charleston, South Carolina.

that this society was dominated by the Christian tradition, and so, willy-nilly, as a Jew, he remained isolated and even alienated from the total community. This made him aware of the need to seek common cause with his coreligionists even in matters beyond the purely religious. But America presented him with many anomalies. Thus, while he fiercely asserted and believed in his American nationality, he could not completely give up a hold on his ties to the Jewish community. This resulted in a somewhat disjointed approach: radical in its desire to adjust Judaism to American ways of life, yet inconsistent in the practical measures it suggested.

As an example of this ambivalence, we have chosen to examine the editorial policy of the *Jewish Tidings*, a radical Reform weekly which appeared in Rochester, New York, in the last years of the nineteenth century. The editorial comment ranged over a number of interesting areas, many of which still shed light on the dilemma of the American Jew of our day, but most particularly illuminate the problems confronting the nineteenth-century native American Jew.[2]

An analysis of the editorial policies of the *Jewish Tidings* gives us an insight into the searching of many Reform laymen of the period, for it was an independent journal which reflected lay rather than rabbinical thinking. To be sure, the journal quoted rabbis and scholars when they supported the viewpoints it espoused, but it was free from direct influence of rabbis. We detect, from time to time, an attempt at definition and philosophical speculation. Most often, however, it reacts quite directly, in terms of the immediate problem at hand, and with the usual inconsistency that characterizes men of action who try to justify their acts with the rationales of afterthought.

AMERICANISM AND JUDAISM

The late nineteenth century in America was an era of "social progress." This was the time of Bellamy's *Looking Backward* and George's *Progress and Poverty*. The quest for a utopia through democratic social reform was a live issue. It is no wonder that the editors of the *Jewish Tidings*, in common with Reform Jews elsewhere, should have seen the function of Jews as being "in the vanguard of human progress in every sphere," and as sympathizing with "every effort for human betterment." American

[2] Copies of the *Jewish Tidings* were found by the writer in connection with his search for material on *The Jewish Community in Rochester*. The only extant issues seem to be Vol. 1, No. 1 (February 5, 1887) through Vol. 14, No. 26 (January 26, 1894).

democracy became for them synonymous with Judaism. The goal of Jewish religious existence was clearly to be in harmony with the goals of the democratic ideal. Good government, liberty, freedom of conscience—these were the basic fundamentals of the new Jewish "theology." To help achieve these goals Jewish social separatism must be destroyed as best it could. Certainly, in their view, specifically Jewish religious practices were of little help in attaining this hope. They predicted that

> Old customs and ceremonies that hinder Jewish progress are dying out and will, before the century closes be pleasant memories of bygone days. Disagreeable habits and customs that prevent the Jew from occupying the social station he deserves will drop away with his increasing merit, and the American Jew of the future will be a polished and cultured cosmopolitan.[3]

This ambition to help bring about social progress was strongly coupled with the desire to "progress as Jews" by destroying any trace of Jewish distinctiveness. "The Jews of the world have a proper appreciation of what they have done for mankind," wrote the editors, "but they do not glory in the fact that they are a distinctive people."[4]

Nevertheless, they were confronted with a dilemma. While they had no desire to be a people apart on religious grounds—their basic rationale for separatism—they found that America did not always accept them as coequals. There is an echo of frustration in their voice as they wrote:

> Church and state, in this country, are fortunately separated by the sentiment of the people and by the constitution of the land. . . . There is no man of intelligence who will gainsay that these principles of self-sacrifice and personal morality embodied in the teachings of Jesus Christ are of everlasting truth. . . .
>
> The Jewish mind . . . recognizes gratefully all that Christianity has done for humanity's cause. But it rebels, naturally, from having its virtues and faults alike called Christian, and from being obliged in all public places and public occasions to listen to the promulgation of Christian religion. Attention to this matter by Christian ministers might frequently avoid embarrassment to those Jewish people who lend their efforts to the achievement of some practical public measure of charity or benevolence.[5]

They deeply desired to be accepted by a democratic nation which recognized their rights as fellow citizens who differed from the majority only as religious dissenters.[6] The Jews were patriotic Americans, they asserted. This driving force for acceptance was placed by them as "above all things." Defending Jewish patriotism, they wrote:

[3] *Jewish Tidings*, September 24, 1887.
[4] *Ibid.*, November 30, 1888.
[5] *Ibid.*, July 16, 1887; see also February 28, 1890; March 21, 1890.
[6] *Ibid.*, April 11, 1890.

The statement has been made that "the Jew is at home in no country." To a born American Jew nothing could be more aggravating than a taunt like that. The love for home and country is strong and deep-seated and abiding above all else. . . . Who will say that today they [the Jews] are not as loyal and true to the stars and stripes as any people in the great republic?

There is a reason why this love should exist, too. It is not a mere spontaneous feeling but a deep love for home, wherever that home may be, that causes the Jew to adore his country.[7]

They prodded their readers into political action, from time to time, basing themselves on the position that the

Jew should follow in the illustrious steps of his ancestors, who were always foremost in the cause of good government and liberty. The Jewish religion teaches the immortal principle that we should care for the interests of our fellow-beings, and in no more effective manner can this principle be applied than in a participation in all momentous public questions.[8]

Yet they fought the banding of Jews into political leagues on the ground that religion and nationality were distinct and separate. Their apparent inconsistency is revealed in this rejoinder to the editors of the Cleveland *Hebrew Observer*, who had advocated such Jewish leagues on the ground that Germans and Irishmen do so:

That because Germans and Irishmen band themselves into political leagues the Jews have an equal right to do so . . . is an illogical assumption. Does not our esteemed Cleveland contemporary recognize the distinction between religion and nationality? The Jews are such because they are of one religion; worship but one God. . . . There can be no possible objection to German-American or Irish-American leagues for whatever good purpose. But to band together the adherents of one religion for political purposes is wrong and in conflict with the spirit of our institutions.[9]

If, as the editors often asserted, Americans had only one nationality but many religions, by what ideological right could Americans of German or Irish extraction band together for political purposes? They were willing to grant other citizens political rights which they wanted to deny themselves, if only to achieve their desire of not appearing different. Again we note: theirs was not an ideological program as much as it was born of practical desires. And this desire was to rid the Jews of any obvious signs of clannishness. "The feeling of Jewish clannishness existing in the community," they wrote, "will not die out until the Jews themselves cease to show symptoms of it, until by their practice they prove how they appreciate living in a country where civil rights have nothing to do with

[7] *Ibid.*, October 11, 1887.
[8] *Ibid.*, February 26, 1887.
[9] *Ibid.*, September 20, 1889.

religious opinions, and recognize that with regard to political affairs they are only Americans."[10] It goes without saying that Irish- and German-American newspaper editors were not concerned with such desires as these.

"Here the Jews are free; free to live as they please; free to worship as they will; free men in every legitimate sense of the word. That they are good citizens is the universal testimony." These editorial comments give us a clear insight into their dilemma.[11] They worshipped freedom as they would their own God. But to be "good citizens" was an even more important social goal for Jews. When freedom of Jews to "live as they please" seemed to conflict with "good citizenship" they preferred to abridge their own freedom. In this respect they paralleled the history of the early reformers in Germany, who some eighty years before had proclaimed "usefulness to the state" as the purpose and function of the Jewish community and of its religious officials.[12]

ANTI-SEMITISM

The ambivalence which the editors revealed regarding their attitudes toward American democracy and Judaism is found again as one examines their position on the problem of anti-Semitism. They sometimes blamed this failure of democracy on Jews themselves, as when they wrote:

> Jewish isolation is too much on the Jewish side. If Jews themselves would but endeavor to secure entree into good society by merit, instead of waiting to be sought, there would be a great deal less complaint. No man is excluded from the society in which he deserves to mingle, and the statement holds true for the Jew.[13]

Yet they were less than forthright in decrying the social anti-Semitism they sought to place at the door of some Jews. What was the advice they gave to those who felt injured by the shafts of intolerance?

> The *Tidings* advises every Jew to keep away from those places where he is not wanted. There are so many summer resorts in this country where the residents and hotel proprietors are glad to have Jews as guests that it is folly for Israelites

[10] *Ibid.*, December 30, 1887.

[11] *Ibid.*, July 6, 1888.

[12] Israel Jacobson, an early reformer, preaching the wedding sermon at the marriage of his daughter, is quoted as saying: "I want you so to live that people will say 'These parents have reared good children; they have given the state useful citizens.'" See Jacob R. Marcus, *Israel Jacobson*, in Central Conference of American Rabbis, *Yearbook*, XXXVIII, 450; see also *Jewish Encyclopedia*, Article on "Consistory," Vol. IV; Israel Cohen, *Jewish Life in Modern Times* (New York, 1914), p. 272.

[13] *Jewish Tidings*, May 4, 1888.

to cry out against hotel keepers who put out the sign "No Hebrews need apply. . . ."

They did not see anti-Semitism as a problem which required social or political action. In their view, Jews should be careful not to create unnecessary anti-Semitic feelings by improper conduct and misbehavior, but one could not expect the American community, as a democratic community, to do anything about it. Through education, as the only hope, would prejudice against the Jew be eradicated. "The sun of knowledge" would rise and anti-Semitism would "find its grave by the same road as all other prejudices that the world has known."[14] In the meantime, despite their recognition that "there are many men and women who move in the best circles whose antipathy to Jews is made apparent at every opportunity," the best strategy they had to offer was for Jews to sit tight and wait, since "this feeling is rapidly passing away and liberality and a spirit of brotherhood are succeeding it."[15] Again the *Zeitgeist* at work: progress, social improvement, and education were the essence of the new eschatology. Education, not legislation, was the necessary requirement, they felt. This, in spite of their ardor for the democratic system and the citizens' need for political alertness.

ATTITUDES TOWARD CHRISTIANITY

Nonetheless, they considered themselves firm Jews, albeit in a religious sense. At every opportunity they decried the nationalistic approach to Judaism. "The Jews have no national characteristics. There is no Jewish nation," they proclaimed.[16] As Americans they saw themselves as religious dissenters and quite properly recognized room for such dissent within a democratic nation.[17] And as dissenters from Christianity they did speak out forcefully, from time to time, to explain why they held such a position. This is the way they summed up the "differences between the two religions":

> Christianity is essentially an active, proselyting religion, eager for converts and ardent to hold them. Judaism is quite the contrary. No sudden inspirations to join the church seize its believers, nor is its course marked by any attempts whatever to secure converts.
>
> Judaism has no offers to hold out of redemption or of eternal life, secured by

[14] *Ibid.*, April 11, 1890.
[15] *Ibid.*, April 26, 1889.
[16] *Ibid.*, November 30, 1888.
[17] *Ibid.*, May 11, 1890.

belief in doctrine. And it is principally in this that the chief difference finds its origin.

Both religions teach morality and charity. . . . Christianity lays the greater stress upon faith and in its principles. Judaism secures the practice of the two great virtues. A blind faith, an uncompromising faith, in a set of doctrines and in a form of belief, may go hand in hand with a total unconsciousness of religious conviction. But the man who follows the old teacher's interpretation of Judaism, "Love thy neighbor as thyself," is not apt to wander far from righteousness. Christianity proselytes by revival meetings: Judaism by its example.[18]

They were obviously annoyed by the attempts at conversion of the Jews to Christianity and asserted "that Israelites can not be proselyted has been proven by the many unsuccessful attempts, costing many thousands of dollars."[19] They claimed that "of the many marriages that occur between Jews and Christians, it is rare that a Jew abjures his faith. It is much more common for the Christian to renounce his religion than it is for the Israelite to turn his back on the faith of his fathers." And with an obvious show of pride, they added: "The cynics may continue to grumble, but it is an undeniable fact that fealty to religion has not departed from the House of Israel."[20]

Yet there are some noteworthy paradoxes that emerge even in the religious loyalty which they professed. On the one hand they spoke out clearly against Jews who celebrate Christmas, calling these people "weak and squeamish."[21] And yet they quoted with favor a sermon by Rabbi Joseph Silverman of Temple Emanuel who prayed that "Christmas may yet become a universal festival of peace and charity and love among mankind."[22] Similarly, regarding intermarriage, they recognized that "the marriage of a Jew outside the pale of religion is as much the cause of odium and repugnance as it was in the days of our forefathers," yet they did not want to "enter a plea for the law or rather custom, which forbids the marriage of a Jew with a Christian."[23] Indeed, they went so far as to insist that a clergyman had the "duty to marry those who come before him, unless objections are entertained other than those of a religious character. If a Jewess and Christian wish to be united the regard of either person for their creed can not be very high, so what influence can

[18] *Ibid.*, March 26, 1887.
[19] *Ibid.*, July 1, 1887.
[20] *Ibid.*, August 30, 1889.
[21] *Ibid.*, January 6, 1888.
[22] *Ibid.*, December 28, 1888.
[23] *Ibid.*, August 6, 1887; see also April 4, 1890.

wedded life have upon their religion or religion upon them?"[24] Here again we see the lack of a philosophical program. To dissent religiously they had to maintain a religious point of view. But because they were interested in a practical adjustment to American conditions they were prepared to surrender the hallmarks of religious differentiation. This dilemma appeared most significantly in the position they took, in 1891, regarding the conduct of a New York City judge, who because he was Jewish refused to serve on the bench on Saturdays. With characteristic confusion they stated: "Men of all creeds are welcome to become citizens of this country, and to worship on any day they please, but if any of them are elected to public office they must serve on every day of the week except Sunday, or else resign their positions." The New York City press had taken the same position, and the *Tidings* agreed, but went a step further, advising the judge "to perform his work on Saturday."[25]

ON JEWISH CREEDS AND PRACTICES

It is precisely this driving desire to adjust to America and to become an integral part of the country that led these men to reform the religious teachings and practices of Judaism. The editors of the *Tidings*, quoting David Philipson, put the matter quite clearly:

> If the Jew of America has a mission, and he has one, it is this: To remove all past false traditions regarding the Jew; to in every way make himself one with his neighbors; to stand off from them only in his religion.[26]

The *Tidings* approved. "This is no Utopian dream fancy," it said, but "a real, live desire in the breast of every true American Jew."[27]

It was the "spirit of progress and liberality which should be breathed into Judaism."[28] It was the duty of every Jew to "free our religion from ceremonies which still cling to it by eliminating the necessity and cause for which have long since gone by."[29] They had little "use" for *sentiments* which, in their judgment, attached themselves to Jewish religious practices. Concerning the dietary laws they wrote that

> nothing is more amusing than the attempt . . . to refuse the aid of chemistry and of optical instruments to decide whether or not food is fit for the Jewish table. Had the writers of the almost extinct dietary laws been in possession of chemical

[24] *Ibid.*, December 6, 1889.
[25] *Ibid.*, January 23, 1891.
[26] *Ibid.*, February 24, 1888.
[27] *Ibid.*, February 24, 1888.
[28] *Ibid.*, November 22, 1889.
[29] *Ibid.*, November 22, 1889.

knowledge and microscopes, one may safely assume that they would have proscribed every article of food which is today on the table of orthodox Jews.[30]

So it was that their distaste for the Jewish dietary laws found its mark in the attack of the *Tidings* upon Jewish hospitals that adhered to this "antiquated" practice. "Jewish hospitals," they asserted, "which admit patients of every creed ... can not be conducted on the strict dietary principle of orthodox Judaism. It is *impractical* as it is unnecessary to observe the rigid demand of the old law."[31]

The practice of cremation was recommended by the editors since they claimed that "competent authorities have shown the dangers attendant upon burial to the living, and its horrors are more fearful to contemplate by far than those incidental to incineration.... Let us consider the living first, and so dispose of the beloved dead that humanity may not suffer from a sentiment."[32]

By far the greatest attack upon traditional Jewish religious practice was made upon the Saturday Sabbath. For a number of years the *Tidings* led the way among Anglo-Jewish journals in calling for a transfer of the Jewish day of rest from Saturday to Sunday. Their reason is summed up in their own words:

> The necessities of social and commercial life seem to require the day of rest be celebrated on Sunday rather than on Saturday. ... by far the greatest number have chosen Sunday as their day of rest, it can be but a matter of time when all Jews will find it a matter of necessity, as well as a measure of "convenience" to change their day of rest to that of their Christian neighbors.[33]

When it encountered serious opposition, the *Tidings* again fell back upon a "practical" approach by preferring to go slow. It suggested a "temporary" solution: "To have Sunday service for those who cannot attend on Saturday, and Saturday services for those who can conveniently come on that day."[34] It slowly abandoned its passionate attack upon the traditional Jewish Sabbath, but not without a strong impact upon the American Jewish community of its day.[35]

Nor was the practicality of convenience the only motive for abandoning many traditional Jewish religious practices. In addition the writers were impelled by a self-serving practicality. They wished to avoid the label of

[30] *Ibid.*, April 20, 1888.
[31] *Ibid.*, April 6, 1888, italics supplied; see also July 4, 1890; August 8, 1890.
[32] *Ibid.*, May 11, 1888.
[33] *Ibid.*, April 20, 1888.
[34] *Ibid.*, July 27, 1888.
[35] For a more complete discussion of this question see the present writer's "The *Jewish Tidings* and the Sunday Services Question," *PAJHS*, Vol. XLII, No. 4 (June, 1953).

"foreigner." That is why they sought to westernize Judaism. They looked upon the Judaism of Eastern Europe as something foreign and strange to American life. Rabbi Joseph Charif, who was chosen "Chief Rabbi" of New York City, became the target of their wrath, and the symbol for them of all that was distasteful in the "dark" areas of non-Occidental Jewish life. Scornfully they lashed out:

That representative of bigotry, of ignorance and of darkness, Joseph Charif, who was recently chosen Chief Rabbi of the Polish Jews of New York, has begun to assert his authority. . . . What sense is there in importing an ignorant, prejudiced Russian to the enlightened country of America to dictate religious affairs? ... [He] should return to Russia, where his services will probably be better appreciated.[36]

RUSSIAN-JEWISH IMMIGRATION

Yet they could not stand idly by while the blood of their brothers flowed as persecution mounted in Russia. They spoke out, from time to time, in behalf of these downtrodden coreligionists. "Immigration to this country should be encouraged," they recommended.[37] They called upon the "leading men of the community to take the matter in hand at once."[38] But while they sympathized with these people they actually felt estranged from them. Russian Jews "lived in filth" after arriving here. They saw this as a barrier and perhaps even as a deterrent to their own position as Jews in America.[39] As a way out of their dilemma they offered the following suggestion, which gives us a strong clue to their thinking:

This paper takes the ground that colonization is the only effective solution of this problem; that the oppression galled people who fly from the persecution and tyranny of Russia and Rumania should obtain a haven of peace and protection in the far West, the untilled soil of which is welcome to their cultivation. The swarms of people who throng New York and who eke out a wretched existence by the pursuit of small trade and other precarious modes of making a living should be taken to the West, there to live in peace, prosperity and happiness by their own exertions.[40]

Again, it is not difficult to see how vexed they were with the practical problems entailed in maintaining their position in the American community. These foreign Jews were a challenge to their merciful impulses. But they were also a threat to the achievement of the goal of a Jewish

[36] *Jewish Tidings*, August 10, 17, 1888.
[37] *Ibid.*, April 23, 1887.
[38] *Ibid.*, April 27, 1888.
[39] *Ibid.*, July 18, 1890.
[40] *Ibid.*, April 16, 1887.

community in America which resembled the larger community in its mores, customs, and outlook and differed only in theological matters.

Undoubtedly it was such a motivation that led them to decry the activity in America of the "Lovers of Zion." When such an organization was established in Pittsburgh, they chided the movement in these words:

Such foolish action is to be deplored. What possible charms residence in Jerusalem can have for American Jews it is hard to say. The sensible Jews of today have no desire to return to Palestine; those that live in civilization are satisfied to remain where they are. . . . It is childish and absurd for any person to agitate the removal of the Jews to Palestine. What possible inducement can there be for such a step?[41]

It would be hard to improve their condition in this country.[42]

CONCLUSION

Life is stronger than logic. And the life of the broader community in which these Reform laymen lived had not as yet developed a recognizable pattern of culture which could be denominated as American. One should not, therefore, expect that they could have developed a tightly-knit program ruled by consistency. Perhaps the saving of this community consisted in just this fact, that they were not so inflexible as to have their attitudes frozen into a fixed viewpoint. In a situation so new for them, had they then been doctrinaire rather than pragmatic the Procrustean bed might have become their deathbed as Jews in America.

But the Reform movement in the twentieth century has been victimized by its earlier history. In some respects it has continued its pragmatic approach to the problems created by modern American and Jewish life. In others, it has tended to crystallize its program too soon, hardening into a new orthodoxy the attitudes developed in response to nineteenth-century American conditions. But one wonders how long it can continue with such an approach. For many of the questions it faced no longer exist, and many of its most ardent answers are themselves no longer relevant nor even practically sound.

Has the time come when Reform must retrace its steps by looking at Jewish experience in America from the eyes of contemporary observers and by reevaluating its needs from that point of view? After all, the theme of nineteenth-century Reform was the Americanization of the Jew. Does it not seem clear that the new need is the Judaization of the American Jew?

[41] *Ibid.*, October 18, 1889.
[42] *Ibid.*, July 27, 1888.

ON THE CULTURAL HISTORY OF YIDDISH RIME

By Uriel Weinreich

YIDDISH POETRY RANKS among the outstanding cultural accomplishments of the Jewish people. It expresses traditional themes as well as individual Jewish experience through literary techniques both inherited and more recently adopted; in so doing it explores and exploits in full the structural originality and the esthetic possibilities inherent in the Yiddish language. The history of Yiddish poetry is the typical history of all Jewish culture: the never-ending creative innovation of the heritage.

When this body of writing is analyzed not as philosophy or ideology, but specifically as poetry, one is struck by various of its technical aspects. Its word coinages, for example, have brought to fruition the many enrichment patterns available in Yiddish; its rhythmic diversity has been progressively attuned to the sound and stress organization of the language. Even the form of its rimes has not remained inflexible: here, too, Yiddish poetry has sought to incorporate the achievements of other literatures while feeling out the individuality of its own linguistic medium. It is the purpose of this paper to set the problem of rime in the larger comparative framework which Benjamin Hrushovski, of the Hebrew University, has just so brilliantly erected for the study of Yiddish poetic rhythm.[1]

Since my task is only orientational, I have cited examples from many authors sometimes at random, and have simplified the identification of sources as much as possible, often dispensing with the titles of poems and quoting from collected volumes or even from anthologies rather than from journals where the same poems might have been published for the

[1] Benjamin Hrushovski, "On Free Rhythms in Yiddish Poetry," in *The Field of Yiddish: Studies in Yiddish Language, Folklore and Literature Published on the Occasion of the Bicentennial of Columbia University* (New York, 1954), pp. 219-66. For an over-all sketch of Yiddish poetry, see now U. Weinreich, "Yiddish Poetry," in *A Dictionary of Poetry and Poetics*, ed. Alex Preminger and Frank J. Warnke (New York, 1957).

first time. When the identity of the author is of subordinate importance, I abbreviate his name to an initial.[2]

I have not tried, on the whole, to evaluate the effectiveness of particular rimes in particular poems. It is rather the over-all riming possibilities and limitations inherent in the Yiddish language and its changing poetic conventions that are discussed. Also, digressions into problems of poetic vocabulary in general have been avoided. To be sure, when the state name *Arizone* is rimed with a traditional word like *kavone* 'intention' (L 227), some readers may be impressed by the American local color of the poem; the appearance of a bold new coinage like *akhzerayen*[3] 'cruel acts' riming with the ordinary word *klezayen* 'arms' (L 226) reflects modern Yiddish poetry's penchant for neologisms; while the riming of plain *klyamkes* 'doorknobs' with so choice a word as *amkes* 'profundity' (L 55, 136) illustrates the absorption by Yiddish poetry of the intellectual vocabulary of traditional Jewish scholarship and philosophy. But in all these cases the rimes only highlight lexical processes which are equally prevalent in the rimeless interior of lines, away from the conspicuous line ending. This paper, on the other hand, concentrates on the riming relationship as such.

RIME AND LINGUISTIC FUSION

The riming possibilities of poetry are determined by two factors: the stock of words in the language and the conventions on what constitutes

[2] The following abbreviations are used: **B** = M. Basin, *Antologye; 500 yor yidishe poezye* (New York, 1917), Vols. I and II; **C** = Y.-L. Cahan, *Yidishe folkslider* (New York, 1912), Vols. I and II; **Gl** = Yankev Glatshteyn (Glatstein), *Gedenklider* (New York, 1943); **GlF** = *idem*, *Fraye ferzn* (New York, 1926); **GM** = S. M. Ginzburg and P. S. Marek, *Jevrejskije narodnyje pesni v Rossii* (St. Petersburg, 1901); **Gr** = Khaim Grade, *Shayn fun farloshene shtern* (Buenos Aires, 1950); **GM** = *idem*, *Der mames tsavoe* (New York, 1949); **K** = Moyshe Kulbak, *Geklibene verk* (New York, 1953); **L** = A. Leyeles, *A yid oyfn yam* (New York, 1947); **LF** = *idem*, *Fanye* (New York, 1954); **LFL** = *idem*, *Fabyus Lind* (New York, 1937); **Li** = Mikhl Likht, *Letste lider* (Buenos Aires, 1954); **Lk** = *Ale verk fun H. Leyvik* [Leivick] (New York, 1940), Vol. I; **Ma** = Itsik Manger, *Lid un balade* (New York, 1952); **MaM** = *idem*, *Medresh Itsik* (Paris, 1951); **Mk** = Perets Markish, *Stam* (3d ed., Warsaw, 1922); **N** = Leyb Naydus, *Litvishe arabeskn* (Warsaw, 1924); **Sb** = Eliezer Shteynbarg (Steinbarg), *Mesholim* (2d ed., Bucharest, 1935); **Sf** = Nokhem Shtif, *Di eltere yidishe literatur* (Kiev, 1929); **Su** = Avrohom Sutskever, *In-fayer-vogn* (Tel Aviv, 1952); **SuV** = *idem*, *Valdiks* (Vilna, 1940); **Y** = Yehoyosh (Yehoash), *Fablen* (New York, 1912). Number following initial refers to the page; e.g., Sb 99 = Shteynbarg, p. 99.

[3] Formed by adding the suffix *-ay* to the existing word, *akhzer* 'tyrant,' on the model of the existing *khazeráy* 'filth; contemptible act' (from *khazer* 'swine'). Yiddish forms are cited in the widely used YIVO transcription, in which *y* corresponds to the sound

an adequate rime. Let us for the moment accept the narrowest view of rime as repetition of sounds, usually at the end of a verse, beginning with the last stressed vowel and including all that follows it. Within this definition, then, the riming possibilities of a language depend on the existence of words of similar terminations.

Evidently the rime resources of Yiddish have benefited from the fusion history of the language.[4] Each stock language has contributed rime schemes to Yiddish which do not exist in the other stock languages: for example, all Yiddish rimes in *-ovim* listed by Stutchkoff's Rime Lexicon[5] are of the Hebrew component of the language ("Hebrew" here is an abbreviation for "rabbinical Hebrew-Aramaic," or, in Yiddish terms, for *loshn-koydesh*); all rimes in *-enye* are of Slavic origin; rimes in *-ukhe* are of mixed Slavic and Hebrew descent, but not Germanic. Even more characteristic of Yiddish fusion are the rime schemes to which all major stock languages have given their share; these may well hold a majority. When we find poems riming *fakh* 'layer': *shlyakh* 'highway': *tanákh* 'Bible' (L 195) or *svore* 'supposition': *nore* 'den': *vore* 'true' (L 41), we have the fusion history of the language manifested in actual poetic practice. (In the first trio, the rime words are of Germanic, Slavic, and Hebrew origin, respectively; in the second, the order is Hebrew, Slavic, Germanic.)

A comparison of the rime schemes of Yiddish with those of the stock languages should prove rewarding. For example, when we compare the Yiddish *-akh* scheme with the German *-ach* and *-ache*,[6] we find that Yiddish lacks cognates of a number of German words (e.g., *brach* 'fallow,' *Drache* 'dragon,' *Rache* 'revenge'), but has about a dozen words of Hebrew origin (e.g., *krakh* 'large city,' *shvakh* 'praise,' etc.) and three or four words of Slavic origin (e.g., *monákh* 'monk,' *lyakh* 'Lachite, Pole') which German lacks. *Mensch* is a notorious example of a German word which has no rime altogether;[7] Yiddish *mentsh*, on the other hand, rimes both with *bentsh* 'bless,' contributed by Southern Loez (medieval

---

y of English *yes;* consequently *ay* stands for a diphthong similar to that of English *my*, and *ey* for a diphthong similar to that of English *day*. *Zh* corresponds to the *s* of *measure*, while *kh* is similar to the German *ach* sound. The stress falls on the next-to-last syllable of a word except where otherwise indicated by a stress mark (e.g., *kávene*).

[4] On the fusion character of Yiddish, its components, and its relation to the stock languages, see Max Weinreich, "Prehistory and Early History of Yiddish: Facts and Conceptual Framework," in *The Field of Yiddish*, pp. 73-101.

[5] N[okhem] Stutchkoff, *Yidisher gramen-leksikon* (New York, 1931).

[6] Willy Steputat, *Deutsches Reimlexikon* (Leipzig, n.d.).

[7] Solutions to this dilemma by rimesters of various degrees of seriousness are discussed

Judaeo-Italian)—a hackneyed rime pair since around 1500[8]—and *paréntsh* 'banister,' of Polish provenience (e.g., Li 25). It would be worth while to investigate how the riming possibilities of Yiddish and its stock languages have diverged as a result of both disjunctive phonological developments (e.g., Yiddish *hot* 'has': *got* 'God,' but German *hat* ≠ *Gott*: Yiddish *Avróm* 'Abraham': *thom* 'abyss,' but Hebrew *Avrahâm* ≠ *tehôm*) and the selective adoption and elimination of words (e.g., *brach*, which Yiddish failed to adopt from German; or *sayâḥ* 'young ass,' never adopted from Hebrew).

While the Slavic component in literary Yiddish does not become important until the modern Yiddish period (eighteenth century and onward), the Hebrew, like the Romance component, has always been present, and although the use of Hebrew-origin rime words of this component may not have been as frequent formerly as it became in the nineteenth and the twentieth century (statistics wanted!) it would be hard to prove that the riming of Hebrew-origin and other words was ever intentionally avoided. On the contrary, the famous *Bovo-bukh*, completed by Elye Bokher in 1507,[9] rimes *hof* 'court': *tof* 'letter tav' (stanza 285), *zol* 'should': (*hamavdil ben kodesh*) *lekhól*: *fol* 'full' (st. 335), *Bove* 'Bovo': *krove* '(fem.) relative' (st. 384), and also rimes Hebraisms with each other, like *bore olem* 'Creator': *sholem* 'greeting' (st. 386). Even earlier examples are cited further on.

But the full enjoyment of the fruits of fusion in rime has been impeded by the retention of the traditional spelling of Hebrew-origin words in Yiddish. Although this is justified, culturally, by the special status which *that* stock language has preserved for the users of Yiddish, linguistically it is an anomaly which already troubled such a nineteenth-century master of Yiddish and Hebrew prose as Mendele Moykher-Sforim, and was bound to irritate much more seriously the modern Yiddish poets. Continuing familiarity with the stock languages of Yiddish by its users and many decades of Maskilic and post-Maskilic vilification of Yiddish

---

by Erich Schmidt, "Deutsche Reimstudien. I," in *Sitzungsberichte der kön. preussischen Akademie der Wissenschaften zu Berlin* (1900), pp. 430-72; esp. pp. 441 and 453 f. On German riming difficulties, cf. also Ernst Bednara, *Verszwang und Reimzwang* (= Beilage zum Osterprogramm 1912 des kön. kathol. Gymnasiums zu Leobschütz, Trebnitz i. Schl., 1912).

[8] See Max Weinreich, "*Yidishkayt* and Yiddish: On the Impact of Religion on Language in Ashkenazic Jewry," *Mordecai M. Kaplan Jubilee Volume* (New York, 1953), pp. 481-514; p. 509, footnote 42.

[9] Elye Bokher (Elia Bachur), *Poetishe shafungen in yidish*, Vol. I (New York, 1949); reprinted from the first edition (Isnae, 1541) and provided with an introduction by Judah A. Joffe. Cf. the introduction, p. 21.

hybridity have tended to make every Jew his own etymologist, ready to decompose the delicate fusion that is Yiddish into its components. The modern poets, who have been concerned precisely with the total integration of the language, could not help but find that the disparate spelling systems for words of different components only aggravate the unhealthy analytic attitude. Nowhere has the orthographic dualism been as vexing as in riming position. There it obscures intended parallelisms by differing spellings of rime words (e.g., *vide* 'confession': *meride* 'rebellion'—ווידוי: מרידה) and occasionally yields unwanted "eye rimes" (e.g., ווער *ver* 'who': צער *tsaar* 'sorrow').

The special spelling of Hebraisms was proclaimed outmoded in 1920 by the particularly self-conscious and advanced group of poets, *In zikh.* "All Yiddish words are equal," they wrote in their manifesto. "As poets—not as propagandists—we shall spell all Yiddish words alike, regardless of their pedigree."[10] Their example was followed widely even by poets outside the group. As B. J. Bialostotzky put it, "Why should the visual obstruct our free riming of words and our finding of additional word and image relations?"[11]

The iron logic of spelling unification might well have prevailed were it not for the fact that a similar reform, undertaken in the Soviet Union in absolute rejection of the Jewish past, had become a symbol of a vulgar antitraditionalism which was unpalatable to the majority of Yiddish users. Until 1939, the poets in and about the *In zikh* group held out; but the political events of that year, and the discontinuance of the journal *Inzikh*, apparently made it impossible for them to continue publishing in a unified spelling. Now Yiddish writing—in any orthography—has been suppressed in the USSR since 1949; but not until the association between Soviet Communism and Yiddish spelling reform is forgotten is the unification of the orthography likely to be considered again. However, such uniquely Yiddish riming possibilities as *kediboe* 'properly': *Elyoe* 'Elijah' (כּדבעי: אליהו) might never have been discovered or accepted if not for the episode of a unified orthography.

[10] *In zikh: a zamlung introspektive lider* (New York, 1920). Introductory essay by Yankev Glatshteyn, A. Leyeles, and N. B. Minkov, pp. 21 f.

[11] B. J. Bialostotzky, "Di shaykhes fun vort tsu vort," in his *Lider un eseyen*, Vol. II (New York, 1932), pp. 77-130, p. 114. On orthographic parallelism as a rime criterion in English and French, see Henry Lanz, *The Physical Basis of Rime* (Stanford University, 1931), pp. 146-51; on orthographic riming in Russian, see Viktor Žirmunskij, *Rifma, jeje istorija i teorija* (Leningrad, 1923), and now B. V. Tomaševskij, "K istorii russkoj rifmy," in Akademija nauk SSSR, Institut russkoj literatury, *Trudy otdela novoj russkoj literatury*, I (1948), 233-80, esp. pp. 235 ff.

The relationship between Yiddish words of Hebrew origin and between the same words as units of an integral Hebrew language has recently been described as one between "Merged" and "Whole" Hebrew.[12] For example, the word for 'bride' has the form *kaló* in Ashkenazic "Whole" Hebrew, but is *kale* in the Hebrew that is "merged" with Yiddish; 'rich man' is *oshír* in Whole, but *oysher* in Merged Hebrew. Since words in the two forms of Hebrew often differ in stress and vowel makeup, a given rime usually admits only one, but not both forms. One would expect Yiddish verse to resort only to Yiddish (i.e., Merged Hebrew) forms; indeed, this is universal practice today, and is supported by a tradition that goes back at least to the *Bovo-bukh*, as the previously cited examples show. On the other hand, the *Shmuel-bukh* (fourteenth century?) contains such Whole Hebrew rimes as *Pninó* 'Peninah': *fro* 'gay' (st. 19); *kohen-godól* 'High Priest': *vol* 'well' (st. 26), *sefer Shmuél*: *kol yisroél* (epilogue),[13] all implying a final stress and full vowel in the Hebrew-origin rime words, i.e., a choice of the Whole Hebrew form. A chronology is hard to establish; in the older (i.e., pre-nineteenth century) period, a correlation may perhaps exist between Whole vs. Merged Hebrew and the familiarity vs. reverence with respect to the Hebrew language typical of secular as against religious poetry.[14] In the nineteenth century, the secularity of Yiddish poetry and the hunger for new rime words in the verse of the *badkhonim* (wedding jesters) and "folk poets" make the use of the Merged Hebrew forms in riming position almost universal, while in the twentieth century this practice becomes a matter of principle with the growing recognition of the integrity of Yiddish. Statistics would probably also reveal a great increase in the riming of Hebraisms of different morphological construction in the stock language (e.g., *nakhes* 'joyous satisfaction' < *naḥat* with *lehakhes* 'for spite' < *lehak'is*) at the expense of analogically constructed words (*shures* 'rows': *tsures* 'faces,' etc.).

THE RHYTHM OF RIME WORDS

From a rhythmic point of view, rimes are classified as (a) masculine if the stressed syllable is the last (e.g., *bold*: *behold*), (b) feminine if the stressed syllable is followed by one unstressed (e.g., *better*: *letter*, symbolized – ᴗ),

[12] See pp. 85-87 of M. Weinreich's study cited in footnote 4.

[13] Cited from the excerpts in Max Weinreich, *Bilder fun der yidisher literatur-geshikhte fun di onheybn biz Mendele Moykher-Sforim* (Vilna, 1928), pp. 68-111.

[14] For example, a religious poem by Ayzik Valakh (d. 1632) rimes *alzó* 'thus' with

and (c) dactylic (trisyllabic or "triple") if two unstressed syllables follow the stressed one (e.g., *attitude*: *platitude*, symbolized – ◡ ◡).

(a) The dropping of final unstressed *e*'s in many words of the Germanic component has considerably increased the stock of Yiddish masculine rime words as compared with German (cf. German *Sache* with Yiddish *zakh*; German (*ich*) *sage* with Yiddish *zog*, etc. Statistics would be helpful). As a result Yiddish poets need not resort to the hard-to-suppress habit of German poets to multiply apocopated forms.[15] Whereas in German verse *Sach'*, *sag'* occur as products of poetic licence, in Yiddish their equivalents are not only legitimate, but the only ones possible. (On the other hand, Yiddish has its own original apocopes in words of non-Germanic descent.)[16] Moreover, modern Yiddish has favored the coinage of new nouns directly from verbal stems far more than German[17] and has thus further enriched its repertory of masculine rimes.

(b) The transfer of many words from the feminine to the masculine rime group has probably been more than offset by the increase of "masculine words" of non-Germanic stock. The stock of feminine rime words has also been increased by the elimination of secondary stresses on syllables adjoining the primary stress[18]—a development attributed by Hrushovski (p. 241) to the influence of co-territorial Slavic languages. Older Yiddish poetry could base masculine rimes on secondary stresses, e.g., *shlekht* 'straight': *únrèkht* 'injustice' (in a recently discovered poem dated 1382),[19] *end* 'end': *élènd* 'misery' (1616, *Megilas Vints*, st. 43), much as older German poets did.[20] Contemporary Yiddish verse, however, has

---

the phrase *ki govar* [?] *oleynu khasdó*, in its Whole Hebrew version, as it would be read in the liturgy (B I 35), while a contemporary historical poem, *Megilas Vints* (ab. 1616), rimes *ore* 'pray': *tsore* 'trouble' (st. 17), *skhore* 'wares': *ferlore* 'lost' (st. 34), in Merged Hebrew forms. (Citations according to reprint in Max Weinreich, *Shtaplen* [Berlin, 1923], pp. 140-92.)

[15] See J. Minor, *Neuhochdeutsche Metrik* (2d ed., Strassburg, 1902), pp. 171-73.

[16] A folk song (C II 251) rimes *padlóg*' 'floor': *astróg* 'jail' (normally *padloge*). Sutskever (SuV 18) playfully tries *yodl*' 'fir': *nodl* 'needle' (normally *yodle*); Glatshteyn toys with *khalát* 'long coat': *gele lat*' 'yellow patch' (normally *late*).

[17] On this trend in Yiddish, see Yudel Mark, "Vegn neologizmen," *Yidishe shprakh*, XII (1952), 37 f., and *idem*, "Vortshafung in H. Leyvik's lider," *ibid.*, XIV (1954), 13 f.; on the corresponding conservatism of Standard German, cf. Walther Henzen, *Deutsche Wortbildung* (Halle, 1947), p. 128.

[18] On the modern Yiddish stress system, see Uriel Weinreich, "Stress and Word Structure in Yiddish," in *The Field of Yiddish*, pp. 1-27.

[19] L. Fuks, "The Oldest Literary Works in Yiddish in a Manuscript of the Cambridge University Library," *Journal of Jewish Studies*, IV (1953), 176-81. See also the same writer's "On the Oldest Dated Work in Yiddish Literature," in *The Field of Yiddish*, pp. 267-74.

[20] Minor, *Neuhochdeutsche Metrik*, pp. 126-31.

emancipated itself from traditional vestiges and, in conformity with the structure of the language, uses such words for feminine rimes: *kozak* 'Cossack': *blozzak* 'bellows' (B II 318), *blozzek* 'bellows' (pl.): *glozik* 'glassy' (Mk 142), *khumre* 'difficulty': *umru* 'anxiety' (LF 35), *hayor* 'this year': *shtayer* 'tax' (Gr 171). (The discrepancy in the unstressed vowels does not invalidate the rhythmic harmony of the feminine stress patterns.) As a consequence of the elimination of secondary stresses there has been a trend in colloquial Yiddish to neutralize the difference between various vowels in unstressed position. Yiddish poets seized on this trend and exploited it—as the unsophisticated folk songs had done[21]—to broaden the resources of feminine rimes; note such pairs as *altmódish* 'old fashioned': *kodesh* 'holy' (L 54), *novis* 'prophet's': *soves* 'owls' (L 118), *oylem* 'crowd': *oylim* 'immigrants to Palestine' (Su 12), *logik* 'logic': *milkhemes-Gog-u-Mogeg* '(eschatological) war of Gog and Magog' (Sb 68), and the like. In its leaning on the "allegro forms" of colloquial speech, Yiddish poetics proved itself to be far ahead of the orthoepic suggestions made for the standard pronunciation[22] and demonstrated that poetic phonology need not be conservative in every literature.[23]

(c) Dactylic rimes manifest Yiddish independence from the patterns of the stock languages even more clearly. Rimes of this type seem to be oddities even in those European literatures in which they are linguistically possible.[24] In German dactylic rimes are restricted to unusual genres or have associations of levity.[25] Also, true dactylic rimes are hard to form in German because secondary stresses tend to reduce them to shorter forms: *Gróssvater* (– ⌣ ⌣) easily becomes *gróssvàter* (– – ⌣), which is feminine, not dactylic.[26]

In older Yiddish poetry, dactylic rimes are as rare as in German;

[21] E. g., *kholem* 'dream': *hevl-havolim* 'vanity of vanities' (GM No. 124), *Rashi* 'RaSHI': *kashe* 'porridge' (GM No. 45).

[22] Cf. Yudel Mark, "Vegn a klalishn aroysreyd," *Yidishe shprakh*, XI (1951), 1-25, §§ 26-29. See also the paper cited in footnote 32.

[23] On the conservatism of poetic phonology, cf. J. Vendryes, "Phonologie et langue poétique," *Proceedings of the Second International Congress of Phonetic Sciences* (London, 1935), p. 106; with special reference to English, Kurt Stryjewski, *Reimform und Reimfunktion* (= *Sprache und Kultur der germanischen und romanischen Völker, Anglistische Reihe*, 36), 1940, esp. p. 100. The introduction of allegro forms in modern Russian rime is discussed by Tomaševskij, "K istorii russkoj rifmy," in Akademija nauk SSSR, Institut russkoj literatury, *Trudy otdela novoj russkoj literatury*, I, 267.

[24] Žirmunskij, *Rifma*, pp. 36, 98 f.

[25] Minor, *Neuhochdeutsche Metrik*, pp. 401 f.

[26] *Ibid.*, pp. 123-26. Even suffixes of little weight tend to receive a secondary stress, so that in older German poetry, at least, *Prédigèr* could be rimed with *Herr* or with *Schlésièr;* cf. *ibid.*, pp. 122, 400.

presumably a more German-like accentual structure with prominent secondary stresses, and possibly an explicit German literary model, hindered their development.[27] Yiddish folk song—which has in some rhythmic respects been more sensitive to the stress structure of the language than has literary poetry[28]—on this point has been rather conservvative; such linguistically dactylic words as *ópsheydn* 'to separate' (– ◡ ◡) are found to function as feminine rimes (... – ◡), e.g., with *reydn* 'to speak' (GM no. 36). Nineteenth-century poets often adhered to this tradition (cf. Mikhl Gordon's *ganéydn* 'Heaven': *óysrèydn* 'utter'; Sf 166), but contemporary Yiddish writing has eliminated such rimes almost entirely and has thus further attuned itself to the structure of the language.

The use of suffixes of dactylic words for masculine rimes has also become an archaism. While Berl Broder (1817-80) could still rime *aráynkumèn* 'enter': *váremèn* 'warm' (Sf 202), contemporary poetry has rather given such words their deserved freedom to rime as full-fledged dactyls; and while in English we associate such rimes with low comedy (Byron's *Don Juan*, Gilbert's operettas), the Yiddish reader thrills to the solemn fervor of such dactylic rimes as those written by Leyvik in 1917 (Lk I 7): *Ergets vayt, ergets vayt/ ligt dos land dos farbótene./ Zílberik bloen di berg/ nokh fun keynem batrótene...* ('Somewhere far, far away lies the forbidden land. Silvery blue are the mountains still untrodden by anyone...').[29]

Occasionally Yiddish poets have even introduced rimes where the stress falls on the fourth syllable from the last (hyperdactylic), e.g., *óvesdike* 'ancestral': *katóvesdike* 'jocular' (Su 34). Such contrivances remain humorous even in Yiddish,[30] but they do illustrate the peculiar increased distance between stresses which has made it possible in Yiddish, as Hrushovski has shown (pp. 240 ff.), to write entire poems in quadruple meter (paeons).

A noteworthy experiment in the use of dactylic words as masculine rimes has been the recreation in Yiddish of the Russian folk epos (*bylina*),

[27] In Russian verse, especially serious poetry, subservience to West European models is known to have delayed the introduction of dactylic rimes well into the nineteenth century; cf. Žirmunskij, *Rifma*, pp. 36-38.

[28] Hrushovski, "On Free Rhythms in Yiddish Poetry," in *The Field of Yiddish*, pp. 230 f., 241 (footnote 68).

[29] The first explicit condemnation of rimes based on a secondarily stressed ultimate as un-Yiddish seems to have been made by Arn Tseytlin (Zeitlin), "Fragn fun yidisher poetik," *Yidishe velt*, 1928, No. 1 (April), p. 111.

[30] In Russian, hyperdactylic and even longer rimes have also remained experimental; cf. Žirmunskij, *Rifma*, pp. 23 f.

where such rimes are common.[31] Leyeles, in "Di almone un er," rimes *zátikèr* 'satiated': *mútikèr* 'courageous,' *khmúrikèr* 'clouded': *tróyrikèr* 'sad' (LFL 105). We see a rime pattern which had existed in older Yiddish poetry and had been eliminated because of the increasing linguistic and poetic autonomy of Yiddish reintroduced as a stylistic device. Originally of Germanic origin, the pattern now comes back—but from an archaic Slavic source. Here is another instance of the complexity of cultural currents in the history of Jewish culture.[32]

COMPOSITE RIME

One of the characteristics of modern Yiddish verse has been the rapid development of composite rimes, in which at least one of the riming elements consists of more than one word (e.g., *illicit*: *miss it*). In its simplest form, where the match is phonetically exact and forces no unusual inversions of word order, this rime has existed in Yiddish at least since the sixteenth century;[33] it also occurs in folk song (e.g., *broygez* 'angry': *toyg es* 'it is suitable'; C 128) and was used even by conservative rimers up to World War I. In its contemporary period, Yiddish poetry also introduced more complex composite rimes which are phonetically or syntactically strained, or both: *zay nit* 'don't be': *taynet* 'argues' (Sb 192) is phonetically inexact, while the riming of *fayer* 'fire' with *tsi iz dem balbós azóy getráy er* 'whether to his master so faithful is he' (Sb 56) requires unusual liberties in syntax.

Composite riming of these more complex types, it seems, entered Yiddish verse through two separate channels: as a humorous device, in a Byronian vein, it is common in the satirical fables of Reb Mordkhele, Yehoyosh, and especially Eliezer Shteynbarg.[34] The other impulse has come from certain German expressionists, and especially from those Russian modernists who strove to rejuvenate the concept of rime.[35] The boldest innovator along these lines was probably Perets Markish; his books of the period immediately following World War I abound with

[31] *Ibid.*, pp. 263 ff.

[32] I have discussed Yiddish polysyllabic rimes in greater detail in a separate paper, "Vegn filtrafikn gram," *Yidishe shprakh*, XV (1955), 97-109.

[33] The use of composite rimes in the *Bovo-bukh* was pointed out by Israel Tsinberg, *Die geshikhte fun der literatur bay yidn*, VI (Warsaw, 1935), 91.

[34] Composite rimes have been classified and analyzed in the paper mentioned in footnote 32.

[35] On Russian, see Žirmunskij, *Rifma*, pp. 92, 179, 187, and footnote 95; on Yiddish interest in German and Russian experiments on this point, see F. Shames, "Der nayer gram in yidishn ferz," *Di royte velt* (December, 1926), pp. 108-14, esp. p. 111 (footnote).

such contrivances as *khalef* 'slaughtering knife': (*efn* ... *dayn* ...) *zal oyf* 'open your hall' (Mk 112), *meshugoim* 'madmen': (*shlaydert* ... *zey* ...) *azóy um* 'hurl them around thus' (Mk 127). In a less extreme form, such rime patterns became a hallmark of serious Soviet Yiddish poetry.[36] This is a more advanced stage of composite riming, for its purpose is solemn; the punning connotations have been overcome, as they were gradually surmounted in Russian verse in the course of the nineteenth century.[37]

RIME AND THE "INTERNATIONAL" OUTLOOK

Yiddish poetry, like all aspects of Jewish culture, was caught up in the vast modern broadening of the Jewish intellectual horizon. To encompass the totality of the present-day Jew's experience, without antiquated compartments for an "outside" non-Jewish, and an "inside" Jewish, world, became a guiding principle for many Yiddish poets. "Wars and revolutions," ran the 1920 manifesto of *In zikh*, "Jewish pogroms and the labor movement, Protestantism and Buddhism, ... all of these may or may not move us.... [If they do,] we write poetry about them" (p. 17). One of the *In zikh* leaders, A. Leyeles, characterizes "modernism" as "the attitude which accepts the entire experience of mankind": from science, the discoveries of astrophysics or psychoanalysis; from the Jewish tradition, the central messianic idea of justice and salvation. "With reference to the Yiddish language, modernism is an attitude according to which ... all the highest accomplishments reached by other languages in poetic culture are possible in Yiddish. Modern in literature means: the most exact word, the most adequate expression."[38]

The search for the "exact word" meant, for those poets who gathered under the banner of modernism, a rapid increase in vocabulary and a blurring of the distinction between poetic and "unpoetic" terms. To be

[36] Shames, "Der nayer gram in yidishn ferz," *Di royte velt*, pp. 110 ff. M. Khmelnitski has suggested that the new inexact rime patterns, created in revolt against hackneyed tradition, themselves became a rut for Soviet Yiddish poets ("Bamerkungen vegn tsvey iberzetsungen fun [Shevtshenko's] lider," *Yidishe shprakh*, II [1942], 118). Few contemporary Yiddish poets have been able to reject the resulting expansion of the riming repertory, but some have used composite rimes more boldly than others. For example, Khaim Grade—one of the leading present-day practitioners of the art—attains the greatest "juncture strain" possible by ending a sentence and beginning a new one in mid-rime: *Reb Yankev nemt mikh bay der hant un* PAMELEKH */ er firt tsu der tir mikh, un biz tsu der* SHVEL. IKH */ derhér fun zayn bet*... (Gr 138) ('Reb Y. takes me by the hand and slowly he leads me to the door, and as far as the doorstep. I perceive from his bed...').

[37] Žirmunskij, *Rifma*, pp. 178 ff.

[38] A. L[eyele]s, "Vegn eynem a durkhfal," *Inzikh*, No. 31 (January, 1937), pp. 27-31.

sure, literary Yiddish had never been plagued by the xenophobia which is cultivated toward *Fremdwörter* in Germany, for example. But under the influence, perhaps, of the completely open-minded view toward new words prevalent in English, modernist Yiddish poetry—despite the uneasiness of some conservative critics—could absorb a host of internationally current words in one big swallow without suffering lexical indigestion.

Since a fair share of the new internationalisms in poetry turned up at the end of lines, they brought with them fresh riming problems. Many of them, it turned out, terminated in sound sequences which were absent in traditional Yiddish vocabulary. To rime them exclusively with other internationalisms having similar novel terminations would place them in precisely that isolation which the modernist poets hoped to avoid. Consider words ending in *-ado*, for example: in a strict interpretation, *bravado* could only rime with *eldorado*, *mikado*, and other novelties. The solution adopted by most poets has been quietly to "hasten" the familiarization of these words. In the rime *avade* 'certainly': *mikado*: *Granade* (Sb 199), Shteynbarg is only subjecting *mikado* to the same reduction of the final full vowel to *e* which the Spanish city name, *Granada*, underwent when it became familiar in Yiddish at an earlier stage.

By such precipitate adaptations (which are again ahead of conservative orthoepy; cf. footnote 22), Yiddish poets have helped to repeat a trend which has always been a part of the history of Yiddish. As in the case of the Hebrew-origin words, we may view the choice between *mikado* and *mikade* as one between "whole" and "merged" internationalisms. It is another example of the perennial tension between the foreign and the adapted in Jewish history.

BIBLICAL ECHOES

Rime has not been the only form of sound effect cultivated in Yiddish poetry. Assonances, for example, were developed into a systematic method by most Soviet and many American Yiddish poets.[39] The repetition of consonants combined with a variation of the vowel (so-called consonance: e.g., *flint—flaunt*) met with particular hospitality in Yiddish because the language has experienced the convergence of

[39] Cf. Shames's analysis of such rimes in the study cited in footnote 35; cf. also Bialostotzky, "Di shaykhes fun vort tsu vort," in his *Lider un eseyen*, II, 127. Possible American English influences remain to be investigated.

grammatical "ablaut" paradigms not only of Indo-European and Germanic origin (e.g., *toyt* 'death'—*teyt* 'kill'), but also of Semitic descent (e.g., *mies* 'ugly'—*moes* 'disgusting').[40] A. Leyeles in particular has not only organized entire poems by consonance (e.g., L 176), but has taken the device one step further and made it an echo of the Hebrew of the Bible, where consonance is a favorite pattern of "poetic etymology." Let us recall such playful etymologies as *Bavel* 'Babel' < *balal* 'confuse' (Gen. 11 : 9) or such consonances as *yoruhu* 'they will shoot him': *yerau* 'they will fear' (Psalms 64 : 4). In one poem (L 85), Leyeles has Reuben say: *nite aykh in ayer* SHTARKKAYT *tsu* SHTREKN *a hant oyf dem yung* ('you must not in your strength raise your hands against this lad'); and later: *hot er far*KÍLT *in zayn* KEL *dos* KOL *fun zayn* KLÉMENISH ('then he congealed in his throat the voice of his distress'). By combining consonance with the syntax and diction characteristic of Yiddish Bible translations, Leyeles has truly recreated biblical poetry in a new Jewish medium.[41]

RIME AND THE STANDARDIZATION OF YIDDISH

Written Yiddish has for centuries functioned as an effective medium of Europe-wide, and later world-wide, communication between Ashkenazic Jews. In its vast territorial expansion the language was bound to develop dialectal differences, but the spelling system has been such that in many cases it could serve several dialects equally well. For example, the rime *krum* 'crooked': *skhum* 'amount,' written קרום: סכום, is a rime also to those who read *krim, skhim.*

However, because the vowel differences are not always quite that regular, many sets of words which rime in one dialect do not rime in another, or those that match at one period of the language may not correspond later. The evidence of rimes in older Yiddish poetry can therefore be used, with appropriate safeguards against generalization, in dating and localizing texts by the pronunciation which they imply, or conversely, where the genesis of a poem is known, the text may be used to unravel the unknown pronunciation.[42]

[40] Proverbs also make use of consonance; cf. *a melokhe iz a melukhe* 'a trade is [worth] a kingdom.'

[41] As Glatshteyn put it (*In tokh genumen*, I [New York, 1947], 101), Leyeles discovered in Yehoyosh's modern Bible translation "the Hebrew potentialities of Yiddish. . . . Yehoyosh revealed to him a new original." On Leyeles's sensivitity to biblical rhythms, see also Hrushovski, "On Free Rhythms in Yiddish Poetry," in *The Field of Yiddish*, p. 266.

[42] Note, for example, the subtitle of Bruno Kormann's *Die Reimtechnik der Esther-*

But when rime makers desire to escape regional restrictions, they must choose between two solutions. One is simply to avoid rime schemes which would not work beyond their dialect. This procedure, however, although it was recommended to modern Yiddish poets by Stutchkoff's rime lexicon (pp. 17-20) as late as 1931, excludes large masses of words from riming position; for example, a Southeastern ("Ukrainian") Yiddish writer could not rime such common words as *bobes* 'grandmothers': *shobes* 'Saturday,' because elsewhere the pair would be *bobes* ≠ *shabes; nukh* 'after': *bukh* 'stomach' (elsewhere *nokh* ≠ *boykh, nukh* ≠ *boukh*); *nuvnt* 'near': *uvnt* 'evening' (elsewhere *noent* ≠ *ovnt*), and so forth.

The other solution is the achievement of a uniform literary language with standardized pronunciation norms valid for all regions.[43] This in fact has been the path followed by Yiddish writers at two separate stages of its development: first on a Western-Yiddish basis, and when the old literary standard crumbled about 1800, again in Eastern Europe. Yiddish represents a remarkable case in the sociology of language, for twice it was unified without the coercive apparatus of a state, a centralized system of schooling, or a prestigious capital or social elite to imitate. The modern standard pronunciation—some dissenting voices to the contrary[44] —is a unique compromise between the dialects, an autonomous system based on the firmly established features of the spelling in such a way that, ideally, every graphic symbol corresponds to one sound.[45] While occasional nonstandard (i.e., dialectal) rimes still occur in contemporary poetry, they are surprisingly rare in comparison with other languages having longer histories of standardization.[46] No poet of *litvak* origin would today be caught dead riming *zeydes* 'grandfathers': *ruakh-*

Paraphrase Cod. Hamburg 144: Beitrag zur Erschliessung des altjiddischen Lautsystems (Diss. Hamburg, 1930). See also the use of rime testimony by Judah A. Joffe in "Dating the Origin of Yiddish Dialects," in *The Field of Yiddish*, pp. 102-21.

[43] A third solution—the switching of dialects in the middle of a poem for the purposes of forcing a rime—has of course repeatedly been ridiculed as far too cheap; cf. Tseytlin, "Fragn fun yidisher poetik," *Yidishe velt*, 1928, No. 1, p. 118; Stutchkoff, *Yidisher gramen-leksikon*, p. 21; N. P. [Noyakh Prilutski], "Di shprakh fun Yekhiel Lerers *Mayn heym*," *Yidish far ale*, No. 4 (June, 1938), pp. 106-18; p. 106.

[44] Cf. Chaim Gininger's review of Uriel Weinreich, *College Yiddish*, in *YIVO Bleter*, XXXIII (1949), 208 ff.; Solomon A. Birnbaum, "Two Problems of Yiddish Linguistics," in *The Field of Yiddish*, pp. 63-72: pp. 71 f.

[45] See Uriel Weinreich, "Tsu der frage vegn a normirter oysshprakh," *Yidishe shprakh*, XI (1951), 26-39, and Yudel Mark's paper cited in footnote 22, pp. 10-12.

[46] Some none too recent examples are cited by Stutchkoff, *Yidisher gramen-leksikon*, pp. 20-22. On substandard rimes in German, see Friedrich Neumann's excellent *Geschichte des neuhochdeutschen Reimes von Opitz bis Wieland* (Berlin, 1920), and on more recent German dialect rimes, Heinrich Stürenberg, "Mundartliche Reime,"

hakoydesh 'Divine Inspiration' (dial. *-hakeydes*), as Yehude-Leyb Gordon permitted himself to do in 1886 (Sf 183).

It is important to appreciate the constructive effort involved in the creation of supraregional rimes. When Itsik Manger, for instance, rimes *Stoptshét* (place name): *zet* 'sees' (Ma 376), which in his native Southeastern dialect is *zeyt*, he is following and at the same time reinforcing the normalized literary pronunciation; similarly, when Moyshe Kulbak, a native Northeastern ("Lithuanian") speaker, rimed *aróys* 'out' with *groys* 'big' (K 243), which in his dialect is *greys*. The resulting uniformity has helped to raise Yiddish literature to the general European level.

AUTONOMOUS RIMING CONVENTIONS

By establishing its own requirements of exactness in riming, every literature seems to regulate its rime resources so that, for the greatest artistic effect, riming should be neither too easy nor too difficult. For example, in Russian, where words ending in stressed vowels are superabundant, poetic convention makes their riming more difficult by requiring the preceding, "supporting" consonant to be different in each rime word: thus *oknó*: *vinó*, which in other languages would be a "rich" rime, is in Russian merely adequate, while *oknó*: *bjuró* is inadequate. German permits the riming of *ü* with *i* (*grün*: *Wien*), thus enlarging the "riming valences" of *ü* words.

Yiddish poetry has not adopted the Russian restriction, matching *gedréy* 'whirl': *arméy* 'army': *vey* 'pain' (L 52) without scruples. Nor has it shared the Anglo-German distaste for "rich" rimes (e.g., *nation*: *damnation*);[47] on the contrary, Yiddish poets seem to enjoy exploring the accidental identities in word terminations which have resulted from fusion in Yiddish: note such rimes as *bule* '(papal) bull': *takhbule* 'remedy' (Gr 39), *palmes* 'palmtrees': *tsepalmes* '(progressively intensive) post-mortem' (Su 141), *beygl* 'doughnut-shaped boiled roll': (*zenen*) *khoyte-beygl* 'commit a sin (of worshipping the Golden Calf)' (Sb 145).

One variety of phonetic freedom allowed by modern Yiddish riming

---

Muttersprache, XL (1925), 299-303 and XLI (1926), 171 f. On uncertainties in Russian, cf. Žirmunskij, *Rifma*, pp. 129 ff.

[47] Žirmunskij, *Rifma*, p. 104 (German); on English, Jane Shaw Whitfield, *The Improved Rhyming Dictionary* (New York, 1951), p. v. In languages like Hungarian, where there are many frequent automatically riming suffixes, rime as a poetic device becomes subject to special syntactic restrictions; cf. George Herzog in *Funk and Wagnalls Standard Dictionary of Folklore, Mythology and Legend* (New York, 1950), p. 1038.

convention is the equivalence of final voiced and unvoiced consonants: *glants* 'glow': *gandz* 'goose' (Su 126), *gendz* 'geese': *inteligénts* 'intelligence' (Sb 102), *shoys* 'lap': *hoyz* 'house' (GrM 78), *shliakh-myukhed* 'special emissary': *geskrukhet* 'shuddered' (Y 90), *koved* 'honor': *óysgekhovet* (Gr 173), *tayneg* 'enjoyment': *vaynik* 'winy' (SuV 51, Su 29).[48] The unvoicing of historically voiced consonants has actually occurred in one of the dialects (Central Yiddish), but writers from other regions have, in varying degrees, taken advantage of this extra tolerance to expand their riming resources, as the above examples, all drawn from the works of Northeastern writers, show.[49] It would be interesting to analyze the advantages accruing from this convention to particular poorly endowed rime patterns of the language in order to show the structural motivation behind the convention.

THE PUZZLING YIDDISH WORD FOR RIME

We have seen that many aspects of Yiddish rime, although their sources can be conjectured, are uniquely Yiddish in their configuration. This is also true of the mysterious Yiddish word for rime itself—*gram*. It is apparently composed of a prefix, *g*(*e*)-, and a root, *-ram*. Now in German, a prefixed form—which, incidentally, is a neuter while Yiddish *gram* is consistently masculine—is attested in the medieval and early modern period only in the meaning 'collection of rimes, rimed poem,' especially in a disparaging sense. Obviously the Yiddish word—though ultimately of Germanic origin—developed, like the poetic tradition, in complete independence of German, shifting its meaning from 'rimed poem' to rimed 'line of verse' to 'rime.'[50]

But while the prefix symbolizes Yiddish autonomy from German, the vowel of the root involves some internal Yiddish puzzles. The vowel being derived from a medieval long *i* (cf. Middle High German *rîm*, *gerîme*), we would have expected Central Yiddish to have *graam*, which

[48] For a normative statement, see D. Hofshteyn and F. Shames, *Literatur-kentenish* (*poetik*), I (Moscow, 1927), 22; also Stutchkoff, *Yidisher gramen-leksikon*, p. 16.

[49] A case of tolerance practiced by Yiddish writers of the Central and Southeastern regions, but obscured by the spelling, is the riming of short and long *i;* cf. M. M. Varshavski's *ki*(*i*)*kn* 'look': *kvikn* 'refresh' (B I 208), Gotlober's *shmi*(*i*)*st* 'chats': *imzist* 'in vain' (B I 149), and the examples given by Prilutski in the paper cited in footnote 43. Stutchkoff, himself a non-*litvak*, makes no distinction between *i* and *ii* words and does not even mention the problem in his riming dictionary.

[50] Yiddish *gram* thus duplicates, without directly participating in, the semantic evolution of the German terms *Vers* and *Reim;* cf. F. Kluge and A. Götze, *Etymologisches Wörterbuch der deutschen Sprache* (15th ed., Berlin, 1952), where the German research literature is cited.

it does, but Northeastern Yiddish should have had **graym*, whereas it generally has *gram*. This would suggest that the word was diffused from Central Poland—perhaps by riming wedding jesters—to Lithuania and Belorussia. But why and when? The puzzle is deepened further by the Western Yiddish equivalent which is attested in the form *raam*,[51] where **graym* was to be expected. The attested form is German in its lack of a prefix but Central Yiddish in its vowel. Could it be due to a contamination of the two? If so, where did this take place? Perhaps the unusual vocalism of this word was supported by the rime with *taam* in the locution *on taam un on raam* 'without rime or reason'—itself a rimed version of the French alliterative *sans rime et sans raison*, which is possible in Yiddish but not in German... But here we are completely in the domain of speculation.

FUNCTIONS AND THEORIES OF RIME

An examination of rime arrangements would lead us afield into the history of Yiddish stanza forms. Suffice it to say roughly that oldest Yiddish poetry depended mostly on the use of alternately rimed and unrimed lines (*xaxa*), and that this quatrain pattern, as Hrushovski has shown (pp. 225 f.), has remained basic in Yiddish folk song. However, at the beginning of the sixteenth century, Elyohu Bokher introduced from Italy the elaborate *ottava rima* riming *abababcc*, which he used in the 650-stanza *Bovo-bukh* and elsewhere, and which did not appear in German poetry until more than a century later.[52] It is curious that not only were Italian-Yiddish poetic relations more lively than Italian-German ones in the Renaissance period, but that Italy had by then replaced Germany as a source of Yiddish literary innovation.

The nineteenth century saw the wide spread of badkhonic couplets (*aabb*) and of *rimes couées* (*aabccb*), favored in satiric popular verse. But as part of modernist experimentation, such poets as Broderzon, Naydus, and Leyeles introduced almost every strict rime scheme known in European literature, not only the sonnet and sonnet ring, but also Romance and oriental forms—triolets, rondeaux, villanelles, ghasels, and the like. Rare patterns, such as systematic "following rime," in which

[51] Thus Abraham Tendlau, *Sprichwörter und Redensarten deutsch-jüdischer Vorzeit* (Frankfurt, 1860), Nos. 419, 734; *es hot ka taam un ka raam*, communicated to me by Professor Ezekiel Kutscher from Slovakia. For one Prussian and several East European outcrops of the form *raam*, see Max Weinreich, *Shtaplen*, (Berlin, 1923), pp. 219 f., and the discussion by D. Leybl in *Filologishe shriftn* [*fun Yivo*], I (1926), 74.

[52] Max Weinreich, *Bilder fun der yidisher literatur-geshikhte*, p. 156.

the end of each verse rimes with the beginning of the next, were also successfully tried (e.g., Leyeles's "A tfile," L 28).

On the other hand, sporadic riming and completely rimeless lines also came into their own in contemporary Yiddish writing. In the twentieth century, when "Yiddish poetry undertook ... to catch up with Europe's deepened appreciation of the classics and the modernistic trends of recent generations" (Hrushovski, p. 219), it toyed with rimeless hexameters, iambic pentameters, and vers libre. Even today, when most Yiddish verse has returned to the use of rime, some poets (most notably Yankev Glatshteyn) continue to use the freer forms.

The theory of rime itself underwent scrutiny in Yiddish much as it did in other contemporary literatures.[53] The serious poets of the late 1800's, the American *Yunge* of the early 1900's, and their conservative followers to this day have worked hard to restore the seriousness of rime which, they felt, had been violated by the extravagant rimings of their predecessors. An elaborate statement of what might be called the "romantic" theory of rime was published by the poet-critic B. J. Bialostotzky in 1932 (cf. footnote 11). This theory, which makes semantic relevance a criterion of good rime, claims to carry forward the subliterary (folk) conception of rime as it functions in folklore. It sees in rime and other sound repetitions a network of association paths which operates as an organizing principle of a vocabulary.[54] The finding of nonobvious semantic relations between riming words becomes the task of the poet's imagination. Other contemporary Yiddish poets, on the contrary, have joined the modernistic world-wide trend to "dethrone" rime by depriving it of semantic relevance while intensifying its euphonic value.[55] The search for "exotic" rime words

[53] For a review of European theories of rime, see Lanz, *Physical Basis of Rime*, chap. V, where additional literature is cited.

[54] The operation of the factor of sound similarity in lexical structuring has been analyzed for English by Dwight L. Bolinger, "Rime, Assonance, and Morpheme Analysis," *Word*, VI (1950) 117-36. Material from many Indo-European languages is presented by Francis A. Wood, "Rime Words and Rime Ideas," *Indogermanische Forschungen*, XXVII (1907-8), 133-71. Ber Shnaper expressed this rime theory poetically when he wrote (*Mayse un lid* [Warsaw, 1934], p. 11): *...nemt lemoshl—broyt! / ...vi "shtram" as gramt zikh mit—noyt! - Un beyde in eynem mit—toyt!* etc. ('Take, for example, *broyt* "bread": how neatly it rimes with *noyt* "need, poverty"! And both together with *toyt* "death"!') Glatshteyn refers to this theory of rime ironically in a line full of poetic ambiguity (GlF 78): *di gramshtegn fun broyt firn tsu noyt* 'the rime-paths of bread lead to poverty.'

[55] On the Russian aspect of post-romantic rime theory, cf. Roman Jakobson, *Novejšaja russkaja poezija* (Prague, 1921), p. 63; for a recent American statement, see W. K. Wimsatt, Jr., "One Relation of Rime to Reason," *Modern Language Quarterly*, V (1944), 323-39. Explicit statements by Yiddish poets or critics seem to be lacking

associated with Naydus (e.g., *emune* 'faith': *fortune* 'Fortune' N 38, *tsaar* 'sorrow': *penyuár* 'peignoir' N 51); the use of colloquial allegro forms; the breakup of symmetry by the cultivation of composite rimes; the use of assonance to dodge predictable rime words; the riming of semantically "trivial" words, e.g., prepositions, and the use of "broken rimes" (i.e., the breaking up of compounds between lines);[56] and finally, the use of unfinished words in rime to signify interrupted speech[57]—all these devices have served to lighten the semantic role of rime at the expense of the euphonic.

In the hands of masters, contemporary Yiddish rime has become an instrument of unprecedented subtlety. One example will have to suffice. In a prologue introducing his volume of Israeli poems, Sutskever rimes (*dos glik un*) *vey do* 'the happiness and pain here': *khevle-leyde* 'birth pangs': *akeyde* 'sacrifice (as of Isaac)' (Su 9). In the composite rime *-ey do*: *-eyde* there is not only the usual tension of inexact rimes, but the full *o* of *vey do* brings out, like an otherwise imperceptible overtone, the "Hebrewness" of the following two rime words in *-eyde.* (In Whole Hebrew—Ashkenazic, to be sure!—these words end in *-eydo.*) This "Hebrewness," which would not be apparent in a phonetically exact rime scheme, is kept from going out of control by the incontrovertible Yiddish *e* of the last rime word, *zeyde.* But once the two middle rime words are viewed, under the pressure of the rime, as genetically Hebrew, the *-e* note of the same rime scheme in turn underscores their Yiddishness; more generally, it suggests the "mergedness" of the Hebrew component in Yiddish and, symbolically, of the Zion theme in Diaspora culture. Now this unity of Zion and the diaspora is precisely the burden of Sutskever's book! To render it so completely by a single rime chord of the overture is a stroke of genius.

Where did Yiddish rime come from? At its beginnings, Yiddish poetry could have adopted it from several sources: from German oral literature, on which it leaned heavily for forms and themes (in de-Christianized

---

so far; but P. Markish's role as a pioneer of assonance was indicated by Arn Tseytlin, "Fragn fun yidisher poetik," *Yidishe velt*, 1928, No. 1, pp. 112 f.

[56] Insignificant rime word: *min* 'kind': *eyn mol in / di teg...* 'once during the days' (Y 23). Broken rime: *nafke- / mine* 'difference' (Sb 188).

[57] For example: *papá* 'daddy': "*zent ir dos frayln Ra...*" / "*Un ir zent Yakob, mayn kuzén*?" ('Are you then Miss Ra...[chel]?' 'And you are Jacob, my cousin?' MaM 58); "*Vi bistu óyfgeshtanen tkhies-...*" / *Un zi hot óyfgeshmeykhlt mit di fiolete vies* ('"How did you arise... [from the dead = *-hameysim*]" And she broke into a smile with her violet eyelids' Su 138).

versions); from Hebrew *piyyutim*, in which rime had been obligatory since the seventh century C.E.;[58] and possibly even from Loez (medieval Judaeo-Romance) poetry. There are still many missing links in this construction, but potentially Yiddish rime could be seen as a poetic equivalent of the fusion which culturally became Ashkenaz and yielded the Yiddish language itself. Over the centuries Yiddish poetry became increasingly independent, especially of German models. It looked to Italy for innovations during the Renaissance, and remained completely aloof from the German controversies about the use of rime in the classicist eighteenth century. In the modern period, Yiddish poetry discovered in word derivation, rhythm, and rime the full richness and linguistic specificness of Yiddish. Secure in its mastery of its linguistic medium, it assumed a posture of self-assured universality, reinterpreting formal traditions from as far back as the Bible and creatively adapting patterns from new sources in Europe and America. Centuries older than Russian rime, Yiddish rime was rejuvenated by modern Russian experimentation. In its increasingly supraregional nature, Yiddish rime today reflects the use of literary Yiddish as an instrument of world-wide communication and as a medium of a mature art.

[58] Israel Davidson, "Rhymes in Hebrew Poetry," *JQR*, XXX (1939-40), 299.

"IT CAN'T HAPPEN HERE!"

AN EPISODE IN THE FAILURE TO ACHIEVE TERRITORIAL UNIFICATION OF FRANCONIAN JEWRY IN THE MID-FIFTEENTH CENTURY

By Arthur J. Zuckerman

THE RECONSTITUTION of Würzburg and Franconian Jewry as a governmental entity made swift progress in the 1440's after a lapse of about twenty years.[1]

In August, 1442, King Frederick removed Duke Sigmund of Saxony from the Würzburg See for maladministration and appointed Gottfried von Limpurg to be *Pfleger* of the bishopric. Gottfried was the most striking personality among the ecclesiastical princes of his day in Germany. Of peaceful temperament and considerable ability, he instituted an efficient administration of his domain and laid the foundation for a new era of peace and order. Under his predecessors, John II of Brünn and Sigmund, economic conditions had so deteriorated that the total net income of the bishopric was not over 10 florins per annum in September,

[1] In 1422 the Jews left the territory of Würzburg and Franconia following their payment of a "ransom" of 60,000 florins. Cf. S. Haenle, *Geschichte der Juden im ehemaligen Fürstenthum Anspach* (Ansbach, 1867), p. 207; M. A. Szulwas, *Die Juden in Würzburg während des Mittelalters* (Berlin, 1934), pp. 67 f.

For several years thereafter no organized Jewry existed in Würzburg although individual Jews probably resided in the Bishop's domain. A list of communities which the imperial tax collector and hereditary Chamberlain Conrad v. Weinsberg considered taxable on February 2, 1434, does not mention the Jews of Würzburg or Franconia. However, in the same year, Jews in Würzburg were credited with paying 315 florins imperial coronation tax. D. Kerler, "Zur Geschichte der Besteuerung der Juden," *Zeitschrift für die Geschichte der Juden in Deutschland*, III (1898), pp. 115, n. 3, 123 ff.

On November 6, 1437, Bishop John II of Würzburg gave a five-year franchise to a group of Jews. This signals the reconstitution of Würzburg Jewry. Ludwig Rockinger, "Magister Lorenz Fries zum fränkisch-wirzburgischen Rechts- und Gerichtswesen," *Abhandlungen der Historischen Classe der Königlich Bayerischen Academie der Wissenschaften*, X, section 3 (Munich, 1870), 245. However, this communal organism made but little progress. Although an imperial listing of May, 1438, suggested that the sum of 600 gulden be raised from the Bishop of Würzburg's Jews, 4,000 gulden were anticipated from those under other sovereigns in Franconia. Kerler, "Zur Geschichte der Besteuerung der Juden," *Zeitschrift für die Geschichte der Juden in Deutschland*, III, 128.

1444, and Gottfried had to request a moratorium on the payment of papal annates.[2]

Gottfried's Jewish policy was also directed toward repairing the wretched state of his realm. Less than three months after his appointment and shortly after his recognition by Pope and Anti-Pope, Gottfried issued a license on November 11, 1442, to the Jew Seligmann to reside in Würzburg for five years. A few days later, on November 16, Jacob of Coburg secured a six-year franchise with permission to make his home in the capital. Jacob's permit of entry exempted him from courts lay and Christian, inasmuch as claims against Jews might be tried only before the synagogue in Würzburg "in accordance with ancient custom." Four witnesses were needed for conviction—two Christians and two Jews—who were not enemies of the accused. For criminal offences committed by Jacob or his dependents, the ordinary criminal court was declared competent. Jacob's permit recognized the right of the other Jewish residents of the city to decide whether or not to accept him into their guild. From 1442 to 1444 several other Jews were admitted to residence in Würzburg and Franconia, the last few licenses being limited to only a single year's validity.[3]

The culmination of these individual entry permits was a lengthy and highly favorable statute which Gottfried, now Bishop, promulgated on April 24, 1445, with the consent of his Cathedral Chapter. This charter, which was to be valid for seven years, offered protection to the Jews (*Judischeit*) then resident in Würzburg and Franconia or who later would enter the Bishop's domain. The new *privilegium* clearly was intended to attract additional Jews into the territory. Its opening provisions were similar to those of Jacob of Coburg's permit. In general, it also harked back to the franchises at the beginning of the century, while containing important enactments that reflect a territorial organization of the Bishop's Jewry and a centralization of Jewish administration in the capital city, Würzburg. The statute declared:

1. The court convening before the Synagogue in Würzburg had sole competence, "in accordance with ancient custom," in all suits at law brought against Jews. Judgments of other courts were null and void. [This is apparently

[2] Lore Muehlon, *Johann III. von Grumbach, Bischof von Würzburg und Herzog zu Franken 1455-1466* (Würzburg, 1935), pp. 2-3. August Amrhein, "Gottfried IV. Schenk von Limpurg, Bischof von Würzburg und Herzog zu Franken 1442-1455," *Archiv des historischen Vereins von Unterfranken und Aschaffenburg* (*AHVUA*), L (1908), 79.

[3] Amrhein, "Gottfried IV. Schenk von Limpurg," *AHVUA*, LII (1910), 48 f. Jacob and associates "sollen mit andern Juden in der Stadt Wurzburg und im Lande keine Gemeinschaft haben mit leihen noch geben, *es were dann ir wille*."

the Jewry court with Jewish and Christian justices recognized by Bishop John II in his charter of 1412].

2. The Jews might buy and sell merchandise and lend money at interest. The interest rate for denizens of Würzburg was to be three heller for each gulden per week; one heller for each pound per week (21 $\frac{2}{3}$ percent). The rate for aliens was not limited.

3. A Jew might be convicted only on the testimony of four honorable witnesses—two Christians and two Jews—who were to give testimony in the court before the Synagogue.

4. The fines of tried and convicted Jews were not to exceed 10 gulden and could not be levied against any but the guilty parties. Crimes involving life and limb were to be judged according to law and might not implicate others.

5. The Jews might lend on any pledge at any time except broken church vessels, bloody clothes, and undressed skins.

6. The meat provisiners were to sell them meat on a par with other burghers and in accordance with ancient custom.

7. The "Jewry" (*Judischeyt*) might maintain a *Hochmeyster* in Würzburg called *Rabi.* He was exempt from taxation and might have as many students as he wished. He might hale any other Jews in and outside of Würzburg into his court, pronounce judgment in accordance with Jewish law, excommunicate them, and rely on the power of the State to help execute his desicions. Whoever remained unpenitent in the *Hochmeyster*'s ban for thirty days—the Rabbi was to supply the needed information—had to pay a penalty to the Bishop.

8. Synagogue and cemetery were "franchised." The Jews' residences were tax-exempt; the individuals exempt from all land and town taxes except common tax and aid, for which they were liable only to the Bishop's treasury.

9. The Bishop and his officials would help the Jews to collect their loans and come into possession of what the courts assigned them; and promised other such aid and protection.

10. The Jews might leave the territory at any time with or without permission provided their current tax had been paid. For three months after their departure their agent might enter the territory and receive help in the collection of outstanding loans.

11. Litigations between Jews which might be brought before the Bishop or his officials were to be referred to their Jewish court in Würzburg.[4]

[4] L. Heffner, *Die Juden in Franken* (Würzburg, 1855), Beilage W, pp. 61 f.; Beilage L, pp. 48 f. Cf. Amrhein, in *AHVUA*, LII (1910), 50 f. Fries's comment, that of old the Bishop's chamberlains or staff officers were the judges of the Jews, but that then he set up a rabbi as their judge, may refer to this new institution of the *Hochmeister* or Chief Magistrate: *darnach hat man inen ain rabi zu richter verordnet.* Rockinger, "Magister Lorenz Fries," *Abhandlungen der Historischen Classe der Königlich Bayerischen Academie der Wissenschaften*, X, 224. For the composition of such a mixed court later in the same century, Sebastian Zeissner, *Rudolf II. von Scherenberg Fürstbischof von Würzburg* (2d ed., Würzburg, 1952), p. 85. M. Szulwas does not adequately distinguish between this court which had sole competence in suits initiated by Christians against Jews and, on the other hand, the rabbinical court for suits between Jews, *Die Juden in Würzburg*, p. 71. Cf. also, A. Amrhein, "Die Würzburger Zivilgerichte erster Instanz," 2. Teil, *AHVUA*, LVIII (1916), 39 ff. Amrhein unduly limits the competence of the rabbinical court.

Bishop Gottfried's statute was a direct continuation of the charters of his immediate predecessors. It went beyond them in its recognition of a regional organization of Franconian Jewry and a central administration in Würzburg. It also made explicit the close relationship between the new institution of a Jewish Chief Magistrate (*Hochmeyster*) and the executive arm of the State. The Bishop's charter recognized his authority (in all but criminal cases) over the Jews in Gottfried's domain and guaranteed enforcement of his judgments. Other documents, especially the rabbinic writings, enable us to see the Jewish officials in action.

This franchise of 1445 did not mention any Jewish notables who must have negotiated it with Gottfried and participated in its formulation. However, one of these leaders may have been Rabbi Ḥ. Kitzingen, of whom Jacob Weil, a very prominent rabbinical authority of the mid-fifteenth century, wrote as follows:

> The Bishop [i.e., John II v. Brünn] confiscated the cemetery in Würzburg when he banished the Jews, and sold it to gentiles. Now that the Jews have returned they thought to repurchase it. However, a very large sum was required, whereupon the lay leaders [lit., householders] withdrew. Rabbi Ḥ. Kitzingen has inquired if it were permissible to sell the [fruit of the] vines and orchards of the cemetery each year in order to acquire funds to redeem the cemetery.

Weil permitted the expedient. It is possible that Rabbi Ḥ. Kitzingen was then the first Chief Magistrate under Gottfried's regime. The actual bill of sale with which Gottfried restored the former cemetery to Würzburg

---

The fine mentioned in § 7 above went of course into the Bishop's coffers. Similarly, the fiscal interests of the Emperor, to whom the excommunicate and his property theoretically fell forfeit after thirty days, added material force to the already awesome character of the rabbinical ban. Among the items of regular income listed by King Charles IV in 1348 was the ransom which defiant Jews had to pay for remaining excommunicate beyond the thirty-day time limit. Such information reached the King or his officials directly from the rabbis themselves: "ob kein Jude den Judischen pan über seinen rechten zil versizze,... derselbe uns seines lipes und gütes vervallen were, so uns die Judischen meister nach iren rechten beschribent und erteilent." *Monumenta Germaniae Historica*, Legum Sectio IV, Constitutiones et Acta Publica T. VIII, *Acta Regni Karoli IV* (Hanover, 1910-26), No. 642, p. 648 (1) (September 9, 1348). Cf. S. W. Baron, *The Jewish Community; Its History and Structure to the American Revolution* (Philadelphia, 1945), II, 230-31, also for similar conditions in thirteenth-century England where confiscation followed after a forty-day waiting period. Medieval Jewish law specifically allowed such recourse to the secular authorities:

ואם ישב (המנודה) במרדו חדש ימים מותר למסור ממונו למלך.

L. Finkelstein, *Jewish Self-Government in the Middle Ages* (New York, 1924), p. 231; Joseph Colon, שאלות ותשובות (Responsa)(Venice, 1519) No. 169: הדבר ידוע ומפורסם שכל מי שהיה בנדוי שלשים יום ממונו מוכתב למלכות.

Cf. M. Frank, קהלות אשכנז ובתי דיניהן (German-Jewish Medieval Communities and Their Courts) (Tel Aviv, 5698), pp. 37 ff.

Jewry has been preserved. It is dated May 12, 1446, and indicates that for a cash payment of 300 florins the Jews reacquired their communal property while obligating themselves to an annual tax of 35 florins for the continuous possession of it. They refused, however, to pay the tithe hitherto due from the property to the Provostship of the Cathedral. They carried their point, when on November 7, 1446, Gottfried declared the Jewish cemetery tithe-free. Like the Court of the Chief Magistrate (*Hochmeyster*) in Würzburg, their burial ground too was designated a regional institution to which the Jewish dead might be brought toll-free from outside the capital city.[5]

As Bishop Gottfried had hoped, several persons were in fact attracted to Franconia by the generous guarantees of his statute. Between 1446 and 1450 the episcopal office issued a number of new residence permits to Jews, the validity of each limited to a single year, and for which every immigrating family was assessed approximately ten florins or a multiple thereof. Among these is to be noted a tax-exempt permit for David the Jew to reside in the episcopal town of Ebern. Probably the same David was the one who, a year later, was received explicitly as a Rabbi in Würzburg and placed under episcopal protection with family and property, August 26, 1447.[6]

The Würzburg community grew substantially. Evidence of such growth is the number of rabbis who made their home here at this time, Moses Minz being the most prominent among them. He was undoubtedly the Mosse *Homeister* who signed a writ of withdrawal from the bishopric

[5] Jacob Weil, שאלות ותשובות (Responsa) (Venice, 1549), Appendix, *Dinin V'Halakhot*, No. 50, p. 94a. Gottfried's statute of 1445 declared: "Wir fryen auch der genanten Judischeyt Ire schule vnd freythoff, den sie yetzund haben oder zukunftigen zyten gewinnen mochten vnd was dinstlewte in darzu notdurftig ist, als von Alter herkomen." In 1429 Bishop John II had sold the confiscated Jewish cemetery to Hans Wenzel, burgher and meat dealer in Würzburg, for 900 florins accumulated debts. Bishop Gottfried acquired the property in 1445. Amrhein, "Gottfried IV", *AHVUA*, LI (1909), 22 f., LII (1910), 56. Cf. Szulwas, *Die Juden in Würzburg*, pp. 73 f.

[6] Heffner, *Die Juden in Franken*, Beilage BB, pp. 67 f. Amrhein, "Gottfried IV," *AHVUA*, LII (1910), 53 ff.; p. 56, incorrectly, August 28. Szulwas, *Die Juden in Würzburg*, p. 74, unaware of Ḥ. Kitzingen's correspondence with Weil, thinks David became the first Würzburg *Hochmeister*. The only *Hochmeister* named in episcopal records of this period was Mosse *Homeister*, who left Würzburg September 25, 1450; while David Frank, without title (very likely our David), signed his writ of departure on September 30 of that year. Amrhein, "Gottfried IV," *AHVUA*, LII (1910), 61. David Frank became burgher in Nuremberg July 2, 1451, for the sum of 32 guldens. Here he came into conflict with a former teacher, David (Tebele) Sprinz, over the matter of exclusive rabbinical prerogatives. M. Stern, *Die israelitische Bevölkerung der deutschen Städte* (Kiel, 1894-96), III, 296; Israel Bruna, שאלות ותשובות (Responsa) (Salonika, 1798), No. 254, p. 103b.

on September 25, 1450. One of Moses's contemporaries in Würzburg was Rabbi Zalman Kitzingen, who may have preceded Minz in the capital city (if, indeed, he is not the Rabbi Ḥ. Kitzingen above). Zalman remained behind after Moses left and may even have succeeded to the office of Chief Magistrate.[7]

Episcopal permits continued to be issued for a year's residence until February 5, 1450. Then on February 16, Smohel and Meyer, both of Lauda, were admitted for only a quarter-year, until Pentecost, May 24, 1450. The reason for this limitation is probably related to Bishop Gottfried's action a week later, on February 23, when he declared a moratorium on interest in behalf of insolvent debtors of the Jews and legislated at length regarding easier repayments of their loans: "Because of the great distress under which burgher and peasant suffer in consequences of debt these days: The roads being closed, they cannot ply their trade in wine and other merchandise in Würzburg and secure the means to pay their debts."[8]

The sad state of affairs described by Gottfried was caused by a ravaging war between towns and nobility in Franconia. In June, 1449, Margrave Albert of Brandenburg and Bishop Anton of Bamberg declared war on the Free City of Nuremberg. The town was supported by the Swabian League and Bishop Gottfried of Würzburg. This conflict devastated the country and brought trade and commerce in the Bishop's territory to a standstill. Unable to pay their outstanding debts, peasant and burgher suffered heavy losses through executive court decree. A bitter cry arose, "The Jews are ruining the country!" Bands of "Enemies of the Jews" sprang up, whose threats of violence added force to their complaints. The Bishop's moratorium and refinancing may have been intended to still the agitation and serve as a stopgap measure until an armistice permitted attention to a more thoroughgoing solution. For the chaotic economic

[7] In his שאלות ותשובות (Responsa) (Cracow, 1617), No. 1, No. 86, Moses Minz refers to his Würzburg residence. On Zalman, see No. 86; also Bruna, *Responsa*, No. 257; and No. 218, p. 86a; No. 221, p. 88b, where records of testimony taken in Kitzingen's court are dated in the year 1447. Bruna, No. 151, names three rabbis probably resident in Würzburg at this time. Herz and Simon Bamberger, *Geschichte der Rabbiner der Stadt und des Bezirkes Würzburg* (Wandsbek, 1905), Anhang III, published a bill of divorce dated Würzburg, November 4, 1448, which must have required the presence of three rabbis. Minz, *Responsa*, No. 64, p. 85a, reports that Zalman Kitzingen authorized the issuance of a divorce in Würzburg.

[8] This legislation is incompletely dated *Montag nach Petri cathedra*, omitting the year. Amrhein, "Gottfried IV," *AHVUA*, LII (1910), 57 f., set it in the year 1450, because he found several departures from the Bishop's territory between August and December, 1450.

situation, coupled with the insistent pressure of certain advisers, was forcing Gottfried to the decision not to renew the Jews' charter after its expiration in April, 1452. This was of course tantamount to banishing them from his domain. The final step was held up pending a cessation of hostilities, which Gottfried effected June, 1450 (May, 1451).[9]

Secretly apprised of the intention of Gottfried and his counselors, the Jewish officials of Franconia were galvanized into action. They called a meeting of representatives of Franconian Jewry in Würzburg. The conference determined to secure a renewal of their charter. This was essential if they were not to suffer considerable loss on unpaid loans and possible violence. For otherwise, as Moses Minz wrote, they would have to rely upon court action to extract early payment. By inducing the Bishop to renew the expiring franchise, they could allow their debtors more time to pay their debts, and thereby forestall an explosive situation. The representatives at the conference agreed "to maintain the District" and obligated themselves to provide the needed funds. They charged certain persons, "the *Parnassim* [Provosts] of Franconia," with the task of maintaining the *status quo*. Finally, the decisions of the conference were embodied in an "Ordinance of the District of Franconia and Its Environs."[10]

[9] Amrhein, "Gottfried IV," *AHVUA*, LI (1909), 119 f., LIII (1911), 71, 103 ff.; F. Stein, *Geschichte Frankens*, I: *Das Mittelalter* (Schweinfurt, 1885), 418. Minz, *Responsa*, No. 1, acknowledged the right of the Bishop not to renew his franchise, but as long as it lasted he expected that Bishop and canons would fulfill their pledges to the Jews:

ההגמון . . . רצה לגרש את כל היהודים אשר במדינתנו כאשר יש לו כח ורשות לעשות דבר זה מדינא דמלכותא . . . ואחר כך דנגמר הגרוש הם (ז. א. יהודי היידינגספלד) בסכנה לכל הפחות או יותר מהק״ק פה בגבית חובות כי יש לק״ק פה קיום מההגמון ומהגלחים שקוראין טומהערן שלא לנגוע בהם ולהציל ממונם.

Clearly, Minz wrote this before the armistice of June, 1450. Apparently, quoting from the charter, he wrote:

אם יקח שום יודי רשות שיתנו לו עיזר עד שיגבו חובותיהם

This is a quotation from the statute: "...welicher also von Vns getzogen were... darzu sollen wir vnd vnser amptleute in Ire schulde... helfen." Minz's quote that "the Jews are ruining the country" and that the Bishop intended to banish them is likewise found in a contemporary document: "...clagten die vnterthanen allenthalben im stifte, wie si so merklichen von den juden beschwerdt vnd verderbt wurden, darum name Bischof Gottfried von Limpurg ein ernstlich Ordnung und satzung fur, alle juden aus dem stift zu vertreiben." Rockinger, "Magister Lorenz Fries," *Abhandlungen der Historischen Classe der Königliche Bayerischen Academie der Wissenschaften*, X, 245. Muehlon, *Johann III. von Grumbach*, p. 203.

[10] Minz, *Responsa*, No. 1; No. 61 (4); Bruna, *Responsa*, No. 257. These documents are undated. However, Israel Bruna's reference to Rabbi Zalman Kitzingen's residence in Würzburg helps to date Israel's mandate No. 257 at the middle of the century.

Würzburg Jews proceeded to make good their pledge, but called on the neighboring Jewry of Heidingsfeld to participate in the cost. Heidingsfeld's Jews refused to cooperate. Since 1431, Heidingsfeld had been a fief of Nuremberg, when King Sigmund privileged the latter town to settle Jews there and to endow them with the same rights enjoyed by other Israelites in Free Imperial Towns. Standing as an enclave in the Duchy of Franconia, Heidingsfeld Jewry was not included in Bishop Gottfried's Jewry charter; nor, as Moses Minz admitted, was it practicable to include it in any new episcopal franchise. True, since October, 1442, Bishop Gottfried had exercised a measure of protection over Heidingsfeld on a year-to-year basis at the request of Nuremberg Town. But when he introduced a cattle tax in 1450, the Town asked the Bishop, on September 4, 1450, to spare Heidingsfeld's residents therefrom. This position of Nuremberg and, in addition, the fact that Heidingsfeld had paid no tax to the Bishop of Würzburg for the past two years (indicating his protection had stopped) doubtless helped to stiffen the determination of Heidingsfeld's Jews not to participate in the Würzburg levy.

Obviously relying on the powerful protection they anticipated from Nuremberg Town, Heidingsfeld Jews declared they were immune to any fate that might overtake their fellow religionists in Franconia. "IT CAN'T HAPPEN HERE!" they insisted. Even should the Bishop of Würzburg banish his Jews, they declared they would nevertheless be able to survive and to continue transactions with their present clients, who were residents of Franconia. Hence, Heidingsfeld Jews refused to contribute to the Würzburg levy for the purpose of securing a renewal of the charter. The case came before Rabbi Moses Minz in Würzburg for adjudication. His decision, in summary, follows:

Zalman Kitzingen was *Hochmeister* Minz's associate in Würzburg before Minz left in 1450; by 1457, Kitzingen was there no longer. In fact, the community was without a rabbi, Heffner, *Die Juden in Franken*, p. 73. In Minz's order, contained in Responsum No. 61 (4), he directed an adjudication of the dispute under discussion there before Rabbi David (Tebele) Sprinz in Nuremberg. The latter became a burgher in Nuremberg on May 26, 1449, was involved in conflict over rabbinical prerogatives with David Frank after the latter's arrival in Nuremberg on July 2, 1451, had to leave the town temporarily in 1457, and was restored on March 3, 1458, Stern, *Die Israelitische Bevölkerung der deutschen Städte*, III, 77, 296 f. Consequently, Sprinz was in Nuremberg between 1449 and 1457. It is obvious from the contents of Minz's mandate No. 61 (4) that he was no longer in Würzburg at the time. Hence he wrote it after September 25, 1450. From its contents, it is clear that *Responsa* No. 1 was written before this date while Minz was still Chief Magistrate in Würzburg. These dates dovetail with the anti-Jewish legislation of the Synod convened by Cusa in Würzburg on May 20, 1451, and the חוקים אשר לא טובים שנתחדשו mentioned by Minz, No. 61, p. 81d. (See note 12 below.)

The Bishop has not demanded any tax levy from the Würzburg *Kahal* [Moses Minz pointed out in his court judgment], but he wishes to expel all the Jews in his entire domain and in all places where his spiritual authority extends, as he has the power and the legal right to do [as soon as the Jewry charter expires]. Many accusers among his inner councilors have been urging this for a long time. But no decision has yet been reached because of the conflict now taking place in this area. This was revealed to us in secret. Yet is is possible to forestall the evil. The expulsion will be very hard for us as we all know. The Jews of Heidingsfeld will not be able to collect their debts at all, while our [Würzburg] community holds a charter from the Bishop and his canons pledging not to injure them but to protect their claims and to help every Jew collect his loans when he leaves the country.

Heidingsfeld Jews claim that their burghers will manage to hold on to them even if not a single Jew remains behind in Würzburg. But Heidingsfeld is weak, virtually within the limits of Würzburg and under the control of the Bishop. It could not survive for an hour in the present war between barons and towns but for the protection of the Bishop of Würzburg. It would then be impossible for the Heidingsfeld burghers to oppose his will if he decided to carry out the expulsion of all Jews who "are ruining his country" even though they offer him considerable sums of money to remain. But if Franconian Jewry should succeed in remaining, Heidingsfeld Jews would likewise be enabled to stay, while banishment of the former also means exile for the latter without any doubt. . . . They are therefore obligated to forestall the calamity together and to contribute to the levy and "let each man help his brother."

The Jews of Heidingsfeld are equally responsible for the outcry "The Jews are ruining the country," which is the cause of the expulsion. . . . Furthermore, we have reason to fear that the villagers will join "the Enemies of Israel" and attack us as they are threatening to do. . . . The present plan to secure permission to remain or an extension of time will also save the outstanding loans of Heidingsfeld's Jews. . . . Therefore do I say that Heidingsfeld must involve themselves in this Würzburg project. But since they cannot be included in a new charter of the Bishop, they must pay in such a proportion that if each member of the Würzburg community gives 2 percent [of his wealth], then Heidingsfeld's members need contribute only approximately 1 percent. In this manner are all expenses to be covered.[11]

Franconian Jewry seems to have carried its project through to a successful conclusion, but only temporarily. Although about twenty-five heads of families signed writs of withdrawal from the Bishop's territory in the period August 24 to December 23, 1450—presumably, their

[11] Wilhelm Altmann, *Die Urkunden Kaiser Sigmunds*, Vol. II (Innsbruck, 1897-1900), No. 8322, p. 156. Cf. Amrhein, "Gottfried IV," *AHVUA*, LII (1910), 5; Heffner, *Die Juden in Franken*, Beilage U, pp. 60 f.; Minz, *Responsa*, No. 1. How accurate Minz was in his analysis of the situation is apparent from the proposed edict of expulsion which required the Bishop to call on other lords under his spiritual authority, including Free Imperial Towns, to banish their Jews too under penalty of excommunication. Heffner, *Die Juden in Franken*, Beilage CC, p. 71.

residence permits had expired and the unsettled conditions in the country made it unwise for them to stay—the Jewish leaders must have secured a renewal of their charter in some form and thus prevented the breakup of the community. We find Jews in the country for several years; in June, 1453, the organized Würzburg community was clearly in possession of its cemetery. In the end, the Jewish authorities even won Bishop Gottfried over to an active policy on their behalf. This was fortunate because before long they were threatened with economic strangulation and the danger of expulsion from a new quarter, none less than the papal legate, Cardinal Nicholas of Cusa.[12]

On April 30, 1451, Cusa summoned a diocesan synod in neighboring Bamberg which legislated against the Jewries of Bamberg, Nuremberg, and the Würzburg bishopric. In mid-May, the Cardinal legate came to Würzburg. On May 20, the synod he convened there ordered the parishes of the Würzburg bishopric, under pain of the interdict, to ban money-lending at interest by Jews in their territory. Cusa was also the leading spirit in the agitation for the expulsion of Franconian Jews. However, on receiving word of the action of the Bamberg synod against Nuremberg Jewry, Emperor Frederick III appealed to the Pope on their behalf. Doubtless, the prime movers in this action were the Jewry of that Free Town. Spurred by such example, and acting on the same supposition that what a papal legate binds, the Pope himself may loose, the Jews in Bishop Gottfried's territory undertook similar action. The leaders appear to have made a surprising coup right at the start. They gained Bishop Gottfried himself for their plan; Gottfried then applied to Pope Nicholas for the annulment of Cusa's action. Obviously, then, he must also have committed himself to a renewal of their charter before its expiration in April, 1452.

It seemed only a matter of time before Cusa's edict would be voided for Franconian Jewry as it was being annulled in other parts of the Empire. On September 20, 1451, and again on March 22, 1452, Pope

[12] Among the emigrants were Mosse *Homeister* (September 25, 1450), David Frank, Simon the Provost (*Judenvoit*). Amrhein, "Gottfried IV," *AHVUA*, LII (1910), 61 f., 63 f. That considerable numbers of Jews remained in the country is evident from the plan to banish them by March, 1454. Johann Uebinger, "Kardinallegat Nikolaus Cusanus in Deutschland 1451-1452," *Historisches Jahrbuch*, VIII (1887), 641 ff. Contemporaries directly associated Cusa with the effort to expel the Jews from the Würzburg bishopric: "Vnd kame solchs furnemen am maisten avf anhalten vnd gebote cardinals Nicolai de Cusa, bapst Niclausen des funfften legaten, der vmb vertreibung der juden hefftig arbaite." Rockinger, "Magister Lorenz Fries," *Abhandlungen der Historischen Classe der Königliche Bayerischen Academie der Wissenschaften*, X, 245.

Nicholas V removed such restrictions from the Jewries in Emperor Frederick's dynastic territories. In behalf of Nuremberg's Jews the Emperor also secured a papal annulment, dated May 1, 1452, voiding the Bamberg synod's ban on financial transactions at interest and its prescription of the Jew-badge. Likewise, letters patent of Pope Nicholas V, drawn up on March 20, 1453, "in response to the appeal of Bishop Gottfried of Würzburg," annulled the decree of Cardinal Legate Nicholas Cusa and placed the Bishop's Jews under the general law. Franconian Jewry too was about to score its triumph. But a combination of new events with old dangers imperiled the entire undertaking and caused a break in the determination of Franconian Jewry to "maintain the *Medina*."[13]

Pope Nicholas's document reached the papal chancellery but was not executed. Can it be that the capture of Constantinople by the Turks on March 29, 1453, which stunned Pope Nicholas, unnerved Western Christendom, and plunged the papal office into frenzied plans for a crusade, blocked the issuing of this privilege for Franconian Jewry? In any event, for the remaining two years of Nicholas's life (until March 25, 1455) the bull remained pigeonholed in the chancellery. Of this situation, apparently, Moses Minz wrote: "I have heard that in but a short while the matter would have been brought to a happy conclusion, only that additional funds are required for the documents which have already reached the chancellery from the Pope."[14]

Meanwhile, back in Germany and Franconia, one blow after the other was being struck at the continued existence of Würzburg Jewry. The work undertaken by Nicholas of Cusa to undermine the economic foundations of Jewish life in the Empire was carried on even more force-

[13] Moritz Stern, *Urkundliche Beiträge über die Stellung der Päpste zu den Juden* (Kiel, 1893), No. 49, pp. 54 ff. (September 20, 1451); Joseph Chmel, *Regesta chronologico-diplomatica Friderici IV. Romanorum Regis (Imperatoris III)*, Vol. II, 1452-1493 (Vienna, 1840), No. 2804, p. 287 (March 22, 1452); Friedrich Kayser, "Papst Nikolaus V und die Juden," *Archiv für katholisches Kirchenrecht*, LIII (1885), 212, 217 f. Uebinger, "Kardinallegat Nikolaus Cusanus," *Historisches Jahrbuch*, VIII, 639. At the request of the Archbishop of Salzburg, Pope Nicholas lifted the ban also from the Jews of that territory on October 15, 1453. J. E. Scherer, *Die Rechtsverhältnisse der Juden in den deutsch-österreichischen Ländern* (Leipzig, 1901), pp. 423, 436 ff.

[14] Minz, *Responsa*, No. 61, p. 81d:

וגם אני שמעתי שכמעט בא הדבר לגמר טוב׳ רק שחסר מעט ממון
שצרי׳ להוציא עבור הכתבים שכבר [ב]הקצ״ל מו האפפייר.

Cf. Amrhein, "Gottfried IV," *AHVUA*, LII, (1910) 63; Wetzer und Welte, *Kirchenlexikon*, IX (2d ed., Freiburg i.B., 1895), "Nicholas V," 296 f.

fully and with tremendous mass appeal by the papal legate, John Capistrano.

Entering Germany in June, 1451, via Austria, this Franciscan preacher swayed vast crowds with his Latin sermons, translated by an interpreter. By way of Bohemia and Moravia, he reached Nuremberg bordering on Franconia. Here Capistrano preached daily from July 18 to August 13, 1452. In ten consecutive sermons delivered in powerful rhetorical style, he treated at great length his favorite theme—lending money at interest. He insisted on the presence of Nuremberg's Jews in a special stall. He attacked violently the legislation of towns and princes permitting "usury." In order to drive home his point and to leave a lasting impression, he devoted his last sermon in the Free Town to the same subject, stressing its legal aspects.

Capistrano's clear intent and often-expressed aim was to secure the strict enforcement of the Church's legislation against the Jews, and, in particular, the decrees against moneylending. He directed unrelenting attacks against the Jewry charters of princes and towns. He was firmly determined to win over spiritual and lay authorities to the strict execution of such anti-Jewish legislation and the nullification of royal and local privileges, which in effect voided the Church's decrees. Capistrano's influence was irresistible.[15]

In the spring and early summer, 1453, during the trial which led to the banishment of Silesian Jewry as the result of Capistrano's two-and-a-half-

[15] From Nuremberg, Capistrano went to Erfurt, where he sermonized four weeks. His final sermon on September 24, it was reported, attracted 60,000 to 100,000 persons who streamed into the town from every direction. In Halle, he "shouted fearfully" in his attacks on interest taking. At Leipzig he gave five talks on this favorite theme and added special lectures on the same subject for the University staff and students. He carried on his agitation in Breslau for over two months, from February 13 to April 30, reaching a climax in his hours-long sermon on the Passion, Good Friday, April 14. On May 1, Breslau Jewry were arrested on the charge of host desecration and ritual murder. Capistrano returned to the town, became a judge in the trial, and exerted decisive influence on the sentence of conviction which led to the execution of several Silesian Jews and the banishment of the rest during July and August, 1453. Johannes Hofer, *Johannes von Capestrano, Ein Leben im Kampf um die Reform der Kirche* (Innsbruck, 1936), pp. 433 f., especially pp. 494, 499 f. To his vast, highly responsive audiences, Capistrano described the Jews as the offspring of an accursed tribe of regicides and Christ-killers who inherited their ancestors' hatred of Christ. This hatred was given full play so long as they could escape punishment. "We are justified in remaining suspicious of them. They are our enemies as is openly known. They crucified our Lord, Jesus Christ!" Hofer, *Johannes von Capestrano*, p. 500. Cf. M. Brann, *Geschichte der Juden in Schlesien* (Breslau, 1907), IV, 124 ff. An interesting polemic of Capistrano was the warning to his hearers against "the Jewish theory" that one might gain salvation in every faith. Were that so, he retorted, there would have to be as many religions as persons.

months' agitation in Breslau, matters also came to a head in Würzburg. Taking advantage of Bishop Gottfried's trip to the Imperial Court of Frederick III of Vienna for the purpose of finally terminating the feud between towns and nobility, a group of highly-placed conspirators plotted to take over control of the city during his absence. The *coup d'état* was set for St. Kilian's Day, July 8. But word leaked through to Gottfried. The Bishop, defying a forewarning at an attempt on his life, returned to Würzburg. He instituted an investigation in early August. This implicated his chancellor, Frederick Schultheiss, whom he imprisoned, and the Cathedral Canon, soon to succeed him, Johann v. Grumbach. Characteristically, the plot against Gottfried also involved a plan to banish the Jews from the bishopric.

This conclusion seems warranted on the basis of a lengthy document containing a series of demands on the Jews by "our lord, the lord of Würzburg," so timed as to go into effect during the week following St. Kilian's Day, 1453 ("between this date and the next Sunday after St. Kilian's Day"—July 15). These proposals called for cessation of banking transactions by the Jews of Franconia within eight days, provided for an extended collection of their loans, demanded the sale of all real estate in their possession, and decreed their expulsion from the territory by March 8, 1454, "since his Grace wishes to have no more Jews in his bishopric."[16]

[16] Heffner, *Die Juden in Franken*, Beilage CC, p. 68. Amrhein, "Gottfried IV," *AHVUA*, LII (1910), 59 ff., erroneously dated this document 1450 because of the several departures of Jews in late summer and fall, 1450. But then he could not account for the fact that as late as January 7, 1453, a bond of indebtedness attests to their economic activities. Amrhein, "Gottfried IV," *AHVUA*, LIII (1911), 142. On June 15, 1453, a mandate of Gottfried shows them still paying the annual rent on their cemetery at that time, Amrhein, "Gottfried IV," *AHVUA*, LII (1910), 63, LI (1909), 150. One of the matters Gottfried might have taken up at the Imperial Court was to secure Frederick's support in behalf of his appeal to Pope Nicholas against Cusa's anti-Jewish legislation. It must be remarked that, except for the explanatory statement of the copyist, who transcribed this document into the codex where it is now found, Gottfried's name does not appear in the edict at any place. Actually, the proclamation is drawn up in the third person throughout. "In every town where our lord has Jews..."; "Similarly in other possessions of our lord and of his institution..."; "Our lord shall require towns, counts, lords, knights and imperial towns [to banish their Jews too]...." Obviously, the "lord of Würzburg" might easily be the Bishop who, the conspirators planned, would replace Gottfried. The banishment of the Jews of Franconia would then constitute one of the very first acts of this new lord of Würzburg Town and bishopric. This proclamation cannot have represented the views of Bishop Gottfried who was involved in behalf of his Jews at the Papal See and was probably seeking the assistance of Emperor Frederick for that effort in Vienna. The expulsion edict was, of course, never promulgated since the coup was nipped in the bud. There can be no doubt that Gottfried did not banish his Jews in 1453; nor could the expulsion

The delay in getting the papal bull through the chancellery and these discouraging events in Würzburg broke the morale of sections of Franconian Jewry. Certain individuals, including the community of Mergentheim, refused to see the project through, and decided to withdraw from further financial responsibility for the effort "to maintain the District."

The *Parnassim* of Franconia, however, insisted on fulfillment of the obligation originally assumed at the Würzburg meeting. Rabbi Zalman Kitzingen, possibly now *Hochmeister*, likewise ordered implementation of that ordinance. Encountering resistance, these leaders called upon Moses Minz and Israel Bruna for aid. Minz declared in a mandate addressed "To all the inhabitants of the District (*Medina*) of Franconia who are under the dominion of the Bishop of Würzburg (God exalt his majesty) . . . and at their head the Provosts of the District" that withdrawal from the agreement was no longer possible. He ordered the parties in the dispute—"all who were together in the beginning"—to reconvene in Würzburg within fourteen days and try to reach an agreement so that the efforts undertaken thus far might not be frustrated. Should they be unable to come to an understanding in Würzburg, Minz commanded both sides in the conflict to present their case within the same fourteen days before the court of Rabbi David Sprinz in Nuremberg and the Provosts (*Parnassim*) there.

Rabbi Israel Bruna in Ratisbon also replied in similar vein, but his order was ignored. Whereupon, Rabbi Israel repeated his mandate and, calling the Jewry of Mergentheim in Franconia by name, commanded them under threat of the ban to pay their share of the levy according to the rate agreed upon. Afterwards, he wrote, the contending parties might go to court in Worms or Ratisbon, as the Franconian leaders had suggested, and Mergentheim could present their case at such time.[17]

Not until after the death of Nicholas V on March 25, 1455, did Gottfried succeed in getting papal remission of Cusa's decrees. Pope Calixtus

---

edict have originated with him as Graetz, *Geschichte der Juden*, 4th ed., VIII, 194 f., and all historians following him have maintained (except most recently, Szulwas, *Die Juden in Würzburg*, p. 76, cf. p. 79). On the contrary, the Jewish officials clearly won Gottfried back to his primary policy of favoring the residence of Jews in his realm. The plot against Gottfried in 1453, for which no explanation has been given, may even be related to his pro-Jewish policy against the insistence of intimate advisers and powerful nonlocal forces like Cusa and Capistrano. It is possible, of course, that the edict of expulsion was first drafted in 1450 but pigeonholed at that time. Cf. Minz's statement at end of note 10.

[17] See note 10.

II confirmed the Jewry patent of his predecessor on April 20, 1455. But now Gottfried was no more. He had died on April 1 of the same year. It was left to his successor, Bishop John III v. Grumbach, to give the *coup de grace* to Cusa's anti-Jewish program. On December 10, 1455, John III annulled the legislation of the Bamberg Synod against the Jews of his bishopric, removing the requirement of wearing the Jew-badge and voiding the ban on moneylending at interest.[18]

By this time, however, the Jewish community had dwindled. Finally there came the day, presumably after the departure or death of Rabbi Zalman Kitzingen, that Würzburg Jewry was without a rabbinical magistrate. Doubtless in response to their request for a rabbi, Bishop John III v. Grumbach ordered Jacob in Rothenburg on March 13, 1457, to serve as Würzburg rabbi while resident in Rothenburg:

> Whereas our Jewry in our bishopric has been privileged and franchised by our predecessors to the extent that they should and may have a *Judenmeister*, known as a Rabbi, in our city of Würzburg who may judge them according to Jewish law for their crimes, this being found in their franchise; and since at this time they are unable to keep a rabbi in Würzburg, we command you [i.e., Jacob] to function in that office, until recall, just as if you were resident in Würzburg, with reservation of the fines and penalties due to us according to the aforementioned franchise. Therein you will do us especial favor which we will graciously acknowledge to you.

In all likelihood, Würzburg Jewry first completed their arrangements with Jacob and then requested Bishop John to make the "appointment" in accordance with their franchised rights, referred to by the sovereign. The Jewish *Judenmeister* or *Hochmeister* was an official of the Bishop. Rabbi Jacob (perhaps surnamed Eisenstadt), resident in Rothenburg, appears in rabbinic documents of the period 1455-57.[19]

[18] Amrhein, "Gottfried IV," *AHVUA*, LII (1910), 63; Szulwas, *Die Juden in Würzburg*, pp. 76, 80; Muehlon, *Johann III. von Grumbach*, p. 182. John had previously been implicated in the conspiracy against Gottfried; see p. 000.

[19] Heffner, *Die Juden in Franken*, p. 73. Minz, *Responsa*, No. 64 and No. 86 refer to Zalman as deceased. At the time of No. 64 Minz was in Landau where he seems to have gone some years after having left Würzburg. On Rabbi Jacob, cf. the similar action of the Nuremberg Town Council, which on February 28, 1448, responded to the request of their Jewry for a *Hochmeister* to succeed the deceased Rabbi Symon(?), by telling them to invite a *Hochmeister* to Nuremberg and then to bring the matter before the Council. On May 26, 1449, David Sprintz was received as a burgher in Nuremberg. Stern, *Die israelitische Bevölkerung der deutschen Städte*, pp. 293 f. Cf. Ludwig Oelsner, "Schlesische Urkunden zur Geschichte der Juden im Mittelalter," *Archiv für Kunde österreichischer Geschichtsquellen*, Vol. XXXI, 1 (1864), No. 32, p. 130, for the related action of the Duchess Agnes of Silesia on March 21, 1370. Heinrich Epstein, "Ein Beitrag zur Geschichte der Juden im ehemaligen Herzogthum Ostfranken," *Monatsschrift für Geschichte und Wissenschaft des Judenthums*, XXIX (1880), 458. On Rabbi Jacob, see Israel ben Petahia Isserlin, פסקים וכתבים (Decisions)

Therewith ended, at least momentarily, the effort to establish a Jewish self-governing entity throughout the domain of the Bishop of Würzburg in the Duchy of Franconia.

(Venice, 1546), No. 142; M. Stein, "Beiträge zur Bibliographie der Eisenstädter Rabbiner bis 1670," *Jüdisches Archiv*, II (1929), 55. Moses Minz, *Responsa*, No. 21, No. 9. Close relations had existed for a long time between Rothenburg Jewry and the Bishop of Würzburg, Karl Weller, ed., *Hohenlohisches Urkundenbuch*, II (Stuttgart, 1901), Nos. 192, 198 (June 28, 1349; September 29, 1349); cf. Meir Wiener, *Regesten zur Geschichte der Juden in Deutschland während des Mittelalters*, Vol. I (Hanover, 1862), No. 218, p. 132 (September 30, 1353).